Community Learning & Libraries
Cymuned Ddysgu a Llyfrgelloedd

This item should be returned or renewed by the last date stamped below.

Newport
CITY COUNCIL
CYNGOR DINAS
Casnewydd

To renew visit:

www.newport.gov.uk/libraries

THE NORTH BRITISH RAILWAY
A HISTORY

David Ross

Holmes 0-6-0 locomotive No. 679, built 1892, with a passenger train leaving Fort William.

Stenlake Publishing Ltd

© 2014 David Ross
First Published in the United Kingdom, 2014
Stenlake Publishing Limited
54-58 Mill Square, Catrine, KA5 6RD
01290 551122
www.stenlake.co.uk

ISBN 978-1-84033-647-4
Printed in China

"The rise and progress of the North British Railway are additional proofs, if any were awanting, that truth is stranger than fiction." *Glasgow Herald*, 13 November 1866

The Borderer
No 808, North British Railway

There's a crowded railway platform where I meet a friend of mine;
She bears the proud name 'Borderer' in letters bold and fine;
And when she slows and settles like some great winged bird of green,
I love to ride in fancy down the roads that she has been.

For when she stands beside me with her fire-doors open wide,
And all her pulses throbbing with the glory of her ride,
I can see the hills she rounded, and the fields she flung behind,
As she sped across the Border with her white locks on the wind.

I can see her gliding grandly from the platform at Carlisle
With the waving hands behind her: see her climbing mile by mile,
Up from English stream and meadow, over English moor and fell,
Till she kisses Cheviot heather in the land she loves so well.

Teviot whispers at her shoulder as she passes; Eildon cries
Something of an older message where a long-dead Empire lies;
Dreaming in its sunlit valley sleepy Melrose wakes and calls,
Winding round her half the glamour of its crumbling Abbey walls.

So she climbs by Gala Water, wood, and wold, and moor and glen,
Flinging back her whistling challenge to the toiling Border men;
While in afternoons of winter 'neath a cloud of rosy sheen,
She goes groping through the darkness picking up her lights o' green.

Here's luck to you, brave 'Borderer', with all the freight you bring,
Of Border winds in winter-time and Border scents in spring!
Safe journey through from Cheviot by mead and moorland brown!
You seem to bring the Borders near when you come in to town.

Will H. Ogilvie (1869-1963)

Also by David Ross
George and Robert Stephenson: A Passion for Success
The Highland Railway
The Caledonian: Scotland's Imperial Railway
The Glasgow & South Western Railway A History

Front cover: Hawick Station.

CONTENTS

MAPS

FOREWORD

The North British came to be Scotland's largest and the United Kingdom's fifth-largest railway company. How it achieved this position makes a remarkable story and reveals a great deal about the commercial and industrial life of the time.

Two previous histories of the North British have been published: by C. Hamilton Ellis in 1955 (revised 1959), and John Thomas's two volumes of 1969 and 1975. Ellis remembered childhood journeys on the Waverley Route; Thomas grew up in Springburn in the 1920s, where the railway scene was still very much as it had been in North British days. Both authors were able to draw on the personal recollections of men who had known the NBR. The present book is however the first to provide a continuous chronological account of the company, from its 'pre-history' to its incorporation as a joint stock company, and of its important role in the unevenly expanding economic life of Scotland in the nineteenth and early twentieth centuries. The author first saw North British engines in the early 1950s, on a visit to Edinburgh from the remote north, when he joined other youthful observers on the lattice bridge spanning the railway cutting just west of the Mound, a fine vantage point. More than a few veteran locomotives from pre-1923 were still in action, by that time wearing the paintwork of British Railways.

As one of the five large Scottish railway companies, the North British had dealings with all the others, but its most important, and most difficult, relationship was always with the Caledonian Railway. From start to finish the two companies were rivals, and though a more co-operative spirit gradually emerged, mutual suspicion and competitiveness died hard, the antagonism sharpened by their respective 'East Coast' and 'West Coast' affiliations with English railways. In *The Caledonian: Scotland's Imperial Railway*, the author traces the growth of each, with comparative statistics. From the North British headquarters in Edinburgh, and the Caledonian's in Glasgow, they watched and schemed against each other, and copied each other's innovations.

Many of the railway companies absorbed by the North British, and several North British branch lines, as well as the West Highland Railway and the two great bridges, have been the subject of monographs. Those read by the author are listed in the bibliography and, if used for quotation or reference, credited in the notes. References taken from secondary sources have been double-checked as far as possible. The text is based very largely on primary sources, referenced in the notes (where numerous items of supplementary information can also be found). A comprehensive time-line is included. Dates have been checked in contemporary sources, though even these sometimes conflict by a day or two. Corrections to points of detail will be gratefully received.

To write the history of a large railway company as a chronological narrative and maintain readability, with smooth transitions between topics, is a challenge. As Scotland's biggest joint-stock company, the North British sprawled across many aspects of public life, and was hugely influential in a range of ways. Naturally, events occurring at any particular time might be linked only by their connection with the company. I hope readers will tolerate occasional abruptnesses in the interest of having things situated in their own time and context. But a clear narrative thread traces a company that from the beginning set out to punch above its weight, absorbing other railways, sometimes bigger than it was itself. Despite passing through several desperate crises and sudden changes of management, it somehow kept a momentum of its own. Three notable men were among the four chairmen of its board of directors up to 1882, and did much to give the North British its distinctive tone and style. Although often penny-pinching and slow to modernise its rolling stock, systems and stations, it was nevertheless the line that saw the mammoth projects of the Tay and Forth Bridges through to completion. Its fluctuating fortunes mirrored those of the wider economy. Study of its relationships with the coal and iron companies of Central Scotland and Fife, of its attitude to its ever-increasing number of employees, and of its provision for the travelling public, adds valuable detail to the chart of industrial and social history between 1845 and 1923. After heavy war service in 1914-18 the North British fought a tenacious battle with the government of the day to reclaim what it considered its rightful due for wear and tear, a campaign which ended only a short time before the great 'Grouping' of 1923, when it became a constituent part of the new London & North Eastern Railway.

Note on currency and measurements

Sterling currency during the NBR's existence was in pounds, shillings and pence (12 pence to a shilling, 20 shillings to a pound. The old penny (abbreviated to 'd') was divided into two halfpence, and four farthings. At a time when skilled men earned a pound a week, farthings were significant. Guineas (21 shillings) were often quoted in directorial and professional fees. Measurements were in miles, furlongs, chains, yards, feet and inches (8 furlongs to the mile, 10 chains to the furlong, 22 yards to the chain). Ground measurements were in acres (1 acre=4,840 square yards). Heavy weights were measured in hundredweights (112 lbs) and tons (2,240 lbs).

ACKNOWLEDGEMENTS

This book was researched primarily in the Historical Research Room of the National Records of Scotland at Register House, Edinburgh, and the author is again grateful to its ever-obliging and helpful staff. The Glasgow University Archive Service, the Mitchell Library, Glasgow, the National Library of Scotland, the National Railway Museum, York, and the Post Office Museum, London, have been further important sources of documents and publications, and I have also been grateful to examine the C.J.A. Robertson Collection in St. Andrews University Library, the J.F. McEwan Collection held in the James Patrick Library, Kirkintilloch, and the North British materials held by Glasgow Museums Resource Centre. The range of newspapers and official documents studied would have been virtually impossible to peruse only a few years ago, and has been made feasible by the National Library of Scotland's provision of access to the on-line archive of nineteenth century British newspapers, and to the *Scotsman* and Parliamentary Papers archives. The NLS on-line map archive is a further boon to the railway history researcher.

Donald M. Cattanach, chairman of the North British Railway Study Group, has generously allowed me to read, and to quote from, the text of his unpublished *G.B. Wieland of the North British Railway*, which sheds much light on that remarkable man and his colleagues. He also read an early draft of the present text and has given invaluable advice and help in many other ways. Dr. John McGregor, author of *The West Highland Railway: Plans, Politics and People*, kindly read my account of the West Highland. I am very much indebted to both for their corrections and suggestions. Mistakes, as well as opinions expressed, are entirely the responsibility of the author. For helpful pointings in the right direction, thanks are also due to John Yellowlees of Scotrail and John Messner of the Riverside Museum, Glasgow. Dr. Warwick Wolseley kindly provided articles from the Proceedings of the East Lothian Historical Association on the Aberlady & Gullane and Gifford & Garvald lines.

The range of illustrations was made possible by the help of Ed. McKenna, Archivist of the North British Railway Study Group, of John Alsop, Richard Stenlake and Donald Cattanach from their collections, of Glasgow Museums Resource Centre, and of the National Records of Scotland and the BRB (Residuary), all of whom are gratefully acknowledged. For looking out the portrait of John Stirling of Kippendavie, which has never been reproduced before, and allowing me to use it, I am particularly indebted to Mr. and Mrs. Stirling-Aird, of Kippendavie House, Dunblane. Thanks are due also to Allan Rodgers for checking the maps, and allowing adaptation of one of his superb Waverley maps.

On-going research into all aspects of the North British is maintained by the North British Railway Study Group, which publishes a regular Journal. It welcomes new members and its web site gives full details of its resources and activities.

6

Wormit Station and the second Tay Bridge.

Wagons at Whifflet

The North British Railway System

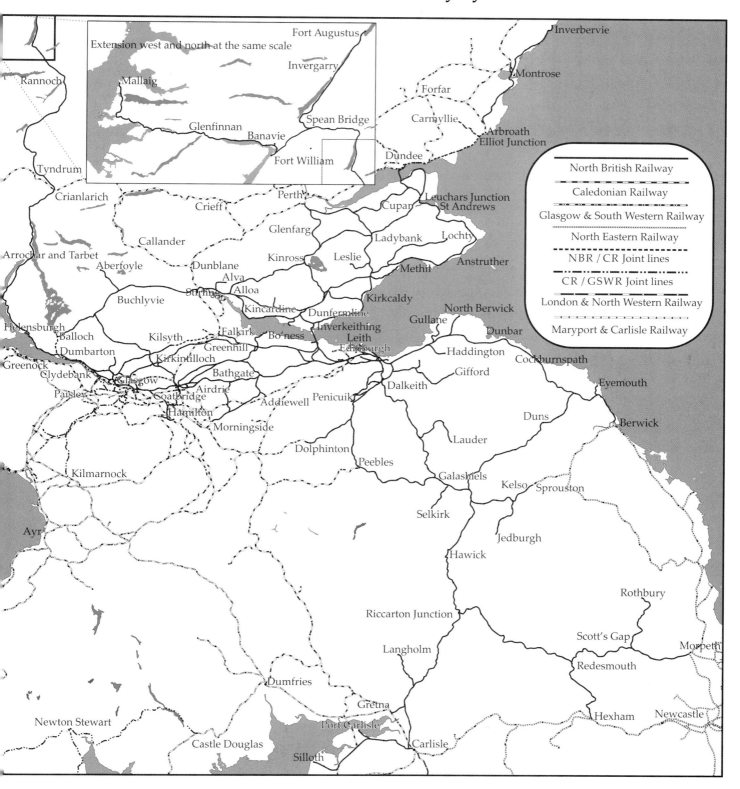

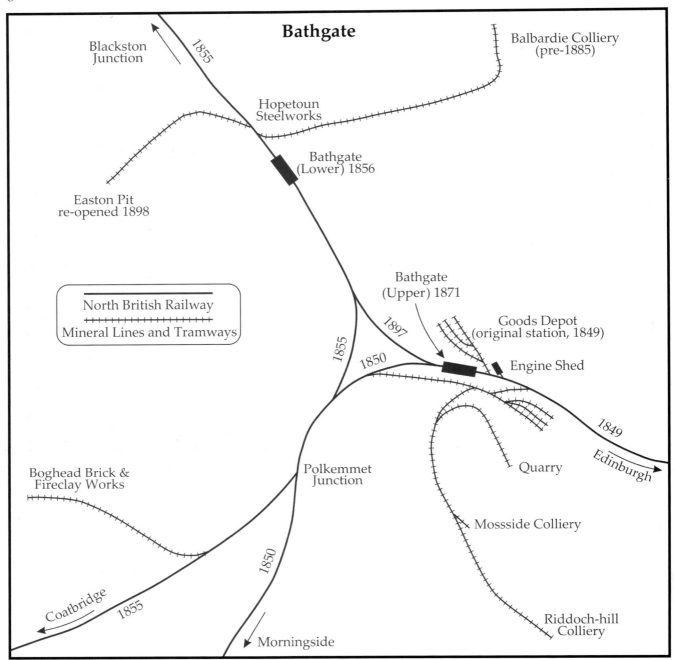

Bathgate

Blackston Junction

1855

Balbardie Colliery (pre-1885)

Hopetoun Steelworks

Bathgate (Lower) 1856

Easton Pit re-opened 1898

Bathgate (Upper) 1871

Goods Depot (original station, 1849)

North British Railway

Mineral Lines and Tramways

1897

Engine Shed

1855

1850

1849

Edinburgh

Quarry

Boghead Brick & Fireclay Works

Polkemmet Junction

Mossside Colliery

Coatbridge

1855

1850

Riddoch-hill Colliery

Morningside

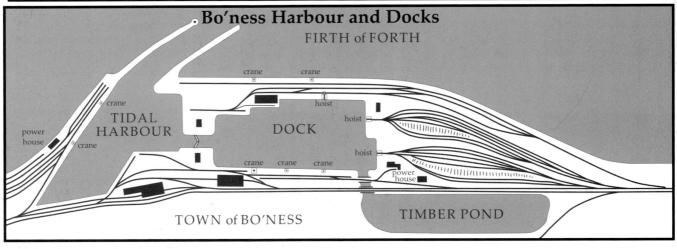

Bo'ness Harbour and Docks

FIRTH of FORTH

crane

crane

hoist

power house

crane

TIDAL HARBOUR

hoist

DOCK

crane

hoist

crane

crane

crane

power house

TOWN of BO'NESS

TIMBER POND

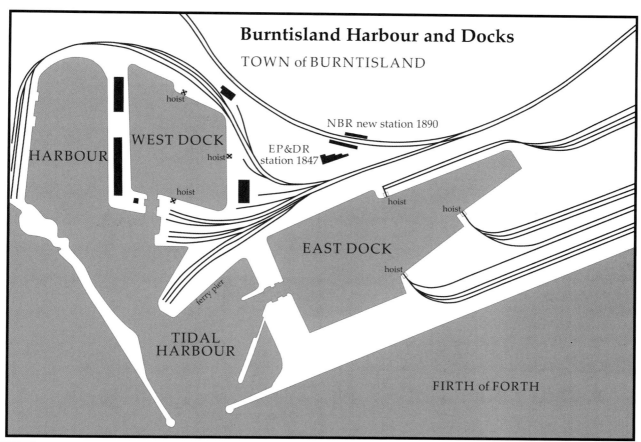

Burntisland Harbour and Docks

TOWN of BURNTISLAND

hoist

WEST DOCK

HARBOUR

NBR new station 1890

EP&DR
station 1847

hoist

hoist

hoist

hoist

EAST DOCK

hoist

ferry pier

TIDAL
HARBOUR

FIRTH of FORTH

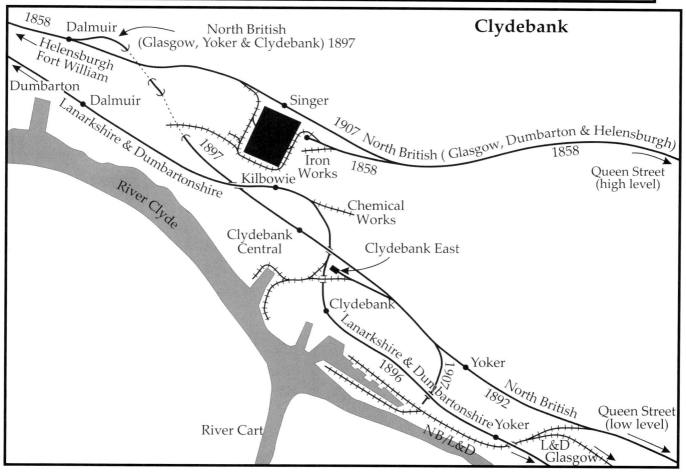

Clydebank

1858 Dalmuir

North British
(Glasgow, Yoker & Clydebank) 1897

Helensburgh
Fort William

Dumbarton

Dalmuir

Lanarkshire & Dumbartonshire

Singer

1907 North British (Glasgow, Dumbarton & Helensburgh)

1897

1858

Kilbowie

Iron
Works

1858

Queen Street
(high level)

River Clyde

Chemical
Works

Clydebank
Central

Clydebank East

Clydebank

Lanarkshire & Dumbartonshire

1896

1907

Yoker

North British

1892

Queen Street
(low level)

River Cart

NB/L&D

Yoker

L&D
Glasgow

10

Coatbridge and Airdrie

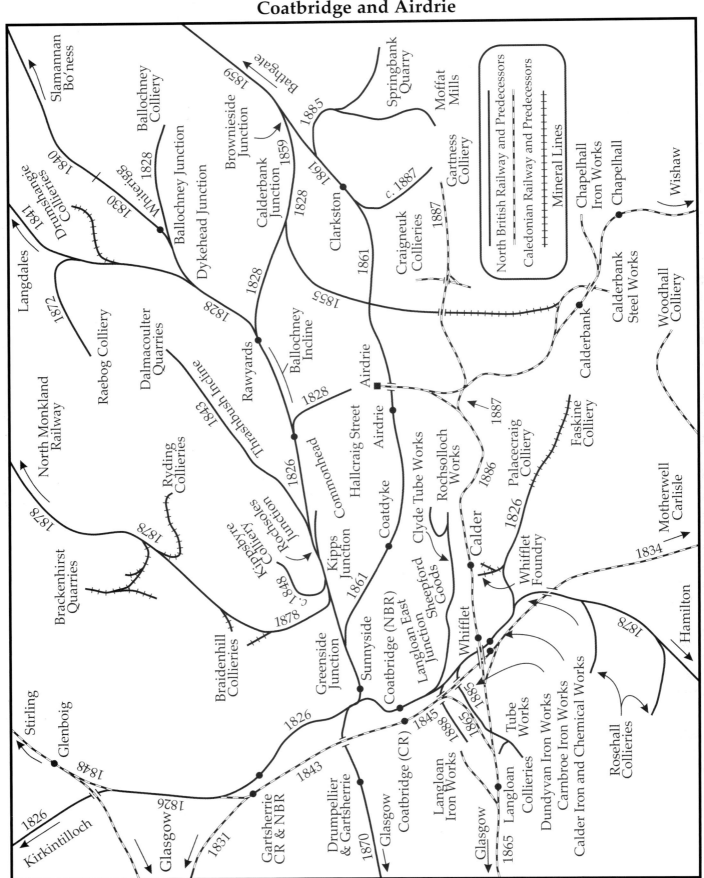

Dalkeith, Penicuik and the Esk Valley lines

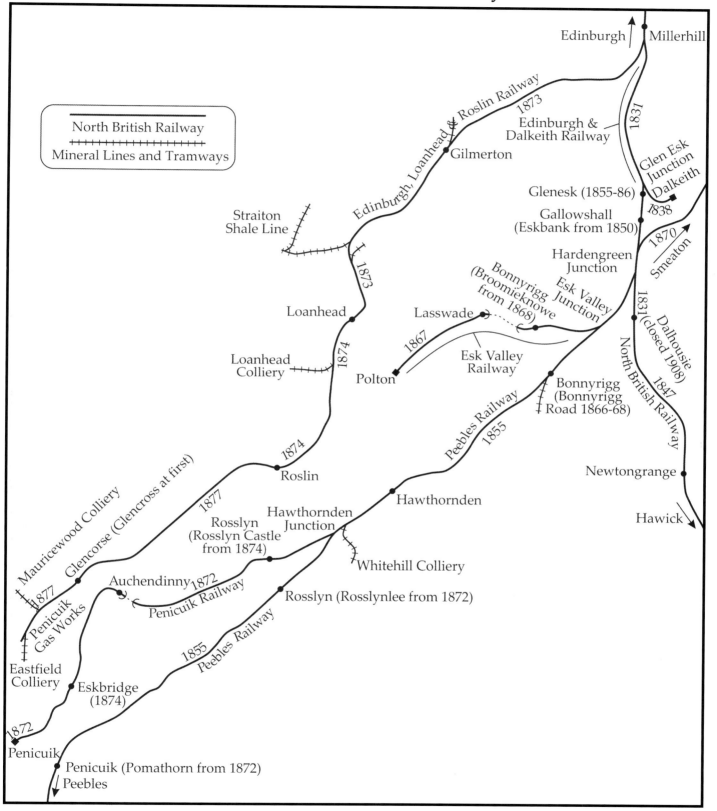

North British Railway
Mineral Lines and Tramways

Edinburgh
Millerhill

Edinburgh, Loanhead & Roslin Railway
1873

Edinburgh &
Dalkeith Railway

1831

Glen Esk
Junction
Dalkeith

Gilmerton

Glenesk (1855-86)
1838

Straiton
Shale Line

Gallowshall
(Eskbank from 1850)

1870
Smeaton

Hardengreen
Junction

1873

Bonnyrigg
(Broomieknowe
from 1868)

Esk Valley
Junction

Loanhead

Lasswade

1867

1831 (closed 1908)

North British Railway

Loanhead
Colliery

1874

Polton

Esk Valley
Railway

Bonnyrigg
(Bonnyrigg
Road 1866-68)

1847

Peebles Railway
1855

1874

Newtongrange

Mauricewood Colliery

Roslin

Hawthornden

Hawick

1877

Glencorse (Glencross at first)

Hawthornden
Junction

Rosslyn
(Rosslyn Castle
from 1874)

Whitehill Colliery

1877

Penicuik
Gas Works

Auchendinny 1872
Penicuik Railway

Rosslyn (Rosslynlee from 1872)

Eastfield
Colliery

1855
Peebles Railway

1872

Eskbridge
(1874)

Penicuik

Penicuik (Pomathorn from 1872)
Peebles

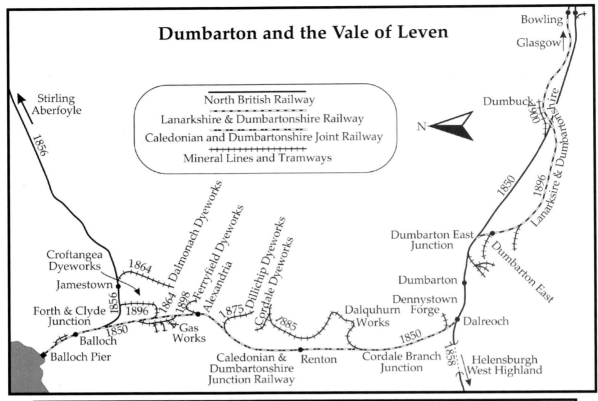

Dumbarton and the Vale of Leven

North British Railway
Lanarkshire & Dumbartonshire Railway
Caledonian and Dumbartonshire Joint Railway
Mineral Lines and Tramways

N

Bowling
Glasgow
Dumbuck
1900
1850
1896
Lanarkshire & Dumbartonshire
Stirling
Aberfoyle
1856
Dumbarton East
Junction
Dumbarton East
Croftangea
Dyeworks
1864
Dalmonach Dyeworks
Ferryfield Dyeworks
Dillichip Dyeworks
Cordale Dyeworks
Dumbarton
Jamestown
1859
Alexandria
Dennystown
Forge
Dalreoch
Forth & Clyde
Junction
1896
1864
1898
1875
1885
Dalquhurn
Works
1850
1858
1850
Balloch
Gas
Works
Caledonian &
Dumbartonshire
Junction Railway
Renton
Cordale Branch
Junction
Helensburgh
West Highland
Balloch Pier

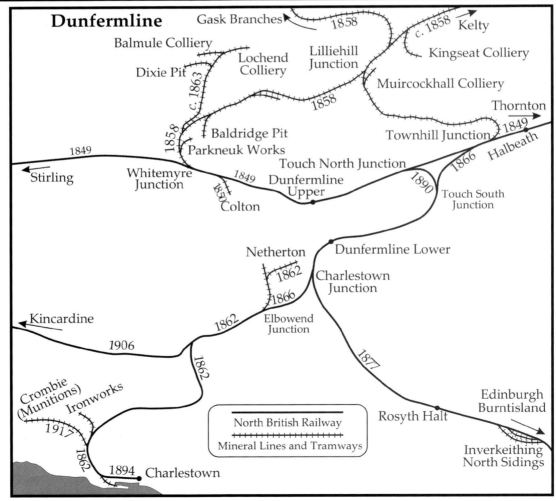

Dunfermline

Gask Branches
1858
c. 1858
Kelty
Balmule Colliery
Lilliehill
Junction
Kingseat Colliery
Dixie Pit
c. 1863
Lochend
Colliery
Muircockhall Colliery
1858
Thornton
1849
Townhill Junction
1849
1858
Baldridge Pit
Parkneuk Works
1866
Halbeath
Stirling
Whitemyre
Junction
1849
Touch North Junction
1890
Dunfermline
Upper
Touch South
Junction
1850
Colton
Netherton
1862
Dunfermline Lower
Charlestown
Junction
1866
Kincardine
1862
Elbowend
Junction
1862
1906
1877
Crombie
(Munitions)
Ironworks
Edinburgh
Burntisland
1917
Rosyth Halt
1862
1894
Charlestown
Inverkeithing
North Sidings

North British Railway
Mineral Lines and Tramways

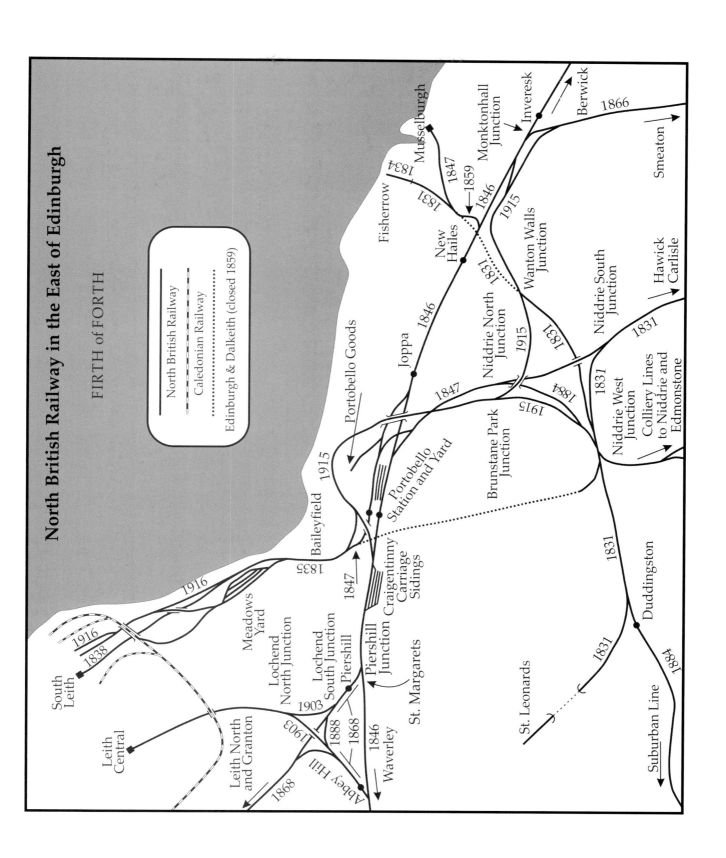

North British Railway in the East of Edinburgh

FIRTH of FORTH

Legend:
- North British Railway
- Caledonian Railway
- Edinburgh & Dalkeith (closed 1859)

13

North British Railway in the East of Glasgow

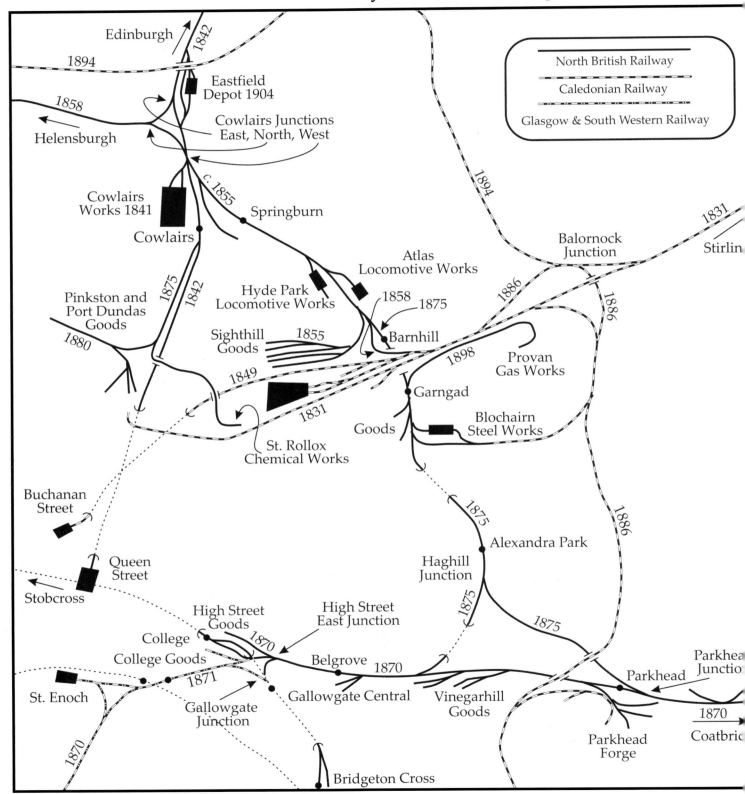

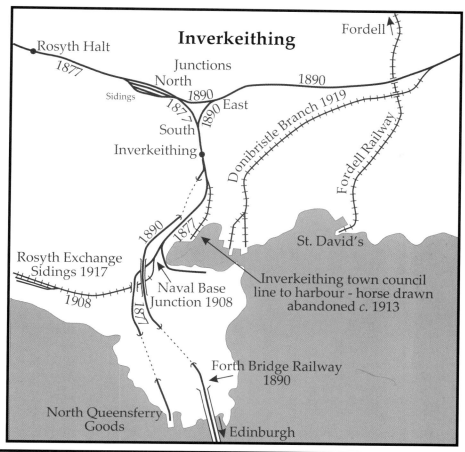

Inverkeithing

Fordell

Rosyth Halt
1877

Junctions
North
1890 East
1877 *1890*
South
Sidings
1890

Inverkeithing

Donibristle Branch 1919

Fordell Railway

St. David's

Inverkeithing town council
line to harbour - horse drawn
abandoned *c.* 1913

Rosyth Exchange
Sidings 1917
1908
1890 *1877*

Naval Base
Junction 1908

1877

Forth Bridge Railway
1890

North Queensferry
Goods

Edinburgh

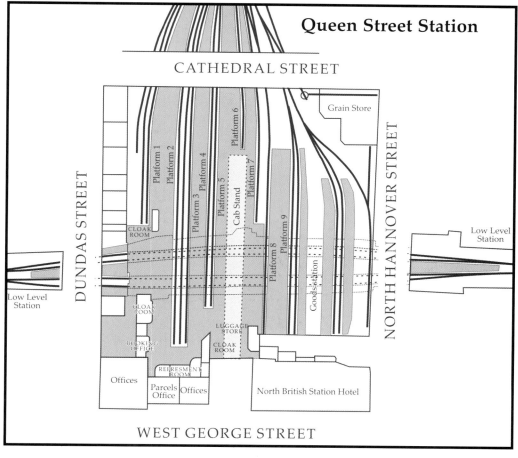

Queen Street Station

CATHEDRAL STREET

Grain Store

Platform 1
Platform 2
Platform 3
Platform 4
Platform 5
Platform 6
Cab Stand
Platform 7
Platform 8
Platform 9
Goods station

DUNDAS STREET

NORTH HANNOVER STREET

Low Level
Station

Low Level
Station

CLOAK ROOM

CLOAK ROOM

BOOKING OFFICE

LUGGAGE STORE

CLOAK ROOM

Offices

REFRESHMENT ROOM

Parcels Office

Offices

North British Station Hotel

WEST GEORGE STREET

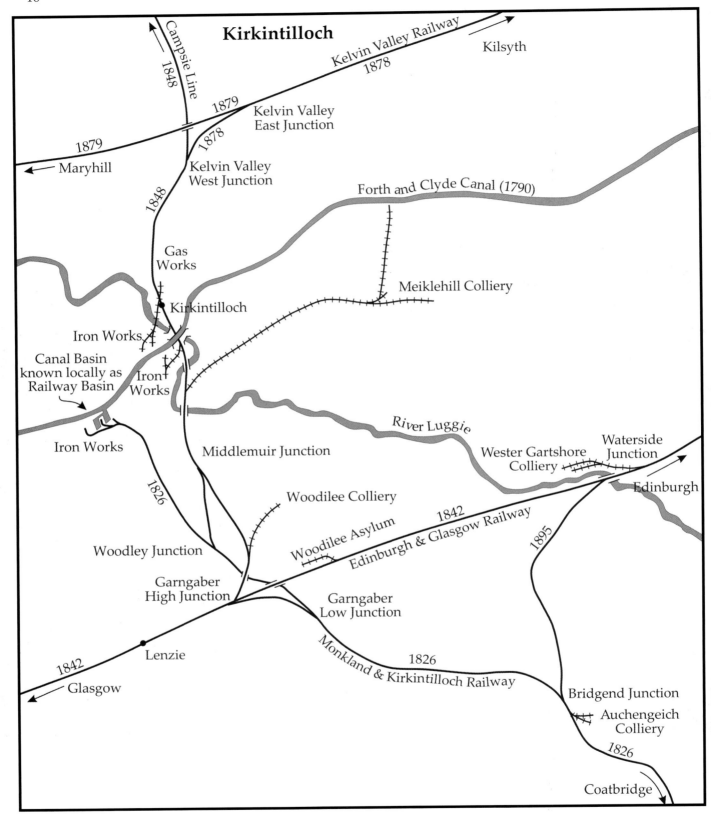

Kirkintilloch

Campsie Line 1848

Kelvin Valley Railway 1878

Kilsyth

1879

1879

Kelvin Valley East Junction

1878

Maryhill

Kelvin Valley West Junction

1848

Forth and Clyde Canal (1790)

Gas Works

Meiklehill Colliery

Kirkintilloch

Iron Works

Canal Basin known locally as Railway Basin

Iron Works

Iron Works

River Luggie

Middlemuir Junction

Wester Gartshore Colliery

Waterside Junction

Edinburgh

1826

Woodilee Colliery

Edinburgh & Glasgow Railway 1842

1895

Woodley Junction

Woodilee Asylum

Garngaber High Junction

Garngaber Low Junction

Lenzie

Monkland & Kirkintilloch Railway 1826

1842

Glasgow

Bridgend Junction

Auchengeich Colliery

1826

Coatbridge

Leven and Methil

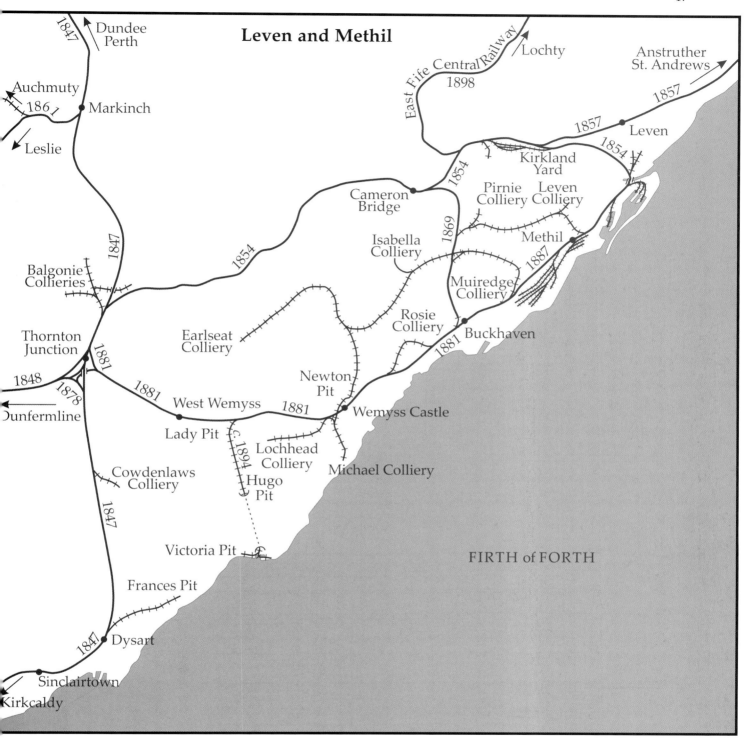

1847 → Dundee Perth

Auchmuty
1861 ● Markinch
→ Leslie

East Fife Central Railway → Lochty
1898

Anstruther St. Andrews →
1857

1857 ● Leven

1854
1847

Kirkland Yard
Pirnie Colliery   Leven Colliery

Balgonie Collieries

1854

Cameron Bridge

1869

Isabella Colliery

Methil

1887

Muiredge Colliery

Thornton Junction

1881

Rosie Colliery

Buckhaven

1848
1878

1881

Earlseat Colliery

1881

Dunfermline

West Wemyss

1881

Newton Pit

Wemyss Castle

Lady Pit

c. 1894

Lochhead Colliery

Michael Colliery

Cowdenlaws Colliery

Hugo Pit

1847

FIRTH of FORTH

Victoria Pit

Frances Pit

1847

1847 ● Dysart

Sinclairtown
Kirkcaldy

18

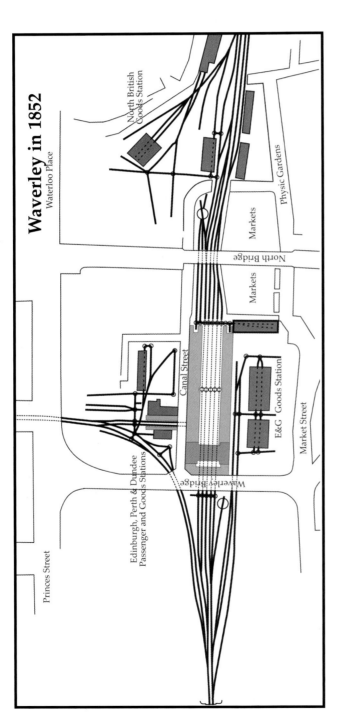

Waverley in 1852

Waterloo Place

North British Goods Station

Physic Gardens

Markets

North Bridge

Markets

Canal Street

Edinburgh, Perth & Dundee Passenger and Goods Stations

E&G Goods Station

Market Street

Waverley Bridge

Princes Street

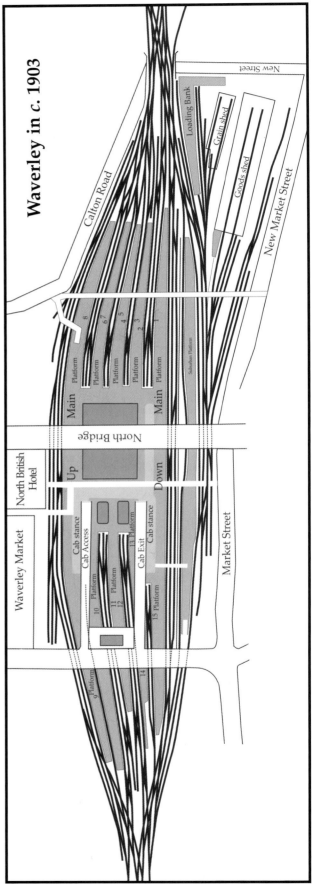

Waverley in c. 1903

Calton Road

New Street

Loading Bank

Grain shed

Goods shed

New Market Street

8

6 7

4 5

2 3

1

Platform

Platform

Platform

Platform

Platform

Main

Main

Suburban Platform

North Bridge

North British Hotel

Up

Down

Waverley Market

Cab stance

Cab Access

Cab Exit

Cab stance

13 Platform

10 Platform

11 Platform

12

15 Platform

14

9 Platform

Market Street

1. LEARMONTH'S RAILWAY 1, 1842–1844

The City of Edinburgh entered the steam railway age on 18 February 1842, when the Edinburgh & Glasgow Railway opened between a terminus at Haymarket at the outer edge of Edinburgh's 'New Town', and another at Dundas Street (soon renamed Queen Street) Station in Glasgow. A railway had been in operation between St. Leonards, south-east of the city centre, and Dalkeith, for just over ten years, but though its act had allowed for locomotives, it was horse-worked, more akin to the old colliery tramways, primarily concerned with bringing coal from the Dalkeith collieries down to the fires of Auld Reekie and the port of Leith. The new line was very different. Built to George Stephenson's 4 feet 8½ inch gauge (not yet confirmed as standard), it was double-track, almost level for nearly all its route, worked by steam locomotives, and intended to carry passengers at speeds never before experienced in Scotland. From the first, it was a success.

The origin of the North British is displayed in its emblem, which combines the arms of the City of Edinburgh and the Borough of Berwick upon Tweed.

Promoters from both cities created the Edinburgh & Glasgow company, proposed in 1835 and incorporated in 1838. At that time, some of the capital's leading citizens were concerned about their city's future. It had few industries apart from brewing, although coal pits were being sunk quite close by. For centuries it had been Scotland's most populous town, but within living memory, it had been overtaken by Glasgow, where new factories were going up constantly, new residents were streaming in, and a strong sense of civic ambition was looking to the future. Edinburgh was faced with the prospect of genteel decline unless it too embraced the new forces of coal, iron and steam. A railway link to Glasgow was seen both as a token and a powerful agent of regeneration. The project was taken up vigorously by John Learmonth, a prominent citizen and former Lord Provost, owner of the Dean estate just west of the New Town, who became chairman of the Edinburgh Committee and deputy chairman of the whole venture. His family business had been coach-building[1], which perhaps enhanced his interest in railways. Head of the Glasgow Committee, and company chairman, was John Leadbetter, born in Penicuik but long a Glasgow linen merchant. But other, equally ambitious railway schemes were also being contemplated in Edinburgh. In 1836 plans had been introduced for a railway leading south-east from the city, the Edinburgh, Haddington & Dunbar Railway and a public meeting in November backed a proposal for another line, via Jedburgh and under Carter Fell, to Newcastle[2]. These ventures were not taken further. Then on 24 October 1838 a large meeting unanimously supported a new proposal for a 'Great Northern Junction Railway', and in February 1839 its prospectus was published, renamed 'The Great North British Railway', and looking to raise capital of £2,000,000 in £50 shares for a line to link Edinburgh, Berwick and Newcastle. Learmonth was a member of its Provisional Committee, though he did not play a leading part[3]. There was also a strong Newcastle Committee. The route had been surveyed by George Stephenson, who remarked that "I must say that, in the whole course of my experience, I never examined a country for a line of railway of the length this will be, where the works to be executed were of an easier description, or the levels and inclination of a more favourable nature"[4]. Local committees had been formed in Berwick, led by the town's M.P., Richard Hodgson, a future chairman of the North British, and in Dunbar, and the plans were "nearly ready to be deposited". At another well-attended promotional meeting in Edinburgh in July 1839, it was noted that a "midland" line had also been surveyed, to run from the Newcastle and Carlisle Railway (completed that year) at Hexham north to Melrose, Galashiels and Edinburgh, with a three-mile tunnel under the Cheviots[5]. Surprisingly, no mention was made of the active promotion on the west side of the country of two potential routes between Carlisle and Glasgow. John Miller, of the leading Scottish engineering partnership Grainger & Miller, had surveyed one of these, via Dumfries and Nithsdale. Grainger & Miller were the engineers of the Edinburgh & Glasgow line, and were also named, with George & Robert Stephenson, as engineers of the Great North British Railway.

The general opinion was that only one railway line between England and the two main Scottish cities was needed, whether it came via Berwick or Carlisle. In the event, the Government's appointment in 1840 of a commission to investigate the alternative railway routes between London, Edinburgh and Glasgow put every cross-border scheme on hold, while the commissioners, Professor Peter Barlow and Sir Frederick Smith, R.E., were bombarded with information and propaganda by the competing promoters. (In May 1840, though, the *Newcastle Journal* commented on the "quiescence" of the Edinburgh-Newcastle promoters while "Numberless extravagant puffs" appeared for the Carlisle-Glasgow route[6]). The commissioners' report, on 15 March 1841, recommended the Caledonian Railway route from Carlisle (via Annandale and Beattock), to Glasgow, with a branch to Edinburgh. Although they did not completely close the door on an 'East Coast' route, evidently feeling some doubt about the western side's finances and likely time-scale, the impact was discouraging[7], and the Great North British project sank from sight. During the hiatus on north-south development, construction of the Edinburgh-Glasgow line was going ahead, but there was dissension between the committees at each end. Learmonth accused Leadbetter of betraying the Edinburgh interests, of profligate expenditure, and even hinted at financial chicanery[8]. By late 1841, things had been patched up, but tension in railway matters between the two cities did not go away. Other parties were also interested in the E&G's affairs: a substantial proportion of its shares had been taken up in England, mostly by merchants and traders in Liverpool and Manchester, who had always been supportive of trunk railways between major cities.

John Learmonth, first chairman of the NBR, from 1844 to 1852
(Glasgow Museums)

It soon became clear that the Caledonian promoters were having difficulty in raising the capital they needed. The British economy was in recession, money was tight, and investors cautious. While a multi-million pound railway scheme might be impossible to float, however, a more limited venture could still be possible. In January 1842 John Learmonth convened a meeting of prominent Edinburgh citizens to promote a line from a terminus by the North Bridge, following the coast to Dunbar. By then he was embroiled with Leadbetter on the subject of Sunday trains. Not only the E&G company, but the entire nation, had been rocked by a huge furore over the company's decision to run some trains on Sundays. An atmosphere of religious earnestness scarcely conceivable today cloaked Scotland in the early 1840s, as the national church, hopelessly split on the issue of its relationship with the state, edged towards the Disruption which would take place in 1843. Sunday trains were seen as flouting God's commandment. Leadbetter, a Sabbatarian, resigned the chair when a board majority (urged on by English shareholders) voted for Sunday trains, and Learmonth was elected in his place[9]. This was very far from being the end of the Sunday trains controversy.

Meanwhile, another railway, under separate auspices, was also under construction in Edinburgh. This was the short Edinburgh, Leith & Newhaven Railway, authorised in 1836, which opened on 31 August 1842 between Canonmills (Scotland Street) and a terminus at Newhaven. It was horse-drawn at first. Canonmills was well to the north of the city centre, but the company was building a tunnel from Scotland Street to a central site on the south side of Princes Street, between the North Bridge and the Mound[10]. As originally planned, the Edinburgh & Glasgow Railway was also to terminate at the North Bridge, and the town council approved a station on the site of the Shambles (slaughterhouses) under the bridge. Parliament, however, influenced by petitions against a railway cutting through Princes Street Gardens, while approving the company's Bill, compelled it to terminate at Haymarket[11]. Though some of its Glasgow-based directors thought Haymarket was perfectly adequate as an Edinburgh terminal site, the E&G company did not abandon the desire for a central station. In the debate, the Edinburgh & Glasgow's dual-committee structure – "two kitchens to dress one dinner" – was fiercely criticised by an English shareholder[12].

The Edinburgh & Dunbar committee held its first meeting on 8 January 1842. They hoped to buy the plans drawn up for the 'Great North British Railway' to save the expense of a new survey, and agreed that their own company's name should be The North British Railway[13]. A first prospectus was issued early in February 1842, for a 28 1/2 mile line from the North Bridge to Dunbar, with a branch to Haddington. The cost, exclusive of stations and rolling stock, was estimated at £464,000. The capital required was put at £500,000. Grainger & Miller were appointed engineers, to be paid at four guineas a day (in Scotland) and five when in London, though not to receive anything until the company's Bill was passed by Parliament. In the event of the Bill failing, they would receive only two guineas a day for work done in Scotland, and if the company funds were insufficient, they would get only their costs[14]. From the beginning, the engineers got the message that the NBR was not a company to throw its money about on constructional aspects. Within a month a revised prospectus was issued, to include a line from near Portobello to meet the Edinburgh & Dalkeith's branch to Leith[15]. Dunbar was an important herring port and a new harbour was planned, but Learmonth made it clear that it was only a first base on the route south, and the line kept to the south of the town and did not include a harbour branch[16]. Haddington had been on the line in Miller's early surveys and was not pleased to be relegated to the end of a branch with the further stipulation that of the branch's estimated cost of £30,000-plus, the townspeople would have to raise "a fair proportion"[17]: numerous meetings and representations would follow, to no avail.

Although Learmonth was chairman of the Edinburgh committee of the E&G (and of the whole company from 25 August 1842), the North British was never an offshoot of the Glasgow line, but very much an Edinburgh company. At a public meeting in the city on 8 February 1842, the hope was voiced that it would make Edinburgh "the depot of goods coming from England to all Scotland"[18]. A quick drive to raise capital for the East Coast Route would pre-empt the Caledonian Railway and preferably kill it off altogether. In June 1842 Learmonth and another committee member went to meet the directors of some English railways but came back with a gloomy report on the likelihood of getting financial backing in the then current economic climate[19], though hoping things would improve from August. Efforts went on to build up a list of shareholders and assure the capital, but the response was slow and small. The route was re-surveyed, to allow steeper gradients and tighter curves in order to reduce construction costs, saving £40,000, but the committee was struggling to amass enough funds to be able to lodge a Bill with Parliament which would require the depositing of 10% of the capital. By October 1842, the subscription price of 10s per share had been paid on only 1,905 shares; expenses so far were £877 and the deposits amounted to £952 10s. Even the balance of £75 10s was needed to pay for the Great North British Railway committee's plans[20]. The West Coast promoters were also suffering delay for the same reasons, but the Darlington-Newcastle line was under construction, bringing the prospect of an East Coast link closer. Still, it was decided to suspend the proceedings for a season, with no application for a Bill before Parliament's 1844 session.

In the Spring of 1843, Learmonth became convinced that the project would look better to potential investors if it were an Edinburgh-Berwick line, the Dunbar project being too "local". In this he was influenced by George Hudson, the York-based railway promoter extraordinaire who, with George and Robert Stephenson as allies, was mastermind of the London-Scotland trunk line on the eastern side of Great Britain. Hudson was keen to get the complete line authorised and was still hoping for some Government funding[21]. A circular was published in July announcing a new plan to build all the way to Berwick on Tweed, 56 miles, with a capital of £900,000. To help costs, contractors would be required to take one third of their payment in shares[22]. A memorial despatched to the Treasury, claiming that the West Coast project had "utterly failed" and asking for "every facility that Government can afford", was politely

An Edinburgh & Glasgow Railway milepost at Eastfield. (*North British Railway Study Group*)

rebuffed by Robert Peel, stating that the Government was neutral on the issue[23]. Edinburgh & Glasgow Railway shareholders were urged to put money into the NBR, on the basis that even if it paid no dividend at all, the extra business accruing to the E&G would benefit them[24]. An E&G resolution in August to apply for sanction to extend its line eastwards from Haymarket to the North Bridge was the product of a deal with the Newhaven company for Leith traffic. The chairman said there was "no certainty" of a junction with the Berwick line, but by September this link was agreed, hailed by the *Scotsman* as "a great advance in every way"[25]. John Miller was instructed to make yet another survey of the line with the aim of reducing construction costs further "with due regard to safe operation". At a shareholders' meeting on 14 November 1843, with the Bill for incorporation about to be presented to Parliament, the capital requirement was revised down to £800,000, in £25 shares. There were to be twelve directors, qualified by ownership of at least 20 shares[26]. An initial annual revenue of £109,549 was expected, with working expenses at 33.33% leaving a balance of £73,033 for the shareholders. A sense of purpose was strong. Miller met Robert Stephenson to discuss the Tweed crossing and arrangements were made with John Wilson of the Dundyvan Ironworks, at Coatbridge, to supply rails at £8 per ton, paid for by two-thirds cash and one-third in shares. The Great North British Railway had agreed in April 1839 to pay off half the Berwickshire Road Trustees' debt of around £18,000 on its opening. The NBR did the same, in order to deflect objections to its Bill[27]. Miller's new plan took the line closer to Dunbar but Haddington remained on a branch – a deputation from the town to the promoters said, a little quaintly, that Haddington people did not want a railway at all, but if they must, then the main line "would do less harm" than a branch. A proposal to work the steeply-graded branch by 'atmospheric railway' was considered but not followed up[28].

While the NBR Bill was being scrutinised by a House of Commons Committee in the spring of 1844, the sale of shares speeded up. A deputation from Edinburgh, headed by Learmonth, went to London to oversee their Bill's progress. It was clear that there was relatively little opposition, and advertisements in English papers, offering NBR shares at par, had already warned that the subscription was filling up fast[29]. But the Caledonian project was also warming up, and Learmonth joined the provisional committee of its rival line, the Glasgow, Dumfries & Carlisle Railway, whose chairman was his E&G colleague, John Leadbetter. Although this too would be a through line into England, its great appeal to the NBR was that it did not come anywhere near Edinburgh[30]. John Miller, with Robert Stephenson to back him up, gave evidence to support the relatively low cost of £14,285 a mile for the NBR's double-track line. As an allied company, and foreseeing lucrative English traffic, the Edinburgh & Glasgow company of course supported the North British project. The Dalkeith Railway, having first been co-operative, switched to oppose, anticipating a loss of traffic[31], as did the Edinburgh, Leith & Newhaven, claiming the proposed Edinburgh station would encroach on the land it had acquired for its own central terminus, but the Commons passed the Bill, noting that among property owners or occupiers along the line, 1,308 were in favour, 440 were neutral, and only 58 against it[32]. A price had been paid for this: the London deputation made expensive agreements on land prices with several large proprietors, including the Marquis of Abercorn, the Earl of Wemyss, and Mr. Miller of Craigentinny, in order to avoid their opposition to the Bill. Purchase of the Edinburgh & Dalkeith Railway was also – in part at least – to remove its opposition to the North British Bill. Before Learmonth and his colleagues left for London, the Edinburgh & Dalkeith Railway directors had offered to sell their line for £120,000; in London £133,000 was agreed and Learmonth admitted that the avoidance of a contest "weighed to a certain extent", in a lengthy justification of the purchase to the somewhat surprised subscribers[33]. In anticipation of success a three-year lease was taken on 18 St. Andrew Square, Edinburgh, for offices. By the time the line opened, the NBR had moved to No. 24. The House of Lords Committee passed the Bill with only minor amendments, such as screening to be put between Holyrood Palace and the railway. The Caledonian Railway, though it had entered objections, did not make a formal appearance.

Back in 1843, the York & North Midland Railway, part of George Hudson's empire, had invested £100 in NBR shares, and in May 1844 it obtained powers to raise £50,000 "for the North British Railway". Shares to the value of £21,250 were duly purchased, and later sold by Hudson, who allegedly kept the proceeds[34]. But this is not wholly true: the York & North Midland Railway accounts for January-June 1846 show £10,000 received from sale of NBR shares[35]. The NBR committee had also hoped that the London & Birmingham Railway would take from 2,000 to 4,000 shares and thus become an ally, but it did not do so, though it promised neutrality in the battle between the North British and Caledonian to gain the Anglo-Scottish route[36].

2. LEARMONTH'S RAILWAY 2 1844-1847

The North British Act received the royal assent on 4 July 1844 and the directors held their first meeting of the incorporated company four days later. Learmonth was elected chairman, with Eagle Henderson, an Edinburgh merchant and a director of the Edinburgh-based Standard Life Assurance Co., as deputy. Charles Davidson, a lawyer who had been secretary to the Great North British project, was appointed secretary, at £1,000 a year. Another director was George Hudson, noted as "the English Director", who accepted an honorarium of £50 for his help in establishing the company. A newly-formed railway company had two immediate needs, to start calling in its share capital and to get down to building its line. Grainger & Miller were confirmed as engineers. Building time was expected to be so short that locomotives and carriages were ordered at the start (although they had not been included in the £800,000 capital), as well as rails, at 70lb to the yard, sleepers and chairs. The new board also embarked on hiring staff. The site of Meadowbank Brewery, required by the railway, was owned by the eminent civil engineer James Walker, who demanded £15,000. The company offered £6,300; Walker took the matter to court and was awarded £6,232 and had to pay half the costs[1]. Many shareholders objected to the purchase of the Edinburgh & Dalkeith Railway, which had "hitherto been the reverse of lucrative to its proprietors"[2], though Learmonth assured them that the Dalkeith company's operating costs, currently 54.25% of its revenue, would be brought down to a third once it was converted to locomotive haulage[3]. Like other 'quaint' lines, the Edinburgh & Dalkeith Railway generated stories: passengers were said to be reluctant to confide their destinations to the ticket seller, "yon speirin' loon"[4]. The purchase may have been a tactical one, but soon it became clear that John Learmonth had much more in mind than providing the northern end of a London-Edinburgh railway. Even before the NBR Bill was passed, John Miller had been instructed to take a flying survey of the country south of Dalkeith for a possible extension that would link up at Kelso with a cross-country line from Berwick[5]. On 19 December a special meeting of shareholders was held to consider the company's proposals for a railway to Hawick, and the investing of £25,000 in the Edinburgh & Northern Railway, which was proposing to build a line through Fife from Burntisland to Perth and Cupar. The Hawick line would extend from the Edinburgh & Dalkeith's terminus at Dalhousie Mains. Objectors pointed out that at 52 miles it was almost as long as the Berwick line. Learmonth's motive was widely debated: "We suspect that the Galashiels and Hawick line has been brought forward partly as a rival to the Caledonian"[6]. Describing the line as a "protective" one, he disclaimed any intention of extending it to Carlisle. Rivalry with the Caledonian Railway, which had yet to be authorised by Parliament, was obvious: at a shareholders' meeting called to discuss the board's plans, one shareholder had suggested that opponents to the board's policy were Caledonian stooges. Learmonth informed the meeting that "I think it is not fair for any gentleman to attack estimates which have met with the approval of the directors", and cited the London & North Western Railway which had doubled its capital with the shareholders' approval, and proposed seven new projects, "and the shareholders at once swallowed them all"[7]. Clearly Learmonth intended himself, and his company, to be major players in the development of a Scottish railway system; and for his shareholders to accept what was put before them. A vote was demanded, but the board had a substantial majority.

The original Burntisland terminus building, of the Edinburgh & Northern Railway, built 1847.
(*North British Railway Study Group*)

As a result of this highly proactive approach, while the business of construction went on through 1845, the North British directors, or some of them, were kept busy by inter-company diplomacy and plotting. The feverish atmosphere was heightened by a wild proliferation of new railway schemes, each with its distinguished committee of titled promoters, each requiring capital amounts that were as dreamily remote from the modest scale of most businesses as bank lending, or losses, seem today. In July 1845 the *Glasgow Herald* published a list of 90 persons in Scotland who had subscribed £10,000 or more to new railway schemes. Top of the list was John Learmonth with £108,000. Close behind were Archibald Smith, merchant of Edinburgh, with £107,000, and James McCall of Daldowie, chairman of the Glasgow, Paisley Kilmarnock & Ayr Railway, with £96,970. Leadbetter was in for £67,650. The railway directors usually put their names down for shares on behalf of their companies or committees, with the intention of later making a distribution among existing shareholders: in this way the £400,000 capital of the Hawick line was subscribed by only twelve persons, "directors of the NBR and their friends"[8]. But some of the investors were mere speculators on a rising market, intending to sell on at a higher price before their own payments fell due. This was the time soon known as the 'Railway Mania', when a sense of urgency to establish modern communication links made unholy alliance with the ever-latent human desire to become rich quickly and easily. Learmonth, Henderson and some other Edinburgh & Glasgow Railway directors were involved in other schemes, including the Scottish Western Railway (capital £700,000) to link the two main cities with "Argyll and other North-western parts of Scotland" by a line from Oban to Tyndrum and then alongside Loch Lomond to Balloch, or possibly via Loch Katrine and Aberfoyle. By 1 November the E&G had given notice of nineteen projects for new lines in Glasgow and the Stirling-Falkirk-Grangemouth district, and was seeking amalgamation with the already-established Scottish Central, Monkland & Kirkintilloch, Ballochney and Slamannan companies[9]. Meanwhile, the Caledonian Railway Act was passed on 31 July, ensuring that another railway to Edinburgh from England was just a matter of time.

Despite opposition, the Bill for an Edinburgh-Hawick Railway became an Act on 21 July 1845, along with the Edinburgh & Dalkeith Railway purchase. A special shareholders' meeting in Edinburgh on 18 August empowered the NBR board to raise further capital of £400,000 to acquire the Edinburgh & Hawick company, plus £160,000 (32,000 £5 shares) for the acquisition and conversion of the Edinburgh & Dalkeith. Learmonth now confirmed that the intention was to continue the Hawick line to Carlisle, to get there "as soon as the Caledonian", and the first of numerous Bills to be introduced for this extension was published in October[10]. Work on the

Berwick line was being pushed on, with the work shared in twelve sections by eleven separate contractors. The main works were the 398-yard Calton Tunnel in Edinburgh and a 266-yard tunnel at Penmanshiel, near the summit at 600 feet above sea level where the railway cut through the Lammermuir Hills, with deep cuttings and high embankments on its approaches. There were 150 bridges, mostly single-span. The engine house and works at Meadowbank were going up on the site of a former dairy. Nearby, the company was also having to construct new buildings for the Piershill Barracks, to replace those demolished for the railway line[11].

The Edinburgh & Glasgow Railway had obtained Parliamentary sanction for its extension from Haymarket to the North Bridge on 4 July 1844[12]. With this line also under construction, in March 1845 Edinburgh Town Council noted that within fifteen months "there will be no less than three railway stations in the immediate vicinity of the North Bridge"[13]. The area was not a salubrious one. At each end of the bridge were high buildings, the Princes Street end containing hotels and taverns and the offices and yards of various businesses, including the Croall coaching company and Russell & Macnee's coachbuilding works on its west side; and the Theatre Royal in Shakespeare Square on the east side. Tight-packed tenements rose at the south end. Canal Street ran downhill on the northern slope past the slaughterhouses and markets, under the North Bridge, curving south under the new railway tracks and alongside the former Physic Garden. Some fine old buildings stood to the east of the Physic Garden, including Trinity Hospital and Trinity College Church. Moray House, in the Canongate, had been bought by the North British so that the hospital could remove to there, and the town council had made conditional agreement (despite protests from conservationists) to the demolition of the fifteenth century church, if the NBR would finance a new building. Its acquisition was authorised in an act of 25 June 1846[14].

Though the bull market in railway shares was beginning to ebb, the mood on the North British was still up-beat. A special shareholders' meeting on 9 February 1846 approved the drafts of four Bills to go before Parliament: the first including branches from the main line to Duns, North Berwick, Tranent and Cockenzie (capital £170,000); the second for branches off the Hawick line to Kelso, Jedburgh, Selkirk and Peebles (capital £770,000); the third for the extension from Hawick to Carlisle (£660,000); and finally a branch from that line to Gretna (£80,000). It added up to £1,680,000 of additional capital. Learmonth's initial disclaimer of interest in Carlisle does not seem to have been challenged. Confidence was boosted by a compact made with the Caledonian Railway, that Peebles would be a 'frontier' beyond which neither company would push in a westerly (NBR) or easterly (Caledonian) direction, and all the proposals were unanimously agreed[15]. Further aims were revealed a week later at the half-yearly shareholders' meeting. The NBR was to lease two proposed lines, the East Lothian Central and Tyne Valley Railways, running through farming and mining country between Dalkeith, Ormiston, Haddington and East Linton. Learmonth did not want a non-NBR railway crossing NBR territory, but though authorised, these lines were never built. His wider strategy encompassed the take-over of the proposed Edinburgh & Perth Railway, whose Bill for a line from North Queensferry via Kinross was currently before Parliament. This latter line would be worked by the NBR at a

The stalk of an Edinburgh and Northern lamp stand. (*Cupar Heritage Centre*)

guaranteed annual return of 4% on capital (£800,000), plus a profit share, with the intention of full amalgamation: four paid-up NBR £25 shares to be given for every five Edinburgh & Perth Railway paid-up £25 shares. Not everyone thought this a good idea: Perth was already being aimed at by the Scottish Central and Edinburgh & Northern companies, and Learmonth was defensive, "If we had not taken the Edinburgh & Perth, the Caledonian or some other rival company might have done so, and diverted the traffic…"[16]. He did not tell the shareholders that the North British board had spent £90,000 to buy up half the Edinburgh & Perth scrip (provisional share certificates): 16,000 shares at £5 per share instead of the required deposit of £1 10s. Nor did he mention that during November and December 1845 he had been negotiating an amalgamation with the Edinburgh & Northern Railway (of which he was chairman), and trying to hustle it also into amalgamation with the Edinburgh & Perth. But the Edinburgh & Northern Railway board, with its line across Fife already under construction, wanted nothing to do with the Edinburgh & Perth Railway, and negotiations ended on 17 December[17].

Another new line which might have attracted the interest of the North British was the Stirling & Dunfermline Railway (authorised on 16 July), but the E&G was already in process of trying to acquire it, and Learmonth could hardly compete against himself. The branch plans were re-affirmed at a further special meeting in May[18]. North British £25 shares were valued at £30 10s, while Caledonian £50 shares had slumped to £10 15s and Newcastle & Berwick £25 shares were at par[19]. Reservations and worries were being raised in some quarters: a special meeting of scripholders of the Edinburgh & Peebles Railway company expressed doubt about the NBR's engagement to work their line for a guaranteed 4% per annum on the share capital plus half of any surplus on operating costs, for a 99-year period. Their own Bill was "disapproved" by the meeting, which resolved to build only as far as Penicuik[20].

Miller was an engineer of great ability and the Dunglass Viaduct at Cockburnspath, with its 130 feet main span, foreshadows his later masterpiece at Ballochmyle on the Glasgow & South Western Railway Kilmarnock-Cumnock line, but some of the work done on the Berwick line verged on the perfunctory. Construction of stations varied from permanent to temporary. Berwick and Dunbar both had train-sheds built over the lines, though Berwick's would cause embarrassment by collapsing in 1847 due to inadequate foundations. Some stopping-points had virtually no station at all, nor was there yet a proper terminus in the capital. The Edinburgh & Glasgow's track between Haymarket and the North Bridge was finished in May 1846, but the joint station, also being built by the E&G, was not. A large crowd assembled to cheer on 20 May as a train of first and second class NBR carriages was drawn "from the tunnel at the West Church Manse, and rolled slowly and majestically along the valley of the North Loch", passing beneath the Mound, the recently-completed stone-arched Waverley Bridge (named for the adjacent almost-finished monument to Sir Walter Scott), and the North Bridge, to be displayed at the North British station "in the old Physic Gardens"[21]. This was in fact the goods depot, which was adapted for passenger use for a few weeks until goods services began on 3 August. Passengers then transferred to a single platform partly under the northernmost of the North Bridge's three wide arches[22].

General Pasley of the Board of Trade made a last formal inspection, on 17 June, and "with all the ceremony corresponding to an event of such national importance", the Edinburgh-Berwick line was opened on the 18th. The first train to cross the Border left Edinburgh with eleven carriages, increased to 23 at Dunbar, drawn by four locomotives, with John Miller driving the leader. Some of Edinburgh's councillors arrived late, found their carriages had been bagged by others and had to be found room in a second train[23]. Some 700 guests were conveyed. The day was proclaimed a public holiday in Dunbar and Berwick. Eagle Henderson presided over a collation served in the carriage shed at Berwick, "sherry and champagne being dealt about in great abundance"[24]. The return was marred by a fatal accident when a railway employee, Matthew Howat, engaged in setting pot-lamps into the carriage roofs, was struck by a bridge[25]. Five trains a day, each way, were timetabled, with ten short-run trains between Edinburgh and Inveresk (for Musselburgh). While other railway companies in Scotland provided third class carriages that were no better than trucks, the NBR provided windowed carriages with wooden bench seats round the sides, although unroofed seatless trucks may have appeared later[26]. Signalling was rudimentary or non-existent: a head-on collision between two trains on the Haddington branch (opened on 22 June) was narrowly averted in August[27].

Thornton express passenger locomotive No. 38. Built by R&W Hawthorn in 1847 as a 2-2-2, it was rebuilt in 1869 to become a 2-4-0. (*John Alsop*)

On 26 June 1846 the NBR branches Bills were given the royal assent, but the Peebles line and the Carlisle extension were rejected, as were the Edinburgh & Perth Railway, and the East Lothian Central and Tyne Valley lines (later authorised in 1847). At a meeting held to discuss the situation, Learmonth argued forcefully for resubmission of the Carlisle and Perth Bills, and this was agreed. The first half-yearly meeting since opening of the line was held on 27 August. At that point the company had capital of £1,528,002 19s 11d and had expended £1,459,957 9s 1d. Receipts from train services between 22 June and 31 July came to £9,933 11s 10d. Additional capital of £600,000 was to be sought. A lot of revenue would have to come from somewhere in order to make it a viable concern. Meanwhile, as a result of the Carlisle Bill's rejection, the directors felt obliged to reduce the stock issued for it, and for the branches (whose acts had been passed) to £12 10s quarter-shares. But if the Carlisle Bill were re-entered, the board would issue the holders with further quarter-shares in proportion to their holdings. It was also announced that the board, still keen on securing the Edinburgh & Perth as a feeder-line from the north, had committed the company to spend up to £25,000 "on the suggestion and behoof of the Edinburgh & Perth Railway" to acquire the Halbeath Railway, a horse-worked coal tramroad of 4 feet 4 inch gauge, between collieries at Halbeath and the harbour of Inverkeithing, as a potential section of the Perth line. A down-payment of £10,000 was made[28]. An increasingly vocal number of shareholders were sceptical about the value of supporting a new Bill for the Edinburgh & Perth Railway, though Learmonth, who had arranged that John Miller should supplant the Edinburgh & Perth Railway's previous engineer, remained bullish about its prospects. He suffered a set-back when a Liverpool shareholder, Matthew Wotherspoon, protested against the investment in the Edinburgh & Perth, a body "with no legal existence", the share-altering, and the directors' practice of making financial commitments on the company's behalf in their own names and not under the company's seal. Wotherspoon's amendment ensured that the meeting gave only a partial acceptance to the directors' report, remitting the share-reduction and Edinburgh & Perth Railway involvement to the board for reconsideration. A short time before, Learmonth had assured an Edinburgh & Perth shareholders' meeting that the North British considered their line to be of the greatest importance to it[29]. It was typical of the period that two-thirds of the NBR meeting's time were taken up by long speeches against and for Sunday trains. The board had agreed to run Sunday trains to carry mail but not passengers[30]. Learmonth may have been relieved that rambling arguments about the Jewish Sabbath distracted his shareholders from other controversial issues; he was quite capable of cutting the Sabbatarians short at other times. The half-year's accounts showed that the company had borrowed £279,110; arrears of calls on shares amounted to £66,807 10s; £32,007 16s 10d had been spent on Parliamentary expenses and payments for land purchase and compensation for loss of amenity amounted to £278,285 9d 2d[31]. Learmonth was under attack on other fronts: Edinburgh & Glasgow shareholders protested about that company's acquisition of the Union Canal, and his involvement with other railways was criticised; it was complained that he was sacrificing the E&G's interests to those of the North British[32].

In September the NBR bought for £1,600 the Leith and Edinburgh terminal sites of the Edinburgh & Leith Atmospheric Railway Company, a venture whose Bill had failed (the Edinburgh site being adjacent to the North Bridge Station). Twenty-six engines had originally been ordered to work the line – enough for some to be hired to the E&G company at first, but now Miller was asked to arrange with Hawthorns for sixteen additional tender locomotives at £2,375 each, to work the Hawick line[33]. Hawthorns, a Newcastle firm, had bought the Leith Engine Works in 1846 and supplied almost all the NBR's original motive power. Some economies were effected: the plan to set up a telegraph system along the Berwick line was dropped, except for the section between North Bridge and the locomotive depot at Meadowbank, now called St. Margaret's[34], and a request from Eyemouth for a branch line was deferred. Nevertheless the company needed to borrow another £200,000 from its bankers[35]. John Learmonth was an embattled man: sustained pressure from English shareholders forced his resignation as chairman of the Edinburgh & Glasgow Railway, along with the other directors, on 22 September. Most of his opponents were the same men who were challenging his policy in the North British[36]. His strategy now changed; no longer having to consider the interests of the Edinburgh & Glasgow company, he could focus on the North British (though he was still also chairman of the Edinburgh & Northern Railway).

One contractor, Rush & Lawton of Newcastle, had been responsible for the Houndwood (from Penmanshiel east) and Reston sections of the line, with many earthworks and seven bridges across the Eye Water. Between Dunbar and Berwick the route included cliff-top sections with fine views out to sea and closer glimpses of rocky coves and stony beaches far below. These were separated by the inland climb over the Lammermuir Hills. During inspections of construction, concern had several times been expressed about the stability of embankments on the clifftops. The standard of work on different sections varied from sound to slipshod. John Miller, as the company's engineer, must bear responsibility for poor supervision: he was a very busy man during the 'mania' period, but he had been working for a board which insisted on economy. One historian commented, "The NB, however, managed a fortunately unique degree of incompetence … Their costs at £34,123 per mile were above average (£32,113) and for their money they received a line that was in many places badly built and in some positively dangerous"[37]. Though most of the bridges were of stone, foundations had often been skimpily laid and earthworks had been cut or heaped up in a hurried and perfunctory manner. Heavy rain in August and September destabilised many embankments and on 30 September floodwaters washed out five bridges, among them the Tyne Viaduct at East Linton, and damaged others, including six over the Eye Water, leaving the line unusable between East Linton and Grant's House. Makeshift connecting services had to be arranged with consequent long delays. Full service was not restored until early November. The cost of making good was £11,949[38].

George Hudson's helpfulness to the North British had probably always cloaked an intention to gain possession, and now the "wretched condition" of the North British permanent way, and the alleged incompetence of its management were condemned in propaganda from York. It was suggested that the Newcastle & Berwick would abandon the link with the NBR at Berwick and build its own direct line to Edinburgh from its proposed Tweedmouth-Sprouston branch[39], but these were simply gambits to soften up NBR directors and shareholders for amalgamation. With the resumption of services to Berwick, Pickfords the carriers provided a daily wagon-link to Newcastle, enabling merchandise to be shipped southwards, as did Thomas Howey & Co. The first NBR goods manager was Archibald Scott, later general manager of the London & South Western Railway; in 1881 he recalled how he had had to work out a way of organising through traffic to England: "I had myself to arrange with Messrs. Pickfords to come to Edinburgh; that was the first time that Messrs. Pickfords came down to Scotland". Goods services had started on 3 August[40].

While backers of the Edinburgh & Perth Railway went ahead with a new Bill for their line, on 30 October a reluctant Learmonth had to announce to a special NBR meeting that, because of the extent of opposition among shareholders to the company's further involvement with the Edinburgh & Perth, the board had resolved not to pursue it. Wotherspoon as spokesman of the antis graciously accepted the climb-down. It was agreed that the Edinburgh & Perth Railway scrip should be sold (it was worthless) and the directors relieved of any responsibility for repaying the £90,000 it had cost. Legal wrangles began immediately as to whether the NBR could lawfully annul its lease/amalgamation agreement with the Edinburgh & Perth Railway Committee, and for a time the Perth party obtained an interdict against the NBR issuing new shares until the rights of Edinburgh & Perth Railway scrip-holders were established (the agreement with the Edinburgh & Perth had stipulated that its subscribers should participate in any NBR share issue). But the NBR, using its dominant holding, effectively forced the dissolution of the Edinburgh & Perth project at a subscribers' meeting[41]. This did not mean instant repayment of cash deposits. The Edinburgh & Perth promoters promptly set about forming a new provisional committee, which, if it had no formal backing from the North British Railway Company, still had the goodwill of John Learmonth. Completion of the Halbeath Railway purchase was made in January 1847, between Donald Peddie, trustee for the owners, and Learmonth, Eagle Henderson and "the whole other partners of the North British Railway Co.", though according to the contract "the real right thereto belongs to the Edinburgh & Perth Railway Company"[42]. Learmonth perhaps thought he knew better than shareholders from beyond the Border what was good for the NBR, or perhaps he was trying to ensure value in his investment in the Edinburgh & Perth: NBR shareholders were informed that the Halbeath line had been sold to the "new" Edinburgh & Perth committee and that payment would be made in August[43].

Meanwhile the Stirling & Dunfermline Railway was under construction, to meet an Edinburgh & Northern branch from Thornton (still a rural hamlet) at a shared station in Dunfermline. In the North British's own affairs, tenders were accepted for constructing branches to Kelso, Roxburgh, St. Boswells, Duns and North Berwick[44]. Forced (temporarily) to drop its interest in Fife, the company was claiming the south-east as its own, and acting to develop it before any other company did. The focus of discussion moved on to George Hudson's desire to merge the NBR with his York-Newcastle-Berwick companies. Learmonth rather loftily claimed that "there was more than one bidder for the company"; who the other might be was never made clear, though "it was also whispered that the influence of the Great Northern Railway made itself felt in their counsels"[45]. As a result, NBR shares remained buoyant, the £25 shares at £35 10s 6d, while Caledonian £50 shares stood at £23 15s 6d. Edinburgh & Glasgow Railway £50 shares were at £77, and the Newcastle & Berwick's £25 shares were at £34 10s. When Hudson eventually made an offer it was to lease the NBR at 8% on the capital for the main line and 5% on the branches. Stiff conditions were attached, including abandonment of the Hawick-Carlisle extension and deferral of branches not in construction. There was an option for full amalgamation with the York & Newcastle and Newcastle & Berwick Railways within three years[46]. It was generally considered a reasonable, even a generous, offer, but hostile letters soon began appearing in the Scottish press about English takeovers and the resultant application of "English rates" for fares[47]. The board's rejection of Hudson's offer was endorsed by a special general meeting on 10 February 1847. It was evident that the 'Railway King' was interested only in the Berwick-Edinburgh line, and John Learmonth had too many ambitions of his own to let the NBR slip into

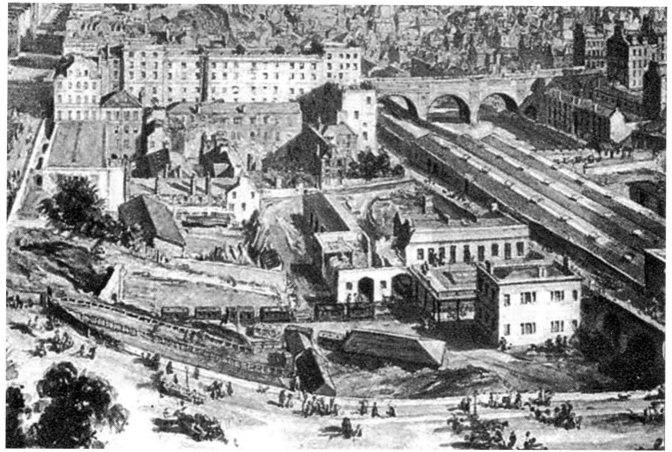

J.W. Ebsworth (1824-1908) painted four views of Edinburgh from the Scott Monument in August 1847. This detail from the eastern view shows Canal Street and Waverley Stations.

Hudson's control. The future of the North British, with its proposed line to Carlisle as well as the line to Berwick, was talked up and Hudson's offer talked down. Hudson, a hard man to repress, introduced a Bill in March for amalgamation of the NBR with the York-Newcastle-Berwick Railways, which the NBR vigorously opposed[48]. An official report on the condition of the repaired North British line was published in 31st March, written by Captain Coddington of the Board of Trade and the engineer James Walker: essentially favourable but still considering the clifftop lines at Lamberton as "a bold measure", although they had been relaid further from the brink. The resident engineer on Rush & Lawton's sections was held up for blame rather than Miller.

From 17 May 1847, the jointly-owned passenger station at Waverley Bridge came into use, with North British and Edinburgh & Glasgow services. Building work was still not finished and a temporary booking office was provided. The goods stations were separate, the E&G's alongside the passenger station, on the former Shambles site, and the NBR's east of the North Bridge. On the same day the Edinburgh Leith & Granton (ex-Newhaven) company opened its tunnel line from Scotland Street to a terminus on Canal Street, at right angles to the joint station. Rails curving through a skew arch in the Waverley Bridge linked the Edinburgh Leith & Granton Railway to the Edinburgh & Glasgow line, but there was no connection to the North British. The NBR continued to refer to the station as Edinburgh or "North Bridge".

1847 was a very difficult year for industry and business. Borrowing costs were high and the climate of expansionism of 1845 had given way to caution. New railway projects were closely scrutinised by investors and Parliamentary committees and once again a NBR Carlisle Extension Bill was refused, as was a revived proposal (without NBR involvement) for the Edinburgh & Perth, which failed by a single vote[49]. The East Lothian Central Railway was approved, but its committee decided to hold off incorporation for the time being, because of the high cost of money and the hope of getting a "more intimate arrangement with the North British"[50]. But the NBR's short Musselburgh branch opened on 16 July, with Fisherrow becoming a goods depot. At this time the company had 624 goods wagons; a further 1,000 were ordered[51]. It was earning money, though not on a large scale. A dividend of 2.5% for the period August 1846-February 1847 was claimed to be based on earnings.

Revenue from February to July 1847 was £47,187 16s 1d, less than in the preceding six months which had included the suspension of train services. After deduction of working expenses and interest, the "free revenue" was £21,700 12s 11d. The dividend of 12s 6d on each £25 share was larger than it should have been – a one-off, in anticipation of better earnings to come, according to Eagle Henderson, who presided at the half-yearly meeting, though far more probably intended to keep the shareholders (many of whom were thinkingly wistfully of Hudson's 8% offer) on side. A second offer from Hudson, of a flat 8% per annum on the North British capital, was turned down on the ground that it was too low – the value of the NBR was "not yet fully ascertained"[52]. Little or nothing was available for maintenance of locomotives and rolling stock. The £95,539 9s 8d locked up in the Perth and East Lothian projects, and the £25,153 8s 8d paid for the Halbeath Railway, remained elusive. Parliamentary expenses for the half-year to 31 January 1847 were £59,120 7s 5d[53]. By October, the *Aberdeen Journal* observed that the North British directors were delaying the issue of contracts for new branches, "in consequence of the derangement of the money market and of the distressed state of all classes in the country." The Selkirk and Jedburgh branches were put on hold. The North Berwick Branch, originally intended to reach the harbour, was now to terminate outside the town. Some expenditures had to be made: a telegraph system was now going ahead, with £5,000 advanced to the Electric Telegraph Co. for installations at Joppa, Tranent, Longniddry, Drem, Linton and Dunbar; £5,722 was allowed for construction of carriage sheds at St. Margaret's, and two fire engines at £100 each were ordered[54]. The share price was sliding downwards: £25 shares were at £27, while the Caledonian £50 shares were worth £37 5s, the Edinburgh & Glasgow's £100 share stood at £94, and the York, Newcastle & Berwick, as it now was, rode high at £33 for a £25 share. With the opening of the Newcastle-Berwick line to Tweedmouth in October, a "through service" was announced between Edinburgh and London, via Newcastle, York, Normanton, and Rugby, taking thirteen hours and ten minutes. By now the Caledonian was open from Carlisle to Beattock, and Croall coaches were being run from Edinburgh to connect. NBR passengers had to change trains twice, using coaches between Berwick and Tweedmouth, and Newcastle and Gateshead. At least the NBR could stop paying a subsidy to the coach operators between Berwick and Newcastle[55]. During this problematic time, railway companies engaged in a series of tentative, half-unwilling approaches at amalgamation. Following receipt of a letter from Peter Blackburn, new chairman of the Edinburgh & Glasgow Railway, the NBR directors felt that a merger between the companies would be "expedient", but nothing came of it. Discussions with the new Edinburgh & Perth committee dragged on in the hope of getting its lawsuits against the NBR withdrawn, and of retrieving the money paid for the Halbeath Railway[56].

The Edinburgh, Leith & Granton Railway was negotiating amalgamation with the still unfinished Edinburgh & Northern, which would create a single-company line (via the Granton-Burntisland ferry) from central Edinburgh to Perth and Cupar. An act of 27 July authorised the merger, though it was not completed until 1848, when the Edinburgh & Northern Railway could show that half its capital was paid up[57]. Its line from Burntisland to Cupar formally opened on 17 September. In Edinburgh the NBR laid a short connection at Niddrie in 1847 between the Berwick and Dalkeith lines. St. Leonards ceased to be a passenger terminus on 31 October, though it remained a busy coal and goods depot. Dalkeith trains now used North Bridge Station. At Hawick Junction two crossbar signals were set up to protect the main line, about 50 yards each side of the pointsman's box. Wearying of the walks, the signalman, Robert Skelden, set up a system of wires and weights so that he could work the signals from his chair. Later the system was used to operate a distant signal 250 yards away. For his invention he was awarded a silver medal and £5 by the Royal Scottish Society of Arts[58].

3. LEARMONTH'S RAILWAY 3, AND INTERREGNUM, 1848–1855

On 1 December 1847, Charles Davidson reported on a meeting convened at Euston Square, London, by Mark Huish, manager of the London & North Western Railway: the first of many attempts to regulate fares and services between London and Scotland[1]. A further meeting took place on 11 January 1848, but no agreement was reached. The interested parties were the LNWR, Midland, and York, Newcastle & Berwick companies in England, and the North British, Caledonian, and Edinburgh & Glasgow companies in Scotland. Under its new board, the E&G was beginning to feel the stress of hostile competition from the soon-to-be-completed Caledonian and its decision to stop Sunday passenger services had aroused much hostile publicity as well as praise from the Sabbatarian lobby (fast days, though, were a lost cause. Though Edinburgh's sacramental holiday at the end of April was observed with "respect and decorum", 4,000 people went off on train trips and "the unusual length of the trains excited considerable attention")[2]. For the half-year between August 1847 and February 1848 the NBR again managed to pay a 2.5% dividend. Following the formal opening of the finally completed joint station on 22 February, with its single-storey pavilion-style booking hall on the Waverley Bridge, the *Scottish Railway Gazette* carried a complimentary account of the "union station – elegant, but by no means extravagant, with pillared booking hall, waiting rooms, washrooms, etc."[3]. Already the North British was feeling its accommodation to be distinctly cramped.

Edinburgh Town Council had originally taken a positive view of railway developments in the city, but relations with the North British soon became frosty. Successive NBR attempts, in 1846 and 1847, to get compulsory acquisition of Trinity College Church (by 1846 hemmed in by railway lines) and the city's fruit and vegetable market, were thrown out due to town council opposition. The council wanted the church re-erected on a suitable site at the railway company's cost, but the NBR refused. Matters came to a head in January 1848 when Lord Provost Black exposed Learmonth's propaganda campaign conducted in the *Caledonian Mercury* against the council, and gave a damning analysis of the company's behaviour in the acquisition of Trinity Hospital. He accepted that the North British needed more space, and claimed that the city was not looking for money, but simply for suitable alternative ground to be provided. Re-siting of the Fruit and Vegetable Market would become an almost-20 year saga[4]. By May 1848 the North British finally agreed to pay £16,300 to rebuild the church on a new site, and dismantling of the 380-year old building began. But deadlock with the Council, plus the company's tight finances, forced it in October to withdraw its plan for enlargement of the Edinburgh station, which also involved acquisition of Shakespeare Square[5].

To get a share of mail traffic was a priority for any railway company, and the NBR had been in touch with the Post Office from the start: an advertisement in July 1846 informed the public that "By order of the Postmaster General" the departures of southbound mail trains would be advanced by nine minutes, to 4.26 am and 11.36 am[6]; and in September 1848 the NBR rented a room at Berwick Station to the Post Office, for the sorting of mail to

**Thornton's heavy-goods 0-6-0 type of 1848, built by R.&W. Hawthorn. No. 50 was
renumbered 50A in 1890, 830 in 1895, 1030 in 1901, and was withdrawn in 1910. (*John Alsop*)**

Edinburgh[7]. In September the NBR declared a 5% dividend on the £25 ordinary shares, but the Directors' Report was not encouraging. Fewer passengers had been carried than in the same period of 1847 – 531,867 compared with 567,716. Bills for enlarging the Edinburgh station and converting the Leith Branch to locomotive haulage had been rejected, as had the renewed attempt to get an Act for the Hawick-Carlisle extension. Twenty miles of the Hawick branch were now open but completion was much delayed because of the difficulty of collecting share instalments. Eagle Henderson, deputising for the chairman at the half-yearly meeting on 13 September, admitted that had the directors read the future correctly, they might have given Hudson's second offer a different answer. Yet the board was seeking authority to raise a further £600,000 of capital. Angry shareholders forced an adjournment of the meeting. When it resumed on the 18th, Learmonth had to tell them that Hudson had been approached a few days earlier and had refused to make any new offer, even a reduced one, to lease the NBR. No mention was made of other bidders. The company was thrown back on its own resources. The Carlisle extension scheme was to be wound up. Subscribers could either put their share subscription towards the £600,000 or get back whatever was left after two sets of substantial Parliamentary expenses had been deducted. Tension and concern increased when the meeting was changed to a Special one, to approve of the NBR taking £113,000 of preference stock in the financially-stricken Aberdeen Railway, which was seeking to complete its line north from a junction on the Arbroath & Forfar Railway. The Edinburgh & Northern would also find £113,000, and the York & North Midland £50,000, to ensure that the Aberdeen Railway would form part of the East Coast Route, to be worked for its first 21 years by the combined North British – Edinburgh & Northern – York & North Midland railway companies.

North British shares no longer stood at a premium: a £25 share was priced at £12[8], though most other Scottish railway shares were similarly depressed. The company's share capital by now had grown substantially: with the original £800,000 of the Berwick line had to be reckoned the capital cost of buying and converting the Dalkeith Railway, £160,000; 32,000 £12 10s shares in the Hawick Branch plus 78,000 'thirds' at £8 6s 8d, making £1,053,000; and 96,000 quarter-shares in the Kelso and other branches, making £600,000. These totalled £2,216,333 before the new capital of £600,000 was added. Dividends were separately payable on all these issues. Thus in March 1849 the company paid 10s per £25 share on the main line, 2s on the Dalkeith shares and 1s on the Hawick 'thirds' (the opened section of line, to Galashiels, had earned a surplus of £4,049 13s 4d[9]). Perhaps most alarming to shareholders was that the working expenses of the North British, far from being Learmonth's 33.33%, were well over 50% of gross receipts. At the half-yearly meeting on 8 March 1849 the chairman announced that the

Aberdeen proposal had been abandoned in view of the divisions on the Aberdeen Railway board, and, for the first time, he revealed the real amount of land purchase for the main line as £350,000, over three times the estimated £112,000. The company's Parliamentary expenses for the half-year were £71,000. A further £25,000 had been spent on legal cases. Calls for a shareholders' committee of enquiry could be deflected only for a few weeks: on 10 May the board finally and "amicably" accepted a committee of eight (six of them from England) to examine the company's affairs[10]. They did not probe very deeply and their report, published on 2 August, was not a killer. The directors were found to have made bad judgements and decisions but were exonerated of anything more untoward. The company's track and plant were recorded as being in good condition. Learmonth's coach-building business had been sold to or merged with another, Russell & Macnee, in 1838, but he still owned the 'Old Coach Yard' at 4 Princes Street, which he had sold to the North British[11] for £22,500, a price which the committee accepted as the market rate. North British directors, acting for the company, had bought shares in the Edinburgh & Northern, Tyne Valley & East Lothian, Edinburgh & Perth and Lancaster & Carlisle Railways: the Edinburgh & Northern Railway shares had been sold again at a profit of £1,340 15s but the loss on the Edinburgh & Perth Railway was £84,954 5s 8d, and on the East Lothian lines £2,937 10s. The secretary's increase in salary in 1848, from £600 to £1,000 a year, was attacked but the committee observed that he was in effect the manager and so deserved the rise. Otherwise, economies and staff cuts were recommended, as was the appointment of three or four English directors, to reflect the 75% English ownership of the shares. On the whole the board could feel that its stewardship had been approved. There were no calls for resignations, but some shareholders felt that the committee had been insufficiently probing, and too lenient[12].

Initially passenger revenue had been greater than goods revenue, but the half-yearly report in September 1849 showed passenger receipts at £34,745 15s 3 1s 2d, up from £29,800 13s 2d in the half-year to July 1848; but goods receipts at £37,957 17s 7d, up from £22,491 13s 2d. Tonnage carried was 195,183, an increase of 57,628 tons. One reason why North British long distance passenger receipts remained comparatively low was the fact that Leith steamship companies kept much of the traffic, having reduced their fares in order to compete. For passages to Newcastle, Hull or London, they offered rates below the railway fare. Well aware of this, the NBR management kept an eye on steamer rates and strove, as much as possible, to match them or to negotiate a joint rate[13]. On 29 October, with the final section from St. Boswells, the Hawick Branch was at last completed. Its free revenue, after expenses, in the half-year to 31 July, had been only £1,984 8s 1d, and a dividend was held over. Working expenses were 66% of gross revenue. In December a short coal line was opened from east of Tranent Station (Prestonpans from 1858) to Tranent Colliery.

That month the board began to implement pay cuts for its employees, with porters losing from 2s to 1s a week: a 10% or more reduction for most. The locomotive men, faced with a pay cut, demanded instead an increase from their 6s a day average to 7s (drivers) and from 3s 4d to 3s 6d (firemen), and informed the board that they would quit work on 1 April 1850 unless the demands in their petition were complied with. The board accepted their resignations, and also resolved to take the necessary steps to resist "combination" among its staff. While these exchanges were taking place, the directors took out a 4% loan from the Union Bank, signed by all of them, in order to reduce their existing obligations[14] and also resolved to prosecute any engine-man who left the company without giving due notice (at least two got three weeks in jail[15]). A week before the deadline, Robert Thornton, locomotive superintendent, paid off 38 men at St. Margaret's. By 4 April, only two of the former footplatemen were still employed. Mechanics and new recruits were used to replace the others and a string of mostly minor accidents ensued through 1850. Typical was an incident at North Bridge Station when an inexperienced driver applied too much steam when starting the London mail, the resultant stress breaking a crank axle on the locomotive. A porter was despatched to St. Margaret's to summon a relief engine, which was driven by a mechanic with the porter as fireman. Arriving too fast, it collided with the train, which was formed of a cattle van loaded with pigs, a York, Newcastle & Berwick brake, one first class and three second class coaches. A pig was killed and several passengers slightly injured[16]. The company was unmoved – "No concession", proclaimed secretary/manager Davidson. At this time the company had 42 drivers, six of them former staff returned, nine experienced drivers from other railways, and 21 mechanics without driving experience[17].

1850 should have been an auspicious year for the North British, with the opening of the Royal Border Bridge (though not a NBR project) completing the route to London. Instead it saw financial stringency, forced economies, bad industrial relations, customer complaints, dissension among the directors, and increasing agitation among the shareholders. At the end of May, the company's obligations were £395,405 19s 3d, in debts, interest, etc., and its assets were £275,623 15s 2d, including the uncertain elements of unpaid-up shares, £111,410 11s 8d; and £36,733 15s 2d still tied up in Lancaster & Carlisle shares and the Halbeath Railway. The Edinburgh & Perth committee had lost a third Bill in 1848 but had not quite faded from the scene: three of its members were involved in dealings between the North British board and the owner of Townhill Colliery, near Dunfermline, in February 1850[18]. On

7 June the Kelso Branch opened to a temporary terminus at Wallace Nick west of the town, and the branch from Drem to North Berwick opened on the 17th. In 1846 the company had been empowered to raise £513,000 in shares and £170,999 in loans for branch construction. Only 4 ½ miles long, the North Berwick Branch's total cost was £116,766 6s 0d; land purchase, estimated at £7,083, was in actuality £18,949 and it (like the other branches) had been laid as double-track. Four mixed trains a day formed the initial service, but the line was not profitable. The committee of investigation had regretted that the directors should ever have undertaken the project. In line with Learmonth's 'protection' policy, the branch was only made to prevent any other company from doing so[19].

The NBR had dire need of further capital but the banks would lend it money only against personal guarantees from the directors (their liability to be in turn assured by the company). A bank Bill for £51,000 also had to renewed, but three directors, including Mark Sprot, refused to give further guarantees, and resigned. At a special shareholders' meeting on 4 July, Learmonth and his reduced board of nine faced angry and anxious questions. The chairman accepted that the North British had over-extended itself in previous years but "they had now awakened from the dream" and he was confident they were at the lowest point and could only rise. The directors had reduced their own allowance to £600. Davidson's salary was cut to £750 plus the dividend payable on £5,000-worth of stock[20]. All board committees were scrapped and all directors would give their attention to all aspects of the business. Learmonth's combination of humble pie and future prospects ensured him a majority for a further borrowing of £250,000 on top of the already-authorised £200,000 debenture issue[21]. Extra funds were needed not only to help out in the immediate emergency – substantial new expenditure had to be faced. Traffic was building up, and the company was hindered by a shortage of locomotives and rolling stock – an order to Mr. Begbie of Haddington for 20 double-deck sheep wagons at £48 each[22] was a mere gesture in the face of what was needed.

With the English main line complete, the North British had two options for through traffic south of York: the original route via Rugby and the London & North Western into Euston Square, or the new and shorter route via the Great Northern to Kings Cross (where a temporary station preceded the terminus of 1852). Though anxious not to offend the LNWR, whose goodwill, if the Carlisle Extension should ever be achieved, was vital, the board decided to go with the Great Northern[23], on a provisional week-by-week basis. The London express, first class only, took twelve hours – half an hour less than the Rugby route; and the NBR perhaps also preferred not to share a London terminus with the Caledonian. But the Caledonian, and with it the Edinburgh & Glasgow Railway, were firm members of what was known as the 'Euston Confederacy', and there was no chance of the North British being able to offer a through connection beyond Edinburgh to Glasgow or Stirling[24].

Kelso Station, in the early twentieth century. Empty stock being brought in. (*John Alsop*)

The purchase of the old coaching yard at 4 Princes Street had been to allow for linking tracks between the North Bridge and Canal Street Stations (the Edinburgh & Northern had changed its name in 1849 to the Edinburgh, Perth & Dundee Railway). Town council objections had prevented this along with other proposals to extend the station, but in September 1850 the council gave its approval to the link line "across property formerly owned by Mr. Learmonth" and East Canal Street, and leased three of the North Bridge's small arches to the NBR for a rent of £125 a year. Intensive discussions followed with the City Paving Board about laying access lines under the bridge and adjacent buildings, with the company accepting all the council's conditions in order to ensure the uncontested passage of its new Bill for station enlargement[25]. Devoting some attention to development of its passenger traffic, the company found that by reducing fares and putting on extra trains between Edinburgh and Musselburgh, revenue on that section rose by 58%[26]. Efforts this year to sell the Halbeath Railway by public auction came to nothing even though in November an advertisement announced "upset price still further reduced". At an uneasy half-yearly meeting on 17 September, Learmonth assured the shareholders that the capital account was about to be closed. Another £200,000 was due to be spent, but after that "no new works." By now, the capital account stood at £4,266,757, a horrifying figure for a company earning only £3,000 - £4,000 a week, with high operating costs. At this time the chairman was in the curious position of conducting a lawsuit against himself, on behalf of the shareholders. He and other directors had purchased a block of Lancaster & Carlisle Railway shares, on behalf of the North British but in their own names, in the hope of running traffic over the Lancaster & Carlisle Railway to and from the Carlisle Extension. Half had been sold when the Carlisle Bill failed, but the sum of £20,000 remained outstanding and the shareholders wished to reclaim this from him and his fellow directors. The loss incurred had been charged against the individual directors, "but he certainly thought it would be shabby if the company did saddle them with that loss"[27].

On 28 March 1851 the Edinburgh, Perth & Dundee Railway opened the new harbour at Tayport (as it had renamed Ferryport on Craig), the Dundee & Arbroath Railway laid a connecting line to the slipway at Broughty Ferry, and the new train ferry *Robert Napier* began service. A six carriage special train crossed the Forth on *Leviathan*, then the Tay: "The sensation of sitting in a railway carriage on board of a vessel breasting the turbulent waves was certainly a peculiar one, and the passengers generally enjoyed it"[28]. At the NBR half-yearly meeting held on the 29th, a critic pointed out that when the company had only 89 miles of track its revenue was £39,304. Now it had 146 miles, and the revenue was £39,967. Part of the reason was simply its inability to cope with the traffic, as Learmonth frankly admitted. There were only 65 locomotives, of dubious reliability, with many out of service, and 75 or 80 were needed. The lack of wagons and vans was another limiting factor. Many stations were inadequate: Dalkeith had a single platform for arrivals and departures, only "a few inches high and three feet broad"; there was no waiting room, and a grain shed was also badly needed[29]. Falling back on a chairman's staple excuses: fodder for horses was very cheap, enabling carters to cut rates, trade was still low, etc., Learmonth insisted that the future was still bright, and the company got authorisation to raise £350,000 in preference shares and another £110,000 in loans. Arrears of subscriptions amounting to £72,582 12s 6d were written off, as was some £16,000 - £17,000 on the Lancaster & Carlisle shares. An Act for the enlargement of the Edinburgh station and the improvement of the Leith Branch (still horse-drawn and 4 feet gauge) was given the royal assent on 5 June[30], and the board also proposed to spend £2,000 on building smiths' shops at St. Boswells. A modest source of income was arranged in a five-year contract with Messrs. Smith for bookstalls at various stations, for a rent of £60. More importantly, at the end of July the company signed and sealed the 'Octuple' traffic agreement on traffic to London, with the Caledonian, Lancaster & Carlisle, London & North Western, York Newcastle & Berwick, York & North Midland, Midland, and Great Northern companies[31]. This five-year agreement, made on 17 April, shared the London-Edinburgh traffic (excluding mails and minerals) in equal division between the East Coast and West Coast companies on the three Anglo-Scottish routes: Euston-Preston-Carlisle-Edinburgh; Euston-Rugby-York-Edinburgh, and Kings Cross-Doncaster-York-Edinburgh[32]. The NBR formed the northern section of two of these routes, and all traffic from places between York and Edinburgh was to be carried by the East Coast lines. Receipts from the Berwick-Edinburgh section went to the North British. The NBR also became a party to the 'Sextuple' agreement, backdated to 1 January 1851, with the same companies except the Great Northern and York & North Midland, allocating shares of all traffic except mails from Birmingham northwards to Edinburgh, with a 50/50 East Coast/West Coast split on through traffic between these cities. Traffic forwarded from Great Northern stations south of York to Edinburgh and Glasgow would be 100% East Coast[33]. These arrangements were not unfavourable to the North British, though it still hoped to break the Caledonian monopoly of all traffic through Carlisle, including that to and from Leeds and Bradford, passed to the West Coast via the 'Little North Western' Railway between Skipton and Lancaster. The prime effect of the agreements was to introduce a degree of stability rather than "ruinous competition". The Railway Clearing House took on the task of computing shares and allocating receipts.

In September work was started on the Waverley Station extension, following the Stations Enlargement Act of 13 June[34]. Two new lines were to be laid under the North Bridge, into the old coach yard, where three passenger platforms would be built. This was a purely NBR project, not part of the joint station, and, extended to meet the Edinburgh, Perth & Dundee Railway lines, would have relieved the joint station of much traffic. Despite its efforts, however, the board by now was a lame-duck one, prisoner of its past excesses and struggling to maintain a semi-satisfactory service. In the face of calls for a new set of directors, Learmonth insisted that he and his colleagues could not resign as long as their signed commitments to guarantee company loans remained in force. North British £25 shares stood at £6 in October 1851. Wrangles within the company were frequent. Robert Thornton resigned as locomotive superintendent on 3 November, after a campaign of criticism about his management, and a stock-taking at St. Margaret's. He was given a quarter's salary and a letter with Learmonth's personal regrets. After his departure he attached himself to a scheme for a "Direct North Railway" intended to supplant the North British[35]. Fifty-three people applied for his job, and an engineer from London, William Smith, was appointed at £300 a year plus a free house[36]. Shareholders gathering in London on 7 January 1852 reiterated all the criticisms and formed a committee of nine to meet the board[37], which continued its rather belated attention to the nuts and bolts of running a railway with a consideration of coal haulage rates, based on a long report from Davidson. Though rates were published, discounts to steady customers, known as 'drawbacks', could be as much as 25%. Different prices were quoted for different grades of coal, from 'great coal' to dross, but some coalmasters were not above mis-representing their shipments to get the cheapest rate. At many collieries the company was competing with road carters, and the general manager and goods managers were authorised to maintain the drawback policy but not to exceed 25% without board permission. The question of coal sales by stationmasters (known as station agents) was also considered. Agents could act as retailers for more than one coalmaster, but coal sales were considered part of their brief and they were not supposed to profit from the activity. The NBR charged the supplier 6d per ton on sales from stations. Doubtless recognising that here was a rich area for bribes and paybacks, Davidson recommended that a portion of the 6d per ton should be passed on to the station agent. To formalise its own position, the company's Bill later in the year provided for authorisation to purchase and resell coal[38]. But the atmosphere of crisis intensified. A meeting of shareholders in London on 7 January 1852 protested about extravagant working expenses, the "unwarrantable reduction of fares and introduction of fourth class" and a general want of care and energy in developing the traffic; and appointed a committee of nine to represent their interests. They claimed introduction of fourth class carriages in 1850 had depressed the revenue per mile:

> 1848 (no fourth class): £206 10s per mile for the January half-year
> 1850 (with fourth class): £141 14s per mile for the January half-year
> 1851 (with fourth class): £107 19s per mile for the July half-year[39]

The half-yearly report noted that fourth class were merely passengers paying the parliamentary fare of 1d a mile, on Parliamentary trains only (enabling the third class fare on other trains to be higher). Gross revenue for the half-year to January 31 1852 was £98,288 12s 7 1s 4d, but after all deductions for operating costs and interest, only £23,437 15s 5½d was left over, enough to pay the No. 1 preference shares at 6% and the No. 2 (as far as issued) at 5%, but there was no ordinary dividend. The directors fell back again on their "pecuniary responsibilities": if the shareholders would like to take over their personal pledges for £300,000, they would be happy to make way for a new board[40]. The No. 2 preference share issue flopped, with only £10,922 10s taken up out of £350,000[41], and the plan for workshops at St. Boswells was dropped. Finally, at the half-yearly meeting on 18 March, it was announced that Eagle Henderson and two other directors were leaving the board, in favour of three members of the London Shareholders' Committee, and Learmonth himself would resign "in due course". Richard Hodgson rose to protest that the committee knew nothing of the NBR or its circumstances and had said nothing about what it planned to do[42]. In April, the board tried to register £130,000 of No. 2 preference stock in the name of the Royal Bank of Scotland; the Bank declined, saying it merely held the shares as security against the directors' signed obligations[43]. Learmonth held on for a few more weeks, but on 13 May he and two other directors resigned, and James Balfour, his deputy, was elected chairman. Mark Sprot returned to the board, which now also had a posse of English shareholders.

John Learmonth had clung to his chairmanship through eight stormy years, and also to his policy of enlarging the North British and fending off all efforts to compete. At one time chairman both of the Edinburgh & Glasgow, and the North British, and of the Edinburgh & Northern, and closely involved with the Edinburgh & Perth, the Edinburgh & Bathgate, and Glasgow, Dumfries & Carlisle, among other railways actual and potential, he might have seen himself as a sort of Scottish George Hudson, though he failed to make combinations, and personal enrichment and a flamboyant lifestyle were not among his aims. To achieve his great idea of a national railway system centred on Edinburgh, he relentlessly pushed the North British beyond its means. Investment in locomotives, wagons, carriages, track, stations, and signalling was starved while vast sums went on Parliamentary Bills, legal costs, share purchases and interest payments on the company's ever-increasing loan burden. After his ousting, he continued to attend shareholders' meetings, but purely in order to safeguard himself and his fellow ex-directors against financial claims. He still owned property above Canal Street, by the station.

The reconstituted board set about implementing the reforms and economies that had long been demanded. An Edinburgh accountant, Archibald Borthwick, examined the accounts and found that £33,872 9s 0d had been erroneously charged to capital rather than revenue between 31 January 1849 and 31 January 1852. The company's debts remained, as did the ex-directors' obligations. In his letter of resignation, Learmonth hoped it was understood that the new board would relieve him and his colleagues of these without delay; Balfour replied that they would use all the assets at their command to this end, subject to the interest of the company[44], and began negotiations with the Union Bank. Some of the new men were keen to get to know the railway: a fine imposed on driver John Fairny for letting passengers on his engine was remitted, "the passengers being Directors"[45]. New board committees were set up. Charles Davidson, his health destroyed through overwork, had been allowed extended sick leave in March, but in June the new board decided to pay him off with a quarter's salary. One of the new directors, Henry Chaytor, was appointed managing director on an interim basis, with no salary specified, but it was found that under the company's articles a director could not act as manager and Chaytor relinquished the executive role to become deputy-chairman[46]. A new general manager, Thomas Rowbotham from the Lancashire & Yorkshire Railway, was engaged.

To save money, work on the station extension at Edinburgh was halted, with the original single platform under the North Bridge brought back into use from the end of the year[47]. An agreement was made with the promoters of the Peebles Railway, whose line would branch off from the Hawick line. It was to be "made on the cheap principle", an approach developed and promoted by the civil engineer Thomas Bouch. Having burned its fingers badly on earlier branches, the NBR was now operating a policy of letting towns find the capital for their own branch lines (as with Peebles, Jedburgh and others) and then setting up a working agreement. The same policy was adopted by the equally hard-pressed Edinburgh, Perth & Dundee company with the St. Andrews Railway,

The General Station in Edinburgh in 1850, looking north along the North Bridge. *(Stenlake Collection)*

which opened on 29 May 1852. Engineered by Bouch, it used lightweight 60lb rails, sleepers 4 feet rather than 3 feet apart, wooden bridges and other skimpings which would soon require upgrading[48].

Having come in primarily to protect the interests of the ordinary shareholders, the new regime at first tried to avoid further issue of preference shares by issuing debentures, in effect a form of loan, repayable by a specific date. Ordinary shares were still slumped around the £7 mark and there was no chance of a fresh issue. Before long the new directors were finding that their freedom of action was hemmed in by the NBR's poor reputation in the financial markets, by its lack of working capital and by its need to compete not only with railways but with road carters and shipping interests, while the Scottish commercial and legal context was unfamiliar to several of them. Owners of preference shares did not take long to complain that the board was neglecting them in the interests of ordinary shareholders. Preference dividends were in arrears and a protest meeting was organised by London shareholders[49].

In October 1852 completion of Kings Cross Station enabled Edinburgh-London passenger services to run in eleven hours, an hour less than the West Coast, and also speeded up goods traffic to London. But the English companies were increasingly critical of the NBR rolling stock: after several instances of broken axles the Great Northern complained about "the deteriorated state of the stock of the North British Railway Company". An accident at Rossington on the GNR on 15 November 1853 was caused by a broken axle and subsequent derailment of an NBR wagon on an express goods, and North Eastern inspectors at Tweedmouth began rejecting suspect vehicles from the NBR. In January 1854 the GNR also banned North British carriages, after a passenger clambered over the carriage roofs to tell the driver about a broken axle on a NBR third (he was awarded £5[50]). The NBR was compelled to hire vehicles from the English companies.

Balfour (father of the future prime minister A.J. Balfour) was a cautious chairman, of conservative instincts, and his board had no grand ambitions, intending to concentrate on developing traffic on the existing lines while cutting down expenditure to a point where a dividend on the ordinary shares would be possible. It did introduce a Bill in November for a Hawick-Langholm-Carlisle line, which failed[51], but the purpose was only to counter the 'Direct North Railway' being promoted at that time. There was plenty of housekeeping to do. Davidson's hand on the staff had been light and numerous cases of agents and clerks defrauding the company had been exposed: new systems and requirements for security payments were introduced. Working expenses were brought down to 48.85% by January 1853 – still high by comparison with other lines[52], and the economy drive was pushed on through the year. Learmonth's Canal Street property was bought for £1,400 for conversion to new head offices, with the St. Andrew Square office to be sold[53]. One victory for the company, or its customers, was the inclusion of third class carriages on the Edinburgh-London night express, on two nights a week; but this only lasted until 1855, when the train was accelerated to eleven hours, and reverted to first and second class only (the third class service took thirteen hours). From 1 November 1853 the night train also carried new postal carriages between York and Edinburgh[54]. September's half-yearly report noted that working expenses were still too high and maintenance and replacement of plant and equipment still needed investment, but it was "satisfactory to be able to record a decrease in our locomotive depot"[55]. In November the NBR obtained a court interdict against an attempt by the Edinburgh & Glasgow company, currently working with the Caledonian through a joint committee, to have Caledonian trains running into the Waverley Bridge Station, and a Caledonian booking office there[56], but the board was struggling. In March 1854 one of its most trenchant critics, Richard Hodgson of Carham Hall, Northumberland, was elected a director in preference to the board's own nominee.

With traffic increasing, the nine directors were confronting a drastic shortage of rolling stock. Apart from the need for additional locomotives, many of the existing ones were in

Richard Hodgson, chairman of the NBR from 1855 to 1866
(*Glasgow Museums*)

Saddle tank No. 1034 was built by Hawthorns of Leith in 1857 as an 0-4-0 tender engine for the Fife & Kinross Railway, named *Loch Leven Castle*. Rebuilt as NBR No. 312 in 1884, it was renumbered in 1901 and scrapped in 1906. (*North British Railway Study Group*)

need of repairs and almost all were obsolescent in design. Of the wagons and carriages, many were in decrepit condition. Amidst these major issues, the board dealt with a steady range of lesser and simpler matters: £33 2*s* 9*d* was granted to the staff insurance fund; the Bible Society wished to place Bibles at certain stations ("cordial permission" given); a rabbit catcher was badly needed to prevent burrows from destabilising embankments and cutting slopes: Mr. Edington of North Berwick was appointed at £5 a year plus the rabbits, on condition he did not use a gun[57]. From October the head office staff moved into their new premises in Canal Street, under the Rainbow Tavern, though the more prestigious address of 4 Princes Street was also used. The goods office, and sack store, was at the shore, in Leith, by the branch terminus. In an ongoing dispute over the price of the mail contract, the company refused to allow Post Office staff on its trains and the GPO had to advertise for road carters to take the post between Edinburgh and Berwick[58]. William Smith had been discharged as locomotive superintendent in January following a committee of inquiry into his methods of maintenance and administration. To keep the NBR's locomotives running was not easy, but among other things, he had ordered an engine driver to pass a red light. Edmund Petre, the new locomotive superintendent, joined in March and was allowed to employ an assistant at £130 a year plus a free house, but by the end of the year, following reports of his being drunk on duty and with the locomotive department still in disarray, it was decided to sack him, and Rowbotham was delegated to consult with his former Lancashire & Yorkshire Railway colleague, William Hurst, on a replacement. In December Hurst himself was appointed to the job, at £500 a year for three years. He was able to boost the locomotive stock quickly by arranging the purchase of four new Lancashire & Yorkshire Railway engines for £11,850 and hiring a further six from the Great Northern Railway, at the rate of 5 $\frac{1}{2}$*d* a mile[59].

Better relations with the Edinburgh & Glasgow and Scottish Central companies led to an agreement that the E&G and Scottish Central Railway would give the East Coast railways the same through-traffic facilities to Perth as the LNWR and Caledonian were getting. Edinburgh-Perth trains began to run via Stirling[60]. Richard Hodgson was much the most active and energetic director, taking responsibility for such issues as the relationship with the Edinburgh & Perth Railway promoters and the associated question of the Halbeath Railway, unresolved since 1848. Balfour was less and less in evidence and finally sent in his resignation as chairman (from Madeira). Hodgson was elected in his place[61]. He was very much a public man, Tory M.P. for Berwick from 1837 to 1847, and this was not his first chairmanship of a Scottish railway board: he had been chairman of the ambitious Ayrshire & Galloway Railway, formed in 1847 but which built less than three miles of its line before its dissolution in 1853.

4. HODGSON'S RAILWAY – 1, 1855-1858

An accident happened in the Calton Tunnel on 9 December 1854, when a passenger train from Hawick, wrongly admitted into the section, hit a Duns to Edinburgh goods being banked up the incline; the shock broke a coupling, four carriages and the guard's van ran backwards to collide with a light engine and a passenger was killed. This resulted in not only the errant signalmen, but also Rowbotham and the (by now dismissed) Petre being put on trial, in March, for culpable homicide. Two signalman, Jeffries and Macintosh, were jailed (eighteen months and two years). The officials, accused of making an unsuitable appointment and lack of supervision, were acquitted[1]. Juries of the time liked to punish railway officials for accidents: William Paton, first locomotive superintendent of the Edinburgh & Glasgow, spent a year in jail, 1845-46, following an accident for which he had no responsibility. Incidentally, the North British had a system of communication between guards and drivers, "at least on their through trains", in 1855[2].

In the half-yearly report the shortage of motive power was admitted, many engines having "unexpectedly failed", and motive power was hired from the North Eastern and Great Northern companies, the latter supplying six goods engines and drivers for two months from 2 December 1854[3]. Between 1844 and 1855 the NBR had spent at least £122,375 on Parliamentary costs, vastly more than on locomotives or rolling stock[4]. At the half-yearly meeting, Henry Chaytor, having resigned from the board, tried unsuccessfully to get places for three nominees of his own, but the forceful new chairman was having none of that. Hodgson had to impose himself on a disunited board, with support from a new director, Col. George Kinloch, of Meigle. No dividend was paid on the ordinary stock. They had to find savings – one wheeze was to invest £5,000 on 80 coke ovens to produce locomotive fuel, with an annual saving of £3,500 on coke prices and the freeing up of £8,000 worth of coke wagons for revenue-earning mineral traffic. But good men had to be kept: the secretary, James Nairne, got a pay rise to £400 and Rowbotham went up to £700. Chaytor's involvement in railway management ended when the adjourned half-yearly meeting failed to re-elect him[5]. The dispute with the Post Office was resolved and the mail speeded up: the London mail due to arrive in Edinburgh at 12.20 p.m. would leave at the same time but arrive at 11.05 a.m., while the southbound train would leave Edinburgh at 2.10 p.m. instead of 12.39, and arrive at the same time as before. A special category of passenger was covered in an agreement with the Prison Board for Scotland: convicts to be carried between England and Scotland at a penny a mile, with escorts allowed to return in second class; but the company declined to provide "the utensil named in Mr. Burton's letter", perhaps to the inconvenience of the convicts[6]. The locally-promoted Peebles Railway opened on 4 July, from Hardengreen Junction on the Hawick line, choosing to run its own services, three trains daily each way, at first using a hired NBR engine and carriages. The first train had run on 29 May, but the Board of Trade required a loop to be installed at Penicuik Station before public opening.

Richard Hodgson's chairmanship was to last eleven years, and perhaps much of the style and strategy of his time in office was formed in the first months. The company was in disarray, its directors at loggerheads with one

Beyer Peacock 2-2-2 No. 213 at Waverley West in the 1890s. Built 1856, originally No. 82, *Polmont*, of the E&GR. (*North British Railway Study Group*)

another, reflecting the conflicting claims of preference and ordinary shareholders; its locomotives and rolling stock were mostly obsolescent, its stations and depots were often inadequate, and its permanent way, especially sleepers and timber bridges, needed renewal and replacement. It had some effective senior officials, including Rowbotham and his assistant, James McLaren. Substantial amounts of new capital were required to get it into better operational shape, but the NBR was not in a good position to raise funds, unless the money was applied to growth rather than consolidation. So Hodgson enrolled himself as Learmonth's heir, his mission to acquire or establish new and lucrative routes which would pull back the North British's ever-receding profits. He had been involved with George Hudson, by now a discredited figure, in the 1848 takeover bid for the NBR, and Hudson's managerial style and approach found no better imitator than Hodgson. Hodgson was a Borderer; he knew that region, he had influential and wealthy contacts as far as Newcastle – it was hardly surprising that he should look at the area's possibilities for railway expansion. Had he been a Fife laird, much later history might have been different.

His second half-yearly meeting was held in London, at the London Tavern, a favourite venue for such gatherings, as a gesture to English shareholders, though again no dividend was paid on the ordinary stocks. Hurst reported progress: apart from hired locomotives, three new goods engines were working; of fifteen sent out for repairs, seven were back at work, eighteen others had had repairs completed in the company's works and a further 20 were back on the road after light repairs. Eight new goods brakes, two new first class carriages and ten new mineral wagons had been added to stock. At the same time, under board instructions, he was reducing staff, and by early 1856 St. Margaret's had lost 130 men and boys, with numbers down to 605[7]. Hodgson got consent to raise £150,000 in additional share capital, plus £50,000 in loans, refusing demands for a renewal fund (present savings against future needs) or a suspense fund (present expenditure to be financed from future savings): the company must pay its way properly from revenue and capital for specific projects[8]. But the chairman's eye was fixed on the alluring prospect of completing the line from Hawick to Carlisle, so making the North British an East Coast *and* a West Coast main line company. At a special shareholders' meeting in Edinburgh he failed to get support for investment of £125,000 in this line; Scottish shareholders were more willing than English ones to back it, but all were more concerned that the NBR's working costs appeared to be around 66% of revenues[9]. An attempt to unseat and replace the board was faced down at a special meeting on 15 January 1856, though the directors pledged themselves to put their seats at the shareholders' disposal "in fair battle" once the current Money Bill was passed by Parliament. The board's chief adversary was Robert Walker, a Glasgow shareholder with numerous allies, all hostile to the Carlisle Extension[10].

At this time the Caledonian Railway was also promoting a Carlisle-Hawick line, to meet the NBR at the latter town. Public debate centred on the relative desirability of the CR's single-track line via Langholm or the NBR's revised scheme, a double-track line through Liddesdale, meeting the Caledonian between Floriston and Rockcliffe, with a branch to Langholm, and other branches to the Port Carlisle Railway and to the CR at Gretna[11]. Scottish railway affairs were in confusion, not for the first or the last time. A newspaper letter branded Walker as an agent of the West Coast companies and suggested that since renewal of the "Octuple Treaty", the Caledonian and North Eastern Railways were in "close and secret alliance" against the North British[12]. From 1 January 1856, the Octuple and Sextuple Agreements had been succeeded by a single 'English & Scotch Traffic Agreement' made between the LNWR, Lancaster & Carlisle, Caledonian, Midland, Great Northern, North Eastern and North British companies, covering the same three routes as the 1851 agreement, again excluding mail and mineral traffic, and to last fourteen years. A clause enabled the Scottish Central and Edinburgh Perth & Dundee companies to join within seven years, extending the range of territory covered to Perth and Dundee, it also provided for the Edinburgh & Glasgow Railway to join, once its current hostilities with the Caledonian were settled. From 1856 the Dundee Perth & London Shipping Co. was also a party to the alliance, having agreed to align its passenger and freight charges with the railway companies'[13].

In April 1856 the Selkirk & Galashiels Railway was completed and the NBR undertook to work it for 45% of the gross receipts, with a minimum payment of £1,700 in the first year and £1,850 subsequently. With the Money Bill looking secure, Hodgson announced that the directors' pledge to put themselves up for re-election was now void, since the offer had been made to Walker, and rejected by him. This disturbed many people who had taken it as a pledge to all shareholders. Walker and his associates had maintained a barrage of criticism against the board, and Hodgson announced that the board "had no intention whatsoever of throwing away any of the company's funds in support of the Hawick Extension Scheme"[14]. By mid-July the Money Bill was passed, and the Walker party sold their NBR shares. Hodgson was triumphant, announcing at the September half-yearly meeting, again held in London, that the company was now free from debt – meaning overdue payments to creditors and short-term loans. A dividend of 2.5% on the ordinary stock was announced. Economies were still being pursued, with the Haddington and Duns Branches, built double-track, being singled; and the overall working expenses were claimed to be down to 44% of gross receipts[15].

In September 1856, the chairman confidently looked forward to the time when the Hawick-Carlisle railway would be in operation. He was not to know it was still six years away. His Liddesdale line had a further dimension. In 1853, a railway had been promoted from Hexham, on the Newcastle & Carlisle Railway, northwards into the Border hills to meet the NBR at Hawick. It was an engineers' speculative line, but was quickly taken up by local proprietors, initially as a 26-mile branch from Hexham to tap substantial coal deposits at The Plashetts, and ironstone reserves at other places. On 1 July 1854 it was incorporated as the Border Counties Railway, between Hexham and the hamlet of Belling. Laid out as a double-track line, except for its viaduct at Hexham, its construction was slow, mainly due to lack of capital. From an early stage, its directors were in touch with Hawick Town Council, then striving to break the impasse on getting a railway line to the south[16]. Extension to Hawick of the Border Counties Railway seemed the answer, giving access to both Carlisle and Newcastle, and conferring main line status on what was otherwise a mineral railway of uncertain prospects. Naturally the North British was interested, as was the Newcastle & Carlisle company[17]. The Caledonian company did not consider the Border Counties line to be of interest. The whiff of rivalry with the Newcastle & Carlisle Railway encouraged Richard Hodgson to get involved, though he considered the Border Counties Railway an alternative not to the Carlisle line but to the North Eastern, as part of an all-North British route to Newcastle. A branch from the NBR's Liddesdale line at Riccarton Burn Head to the Border Counties at The Belling became part of his strategy, and the NBR board gave a contribution of £400 towards the Border Counties Railway's parliamentary expenses[18]. But both Carlisle Bills, and the Border Counties Railway's, would be rejected in the 1857 session.

In January 1857 a reading room for employees was set up at St. Margaret's, with fines levied on locomotive department staff to go towards its book fund. This was formalised as a lending library on 10 February, with a quarterly fee of 6d (3d for appprentices[19]). Economies were still being effected: the clerk at North Berwick was dispensed with but it was resolved that "boy remain in the meantime till the driver can manage to dispense with a Guard and so free the Porter from his attendance as Guard". Sleepers from the second lines of the Haddington and Duns Branches, currently being lifted, were to be reused on other lines if in good condition[20]. Early in 1857 the company was presented with a claim for £65,000 from the Edinburgh & Glasgow Railway, as its share of expenses and works at the Waverley Bridge Station[21]. The name of 'Waverley' was coming into public use, though the NBR continued to refer to North Bridge. Official 'Badge Porters' there had to be robust and under 40 on appointment. They paid an entrance fee of 10s, and lived off tips; but could be sacked if they made excessive demands on passengers[22]. At this time the NBR had 212 passenger carriages, of which only 57 were third class; a modest number considering that in Scotland over 70% of passengers travelled third: a Board of Trade report in

A 1907 view of Riccarton Junction, showing the extensive layout and locomotive facilities. (*Stenlake Collection*)

1856 noted that 72% of Scottish passengers were third class against a UK average of 54%[23]. It is not surprising that there were frequent complaints of third class passengers invading the higher class carriages. Though the number of carriages scarcely seems excessive, in June Hurst was authorised to sell up to 30 to the Scottish North Eastern Railway, and Rowbotham was instructed to sell "the omnibus formerly run between Eskbank and Lasswade" for £50[24].

Transport of coal and iron was becoming ever more important and a typical arrangement was made with Messrs. Christie for serving Gladsmuir Ironworks and Dolphinston Colliery near Wallyford. New sidings would be laid at the customers' expense but the NBR would pay to instal the junctions. The coal rate from Wallyford to Gladsmuir would be 1s 3d per ton; to Leith 1s 9d per ton; iron from Gladsmuir to Leith would be 2s 7d per ton. A drawback of 33.33% would be given if 80-ton trainloads were made up and run at regular intervals, and if coal shipments reached a minimum of 1,800 tons a month. The agreement was for ten years, renewable for a further 21 with the same discount on whatever rate might be fixed[25]. A new mail contract was agreed from 30 March 1857, for £3,960 a year, plus 1s per mile for any additional train requested by the Post Office. This was a standard agreement, based on the one made by the Post Office with the Lancashire & Yorkshire Railway, but soon it was being tweaked. Sunday trains attracted higher charges and from 26 April the Post Office discontinued the Sunday day mail between Edinburgh and Berwick, paying a retrospective 2s per mile for its use up to that date[26]. James McLaren was appointed passenger superintendent in August, at a salary of £200 a year. One of his first tasks was to reprimand a guard for insolence to a passenger, the Rev. Mr. Parkinson, but he was not sacked since eye-witnesses reported "considerable provocation"[27].

Competing Bills were again in preparation, for the Carlisle, Langholm & Hawick Railway (CR), and the Hawick & Carlisle Junction Railway (NBR). The North British Bill provided for a junction with the Border Counties Railway at Riccarton, but the Border Counties Railway had also entered its own Bill for a different route from The Belling, bypassing Hawick to a junction near Belses, with a branch to Jedburgh. This disparity led to the withdrawal of both Bills in February[28]. The Langholm Bill was rejected in June. Across the Borders, the summer and autumn of 1857 were filled with discussions of known railway proposals and rumours of others. Richard Hodgson was negotiating with the North Eastern Railway on a possible NER/NBR merger, and deputations from each company met several times without a positive result. The North British suspected that the NER and Caledonian had a secret agreement on dividing Newcastle-Glasgow traffic, but the sticking point was the NER's insistence that net receipts, not gross, should be the basis of apportioning the combined revenues[29]. The Carlisle-Hawick line was the prime focus of attention, however; Hodgson wanted a double-track main line (except for the

Plashetts Station. Colliery spoil heaps can be seen on the hillside above. (*John Alsop*)

Riccarton-Canonbie section) linking Edinburgh, Hawick and Carlisle, preferably running through Liddesdale so that the Border Counties could link up with it. He did not mind who built it so long as it was an "open line" on which the North British would have guaranteed running powers, with facilities to take up and send on traffic at Carlisle, at rates and fares agreed with the other operators. The Caledonian's proposal was for a single-track line of a local nature, bringing coal from the Canonbie field to the Hawick mills. A special meeting of NBR shareholders on 17 August was told by Hodgson that it was a moment of crisis: was their company to be "shut up at Hawick" or allowed to expand? The proposed line would cost £450,000, of which £337,500 would be raised by shares and £112,500 by a loan. The meeting voted in favour[30]. A month later there was an up beat half-yearly meeting, with a dividend announced of 2.75% on the ordinary shares. The Edinburgh & Glasgow's claim on the joint station was going to arbitration, and the NBR had set £41,000 aside against this[31].

Lt. Col. Thomas Salkeld, vice-chairman of the Caledonian, with his allies John Scott Chisholm of Langholm and John Gibson, agent for the Duke of Buccleuch, held a meeting with Hodgson on 24 September. Though he referred to the Hawick-Carlisle line as an "open highway" for other companies' traffic, Salkeld insisted that the Caledonian should be the only company to build it and work the traffic. John Thomas called this "Caledonian arrogance at its worst"[32], but Salkeld was only doing exactly what Hodgson (as he later admitted) would have done if their roles had been exchanged: protecting the Caledonian's monopoly of Anglo-Scottish traffic through Carlisle. Already the East Coast companies, abetted by the Edinburgh & Glasgow Railway, were drawing off traffic from the West Coast. If the NBR got a foothold in Carlisle, it would demand and manoeuvre for a share of the West Coast traffic. The Caledonian had good reason to try to keep the North British "shut up" at Hawick.

The Border Counties directors had passed their surveys to Hodgson, but there was no likelihood of the NBR abandoning the Liddesdale line and the final route plan confirmed the junction location at Riccarton Burn Head. It was agreed that the Border Counties should introduce a Bill for extension of their line (none of it yet opened) to this spot[33]. Much of the argument revolved around the respective merits of Canonbie and Plashetts coal. In typical nineteenth century style, a Langholm versifier mocked Hodgson's praise of Plashetts:

Oh, Plashets, Plashets! 'Phoebus, what a name!'
To fill the speaking trump of Hodgson's fame!
Seams sixteen inches, mileage 29;
This age sure never heard of such a mine!
These coals are cheap as dirt to Hawick and Silloth,
Langholm may have them too, just as she willeth,
But Langholm spurns the gift. The proffered coal
Is just a dodge, like terminals and toll.
Oh, Hodgson, Hodgson! leave that prating style,
Go, carry coals at something less per mile.
The Caledonian is, though stern, yet true;
The only line for us, if not for you[34].

It was observed that "Mr. Hodgson is very fond of a monopoly at Hawick, but a monopoly at Carlisle is a dreadful thing" – protests from Hawick traders against overcharging by the NBR had resulted in the company having to drop its goods rates by 20-25%[35]. Through the winter, statistics and counter-statistics were brandished by the rival lines. At the NBR's half-yearly meeting on 21 February 1858, Hodgson announced that negotiations for amalgamation with the North Eastern Railway had failed, because of disagreement on the value of the North British company, which would, he said, be much greater once the Carlisle Extension was in place. The half-year's results were "good in the face of economic difficulties", though expenditure was rising faster than revenue:

	Half-year to 31 January 1857	Half-year to 31 January 1858
Passenger receipts	£59,705 8s 2 1/4 d	£61,911 14s 10 1/4 d
Goods receipts	£74,062 17s 11d	£75,105 2s 2d
Horses, mails	£2,794 2s 1d	£2,459 18s 3 1/2 d
Selkirk & Jedburgh	£1,717 19s 11d	£1,772 1s 3d
Miscellaneous	£1,173 1s 2d	£1,020 2s 8d
Total	£139,453 9s 3 1/4 d	£142,568 19s 2 3/4 d
Expenditure	£87,500 17s 1d	£82,904 12s 3 1/2 d

Goods revenue was pulling steadily ahead of passenger, a gap that would widen with the expansion of mining and heavy industry.

A considerable amount of the company's motive power was supplied by horses, which did the shunting at most places. Downie of Inveresk got 1s a day for a man and horse to move wagons at Inveresk and Fisherrow Stations[36]. Horses were both owned and hired. The NBR usually provided stable accommodation and feed. A horse could be hired from 6s a week, but at busier stations the company preferred to use its own. A contract for shoeing horses at Edinburgh, Leith and Berwick denotes ownership[37]. For additional horses for the Leith Branch, £634 15s was charged to the capital account in 1857. Horse hire, keep and harness cost around £590 in a half-year, with wages of horse drivers and pilotmen around £200. In August 1858 the board resolved that grass on NBR-owned slopes should no longer be let, but used as fodder for the company's horses[38]. Horses were part of the responsibility of the multi-tasked stores superintendent, John Lingard. Also, of course, all merchandise deliveries and collections used horse-drawn transport provided by customers or local contractors. The heavily-congested Leith line was still horse-worked. Its passenger horse-bus had been taken off in the autumn of 1856 and put to use for the winter service of the North Berwick Branch[39]. Horse manure was a saleable commodity and the NBR had a contract with Mr. Henderson of Longniddry to purchase it all, except at Kelso[40].

Despite Hodgson's comments in February, discussions with the North Eastern company were not dead. At the board meeting on 23 March a letter from York inquired what the NBR's "leading conditions" for an amalgamation would be. In the ensuing exchanges of letters, it emerged that the NER had wanted to measure the North British's worth by using its results in 1855-56-57; Hodgson wanted to include the current half-year. Finally in June Hodgson wrote to the North Eastern that he was "reluctantly compelled to terminate the negociation"[41]. In 1858 the NBR received a perhaps unexpected tribute to its punctuality. In 1857 it had been the only railway company to participate in a scheme whereby extra payments under the mail contract were made for regularity of service, and deductions taken for delays. The company was earning an extra £200 a quarter, though the Post Office did comment that the NBR mail trains ran at an average of only 25.5 mph, including stops. The scheme applied only to the night mail expresses[42], and it is likely that a special effort was ordered to keep these to time.

5. HODGSON'S RAILWAY – 2, 1858-1861

For the 1858 Parliamentary session, the company introduced a drastic-sounding Bill "to dissolve the North British Railway Company, and incorporate a new company"[1]. This measure was to consolidate previous Acts, and to simplify the negotiation of new agreements. The Act was passed on 23 July 1858 but there was no formal re-incorporation. Yet again, competing Bills for the Hawick-Carlisle route were also presented. Reviewed by the same House of Commons committee, the Langholm Bill was passed by three votes to two, and the Liddesdale Bill was rejected by the same margin, on 5 May[2]. The NBR counsel then tried to get a Hawick-Riccarton line approved, to effect the link-up with the Border Counties, but this was also rejected. Caledonian triumph was short-lived, however, as the Langholm Bill was rejected by the Lords committee in June. Another year and still no railway – angry meetings were held in Hawick, Langholm and Hexham, and both companies pledged a return in the next session. A monster dinner was organised in Hawick in early August as a tribute to Hodgson, described as "an immense sensation" with a trainload of guests from Edinburgh and points between, and a banner inscribed:

> Welcome to Hodgson!
> Come, let us dine;
> We're resolved yet to gain
> The Liddesdale line[3]

Opponents pointed out that opinion in Hawick was by no means 100% pro-North British and suggested that 600 "strangers" were brought to the feast in first class carriages by the NBR, at only 1s per head. The board had indeed approved a special rate of 1s from all stations to Hawick[4].

Work was underway on the Border Counties Railway, which opened its first ten miles, as far as Chollerford, on 29 August 1858 and by 2 December it would reach Countess Park. While the Liddesdale line remained in abeyance, under the NBR engineer, Charles Jopp, works were in progress in and around Edinburgh. A new link to the Musselburgh Branch, diverging from the Berwick line at New Hailes, would replace the steep section of the old 1831 line from Niddrie (built over an even older wagonway). At last the Leith Branch was being rebuilt, with Hurst instructed to have a new locomotive to work it by 1 March 1859[5]. The NBR had long needed to upgrade the branch, but its financial problems and difficulties with the road commissioners had delayed matters. It was only in 1857 that the Leith Docks Commission approved the use of steam by the North British from the branch into the docks. By now, too, telegraph communication extended over the whole North British system[6].

Richard Hodgson used the half-yearly shareholders' meeting on 4 September to propose to the Caledonian company that the Carlisle-Hawick railway should be a joint venture, with each company building half the line, free interchange of traffic at each end, and local traffic proceeds shared equitably. He would even accept the Langholm route and allow the CR to set the through traffic rates. Lack of any agreement for the English traffic at

Chollerford Stattion, circa 1900. (*John Alsop*)

Carlisle was a serious worry for the NBR board. But the Caledonian was not swayed and a new Liddesdale Bill was drafted[7]. Walter Wilson of Hawick led a movement to have a Royal Commision appointed to rule between the two routes, in order to avoid another Parliamentary contest, but a contest was unavoidable. Another winter of stormy meetings and demonstrations ensued, perhaps the most notable being at Kelso on 12 November. Both Hodgson and John Scott Chisholm (for the Langholm line) were Billed to speak, but each side had brought in non-Kelsonian supporters. Chisholm's speech was lost in disorder and he departed. Hodgson remained, to promise the same coal rate, of $1\frac{1}{2}d$ per ton-mile, as the other side, and to enlarge on the qualities of Plashetts coal and the excellence of Silloth Harbour[8]. He was forcefully backed up by Wilson, of whom another local rhymer wrote, "… though he gave no blows … he held a stick within an inch of his opponent's nose"[9]. After that there were no more shared meetings. At Jedburgh on 30 November another scheme won strong support: an extension of the Border Counties line from The Belling to meet the Jedburgh Railway. This up-and-over route, with a fork to Hawick, had been surveyed by Thomas Bouch, and costed at £250,000. No-one from the North British was present, but Scott Chisholm of Langholm came to express support. The Langholm line's backers were keen to see any Border Counties extension diverted well away from Hawick[10].

Finding it still had 25 tons of old fish-bellied rails from the original Dalkeith line, the company sold them to Hawthorns at £4 17s 6d a ton, to make them into axles at £15 a ton. Sleeper renewal was an ongoing problem; most of the original sleepers were decrepit, and also had been laid at a ratio of four to a 16-yard rail: five were now deemed essential. A creosoting plant was set up at Fisherrow, operative from the beginning of 1859, to help preserve new sleepers[11]. An NBR special meeting on 17 December 1858 approved purchase of the Selkirk & Galashiels Railway. A Board of Trade report on this Bill observed that it did not specify for what purposes money was to be raised and that it sought to repeal clauses in the original Selkirk & Galashiels Railway Act which restricted capital raised to use on the named undertaking only. On the North British Bill, it noted that while it allowed the NBR to raise shares to the value of £495,000, to be held separate from NBR shares, it allowed the company to guarantee 5.5% on these shares from its general receipts[12]. Richard Hodgson was already embarked on financial machinations. Mutual agreement saw Edinburgh connections improved: it was noted in January 1859 that the E&G and NBR "having agreed to allow the Caledonian Railway Company to bring in trains to the General Station, the latter company have undertaken to open their branch line, made a considerable time ago, betwixt their main line and Haymarket Station". A connection at Granton between the Caledonian and Edinburgh Perth & Dundee lines was also to be laid[13]. A grand – and for the NBR unusual – gesture celebrated Robert Burns's centenary by selling return tickets on the 25th at the single rate from all stations on the system, for all classes[14]. The company rarely made concessions to passengers: more typical was a refusal to build a footbridge at the new suburban station of Joppa and a grudging agreement, at the Great Northern's request, to put cushioned seats into second class carriages – but only on through trains into England[15].

Reedsmouth, where the Border Counties and Wansbeck Valley lines met. The large tank held 60,000 gallons of water. (*John Alsop*)

Not since the battle between the Nithsdale and Annandale routes to Glasgow, 20 years before, had there been such vociferous public engagement with competing railway projects as there was between the Langholm and Liddesdale lines. Even a Parliamentary committee in London might understand that in 1859 one or other must be approved. A range of Scottish railway Bills was up for scrutiny that spring. Apart from the Hawick-Carlisle proposals, they included a new Border Counties Railway Bill for its "Liddesdale section" between Plashetts and Riccarton; a railway between Peebles and Innerleithen and, not in Scotland at all, the Wansbeck Railway – a line in Northumberland which would run from Reedsmouth, on the Border Counties Railway to Morpeth. At Morpeth there was not only the North Eastern main line, but an independent railway, the Blyth & Tyne, with its own line to Newcastle. Its capital was set at £120,000, in £10 shares. As a generator of local traffic, the Wansbeck Railway's potential was modest, though vigorously talked up by Hodgson. As a link in a wholly North British controlled route between Edinburgh and Newcastle, he saw it as very important indeed, though not all his colleagues agreed and a petition from the Wansbeck promoters, "craving assistance", was turned down[16]. The historian of the North Eastern suggested further considerations: the Wansbeck was a lever to force the NER into paying the North British a greater share of the East Coast revenue, or to give better amalgamation terms[17].

A resonant name had been found for the Liddesdale line, the Border Union Railway. At its southern end, it was now to cross over the Caledonian to a junction with the Port Carlisle Railway, which had its own station, Canal, in Carlisle, and meet the Silloth Railway at Drumburgh. The Bill provided for the North British to lease both the Carlisle railways, as well as to have running powers for a last mile and five chains into the Caledonian/Lancaster & Carlisle Citadel Station, and to make use of it. A document of amalgamation with the Carlisle companies had been approved by the NBR board back in September 1857. It included a clause committing them to subscribe £30,000 to the Hawick line[18]. This was shrewd planning, not only minimising use of the Caledonian tracks, but also giving the North British the port of Silloth from which, if railway connections southwards were refused, traffic could be sent on by sea. The Commons Parliamentary committee had to decide, in effect, between the NBR's trunk route and the Caledonian's local line. On 22 March it opted for the trunk line through Liddesdale, and the Caledonian Bill was thrown out. The Bill still had to be passed by the Lords, but it was a triumph for Hodgson after a long, hard campaign, and he told the NBR half-yearly meeting on 24 March (specially delayed for the news) that:

> "Had the North British been shut up between the Caledonian and the North Eastern Railway, it would have been totally dependent on these companies … and it was the duty of the directors of these companies to bring the screw to bear on the North British Company … He would have done so himself had he been a director of these companies".

Now, the NBR "instead of being a mere puppet in the hands of the companies around it, was able not only to hold its own but to exercise an influence on the railway system on the borders of England and Scotland"[19]. The stock market was unmoved. North British £100 ordinary shares stood at £61 10s, compared to Caledonian at £84 12s 6d and Glasgow & South Western at £93 15s. It was not a good year for railway shares and two months later the prices were £53 12s 6d, £77 10s, and £91 – the NBR was almost invariably the lowest quoted of the three companies[20]. Despite an attempt by a shareholder, Mr. Barstow (a former CR director and "Caledonian tool or dupe" according to Hodgson) at a Wharncliffe meeting, to stop the Bill in the Lords, the NBR's fifth attempt at the Hawick extension got the royal assent on 21 July. The Border Counties Railway's Bill was also passed[21]. Under a banner inscribed 'Vive le Hodgson', his wife cut the first sod of the line at Hawick on 7 September.

The Border Counties Railway Act of 5 August 1859 gave the North British powers to contribute funds, guarantee loan interest, and put a director on the board. £50,000 of capital was provided and building of the Riccarton line got under way. The Wansbeck Railway Bill was also passed, and an agreement was made to establish traffic between the North British, Border Counties, Wansbeck, Port Carlisle, Silloth Bay (the Marshall Dock at Silloth had opened on 3 August), and Blyth & Tyne Railways[22]. The North British was over the Border, which did not please the North Eastern company. Hamilton Ellis observed, "Noteworthy was the way in which these lines were built not as offshoots of the North British, but *extended towards it*. Thus the North British Company kicked its way into holy Northumberland, whether the North Eastern liked it or not"[23]. Though there had been a continuous line between Kelso and Tweedmouth since 1851, there were no through trains and passengers had to rebook at Kelso[24]. The Border Union Railway was authorised to raise capital of £495,000 and loans of £165,000, and tenders were promptly sought for construction, in nine sections. In all cases the lowest bid was accepted, to a total of £306,319 18s 6d. Very soon some contractors regretted their low tenders and tried to back out[25]. While Border Union shares were going on the market, the NBR had to confront its own needs for expenditure. It still had only 72 locomotives, of which nineteen were "non-effective", and in September orders for £68,950 worth of plant were placed, including one powerful tank engine, four "very powerful express engines", two small express tank engines, and two heavy goods engines. 300 hopper-bottomed coal or lime wagons, 100 merchandise wagons, 40 cattle trucks and 12 first class carriages were also ordered. A tender of £25,937 10s for 150,000 Baltic wood sleepers, ready-creosoted, was accepted, from Gleddon of Northallerton. The directors' remuneration pool was raised from £600 to £1,000 and the board reinstated its law committee (in abeyance for some years), of four directors including the chairman[26]. There were ever more legal issues: claims from passengers injured in accidents, thefts from goods trains and depots (fruit, cheese, grain and spirits the main commodities affected), disputes relating to land acquisition, company liability to pay poor rates and other local taxes. Between October 1859 and December 1860 the law committee would deal with 549 claims, of which 376 were against items damaged in transit. Not least was the question of coal or mineral reserves lying under railway lines. Rights to minerals were always reserved by landowners. Since mining often led to surface subsidence, railway companies did not want diggings beneath their lines. Proprietors claimed a right to receive the value of the "stoops" of un-mined coal, and railways might have to compensate both a tenant for loss of revenue and the landowner for loss of royalties. Except where viaducts were involved, the companies often risked subsidence rather than pay out. The board had long discussions in 1860 about whether to buy a stoop at Drummore Colliery, near Musselburgh, and eventually decided on payment, but nine years later encroachment of coal workings there was still an issue[27].

In November 1859 the NBR directors met a deputation from the board of the Edinburgh, Perth & Dundee Railway, and both sides agreed that a closer connection between the companies would be beneficial. A proposition was to be made by 1 January, but no action resulted at this time. With his southern routes established, or in projection, Hodgson was turning his attention northwards. After cutbacks and neglect, there was some investment in St. Margaret's, with a 30 cwt steam hammer and a 1¼ inch punching machine ordered. It had built two tender and two tank engines in the half-year to 31 January 1860, and by then employed 686 men and boys, an increase of 120 on the comparative half-year. Hurst's report also contained a list of the Carlisle companies' stock, which the NBR had already taken over: three locomotives, two tenders, three first class carriages, six seconds, two composites, one horse carriage, two passenger guard's vans, 125 goods/mineral wagons, six cattle trucks, nine covered vans and one goods guard's van[28].

In an improving economic climate, railway expansion was hotting up again. The Parliamentary session of 1860-61 had 260 railway Bills, the most since 1846. Seven were from the NBR, including acquisition of the Border Counties and the Peebles and Jedburgh Railways, at guaranteed annual payments for the latter two of 3.5% of capital for three years, and 4% in perpetuity thereafter; the capital being £70,000 and £30,580 respectively. Following representations from the Peebles chairman, Sir Graham Montgomery, the proposed guarantee was raised to 4.5% of gross proceeds, "… the permanent interests involved in the settlement of some point where a limit should be placed on the encroachment of the Caledonian Company on the ground legitimately occupied by the North British, renders the concession of 0.5% per annum in a £70,000 stock, comparatively of small account." A Wharncliffe meeting of Peebles shareholders, however, decided that the terms were still too low, and the Peebles company remained independent[29]. Montgomery resigned. With traffic rising fast, and the Carlisle line to come, the NBR also had a Bill entered for acquisition of the site of Edinburgh's fruit & vegetable market, adjacent to Waverley Station on the south side, extending underneath two of the three main arches of the North Bridge. As with all issues between the railway company and Edinburgh's city councillors, it was to be a long drawn out affair. In 1858 the council had refused a low offer of £4,290 from Hodgson and he rejected a demand for £12,000 from the council. By 1860 the old principle of "ground for ground" was re-established, but the plan (and the Bill) foundered on inability to agree where the new market site should be. Charles Jopp, the NBR's engineer, described the station as it then was: the passenger shed was 170 yards long and 39 $\frac{1}{3}$ yards wide, with a platform 33 feet wide on the north, and 30 feet wide on the south side. There was a cab-stand 130 yards long and 22 feet wide. Five lines of rails ran through the shed, of which the centre one was kept clear for transfer goods to the Edinburgh & Glasgow and Edinburgh, Perth & Dundee lines. Under the Waverley Bridge was another platform, 45 yards long and in places only 3 feet wide. Apart from special trains, 86 scheduled passenger trains used the station daily, 59 of them being North British, and the need for enlargement was vital[30]. Between May and September 1860 a Dalkeith passenger service was again run from St. Leonards, in addition to that from Waverley. As a separate issue, arbitration on the North British share of Waverley Station building costs awarded £55,411 12s 2d to the Edinburgh & Glasgow. The NBR had already paid £40,000 but now had to pass on the extra amount.

In 1857 a correspondent in the *Fife Herald* had noted, "I went down to Charlestown in the omnibus by the Elgin Railway. We started at 2.25 pm and after nearly three quarters of an hour's hard riding by horse and partly by steam, we found ourselves about 300 yards from the Dunfermline Station. It was a stand every other half-minute, or a run back, or a shift of some kind …"[31]. The Charlestown Railway & Harbour Act of 1859 recorded that the company had four locomotives, one tender, two coal trucks and 223 coal wagons, 35 goods trucks, one covered van, and two passenger carriages. It would seem that around 1860 local services in Fife left a lot to be desired. Three rival schemes were seeking to close the railway gap between the Forth Ferry and Dunfermline. The Edinburgh & Dunfermline Railway was backed by local interests on the Fife side, including the West of Fife

The east side of Waverley Station before the remodelling of the 1890s. (*North British Railway Study Group*)

Mineral Railway, and by the North British, which would put up £36,000 and supply working plant and ferry-boats; the West of Fife Mineral Railway, would subscribe £40,000. Thomas Bouch, lately of the Edinburgh & Northern, now a freelance, was retained as engineer. Its Bill, drafted by the NBR, included a clause authorising the North British to sell the Halbeath Railway to it. The Edinburgh & Glasgow Railway proposed a branch line to Port Edgar, with a ferry to a 'Dunfermline & Queensferry Railway' on the north bank. Finally, the Edinburgh Perth & Dundee company was seeking authorisation for a line between its ferry terminal at Burntisland, and Dunfermline. The fight for Fife was well and truly on. At this time, a merger between the Edinburgh & Glasgow, Scottish Central, and Caledonian Railways was again being mooted, and the hand of the Caledonian was seen behind a wider scheme. The Fife & Kinross Railway was to apply for running powers over the Edinburgh Perth & Dundee, Kinross-shire, and West of Fife Mineral Railways. All that then would be needed was a new line between Kinross and Perth, "and with the Caledonian amalgamation carried, one of the happiest families would be constituted which we know of"[32]. Not if the North British could stop it. Seven NBR board sub-committees were set up to watch over its Bills; Hodgson chaired all of them. But none of the Dunfermline schemes was passed. Perhaps in connection with these plans, Rowbotham and two colleagues inspected the Halbeath Railway on 20 September 1860, still running coal from Halbeath and Townhill Collieries to Inverkeithing. From May 1858 to May 1859 its receipts were £894 0s 4d and its expenses were £867 6s 2d: gross profit £26 14s 2d. It owned 72 wagons and employed 28 horses. Donald Peddie, still its manager, informed Rowbotham that arrangements with customers were purely verbal, with no written records[33].

The NBR acquired the Jedburgh Railway in an act of 3 July. The same determination to block Caledonian expansion that lay behind the company's interest in the Peebles line was evident in a new agreement with the local promoters of a line along the Tweed from Peebles to Innerleithen and Galashiels, 18.5 miles, to cost £70,000, and to be worked by the NBR at 43% of gross revenue. The NBR would also invest £44,000. The half-year report in March noted that the Caledonian was seeking to extend its Symington-Broughton line to Peebles, and foresaw the probability of "invasion" of the lower Tweed valley. But the Bill was rejected[34]. From 13 August 1860 the Border Counties Railway was duly vested in the North British, its enlarged share capital of £280,000 converted on an equal footing into NBR consolidated stock, and presenting its new owner with a useful dowry of £120,000 in newly-raised preference shares[35]. But the NBR was committed to a further investment of £70,000 in the Border Counties Railway, on top of £50,000 subscribed in 1859.

In 1860 the North British was the fourth-largest railway company in Scotland. In the half-year to 31 January 1860 it had a gross revenue of £157,516, and paid a dividend of 3% on the ordinary shares; the Edinburgh & Glasgow had a gross revenue of £188,625 and paid 4%; the Glasgow & South Western had a gross income of £198,950 and paid 5.5%. The Caledonian gross revenue was £381,410 and its dividend was 5%. The working expenses of the North British Railway were 40.6% of revenue; of the Edinburgh & Glasgow Railway, 38%; of the Glasgow & South Western Railway, 37.75%; the Caledonian Railway's were 70%.

The Leith Branch, now steam-powered, was very busy. On 14 May 1860 the NBR completed a drawbridge to extend tracks to the South Quay, where a steam crane could hoist and discharge open-ended coal wagons[36]. Baileyfield had become a corner of industry, adding to the smokes emanating from nearby St. Margaret's. The NBR had set up a corn-bruising and hay-cutting plant, presumably on its customers' behalf, and five furnaces were to be made for steeling rails according to Dodds's patent[37]. Frequent complaints about smoke were regularly rebuffed by the company. This year Edinburgh's one o' clock 'time gun' was instituted, and the NBR contributed £5 to its cost. By now Richard Hodgson was the darling of the shareholders, delivering regular half-yearly dividends of 2.5% to 3%. Though he dominated the board, three members were of sufficiently independent mind to oppose him on occasion. George Kinloch deplored a motion for the company to invest up to £30,000 in railways proposed in the hilly country between Edinburgh and Penicuik: "making branches had been ruinous to the North British Railway". Mark Sprot, the vice-chairman, and Benjamin Craven (one of Robert Walker's nominees, now a director) also opposed. But these were only part of Hodgson's agenda; reporting local interest in an extension of the Duns Branch to Melrose, a 22-mile line to cost £100,000, he proposed the NBR should put up half the capital and work the line for 50% of gross proceeds. He wanted to proceed with purchase of the Port Carlisle and Silloth railways and to lend £20,000 to the Silloth company for dock works[38].

By December an initial agreement with the two Carlisle companies had been worked out: the NBR would work both for four years. The advance to the Silloth company was cut back to £10,000. Numerous local lines, in theory independent schemes, were having their initial deposits, payable before a Bill could be lodged, funded by the NBR, including the Esk Valley (to Polton from a junction on the Peebles Railway, with a long tunnel under Lasswade), Edinburgh & Dunfermline, and Innerleithen & Peebles companies. The total sum required, £28,000, could only be raised by new bank Bills in the directors' names[39]. The Carlisle arrangements were in anticipation of the Border Union Railway being up and running. But the news from the construction sites was of difficulties and delays. Particularly on the hill sections, the contractors had been having trouble in getting the work done within their prices. Unquestionably it was a tough route, but there were no topographical features to contend with that had not already been met by railway builders elsewhere in Britain, and the delays had much to do with the low tenders accepted and the lack of determined engineering supervision. In March 1860 James Douglas of Cavers gave a soirée to over 200 navvies on the Hawick section, with tea, beef, bread, songs and music – a "love feast" in the interest of the temperance movement. But in August the Hawick magistrates had to swear in special constables because of riotous goings-on among the workers[40]. In the Stephensons' time, almost a generation before, the engineer would have been far more in evidence, but the engineer of the Border Union (and of the Border Counties line), Hodgson's friend J.F. Tone, was far from being a Stephenson or a Locke. The most testing sections were the Whitrope, Riccarton and Hermitage lengths, and Anthony Ritson's Whitrope (with the 1,208-yard tunnel and viaduct) and Riccarton contracts became a saga of delays, demands for advances by him – £6,000 was authorised by the urgency committee in June – and warnings from the company, until he was compelled to sign a document by which the NBR could give him one day's notice of taking possession[41]. He was eventually ousted and the company took over. Davidson & Oughterson, on the Carlisle section, went bankrupt, and by a majority board decision, Charles Jopp was instructed to complete the section by direct labour[42]. Exceptionally heavy rain was blamed, but cut-price contracts and poor management played their part.

Perhaps in order to make the North Berwick Branch pay better, the company took an interest in the North Berwick Hotel Company, and contributed a loan of £600 at 5% interest for new furnishings. In 1860 the NBR and NER agreed with the GNR's proposal to provide a special range of carriages for the East Coast expresses. Known as the East Coast Joint Stock, they were handsome vehicles with a teakwood-finish, with 50 built initially, of which the North British was responsible for four first class carriages at £310 apiece, two second class at £245 and one brake at £215. From August 1861 Great Northern guards worked right through to Edinburgh[43]. In early 1861 the pay of NBR goods guards was put up to a scale of 21s-25s a week. William Hurst's pay went up to £100 a year. He also got 2.5% commission on sales of scrap material. At the end of 1860 a directors' Plant Committee had recommended the ordering of 308 assorted wagons, nine first class carriages and six new locomotives, together with installation of the Newall continuous brake system on 60 trains. This added up to £46,472 and might have kept Hurst busy, but in 1861 he joined with J.P. Lythgoe (the company accountant) and others to set up the Scottish Waggon Company, its function "to supply railways and mineral companies with waggons on hire for terms of three years and upwards". Its offices were very close to the NBR's at 63 North Bridge, Edinburgh (moving a little distance to South St. David Street in 1865), and Hurst was openly listed as a director in its notices[44]. The Newall brake was one aspect of modernising the working. Another was in progress with the abandonment of loading luggage on to carriage roofs[45]; but the inadequacy of many stations and the poor condition of the rolling stock drew complaints. Portobello Station was "a wooden shed with a room boarded off at the end", and at Edinburgh a fastidious passenger complained of puddles, dirt and "having to pass through, and rub shoulders with, the fisherwomen pulling their buckets of fish along the platform"[46]. A subway linking the Leith and main line platforms was actually being made at Portobello, but the board was more interested in making economies in working than in spending money on improvements – the chairman by now knew how little real money was available after guaranteed payments, dividends, subscriptions to new companies and legal/parliamentary fees had been met. But he kept silent about this. Improvements were made when essential, like three iron bridges to replace worn-out wooden ones on the Hawick line. In the hope of stemming the constant drain of claims against pilferage, it was decided that "the Manager should appoint a Detective privately". Unlike other companies, incidentally, the NBR board minutes did not record deaths of staff due to accident or negligence. But dismissals, normally for theft or drunkenness, were regularly noted. Money could still be found for expansion of the system. At a special general meeting of shareholders in August 1861 the board was authorised to subscribe £50,000 towards the Wansbeck Railway (62.5% of its capital) and to work the line at a guaranteed 4% on the capital. The sum of £296,820 was to be raised by a £10 share issue, guaranteed a 5% dividend for ten years, after which the company could redeem them at a 10% premium[47].

A new arrangement with the Peebles Railway Company had to be made and in January 1861 the North British agreed to permanently lease the line, with a guaranteed dividend raised to 5% of the capital. Pending an act of Parliament, a temporary agreement was effected from 1 February, and the NBR purchased the Peebles Company's rolling stock for £20,000[48]. The Peebles Railway (Lease) Act was passed on 11 July[49], but both Bills for the Edinburgh-Dunfermline route were thrown out: the five-mile gap between North Queensferry and Dunfermline remained. At this time, the NBR also had a Bill in Parliament for a wholly English railway, from Newcastle to the Derwent Valley and into Weardale, competing with a North Eastern proposal for the same route. Hodgson however expressed the hope that the NER would see the North British as "its true and natural ally" and that it would no longer seek to occupy "too exclusively" the district which divided the NBR from "the great railways to the south"[50]. The NBR Bill was rejected. In April 1861 Hodgson was returned to Parliament in a by-election, as Conservative member for Tynemouth & South Shields, which he would represent until 1865. Having lost his seat at Berwick in 1847, he had failed there again in 1852 and 1853, and by a single vote in 1859: in that election both sides were found by a Select Committee of Parliament to have bribed voters, in Hodgson's case using job promises on the NBR as well as money. Hodgson was listed as guilty of bribery but no action was taken against him[51].

From 11 October 1861 goods trains were running between Carlisle and Scotch Dyke but delays on other Border Union sections were still a concern. Captain Tyler of the Board of Trade refused to allow passenger trains until the Caledonian doubled 500 yards of the track of its Port Carlisle Branch to meet the Caledonian line – this was done by 7 March 1862. The Caledonian refused to carry NBR wires on its telegraph poles: as full opening drew nearer, the impasse was as great as ever.

Significant developments in Fife were suggested in the half-yearly report of the Edinburgh Perth & Dundee company on 1 September 1861, which revealed that negotiations were going on with the North British for either amalgamation or joint working of their systems[52]. The Edinburgh Perth & Dundee had just taken over the new Kinross Railway, traversing an area of coal pits between Lumphinnans, on the Edinburgh Perth & Dundee Railway main line, and Kinross, where it shared a joint station with the Fife & Kinross Railway, which had opened between Ladybank and Kinross on 15 March 1858, and was worked by the Edinburgh Perth & Dundee from 5 April 1861. Other mergers had already taken place in Fife that year: the East of Fife and Leven Railway companies amalgamated on 22 July, with plans to extend eastwards to Anstruther; and on 1 August the West of Fife Mineral Railway, Charlestown Railway, and Elgin Railways combined to form the West of Fife Railway & Harbour Co. A short new line, the Leslie Railway, had opened on 1 February from Markinch, with a branch to the Auchmuty paper mills. A strategic eye could readily perceive further opportunities for amalgamation.

To the disquiet of some North British directors, large sums of money were still being committed to new railways which were finding it hard to raise their own full capital: £10,000 to the Esk Valley Railway; £50,000 to the Berwickshire Railway's line from Duns to St. Boswells[53]. A board motion to build no more branches south of Edinburgh until the Border Union and Border Counties lines were finished, was lost by five votes to four, but Hodgson promised not to propose any more without the concurrence of eight directors[54], and when the working agreement with the Leadburn, Linton & Dolphinton Railway was approved, it was stated that the NBR was not subscribing any capital[55]. Current ideas among railway promoters were expressed by Charles Wilson, chairman of a Berwickshire Railway support meeting held in Earlston, stating "a well ascertained fact that any line of railway would pay having ten miles on both sides of it not interfered with by any other company … and a fair population in need of coal, lime, etc."[56]. This referred to the parallel NBR-NER line between St. Boswells and Tweedmouth, only ten or twelve miles to the south of his proposed railway.

Trains cross at Earlston, 1907. (*John Alsop*)

By now the North British was Scotland's third-biggest railway company in terms of receipts, after the Caledonian and the Glasgow & South Western; comparative gross revenues for 1860 were: Caledonian: £789,941; Glasgow & South Western £418,436; North British £322,622; Edinburgh & Glasgow £209,701; Scottish North Eastern £199,581; Scottish Central £195,120[57]. The North British was still hungry for expansion. At the half-yearly shareholders' meeting on 27 September 1861, Hodgson noted a big jump in passenger numbers, from 745,868 in the half-year of February-July 1860 to 860,046 in the current half-year. Of those, 125,145 travelled first, 178,825 second, 96,959 third, and 449,116 fourth (this being the penny-a-mile fare on 'Parliamentary' trains). He spoke up for the merger with the Edinburgh, Perth & Dundee company: what the NBR wanted was "an East Coast Route to Perth". The Edinburgh, Perth & Dundee Railway was paying a dividend of only 0.5% and the basis of amalgamation was three of its shares for one North British. One influential shareholder, John McGavin, said the Edinburgh, Perth & Dundee directors were mad to accept these terms and warned that Hodgson's schemes were "bold and perilous"[58]. Bills were being lined up for the new Parliamentary session, including a line from Monktonhall, on the Berwick line, to Smeaton, where it would divide into an eastward branch to Ormiston and Macmerry, and a southern line passing east of Dalkeith to Hardengreen, giving access to the Border Union and Peebles lines and the proposed Esk Valley Railway to Lasswade and Polton. Another attempt at Edinburgh-Dunfermline was to be made (the Edinburgh & Glasgow Railway also was renewing its proposal), plus a line from Dunfermline to Perth; also a Bill to compel the Glasgow & South Western to accept through bookings between the Border Union and the 'Port Line' to Portpatrick, and another for vesting of the two Carlisle-Silloth companies in the NBR. With so many new plans, some agreed projects were deferred, and the Peebles-Galashiels line was put on hold[59].

On the footplate: driver Wilson of Haymarket at the regulator. (*John Alsop*)

6. HODGSON'S RAILWAY – 3, 1861-1864

One of John Learmonth's ambitions for the NBR had been to invigorate Edinburgh's commercial life, and a sketch of the city's activities is given in Measom's 1861 '*Official Illustrated Guide*'. There were still few large industries other than brewing, but thirteen life assurance offices with an aggregate annual income of £2 million, and funds realised and invested of upwards of £11 million. Among the larger factories were James Milne's Gas Metre [sic] and Appliance Works, the Holyrood Glass Works, Tennant's Steam Engine Works and the Corrugated Iron Works. The coal trade was not mentioned. Best hotel was the Waterloo, hard by Waverley Station. Big factories were on the tourist itinerary. Moving on to Glasgow, Measom reports of the Tennant Chemical Works, near Cowlairs, that "we can promise strangers a courteous reception at these important works". He also refers to "the green fields of Stobcross", on which the North British would soon have designs[1].

Thomson, contractor for the Border Union's Hawick section, with three viaducts, was far behind, and the board agonised over whether to spur him with a bonus or sack him[2]. In the end he completed the task. Hodgson acknowledged the delays and spending increases on both the Border Union Railway and Border Counties Railway lines, blaming the weather mostly, and illegal sale of alcohol to navvies partly; but compensation to landowners and Parliamentary/legal charges had brought the costs up by £122,799 8s 6d, apart from extra charges on the actual works. The Bill for the 'Edinburgh, Perth & Dunfermline Junction Railway' was lost through not conforming with the Commons' Standing Orders, but the NBR proposed to reintroduce it. Sales of lately-issued shares were slow, and the directors underwrote loans of £40,000 to the company from the Royal, National and Union Banks. But another dividend of 3% was duly announced[3] and a special meeting on 23 May approved the takeovers of the Edinburgh Perth & Dundee and the West of Fife Mineral Railways, also the £50,000 investment in the Berwickshire Railway[4]. James Nairne, the secretary, negotiated an overdraft of £100,000 from the Union Bank, repayable in August 1863, again backed by directors' guarantees. By now they were getting increasingly nervous about their commitments. Only Kinloch had not signed the guarantees, which now covered more than £300,000 of loans[5].

The entire Border Union line was opened for goods trains on 23 June and for passengers on 1 July 1862. From the first it was named and promoted as the Waverley Route[6]. Work was not finished; the telegraph line was not installed, and the Riddings-Riccarton section was only a single line. The Border Counties line was completed with the opening of the Riccarton-Plashetts section on the same dates. Railway politics along the Border changed on 17 July, when the North Eastern and Newcastle & Carlisle Railways amalgamated. North British opposition was withdrawn when it was guaranteed running powers between Hexham and Newcastle Central. A reciprocal bestowal of NER running powers between Berwick and Edinburgh perhaps seemed only a gesture, but would later generate a long dispute. With this arrangement, the NBR no longer needed the Blyth & Tyne's line into Newcastle, and the strategic value of the Wansbeck Railway, newly part-opened between Morpeth and Scots

**Silloth Convalescent Home, opened in 1862, with its platform and invalid train.
The siding also served a saltworks. (*Stenlake Collection*)**

Gap, evaporated. The junction at Reedsmouth was altered to face south to Hexham instead of north to Riccarton[7]. Arrangements for a 999-year lease of the Carlisle & Silloth Bay Railway & Dock from 1 August were also authorised, at a fixed annual rent of £2,000 from 1 February 1863 plus a half-yearly dividend on their capital of £165,000 at the same rate as the NBR ordinary dividend. The Port Carlisle Dock & Railway was leased for 999 years at a fixed annual rent of £3,100 plus, if the NBR ordinary dividend should go over 4%, the excess above that figure to be paid also on the Port Carlisle Dock & Railway ordinary shares of £70,600[8]. These were generous terms for the struggling Cumberland companies. While the Bill was under consideration, Lord Redesdale commented, "The North British Company are the best hands in the world that I know of for making bad bargains, and they certainly have made a most decided hit on this occasion"[9]. On 1 August the opening of the Waverley Route was celebrated, with a special train from Edinburgh and a feast in the carriage shed at Carlisle for around 700 guests. Hodgson in his speech looked back to 1857 when the North British was a small company with only 150 miles of line. Now it had 500 and was set to expand even further. On this expansive occasion, the NBR's horizons seemed wide: George Kinloch hinted heavily that the company might take over the still-building Inverness & Perth Junction Railway "at no distant day"[10]. Thomas Bruce, Lord Elgin's brother, chairman of the Inverness & Perth Junction Railway, was present and briefly joined the North British board (1862-63). But the Highland lines had a solid and long-standing relationship with the Caledonian.

With the opening of the Waverley Route, East Coast goods traffic from Edinburgh to London fell from 4,045 tons in 1861 to 624 tons in 1863[11]. The North British was doing its best to use its new line. But the Carlisle speeches glossed over the fact that, although it had running powers into the Citadel Station, the North British had no facilities for through bookings of goods or passengers south of Carlisle. There would be no traffic for it, except for what was specifically consigned via the NBR. And although it now offered an alternative route from Edinburgh, passengers and goods consigners from Edinburgh to cities like Liverpool or Manchester would still find it more convenient to use the Caledonian line, as before. As a result, the Silloth Harbour connection assumed great importance. In June Rowbotham had been instructed to advertise for a paddle boat to operate between Silloth and Ireland; and a Mr. Jacob was appointed goods manager south of Hawick and superintendent of Carlisle-Silloth at a salary of £350 plus 2.5% commission on tonnage revenue over £10,000 (the current level was £7,000). He proved more interested in his own affairs and was paid off with £100 in October[12].

An Act was obtained on 3 June 1862 for the branch from Monktonhall to Ormiston and Macmerry, and to Hardengreen Junction, involving purchase of an 1840 horse tramway owned by the Duke of Buccleuch, carrying coal from Thorneybank to Dalkeith. It was to be double-line between Inveresk and Dalkeith, except for a viaduct over the South Esk. Difficulties with two local landowners, Sir John Don Wauchope and Mr. Dick, had to be bought off with an annual wayleave payment of £1,000 each[13]. The board could also congratulate itself on receiving the royal assent, on 29 July, to its acquisition of the Edinburgh, Perth & Dundee (including the Kinross and West of Fife Railway & Harbour companies). The terms reflected their relative strengths: West of Fife Railway & Harbour shareholders were guaranteed 5% on their company's capital of £130,000. Edinburgh, Perth & Dundee Railway shareholders would receive nothing unless the NBR ordinary dividend exceeded 2%, with any further amount to be applied equally, so that if the North British Railway stock paid 2.25%, Edinburgh, Perth & Dundee Railway would pay 0.25%, and so on[14]. The North British was now the prime railway operator in Fife, though there was no physical connection apart from the train ferries between Granton and Burntisland. On the former Charlestown Railway, work was almost completed on a new locomotive-worked incline down to the harbour at Charlestown, replacing the rope-worked Pittencrieff incline. It opened on 27 October, and the North British also put in hand plans to improve the harbour. Thomas Bouch designed coal drops (seven eventually) and four shunt horses were bought from the Elgin Estates.

The NBR also now owned Edinburgh's Canal Street Station, at right angles to Waverley, with its tunnel, engine-house and smokestack, and renamed it Princes Street. A news item in January 1863 foresaw a short future for it, as the NBR was planning "a large station on the site between Princes Street and Canal Street, partly occupied at present by the Edinburgh, Perth & Dundee Railway Station. The North British will retain their share of right to the joint station at Waverley Bridge" and would also take a portion of the vegetable market, in return for new accommodation, currently under arbitration[15]. By now the company possessed 102 engines, of which eighteen were non-effective; to which were added the Edinburgh, Perth & Dundee stock of 20 passenger and eighteen goods engines, and nine "four-wheeled engines". Among the staff taken into NBR employment was John Walker, Edinburgh, Perth & Dundee Railway interim secretary, born in Cupar, who became company registrar (treasurer from August 1863) and would be a key figure in its operations for many years. But the two rival Bills for Dunfermline-Queensferry were both thrown out; the North British one because of bad drafting: the Bill specified compulsory powers to take over the Forth Ferry while the preliminary notice had only allowed for permissive powers. This was bemoaned but the failure of the E&G's Bill was greeted with glee in Dunfermline and Inverkeithing, where it was believed to be a phantom scheme which would never have been built. Both companies pledged to re-enter their Bills in the next session.

Additional capital was badly needed and a special meeting of shareholders was held on 31 August to approve the board's issuing of £220,000-worth of 5% preference stock, redeemable in 1872 or later at a 10% premium. It emerged that expenditure on the Border Union, to date, was £847,000 – exceeding the capital raised by £199,000.

A view east towards the North Bridge, the sheds of the Edinburgh and Glasgow Railway's goods station are in the centre and to their left is the roof of the Joint Station.

A further £300,000 was needed. No shipping company appeared keen to start an Irish service from Silloth. Railway companies were unable, under their acts of incorporation, to purchase or operate ships, but this legality was circumvented with the purchase through nominees of the paddle-steamer *Ariel*, to work between Silloth, Ireland and Liverpool[16]. The Glasgow steamship owners G.&.J Burns tried and failed to get a court interdict on the use of the *Ariel*[17]. To legitimise its steamer ownership, the company put forward a Bill to allow it to build and operate steamships on sea routes (it was already the legitimate owner of ferryboats). *Ariel* ran a weekly Belfast service, advertised as "in connection with the North British and North Eastern Railways", and Newcastle-Belfast through tickets could be bought[18]. As Silloth Harbour proprietors, the NBR also had to maintain the Solway Lightship, paying its master 25*s* a week and his crew £1.

Tenders were requested for the Langholm Branch, Peebles-Galashiels, and the Berwickshire Railway. With the Edinburgh, Perth & Dundee Railway safely incorporated, Hodgson informed the half-yearly meeting that he was keen to effect a merger with the Edinburgh & Glasgow company. But the much-enlarged NBR could only reward its shareholders with a 1% dividend for the first half of 1862. Hodgson promised better things to come and all the directors, having put themselves up for re-election, were duly re-elected[19].

Amalgamation of the Edinburgh & Glasgow Railway with the Caledonian and Scottish Central companies had been proposed several times and refused by Parliament. In January 1863 the East Coast companies, including the North British, had a go, with a Bill for the 999-year lease of the E&G at an annual 5% of its ordinary share capital of £2,218,929. The Bill was thrown out in February, and the Edinburgh & Glasgow re-committed itself to the embrace of the Caledonian. A NBR Bill to enable the raising of £500,000 in shares and £165,000 by new loans was successful. Preference shares at 5%, amounting to £300,000, were to be based on Border Union revenue, and Border Union stocks and accounts were to be incorporated with those of the North British. That would spare Hodgson from future disclosures such as that in its first six months, the Waverley Route had an excess of revenue over costs of only £1,165 6*s* 0*d*[20]: much would have to change if it was to fund 5% on £300,000, on top of the original capital. The dividend on NBR ordinary shares in March 1863 was 0.75%, and Hodgson fell back on the old excuse of bad trade, in this case the failure of the Lothians potato crop. Nothing had happened to improve or enlarge the overcrowded Edinburgh station, still jointly owned by the NBR and the Edinburgh & Glasgow, and Hodgson pledged not to start until funds were available.

Station amenities were few, but by 1864 refreshment rooms were leased at some: Ladybank, Thornton, Princes Street (i.e. Canal Street), Waverley, Galashiels, Melrose, Newtown (St Boswells), Kelso and Berwick. All were termini or junctions where long waits might be endured. Bookstalls were set up in some stations; in November 1862 John Menzies had taken a five year lease of the Waverley stall at £180 a year, beginning a long connection

Beyer Peacock 0-4-2 No. 329, originally No. 83 of the Edinburgh & Glasgow Railway. (*John Alsop*)

Knowesgate Station on the Wansbeck Valley line, *circa* **1900. (***John Alsop***)**

with the NBR and its successors[21]. Passengers were irritated by a quirk of policy at this time: the North British stopped issuing return tickets. A return fare conventionally cost less than two singles and it was suspected that return-half tickets were being sold on at a profit. This did not apply on worked lines: the Glasgow & Milngavie Junction Railway, opened for both goods and passenger services on 20 April 1863, offered return fares between the termini of 1s 3d (first) and 9d (third). The unpopular policy was dropped in September 1864[22].

Back in January 1862 the NBR had identified a site at Tyneside Terrace in Newcastle for a goods station, alongside the Carlisle line, and purchase was completed in March 1863, by which time running powers had been granted, for £16,166 7s 11d. The seller – by coincidence perhaps – was John Hodgson Hinde, elder brother of Richard Hodgson, a fellow-director of the Wansbeck Railway and one-time vice-chairman of the Caledonian company[23]. The charge was set against the Border Counties Railway, whose costs by 31 January 1863 had reached £457,153 0s 10d, after deduction of the £94,000 of its paid-up share capital[24]. NBR traffic into and out of Newcastle brought about a dispute with the Corporation over tolls. It was a contest between Hodgsons, the city being represented by Alderman John Hodgson (a NER director[25]). Richard Hodgson was a shareholder and director in another railway company, incorporated on 28 July as the Northumberland Central Railway, 49 ½ miles long, to run between the Wansbeck Railway and the locality of Ford in Northumberland, with an extension from Ford to Cornhill on the North Eastern's Tweedmouth-Sprouston line. For this quite substantial project it sought a capital of £270,000 with borrowing facilities of £90,000. Once again it seemed as if the Wansbeck line, or at least its eastern section, might acquire something approaching main line status (the Blyth & Tyne was not yet absorbed into the North Eastern).

Anxious voices were being raised, particularly by ordinary shareholders, about the plethora of amalgamations, leases and extensions being undertaken, and their financing through preference share issues. Hodgson's response was that ordinary shareholders always got priority when preference shares were issued, but he sidestepped the question of consequent depreciation of the value of ordinary shares. In June 1863, at a time when railway shares were buoyant, NBR £100 ordinary were at £51 17s 6d, while Caledonians stood at £117 5s, and G&SWR at £109. Hodgson's tone was increasingly defensive, and at an unusually restive Wharncliffe meeting on 11 June 1863, to consider Bills in progress, he said that a 3% dividend would be resumed once receipts reached £2,000 a week[26]. Both the NBR and the Edinburgh & Glasgow had re-entered Bills for lines to Dunfermline, with a ferry link. The North British project, as in 1862, was a railway right across North Edinburgh, branching from the Berwick line at Piershill to run via Granton to Queensferry. This line was intended to replace the Princes Street-Scotland Street tunnel, which would be closed, with the former Canal Street Station, to allow for the enlargement of Waverley. In a 'judgement of Solomon' decision, Parliament granted only the Piershill-Granton section, and gave the South Queensferry line, from Ratho, to the E&G, though the North British was to have running powers over it; as well as a two-year period to acquire the ferry, failing which the E&G could do so. The NBR was also authorised to build the North Queensferry-Dunfermline railway, and onwards via Glenfarg into Perth, bypassing the Caledonian's Moncrieff Tunnel, with associated double-tracking of the former Fife & Kinross and Kinross-shire lines. For the 22 miles, a capital of £400,000 plus loans of £153,300 was approved. The two previous, failed Bills for this line had included a provision to sell the Halbeath Railway to the new company; this had been dropped. As approved, the crossing at Queensferry was to be by train ferries for both passenger and goods trains – incautious remarks by both Rowbotham and Thomas Bouch suggested that the Burntisland-Granton ferries would be dispensed with, causing consternation in these places, though Hodgson hastily denied it[27]. No mention of a Forth Bridge arose at this time.

Also on 20 July the North British (Steamboats) Bill was passed, though it restricted services to the Silloth-Belfast route. Imposition of this limitation had been foreseen for some months, and arrangements were made for carriage to Liverpool by the Silloth Bay Steam Navigation Co. Another Act of 20 July permitted amalgamation of the Scottish Central and the Dundee & Perth & Aberdeen Junction Railways and gave the North British running powers between Broughty Ferry and Dundee[28]. It was only a toehold north of the Tay, but in a climate of mergers and inter-company pacts, it was valuable.

At the half-yearly meeting on 24 September 1863 Hodgson announced – somewhat prematurely as it turned out – that the dispute between the company and Edinburgh Town Council over the siting of the new vegetable market had been resolved, through arbitration. One of his more awkward shareholders, Mr. Arklay of Forfar, pointed out that receipts were now exceeding £2,000 a week but the ordinary dividend was only 1.25%; Hodgson replied that he had meant a permanent level exceeding £2,000 a week[29]. Others joined in protest, but three weeks later a special general meeting authorised the board to raise £990,000 in new preference shares with a dividend not to exceed 5%. Major Hall, another protestor for the ordinary shareholders, was not appeased to be told that ordinary shares had no 5% dividend ceiling[30].

Rather than resolving matters, the parliamentary decision on Queensferry led to further controversial proposals. Another Bill for amalgamation of the Edinburgh & Glasgow and Caledonian companies was published in November, and the NBR responded with a Bill for a completely new line between Edinburgh and Glasgow, the Glasgow & North British Railway. It would have a branch to Grangemouth, but would also be connected to the North British in Fife by a great bridge over the Firth of Forth[31]. This 'Glasgow & North British' project was generally seen as a lever to obtain running powers for the North British on the Edinburgh & Glasgow company's line[32], but simultaneously, a rival Forth Bridge Railway Bill was presented, to build a railway from the Edinburgh & Glasgow main line, crossing the firth at almost exactly the same location, between Blackness and Charlestown[33]. Meanwhile, nothing was done about the Dunfermline and Perth lines.

In January 1864 the NBR acquired the two vessels, *Queen* and *Silloth*, of the Silloth Bay Steam Navigation Co. for £11,350, running services to Annan, Dumfries and Liverpool as well as the *Ariel's* Belfast route[34]. To circumvent the route limitations imposed by the NBR Steamboat Act, and also its capital limitation of £30,000 plus £10,000 loans, a new body, the North British Steam Packet Company, was formed around this time, not as a joint stock company but as a partnership, theoretically independent but funded and controlled by the NBR, and whose "owners" were members of the NBR board. It was established at 4 Princes Street, with Robert Darlington as secretary.

With his attention very much focused on potential developments north and west of Edinburgh, Hodgson said little to soothe the Wansbeck Railway shareholders at their half-yearly meeting. Their line was not yet fully open, the contractors were dragging their heels, and there was no dividend. They felt that the North British was not doing enough to develop their traffic[35]. Hodgson spoke with enthusiasm about the Forth Bridge at the NBR's half-yearly meeting in March – he would rather put £200,000 into that than spend £150,000 on terminals and ferries (the estimate for the bridge was in fact £500,000[36]). At this time the board was wondering if the Kirkcaldy Harbour Branch was worth keeping on, but decided to retain it[37]. The ordinary dividend was marginally up at 1.75%; average weekly revenue increase on the same previous half-year was £993. Shareholders might remember that the chairman had held out great things from the opening of the Carlisle line and the acquisition of the Edinburgh Perth & Dundee company – now it seemed that a new railway to Glasgow, another to Perth, and a monster bridge across the Forth were needed before their dividends would be restored to former levels. A modest boost to revenue was given by a new contract with the Post Office, for £2,606 a year from 1 February. This related only to mails on the Berwick and Fife lines, from York; the West Coast had the Perth and Aberdeen mails; and the Border Union carried local mails only.

The Border Union branch from Riddings Junction had opened to Canonbie in May 1862, but the 5¾ miles to Langholm took a further two years, while a twelve arched viaduct was built over the Tarras Water. Within a week of the eventual opening on 18 April 1864, another viaduct, over the Byreburn just south of Gilnockie, partially collapsed. Charles Jopp blamed wet weather and poor brickwork; the contractors, Mathieson & Gillespie, blamed underground coal workings. The citizens of Langholm fumed about their renewed isolation until reconstruction, by a new contractor, was finished on 2 November[38]. A station at Gilnockie was added in December. Other new connections in 1864 were the Leadburn, Linton & Dolphinton Railway, opened on 4 July, prophesied as "shortly to form a central part of an important trunk line"[39]. During construction there had been an accident when five ballast trucks broke away and ran backwards down the Leadburn-Dolphinton incline, through the junction and on to the Peebles Railway, colliding with a passenger train near Penicuik Station, causing the death of the young son of Sir Charles Tennant, a future NBR deputy chairman, and injuring numerous others[40]. The Peebles-Galashiels line opened as far as Innerleithen, on 1 October, with a new through station in Peebles replacing the old terminus which had been inconveniently sited beyond the northern edge of the town.

The board had an urgency committee which dealt with immediate issues. The Edinburgh & Glasgow/Caledonian merger Bill had failed and on 20 May 1864 it considered a letter from John Jamieson, secretary of the E&G, which emphasised the mutual usefulness of the E&G and North British, and deplored the antagonisms which had led to the Glasgow & North British Bill (now before Parliament). Noting that the current English and Scotch traffic agreement still had six years to run, the E&G board was willing to make a permanent reciprocal arrangement for free exchange of traffic with the NBR, and proposed a meeting. The board returned a rather frosty answer: having looked at the various agreements entered into by the E&G (documents helpfully provided by that company), particularly with the Caledonian, which included a joint purse arrangement on traffic revenues, "the Directors feel it is to be quite incompetent for the Edinburgh & Glasgow Company to make any satisfactory arrangement with the North British Company without breach of their engagements already

Leadburn Junction Station. The point rodding from the high signal box is wholly enclosed, probably as a protection against snow in this exposed location. The dumb-buffered Loco Coal wagon has a wheel spragged to prevent movement. The elevated signal box was built in the 1900s. (*Stenlake Collection*)

0-4-0 locomotive No. 268 at Garnqueen North, originally built in 1864 by R&W Hawthorn for the Monkland Railways. (*North British Railway Study Group*)

made which preclude free agency or independence on the part of the Edinburgh & Glasgow Company." The E&G's current arrangement with the Caledonian and Scottish Central companies would expire on 1 March 1866, but in anticipation of this, a further agreement was already in place to continue from that date[41]. Borrowing on the short term continued, with a loan of £30,000 for one year from the Imperial Finance Co. at 5% plus 0.5% commission, against a certificate for £40,000 of preference stock (1863) as collateral security. If the value of the stock were to fall below 10% above the loan amount, the company would pay the difference in cash or securities.

Questioned by the Commons Committee considering the Glasgow & North British Railway Bill, Hodgson said he believed the North British and Edinburgh & Glasgow companies should merge. He claimed that his Glasgow line was an independent enterprise, not a North British scheme, though the NBR wished to subscribe to it; and added that he had always been of the opinion that the North British would never flourish unless it got to Glasgow[42]. It was evident that things were on the move between the North British and the Edinburgh & Glasgow companies. An extraordinary general meeting of NBR shareholders on 25 May had been told that heads of agreement had been established for "a more intimate arrangement" with the E&G, and at a further meeting in Edinburgh on 9 June, chaired by George Kinloch, it was stated that the E&G company had made a pledge to the North British not to be party to any extension of their joint purse arrangement with the Caledonian after 1 March 1866, and on that understanding, the Bills for the Glasgow & North British, and the Forth Bridge, were to be withdrawn[43]. At a further extraordinary general meeting on the 30th, an exciting package was unveiled. The Edinburgh & Glasgow company would merge with the Monkland Railways and that combination would immediately amalgamate with the North British. The Wansbeck Railway, of which only three miles were open, was also to be acquired by the NBR. Hodgson told the meeting that agreement with the Edinburgh & Glasgow was reached easily, "he might say in half an hour" once its "unnatural combination" with the Caledonian was accepted as ended. At a simultaneous E&G meeting in Glasgow, Henry Dunlop, the vice-chairman, had to explain his company's *volte-face*. He pointed out that three attempts to amalgamate with the Caledonian had failed, and noted dissensions with the CR on the joint-purse agreement[44]. From 1 August the NBR and E&G set up their own joint-purse arrangement, in anticipation of the merger, and a joint committee was set up to regulate fares, train arrangements, and the division of revenues. Gross earnings were to be split in the same proportion as the aggregate gross receipts of each bore to the whole for the year ending 31 January 1864[45].

The Monkland Railways company was an amalgamation, from 1848, of the Monkland & Kirkintilloch, Ballochney, and Slamannan Railways. With revenue of around £100,000 a year, it was a profitable concern despite high operating costs, and at its half yearly meeting in August 1864 a 5% dividend was announced. The agreement with the E&G (to be honoured also by the North British) was for 6% per annum on Monkland ordinary stock[46]. The North British half-yearly report for February-July recorded the largest receipts of any half-year in its history, up £36,347 on the corresponding period in 1863, while working expenses had risen only by £4,513. A dividend of 2% on the ordinary shares was announced. The Border Union line was now double-track throughout and Border Union Railway ordinary shares received a 3% dividend, though information on that line's actual earnings was not provided. In Carlisle, Border Union Railway trains which had terminated at the Canal Station ran to the Citadel Station from 1 July, and the NBR had a carriage shed there[47]. Edinburgh Perth & Dundee ordinary shares were paid 0.625%. The chairman's report noted some large capital expenditures: £26,125 on locomotives, carriages and wagons; £9,000 on station improvements; £46,351 on the Border Union. To the disappointment of Dunfermline, he announced the deferral of work on lines from there to Inverkeithing and Perth. The Ormiston Branch was also further delayed. In bullish form, Hodgson hoped that a 3% dividend was "not too far distant", and Sir John Don Wauchope, now a prominent supportive shareholder, carried a unanimous motion to award him £1,000 a year while he remained as chairman[48]. Some minor board items show the directors in good mood: use of the engine shed at Riccarton for divine service on Sundays was approved, and William Campbell, "a Highland piper" was allowed to make himself a seat by the paling on Waverley Bridge. But a pass for a boy fiddler on the Granton ferry was refused, and one previously given to a blind fiddler was withdrawn. Local promoters of a branch line to Eyemouth were informed that the NBR would work it, if they built it, for 50% of gross receipts: nearly 30 years would pass before the line became a reality[49].

Delay on construction in Fife was related to the Forth Bridge project. Thomas Bouch, designated as engineer, had been authorised to spend up to £300 on testing the foundations on the E&G's proposed crossing between Pardovan (Blackness) and Charlestown. Bouch, who had been paid £2,000 for survey work on the 'Glasgow & North British'[50], was engineer of choice to the NBR and satellite companies. Within its own established operations, the North British was keeping up with modern developments and (to a degree) with traffic requirements. An apparatus was installed at Edinburgh in connection with lighting trains by gas, and Hurst was instructed to extend gas lighting, in consultation with Rowbotham. In June he indicated that increased traffic required new plant: six goods brakes vans, 20 first class and 30 third class carriages, and a new goods ferry boat for the Firth of Tay. A new boat for the Forth was also urgently needed and a tender from A.&J. Inglis was accepted at £19,654 for a vessel that would do 10 mph. A wagon repair shop at Thornton Junction was approved,

Broomlee: details of the signal post and crossing date. The lamp has been wound down and the winding handle of the windlass can be seen. (*North British Railway Study Group*)

and a joint committee with the Scottish North Eastern Railway acquired ground for a new shared goods station at Dundee East. A modest addition to Border Union revenue was made by a contract with the Post Office for a mail carriage on the line, backdated to 15 June 1863, at £500 a year[51]. A programme of replacing timber bridges with malleable iron was in hand in the southern district, and the train staff working system had been installed on the former West of Fife lines.

An important private meeting was held at the NBR offices on 23 October, with the chairmen and general managers of the Edinburgh & Glasgow and Glasgow & South Western Companies, to consider joint action against the expansionism and "threatened aggression" of the Caledonian company. The Caledonian was again seeking to take over the Scottish Central and the others agreed not to oppose this if suitable concessions were made and facilities provided. The companies revealed some of their future plans, and agreed on free transfer of traffic at Gretna, Annan and Glasgow, with access to Greenhill on the E&G for the Glasgow & South Western Railway. The Glasgow & South Western party then left, and Hodgson showed the E&G visitors his list of 22 projects, including new lines between Portobello and Penicuik, the leasing of the Leadburn, Linton & Dolphinton, power to subscribe £9,000 of the Esk Valley's £27,000 capital (to counter a Caledonian bid for a Slateford-Penicuik-Dalkeith railway), independent access to Carlisle (Citadel), enlargement of Waverley Station, investment of £40,000 in the Devon Valley Railway to forestall a Caledonian/Scottish Central Railway attempt to build a line into Fife from Gleneagles (the E&G board however refused their proposed subscription of £40,000 towards this line); and, if the ongoing tests should prove satisfactory, the Forth Bridge. Discussion resumed on the 24th, with Thomas Bouch in attendance, mostly on new lines in the Monklands district and in Fife, agreeing to invest if local promoters also put up funds. They noted new lines between the Morningside Railway and Newmills, Shotts and Airdrie, Dolphinton and Douglas (right into CR territory, and the meeting felt this might better be a G&SWR venture); Cowdenbeath and Burntisland, and, in Cumberland, Longtown to Brampton. The Edinburgh & Glasgow's Morningside line would be extended to Strathaven as "retaliation on the Caledonian aggression at Ayr" (the Caledonian was backing a line which would give it access to Ayr, a South Western stronghold). The E&GR already had lines planned between Coatbridge and Glasgow, and from Maryhill to Stobcross; and was involved with the G&SWR in building the City of Glasgow Union Railway, linking their systems in the city. It was a huge plan requiring huge investment, though several of the lines were perfectly sensible in their own right and would serve known mineral districts.

In Edinburgh the company's stables at Waverley were taken over to accommodate the Northern Section goods clerks, and a committee was set up to report on new housing for the horses[52]. Perhaps the hardest-worked official in the company was Lingard, who was not only stores (and horses) superintendent but superintendent of Waverley Station, in charge of tramway traffic at Leith Docks, of cattle market traffic, and manager of a 'flying gang' of fourteen grain porters who moved between stations in East Lothian and the Borders. In November his salary was raised from £165 to £200 a year, plus £61 a year commission on the sale of English coal[53]. Some directors thought Lingard had too many jobs, but he appears to have kept them all until he retired as stationmaster at Waverley in 1874, though he stayed in harness as horses superintendent until his death in November 1899. The increasing volume of traffic spurred Hodgson to request tenders for a thousand new wagons, on extended terms of payment, up to five years. These would replace the many wagons on hire from the Scottish Waggon Co. and others. Locomotives were also in short supply. Robert Stephenson of Newcastle were very late with an order for ten, but six had recently arrived, two more were due by the end of November and the last two in December. Meanwhile a new tender from Dübs of Glasgow was accepted for six passenger and twelve goods engines for delivery between July and December 1865, at an average cost of £2,225. A 'rulley wagon' to carry marine boilers was also ordered, at a cost of £215[54].

7. HODGSON'S RAILWAY - 4, 1864-1866

Hodgson might have felt he had enough plans in his portfolio, but there was always room for more. He had been negotiating with the St. Andrews Railway about a take over, and without informing it, introduced a Bill for a merger or lease. This was successfully resisted by the St. Andrews company, which did not pass into the NBR fold until 1877[1]. Bouch's striking suspension design for the Forth Bridge was revealed in November 1864, by which time Hodgson was also discussing the project for a Firth of Tay bridge with a group of Dundee promoters. A Tay Bridge and Dundee Union Railway Bill was prepared, and the Tay Bridge committee attended the NBR board meeting on 19 January 1865, but the Bill was later withdrawn for redrafting[2]. Sunday trains were again an issue, with a stream of around 200 memorials reaching the office in what was clearly an organised campaign. The Sabbatarians were not just a pressure group of ministers, formidable as that would have been in the mid-1860s, but included prominent industrialists and men of commerce, including perhaps the richest, Sir James Baird, who led a deputation to the board[3], but Hodgson made no concessions. The half-yearly report in March 1865 announced a 2.5% dividend, plus a *pro rata* bonus of 3s 9d per £100 in respect of penalty payments recovered from the Hawick and Hermitage section contractors of the Border Union. At the subsequent shareholders' meeting the chairman defended the plans for lines south of Edinburgh taking in Liberton, Gilmerton, Lasswade, Penicuik, Roslin, Newington, Morningside and The Grange as necessary in their own right and to forestall Caledonian plans to invade North British territory. To fund these, £565,700 was to be raised in a mixture of ordinary and preference shares, the latter not to exceed a 7% dividend. A conditional agreement had been made to lease the Esk Valley line. He announced that the board, in association with the E&G directors, had agreed to subscribe half the capital of the Tay Bridge, £187,000, if the promoters raised the other half. There was also a gleam of hope for Border Union revenues: the Midland Railway was planning to build a line which would link Leeds with Carlisle. Commenting on "that very inconvenient and dangerous station at Waverley Bridge", Hodgson attacked Edinburgh Town Council for "higgling and haggling" to extort money from the NBR. By now it was agreed that the Canal Street Station site would be exchanged for that of the vegetable market, and the council was contemplating a grandiose plan for a rebuilt Waverley with a new town hall alongside[4]. Reminded again by Arklay of his 3% dividend pledge, Hodgson protested that it was unfair to bring up remarks made years ago and convert them into accusations[5].

Three companies were aiming at Penicuik, whose station on the Peebles line was some way east of the town, but the Esk Valley Railway withdrew its Bill for an extension, on agreeing a perpetual lease of its not-yet finished line to the NBR, at £1,350 a year, equivalent to 5% on its share capital of £27,000[6]. The North British won the battle for Penicuik and other lines with an act on 23 June, but Penicuik would have to wait seven years for a better rail link. In May the Wansbeck Valley line finally opened between Scots Gap and Reedsmouth, where a two-road engine shed and turntable were installed. A short mineral branch to Armstrong's ore and limestone field helped the line's precarious finances.

Hawick Station approach and goods yard, around 1907. (*John Alsop*)

To the English East Coast companies, the North British was by now a distinctly shaky ally, and the prospect of Midland trains running over a Forth Bridge added to their unease. The position was not helped by a joint Midland-North British Chancery suit that summer against the terms of the Sextuple Agreement of 1856, which did not include the Waverley Route – the NBR occupying "the peculiar position of being a co-defendant on one side and a sub-plaintiff on the other"[7] – and this prompted both the Great Northern and Great Eastern companies to insist that running powers for them all the way through to Perth be included in the NBR-E&G Amalgamation Bill then being considered in Parliament. On 20 April shareholders' meetings approved the merger, with Hodgson emphasising the financial strength of the combined concern. E&G ordinary shareholders were to receive a guaranteed minimum dividend of 4.5% per annum, and he held out the prospect of faster increase on the NBR ordinary dividend. Despite all the hostile talk, the NBR, E&G and Monkland directors met representatives of the Caledonian and Scottish Central boards in London, on 12 May, and made a formal covenant, the 'Scotch Territorial Agreement', not to oppose the amalgamations of the Caledonian-Scottish Central Railways, and of the Monkland-Edinburgh & Glasgow-North British Railways; the E&G's Bill for a Coatbridge-Glasgow line, the Forth and Tay Bridge Bills, and two Bills for Caledonian branches[8].

Full union of the E&G-plus-Monkland with the North British was authorised on 4 July, along with the Forth Bridge Railway and the Coatbridge-Glasgow line, now inherited by the NBR[9]. In East Lothian the idea of a Tyne Valley Railway was revived, to run from the NBR Ormiston branch (still unbuilt) to Haddington and on to meet the Berwick line at East Linton. Not backed by the North British, the proposal fell from sight.

Many people were surprised that the Edinburgh & Glasgow had been swallowed up by the NBR, rather than *vice versa*: a commentator in the *Dundee Courier* remarked of the E&G chairman Peter Blackburn, "Had he possessed the far-reaching sagacity and comprehensiveness of intellect Richard Hodgson has exhibited, he might have stood today where Richard Hodgson does. Instead of the North British absorbing the Edinburgh & Glasgow, the tables would have been turned"[10]. The amalgamation was effective from 1 August, and on the 16th a special meeting was held in the Music Hall, Edinburgh, to elect new directors. Hodgson, presiding, commented that for ten years the NBR had been what people called an aggressive company, but it had been fighting for its independence and its life. Aggression did not seem to be at an end: he warned the Caledonian company that "competition between Edinburgh and Glasgow at sixpenny rates meant corresponding rates between Glasgow and Carlisle", and was applauded. He hoped that an early amalgamation with the Glasgow & South Western Railway would now happen, though the chairman of the G&SWR, who was present, might well have taken note of strong E&G protests about the formation of the new board, with thirteen NBR and only two ex-E&G directors,

Henry Dunlop and John Orr Ewing. Only Dunlop could be considered as representing Glasgow's interests, while four or five of the directors were from Fife[11]. From the beginning, there was a disgruntled Glasgow faction. But Hodgson was riding high, and his chairman's allowance was raised to £1,200 a year. North British officials were to be in charge: Latham, the E&G general manager, was to leave at the end of the year, and Jamieson would depart at the end of January 1866. Hurst was the new supremo of the E&G's Cowlairs Works, though he remained at St. Margaret's. At Cowlairs the company inherited the newly-built set of four handsome tenements for workmen's families, designed by Andrew Heiton of Perth: 143 dwellings of one or two rooms plus kitchen[12]. The numbers and condition of Monkland, E&G and NBR combined rolling stock had to be ascertained, but meanwhile 50 pairs of timber wagons were to be built at St. Margaret's and 50 iron wagons were to be put out to tender[13].

On 29 August the new lines & works committee met with Caledonian representatives and an agreement was made that for fourteen years neither side should enter into negotiation for possession or privilege over the Scottish North Eastern, Forth & Clyde Junction, and Highland Railways. It was also hoped to achieve co-operation over traders' passes and rates for goods and minerals between both companies and the Glasgow & South Western Railway, and a 'Peace Committee' of the three companies was set up. The North British was also now co-owner, with the Glasgow & South Western Railway, of the City of Glasgow Union Railway, incorporated in July 1864 and now in the early stages of construction, from Pollokshields across the south of the city and over the Clyde to meet the proposed E&G Coatbridge-Glasgow line at Sighthill, and with a spur to a large new terminal station at St. Enoch Square. For the North British, as for the E&G, one attraction of the City of Glasgow Union Railway was that it had power to build a branch to join the General Terminus line, giving access to the South Clyde quays. The new lines committee noted that the City of Glasgow Union Railway, under acts of 1864 and 1865, was estimated to cost £754,000 exclusive of buildings. Its authorised capital of £1,050,000 in shares and £350,000 in loans would have to be raised by the NBR and Glasgow & South Western Railway as joint owners. The committee wanted St. Enoch put on hold – the NBR had its own idea for a new Glasgow terminus. Also put on hold was the NBR's goods station in Newcastle, ostensibly due to tollage demands from the Corporation[14]. Hodgson had visited Silloth and gave a highly favourable report: the ships were paying their way, except for the Belfast route, which would be dropped[15]. At the 1865 September general election, he lost his Tynemouth seat to a Liberal. That marked the end of his Parliamentary career, though not of his influence in Northumberland Tory politics.

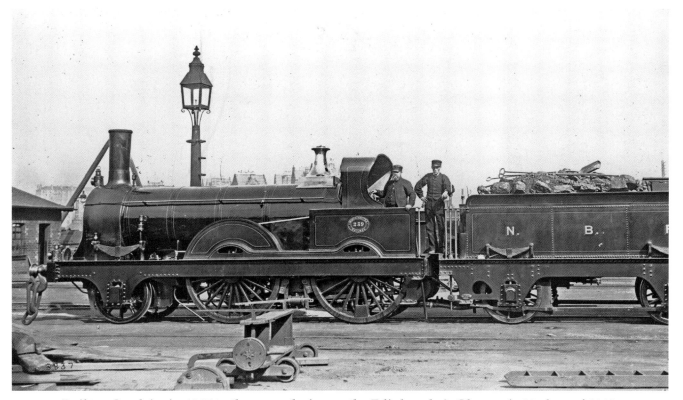

Built at Cowlairs in 1867 to the same design as the Edinburgh & Glasgow's 40-class of 1860, 2-4-0 express engine No. 239 is shown here in original condition. The wheeled frame in the foreground is perhaps a rail-gauge. (*John Alsop*)

Waverley Station was now wholly a North British domain, though carriages of the North Eastern, Scottish Central (soon in Caledonian livery) and the newly-formed Highland Railway companies could be seen there. Its much-delayed expansion was finally in sight, with the passing of the Edinburgh Vegetable Market and Station Enlargement Act on 29 June, providing for the fruit and vegetable market to be moved to a new position on a 'raised platform' on the site of Canal Street Station. Granton and Leith would be served from the east side of Waverley, via the new line from Piershill. William Chambers, Lord Provost of Edinburgh and chairman of the Peebles Railway (currently justifying its independence by paying a 6.5% dividend) helped greatly to finalise the deal. Plans for Waverley expansion could get under way (a prize of £350 was offered for the best plan for extension) though the market site remained a source of argument, with truculent voices on the council: "The NBR people might rest assured that they would not juggle or jostle the council out of its rights."[16]. The NBR also now owned the terminus at Glasgow Queen Street, centrally placed, but squeezed into a narrow site at the end of a thousand-yard tunnel, on such a steep gradient, 1 in 42, that trains were hauled out with the help of a cable, worked from Cowlairs at the top of the incline. Incoming engines were detached here, and trains ran down controlled by specially-built brake-trucks. There were only two passenger platforms. The Edinburgh & Glasgow's offices, in a former church alongside, were retained, but the Monkland offices were leased out. Inheriting an E&G scheme, the NBR set up a committee to pursue the idea of acquiring a hotel in Glasgow. In Edinburgh, Kennedy's Hotel, adjoining Waverley Station, was bought in October for £12,000[17], and rented to a tenant. Elsewhere, the passenger train shed at Hawick was to be turned into a goods shed, and the existing goods shed moved to Silloth. The decrepit locomotive shed at Morningside, which had no turntable, was to be replaced by a new depot at Bathgate[18]. In October the company appointed its first law agent, Adam Johnstone, at £1,200 a year. He had plenty to do, with 33 projects being considered for Bills, including the postponed Tay Bridge Bill. New shares to a value of £563,379 were isssued as Monkland preferred (ordinary) stock at a 6% dividend, against the former Monkland ordinary shares. But the board's main priority was to raise a total of £1,614,810 through the issue of £10 preference (1865) shares[19].

The Edinburgh & Glasgow Railway had made its Campsie Branch to Kirkintilloch and Lennoxtown in 1848, and an extension to Killearn was authorised in 1861, as the Blane Valley Railway, with the E&G to subscribe a third of the capital and work the line. Even before completion, a further extension to meet the Forth & Clyde Junction Railway at Gartness was approved[20]. The Blane Valley company held its ninth ordinary general meeting on 27

Cowlairs Incline, before November 1908: a double-headed train is about to drop the cable. The lead engine is Holmes 592-class No. 598, of 1888. The pilot behind appears to be one of the 574-class of 1884. (*Stenlake Collection*)

Three levels at Kirkintilloch: the railway crosses the River Luggie and goes under the Forth & Clyde Canal. (*Stenlake Collection*)

September 1865, with Richard Hodgson in the chair, and it was resolved that the Blane Valley Railway would be advanced £55,000 in debentures and preference shares at 4.5% interest, and the NBR-E&G would work the entire line for 50% of gross proceeds, with any excess of profits to be divided equally[21]. In Edinburgh, placing of a large clock on Haymarket Station was approved by the board on 9 November, and that month also saw completion of the haggling on the relocation of the vegetable market.

One of the secretary's tasks was to arrange insurance against defalcation by staff. Since 1 November 1863 the NBR had been operating a scheme of mutual insurance with the Guarantee Fidelity Fund, intended to indemnify the company for losses incurred by fraud or theft by officers and agents, at a premium of 1% of the sum guaranteed in each case. The cost was shared between the company and the employee, at rates varying between 50/50 and 75/25. But it was found that the E&G (now the 'Western Section') paid only half as much in premiums. Further checking found that some companies paid the whole premium for their staff, while others including the Caledonian paid half, except for amounts above £300, when it paid the whole sum. The NBR board decided to switch to one of the public guarantee companies, with station agents and booking clerks required to furnish a bond of £100; the company would pay half the premium of staff earning less than £100 a year.

The immediate institution of Sunday trains between Edinburgh and Glasgow, following the amalgamation, brought a new furore of protest, but voices were also raised in support, more than in the 1840s, and the board stuck to its guns, insisting that Sunday trains were a public service, "especially to the poorer classes"[22]. Two trains ran each way. The enlarged company had a daunting range of tasks in the autumn of 1865: not only the preparation of plans and Bills for the new projects, but the integration of three separate railway systems into one. A certain delicacy of feeling for a brief time brought the name 'North British-Edinburgh & Glasgow Railway' into use, but quickly vanished in favour of a blanket North British identity. Wordies, the E&G carters in Glasgow and Alloa, lost their contract and the NBR bought their stables at Grahamston. By September a census of rolling stock had been made and it was apparent that very substantial investment was required. Though Hurst reported 1,280 new goods and mineral wagons added to stock, over 2,300 more were urgently needed. Around 450 wagons on the Monkland and E&G lists were "non inventi" and had to be written off. Currently there were 326 effective engines, running a total of over 5,000,000 miles a year – given their age, around twelve a year would have to be replaced just to maintain current services, at a cost of around £1,500 each. Taking new requirements into account, Rowbotham and Hurst reckoned the needs at 120 engines, 651 carriages, and 6,426 wagons, at a total cost of £596,115. A new boat, *Kinloch*, was now on the Forth run, but boat renewal would need £30,000. A growth of 5% in existing traffics would require even more investment, reckoned at £103,170. And that was just one department's list[23].

For the February-July half-year Hodgson declared a 3% dividend on the NBR ordinary shares, to general gratification. Surely the new big company would do even better for its shareholders. Questioned about Caledonian access to the expanded Waverley, he hedged: "… the amount of traffic exchanged between the Caledonian and North British companies was very small"[24]. A week later he addressed a festival of Western District staff in the City Hall, Glasgow, preceding the usual vocal and music programme with a stern demand for "their whole devotion, their whole time, their best talents, and all their abilities"[25]. New management was not resulting in universal customer satisfaction: a latter from 'Coalmaster' in the Monklands complained that bad as the traffic accommodation had been on the Monkland and Slamannan Railways, it was worse under the NBR, with low priority given to moving traders' wagons[26]. Hodgson returned to the theme of creating more stock at an extraordinary general meeting on 13 October, emphasising the "recent extraordinary rise in the value of money" and the need to pay for works authorised in the 1864 and 1865 Parliamentary sessions, while also announcing a "small branch" to run from the Coatbridge line to Sighthill where it would meet the City of Glasgow Union Railway. The many new Bills for the next session included amalgamations with the Scottish North Eastern Railway (actually achieved by the Caledonian), the Fife & Kinross, Leadburn, Linton & Dolphinton and the Forth & Clyde Junction Railways, as well as link lines to the Tay Bridge, the lease of the Esk Valley Railway, a further £30,000 towards completion of the Berwickshire Railway, branches in the Devon Valley, the Tyne Valley line, and a diversion at St. Margaret's, where the main line ran through the centre of the works, separating the turntable from the engine shed. The Berwickshire line was fully opened on 2 October, with five trains each way between St. Boswells and Berwick, and fourth class fares provided between local stations[27]. Despite the 3% dividend, North British share prices were trailing, with £100 ordinary at £58 10s, compared to the CR's at £124 17s 6d and the G&SWR's at £115. Edinburgh Town Council, allotted shares in the new preference issue, decided not to take them up, though in December it asked the company to provide a siding at St. Margaret's for the loading of 15,000 tons a year of city manure[28].

Earlier in the year there had been a dispute over mail traffic in Fife. The Post Office had been paying £1,760 a year for the use of specified trains, and wanted to change it to £2,000 for the use of "all or any" trains. The NBR demanded £2,250 but the Post Office, backed by the Treasury, refused. From 22 December the Night Mail's stop at Berwick was discontinued and a Post Office sorting clerk joined the train at Newcastle, working through to Edinburgh. The carriages used on what the Post Office called the 'Day Mail' were to be transferred to the night service[29].

Auchtermuchty Station with a Stirling-bound train arriving. (*Stenlake Collection*)

In December a grand plan was unveiled, for a railway from Sighthill to meet the City of Glasgow Union Railway line, then diverge past High Street and along the north side of George Street into a huge new east-west station on the Queen Street site, with eight platforms, fronted by a "palatial" hotel, and to continue westwards to join up with the (as yet uncommenced) Stobcross-Maryhill line, so giving access to Dumbarton and Helensburgh trains. The Queen Street tunnel could be dispensed with, and a circular suburban service could be run from the new central station via Sighthill, Maryhill, and Partick[30]. Coinciding as it did with the Caledonian's plans to build a new central terminus in Glasgow, this prompted a meeting of shareholders in the NBR, CR and Glasgow & South Western Railway to consider, and deplore, the policies being pursued by the directors. In the chair was James Hozier, of Mauldslie. Observing that the total of proposals would require £10,000,000 of new capital, he criticised the "hostile and aggressive character" of most of the plans and estimated that the NBR's schemes alone would need £4,344,000, more than the current ordinary stock. At this time NB ordinary amounted to £4,128,951, guaranteed/preference was £8,828,003, and loans £4,461,684, a total of £17,418,638. Where was all the new money to come from? "Lawyers and engineers" were blamed for pushing the companies into competing schemes. A committee of substantial shareholders was formed, to pass the meeting's views to the three boards. These included a request to withdraw all Bills involving capital investment for twelve months. Hodgson wrote a semi-placatory letter to James White, chairman of the shareholders' committee, insisting that the board, and he, took responsibility for the company's plans, and that he did not expect all of them to come to fruition. For Glasgow, he suggested a Royal Commission should look at the plans for new termini[31]. His intentions became a little clearer in the board meeting of 4 January 1866. Much of the adopted position was a bargaining stance: the NBR would be willing to withdraw from new lines south of Stirling if the CR committed to doing the same. But still there were unyielding issues: amalgamation Bills would go ahead; the NBR had no intention of giving up its 'rights' in the Wilsontown mineral district; major revisions to the City of Glasgow Union project were required. Hodgson had tried unsuccessfully to avoid a meeting with White's committee and it got little satisfaction from a visit to the NBR board[32]. The North British withdrew its Bill for amalgamation with the Scottish North Eastern, though it continued to contest the Caledonian's Bill, and also withdrew its proposal for a Hamilton-Wishaw line when the Duke of Hamilton switched support to a Caledonian line. But there was some co-operation on the ground between the companies. A meeting at Forth to discuss rival NBR/CR lines to the village voted 104 to 81 in favour of the North British (but the Caledonian built the line). At the March half-yearly meeting, Hodgson made disparaging references to "cosmopolitan shareholders" with holdings in several railway companies. James White was there to move a protest against board policy but Hodgson obtained a large majority, emphasising that the company would proceed prudently.

Cattle plague was rife at this time and restrictions on cattle transport lasted into 1867. In January 1866 petroleum was landed at Leith for the first time[33]. Mineral oil was becoming an important commodity and the shale deposits of West Lothian promised valuable traffic for the Edinburgh & Bathgate Railway. In a take-over attempt, the NBR offered a guaranteed 5% dividend on capital, but a faction of Edinburgh & Bathgate Railway shareholders held out for an extra half-percent, staving off the merger and forcing their board to resign. The NBR continued to work the line[34].

Clothing the staff in uniform or suitable attire was a regular expense and the clothing committee in February 1866 issued a large order. For agents, passenger guards and ticket collectors: seven to eight hundred yards of "woaded ground cloth" for coats, waistcoats, caps, etc., at 11s 3d a yard; 500-600 yards of Oxford Mixture Doeskin for trousers at 6s 6d a yard; 3,500 yards of Indigo Kersey for topcoats at 8s a yard. The topcoats were lettered NBR in white on the collar. For porters and pointsmen, 4,500 yards of moleskin cord at 2s 9½d "as for the LNWR" were to be ordered. Jackets had red collars, and red neckcloths were provided. Chance porters were provided only with an armband. Messengers had a single-breasted coat, with trousers and waistcoat as for guards[35]. The half-yearly meeting on 23 March approved the construction of fourteen new locomotives, plus the purchase of two small 0-4-0 saddle tanks, as well as 567 goods/mineral and 36 ballast wagons from outside suppliers, and 120 goods/mineral, eight ballast wagons, and six goods guard's vans from company workshops, including Burntisland[36]. For the isolated community at Riccarton, £600 was provided for a school and dwelling, with £50 a year for the teacher's salary. A special meeting of directors in March picked from 30 entries a plan submitted anonymously under the Latin motto *Sic Donec* ('Like this, for the time being') by their own engineer, Charles Jopp (Jopp was on a retainer, enabling him to work for other companies), as the prizewinning design for Waverley Station. It provided for a new arrangement of lines and platforms, the booking office being brought down from the Waverley Bridge to platform level, the construction of a new Waverley Bridge, and an overall roof as "a broad unbroken series of glass ridges". The grandiose plan for Queen Street was abandoned, however, by agreement with the Caledonian[37].

As usual, when the wider economy was on an upward trend and the company was visibly doing well, pressure came from the work force for a share in the prosperity. There are no recorded instances of a Scottish (or English) railway company giving its workers any concession, whether pay increase or better working conditions, without its being asked for. In the engineering trades, most of the requests from the men centred on a reduction of the 60 hour working week. Employers were resisting it, usually claiming that the demand was just a means of securing overtime pay. On the railways, North British drivers got starting pay of £1 10s a week, compared with £1 4s on the Caledonian, in both cases for a 12 hour day[38].

James Nairne died suddenly on 26 March 1866, and his chief clerk David Crabb was appointed interim secretary by the urgency committee[39]. At the end of May the Lochlong & Lochlomond Steamboat Co. inaugurated the excursion season with a trip for invited guests from the NBR, Caledonian and Forth & Clyde Junction companies, on the SS *Chancellor* from Glasgow to Arrochar, coach to Tarbet, and the saloon steamer *Prince Consort* from Tarbet to Balloch. This outing became an annual event. The North British itself was running excursions as well as regular coastal traffic. From Helensburgh Pier, *Dandie Dinmont* and *Meg Merrilies* ran to Ardrishaig, connecting with trains leaving Edinburgh at 6.15 a.m and Glasgow at 7.35. Trippers had two hours ashore. At the Dundee Fair in June, tickets for a ten-day train and steamer tour of the west were sold. Four double journeys to Rothesay were made daily, and eleven trips across to Greenock. At this time, around 36 passenger steamers were plying the Clyde waters. North British capital expenditure on ships at 31 July was £94,032 14s 6d, of which £78,492 10s had been advanced by banks, with the value of *Ariel* and the newly-delivered *Waverley* set against it as security[40].

As required by Parliament, a special meeting of shareholders was held on 15 June, to consider some company Bills currently under scrutiny. Introducing it, Hodgson mentioned that the first pier of the Forth Bridge was now in position. A long list of Bills was on the agenda:

1. New Works Bill, for Firth of Forth works and the enlargement of Waverley Station (£155,270).
2. A diversion line to take the main line north of, rather than through, St. Margaret's Works (£50,000).
3. Camps Branches, works in Stirlingshire, West Lothian, Edinburgh (£73,000).
4. Glasgow area branches (£60,000).
5. Coatbridge lines (£72,000).
6. Stirlingshire branches, in connection with ex-E&G and Monklands lines (£81,000).
7. Devon Valley branches in the Fife and Clackmannan mineral districts (£95,000).
8. Lease of the Esk Valley Railway, with the NBR taking up mortgage debts not to exceed £9,000.
9. An Act to empower the Devon Valley Railway to raise additional capital to complete the Rumbling Bridge-Tillicoultry section; and for it to amalgamate with the North British.
10. The North British (Tay Bridge) Bill.

Other Bills included the raising of extra capital for the Berwickshire Railway and the Solway Junction Railway, for the Longtown to Brampton Branch, and for the NBR to acquire the harbour and construct a new dock at Burntisland.

Some projects had been dropped and others were not included. The usual voices were raised against yet more capital expenditure and the meeting had to be adjourned to the 25th. In between, in contrast both to the expansive plans and the economic upturn, a board meeting on the 23rd was largely concerned with staving off purchases and payments. Alexanders, Cunliffes & Co. were demanding repayment of a £50,000 loan, or they would sell the £75,000 of stock they held as security. Since "a forced sale of so large an amount of stock at this time would be very injurious to the company's interests", and repayment was impossible, a short-term extension was agreed, on the directors' personal security, a promissory note binding them jointly and severally. To indemnify them, £20,000 of the 1863 stock issue was registered in their names[41]. Hodgson's wife fell ill and he took her to Aix-la-Chapelle (Aachen), leaving Henry Dunlop, as vice-chairman, to preside at the adjourned meeting, at which the board got the necessary majority. Also on the agenda were new terms for leasing the Edinburgh & Bathgate Railway. This company, incorporated in 1846, had been vested in the Edinburgh & Glasgow Railway for 999 years from 31 July 1852, for a consideration of £9,500 a year plus a share of surplus profits after deduction of 33% working expenses. It had had a stormy relationship with the Edinburgh & Glasgow, and had petitioned against the E&G's amalgamation with the North British. Though it had passed into the NBR embrace in 1865, it was currently opposing the North British Camps Branches Bill. Hodgson, with his eye on the burgeoning coal and mineral traffic between Bathgate and Wishaw, was determined to neuter it, and seemed to have agreed terms: a lease of 999 years at a fixed 5% of capital per annum for seven years, and 5.5% thereafter, plus taking on the Edinburgh & Bathgate's debenture debt of £62,700: "We will make the Bathgate line available for all traffic we can put upon it, without the fear of hereafter having to pay a larger sum for it". But strains on the NBR board

Rumbling Bridge Station on the Devon Valley Railway. (*Stenlake Collection*)

were revealed when Dunlop said the directors were divided about the deal, and announced himself as opposed to the motion he was introducing. The meeting failed to give the necessary 75% vote in favour, with £81,592 of share capital supporting, and £69,351 opposing. Hodgson might have swayed the antis, but it is clear that the shareholders were no longer willing to rubber-stamp their chairman's proposals[42]. Dunlop's next meeting with Hodgson must have been sulphurous.

By then Parliament had refused to let the Forth & Clyde Junction Railway amalgamate with the Caledonian, and the NBR withdrew its own amalgamation Bill (obtaining a long-term lease agreement instead). The Bill for a NBR branch to Bridge of Allan was also thrown out, but absorption of the Leadburn, Linton & Dolphinton Railway was approved, along with the lease of the Esk Valley line. Also authorised was the Caledonian Railway's absorption of the Scottish North Eastern, giving it control of the railway to Aberdeen. The East Coast companies had campaigned hard against this, and Hodgson had suggested the NBR might build its own line to Aberdeen if it should happen, but now said the company would not rush into such an ambitious undertaking. Strong running powers to Aberdeen for the NBR, NER and GNR were included in the Act, but the Tay Bridge Bill was withdrawn, despite protests from Dundee, and in August the NBR announced it was also dropping the Forth Bridge project[43].

On 18 June the much-delayed Tweedside line between Peebles and Galashiels was completed between Innerleithen and Galashiels. Captain Rich, making the preliminary inspection for the Board of Trade on 24 May, had observed that though the track of a west-to-south link with the Caledonian's line to Symington had been laid at Peebles, the points had been taken out. The junction was never used and the potential of a railway linking Lanarkshire with the East Coast line was never realised. At the Edinburgh & Bathgate's half-yearly meeting on 10 August 1866 its chairman regretted that "amalgamation" with the North British had been lost through the opposition of a section of NBR directors and shareholders[44]. The Edinburgh & Bathgate kept its identity and remained on guard against North British or other schemes that might adversely affect its traffic.

In his constant struggle to enlarge the company and defend its 'rights' and interests, Hodgson was getting close to the wire. Parliamentary, legal and engineering expenses were very high and the company's liquidity was very low. New share issues, bringing in additional capital, were essential, not to finance new projects, but to pay obligations already incurred, and, crucially to Hodgson, fund a dividend to the shareholders. But NBR share prices still languished far behind those of the Caledonian and Glasgow & South Western Railways and new issues were hard to sell. Tight economy was enforced in operations. One example was exposed by a disgruntled passenger: the timetable showed trains from Balloch and Helensburgh arriving at Queen Street at exactly the same time. The Helensburgh train was supposedly non-stop; the Balloch train stopped at Dumbarton. What actually happened was that the Helensburgh train did stop at Dumbarton. The Balloch train stopped outside the station, and Dumbarton passengers had to get off and walk along the track. Both trains were then combined and went on to Glasgow behind a single locomotive[45]. But positive items led the half-yearly report issued in August: gross traffic receipts were up by £43,586, and £15,000 held in a suspense account during the Chancery suit relating to the Scotch-English traffic agreement was now released. An ambitious Bill for a NBR line from Shettleston to meet the former Wilsontown, Morningside & Coltness Railway west of Wishaw, with numerous industrial branches[46] had been rejected, but the company had got running powers on the Caledonian tracks between Morningside, Wishaw and Coatbridge, and "the directors have already opened friendly negotiations with the Caledonian". A satisfactory agreement had also been made with regard to the City of Glasgow Union Railway: the interchange at Sighthill was now as the NBR desired, no joint funds would be expended on the St. Enoch extension, and NBR capital spent on it so far would be refunded and spent on connecting links. A 3% dividend was proposed[47].

Richard Hodgson never wrote a memoir, and it can only be guessed whether he felt his control of the North British becoming shaky in the late summer of 1866. Hozier, White and their associates were massed like the hosts of Tuscany, but they had the other railway boards to confront as well. In the course of the year, John Walker, the treasurer and cashier, was appointed secretary, at an annual salary of £1,000. He can hardly have failed to be already aware, at least in a general way, of Hodgson's financial manipulations, but now he saw a crisis looming. Finding it impossible to make Hodgson face up to the fact that the company was effectively bankrupt and unable to pay a 3% dividend, Walker wrote to two members of the finance committee, John Beaumont and John Ronald. This resulted in an emergency board meeting on 14 September. Five days later a "supplementary report" was issued. The operating surplus was reduced to £19,285 4s 10d, and the dividend cut to 1%. Blame was put on

renewals needed on the acquired lines, plus the need for urgent increases in the rolling stock. Hodgson appended a personal circular, putting his seat at the shareholders' disposal, but affirming his belief that the company's affairs would progressively improve. A few days later, the NBR informed the stock exchanges that because only £65,000 of the £800,000 preference share issue of 1865 had been taken up, it could not pay both a dividend on shares and the interest on debentures. The board had opted to pay the debenture interest and to issue deferred dividend warrants at 4%. Only certain preference stocks (on minor branches) would be paid. North British £100 ordinary shares, already low, fell by 8% overnight to £40.

Applause and hisses greeted Hodgson at a packed half-yearly meeting of some 1,200 people at the Queen Street Hall on 27 September. His suggestion that the shareholders might take up the 1865 5% preference stock to the extent of the unpaid dividends due was greeted with more hisses and cries of "Oh, no!" Telling them that he alone was responsible for the state of the company's affairs, having concealed them from the board as well as from the shareholders, he informed the meeting that he held £2,700,000 of proxies in his own favour and intended to remain chairman "as long as he had the confidence of the shareholders". James White rose to demand a committee of inquiry. Dividends had been paid out of capital and this had been concealed in the accounts. The directors and auditors could not avoid responsibility. Eventually it was agreed that the directors' report should "lie on the

John Walker, general manager of the NBR from 1874 to 1891
(*Glasgow Museums*)

**No.237 was built at Cowlairs for the Edinburgh & Glasgow Railway as their No. 40.
In 1880 it was named *Alexandria*. (Stenlake Collection)**

table" rather than be approved; and the motion for a committee of investigation was carried unanimously[48]. While this committee picked through the company records, Hodgson remained in office. In October the City of Glasgow Union Railway sued the North British in the Court of Session for unpaid subscription to City of Glasgow Union Railway stock. At a Western District staff soirée on 19 October Hodgson made a speech which said nothing about the company's affairs but in a comment on pay (a hot issue at the time), said "I for one will never dictate to the labourer the price at which he is to offer his services" – he appears to be supporting some form of mutual bargaining, but the NBR was at one with other railway companies in its refusal to allow any sort of collective bargaining on wages or working conditions[49].

The committee, nine strong, led by James White, with Walter Mackenzie and James Wyllie Guild as its accountants, reported at the end of October. "For several years the books of the company … have been manipulated by the Chairman to such an extent that it was with the utmost difficulty that two practised and able accountants … could unravel the truth." The directors, guardians of the shareholders' interests, were characterised as "a sort of honourable dummies". The assets of the North British were set out as £3,912,548 1s 6d, and its liabilities at £4,476,254 14s 11d, leaving a deficiency of £563,706 13s 5d. But after extracting contingent liabilities and assets (works authorised but not contracted for and borrowing powers not yet exercised, stocks unissued, etc.), the real deficiency was exposed as £1,875,625 19s 11d. All that was available to meet this was £95,550 18s 0d in the form of unexercised borrowing powers. The report noted the systematic placing of sums which should have been paid out of revenue, to "capital or suspense accounts where they appeared to be company property rather than debt". Any available source had been plundered, even the loss-making North British Steam Packet Co. In the arrangement made in August 1863, the NBR was to have no receipts until the steamship company's revenues were greater than its working expenses, interest and depreciation charges. This had never happened (and never would happen), but the NBR had taken £21,217 11s 0d out of the NBSP revenues. Dividends had been paid from these various sources to the sum of £304,136 4s – "Under Mr. Hodgson's rule the North British has been very successfully engaged in accomplishing the feat of eating its head off." Also hidden in the accounts were Parliamentary expenses of £181,026 12s, with £79,000 still owed. An adjourned board meeting on 1 November, with Hodgson absent, sought to absolve the directors and put all blame on the chairman[50]. Inevitably, the committee considered that a new board and chairman were needed. It censured Rowbotham, as manager, and Lythgoe as general accountant, but praised John Walker's part in bringing the scandal to light. Rowbotham admitted he knew the accounts were "irregular" and Lythgoe confessed to having made drafts of the true position, which he then revised under Hodgson's instructions[51]. Hodgson contested the report, writing (still as chairman) to Walker on 2 November denying

**Wheatley 0-6-0ST No. 221 of the 229-class at Waverley in the late 1890s. Built in 1872,
it was rebuilt by Holmes in 1895. (*John Alsop*)**

that the accounts had been falsified: "What has been done is to postpone, and place in suspense, until dealt with by the shareholders, a portion of expenditure during a period of constant struggle of enormous proportions"[52]. The revelations aroused huge public concern and debate. A group of former Edinburgh & Glasgow directors wanted to see a criminal prosecution of Hodgson, alleging that the merger had been agreed on false premises[53], but the embattled chairman was not without supporters. The *Railway Times*, always his ally, later denounced "the deceptive statements and false conclusions of parties who avenged their Sabbatarian prejudices and gratified their Caledonian proclivities by casting the noble fabric of the North British to the ground"[54]. A special general meeting was scheduled for 14 November and both sides appealed for support in proxy votes from those not planning to attend. The *Caledonian Mercury* published a special evening edition to record the meeting, noting anti-Hodgson Sabbatarian pickets with placards, "The Lord reigneth" etc. – the man who ran Sunday trains was at last to get his due. But Hodgson was not there. James Balfour presided, explaining that the chairman had had "a painful attack in the head". Hodgson had been in London, in the hope of winning support from English shareholders, but got a frosty reception and suffered the attack on his way home.

James White was the central figure in the meeting, setting out the indictment against the absent chairman. He put the full responsibility on Hodgson, who was voted out of office by a large majority, the reformers holding proxies of £3,709,305 against his £1,536,343. Absolving the other directors of blame, White nevertheless wanted only four to remain, for continuity, on a new eleven strong board. Though some called for a clean sweep, Beaumont, Muir, and Ronald were re-elected, even though they had been on the Finance Committee, and Orr-Ewing was also re-elected. White, for health reasons, refused a directorship (he was awarded a lifetime free pass), and John Beaumont was the new chairman. The new board was all-Scottish, with a strong Glasgow element (not friendly to Henry Dunlop, who resigned his seat in December), though there were calls for four English directors to be added. Even amidst the onslaught on Hodgson, White had to admit that the NBR was earning £27,000 a week and that good management could restore it to genuine profitability. Mackenzie and Guild were elected as new auditors. It was obvious that the company would not be paying dividends for some considerable time, and Peter Blackburn and John Jamieson opened a campaign for the NBR's debts to be met by the pre-amalgamation proprietors only. They had to defend their own action in walking blindly into the merger: Jamieson explained that it was not the practice in railway amalgamations to make "minute examinations of accounts". The procedure was simply to exchange audited balance sheets, with a *vidimus* of the assets and liabilities of each company. Reliance was placed on the good faith of directors and officials[55].

8. THE KIPPENDAVIE YEARS 1, 1866–1870

Quick action was taken by the new board to raise a special preference stock at 5.5% per annum maximum, to the value of £1,875,625, which would outrank all other preference stocks. The money was urgently needed to meet liabilities which included amounts due to banks of £261,543 5s 5d and debts due to wagon-hire companies of £216,242 19s 0d. A balance of £74,027 10s 1d was also due to the North British Steam Packet Company[1]. Shocks and surprises were not over it was announced on 21 December that a new director, John Stirling of Kippendavie, had joined the board and immediately been elected chairman, with Beaumont as his deputy. Stirling had been chairman of the Scottish North Eastern until its amalgamation with the Caledonian, and had since been a director of the Caledonian. To take on the North British was no small challenge, but for a 55-year old veteran of Scottish railway politics this was a unique opportunity to play a leading role. G. P. Neele gave an unflattering description: "very able … but unfortunately lame; he had to support himself on a crutch, in addition to which the dark spectacles he wore to hide some defect in his eyes, did not improve his appearance …"[2]. The self-important Neele felt Kippendavie was too ugly to be introduced to the Queen. At the end of the year, NBR £100 shares were trading at £37 12s 6d, a small increase on the £34 to which they had sunk in November. The Caledonian price was £132 13s 9d, the G&SWR 's £117 12s 6d[3].

John Stirling of Kippendavie, chairman of the NBR from 1866 to 1882; the portrait is believed to date from 1862. (*Courtesy of Mr and Mrs Stirling-Aird*)

Rowbotham resigned on 15 November and Lythgoe on the 23rd, though Rowbotham did not leave until the end of December, and not in disgrace, being paid a £1,000 retainer for the period between June 1867 and April 1869[4]. A complimentary reference was later provided. William Hurst sent the board a "statement as to his retirement" in December[5]. The company already had a short list of potential successors, and the new board could hardly be expected to approve of his highly profitable association with the Scottish Waggon Company, as Hodgson evidently had done. Rowbotham, McLaren and Bell (chief engineer) were also shareholders, and the chairman was Bailie James Falshaw, of Edinburgh, a future chairman of the NBR[6]. In January 1865 it paid a dividend of 11% on a share capital of £30,000. At the beginning of 1866 it owned 2,246 wagons, of

Killearn Station, circa 1900. (*John Alsop*)

which 2,154 were let out on purchase leases, and 92 on hiring leases, and had contracted for 1,037 new wagons. By then its share capital was £120,000 and its dividend 12.5%. But by the end of 1866 the share price was down to £5 18s[7]. The North British was still doing business with it; 100 iron bar wagons were supplied in January 1867[8]. Hurst did not remain in Edinburgh but returned to Lancashire[9]. Thomas Wheatley, of the LNWR's Wolverton works, was appointed locomotive superintendent at £800 a year and began his duties on 1 February 1867. The locomotive committee was now strengthened by two extra members and the duties of the superintendent were to be examined and reported on: it seems the board felt the need to keep a closer eye on the superintendent's activities.

The board revolution overshadowed the opening of the Blane Valley line for goods trains, from a new station at Lennoxtown to Killearn, on 5 November; and on 23 December, of the line from Monktonhall through Smeaton to Thorneybank Siding, outside Dalkeith. Completion to Hardengreen Junction on the Hawick line, including the iron viaduct over the South Esk, would have to wait until 31 July 1870. The other arm, from Smeaton as far as Ormiston, opened on 1 May 1867, and was through to Macmerry on 19 March 1868 for goods and mineral trains only, to the annoyance of the residents. Dalkeith too felt hard done by. When the link line between Smeaton and Hardengreen had been proposed, the town was promised a "main line" station for trains to the south. This had not happened; indeed in 1864 the NBR had first sought to abandon the Smeaton-Hardengreen section, then reduced it to single-track although the act provided for a double line, and it remained little-used[10].

The new men met Caledonian directors at the NBR offices on 8 January (Rowbotham was in attendance, with Walker) and both sides agreed that the territorial agreement had been tacitly broken and both promised better behaviour. The new general manager, Samuel Lack Mason, aged only 30, came in April, from the Great Northern Railway, at a salary of £1,000. After the strings of Bills in previous years, the NBR only had two entered for the 1867 session, one for alterations to the Stobcross line and other matters, including authorisation of agreements on railway and tramway lines with the Leith Harbour Commissioners, and another for separating unexecuted lines and works, with their capital and borrowing requirements, from other company undertakings[11], in the hope that some other body might finance and build them and the North British work them. Finance naturally dominated Kippendavie's first half-yearly shareholders' meeting, on 28 March. Gross receipts were £674,369 2s 1d compared to £663,335 11s 3d in August 1865-January 1866, and expenditure was £422,156 15s 8d, compared to £304,435 4s 2d, the increase explained by the new and proper accounting methods. Dividends were deferred because of the unavoidable application of revenue to the capital account, which had been increased by £259,777 16s 5d. Included in the capital account was £700,000 of "unproductive work", the interest on this being charged to revenue. The Devon Valley Railway Act of 1866 bound the NBR to advance £60,000 on 4% preference stock, for completion of that line and the company proposed to pay this by instalments; it also still had to pay £214,000 of its £300,000 investment in the City of Glasgow Union Railway, now jointly vested in the NBR and Glasgow & South Western Railway. At this time, the Glasgow & South Western Railway was seeking amalgamation with the Midland Railway – the NBR was not opposing the merger but looking for safeguards for its own interests[12]. Rationalisation of the three workshops was announced: all heavy repairs would be at Cowlairs, with St. Margaret's and Burntisland doing only only light repairs.

In the Spring of 1867 railwaymen across Britain continued the campaign for improved pay and working hours. Enginemen of the North Eastern Railway went on strike in May. North British enginemen met in Glasgow and resolved to present a set of resolutions to the directors, including a ten hour day, with any time in excess to be reckoned by the hour, with two hours counted as a quarter-day. Proposed daily pay rates for drivers were 5s 6d for a pilot driver; 6s for a goods driver in his first year, then 6s 6d; 7s for a passenger driver. One hundred miles should count as a day's work on goods trains; 130 on passenger trains. Sunday work should be paid at time and a half, and lodging and refreshment allowances should be given for overnight stays and long distance work. At least nine hours off should be allowed between duty stints, and no-one should be penalised for being a member of the Engine Drivers' and Firemen's United Society[13]. To such requests the company returned a standard response, that any servant with a request or grievance should approach his foreman or department manager. The new board was in no mind to increase the workers' pay; its vital Money Bill had had the "reluctant consent" of the House of Commons and was now with the Lords, and a special meeting of shareholders approved it on 4 June[14]. A few ex-directors, including Col. Kinloch and Walter Wilson of Hawick, made oppositional noises but were shouted down. Hodgson himself made no further appearances.

The 'Queen's station' at St. Margaret's, built for royal access to Holyroodhouse, but long unused and decrepit, was pulled down in June[15]. On 15 April 1867 the short but heavily-engineered Esk Valley Railway, in the hilly country south of Edinburgh, opened to Polton. Its perpetual lease by the NBR had been authorised on 16 July 1866. Passenger services on the Blane Valley line began on 1 July, via a new station at Lennoxtown (Blane Valley); the original terminus, now Lennoxtown (Old) survived in use until 1 October 1881, with trains entering, then reversing out. Hodgson's fall was a blow for the Northumberland Central Railway, still under construction to Rothbury (he remained a director for some years), and which was far short of its capital requirement. With no support now in Edinburgh, it had to apply for an Act to abandon the section north of Rothbury, and to reduce its capital to £75,000. When at last it opened on 1 November 1870 Hodgson had left its board, and was not a guest at the ceremony[16]. It had been built in the cheapest possible manner, thirteen miles for £54,000.

By September there were few signs of progress although the immediate financial gap had been plugged by the passing of the Money Bill (29 July) in an adjusted form: pre-preference stock was reduced to £1,050,000, with debentures of £843,850. This almost exactly matched the company's debts, still around £1,800,000. The shareholders, their dividends still deferred, were not cheered to be told by Kippendavie that the NBR remained committed to some £2,600,000 worth of new construction. An indiscriminate abandonment of works was not advisable, though he hoped that certain projects might be reconstituted as separate undertakings. Locomotive expenditure had been reduced by £9,500[17]. The Glasgow & Milngavie Junction Railway, worked on a 50% of receipts basis by the E&G, then the North British, since its opening in April 1863, was chasing arrears of payment amounting to £1,405 5s 7½d[18]. That year the NBR exercised its option to acquire the Queen's ferry over the Firth of Forth for the sum of £4,700, taking over responsibility for the ferry service, though the money was not paid over until September 1868 and the purchase was not finalised until 30 March 1869[19].

By October NBR £100 shares had climbed to £83 10s[20]. Mason's English connections helped to get monthly return tickets to London via the East Coast, something long-desired according to Kippendavie, and through passenger bookings with the LNWR via Carlisle (his brother was assistant general manager of the LNWR)[21].

A faction of E&G shareholders and ex-directors put forward a Bill in January 1868 for repeal of the amalgamation[22], and though it was withdrawn, they remained unreconciled. Kippendavie, however, had his eye on further union. Building on his connections with the Caledonian company, he signed up on 16 January to a joint-purse arrangement. For 20 years from 1 February the combined revenue would be divided on the basis of each company's gross receipts for the eighteen months prior to 31 January 1868. Allowance was made for traffic that might have been carried on the Waverley Route (were it not for Caley obstruction) and it was agreed that the East Coast Route should be maintained at full efficiency, though present arrangements would have to be revised once the Midland line to Carlisle was completed. A joint traffic committee, with four directors from each company, was envisaged, holding meetings alternately in Glasgow and Edinburgh, and a further committee would manage the Forth & Clyde Canal[23].

Pre-requisite to the improved relationship was an agreement that the Caledonian should give up opposition to various NBR projects whose completion had been delayed by the company's difficulties and which needed Bills for time extension: including the Devon Valley, the Lasswade line, Inverkeithing-Dunfermline, Glasgow-Coatbridge, and the Stobcross Branch. The latter two were inherited E&G projects. The Stobcross line gave access from the Dumbarton line at Maryhill to Stobcross, where the Clyde Trustees had bought the riverbank ground in the winter of 1865-66 and were proposing to build a large dock. Construction involved a 586-yard diversion of the Forth & Clyde Canal, with the rails laid in its former bed, an aqueduct for the canal, and fifteen other bridges, with the approach to Stobcross to be on brick arches, which could be let for storage and other purposes. The Caledonian, as a price for withdrawing opposition, had gained running powers on the line and shared ownership of the Stobcross Goods Station. But matters were delayed by a wrangle over price, when the landowner, Mrs. Gilbert, demanded £55,621 5s for land which the NBR's surveyor had valued at £17,382 4s 9d, inclusive of damage to her amenities; and then thrown into limbo by the NBR's crisis. The original estimate of costs, from the engineers Formans & McCall, was £84,399 12s 2d, with the work to be completed by 1 November 1872[24], but £140,000 had already been spent on property and law fees. Early in 1868, with no sign of the dock being started, the North British introduced a Bill for the line's abandonment[25].

Simultaneous shareholders' meetings of both companies were held on 31 January. Despite many adverse comments on the current state of the Caledonian, the North British meeting gave unanimous consent[26] and a 20-year agreement from 1 February 1868 was made. Strong currents of latent rivalry remained, however, notably at Alloa, where both companies sought to bridge the Forth. The North British was not out of financial travails: warrants for deferred payment were issued against the preference dividend of March. But for the first time in years its share price overtook the Caledonian's: £100 ordinary trading at £83 10s against the CR's £81.

The line from Piershill to Trinity Junction was opened on 22 May, with a west-to-north curve from Abbeyhill Junction giving access from Waverley, and "a set of very handsome first, second and third class carriages, with short buffer springs … and powerful lever continuous brakes" was provided. Granton and Leith trains now left from a new platform "at the foot of Canal Street" and came in to another new platform at the edge of the Green Market. Waverley now had three arrival and four departure platforms[27]. Princes Street Station and the Scotland Street Tunnel were now closed and work began to build up the base of the new Market. Confusingly, the NBR had two stations both known as Leith. The one-time Edinburgh Leith & Granton Railway terminus at

Gorebridge Station, a view taken very soon after the 1923 Grouping. (*North British Railway Study Group***)**

North British lamp post.
(*North British Railway Study Group*)

Commercial Street was often referred to as "the North Leith Station" and the former Edinburgh & Dalkeith Railway terminus as "South Leith"[28]. Around this time company advertisements referred to the station on Commercial Street as Leith (Citadel), though North Leith (later altered to Leith North) quickly supplanted it; and by 1868 the "North" and "South" names were established[29].

Public and official concern at the frequency of railway accidents was strong in the late 1860s. The NBR had its share of these. At Arniston Colliery Siding, near Gorebridge, a goods train from Newcastle ran into a stationary shunting train at 3 a.m on 28 February. Three men were killed. John Stirling and Samuel Mason were arrested at a board meeting, but freed on £50 bail each[30], and no case was brought. Kippendavie's priority was to keep the railway operating effectively and while the dividends were held off, £88,047 10s 7d was spent on new works, and £48,608 3s 5d on locomotives and rolling stock in the half-year from August 1867 to January 1868. Expenditure on the permanent way was up by £26,357 15s 1d. The new chairman also told the shareholders that it was "monstrous" that the company had not a single decent goods station in Glasgow. Despite complaints about new projects being put in hand before any dividends were paid, he announced that the nine-mile Glasgow-Coatbridge line was going ahead, at a cost of £250,000[31]. In May the company's General Purposes Bill was passed, giving extensions of time on Glenfarg and other works and allowing the abandonment of some Dundee and Devon Valley branch schemes, and of the St. Margaret's deviation[32]. Another Bill for further time extensions and abandonments was in Parliament, approved by a shareholders' meeting on 29 May. Bo'ness-Grangemouth and Brampton-Longtown lines were dropped, but there was an agreement with the Baird company for taking over their line from Sunnyside Junction at Coatbridge to the ironworks at Rochsolloch, with the North British working it for 25% of receipts, and guaranteeing Baird's a 5.5% return on capital. Not unreasonably, Col. Kinloch, established as the main but not only voice of opposition, criticised the one figure as too low and the other as too high. Kippendavie defended the deal as "permissive only" at present[33]. The line served other ironworks as well as Baird's, but keeping in with Baird's was a central plank of North British policy. Their industrial interests were spread across the central industrial belt, and they were very large shareholders in the company.

Financial issues dominated the year, with the affairs of the City of Glasgow Union Railway coming under regular scrutiny. Like all cross-city projects, it was costing much more than the original estimates, partly through rises in property prices. The North British had already subscribed £200,000 and another £100,000 was due. Kippendavie considered that the City of Glasgow Union Railway was in "a thorough mess". The two miles from College Station to meet the NBR at Sighthill would cost £250,000 and there seemed no hope of completing that. But the NBR was willing to invest more if the City of Glasgow Union Railway were extended eastwards to meet the planned Coatbridge-Glasgow line at Sword Street (Bellgrove Station) with the Bellgrove-College section as a joint NBR-City of Glasgow Union Railway line. The NBR would also take up half the College ground for a station[34]. In September, half-yearly dividends were again deferred and the board now proposed a scheme for liquidating the warrants by converting them to preference stock from the 1865 issue, of which £1,185,000 was still available. Maintenance and renewal were still absorbing large amounts of cash: many wooden bridges still needed replacement. The Tweed Bridge near Selkirk was being rebuilt in stone and iron at a cost of £6,000 - £7,000. Much of the rolling stock was in an unsatisfactory state, and the signalling installations were inadequate for busier stations and increased traffic. But progress was being made: the NBR's debts were down to £566,348 10s 1d. Gross receipts for the half-year were £681,731 6s 0d, against £658,335 11s 8d; while working expenses, though also higher (£391,105 4s 9d against £383,646 12s 7d) showed signs of being contained. The North British Steam Packet Co. was operating seven ships from Silloth and Helensburgh. The joint-purse arrangement with the Caledonian was said to be operating well. The directors had got rid of £1,000,000 worth of liabilities and hoped to reduce these by a further million, but the board also wanted to raise £1,000,000 in new debenture stock. Some shareholders wanted a committee set up to consult with the directors on financial questions, but this was voted down[35]. By the end of the year, Kippendavie was able to announce that no more deferred dividend warrants would be issued after

Bathgate Upper in LNER days, but details all North British. (*John Alsop*)

January 1869, and that from July, cash would be paid and arrears of interest would be met. The board's financial sights had been raised: it was now proposed to raise £3,000,000 of new capital. The company was currently empowered to issue stocks of three million pounds. This would be cancelled and the new powers would be drawn on "at such times and at such rates as shareholders may agree to". A special meeting approved the plan despite criticisms that the board should spend more time on running the company economically and less on high finance[36].

The NBR was working the Edinburgh & Bathgate Railway on the 999-year lease inherited from the Edinburgh & Glasgow, and the terms were modified as from 1 January 1869 to a yearly rental of £12,500, giving the Bathgate shareholders a regular 5% a year. The stock amounted to £250,000. That relic of earlier days, the Halbeath Railway, continued to be a North British property since no-one would buy it. A company memorandum of January 1869 noted, "a very bad investment but we cannot get rid of it". Between 1861-68 it recorded total losses of £9,166 13*s* 11*d*[37].

Having decided to abandon the expensive Stobcross Branch, the board reversed policy and introduced a Bill to un-abandon it, though a separate company was to be set up to raise the capital[38]. On 1 March Edinburgh's new Waverley Market was formally handed over to the town council, and work on the expansion of Waverley Station, to Jopp's plan, got properly underway[39]. Half-yearly receipts for August 1868-January 1869 were up by £67,000 and working expenses were down by £12,000, but such positive signs were overshadowed by a growing dispute with the Caledonian. Part of the joint-purse arrangement between the companies was a share for traffic via the Waverley Route. Lord Salisbury, already a prominent Conservative politician, was appointed as arbiter in the case of disagreement over amounts and proportions, but the Caledonian company took the view that he should arbitrate only on certain traffics. Dispute on how much revenue should be ascribed to the Waverley Route quickly sharpened. The North British was willing to set £40,000 aside, if the CR did likewise, until the dispute was settled, but the Caledonian board refused, and the NBR sought an interdict against the CR paying a dividend until the issue was resolved. Counsel for the Caledonian claimed that the joint-purse agreement had no legal standing; James White blamed both boards for negligence and feared that the joint-purse would not survive (some NBR shareholders said "the sooner the better"). Mackenzie and Guild were re-elected as the NBR's auditors at the half-yearly meeting on 31 March, despite protests that they were share-brokers as well as accountants, and that they had been "bulling" and "bearing" on both North British and Caledonian share prices (the NB £100 ordinary had risen briefly to over £80 before subsiding to a more usual £34 10s). Bad relations between the companies spilled into the City of Glasgow Union Railway sphere, where Caledonian obstructiveness had forced that company into "expensive litigation"[40]. The Court of Session refused the North British plea for an interdict against the Caledonian dividend on 6 May. It emerged however that the Caledonian and London & North Western companies had concluded a secret agreement on 31 January 1867, on the division of traffic at Carlisle, maintaining the exclusion of the North British. Any traffic not specifically consigned by another company was to go by LNWR/Caledonian, leaving no room for a NBR share[41]. Notice of this agreement had not been given to the NBR when the joint-purse agreement was made. But, as the Caley was quick to point out, during his short time on its board John Stirling had been a member of the committee which made the agreement. He could hardly claim ignorance of it now. In self-extenuation the embarrassed Kippendavie said, "I had totally and utterly forgotten that I had ever heard the heads of it" though he admitted he had been at the meeting where the heads of agreement had been presented. Adding that he could not in honour have passed on to the NBR board things he had been told as a Caledonian director, he also pointed out, as a proof of his good faith, that "when this secret agreement was brought out in Parliamentary Committee, no man spoke more strongly than myself on the subject". If he had remembered the CR board meeting, he would have been "an idiot" to make any such comment. He was still willing to continue the joint-purse agreement if the Caledonian would allow Salisbury to arbitrate on a full Waverley Route share, and suspend the LNWR agreement for five years[42]. The Caledonian was given until 25 May to respond. Kippendavie's position was weakened by these events, and he had to accept a shareholders' committee of consultation to monitor board proceedings. One member was the industrialist Alex Whitelaw of Gartsherrie, a Baird partner and "a warm and constant friend and very large customer to the North British."[43]. His son William, the NBR's future chairman, was a one-year old infant. On 25 May, the committee proposed new terms for a settlement with the Caledonian, but the board was also given authority to terminate the joint-purse if it should so decide. By September the joint purse agreement was dead and relations between the North British and Caledonian had sunk to a new low.

The opening of the Caledonian's new line between Glasgow and Edinburgh via Midcalder in June helped to worsen things, with an immediate fares war. The NBR, still with the fastest route, cut its fare between the termini to 5s 6d to match the Caledonian's, but did not reduce the fares to and from intermediate stations, causing angry complaints. The number of trains was increased and prices lowered further. By mid-July 13 trains were running each way daily, of which two were expresses. The Sunday service remained at two trains. Fares were first class 5s 6d (return 9s 6d); second 4s (7s), third 2s 6d (4s), except for the expresses, first and second class only with a single fare of 6s 6d (first) and 5s (second)[44].

Four years after announcing its intention to do so, from 1 June 1869 the North Eastern Railway began to run the East Coast expresses between Berwick and Edinburgh with its own locomotives, under the powers granted in 1862. At first only two trains were involved, but on 12 July it gave notice that it would run all through trains from 1 August. The NBR-Caledonian joint-purse agreement of January 1868 had restrained the North British from exercising its own running powers to Aberdeen, and thus deprived the East Coast Route of some long-haul traffic, despite a 'Private Agreement' made with the NER on 12 May 1862 binding both parties to maintain the East Coast Route in full efficiency[45]. The Amalgamation acts of 1865 and 1866 had bound the North British, and the Caledonian, to run a train to Aberdeen without change of carriages "in connection with every train which should be run or appointed to be run by the East Coast ... by way of Edinburgh." This effectively deprived the NBR of control of the service, and use of NER engines pre-empted any difficulties. But in any case the NBR acquiesced, paying the North Eastern 1s per mile for the use of their engines north of Berwick, and retaining its share of receipts, an arrangement terminable on three months' notice. At the end of June 1869 the Anglo-Scottish Traffic Agreement came to an end, and was not renewed, but the companies involved agreed to charge the same rates and fares as before. From 2 August the Great Northern and North Eastern laid on a new express train, leaving London at 8 pm and arriving in Waverley at 6.05 am, half an hour ahead of the West Coast, and timed to connect with onward NBR services. Nevertheless the NBR also kept its contacts warm with the Midland and Glasgow & South Western companies for interchange and joint development of traffic via Carlisle. An act for the Settle-Carlisle Railway had been passed in June 1866 but in the Spring of 1869 the Midland, having received an offer of running powers and accommodation from the LNWR, was seeking to abandon the hugely expensive project. But its Bill for abandonment was rejected by Parliament, partly through the opposition of the North British and the Lancashire & Yorkshire Railways, both of which stood to gain considerable new traffic from the Settle & Carlisle line.

Parliament passed the North British (General Purposes) Act at the end of June 1869, and the board resolved to create a debenture stock of £670,000 in order to pay the deferred preference dividends, plus interest. No dividend was forthcoming on ordinary shares, but it was also resolved to raise £400,000 on a second debenture stock, to be allotted to ordinary shareholders if they wanted to take it up[46].

Ladybank Station: when the Edinburgh and Northern Railway first built their station here the area was known as the Lady Bog. To encourage development around their new junction they renamed the place Ladybank.(*Stenlake Collection*)

A boost to NBR Leith traffic was given when the port commissioners opened the Albert Dock on 21 August, served by new sidings from the former Edinburgh & Dalkeith Railway Leith Branch. Transfer of the railway telegraph network to state ownership brought the company a payment of £100,000 from the Post Office along with a maintenance contract worth £2,520 a year. Kippendavie noted that in 1867 the NBR had paid the telegraph companies £3,200 for their services. He had organised the NBR's takeover in time to benefit from selling it on to the Government. He chose the moment of mild euphoria to announce the revival of the Tay Bridge project, justifying the capital cost of £350,000 by pointing out that the NBR paid a toll of £10,229 a year to the Caledonian to run trains from Broughty Ferry to Dundee and that the ferries cost £9,792 a year to run. Opposition was immediate and vocal, however, with the cost estimate ridiculed, and it was not clear whether the motion actually gained a majority, though Kippendavie insisted that it had[47]. Some weeks later he was able to say that a tender of £229,680 for the Tay Bridge had been accepted from Butler & Pitt, of Yorkshire, and that John Waddell of Bathgate, as contractor, would build the railway links for £116,662 – a cost coming out at less than £350,000. The Tay Bridge Company was to be a separate undertaking, and he said no North British capital would be involved. George Kinloch, still opposing, uttered a prophetic warning about the dangers of "a fairy or spider bridge" being damaged by a gale[48]. A new Tay Bridge Bill was presented to Parliament, allowing for repeal of the clause in the previous Tay Bridge Act which restrained the NBR from acquiring a joint interest in the Dundee & Arbroath Railway until the bridge was completed[49].

Railway accidents remained a cause of public concern, heightened by newspaper coverage. Even in the relatively restrained style of the nineteenth century, 'Shocking' or 'Dreadful' were almost automatically coupled to the words 'railway accident'. The *Dundee Courier*, commenting on the number of fatal accidents to rail staff, quoted Richard Hodgson from his days as chairman, "Oh, we think we get on very well if we are below the level of the North Eastern, who kill a man a week" to indicate the relaxed attitude of railway managements to the steady attrition of accidents at work[50]. Samuel Mason informed the Commons Committee on Railway Companies that the NBR had about 120 miles of block working, but admitted much of it was "modified block" in which a driver might be stopped at the start of a section, then allowed to proceed at slow speed even though the previous train had not yet cleared it[51].

A cold snap in January 1870 encouraged curling bonspiels and the NBR ran special trains to and from Lindores Loch, on the Ladybank-Collessie line, to carry 400 players and spectators to a curling match[52]. In Glasgow, the Stobcross line's future now looked highly promising, with the project formed into a separate undertaking, in which the Clyde Trustees were to invest £140,000 (at a guaranteed 4% annual return), and proceed with their dock (work did not start until October 1873). The NBR also introduced a Bill for a harbour at Port Edgar, just west of South Queensferry, and another to get permissive power to convert lien stocks of certain absorbed companies, including the Leadburn & Dolphinton Railway, into consolidated NBR stock.

Competition with the Caledonian Railway was not confined to Edinburgh-Glasgow trains. Another inter-company dispute broke into public print when a letter from Kippendavie to the Caledonian chairman, Thomas Hill, was published. Noting that CR passenger traffic from Glasgow to the north had been worked by the North British between Queen Street and Greenhill for upwards of 20 years (mostly over Caledonian tracks), a traffic worth some £22,000 a year to the NBR, he referred to exchanges between the two company managers about the Caledonian's plans to operate its own northbound passenger trains from Buchanan Street, from 1 January 1871. John Walker, for the NBR, had asked the CR's Archibald Gibson to take North British carriages onwards from Greenhill on certain trains and Gibson had agreed. Since the NBR also wanted to continue with some trains of its own, it was agreed that the Caley could run trains of its own over the North British between Larbert and Edinburgh. But on 24 December the Caledonian had backed away, refusing to convey North British carriages between Greenhill and Perth and so leaving the NBR to run an expensive duplicate service or lose revenue. Meanwhile the NBR was co-operating on the Larbert-Edinburgh trains, including the sale of interchangeable return tickets, something the Caledonian had refused to introduce between Glasgow and Perth. Hill's reply justified his company's attitude by claiming that the North British was making unreasonable demands: to have carriages attached to CR trains *and* run their own trains to Perth would give them a greater use of the line than the Caledonian, which owned it[53]. The North British went to the Court of Session, with a successful request for suspension and interdict on certain Caledonian trains, especially the 4.15 pm from Glasgow to Perth, which duplicated a heavily-used NBR service. Its own treatment of passengers was criticised at this time. A through train from Glasgow to Hawick was advertised, leaving at 7 am, including third class accommodation. But at Edinburgh third class travellers were required to pay an extra 3s 6d to use this train, or else wait for four hours and 45 minutes for the 1.45 Edinburgh-Hawick. Protests were unheeded until one passenger took the matter to court, whereupon the NBR swiftly changed its policy and paid his costs[54]. The company's new contract with the Post Office, from 1 April 1870, provided for payment of £9,500 a year for two years, of which £50 was to be passed to the Peebles, £50 to the St. Andrews, £52 to the Berwickshire, and £5 to the Milngavie companies. A second class compartment was reserved for the Post Office on Edinburgh and Berwick trains; on other lines the NBR guards were responsible for looking after the mail bags[55].

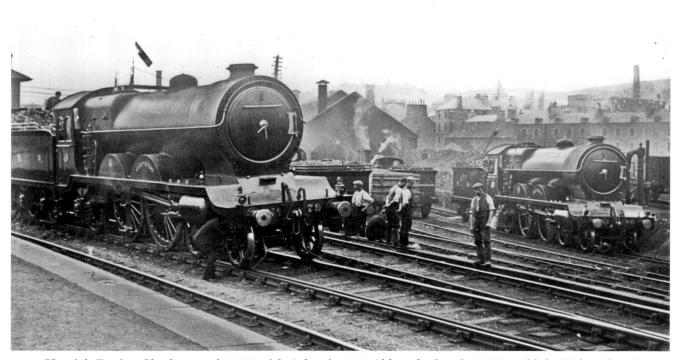

Hawick Engine Shed around 1907, with Atlantics 879 *Abbotsford* **and 880** *Tweeddale*. (*John Alsop*)

Wheatley 4-4-0 No. 224, in original condition. Salved from the Tay Bridge collapse, it was rebuilt as a compound engine in 1885, then restored to single-expansion in 1887. It was withdrawn in 1919. (*North British Railway Study Group*)

Wrangling with the Caledonian went on into 1870, dispute extending into other areas. At the March half-yearly meeting Kippendavie defended a North British-Glasgow & South Western wheeze of sending iron ore from Dalry in Ayrshire to Grangemouth via a long detour by Gretna, at a lower rate than the Caledonian would charge by its far more direct route. He also asserted that the Caledonian was trying to secure business that would prejudice the NBR's almost-completed line between Coatbridge (Sunnyside Junction) and Glasgow, and suggested that complaints from North British shareholders came mostly from those who had larger holdings in the Caledonian (a breakdown of joint shareholdings in 1870 found that 23.3% of NBR shareholders had shares in one or more of the other Scottish railways, compared with 30.75% of Caledonian Railway and 47.12% of Glasgow & South Western Railway shareholders[56]). But many protested when he requested powers to invest £100,000 in the Tay Bridge, having previously said there would be no NBR capital involved and that work would not start until all the £350,000 had been raised. Now only £200,000 was raised, the North British was to plug the gap, and work was to start once the Act was passed (it received the royal assent on 1 August[57]). Kippendavie dealt smoothly with the objections, saying that he was sure "it would only be an arrangement for a short time" and informing the meeting that he had £1,937,000-worth of proxy votes in support of the board. Challenged about the company's still very high rate of working expenses, 51% of gross revenue compared to the Caledonian's 45%, he replied that the NBR had tunnels, ferries, and a large number of branches that needed locomotives to work them, while carrying less mineral traffic than the Caledonian. Besides, the rate was falling, down from 55.8% two years previously[58]. Collaboration was also possible: combined NBR-CR objections put a stop to a scheme for all railways to charge for the use of foot-warmers, being proposed via the Railway Clearing House[59].

Work was progressing on the rebuilding of Waverley Station and tenders for building the new booking office and waiting rooms were invited in April[60]. A perhaps unexpected item of expenditure was £3,500 for an additional locomotive shed at St. Margaret's, to be rented to the North Eastern Railway. The NER remained suspicious of the North British: Hodgson's acquisitive policy in Northumberland had not been forgotten, and the NBR's efforts to set up joint goods facilities with the Midland at Carlisle were further exposing its less than total commitment to the East Coast. For the North British, with its barely adequate locomotive fleet, to have the English expresses worked by NER locomotives was one burden less. Questions of prestige did not arise, or were ignored. The route to Aberdeen was a different matter, however. When the Caledonian Railway absorbed the Scottish North Eastern company in 1865, the NBR had secured running powers from Perth to Aberdeen. As usual, an arbitrator was appointed to rule on disputes. C.W. Eborall, manager of the South Eastern Railway, filled this role and in April 1870 he gave the North British company equal status with the Caledonian in CR stations north of Perth. The North British was to have its own goods office at Aberdeen, and effectively operate it as a North British station for all goods consigned in and out via the NBR. Naturally this heightened competition, with both companies employing canvassers to get business, and doubtless offering 'drawbacks' for regular or bulk loads. The Caledonian, legally obliged to give access to the North British, did not make it easy, and complaints about obstruction, delays, and mis-routing of goods would be endemic until the early 1900s. Eborall gave a further judgement in August. Finding that the Caledonian had been obstructive to the NBR's running powers on the former Scottish Central Railway line between Greenhill and Perth, he ruled that the NBR could run 7.15 am and 4.15 pm trains from Glasgow to Perth, also a 10.35 am Glasgow-Dunblane train, plus other trains so long as the total number of NBR trains and Caledonian trains with NBR "facilities" should not exceed the total number of CR trains on the route, taking 1869 services as a base. The Caledonian was required to accept North British trucks and carriages at Greenhill for combined services and to provide booking facilities for the NBR at Dundee West and also at Aberdeen, "unless the Great North of Scotland Railway can offer lawful objection".

Another constant source of complaint was the Caledonian's habit of sending off trains from Perth without waiting for the North British connecting service. The NBR was not famous for time-keeping but sometimes Caledonian signalmen delayed its trains unnecessarily. Now Eborall ruled that Caledonian departures should be delayed up to ten minutes if the NBR train was late, and longer if the train was signalled as outside Perth Station. Greenhill Upper Junction was another prolific source of delays: "As a remedy for the obstruction of North British trains north of Greenhill Upper Junction, it is directed that the Caledonian shall keep the line clear for five minutes at least before the timed hour of passing of a North British train, and for ten minutes after"[61]. On 10 May 1872, in the course of evidence to the Joint Committee on Railway Amalgamation, Peter Macpherson, the NBR goods manager, gave a detailed account of Caledonian tactics, which he estimated lost the North British £60,000 a year[62]. Not all rulings were in favour of the North British. After representations from the Caledonian, the NBR was instructed not to sell tickets or carry goods to intermediate stations between its own system and Perth[63]. Eborall's rulings were not always obeyed and the fare war between Glasgow and Edinburgh was still going on in September, though the companies by then were engaging in talks to achieve a formal and binding division of traffic. Neither could afford to lose revenue, and the North British gross passenger takings for February-July 1870 had fallen by £11,049 0s 5d from the same period in 1869[64]. The NBR would reduce its Glasgow-Perth trains from seven to two, the CR would drop its Larbert-Edinburgh services, and both would give up competitive advertising of services from Edinburgh and Glasgow to the North. But with the opening of the Glasgow-Coatbridge line, the NBR was about to introduce yet another Glasgow-Edinburgh service, via Coatbridge (Sunnyside), Airdrie and Bathgate[65]. This line terminated at Bellgrove between 23 November and 19 December 1870, then at Gallowgate until College Station was opened on 1 February 1871.

In this atmosphere of mingled co-operation and competition, the NBR had to return to the arbitrator in November 1870. At Aberdeen the Caledonian goods clerks were annexing all traffic that was not specifically consigned 'North British'. Even 'Via East Coast' was claimed by the Caledonian, at least as far as Greenhill. Now it was ruled that all East Coast traffic must be credited to the NBR, and the Caledonian must also stop withholding forwarding notes and invoices from the NBR clerks, and pay the NBR compensation of £300[66]. In that month the company introduced Bills to (among other things) enable it to run workmen's trains, at limited fares and limited liability for compensation in case of accident (£100 maximum); to absorb the Esk Valley Railway; and to support a new line, the North British, Arbroath & Montrose Railway.

Armadale station looking east, in the 1900s. (*Stenlake Collection*)

9. THE KIPPENDAVIE YEARS 2, 1870–1873

All railway companies could make common cause in the matter of land valuation. In June 1870 a Commons Select Committee was discussing the proposed exemption of railways from paying into the poor rates. Every parish was entitled to levy a rate to assist the poor, and from 1854 an official assessor was appointed to value railways and canals. In many parishes the railway was the largest contributor to the rates, especially if there was a station. The assessor established a standard value per mile of track for each company, from which the company was entitled to make certain deductions, including half the actual cost of permanent way maintenance and repairs. Five per cent of the replacement cost of any station or other property was added to the rateable value. The formula was complex and the findings were frequently contested. Mr. Miller, inspector of the poor for the Barony Parish of Glasgow, told the committee that he had more difficulties with the North British than all other companies together (the NBR board would have taken this as a tribute to their secretary, John Walker). It claimed a 40% reduction (against "probable average cost of the Repairs, Insurance and other Expences" of its properties), after deduction of half the permanent way maintenance payment, while the Caledonian claimed only 28%. In most parishes the NBR appears to have simply made a 25% reduction, which was hardly ever contested. The North British claimed £158 0s 6d per mile for maintenance of the line, compared with £150 by the CR and £149 7s 8d by the Glasgow & South Western Railway. Station valuations for rating purposes had risen steeply in the later 1860s. In 1865 Queen Street Station was valued at £1,500 and Cowlairs Works at £875. By 1869-70 the figures were £7,000 and £5,025[1]. This is a direct reflection of the rise in the company's revenues. In addition, the Commissioners of Supply (predecessors of elected county councils) levied a local rate using the assessor's valuations. Under protest, and always trying to minimise the amount, the railway companies were very substantial contributors to the social budget of the country. In addition, of course, passenger duty was payable to the Government on most services apart from the penny-a-mile Parliamentary trains.

North British ordinary share prices remained at a low level through 1870, though preference shares bounced back once dividend payments resumed. Monkland 6% £100 Guaranteed preference traded at £112 while NBR £100 ordinary were at £33 10s and Edinburgh, Perth & Dundee Railway £100 stocks could be had for £16[2]. Shareholders could claim a free pass to attend half-yearly meetings, and it was suggested that "the bulk of the crowds on meeting days in Edinburgh are holders of £50 Edinburgh, Perth & Dundee stock which can be got for about £7 10s. They get a free ride to Edinburgh twice a year"[3]. Among the NBR employees, the issue of working hours had never gone away – and was sharpened by the Fife miners winning an eight hour day from 1 June – though the company had successfully avoided any action and had reduced the total staff numbers from September 1870. Workers at Bathgate and Morningside complained not about twelve hour days but sixteen to eighteen hours, "day after day and week after week" with no overtime pay. Safety of working with exhausted drivers and shunters was also an issue[4]. With criticism of the NBR's high level of working expenses raised regularly at shareholders' meetings, an increase in the pay Bill was not in the board's sights. Between August 1870 and

January 1871 the passenger revenues were again down, by £6,680, on the corresponding previous half-year, and the steady increase in goods revenue was also slowing down. The ordinary shareholders, denied a dividend since the catastrophic days of 1866, were becoming ever more restive. When Kippendavie spoke of improvements to the plant – 25% of all Monklands wagons had been rebuilt since 1865, along with 60 old Edinburgh & Glasgow carriages, and more than 80 engines rebuilt, charged to revenue, in the past four years – Orr Ewing, a former E&G director, complained that all the costs had in effect been borne by the ordinary shareholders, for no reward[5], but the board was more concerned with preference shares and shareholders. A Bill had been introduced in the 1871 Parliamentary session for the consolidation of stocks. Over the years, through acquisitions and new issues, the North British had come to have over 20 different kinds of stock, and 20 separate share registers. Keeping these up to date was a time-consuming and expensive business. By August, most of these groups of preference or guaranteed shareholders had agreed to the proposal to class them all as North British consolidated lien stock at 4%. Such almost-forgotten companies as the Stirlingshire Midland Junction, the West of Fife, Kinross-shire, Jedburgh and Wansbeck Railways, their shares and payments still recorded separately, now agreed to consolidation. Only the Border Union shareholders, led by Walter Wilson of Hawick, dissented. They had always been dissatisfied with the North British's failure to establish their railway as a real Anglo-Scottish trunk line[6]. From here on, the consolidation of absorbed companies' stocks would be a periodic exercise.

The Glasgow & Coatbridge Railway had opened as far as Gallowgate on 19 December 1870, then on 1 February 1871 College became the terminus, ending the NBR's long usage of the Caledonian station at Buchanan Street for its trains to Coatbridge and Airdrie. A rather bare station, College used part of the former University buildings as an office and it was only in July 1872 that a contract was let for an iron roof over the two platforms, at a cost of £8,389. There was also a service of three trains a day each way from College to Manuel (Low Level) from February; the return services went to Queen Street. John Waddell had major works in hand in Coatbridge, where three level crossings on the old Monkland & Kirkintilloch line had become a great inconvenience to the new town (15,802 inhabitants in 1871 compared to 741 in 1831). Under pressure from Alex Whitelaw a new high-level line replaced it, opening for goods trains on 7 August 1871. Costing around £50,000, it changed the townscape, encompassing a canal deviation, new streets, and 'Fountain Place' and altering access to the Rochsolloch line (vested in the North British through the NBR General Purposes Act of 13 July 1868) via the Sheepford Branch from Langloan East Junction. Passenger trains ran every half hour to Glasgow (College) from 23 October, from a rebuilt terminus at Whifflet, through a new Coatbridge Central, at first of wooden construction[7]. At the other side of Glasgow city centre, work on the long-delayed Stobcross Railway was about to start. The contractor was John Mackay, the engineers Formans & McCall, of Glasgow. This partnership would be closely involved with North British projects for the next 30 years.

Coal and sheet iron: Whifflet East Junction around 1920. (*North British Railway Study Group*)

The Caledonian/Scottish North Eastern Railway Act of Amalgamation of 1866 had given the NBR the right to apply, within five years, to extend its line northwards via Montrose to Aberdeen, with the Caledonian restrained from opposing, except to junctions with its own line; and a prospectus was issued in November 1870 for the North British, Arbroath & Montrose Railway, with a capital of £171,580 in £10 shares (£20,580 reserved for NBR directors). The chairman was Hercules Scott, also chairman of the Montrose & Bervie Railway, Thomas Bouch was engineer, and John Walker secretary. It would be single-line though laid out for double, would have a junction with the Bervie line at Montrose, a short branch to Montrose Harbour, and meet the Caledonian above that town at Kinnaber. Gross revenue, after cartage charges, would be split 50/50 between the NBR and the new company, which would also receive 25% of gross revenue on the NBR attributable to traffic originated on its own line. A dividend of 5.5% on the shares was assured, with any surplus going to the North British. It duly obtained its act on 13 July 1871. On the Tay Bridge site Butler & Pitt had faded from the scene and on 1 May the Tay Bridge company signed a contract with De Bergue & Co, who had entered the lowest tender for construction. On 22 July the first stone was laid without ceremony[8]. An independent company on which the North British had had an eye for years, the Forth & Clyde Junction, from Stirling to Balloch, now was willing to accept a 30-year agreement for the NBR to work it at 50% of gross revenue. This began on 1 August (on 1 August 1875 the lease would be extended to 50 years). The Forth & Clyde Junction Railway's four engines were moved to the North British Shore Road Depot at Stirling and the old shed became a wagon repair shop.

A local committee backed by the NBR had entered a Bill for a railway from Hawthornden, on the Peebles line, to Penicuik, in December 1869, prompting rivalry with supporters of another project deferred from the mid-1860s, a line between Penicuik and Millerhill, via Loanhead and Roslin. A firm agreement was made with the Penicuik Railway to work, manage and maintain it in perpetuity for 45% of gross revenue, with a half-share of any surplus profits after the Penicuik shareholders got 5% on their capital of £54,000. All these schemes were approved by the September half-yearly meeting. When a shareholder asked why there was no passenger service on the Ormiston line, the chairman replied that the upgrading required by the Board of Trade was too expensive (but the work was put in hand). There was also a protest about the withdrawal of passenger trains between Scotland Street and Leith. Insufficient demand was the answer. Kippendavie's remarks at this meeting were still critical of the Caledonian Company's attitude[9], but soon afterwards, rumours about a new rapprochement, even an amalgamation, between the companies began to circulate in Glasgow. A letter from 'Suffering Coalmaster' in the *Glasgow Herald* suggested that both companies were equally bad at supplying wagons when needed by the collieries[10] – but not many people had sympathy to spare for coalmasters, even in 1871. Better relations with the Post Office brought agreement that all NBR trains could carry mails, with consequent better postal services in Lanarkshire, to Alva, and out to the Port of Menteith[11]. In the course of the year the Halbeath Railway was finally closed and some of its track was lifted[12].

Amalgamation rumours soon became fact: on 29 November both companies had signed a provisional agreement. From 1 August 1872 dividends in the amalgamated company would be paid in the proportion of relative earnings for the year to 31 July 1871: £711,329 (NBR) and £1,106,691 (CR). Earnings above those combined figures would be split equally for dividend purposes. In order to go through the next session of Parliament, the Bill had to be lodged by 15 December, and special meetings of both companies were convened on 1 December. Kippendavie faced a barrage of opposition. It was obvious that the apparent unanimity of his board was not reflected among the proprietors. Critics arose from all over NBR territory. John Monteath Douglas, from Cupar, pointed out that in the failed joint-purse episode, the NBR had rejected a 45.5% share of the revenues as too small. Now it was willing to accept 39%. Douglas proposed that a committee of shareholders be elected, to confer with the directors before any commitment was made. His amendment was carried by a show of hands but the board was backed up by £4,500,000 of proxy votes and its resolution was declared to be carried. After a private discussion between Kippendavie and Douglas, the chairman announced that if at the necessary Wharncliffe meeting (the timing of these was now set prior to a Bill's second reading), a majority wished to appoint a shareholders' committee, the board would not oppose it[13]. The Caledonian shareholders unanimously approved the plan. A Bill had been listed for the amalgamation, with the possible inclusion of the Glasgow & South Western[14], but both boards now agreed to defer the application for a year. Douglas mounted a vigorous campaign against the merger, sending a circular to all North British shareholders asking for their co-operation. His grounds were that the year's results chosen as basis for a division of revenues (1870-71) were unfavourable to the NBR, that the disproportionate amount of repairs and improvements paid from revenue by the NBR gave a false impression of its net income and that the company, on its own, had excellent prospects. In all he listed eleven points, totalling an annual loss to the NBR of £355,000 "for ever", with no counterbalancing advantages[15]. In January, rumours surfaced that the amalgamation was to be abandoned. The shares of both companies fell slightly (NBR at £61 5s and CR at £122 10s), and finally on 2 February the North British board informed its shareholders that negotiations had been terminated because of "difficulties". Despite claiming "inaccuracies" in Douglas's circular, the board never published a response. The Caledonian company reacted angrily, calling the pull-out an unjustified breach of an engagement, and noting that "we shall, no doubt, have a renewal of the old rivalry"[16].

John Stirling's second and final attempt to bring the two companies together was motivated by a realisation that as separate concerns, they would always and inevitably consume energy and resources in competition. A single large company would be far more powerful and profitable, and of a size to match the big English companies. His opponents did not share this vision. Many of them were industrialists and businessmen, who preferred to have competition between railway companies because it kept fares and carriage costs down. A monopoly such as the combined NBR-Caledonian would be in a strong position to increase fares and reduce services. Pressed at the half-yearly shareholders' meeting in March, Kippendavie refused to give the reasons for the North British withdrawal, saying only the difficulties were "insuperable" and he did not wish to exacerbate the situation with the Caledonian. One of the directors, J.J. Stitt, of Liverpool, went a little further, saying that the Caledonian had put a construction on the [Amalgamation] Acts of 1865 and 1866, relative to the rates they were entitled to charge, "which the North British did not believe to be tenable, and which went to the very foundations of the agreement"[17]. His implication seems to be that the CR was pushing for too large a share of the joint enterprise, but the rapid caving-in of the North British board suggests that their backing had been lukewarm from the start. Whether Parliament would have agreed the merger is debatable, but some form of alliance, perhaps a resumption of the joint-purse, would probably have been welcomed.

The North British had a range of Bills in Parliament, including improvements to Portobello Station, a branch in Glasgow from Cowlairs to the Forth & Clyde Canal at Port Dundas, and other industrial branches including a line from the Blackbraes Branch to a Carron Company mineral field, a four mile branch from Kelty to Auchterderran and other mineral lines in Fife; continuing works at Waverley and absorption of the Coatbridge line with redemption of its stock at a 10% premium. The NBR also proposed to acquire the branch line from Markinch to Leslie, in Fife, where the working agreement was nearing its end. The Leslie company was paying 3.25% on ordinary stock, and the North British was to guarantee 3.5% in 1873, 4% in 1874 and 4.5% after that. It would also purchase £10,000 of the Leslie Railway's £22,000-worth of ordinary stock. At the same time, approval would be sought for agreements to take over the Leven and East Fife companies. A final Bill was for junctions to

Leslie Station, *circa* **1900. (***John Alsop***)**

link the Arbroath-Montrose line with the Caledonian and Montrose & Bervie lines, at Montrose. All these were relatively uncontentious, but the proposed acquisition of the Northumberland Central Railway was fiercely opposed. It had been worked by the North British since its opening in 1870. Defending the purchase against claims that the NCR was effectively a bankrupt concern, Kippendavie agreed that the line had been "a bad speculation" but insisted that it could be made to pay. £9,000 would be advanced to clear its liabilities and its mortgage debt of £21,706 would be converted to NBR 4% debentures, from 1877. Three per cent would be paid on NCR preference stock (only £1,625) for five years, then 4%. On its £72,000 of ordinary stock, no dividend would be paid until 1877 or 1878, then 1%. Any subsequent dividend would always be 1% less than that on NBR ordinary stock. The motion was carried despite the opposition. On exiting, one disgruntled shareholder was heard to say, "It is no use our coming here for you just over-ride us"[18]. At the NCR's final meeting, Richard Hodgson-Huntley (the Huntley a later addition), as a shareholder, complained that the North British was being made a present of the line[19].

That month, long-rumbling discontent among the waged workers came to a head. Thomas Wheatley had a notice put up at Cowlairs Works to say that any man dissatisfied with the 54 hour working week should leave the works at once. Over 200 men went, and a mass meeting of all the Cowlairs workmen resolved to quit work until the notice was removed. Around 1,200 men withdrew their labour, and Wheatley was obliged to take the notice down. In January, guards in the Western District had sent in a request for 2s a week extra pay, a 10 hour day, and overtime pay, and in March signalmen, pointsmen and porters made a similar claim. The board rejected it, claiming that the NBR was paying more than "neighbouring railways" and that the company had already conceded pay rises to the value of £50,000 in 1871[20]. In March, a dividend of 1.25% on the ordinary stock was paid, not an impressive percentage, but the first since 1865. At the time, the *Scotsman* noted that "railway stocks which at present do not yield a net return of 5% are particularly open to speculative influences"[21]. Kippendavie commented that the trade of the country was "in a state of the most unexampled prosperity"[22]. Revenues were still rising:

	August 1871-January 1872	**August 1870-January 1871**
Passenger, parcels, mail	£330,786 6s 3d	£303,529 17s 4d
Goods, minerals	£514,557 9s 5d	£453,194 4s 0d
Total	£845,343 15s 8d	£756,724 1s 4d
Working expenses	£458,851	£423,301

If expenses had risen by 8.5%, gross revenues had risen at a faster rate. The breakdown of working expenses included:

Locomotive department	£101,717	£96,056
Compensation	£8,952	£6,585
Ferries	£12,957	£11,580
Carriage & wagon	£53,075	£45,969
Parliamentary exps	£2,000	£2,000

Compensation included payments made to injured passengers or shippers whose goods had been damaged in transit. It was noted that completion of the Stobcross Branch, financed as a separate undertaking, would put the NBR "in a very good position" in Glasgow. Relations with Edinburgh Town Council were much improved and a rapid agreement was made in April, with the approval of the City Improvement Trust, about further extension of Waverley Station on the south-east side, taking over the site of the Physic Garden. From 2 August 1872 the NBR's mail earnings went up to £12,000 a year in a new three year contract, and it was noted that a Post Office carriage with sorting boxes was needed on the Edinburgh-Berwick Night Mail trains (departing Edinburgh 2.05 pm and Berwick 4.30 am.

Co-operation with the Caledonian did not expire. Joint newspaper advertisements announced that all North British and Caledonian trains would carry third class passengers from 1 April. Newspapers themselves were becoming increasingly important customers and in April the *Scotsman* hired a special early train to carry its morning edition to Glasgow for delivery to subscribers before 8 am also to catch early trains from Glasgow to other towns[23]. The *Glasgow Herald* reciprocated with a train to Edinburgh – rivalry did not exist only among railway companies. But old habits persisted – the Parliamentary Joint Select Committee on railway amalgamation heard a long litany from Peter Macpherson, goods manager of the NBR, of Caledonian obstructiveness on the northern line. Arbitrator's awards were being ignored, letters addressed to the North British were being opened, waybills altered, trains delayed on the pretext of checking wheels. The CR was refusing to put foot-warmers into NBR carriages on cold days[24], and so on.

An independent Bill for a Glasgow & Bothwell Railway was before Parliament. Giving evidence in support, Sir James Baird said it was being promoted because of a Caledonian-North British pact not to build any new lines in the district. In passing he mentioned that he had been instrumental in relieving the NBR of its difficulties (as well as doing much for the Caledonian). The proposed line was to be worked independently, but it would feed traffic into College Goods Station in Glasgow. In June 1867 the NBR had declined to build a mineral line through New Monkland parish[25] and now first opposed an independent Bill for the North Monkland Railway, swinging eastwards from a junction at Kipps to another a mile west of Slamannan, then made an agreement to work it, for 50% of the gross revenue (if less than £20 per mile per week) or 42.5% if the gross revenue should exceed this figure. Its act, of 18 July, included an option for the NBR to take over the new company within three years at cost plus 10%[26]. The North British was also extending its own system in the Stirlingshire coalfield, combating a demand from local proprietors for a regular wayleave payment, as "custom of the district", for an extension of the former E&G Maddiston Craigend Colliery and Blackbraes Branch, to a colliery at Shieldhill. It had already opened a line to the nearby Roughrigg Colliery in 1868 from Bowhouse. Extension to Glencorse of the unfinished Roslin line was approved on 5 August. Its main investor and user was the Shotts Iron Company (John Walker was a director), which put in £10,000, though the North British contributed £6,000. The NBR's acquisitions of the Northumberland Central and Leslie Railways were also authorised, on 18 July. The terms reflected the relative prosperity of these concerns. The Northumberland company was insolvent. Its preference shares, only £1,625, were to receive annual dividends of 3% for five years, then a perpetual 4%, while ordinary stock, £71,985, would receive a preference dividend of 1% only from 1 February 1877, while the NBR paid £9,600 to clear the NCR debts, and (in 1877) converted its mortgage debt of £21,706 into North British 4% debentures. Effectively the North British got the Northumberland Central (not that it wanted it very much) for a tenth of the original cost of the line[27]. The Leslie Railway was to get a preferential dividend of 3% on its £35,000 capital in 1873, half a percent more in 1874, and 4.5% in perpetuity after that[28].

In August 1872 a new postal contract worth £12,000 a year was agreed. The Post Office was experiencing problems at Berwick. A Post Office official telegraphed his chief, Mr. Benthall, "Great difficulties with Fifeshire sorting this morning. Smellie attended train at Berwick and when applying to Guard for compartment he refused, stating he had no instructions. After much arguing he arranged to give a compartment. The boxes could

Rothbury station, Northumberland. (*John Alsop*)

Wheatley's 0-6-0 type: No. 1 of the 251-class, built at Cowlairs in 1870.
Cannibalised parts from withdrawn engines were used in building the first eighteen. (*John Alsop*)

not be set in the manner intended but the porters contrived in a way to put them up and did a great portion of the work. The train was forty minutes late, when it reached Edinburgh Fifeshire train was gone." The difficulty appears to have been that the GNR and NER refused to keep a compartment empty all the way from London to Berwick. The guard would have been a NER man. North British officials at Berwick had to find accommodation for the sorting clerk. Evidently a special Post Office vehicle was needed[29].

Consolidation of stocks continued, with a special meeting on 23 August approving the conversion of a raft of Guaranteed and preference stocks into North British consolidated preference stocks. Into North British consolidated preference stock No. 1 went Granton preference at par, Monkland 6% guaranteed at £150 of the new stock for every £100, Monkland 5% and 4.5% Guaranteed at £125 and £112 respectively, North British Nos. 1 and 2 guaranteed at £125, E&G No. 1 preference at £125, and Edinburgh Perth & Dundee second preference at £100. Taken into North British consolidated preference stock No. 2 were Border Union Guaranteed at £137 10s for every £100, North British guaranteed (1861) at £125, Fife & Kinross at £112 10s, E&G Nos. 2 and 3 preference at £125, and North British preference (1862 and 1863), also at £125. In total North British consolidated preference No. 1 stock amounted to £2,444,128 15s 0d, with a preferential dividend of 4% per annum, payable half-yearly. The consolidated preference No. 2, amounting to £3,856,197 10s 0d, had the same terms. Coatbridge lien stock of £300,000, with a preferential dividend of 5% per annum, was also to be bought up[30]. The exercise was successful and the half-yearly shareholders' meeting in September was told that the market value of the consolidated stocks was higher than the best of the old stocks. At this time, NBR ordinary £100 shares were standing at £80 10s, compared with £113 for the Caledonian and £129 for the G&SWR equivalents. North British consolidated preference No. 1 were trading at £89 and No. 2 at £83 15s. Some of the old stocks remained separate, including Monkland preferred ordinary, trading at £123. Increased carriage rates for goods and mineral traffic, as with other railway companies, had helped the company to a record jump in gross revenue, £90,000, between February and July 1872; NBR ordinary paid £1 10s. Even Edinburgh & Glasgow ordinary enjoyed a dividend of £1 7s 6d[31].

New services, new lines and new plans were in the news that autumn. From 1 September, in conjunction with the Glasgow & South Western Railway, through trains to Edinburgh from Greenock and Ayr could travel across Glasgow and on to Edinburgh via the City of Glasgow Union Railway, Coatbridge and Bathgate. The Penicuik Railway had run goods trains since 9 May, and opened for passengers on 2 September, but the Board of Trade was demanding a covering over the line where it passed the Roslin gunpowder works, to guard against sparks[32]. Some 21 new lines, plus the pier at Craigendoran, were listed in the NBR's 'Additional Works & Powers' Bill[33], also absorption of the Glasgow & Milngavie and Broxburn railways. Major works were proposed, for an extension from the Stobcross Branch across west central Glasgow to a new terminus for Dumbarton and Helensburgh trains at Bothwell Street, thus reducing pressure on Queen Street. This was a truncated and adapted version of the scheme proposed and withdrawn under Hodgson in 1865. A new railway from Shettleston to Bothwell and Hamilton was included: a bold incursion into Caledonian territory. An agreement to proceed was made with the promoters of the Dunfermline-Queensferry Railway; and a new Forth Bridge Railway Bill (nominally an independent project, but mentioning only the NBR as a potential associate) was published[34]. Agreements were also made with the newly-incorporated (1 July 1873) Whiteinch Railway & Tramway Company for it to make a branch from the Stobcross line to the shipyards and factories at Whiteinch. The NBR would work the line with an option to purchase it for £28,400 within four years of completion[35].

Winter was always the main season of complaints. Letter writers who moaned about the Helensburgh service were told by others they should try the Balloch line if they wanted to know what a bad service was like, and others again said the Milngavie line took the prize[36]. But the North British was making some efforts to improve its dismal reputation for passenger comfort and convenience. In February 1873 it tested Britain's first sleeping car, built for it by the Ashbury Railway Carriage and Iron Co., a six-wheeled vehicle 30 feet long, with first and second class compartments separated by a central lavatory. The seats converted to beds. From 2 April it ran each way from Glasgow via Edinburgh to London on alternate nights, for a supplement of 10s. Its usage, closely monitored, was very low, only fourteen passengers in the three weeks up to 15 November. In January 1874 the manager was told to have it made part of the East Coast Joint Stock[37]. Most stations still had very low platforms, making it difficult to get on and off trains, but this was gradually being remedied. A works committee order went out that all new station works must be made to suit 'high' platforms. At this time the company had 81 horseboxes, evidently insufficient for demand, as a further 69, at £213 apiece, were ordered from Ashburys, as well as 26 goods brakes at £245[38].

Buoyancy in the boardrooms and new plans meant renewed anxiety among shareholders. On 5 March 1873 shareholders of the North British, Caledonian and Glasgow & South Western companies met once again to consider the currently proposed schemes, whose aggregate cost was reckoned at £8,000,000. A leading spokesman, John McGavin, familiar at both NBR and CR meetings, criticised managements for too many extensions and a shortage of wagons. A new committee was formed, to put pressure on the directors, and a Scottish Railway Shareholders' Association was set up, with committees in Glasgow and Edinburgh[39]. North British half-yearly revenue was nearing the million-pound mark, £928,229 11s 3d for August 1872-January 1873, but – a warning sign – working expenses were rising faster: an increase of £85,900, ascribed to a surge in coal

Milngavie Station in 1912. (*John Alsop*)

costs of £35,395 and to wage increases (though most pay rises in 1873 were to salaried staff). On 14 March John Walker announced his retirement as secretary and was encouraged by Kippendavie to offer his services as a director[40]. He was duly elected and James Fergusson was made interim secretary. James McLaren, as Superintendent –" raucous in voice and trenchant in expression"[41] – was put in charge of all operating matters and staff, except the locomotive department, at a salary of £800, rising to £1,000 over three years. Kippendavie agreed to the formation of a shareholders' committee (J.M. Douglas was a member) to help the board in reducing expenditure and in negotiations with the Caledonian and Glasgow and South Western on competitive routes and schemes[42].

Shareholder pressure helped produce a ten year agreement between the NBR and Caledonian on Edinburgh-Glasgow traffic, at 80% to the North British and 20% to the CR, with interchangeable tickets. The North British would not exercise its running rights on CR lines north of Greenhill (until the opening of the Tay Bridge in the case of the Dundee-Aberdeen line), and the Caledonian would drop its Bill for a separate line between Larbert and Edinburgh. A junction at Wester Dalry, in Edinburgh, would be made to enable Caledonian trains to use the North British line from Larbert. A five-year moratorium was declared on new lines in each other's territory (excepting the NBR's Bothwell-Hamilton line, rejected by the House of Commons in April but not given up as a NBR proposal). The Bothwell Street Station was approved by Parliament, but J.M. Douglas was rallying opposition, insisting instead on the remodelling of Queen Street, with an underground link to be made "in good time" between Stobcross, Queen Street, and College[43]. Glasgow's new town clerk, J.D. Marwick, was pressing the North British about the state of Queen Street, which still had only two passenger platforms, and travellers were "jostled off the platforms … having to alight in the tunnel and make their way into the station along a narrow ledge". In 1863 1,575,000 people had used the station. In 1873 the number was 3,000,000. The NBR replied that accidents were caused by "want of reasonable care by passengers themselves". In December Captain Tyler inspected the station for the Board of Trade and urged the company to resite the goods station[44].

The locomotive committee was bothered about "bogie wagons". It wanted to get rid of them, but Baird's Gartsherrie company was running similar wagons on the line, "which cannot be dispensed with". There was an accident near the Calder Ironworks in May when a wheel broke on a Gartsherrie bogie wagon[45]. Movement towards "economical and harmonious working" went forward with a wider NBR-Caledonian agreement in June. Covering passenger traffic only, it allocated 57.5% to the CR and 42.5% to the NBR, of all coaching traffic revenue between Glasgow and places north of Lower Greenhill, including Perth, and places north of Forth and south of Tay on the Greenhill-Glasgow section. All trains would be worked by the Caledonian from Buchanan Street, with the CR to receive 15% working expenses before the revenue division. On traffic between Glasgow and Alloa (north and south) 65% of revenue would go to the Caley and 35% to the NBR. Glasgow-Grangemouth would be divided 50/50. Coaching traffic between Glasgow and North British stations east of Stirling, north of Forth, and west of Rumbling Bridge and Bogside would go via Larbert and Lenzie. The North British could exercise running powers between Stirling and Greenhill Upper, and pick up passengers at Stirling, Bannockburn and Larbert, while accepting restricted running powers on other CR lines; and the Caledonian would accept like restrictions on NBR lines, including Edinburgh-Larbert. Looking ahead, the agreement made provision for a division of passenger revenues over the Tay Bridge and Montrose-Arbroath line. There were very detailed provisions for the use of the Dalry Junction link in Edinburgh, for which the Caledonian would pay "a perpetual fixed minimum net sum" in respect of extended running powers and other privileges[46]. Competing proposals were to be withdrawn from current Bills, including a NBR proposal for a line near Larbert, between the former Scottish Midland Junction and Scottish Central lines. The agreement said nothing about the Caledonian-owned line between Montrose and Aberdeen, over which the North British certainly wanted to run trains, but it was a real attempt to resolve some of the problems between the companies[47]. Late in the year the NBR raised its parcel rates on non-competitive routes but referred other routes to the joint committee[48]. Though occasional muscle-flexing still happened, from now on co-operation and mutual consultation became the regular thing.

10. THE KIPPENDAVIE YEARS – 3, 1873-1877

Helensburgh, with a population in 1871 of 8,054, though many more in the summer months, had a mixed opinion of the North British Railway. A sedate residential town, it needed the railway for its role as a resort and Glasgow businessmen's dormitory. But the North British wanted to extend its line from the station to the pier, bisecting the town, in order to improve and increase its steamer services. This proposal was successfully resisted, leading to the Company's plan for a new railway pier at Craigendoran, just outside the town. In turn this was opposed by Helensburgh, which would lose its pier traffic. Controversy was hot in the early summer of 1873, with opinion in the town sharply divided. The Commons passed the North British Bill for a new pier, though it expressed a desire (not an order) that Helensburgh Pier should also remain in use, and have rails laid to it[1]. Further acts that

G.B. Wieland, chairman of the NBR from 1901 to 1905, the Fildes portrait. (Glasgow Museums)

summer authorised the incorporation of the Dunfermline & Queensferry Railway, and the Kelvin Valley Railway. Both would have a difficult relationship with the North British. The Dunfermline company's act provided for a joint committee with the NBR and it quickly became clear that the NBR expected this body, rather than the Dunfermline & Queensferry board, to make executive decisions[2]. Take-up of shares in the Dunfermline & Queensferry's authorised capital of £105,000 was slow, and though the NBR was permitted to subscribe "such sum as has been or may be agreed on", there was no agreement. At the time, the Forth Bridge Railway Bill was before Parliament, and became an Act on 5 August. This was to be an independent concern, with capital of £1,250,000 in £10 shares, and borrowings of £450,000, but with close ties to the North British and Midland (not the East Coast) companies. The North British was vastly more concerned with the bridge than with the Dunfermline & Queensferry line, whose ferry terminus at North Queensferry would lose its traffic when the bridge opened (the idea of train ferries had been dropped). To the Dunfermline & Queensferry Railway backers, the bridge was only a "great Perhaps" (though they protested about being left out of the Forth Bridge Railway Bill), but in a prolonged argument they cannily insisted on their line going through Inverkeithing, against the NBR's wishes[3]. The NBR directors on the Joint Committee were instructed by the North British board in September to "endeavour to delay" commencement of the Dunfermline & Queensferry construction works[4]. Progress on the Tay Bridge was marred by the bursting of one of the hollow piers, No. 54, on 26 August. Six men working inside were drowned[5].

Neither board nor shareholder committees, it seemed, could hold down the North British's working expenses. For February-July 1873 they reached £543,906 9s 9d, compared with £434,989 19s 5d for the comparable period in 1872. Again the rise was greater than the gross revenue increase, £949,691 11s 3d against £873,415 3s 9d. No dividend was available to the ordinary shareholders. Coal and iron prices were blamed, along with wage rises[6]. Though the Bothwell-Hamilton Bill had been thrown out, the NBR General Purposes Bill, which included Bathgate area lines and the absorption of the Broxburn and Milngavie Railways, was passed. J.M. Douglas achieved another victory when a Wharncliffe meeting failed to give a sufficient majority to the proposed Bothwell Street terminus, and the board gave up the plan[7], but his attempt to have all new works halted until the ordinary dividend should reach 5% was voted down at the half-yearly meeting on 31 September. Nevertheless, new construction in 1873-74 was mostly based on traffic requirements rather than modernisation of existing facilities. Thus the old Monklands line between Airdrie and Bathgate was being doubled, new engine sheds at Parkhead and Manuel were approved, as were new stables at Alloa and Haddington, an additional loop on the Benhar line (an extensive system of colliery lines between the former Wilsontown, Morningside & Coltness and Monkland lines, west of Bathgate), a "small engine" for the Broxburn branch, and expansion of Dundee East Goods Station. But signals for the Jedburgh Branch, at £322, were delayed, as was installation of a block system on the Devon Valley line. Pay rises were being made, on a selective basis. When porters and marshalmen in Fife asked for 4s a week more, the superintendent was told to give rises to the best men and discharge the inefficient. Some large sums were spent: 5,000 tons of cast-iron rail chairs were ordered from the Anderston Foundry, at £6 12s 6d a ton, for delivery in 1874 and £25,000 was paid for additional ground at College Station[8]. In September a new name joined the senior management, George Bradley Wieland, an Englishman, came from the London & North Western at Euston to become secretary, at £800 rising to £1,000 over three years[9]. He was a short, dapper figure, bringing with him all of the 'premier line's' grand manner and arrogant style towards lesser companies. He also became secretary of the Forth Bridge Railway, which held its first quorate board meeting on 12 November, with John Stirling elected as chairman.

The much-adapted and altered station buildings at Loanhead, with coal trucks in the foreground, including traders' wagons of the Shotts Coal Co. The adjacent school was built in 1915. (*Stenlake Collection*)

Another delayed project, the Edinburgh, Loanhead & Roslin Railway, opened between Millerhill and Loanhead for mineral traffic on 6 November. Its act had been authorised on 26 June 1870 against hot opposition from the Penicuik Railway. As with the Penicuik line, the North British was to work it, for 30 years for 45% of gross revenue, with powers to acquire it within five years, Bouch was the engineer, and John Waddell of Bathgate was appointed contractor. The two lines were less than a mile apart, on opposite sides of the Esk Valley, at different levels, and tapping different industries. The Penicuik Railway served papermills primarily, while the Loanhead was a mineral line. It would open through to Roslin for all traffic on 23 July 1874, by which time it had also got authorisation for the extension to Glencorse, on the outskirts of Penicuik. The Penicuik Railway renamed its Rosslyn Station as Rosslyn Castle in 1874.

Railway safety continued to be an issue, and Kippendavie gave an update on the North British position in a reply to a circular from Chichester Fortescue M.P. The NBR had "largely adopted the block system and interlocking" of points and signals and was experimenting with continuous brakes, although "on fast trains they lead to rapid deterioration of the rolling stock." Though he did not mention it, the board had ordered a tourniquet to be supplied to every station, and instructions had been given in April 1873 that brake vans must always be the last vehicle in fast trains and have not more than two vehicles behind them in local trains[10]. Accidents were still occurring where the block system was inoperative or not yet installed. On 8 January 1874 a passenger train ran into a goods at Bonnybridge. Busy as it was, on the Edinburgh-Glasgow line the block system was only operative between Queen Street and Bishopbriggs and between Falkirk and Polmont[11]. Seventeen people were killed at Manuel Junction on 28 January in a collision between a passenger train, its engine running tender-first, and a mineral train. Block instruments were in process of being installed. The driver of the passenger train, the signalman, and the guard of the mineral train were all arrested[12]. At the ensuing Board of Trade inquiry at Linlithgow, Col. Yolland of the railway inspectorate was startled to learn that not only was William Cumming, area traffic inspector, in the Manuel signal box at the time, but was assisting signalman Gordon to perform "an operation expressly forbidden by the company's rules and regulations" (shunting across a main line inside the minimum time allowance for the passage of main line trains). Cumming stated that, "It was simply to help him, and facilitate in clearing the line"[13]. Yolland's critical report noted that the passenger locomotive was running tender-first because it was too long for the Larbert turntable (Wheatley said a new one had been ordered in November 1873), and it could take up to two hours to get a path to Greenhill in order to turn on the CR turntable there; also sometimes the Caledonian denied access. Yolland recorded that in 1867 the NBR had 25 miles eleven chains worked by absolute block. In 1874 this had risen to 193 miles 56 chains out of 758 miles of road, and he regretted the company's slowness in the matter[14].

Maurice Mocatta, a Liverpool stockbroker, representing many English shareholders, met NBR directors and John Walker in January 1874 to discuss further share consolidation, now moving on to ordinary shares. It was agreed that Border Union and Edinburgh & Glasgow ordinary stocks should be consolidated with NBR ordinary from 1 February 1875; also that £421,000 of new 5% £100 preference stock be issued at £90% with an option for holders to exchange it for NBR ordinary stock on and after 1 February 1875. This stock would be offered to holders of the three ordinary stocks in the first instance, with any left over to be disposed of as the directors thought fit[15]. Gross receipts were up for the August 1873-January 1874 half year, by £86,301 11s 8d, making it the first time the company recorded receipts of over a million pounds in six months (£1,014,531 4s 11d), but working expenses had risen by £117,813 15s 4d, to £628,728 5s 2d. They included Parliamentary expenses of £23,409 and compensation payments of £16,516 19s 7d following the Manuel disaster. Accepting that these were disappointing figures, the board pleaded "special circumstances". No ordinary dividend was paid – the NBR was the only Scottish railway not paying a dividend on its ordinary shares at this time. "Everything costs more," protested John Stirling: the wage bill was up by £53,000 compared with the same half-year in 1871-72, and the coal bill was up by £48,000. The NBR was using 240,000 tons of coal a year. John Monteath Douglas raised an old claim, that the vocal cohort of Glasgow-based shareholders were more friendly towards the Caledonian than to the NBR (hence their opposition to the Forth Bridge, he implied), and in a contest for a vacant board seat he defeated the Glaswegians' man, Henry Grierson. Douglas admitted that he practised as a share-broker but promised that as a director he would not deal in North British shares. Aware that Douglas had wide support among the shareholders, the board backed his candidacy[16].

Mocatta remained a critic of NBR policy. The shareholders were not rallying behind the Forth Bridge project, which was described as "madness" at a special meeting on 5 March to review current Bills, and the board had to withdraw a Bill to enable the NER and GNR to invest in the Bridge company. Defiantly, Kippendavie informed the meeting he had £1,746,000 of proxy votes in support, but Mocatta asked if £1,100,000 of that was not from the Baird family interests (Scotland's largest ironfounders)? The chairman admitted that "Certainly there was a large number from them". Mocatta described the bridge scheme as got up by engineers and lawyers for their own benefit. The meeting ended abruptly when Kippendavie put on his hat and walked out, with the directors[17]. Now the Dunfermline & Queensferry Railway, stalled by its inability to raise capital, and North British delaying tactics, saw an opportunity and reissued a prospectus. Though Wieland told the Dunfermline & Queensferry board in June 1874 that the NBR was unwilling to see a start made on their line "until it is seen what is to be done as to the Forth Bridge"[18], the Dunfermline & Queensferry Railway went ahead, claiming that the NBR had "intimated their readiness to carry out their part of the agreement"[19]. By September the Dunfermline company had amassed only £58,270 of capital, but now took the view that it only needed £78,7560 plus borrowing powers to reach £105,000. Kippendavie refused any North British contribution[20].

By May 1874 the City of Glasgow Union Railway line between Bellgrove and Sighthill was complete, as a single-track, and the Board of Trade allowed goods and mineral trains to use it. For three years, a powerful group of coalmasters and ironmasters had been pressing for a new railway to run from Shettleston, on the NBR's Coatbridge-Glasgow line, down to Bothwell and Hamilton, to give access to coal reserves in the Uddingston-Bothwell area, but North British Bills had failed in 1872 and 1873. In 1874 the industrialists successfully promoted their own Bill for a Glasgow, Bothwell, Hamilton & Coatbridge Railway, from Shettleston to Hamilton, with a connection from Bothwell to Whifflet, where it would meet the former Monkland & Kirkintiloch Railway line. Coal could thus be shipped to Glasgow or to Coatbridge's ironworks. Running powers over the NBR to Sighthill and Whifflet-Coatbridge-Shettleston were incorporated. When the company's Act was passed on 16 July, the North British was already negotiating a working agreement, speedily transformed into an intention to purchase. This line placed a great fork right across Caledonian territory. It is not unlikely that the project was a conspiracy to achieve a NBR line without the NBR having to confront Caledonian opposition. The Baird family company, prime movers in the affair, preferred the NBR to the CR, because they had more pull on its board. In any case it was a definite *coup* for the North British. A form of compromise with the Caledonian was reached when the NBR dropped a possible extension to Blackwood while the CR abandoned its project for a line into Fife from Alloa. But most of the news in the summer of 1874 was unwelcome to the board. The Stobcross line was not yet ready. De Bergue, contractor for the Tay Bridge, died, and the contract was transferred on 26 June to Hopson, Gilkes & Co., of Middlesborough, who had put in the second-lowest tender. Samuel Mason perhaps did not get on too well with Kippendavie (he would have been handsomely paid off if the Caledonian merger had gone through) and resigned in August, to become a ship-broker in Leith and London. John Walker left the board in September to take up the role of general manager, at £1,750 a year[21]. Mason's prompt departure was at his own request. The

Engine 502, an 0-6-0T built by Dübs & Co. for the Glasgow, Bothwell, Hamilton and Coatbridge Railway as their No. 4. (*John Alsop*)

board gave him £1,000[22], and he appears to have kept up a business relationship with the NBR. Henry Grierson was elected in Walker's place, to the annoyance of Walter Wilson of Hawick, who felt that the "western district" had too much influence (there was no director from his Borders area). Wilson also wanted the wage bill reduced and claimed that it was high time that the management of Cowlairs Works was investigated[23]. At the half-yearly meeting on 30 September, Kippendavie noted that under the Education Act of 1873, the company would face a rise of some £8,000 in its rates Bill to pay for parish schools. Pressed by the shareholders, in November the board raised fares and cancelled the availability of Parliamentary tickets on express trains. In Fife, the collieries' "golden period" was ending, with falling prices and a 20% wage cut followed by a further 15%[24].

By the end of 1874, the rebuilding of Waverley Station was complete. A broad central island platform had terminal bays at each end and a new transverse-ridged roof covering most of the platform area between the two bridges. Waverley Bridge had been completely rebuilt as an iron lattice girder structure, with an access road down into the station from its centre. An ornamental arch on Princes Street next to Waverley Market topped the windy "Waverley Steps" which led down to a footbridge and the station offices. The old buildings on the corner of Princes Street and North Bridge remained intact. Platforms extended eastwards over the old Trinity College Church site, and goods facilities had been rearranged, with one shed tucked below the new post office (1866), and a range of others on the old vegetable market site, leading into the original Edinburgh & Glasgow depot. Canal Street was now a dead end leading to the North British offices.

Among the departments based there was the company's police staff, always busy, their functions being constables, detectives, and watchmen (the last at goods depots), under a superintendent and a varying number of Inspectors. Much of the thieving on goods trains and in depots was done by employees, or by employees in collusion with others. Dramatic actions sometimes happened. One night, two detectives concealed themselves under a tarpaulin in a goods wagon. While the train was on the move, two guards clambered along and opened up the tarpaulin. The policemen chased them back along the moving train to the brake van, and arrested them (they got 60 days in jail[25]). Evidently the detectives were expecting them, which suggests they were acting on a tip-off. Tampering with goods was endemic, but a different sort of handling prompted a complaint about the reckless loading of gunpowder from boats on to NBR vans at the unfortunately-named Frisky Wharf at Bowling[26]. Dubious practices at a higher level were being probed by J.M. Douglas, whose election to the board did not tame his zeal to probe all aspects of management. Though he was not on the locomotive & stores committee, his investigations of doings at Cowlairs Works, aided by an anonymous whistle-blowing letter and backed by the new secretary, led to the resignations in October of Thomas Wheatley, the locomotive superintendent, his brother William, who ran the carriage and wagon side, and Mr. Dunderdale, the stores superintendent[27]. Wheatley stayed in office to the end of the year, then he established himelf as manager of the new Wigtownshire Railway; his relations with the NBR remained good enough for him to be given a free pass for 1875 and to buy engines Nos. 32 and 146, ex-Edinburgh, Perth & Dundee, rebuilt as 0-4-2ST in 1875 for £175 and £300 respectively and the 2-2-2WT No. 31 in 1877, for his rural line.

John Walker, NBR directors, and Forman and McCall joined directors of the Whiteinch Railway Co. in an inspection trip of their newly-finished line on 2 October (it opened on the 8th). From a trailing junction with the Stobcross Branch, it ran to Dumbarton Road, where it converted to a horse-tramway. The NBR, which had sold the rails and chairs to the Whiteinch company, was to work the railway "as part of their own line" as far as the tramway section, on which only animal power was permitted, though it seems that this stipulation was soon ignored[28]. It was goods only, the shareholders in its £18,000 capital all local companies, apart from Hugh Kennedy, the contractor. Total cost was £19,663 18s. A coal depot was also established with materials supplied by the North British[29]. The NBR was very much the dominant railway on the increasingly-industrialised north bank, and extensions were also made on the Balloch line, with a spur to the Dillichip Dyeworks at Renton agreed on 26 November. Its Stobcross Branch and goods depot finally opened on 20 October, though it would not become fully effective until completion of the Queen's Dock in 1877. Caledonian pressure had given it running powers over the line and joint ownership of the goods station at Stobcross[30], the NBR was just as obstructive as the Caley was to it in other places. Eventually the line would become a vital link in the company's Glasgow network. In 1875 an extension was laid to pits at Knightswood, with a spur north to brickworks at Cowdenhill.

From 1 January 1875 the Devon Valley Railway became vested in the North British, with each £100 of its stock exchanged for £62 10s worth of NBR ordinary stock. In February a group of Lanarkshire coalowners brought a case against the NBR, claiming its coal rates unduly favoured Bairds. The argument centred on the Limerigg area, where the NBR picked up wagons from collieries and took them down the old Ballochney Railway incline to Rawyards. In evidence, Walker admitted that Bairds, the NBR's largest shareholders, were charged a lower rate, but claimed that was because they were cheaper to serve. Also the Bairds provided two-way traffic: coal into the

The running shed at Cowlairs, *circa* **1910. (***John Alsop***)**

ironworks and iron out, whereas the colliery owners' wagons were taken back empty. It was also alleged that when wagons were in short supply, Bairds got preference. In March, Bairds agreed to pay the same coal rates as other coalowners[31]. Coincidentally or otherwise, Sir James Baird resigned that month as a member of the NBR audit committee. A board vacancy was filled by the election of Lord Provost James Falshaw, of Edinburgh, a useful ally to Kippendavie not only because of his civic eminence but because of his background as an engineer – the chairman had by no means given up on the Forth Bridge, though progress on share sales and land purchase was very slow. Falshaw was also a director of the Highland Railway, and still chairman of the Scottish Waggon Co., holding the post until at least 1883. Another new arrival was Dugald Drummond, appointed locomotive superintendent from February, at £700 a year. A forthright Scot, he came from the London Brighton & South Coast Railway, but had worked at Cowlairs under William Stroudley in E&G days. This was his first post as supremo, and he set up a census of rolling stock, and identified decrepit engines for sale or scrap[32].

Noting that the NBR had been "miserably paid" by the Post Office under previous mail contracts, Kippendavie welcomed a new two-year agreement worth £16,000 a year, up by £4,000. The August 1875 contract provided for both day and night sorting trains; the previous one made in March 1873 showed a day service only[33]. A short north to east link was built from the City of Glasgow Union Railway line to the NBR Coatbridge line, just east of Parkhead Station, enabling trains to run from Sighthill. Work was also in progress on the line from Shettleston to Hamilton[34]. Walker's management had achieved a reduction in working expenses, down to £573,863 4s 8d, and a dividend of 1.25% was paid to ordinary shareholders in March 1875. The first sod of the Dunfermline & Queensferry Railway was cut by Lady Louisa Bruce on 3 April, in front of 10,000 people. Invited guests sat down to brown soup, turkey, chicken, ham, tongue, rounds of beef, quarters of lamb, beefsteak pies, jellies and cream, fruit and jam tarts, provided at 5s a head by Williamson & Son of Edinburgh. An attempt to cut the soup and get a lower price had failed[35]. Establishment of a horse-tramway to Portobello prompted a cut in fares between there and Waverley, to 4d (First) 3d (Second) and 2d (Third), with a recommendation to increase the number of trains "where it can be done conveniently"[36].

Four people died in an accident on the Northumberland Central line on 4 July, when the drop-bar of a wagon broke on a high embankment between Rothley and Scots Gap, and five carriages and the guard's van of the mixed train went over[37]. However, the fortunes of the North British were looking better again with revenue rising and costs falling (down now to 50.66% of receipts). 4% was paid on the ordinary shares in September. All the ordinary stocks of the absorbed companies were now consolidated into North British shares[38]. NBR share prices rose to £89 5s on £100 ordinary. Caledonian were £101 7s 6d and G&SWR £108 10s[39]. The chairman was able to cite various satisfactory statistics. Receipts per mile of line were up from £48 to £52 a week and per train-mile up from 55.5 pence to 59.95 pence. It was an opportune moment to announce the issue of £3,000,000 worth of 4.5% irredeemable preference stock (£1,600,000 in the first instance) against the redemption of A and B debentures about to become due. At last (on 1 August), the Midland Railway had completed the line between Leeds and Carlisle, and goods services began on the following day. Passenger services had to wait another year, but a taste of things to come was given by the trial run of a Pullman car over the Waverley Route and on to Glasgow. Its return from Cowlairs to Edinburgh was made in 45 minutes, with an average of 65.45 mph for much of the journey. Perhaps in anticipation, the NBR proposed to entirely cover over Waverley Station between its two bridges, hitherto only partially roofed[40].

Springburn was becoming a densely-populated community, with more four-storey tenement blocks being put up by the NBR to house its growing work force. "The blocks" made it the area's biggest landlord. The need for increased motive power and workshop capacity was tackled in 1875. In August an officers' meeting recommended 20 new goods and six express engines, and the board approved the building of a new erecting shop, with six hydraulic traversing cranes; and the building of twelve new goods engines in addition to ten already in hand. A new carriage and wagon shop at Cowlairs was also confirmed, at a cost of £14,000. The colour of NBR carriages was to be teak, or painted imitation teak[41]. In this expansive climate, the directors agreed to set up a superannuation fund for "officers and servants", applicable only to salaried staff, who would pay a small contribution towards it. A scheme for all staff had been urged by J.M. Douglas, but was ignored. There was no trouble in getting shareholder meetings to agree to invest £6,000 in the Edinburgh, Loanhead & Roslin Railway (total capital £36,000) and to make a new 50-year agreement with the Forth & Clyde Junction company to work its line, paying a dividend on its capital of £106,000 at 6% for the year ending on 31 July 1876, then 6.5%, then 7%; thereafter rising *pari passu* with NBR ordinary when the latter should attain a 7% dividend. It was also agreed to pursue amalgamation with the Berwickshire, Peebles and Penicuik Railway companies. One relatively neglected area was Fife, but the NBR was spurred into action when a consortium of local coalowners put up a scheme for a railway from the Cowdenbeath area to Burntisland, and to build a new dock there[42]. Around Cowdenbeath and Lochgelly, new pits were being sunk into substantial coal reserves. Kippendavie considered their action "quite uncalled for" as the NBR had entered a Bill for a railway to run from the not-yet laid Dunfermline & Queensferry line to its terminus at Burntisland[43]. Between August 1874 and January 1875, the company's working expenses slipped just below 50% of receipts, at 49.87%, and a 4.25% dividend was declared on the ordinary shares, whose price for the first time for many years fetched a small premium, £101 5s[44]. With the Fife coal industry expanding, the North British set out to maintain its hold by proposing amalgamation with the Leven and East of Fife Railway, assuring its control of Leven Harbour as a coal exporting port, and prompting its interest in Methil.

Cardenden Station was opened by the Edinburgh & Northern in 1851. The architectural style is unusual. Note also the cast iron urinal. (*North British Railway Study Group*)

Bills entered for the 1876 Parliamentary session show the NBR selling the gas works at Burntisland to the town council[45], and buying the gas works at Silloth; but it owned more property at Silloth than at the Fife port. Other Bills covered the NBR's acquisition of Burntisland Docks, new mineral lines to collieries in Fife, and a time extension (to be much repeated) for the Forth Bridge. The twelve mile Kelvin Valley Railway had obtained an Act in 1873 for a line between Maryhill and Kilsyth, crossing over the NBR's Campsie Branch north of Kirkintilloch, and giving acess to coal mines owned by George Baird of the powerful Gartsherrie-based family. Only two thirds of its £90,000 capital had been raised and a distinct lack of enthusiasm from the NBR had helped to stall it. As far as the North British was concerned, Kilsyth certainly needed a railway, but a cheaper connection from the Campsie Branch would have served. Baird threatened to promote a line to join Kilsyth to the Caledonian at Denny and the NBR then backed an 'independent' Bill for the Kilsyth Railway, diverging from the Kelvin Valley Railway's link to the Campsie Branch, with a separate station at Kilsyth, and meeting the NBR again at Falkirk, but also with a link to the Caledonian at Bonnybridge[46]. However, it did not want any other company to control the Kelvin Valley Railway, especially if the Falkirk line went ahead. It was agreed with Baird that the company would subscribe £30,000 to the Kelvin Valley Railway and work the line in perpetuity at 50% of gross revenue, with a minimum payback of 5.25% on the full capital[47]; and J.&W. Granger cut the first turf on 8 June. The Kilsyth Railway was also to be taken under the NBR wing, but only for a line between Kirkintilloch and Kilsyth. It was agreed that the Kilsyth Railway would be merged into the Kelvin Valley Railway, which would build and use the Kilsyth company's approved line into Kilsyth. Bairds usually got what they wanted. These arrangements were incorporated in a Bill for the 1877 Parliamentary session[48].

While the new workshops at Cowlairs were going up, orders for new engines and rolling stock had to be placed outside, and Neilsons got orders for six goods engines in November 1875, at £2,885 each, and a further 20 in February 1876 at £2,860, when 1,000 new wagons at £70 each were also ordered, from four suppliers. A programme of wagon replacement resulted in 277 old 4 or 6 ton wagons being scrapped and replaced by the same number of 8 ton wagons. Drummond was also authorised to buy a second hand dredger and two barges, for dredging at Dundee. Coalfield development in the Monklands required the doubling of track between Clarkston, Burnieside and Caldercruix, and extended mineral lines, with the Blairmuckhill Branch extended in the Benhar pits area to Dewshill Colliery. A siding to the recently-enlarged Alloa Dock was agreed, but difficulties over replacing the

Forth Ferry *William Muir* discharging passengers at Burntisland Docks, in the 1900s. (*John Alsop*)

Alloa Coal Co.'s high-level tramway would delay it for two years. Key staff got pay rises: Drummond to £850 then £1,000 over two years; Wieland to £1,200, but by mid-1876 the economic boom was slackening and the Plashetts Coal Co., never a good payer, was allowed a 50% reduction in the rental of its sidings.

For three years, large-scale reconstruction work had been going on in Carlisle, in anticipation of completion of the Midland's line from Leeds via Settle. The North British worked closely with the Midland and the Glasgow & South Western in planning their own facilities, hoping that at last a decent share of traffic would come its way. New north-south goods lines were being laid to the west of Citadel Station, passing east of Dentonholme, where the NBR had first acquired powers to build a goods depot in 1865. From late 1865, it had had an agreement with the Midland for "Cultivation and Development and free Interchange of Traffic" at Carlisle, and the South Western had been admitted as partners in the Dentonholme Depot in acts of 23 July 1866 and 13 July 1876. Despite the pioneering work of the North British, the G&SWR took over the Dentonholme Station, completing it in October 1883, while the NBR concentrated its goods working at Canal. The introduction on 1 May 1876 of passenger services over the third Anglo-Scottish route was made without ceremony, though the Midland Railway's new Pullman carriages were a public sensation. There were two daily expresses each way, with Edinburgh portions detached at Carlisle. In response, the East Coast announced a new speeding-up. The ten o'clock express would now run each way between London and Edinburgh in nine hours, at an average speed of 47.3 mph allowing for stops. The West Coast took ten hours and 25 minutes; the Midland ten hours 45 minutes. For a time, the 'Flying Scotsman' became the fastest train in the world. Since 18 June 1862 the 10 am trains between Edinburgh and London had been informally known as the 'Flying Scotchman' or 'Scotch Express', with 'Flying Scotsman' becoming usual from the late 1880s. To help run these trains two, then four, passenger engines at £3,045 each were substituted for goods engines already ordered from Neilsons[49]. At Cowlairs Works, new office buildings were approved, for £3,300 17s 3d. In Edinburgh, the old Edinburgh Leith & Granton works at Heriothill, long disused, were leased out.

On 1 August 1876 the independence of the Peebles Railway Company finally came to an end (Act passed 13 July) and its preference and ordinary shares became respectively 5% and 8% lien stock of the NBR. On the same day the NBR absorbed the Berwickshire and Penicuik companies. Berwickshire shares were exchanged for NB ordinary at £83 10s per £100; Penicuik were exchanged at par. The Forth Bridge project was still languishing – of its £1,250,000 share capital, £1,157,660 was unissued and its funds were only £16,768[50].

The general quality of service at this time is hard to be certain of. Complaints in the newspapers were regular. A Silloth correspondent wrote about North British mixed trains with dumb-buffered goods wagons coupled ahead of the passenger carriages. Another complained about no lighting in some Berwick-Edinburgh local trains and another bemoaned the lack of amenities at Ladybank Junction[51]. Accidents encouraged complaints. Fifteen people were injured on the South Leith Branch on 10 December 1876. Even amenities were criticised: the new underpass at Portobello was described as "a fearful subterranean passage" by a correspondent who wrote, "Sufferance is the badge of all the tribe who come under the tender mercies of the North British Railway"[52]. Then as now, a bad experience brought pen to paper. Nothing had been done to modernise the cramped and overcrowded Queen Street. Far away, general complaint came from Rothbury, which felt isolated at the end of its long branch. A disgruntled public meeting recorded that the mails still came by horse-gig; the connections at Morpeth were very bad because of unfriendly relations between the North Eastern and North British; the NBR carriages were a disgrace and Rothbury Station was in equally disgraceful condition[53]. Of more concern to the board was an evident slackening in the economy through 1876. Between February and August, passenger receipts were static while goods and minerals fell slightly. The ordinary dividend fell to 3.5%.

Financed by loans from the NBR, the new dock at Burntisland opened on 1 December 1876, inaugurated by the North British ferry vessel *Express*. It boasted two hydraulic coal hoists, but a demonstration for the guests failed when a truck was tipped the wrong way and shed its load on to the wharf[54]. Burntisland also had an import trade, of esparto grass, sleepers, pit props, linseed and straw. The Fife coalowners withdrew their Bill for a Cowdenbeath-Burntisland line, placated by the NBR (Fife Railways) Act of 1876, which included the link line between Lilliehill and Townhill Junctions, east of Dunfermline, and the chord between Thornton West and South Junctions, and also provided that if customers were dissatisfied with rail links to Burntisland or Methil, they could require the NBR to provide more direct access[55].

Dugald Drummond arranged for a trial of the Westinghouse and Smith automatic brake systems, on the Edinburgh-Glasgow main line on 12 December. Both inventors were present, with observers from the Midland, North Eastern, and Manchester Sheffield & Lincolnshire Railways. The trains were formed of eight carriages plus a brake van at each end, drawn by new Drummond 4-4-0 engines. One of the brake vans had a Westinghouse instrument to measure speed and braking distance, with an electric link to the driving cab. On greasy rails, tests were carried out at up to 60 mph. With brake applied in the rear van only, the train took 30 seconds to come to a stop from 30 mph. The continuous brake achieved a stop in 10.5 seconds, and in 17.75 seconds from 40 mph. The Smith brake pump failed. Honours, and orders, went to Westinghouse. By the end of 1877 Westinghouse-braked trains ran between Edinburgh and Glasgow, Edinburgh and Carlisle, and on the Glasgow-Helensburgh boat trains[56].

Heavy snow in late December disrupted the Peebles and Dolphinton lines, with their high moorland sections. The North British at this time had a single large snowplough, capable of clearing drifts up to five feet, and Mr. Sutter, assistant locomotive superintendent, travelled on the snowplough engine. However, up to fifteen feet of snow lay in the cuttings between Hawthornden and Eddleston, and eight goods strains were stranded on the Waverley line[57]. Winter slowed but did not stop work on the Tay Bridge, its narrow structure extending across the Firth, and Dundee Town Council and Harbour Trust opened discussions with the Caledonian and NBR on the question of a single new central station. Both companies expressed only lukewarm interest. The Caledonian was perhaps more concerned to minimise the North British impact on a city where it currently enjoyed a monopoly and the NBR wanted to make the most of its opportunities. Supporters of the proposal were themselves divided between a high-level station on arches or a low-level one reached by tunnels. Soon after came reports of a "frightful accident at the Tay Bridge", when two 250-ton girders and adjacent piers were blown down in a fierce gale on 2-3 February. This "may to some extent weaken the public faith in its secure stability"[58], though it was noted that the girders had not yet been fixed in place and had merely been resting on the piers. In May John Waddell got the contract for the NBR's Tay Bridge Station, at £15,750, with its ironwork to cost an additional £6,000[59]. In anticipation of the bridge's opening, the NBR also improved its goods handling facilities at Dundee East, with a hydraulic crane and "shifting table" and new goods shed to cost £13,965 5s 5d. From May, Drummond's new express locomotive class was introduced, for the Aberdeen and Waverley routes. The first four, built by Neilsons, were all delivered by July.

As the years had gone by, the cost of the Dunfermline & Queensferry Railway, originally estimated at £96,000, had reached £130,000. At a special meeting on 15 February its shareholders had to face the fact that they needed £30,000 more capital, which they could not raise themselves. It was explained that the NBR "will only consent to

Dundee (Tay Bridge) Station on 19 September 1912. (*John Alsop*)

find the money required on condition that an amalgamation is effected, on such terms as will diminish the burden to be cast on their company", and on that basis would accept the liabilities of the Dunfermline & Queensferry Railway up to £112,509, for which sum it would acquire the company and accept responsibility for completion. The Dunfermline & Queensferry capital, reduced to £75,000 by a NBR-promoted Act in 1876, would become NBR lien stock at 3% per annum. The North British had done nothing about providing passenger facilities at Port Edgar, on the other side of the Forth, which had had a goods only line since 5 December 1868[60], but now promised to do so and to open an Edinburgh-Dunfermline service without delay. Reluctantly, the Dunfermline & Queensferry shareholders voted for merger, by a majority of eleven[61]. The North British reverted to a 4% ordinary dividend in March. Passenger receipts had risen though goods revenue was still almost static.

At the half-yearly meeting, J.M. Douglas's re-election as a director was blocked on the grounds that he had been jobbing in North British shares. Though he later explained his dealings to the satisfaction of the board, it declined to re-accept him as he had not been re-elected at the shareholders' meeting, though they expressed "their high appreciation of Mr. Douglas's services"[62]. Douglas perhaps saw himself as a better man than Stirling for the top role; but his officious zeal had probably irritated the chairman. In 1878 he issued a pamphlet for shareholders which justified his actions and exposed some of the NBR's continuing shortcomings[63]. 'The North British Railway: Its Management, Maintenance, Accounts and Prospects' is an intriguing glimpse into the role of the railway director and gives his watchwords for success: Peace, Rest and Economy. In particular that "most pernicious thing – capital expenditure" must be cut down. In Douglas's view the railway was the shareholders' property, and their interests, in the form of dividend, should always come first. The shareholders gave approval to the company contributing up to £150,000 to the Arbroath & Montrose Railway, and to an issue of £1,400,000 of NBR preference stock (1875) to be applied partly in redemption of 'B' debentures and partly for the company's purposes, including the long-desired improvement of Queen Street Station. Bank rate at the time was 2% and money could be raised cheaply[64]. In Fife, work was in hand on two new short lines authorised in the Fifeshire Railways act of 1876. The Lilliehill-Townhill line had nine bridges in $1^3/_4$ miles and cost £13,981 18s. Its contractor, Thomas Chalmers of Dunfermline, was using a new Chaplain & Co. steam scoop that shifted 60 cubic yards an hour[65]. Other contractors, including Charles Brand on the Glasgow, Bothwell, Hamilton & Coatbridge line, also claimed to be the first to use steam shovels. The navvy with his shovel and barrow was becoming redundant.

Work also began on constructing a new dock at Leven in June. The North British, about to absorb the Leven & East of Fife company, invested £5,000 in the project. On 28 June the Edinburgh Loanhead & Roslin's extension to Glencorse was passed by the Board of Trade, and though it was primarily a mineral line, some passenger trains worked through to Glencorse from Waverley or Millerhill Junction, where Roslin and Polton trains were often combined or divided. The Edinburgh Loanhead & Roslin Railway was amalgamated with the North British from 31 July, with a preference dividend of 4.5% on its £84,000 paid-up capital in the first year, and 5% thereafter, a good bargain for the shareholders as the final Edinburgh Loanhead & Roslin dividend was only 2%[66]. A final goods extension to the outskirts of Penicuik was completed under NBR auspices on 30 June 1878. Talks were under way on the working agreement for the St. Andrews Railway, due for renewal on 31 July 1877. The St. Andrews company had declined terms of a new lease, and in October amalgamation was agreed on[67], with its share capital of £21,000 exchanged for North British 'St Andrews lien stock' earning a fixed preference dividend of 10.5% per annum. As well as the Roslin company, on 1 August the NBR acquired the Leven & East of Fife Railway and the almost completed Dunfermline & Queensferry Railway. On 23 August a five-year mail agreement was concluded with the Post Office, backdated to 2 August, at £18,500 a year for two years, rising to £19,000, £19,500 and £20,000 in subsequent years, with the company to supply any necessary carriages. Other business included resistance to a claim by the Leith Harbour Trustees for £4,146 11s claimed as tolls for the period October 1864-15 May 1877; a payment to the Earl of Elgin of £1,200 in commutation of an old toll on coal wagons crossing the line of the Elgin Railway; and direct working of the Silloth Dock lines, formerly done by a local contractor, from 1 September[68].

Thoughts of ordinary dividends at 7% or more were receding. The half-yearly report in August 1877 announced 2%. Working expenses had risen faster than receipts. Miners' lock-outs in Fife and Clackmannanshire were blamed. At the half-yearly meeting, Kippendavie said, rather ominously, that the shareholders "had had their cake". It was back to short commons. Labour disputes spread during the year across the basic and manufacturing industries. Despite the rise in the North British wage Bill, its employees still looked for more in terms of shorter hours and better pay. The only NBR workers to have an eight hour day were the Waverley Tunnel pointsmen, but a train passed through the tunnel every three minutes – around 500 a day. The Royal Commission on Railway Accidents had reported that year, finding railway workers more than 33% more likely than other industrial workmen to suffer injury. The Commission made recommendations, but a Scottish newspaper remarked that of 652 members of Parliament, 97 were railway directors and 22 of those were company chairmen[69]. The implication was that reform was not over-likely. The Tay Bridge was unfinished, though its first ever-train, carrying invited guests, was drawn across by the contractor's engine *Mongrel* on 22 September[70]. Money was still being spent on renewing wooden bridges with iron (but only £3,250 in the half-year). With reluctance the board agreed proposals for increased services by both the Midland and East Coast Routes, but refused to stuff the backs of third class seats, even on English expresses, despite requests by its Glasgow & South Western and Midland fellow-operators[71]. This issue would be batted between the board and its committees, none willing to sanction such a revolutionary step, for two years.

On 2 November, the Dunfermline & Queensferry Railway opened, without ceremony. Neither cheers nor bells sent the first train from Comely Park Station (Dunfermline Lower from 5 March 1890) on its way shortly after 7 am. The townsfolk of Dunfermline had waited too long, and it was no longer their railway, but an offshoot of the North British's Fife empire. A branch was built in 1877 to serve Inverkeithing Harbour, laid partly on the Halbeath Railway trackbed. Paid for by the town council, it was little used by the NBR. The derelict Halbeath lingered on. In 1882 43 tons of scrap from it were sold. In 1883 the NBR works committee was still trying, and failing, to sell the abandoned track. By July 1896 all rails had been lifted except 300 yards to Inverkeithing Brickworks, and 377 yards at the northern end[72]. On the south shore, the North British did not open the station at Port Edgar until 1 October 1878. A few miles along the Fife coast, the NBR had acquired the small harbour of Pettycur with the Edinburgh Perth & Dundee line. It had a short, steeply-graded rail spur to the pierhead but was prone to silting and in November the company applied for authority to close the port and take over the adjacent coke ovens and salt works[73].

After years of complaint from users and Glasgow Town Council, the modernisation of Queen Street Station was begun, with acceptance in November of James Young's tender for £34,414 5s 7d, excluding the ironwork, and less £3,500 for the materials in buildings to be demolished. A bonus of £500 would be paid if the work were completed by 30 September 1879. The contract for the arched, glazed roof went to P.&W. MacLellan in September for £17,500. Building costs were overshadowed by the price of land: property purchases for the enlarged Queen Street and for the College Station site were reported at £56,600 and £38,920 respectively, and more were to come. Property could also bring cash. The Royal Hotel, Glasgow, was leased to Wylie & Lochhead for £1,500 a year and Lees' Hotel in Lothian Road, Edinburgh, was leased for seven years on a rising scale from £250 to £325. Edinburgh Town Council had expressed interest in acquiring the semi-derelict Port Hopetoun, terminal of the Union Canal, on Lothian Road, and the secretary was instructed to ask for £45,000[74], which turned out to be more than the City would pay. Ground at Shot Factory Lane, Newcastle (on or by the proposed but unbuilt goods station site) was also to be sold[75].

Officials of the NBR in 1879: Key numbers are under each image. 1. James Walker, general manager (in centre); 2. G.B. Wieland, secretary; 3. Missing: probably James McLaren, superintendent; 4. James Bell, engineer-in-chief; 5. Thomas Bouch, consulting engineer; 6. James Carswell, district engineer; 7. Robert Bell, district engineer; 8. and 9. indecipherable district engineers; 10. Dugald Drummond, locomotive superintendent; 11. D. McDougall, general goods manager; 12. A. Rutherford, district goods manager; 13. David Deuchars, district goods manager; 14: indecipherable district superintendent; 15. George Simpson, general accountant; 16. J. Macdonald, cashier; 17. D. Anderson, audit accountant; 18. A. Bell Scott, registrar; 19. John Cathles, assistant to general manager; 20. John Fergusson, assistant to secretary; 21. David Hunter, assistant to superintendent; 20. John W. Philp, chief clerk to general goods manager; 23. J. McGregor, pay clerk; 24. Peter Wood, law agent; 25. John Hay, district superintendent; 26. James Symons(?), district superintendent; 27. R. Darling, steam packet secretary; 28. A.F. Clement, telegraph superintendent; 29. James Allan, police superintendent; 30. John Stewart, rolling stock superintendent; 31. John Lingard, horse superintendent; 32. A. MacDonald, sack superintendent; 33. Allan Robertson Jr, stores superintendent; 34. Matthew Holmes, assistant locomotive superintendent; 35. A.P. Clark, assistant to locomotive superintendent. (NRS. BR/NBR/4/309, reproduced with permission of BRB Residual)

PRINCIPAL OFFICERS OF THE NORTH BRITISH RAILWAY.

11. THE KIPPENDAVIE YEARS 4, 1877–1881

Following a recommendation from John Walker the board resolved to set up a savings bank for staff, from 1 February 1878, under its own manager[1]. But it was going to be a difficult year on all fronts. A wage squeeze was on. Rather than have the Cowlairs men's pay reduced, Drummond proposed to increase their weekly hours to 54. With a new trade recession – the coal and iron trades were reported as "almost at a standstill"[2] – pressure from Fife coalmasters led to a rebate of 6*d* per ton being granted on coal carried to Edinburgh stations and Portobello from 1 March. In March the Caledonian Railway notified the NBR of termination of the 1865 New Lines Agreement, and the board decided it was "inexpedient to continue the correspondence." Edinburgh Town Council took exception to what it called "the shed" over Waverley Station and demanded its removal[3].

Further stock consolidation into NBR 4% consolidated lien stock in February showed the relative value of NBR acquisitions: Peebles Railway stock was brought in (despite angry opposition) at the rate of £125 per £100 for Peebles No. 1, and £200 per £100 of Peebles No. 2. St. Andrews lien stock was consolidated at £265 for every £100. Fife Nos. 1, 2 and 3 were consolidated at £112 10*s*, £262 and £125 respectively, Loanhead at £125; but Dunfermline & Queensferry lien stock at only £75 per £100[4].

On 1 November 1877, the Glasgow, Bothwell, Hamilton & Coatbridge line opened for goods trains between Shettleston and Hamilton, worked by the North British. Beyond Bothwell it crossed the Clyde on a lattice girder viaduct 728 feet long and 112 feet high, on seven piers. Sir James Baird, its chief sponsor, died shortly before its opening. Passenger services, with carriages "after the model of those in use on the London underground railways" ran from 1 April 1878, to a one-platform terminus at Hamilton, with an overall roof, soon known as "the barn"[5]. Negotiations for its amalgamation with the NBR were concluded on 2 August. In the first week of February, the North Monkland Railway opened[6]. A joint committee with the NBR had watched over construction of its line, which had a junction with the former Monkland Dykehead-Langdales mineral branch at Greengairs.

By March, revenue had fallen by £28,541. The ordinary dividend was 2.5%. (The new City of Glasgow Union Railway, jointly owned with the G&SWR, with a large amount of NBR shareholders' capital invested in it, was paying 5%). Given the choice of a working week extended from 51 to 54 hours or an 8% drop in wages, the Cowlairs workmen went on strike on 29 April. Dugald Drummond informed a deputation that he would keep the gates open until 4 May, after when he "would take whatever steps he thought fit"[7]. Out of 1,700 workers, only 158 mechanics, 133 boys, and 300 labourers were still working on 24 May. Efforts by the company to recruit replacement staff in England failed when two contingents arrived, and were intercepted by strikers. Some were "persuaded" to go home, but scuffles were reported. Across the North British system, surfacemen's wages were reduced from 19*s* to 18*s* a week. Nevertheless, four new 4-4-0 express engines were ordered from Neilson, at £2,845 each[8].

Dundee East Station, terminus of the Dundee & Arbroath Joint Line, in the 1900s.
(*North British Railway Study Group*)

While Cowlairs Works remained largely strikebound, positive things were also happening. Having been certified as suitable for passenger use on 5 March, the Tay Bridge was formally opened on 31 May. Six hundred gentlemen were entertained to lunch in Dundee's Albert Institute. A surprising absentee was Thomas Bouch[9]. Nine years later, a newspaper article would recall that when the first train crossed the bridge, a workmen's platform carelessly left dangling from the transverse girders scraped along the roofs, knocking off the ventilators with such a crashing noise that some people thought the train was falling[10]. The southern access was from Leuchars, where the junction station was moved south to serve the Tayport line (now a branch) as well as the St. Andrews Railway. In June-July the NBR carried 71,930 passengers to Dundee Tay Bridge Station, compared with 28,230 to Dundee East via the ferry route in the same months of 1877. A ruling from the Railway & Canal Commissioners had to be got before the company could resume running powers between Greenhill and Stirling, for trains across Fife to the bridge[11]. Three days after the Tay Bridge, Kilsyth's railway link to the Campsie Branch opened, with a celebratory luncheon[12]. This year also saw a fillip for the Forth Bridge project, with a new Act on 17 June establishing the involvement of the NER and GNR companies with the NBR and Midland, and a lowering of the Forth Bridge Railway's guaranteed dividend to 6%. Money was paid to the owners of Inchgarvie to enable construction of Bouch's lofty central towers to begin, tenders for steelwork were invited and a foundation stone was laid on the island on 30 September[13]. At Alloa, a deal had been struck with the Alloa Coal Co., and the Dock branch opened, with a steam crane to load coal.

On 10 June the Caledonian workmen at St. Rollox, who had been on strike for similar reasons to the Cowlairs men, returned to work, but around 1,000 NBR employees stayed out. In the ninth week of the strike, they sent a memorial to the company offering to open negotiations[14], but the board did not respond. Enough men – "scum and sweep of the country" according to a speaker at the Glasgow United Trades Council – had been recruited to keep the works going. At St. Margaret's the men went on strike in protest at the imposition of a 54 hour week there. Sutter, the assistant locomotive superintendent, informed them that Cowlairs now had a full establishment of 1,750 men and that if they did not return, men would be sent from Glasgow. The Cowlairs workers had now been on strike for 17 weeks. They were getting strike pay of 8s to 10s a week, depending on whether they were single or married, financed by subscriptions from other city trades. Even in Dundee a relief committee was organised. But the company was far from yielding, while committing large sums of money in other ways. At the half-yearly meeting on 27 September, Kippendavie asserted that Cowlairs was fully functioning on a 54 hour week, which, he claimed, was standard in England, so why not in Scotland? But outside suppliers were also needed: 100 carriages were ordered from Ashbury in Manchester, in August, 50 first class, 30 composite, 20 third class, though 20 passenger brake vans were to be built at Cowlairs. £200 was also authorised for a 6-ton accident crane, from Armstrong Whitehead, of Warrington; and 20,000 tons of steel rails at £5 15s per ton were authorised for delivery in 1880-81[15]. Eight new engines, five goods, three passenger, were to be contracted for, and Drummond was instructed to push on for completion of engines now in hand, with all despatch. Motive power was needed by new lines, including that from Bothwell via Bellshill to meet the ex-Monkland & Kirkintilloch at Whifflet, opened for goods trains on 1 November, with branches to collieries at Rosehall. Passenger trains would operate on it from 1 May 1879. Pullman saloon cars appeared on the East Coast from 19 August: two, *India* and *Germania*, were incorporated in the East Coast Joint stock, running first to Edinburgh, then through to Glasgow[16]. A programme of installing station footbridges was also now in hand, with lots of six at a time being ordered from Oliver & Arrol at £190 each[17].

Ordinary dividend that autumn was 2.5%. A petition for NBR involvement with the proposed Anstruther & St. Andrews Railway was declined for the present, but the board approved purchase of the Whiteinch Railway in Glasgow for £19,100 plus £2,500. The North British was to obtain Parliamentary sanction[18]. Then on 2 October the City of Glasgow Bank failed. With the dividend payments due to be made on the 10th, the directors held emergency meetings, and agreed if necessary to advance £59,000 to the company, in exchange for ordinary stock at a 100% premium; also to switch the NBR's funds from the Royal Bank of Scotland to the British Linen Bank. Of £456,750 of consolidated lien stock offered to ordinary shareholders, £208,855-worth had not been taken up, and was now offered to the preference shareholders at 4% discount, with interest backdated to 1 August 1878. A group of brokers including Messrs. Renton of London took up the stock at 93%, with 0.5% commission to Rentons[19]. J.H. Renton, born in Edinburgh in 1821 and also a director of the Forth Bridge company, would continue to play an important part in the NBR's financial affairs. The bank crash exposed a major NBR customer and debtor, the Benhar Colliery Co., and John Walker chaired a committee of investigation into its affairs and played a significant part in its re-constituting. Almost all share prices were falling, and all industries were shedding staff and reducing pay. The North British went on imposing cuts through the rest of the year. In November all outdoor servants earning over 19s a week had their pay cut by a shilling (stationmasters and guards excepted), and in November the surfacemen's pay was reduced again, to 17s. But approval was given to the rules of a workmen's friendly society for the locomotive and carriage & wagon departments, instigated by Drummond, and £100 was donated to its funds[20].

Rumours and veiled accusations about false entries in the NBR accounts met a stout defence from the chairman in December. These centred on the suggestion that rolling stock figures on the balance sheet had been fiddled, and that if enough money had been set aside to maintain the rolling stock, the dividends would have been less than they were. Kippendavie suggested that the comments went back to the committee of inquiry in 1867, which had reported a deficiency of 2,319 vehicles in the stock figures given on 14 November 1866. Since then, he asserted that the NBR had accounted correctly for rolling stock, and had charged considerable sums to the revenue account. He presented comparative figures from NBR and Caledonian half-year balance sheets of 1877:

	NBR	CR
No. of engines	485	684
Cost of repairs per engine	£70.03	£77.22
No. of carriages	1,599	1,629
Cost of repairs per carriage	£19.23	£17.19
No. of wagons	25,285	41,421
Cost of repairs per wagon	£1.55	£1.12
Receipts	£1,082,143	£1,287,515
Expenditure on track	£135,138	£125,312

Drummond 4-4-0 No. 490, *St Boswells,* **built in 1879, at Hawick. (***North British Railway Study Group***)**

– in order to show that both companies' expenditure was broadly the same and that the NBR was not under-charging its revenue account. The number of wagons does not include the very large number of traders' wagons conveyed by both companies. There was more substance in comments about stock jobbing[21]. These are borne out by evidence given to the Stock Exchange Commissioners by an expelled stockbroker, William Wreford, on 13 March 1878. Now operating as a "private speculator", he had opened large accounts, chiefly in North British stock. Over a nine-month period "I made £85,000 in North British alone."[22] This can only have been possible through dealing in large quantities of stock. In the course of 1878, a poor trading year, with the City of Glasgow Bank failure in October, North British £100 ordinary started at £85 10s in January, fell to a low of £79 in March, rose through the summer to a high of £95 in September, fell back to £87 at the end of October, but finished the year at £90 15s. Other railway shares followed the same pattern.

If the townspeople of Helensburgh were divided over railway access to their pier, they were united against the North British, defeating its Bill for a new pier at Craigendoran, just south of the town limits. A new Bill for this purpose was lodged for the 1879 session. The cost of works was estimated at £35,000. Other NBR Bills included the takeover of the Bothwell, Hamilton & Coatbridge Railway, the restructuring of the Dundee & Arbroath Railway as a joint Caledonian-North British line; and a working agreement with the Glasgow Yoker & Clydebank Railway. After the dismal experience of 1878, 1879 seemed to offer a more hopeful outlook. Revenue was growing again, and the ordinary dividend was pushed up to 3.25% (no upward move from the reduced wage levels, however).

On 6 April 1879 the entrance gate to the dock at Silloth collapsed, trapping some 20 vessels, including the SS *Silloth*, which had been employed on the regular Liverpool run, and expensive engineering works were required as well as settlements with the owners of stranded vessels. At Inverkeithing plans for a new dock were in hand and the NBR agreed to extend terms to facilitate works to the value of £71,880[23]. Having rebuffed the Anstruther & St. Andrews Railway in 1878, the board now agreed to contribute £1,000 towards it, in return for use of a small portion of line and the old station at Anstruther as a goods depot[24]. From mid-June the NBR combined with the Midland and G&SWR in using the newly-built and jointly-owned Midland Scottish Joint Stock, 40 vehicles comprising ten 54 feet and two 40 feet composite carriages and ten passenger brake vans. Midland Pullman cars were also still used, and from 21 September the 8 pm night train conveyed a Pullman sleeper for Perth, via Edinburgh and Stirling, arriving at 8.30 am (8.15 am from January 1880)[25].

The Newport Railway opened on 12 May between Newport and a resited station at Tayport, and on the 13th to an off-shore junction with the Tay Bridge. Hopes for a joint Dundee station had come to nothing, but there now was a main line across the city to meet the Dundee & Arbroath Railway. The Bill for joint ownership and management of the latter line received the royal assent on 21 July. On the same date the North British formally absorbed the Glasgow, Bothwell, Hamilton & Coatbridge Railway, the transfer being backdated to 2 August 1878. The bargain was expensive: Glasgow, Bothwell, Hamilton & Coatbridge shareholders, with a capital of £500,000, were to receive dividends on a scale rising from an initial 5% to an annual 8% from 1886. Enlargement works at Queen Street Station included the cutting back of the tunnel-entrance to widen access, but the end-section of the tunnel collapsed on 18 August, blocking all access, and for a time all trains were diverted to College, with consequent delays. Such unforeseen incidents as this and the Silloth collapse added to the company's costs, but in any case hopes of a recovery were dashed. During August the board decided on further pay cuts. The directors' fees were to be reduced; salaries down by 10%; labourers to have a 5% - 7.5% cut. Over 12,500 staff were affected: 5,400 in the traffic department, 4,600 in the locomotive department, and 2,600 surfacemen. The cuts were expected to save some £50,000 in a year[26]. The NBR's action was more drastic than that of the Caledonian and G&SWR, which decided not to enforce a pay cut. Against the trend, the salary of David Deuchars, the able goods manager at Dundee, was raised from £225 to £300 a year because of "special circumstances"; and there were evidently problems in enforcing the pay cuts, since in September the board decided instead on reducing staff numbers. No dividend was paid on the ordinary stock, and the preference dividends were not paid in full. For the February-July half-year, the gross revenue, £1,038,743 10s 11d, was down by £20,361 19s 5d: working expenses at £592,536 13s 0d, were up by £16,814 19s 9d, making a total shortfall of £37,176 19s 2d against February-July 1877, which had itself been a poor performance. After the opening of the Tay Bridge and of other lines for which high hopes had been held out, the shareholders were angry; the board was humble but defensive. Kippendavie was greeted by claps and hisses at the half-yearly meeting on 25 September. His claim of bad trading conditions did not stem criticism. William Ainslie of Fort William asked why 20% had been taken off porters' pay but not directors', and openly accused two directors, Harrison and Robertson, along with Wieland, Walker and Mr. Scott the registrar, of using inside knowledge to sell or buy shares. J.M. Douglas pointed out that the NBR had advanced a total of £66,000 to the Kelvin Valley Railway, not the authorised £30,000; that the directors had illegally bought and sold Kelvin Valley Railway shares, and were charging the loss of £1,400 to the company. "A mistake," replied Stirling, "… a matter of accounting simply." Had Douglas not gone on to raise other issues, more about this murky transaction might have emerged[27]. That summer G.B. Wieland completed the capital of the Arbroath-Montrose line by the sale of £80,000-worth of stock each to Renton Brothers and Brunton & Bourke, stockbrokers of London. The Kelvin Valley Railway opened for passenger trains on 1 October but the NBR treated the one-platform halt of Torrance as the terminus. Until 1886 Kilsyth-Glasgow trains went via Kirkintilloch, earning more revenue for the North British than the 50% rate from the Kelvin Valley Railway, while only goods trains used the Kilsyth-Torrance section. Total cost of the Kelvin Valley Railway was £77,308 18s.

Contractor's engine inside the high-girder section of the original Tay Bridge. (*Stenlake Collection*)

In the summer, steelwork tenders for the Forth Bridge towers had been received and Sir Thomas Bouch intimated his willingness to receive £35,000 in deferred Forth Bridge Railway debentures, in full of all his charges and expenses, except for inspectors' wages. But investment was still far behind requirements, and on 3 October all work on the bridge was suspended with immediate effect. In November the North British board decided to abandon its option to purchase the Forth Bridge Railway company[28]. The difficulty was resolved with remarkable speed by Wieland's connections with London stockbrokers, who took large holdings, and by 22 December the subscription list was closed. Wieland was rewarded with a Forth Bridge Railway salary of £500 a year, backdated to the incorporation of the company.

St. Margaret's Works had been operating with new labourers since the summer. Now the strikers were trying to get their jobs back. Negotiating on their behalf, an Edinburgh civic leader, Bailie Cranston, said they were willing to work reduced hours for less money. Kippendavie regretted that re-hiring was impossible, "the circumstances of the company left them no choice"[29]. To the committee of the Amalgamated Society of Railway Servants, the North British was high on the list for condemnation. At its conference in Leeds, the president said, "Five months ago the directors issued preference stock on which no dividend can now be paid, and it is hard to believe that when this stock was issued, the directors were ignorant of the condition of their affairs"[30]. His suspicion was shared by many people who had no involvement with the workers' cause. He concluded that railway property was "at the mercy of gamblers and speculators". A new railway on which a good profit was anticipated was authorised on 17 October: the Wemyss & Buckhaven, intended primarily to carry coal. On 21 April a working agreement had been made with the NBR, to operate the line for 40% of the gross revenues, and to pay an annual dividend of 4% on the capital of £25,000, with any surplus to be evenly divided. The moving spirit was Randolph Erskine Wemyss, owner of the Wemyss Estate, only 20 years old.

The North British was not the only railway company experiencing difficulties and anxious shareholders were urging them throughout the year to combine in economies and minimise competition. The Caledonian proposed a traffic agreement between itself, the NBR and the G&SWR, but the NBR was cautious, and queried whether such an agreement would have legal force[31]. From the start of through services to Aberdeen, over the Tay Bridge, it had been having difficulties with Caledonian obstructiveness and delays in providing facilities at Aberdeen Station, but a joint committee was still in being.

At the very end of the year, at this already low point in the company's affairs, burst devastating, scarcely believable news. The Tay Bridge had collapsed in a storm, taking a passenger train with it. Cable messages flashed the news around the world. Train disasters were, sadly, almost routine happenings, and 71 deaths by no means a record figure, but this seemed a special event. The longest bridge in the world, so proudly opened little more than a year before, had been wrecked by the wind. The fate of the passengers and train crew, hurled from the bridge deck into stormy waters, with no survivors, gripped everyone's imagination. There was something epic in this tragedy, revealing the frailness of human endeavour against the gigantic powers of nature, which made it into more than a happening – a judgement or intimation. Having occurred in Scotland, there was no lack of voices to point out that it was a Sunday train which had been snatched to destruction[32]. In this sudden, extreme situation, Kippendavie, his board and officials behaved in the most commendable manner, without panic, confusion or recrimination. A meeting of directors on 31 December resolved first of all to contribute £500 to the disaster fund, and then to reinstate the bridge. The necessary actions to maintain and reroute services were taken swiftly, with the Caledonian's ready co-operation, while preparations for inquiry into the cause of the disaster were also begun[33]. Two train ferries sent from Granton resumed their chugging between Tayport and Broughty Ferry.

At this stage, Sir Thomas Bouch, still the bridge's supervising engineer (a task delegated to a junior figure) was very much involved. He believed the train must have become derailed and hit the side-girders – this theory had been advanced as early as 28 December by one William Dow[34] – and would learn from the event how to restore his bridge to full and permanent serviceability. A Board of Trade inquiry began on 3 January, headed by H.C. Rothery QC, Commissioner of Wrecks, with Colonel Yolland of the Railway Inspectorate, and W.H.Barlow, president of the Institution of Civil Engineers. The issue of wind pressure soon became a prime concern, but ugly rumours had been circulating about the bridge's condition even before the storm, and these became more widespread. A Glasgow engineer, John St. Vincent Day, asked in a lecture to the Institute of Engineers and Shipbuilders of Scotland: "Did General Hutchinson really closely inspect the columns? If so, his report is, to say the least, incorrect"[35]. The reputation of the NBR took a further hit when a light engine ran into a passenger train at Dumbarton on 26 January, and fourteen people were injured. Block working still had to be introduced on many sections[36].

The Port Carlisle dandy car, in the 1900s (*Stenlake Collection*).

The Forth Bridge company had suspended building on purely financial grounds, but it now resolved on "a thorough investigation into the principles and details of construction and cost", though allowing foundation work to go ahead, up to £25,000. Its half-yearly report in February defended the Bouch design as being of an entirely different character to the Tay Bridge. Prudently, it resolved to set up a Reserve Fund for the owning companies, to be created from half of the North British share of surplus profits until a level of £250,000 was reached[37]. The *Scotsman* reported that the first sod of the Forth Bridge Railway was cut at South Queensferry on 1 March 1880: a letter from William Arrrol denied that it had happened. Perhaps someone had jumped the gun[38].

The Cumberland lines were prominent among the NBR's Bills in Parliament for 1880. The Port Carlisle Dock & Railway and the Carlisle & Silloth Bay Railway & Dock companies were to be amalgamated with the North British, and a new dock was to be constructed at Silloth. New "passenger sheds" were to be erected at Waverley, by agreement with the town council, and the new Tay Bridge and amendments to the Forth Bridge Act were also included. For the time being, the Tay Bridge Disaster provided a reason for passing a dividend payment: the company needed to set aside £120,000 against likely expenses and claims for compensation. There was no ordinary dividend, and a circular to preference shareholders asked them to accept a reduced amount, cut by £1%, on their holdings. A majority of first class preference holders agreed, but the second class preference holders refused, and the idea, suggested to the board by Wieland, was dropped. Preference dividends were paid down to E&G preference. The ordinary share price, which had fallen to £65 10s after the bridge collapse, recovered as far as £75 7s 6d by March[39].

Plans to complete railway communication round Fife's East Neuk were moving slowly. The committee for the proposed Anstruther & St. Andrews Railway accepted a working agreement with the NBR in March 1880, with the North British to contribute £5,000 towards a new through station at St. Andrews to replace the terminus outside the town, but completion was nearly ten years away. North-east of Dunfermline, the Lilliehill-Townhill connection opened on 1 June.

Not only industrial recession and unrest, and natural disaster, were cited as reasons for yet another dismal set of figures for July 1879-January 1880. Poor potato and grain harvests had also made their negative contribution. Though goods revenue was again slightly down, mineral traffic had gone up by 321,000 tons and would have been greater if more wagons had been available (this comment by Kippendavie at the half-yearly meeting on 30 March might have provoked the question 'why weren't they?' but apparently did not). Applause greeted his declaration that the Tay Bridge must be restored. For a change preference shareholders replaced ordinary shareholders as protesters. With the Tay Bridge provision of £120,000 charged to the past half-year's revenue, the later preference shareholders had to share the loss. Yet if the bridge had made a profit (the Tay Bridge Railway was a separate company, though in effect a NBR subsidiary) they would still have got only their 4%.

Burntisland Harbour was run by a joint committee appointed by the North British Railway and the town council, but railway members were in a majority. This led to a dispute and eventual arbitration by a Board of Trade tribunal, when the majority voted to put the rate for harbour haulage up by a half-penny to 2*d* a ton, and for imported goods to $\frac{1}{2}d$ a ton. The NBR also had an interest in Charlestown and Leven Harbours, and Burntisland Town Council kept a close eye on harbour matters as its main source of income.

At this time the NBR had negotiated a cash credit of £200,000 with the British Linen Bank, renewed in March for six months at 1% above Bank Rate[40]. There was need for additional capital. The North British Railway Act of 1869 had authorised the raising of £3,000,000 worth of stock and in May the company issued a convertible stock 1875 to cover the unraised residue – this was convertible at any time into NBR ordinary stock, and in the meantime attracted a dividend of 4.5% a year. No buyer would have been in a hurry to convert.

In May James Carswell was awarded £1,000 for his enlargement plans for Queen Street Station. It was still assumed that the Tay Bridge would be restored, not rebuilt, to plans made "through Sir Thomas Bouch", and his contract for Tay Bridge works maintenance was continued[41]. A special meeting on 12 June endorsed the plan for renewal of the bridge at a reduced height. The link-lines at each end were void of traffic, but the bookstall and refreshment rooms at Tay Bridge Station stayed open, with the rental waived[42]. Everyone however was waiting for the Commissioners' report, which was published on 30 June. All three members were at one in dismissing the derailment theory and ascribing the fall of the bridge to "the insufficiency of the cross-bracing and its fastenings to sustain the force of the gale." They condemned the workmanship of the piers, and also noted that trains had frequently run over the bridge at speeds much greater than the prescribed 25mph. Barlow and Yolland did not ascribe responsibility, but Rothery (the only non-engineer

St Andrews Station staff in 1910. (*North British Railway Study Group***)**

of the three) wrote in a separate report that the bridge was "badly designed, badly constructed, and badly maintained", and "I do not understand my colleagues to differ from me in thinking that the chief blame for this casualty rests with Sir Thomas Bouch, but they consider it is not for us to say so.". But said it was. Rothery also hinted that General Hutchinson should have been more rigorous in considering the issue of wind pressure. France had a rule requiring structural ability to withstand 55lb pressure per square foot, and the United States 50lb. The British authorities (when questioned by Bouch at the design stage) had made no stipulation at all[43]. Rothery's verdict ensured that the public had a culprit, with Bouch as the man whose incompetence and negligence had made the disaster inevitable. The procurator fiscal of Dundee took no action, but the findings of the report left Bouch's reputation shattered. Speculation about the disaster's cause goes on in the twenty first century. The derailment theory still has support[44], though the Commissioners assured themselves that the track on the bridge was "in very good order".

On 8 July the Edinburgh bakers, fleshers and grocers had their annual holiday and outing. The North British carried 600 people on a grocers' trip to Rumbling Bridge, and 500 on a bakers' jaunt to Stirling. Brass bands accompanied the excursions. Sunday school and temperance society outings were also frequent in the summer months. Such specials were a useful source of income. The directors enjoyed their own annual trip to Loch Lomond on 4 August.

Marshall Meadows, above the cliffs just north of Berwick, had been identified as a tricky section of the main line from the very beginning. Surfacemen had been re-laying the track in late July and a speed restriction of 10-15mph should have been in force. On 31 July the 'Flying Scotchman', formed of eleven carriages and pulled as usual by a North Eastern engine, went off the rails here, killing the driver, fireman and guard. Its speed was estimated at 60mph. The resultant Board of Trade inquiry was severely critical of the North British. The new sleepers had only one spike for each chair on the inner rail of a curve. The company's rules and regulations were branded as inadequate for public safety. Despite pressure from Parliament and the Board of Trade since 1873 for absolute block working, only six or seven miles of the Edinburgh-Berwick railway were worked in this way[45].

Apart from the new, or rebuilt, Tay Bridge, there were several Bills in Parliament presented by the NBR, or in which it had an interest. All were approved by the necessary shareholders' meeting on 15 July[46]. An extension of the Blane Valley line from Killearn was to meet the Forth & Clyde Junction Railway at Gartness, and a branch would be built to Aberfoyle from another new junction on the Forth & Clyde Junction Railway at Buchlyvie; the junctions laid to allow through trains between

Holmes 0-6-0 locomotive No. 82, built 1885, at Newington. (North British Railway Study Group)

Morningside Road Station in Edinburgh. (*Stenlake Collection*)

Glasgow and Aberfoyle. These lines, engineered by Formans & McCall and originally intended to reach Loch Lomond at Inversnaid, would form the Strathendrick & Aberfoyle Railway, with a capital of £50,000. The NBR would work it for the usual 50% of gross receipts, but the shareholders were assured that none of the company's capital would be involved (the Blane Valley put in £11,000). A line from Bellshill to Motherwell and Wishaw was proposed, but, vigorously opposed by the Caledonian, the Bill was thrown out. The Anstruther to St. Andrews line was included, to be worked by the North British for 50% of the gross receipts, so long as these amounted to £12,000 or more a year; otherwise the NBR was to receive its working costs. Also proposed was the Edinburgh Suburban & Southside Junction Railway, from the St. Leonards line at Duddingston, tapping the growing residential districts of Liberton, Blackford and Morningside, and meeting the Glasgow line at Haymarket West Junction, thus providing a bypass route across south Edinburgh (a line first authorised in 1865 but not proceeded with). Its engineer was to be Sir Thomas Bouch, and capital was £225,000 in £10 shares, with borrowing powers of £75,000. Though nominally independent, it was a NBR dependency, with Falshaw as chairman, and the North British was to work it for 50% of gross receipts. Both Bills became Acts on 26 August. Financing of the suburban line was achieved by Wieland in his classic fashion, placing £100,000 of shares with each of Brunton, Bourke & Co., and Rentons, and £21,050 with William Taylor of the Baird company[47].

Following the Tay Bridge report, the Forth Bridge Railway board had withdrawn its current Bill in Parliament and asked W.H. Barlow, with two other eminent engineers, John Hawkshaw and Thomas Elliot Harrison, to revise Bouch's plans. In July it sent their report to Bouch, with a covering note delicately suggesting that "in view of the present state of public opinion he would probably prefer to be relieved of his position as Engineer in charge of the Work, so as to leave the board free to act in the present exceptional circumstances". He was instructed to tell the contractors to discontinue "all further operations of every description". Bouch asked for time to give his own plans further consideration, but the board pressed on and resolved on 4 August to abandon the present contracts. Kippendavie resigned as chairman on the 26th; Falshaw joined the Forth Bridge Railway board and became chairman in September, leading the difficult negotiations with William Arrol, Vickers, P.&W. McLellan, Friedrich Krupp of Germany and others, over the cancelled contracts. Bouch was willing to be paid off with £31,156 11s 7d cash in discharge of his account, but the Forth Bridge Railway declined the claim and said it had no power to relieve him of his allocated shares[48].

The half-yearly meeting on 23 September had a positive feeling. Kippendavie commended the operating figures as better than he had expected, with gross revenue up by £45,000 and working expenses down by almost £20,000, despite the effects of the Tay Bridge collapse. Trade was picking up nationally. This was the first meeting since the Tay Bridge report, and it was announced that W.H. Barlow had been asked to review the plans for reconstruction[49].

In the course of the year it was confirmed that the NBR should acquire the Whiteinch Railway, for £22,000. In 1878 it had paid £1,260 in tollage and no doubt foresaw this going up. It was not an amalgamation and no Bill was raised. The purchase was made in the names of trustees, though the money came from the North British. On 15 October a meeting of Whiteinch Railway shareholders refused a request from John Walker that the payment for their line be deferred until Martinmas[50] (11 November) of 1881.

Sir Thomas Bouch died at Moffat on 30 October, aged 58, following a chill[51]. His Arbroath-Montrose line was almost complete, but Col. Yolland condemned the long South Esk Viaduct at Montrose. Despite some revision of the design, he found the foundations insecure, the general design unsatisfactory, and the cast iron columns of unsuitably narrow diameter[52]. Virtually every Bouch bridge in the country was examined. Many were North British, including the lofty Bilston Glen girder viaduct on the Loanhead line, which was rebuilt, though not until 1892.

By the end of 1880 the sense of renewed confidence within the North British management was stronger. A major crisis had been faced and resolved, the economic slump appeared to be over, and once again the future looked bright. For 1881 the board foresaw Bills for the new Tay Bridge (now to be a wholly new structure) with a capital requirement of £600,000 plus borrowings of £200,000; takeover of the Montrose & Bervie Railway (currently worked by the Caledonian) from 1 August, at £6 10s for each £10 of the Montrose & Bervie Railway's £70,000 capital stock, with the NBR taking responsibility for interest on the Montrose & Bervie mortgage debt of £18,000; and short colliery lines in Old Monklands parish. Reflecting the new mood, NBR £100 ordinary shares rose to £91 7s 6d[53]. But the Forth Bridge project was in dire straits. Deals had been done with Arrol and McLellans, but Vickers, contracted to make the suspension chains, were holding out for £205,000, and their claim, along with Krupps', was under arbitration. Despairing, the Forth Bridge Railway board decided to enter an Abandonment Bill for its own abolition[54].

Reconstruction work on the South Esk Viaduct at Montrose. (*Stenlake Collection*)

12. WALKER'S RAILWAY, 1881-1887

A third hard winter in a row saw Loch Lomond freeze over. Extra trains were laid on to bring 6,000 visitors to Balloch. Special services were not always slickly organised. On 1 March the trains ordered for guests at the launch of the Cunard liner *Servia* at J.&G. Thomson, Clydebank, arrived after the ship was in the Clyde[1].

At a third annual soirée of Glasgow employees in the City Hall, on 25 February, John Stirling gave a talk on the railway situation. He noted that the North British had above 12,000 shareholders, and once a "moderate dividend" was achieved, he hoped to be able to effect improvements for the employees. While many of his hearers might have been members of the Amalgamated Society of Railway Servants, the organisations he commended to them were the Railway Benevolent Society, the company-run savings bank, and the Railway Temperance Society[2].

In March, the Arbroath-Kinnaber Junction line opened for goods traffic, with a short spur to Montrose Harbour. The NBR began to exercise its running powers on the Caledonian line, with its own goods trains to Aberdeen. A dividend of 2% on ordinary stock was announced. An offer of £9,500 against the company's losses in the City of Glasgow Bank crash was refused[3]. Kippendavie, who had been in poor health, told the shareholders' meeting that this would be his last as chairman, and gave a long account of events and achievements under his régime[4].

While the Forth Bridge (Abandonment) Bill was in Parliament, intense discussion went on among the partner companies, prompted by Matthew Thompson, chairman of the Midland[5]. A joint meeting in York on 17 June decided that the bridge must be built, but to a wholly new design. The Abandonment Bill was withdrawn and new contracts were sought. The companies guaranteed to the Forth Bridge Railway an annual amount sufficient to pay the interest and a dividend not exceeding 4% on the cost of the bridge and its link lines (except for Inverkeithing-Burntisland, which was passed to the NBR). It was assumed that the total cost would not exceed £2,000,000, and that surplus profits would go to the North British. The NBR took a 30% share, the Midland 32.5% and the NER and GNR split the remaining 37.5% between them. It was agreed that the North British would apply for fresh powers to construct the unmade direct line to Perth via Glenfarg. An extraordinary general meeting of the Forth Bridge company unanimously approved these decisions[6]. Compared to the despondency of January, everything was bright again. On 18 July the new Tay Bridge Bill received the royal assent, along with the absorption of the Bervie and Blane Valley Railways. 'Wemyss's railway' was opened from Thornton Junction to Buckhaven on 1 August, worked by the NBR.

At the September half-yearly meeting John Stirling again presided as chaiman, explaining to applause that his health had improved and his colleagues had urged him to remain. On safety, without giving figures, he claimed that the block telegraph system was being "steadily increased" and that Westinghouse brake equipment was

NBR workmen at Thornton Junction in the 1890s. Christopher Cumming, Locomotive Foreman at Burntisland, on extreme right. Wheatley 2-4-0 engine No. 427, built at Cowlairs 1873. (*North British Railway Study Group***)**

being fitted to all new plant and to all old plant worthy of the expenditure. On general operations between January and July, passenger numbers had fallen by 130,000 but they had carried increases of 50,000 tons in general goods and 180,000 tons in minerals. Once again he commented that more could have been carried but for a lack of wagons: "They had always been kept short of plant, because unwilling to spend more on it than absolutely necessary". Queen Street he described as "now a most satisfactory station", though the new booking office and waiting rooms were not yet built and this would come "as soon as they could afford it". Financial prudence was his underlying theme, though expansion was not neglected. He cited the Whiteinch Railway and the intention to invest £25,000 in the Glasgow, Yoker & Clydebank line[7], whose act had been obtained on 4 July 1878.

John Thomas notes that a group of 28 NBR employees founded the Springburn Co-operative Society in 1881, using as their emblem a Wheatley 4-4-0. From one small shop the venture became very successful, managed by its founders in their own time. The Traders' Protective Association prevailed on the NBR to sack anyone involved with the SCS's business and six men were given notice to either leave their roles as directors of the Co-op or their NBR jobs. Controversy erupted and after discussions between William Maxwell of the Scottish Co-operative Wholesale Society and John Walker, the dismissal threat was withdrawn[8].

The new Tay Bridge was a wholly North British project. Design was entrusted to W.H. Barlow and his son Crawford, with a Board of Trade stipulation to "adopt no new or untried methods of engineering". It was to be 20 yards upstream of the old bridge, with some of the original girders integrated into the new structure, and double-tracked. Though building methods were very different, it resembled a more massive version of Bouch's design, with 74 spans, eleven of them 245 feet wide over the shipping lane, and 77 feet high. At the end of October a contract for construction was made with William Arrol & Co., of Dalmarnock. At Tayport, again a terminus for northwards services, a passenger train from Burntisland ran into a shunting goods outside the station, killing four people, on 25 November. The signalman was held responsible but the issue of over-long shifts was again raised. Dundee Town Council, concerned for the bridge to be restored as soon as possible, became anxious when work apparently stopped in December, fearing that the NBR was reneging on its "honourable understanding" with the people of Dundee. A deputation met with NBR directors and W.H. Barlow in January 1882. Disagreement between the company and the Board of Trade was the cause of the problem: the Board of Trade wanted the piers of the old bridge demolished and the NBR wanted to avoid this expense. The Provost expressed Dundee's fear that the North British intended to replace the Tay Bridge by its new line from Edinburgh to Perth via the Forth Bridge and Glenfarg, but Kippendavie assured him that was not so. By March, all claims relating to the disaster had been settled, at a cost (including salvage and inquiry costs) of £50,310 3*s* 9*d*[9]. Compensation payments to victims' families amounted to £21,632 4s 6d. What happened to the balance of the £120,000 set aside against costs was never made clear. A public relief fund for victims' families had raised £6,500 but disbursed only £1,910. The NBR reclaimed its £500 donation, as did the directors, who had personally given £560[10].

Sir (since 1876) James Falshaw, deputy chairman of the NBR and chairman of the Bo'ness Harbour Commission, formally opened the new dock at Bo'ness on 5 December 1881 and entertained 500 guests to dinner in the Volunteer Hall. Three hydraulic coal hoists were installed, as well as travelling cranes, said to be capable of shipping a million tons of coal a year; and 3 1/2 miles of railway sidings were laid. The works were designed by Thomas Meik & Co. of Edinburgh, and accomplished for £170,000, £10,000 below the estimate[11]. By the end of the year Falshaw's other board, the Forth Bridge Railway, had settled the Vickers claim (for £25,000), Bouch's (£16,144 2s 2d paid to his trustees, who also retained his shares), and agreed terms with a new engineer, John Fowler, for design, with his partner Benjamin Baker, of a steel girder bridge, at a charge of 3% on the railway works and 5% of the bridge costs, to a total of £75,500 inclusive of his staff, "… and no additional charge to be made on any grounds whatsoever"[12]. By February 1882 the total cost, including Parliamentary costs, was estimated at £1,730,000.

Railway rates and fares were under scrutiny by a House of Commons Select Committee in March 1882. Giving evidence, John Walker emphasised the social benefits of railways. The North British had paid £671,000 to shareholders between 1862 and 1877 and a further £516,000 in local rates and taxes. Traders' tickets at low prices were available to all traders who spent more than £400 a year with the company. A Mr. Barclay of Montrose wrote to the Select Committee on the subject of fish. Cod, landed at Montrose and sent to Billingsgate, was sold there at 1 1/2d per lb. Out of that sum the railway got $^{13}/_{32}$ of a penny, the fish curer $^{17}/_{32}$ of a penny, and the fisherman $^{18}/_{32}$ of a penny. The Billingsgate merchants sold it on at 7d per lb. Yet Parliament was being urged to compel the railway to reduce its carriage price by one third. This would merely push the fish merchants' profits up even further[13].

Despite continued opposition from Helensburgh, the NBR's Bill providing for a pier at Craigendoran had received the royal assent on 12 August 1880 and it opened on 15 May 1882. A short spur from the Helensburgh line ran to two jetties, 109 yards long, the eastern one intended for coal boats and the western one for passenger ships. The new station was of red brick, with white facings, a "tastefully stained and varnished" pitch-pine interior, and covered platforms. It cost £50,000, but now the North British could make a serious effort to get a share of the growing Clyde commuter and tourist traffic, and the new pier was widely advertised. An additional steamer, *Sheila*, was bought to supplement *Dandie Dinmont* and *Gareloch*[14].

**A party inspecting the new Tay Bridge works in 1882. G.B. Wieland and
Henry Grierson are fourth and seventh from left in the back row, John Walker is second from right.
William Arrol is second from left in the middle row, James Falshaw (chairman 1882-87)
and Lord Tweeddale (chairman 1887-99) are third and fourth from left in the front row.**

Shortly after work on the new Tay Bridge began (30 June), on 27 July John Stirling died. He was 71 and had worked tirelessly for the company which he had so surprisingly joined in 1866. The obituaries were more a history of the North British than of the man. Though laird of two Stirlingshire estates, Kippendavie and Kippenross, he had devoted himself to railway matters since joining the committee of the Scottish Grand Junction company in 1845, and had gone almost daily into the NBR Edinburgh office. An Episcopalian in religion, a Freemason (as were many senior railway personnel), and a Conservative in politics, he had also been a director of the Royal Bank of Scotland. The last of the three dominant chairmen who had battled to shape and build the company according to their own vision, he did not live to see the new Tay Bridge, or the Forth Bridge, but he ensured that both were central to the North British Railway's future. Of all the doughty and dedicated men who chaired the Scottish railway companies, his achievement was the greatest. Falshaw was elected as his successor. Born in Leeds, he had made Scotland his home ever since being joint contractor for the Inverness & Nairn Railway in 1855 (in 1882 he was still a director of the Highland Railway). But Falshaw had many other interests and concerns, and under his chairmanship the vastly experienced John Walker, as general manager, became the leading figure in the North British management. From now on the company would be run by managerial rather than visionary men, though often equally dedicated, certainly not lacking their own quirks and oddities, and sometimes capable of sponsoring controversial projects. The vacant board seat was filled in August by the Marquis of Tweeddale.

Also in July, Dugald Drummond resigned as locomotive superintendent, to do the same job, at a considerably higher salary, for the Caledonian. Friction between Drummond and the board has been surmised[15], and is not unlikely. Responsibility for placing orders for new plant was given to Wieland (who had gained a reputation as ace negotiator) and the board was very slow in building a suitable house for the locomotive superintendent. But Drummond was anyway ambitious and in his prime, ready for a new and rewarding challenge. Matthew Holmes, chief inspector at Cowlairs, was immediately appointed as his successor.

The large blank area on the railway map north of Oban had long attracted speculators. Nothing came of an 1863 scheme to link Fort William to the Highland line at Newtonmore. A proposal in June 1878 by Sean McBean CE, for a Glasgow-Inveraray-Fort William-Inverness railway was not taken up[16]. In 1882 the promoters of a 'Glasgow & North Western Railway' put forward a Bill for a line to run from the NBR at Maryhill, along the east bank of Loch Lomond, through Glen Coe and up the Great Glen to Inverness. It included powers for the NBR to work the line at a guaranteed rate, but the NBR had no official involvement, though Samuel Mason, its former general manager, associated himself with the promoting contractors, Wilkinson & Jarvis; and it refused any guarantee. John McGregor suggests, plausibly, that the NBR may have sought to disguise "a more intimate relationship than they wanted to admit"[17]. Opposition from the Highland and Callander & Oban companies helped to get the scheme rejected by Parliament on 29 May 1883, but it was clear that a railway connection was very much desired in Fort William[18].

Industrial development along the north bank of the Clyde had prompted the promotion of a line diverging from the Whiteinch Railway, to the Clyde at Yoker and Clydebank. First suggested in 1872, as the Glasgow, Yoker & Dalmuir Railway, its prime mover was James Thomson of the J.&G. Thomson shipbuilding company. Local industry subscribed £65,000 of its £82,500 capital, the rest provided by the North British, which would work the line. The first Bill, in 1876, had failed but it was authorised in 1877. It had originally been intended to rejoin the NBR system at Dalmuir, but difficulties about crossing the (Caledonian-owned) Forth & Clyde Canal placed the terminus at Clydebank. The Dalmuir link would not be achieved for another ten years. The line opened on 1 December 1882, appropriately with a workmen's train from Partick to Clydebank[19].

The Forth Bridge Railway Company was reconstituted in 1881 with a new Act (12 July). Two directors were nominated by each of the participant companies: North British, North Eastern, Great Northern, Midland, and the Forth Bridge company itself. Falshaw was chairman, Wieland still secretary. Shares were guaranteed at a perpetual 4% per annum. A proviso was made that if the North British should pay 5% or more per annum on its ordinary stock in four consecutive years, it would relieve the other companies of half their guarantees. The great cantilever design of Fowler and Benjamin Baker had already been accepted. Arrol was again contractor, for a price of £1,590,000, agreed on 21 December 1882, but in a consortium with Falkiner & Sir Thomas Tancred and Thomas Phillips, the next-lowest tenderers, known as Tancred Arrol. The work was to be completed within five years[20]. Arrol was in charge of two great projects, fortunately only some 50 miles apart.

Almost as soon as the Kilsyth Branch had opened in 1878, local promoters revived the plan to extend it to Falkirk, and in 1883 the project was briefly part of a grander scheme, the Glasgow & Fife Direct Railway, intended to reach Dunfermline via a tunnel under the Firth of Forth. But its Bill, rather misleadingly entitled "Kilsyth &

Falkirk Grahamston Station, circa 1910. (*Stenlake Collection*)

Bonnybridge Railway" was withdrawn[21]. A cross-city line in Glasgow had often been mooted, authorisation was given to the Glasgow City & District Railway, to cross by tunnel from Stobcross, with an underground station at Queen Street, to a junction with the City of Glasgow Union line at High Street East; and with a separate western section between North and South junctions in Knightswood, to meet the Dumbarton line. Its capital was to be £550,000 in £10 shares, with borrowings up to £183,000, and the North British was to work it, on a novel basis of $2\,^1\!/_2d$ per passenger for every double journey, and $1\,^1\!/_4d$ for every single journey; with goods at $2d$ per ton, and a guaranteed annual minimum of 3% on the paid-up capital. Provision was included for the NBR to purchase it, within five or six years. Big industry was behind it, with William Weir and William Laird of the Baird empire as chairman and a director. The engineers were Simpson & Wilson of Glasgow, Charles Brand was contractor for the eastern part, and James Young in the west. An ambitious engineering enterprise, its cut-and-cover tunnels would turn much of the central area into a construction site for four years[22].

An unusual accident happened near Dunbar on 1 September, when locomotive 465, a Drummond 0-6-0 of 1876, hauling a goods train southwards, burst its boiler, killing three men on the footplate. Another goods coming from the south hit the wreckage. The extra man in the cab had told the guard that he was a locomotive inspector, testing the coal, which was not true. But the driver was reputed to be "not a steady man"[23], and most people assumed he had tampered with the safety-valve levers to get more steam. The subsequent inquiry concluded that the explosion must have been caused by "a sudden generation of very high pressure steam" without explaining how this might have occurred[24].

Now that the economy was picking up again, wagon shortages became an acute issue. The Caledonian and the North British were both again criticised by Lanarkshire coalowners[25]. A different customer complaint arose when McClure, Naismith, Brodie & Co., ironfounders, brought a case before the Railway & Canal Commission against the NBR, claiming that rival companies were being given preferential rates on carriage from Glasgow to London. The North British admitted the charge, but said the amount involved was small, and offered a refund. But the commission found itself confronting a procedural issue. Their base was London, but in Scottish cases, should they follow the practices of Scottish law? English law allowed documents to be ordered from the defendants and Scottish law did not. The Lord Advocate pronounced that in such a case the Railway & Canal Commission was "a Scotch court sitting in England". Eventually the commissioners decided that it would be appropriate to follow the procedures of the Court of Session when dealing with Scottish cases[26].

Shunting operations at Aberfoyle. The Duke's Road to the Trossachs zigzags up Craigmore Hill behind the village. A tramway ran directly up to the slate mines. A Valentine's view from 1907.

The NBR's hegemony of Glasgow's northern hinterland was consolidated with the opening on 2 October of the Strathendrick & Aberfoyle Railway. Aberfoyle's slate quarries were being worked at this time, adding to the goods traffic. An ambitious Forman-inspired Bill for a 27-mile extension through the Trossachs to Crianlarich did not survive[27].

Mail traffic was rising rapidly in volume, and with the Post Office contract expiring in August 1882, Walker put in a request for an increased annual rate of £26,000. The Post Office considered this too high, and a rate of £24,000 was agreed. In an exchange between John Walker and Mr. Baines of the Post Office, the NBR tried to get an extra payment for a "travelling post office" attached to the 10.20 pm Berwick express, but yielded gracefully[28].

With improved trading results, as dawn follows dark the employees of the railway companies began to agitate for better pay and conditions. On 2 October 1882 a North British group had sent in a petition for a shorter day, which met no response. In January 1883 Walker issued a circular to say that he had altered the timings of "certain trains, which would remedy matters very much in future; and much more could be done eventually"[29]. Some Caledonian workers were already on strike and NBR men met to express solidarity and collected for a day's pay to be sent over. The Caledonian strike was a brief one, and meanwhile a deputation from the NBR locomotive department met Walker and Matthew Holmes, the new locomotive superintendent, on 24 January, to re-present a petition for a nine hour day. Currently they were working up to fourteen or fifteen hours with no overtime pay. The meeting was courteous, and Walker promised that the board would consider the request. A signalmen's deputation followed on the 28th, with delegates from Edinburgh, Glasgow, Fife, and Kipps (Coatbridge). Their request was for a six day week, with time and a half for Sunday work, and for a pilot jacket and vest to be provided instead of the present uniform of corduroy jacket and vest. They wanted signal boxes to be graded at three levels, depending on how busy they were, and pay levels from 22s to 24s a week, with for the busiest an eight hour shift instead of the standard twelve hours. An end to the practice of paying signalmen for thirteen shifts a fortnight, while actually requiring them to work fourteen, was requested, along with one week's paid holiday. Again Walker agreed to refer it to the board. The response came with unusual speed, in a circular from the manager on 9 February. The directors, believing that the issue was of pay rates rather than working hours, had decided to revive, from 1 August, the various scales of pay and salaries that were effective in May 1878. Shifts at busy signal boxes would be limited to eight hours. A "reasonable allowance" would be paid to locomotive men on trip work, and clothing arrangements would be altered as requested. This limited set of concessions was accepted by the signalmen, but not the other workers. The circular was denounced as "a masterpiece of equivocation". Walker's suggestion that pay rates, rather than working hours, were the motivation was denied[30], but for years to come, the board would continue to resist efforts to have standard working hours reduced, because it would involve hiring more staff, or paying overtime rates. On the North British in particular, which always had a high level of working expenses, there was a determination to keep the lid on wage costs. When North British servants in Dundee held a first annual gathering in the Buchan Hall on 19 February, Falshaw made a speech recalling comic incidents from the early days of Scottish railways, and kept off the pay and hours issue beyond saying, to applause, that the company should not treat its employees like machines[31]. That spring, shareholders were happier than the workers, with a 5% dividend on the ordinary shares in March, described by Falshaw as the first one paid since the earliest years of the company "without any straining of the accounts". Back in 1875, powers had been acquired to start a superannuation fund, which was only now inaugurated. Intended to help keep "the best of the officers" until retirement, it was financed by company contributions plus 2.5% deducted from the officials' salaries[32].

Pressure on signalmen was at least partly responsible for a string of accidents in the winter of 1882-83. On 5 January 1883 nine people were injured when an Edinburgh express was diverted on to the Cowlairs Goods Station Branch and ran into a goods train which had just left the main line. The signalman had failed to reset the points at the junction[33]. Reporting on a collision at Foulford Sidings, near Cowdenbeath, between a Dunfermline-Kinross passenger train and a Townhill-Burntisland goods, Major Marindin of the Board of Trade assigned blame to the signalman, the driver of the passenger train and the Dunfermline stationmaster, but observed that the accident would not have happened with block working. Not one mile of the NBR lines in Fife, except a few short lengths of recent construction, had block working, and Marindin said that responsibility must rest on the directors if fatal accidents should occur. The lines were "in a state which, considering the amount of traffic upon them, is without a parallel upon any system in Great Britain"[34]. At the March half-yearly meeting Falshaw claimed that block working would be completed before the end of 1884. He could point to the highest-yet half-year receipts, £1,304,937 6s 7d, while working expenses at £621,244 4s 0d were, for the North British, relatively low at 47.6% of gross revenue[35]. The pattern continued through 1883, and though the dividend in September was down to 3.5%, the chairman noted that the average for the year was the highest in the company's history, it might have been doing even better. While the Caledonian had 47 vehicles per mile of line, and the G&SWR had 33, the North British had only 29. It was still short of wagons[36].

On 28 April the Arbroath-Montrose line was opened for passenger services, a single track but with the road structure allowing for a second line, except on the Usan-Montrose section. The NBR took most of Montrose's southbound traffic, but it had a fight on its hands on the north bank of the Firth of Forth. Since 1852 Alloa, with glass, chemicals, brewing and distilling industries, had been an important source of traffic, and in the mid-1870s a short branch had been laid to the recently extended Alloa Dock. Just across the river, the Caledonian, with a station and harbour, had long itched to get access. In 1879 the Caledonian-backed Alloa Railway got authorisation to bridge the Forth just west of Alloa, whereupon the North British put forward a Bill in the winter of 1882 for a parallel bridge and railway between Cambus and Larbert, at a cost of £150,000. Ultimately common sense prevailed, and the NBR agreed to use the Caledonian bridge, with a minimum guaranteed toll of £3,000 a year on goods, mineral and livestock traffic[37]. The CR got use of the enlarged Alloa Station, but the North British was mounting strong opposition to two other schemes, the Caledonian-backed Alloa, Dunfermline & Kirkcaldy Railway, currently before Parliament, and the Seafield Dock & Railway for new lines and a coal dock at Kirkcaldy. Giving evidence against the Seafield Bill, John Walker said he thought its coalmaster promoters "had rather broken faith" with the North British and denied that provision at Burntisland was inadequate – a fourth coal hoist was under construction[38], but the Seafield scheme got its Act on 16 July. Further east, Randolph Wemyss wanted to extend his Wemyss & Buckhaven Railway a further two miles to Methil. The North British resisted this at first, but on 21 April 1883 Wemyss and Walker agreed that "Mr Wemyss should extend the Wemyss & Buckhaven Railway to Methil, to be worked by the NBR as Wemyss & Buckhaven Railway." Work on the steeply-graded line began in August[39].

Late in 1883, the NBR was again before the Railway & Canal Commissioners. Macfarlane & Co., large ironfounders, brought a case alleging overcharging over many years, applying preferential rates and shipping criteria at Possil Park and Sighthill to a rival concern, George Smith & Co. Giving judgement against against the North British and awarding costs to the claimants, the Commissioners criticised Walker and McDougall the Glasgow goods manager, who "did not seem to be alive to the responsibility of their position". Goods rates were a murky area, with many special deals and 'drawbacks', for customers in a position to haggle. The Railway & Canal Commission also had to arbitrate between the NBR and the Caledonian on how much the CR should receive for transferring a 50% interest in the Dundee & Arbroath Railway, under the act of 1879. The Caledonian claimed £431,852: the North British wanted to reduce that by £44,000. The Commissioners eventually ruled that the NBR should pay £136,000 plus 5% interest from 1 February 1880[40]. At the end of the year, North British £100 ordinary shares stood at £106 10s, higher than Caledonian at £104, though the G&SWR as usual was ahead of both at £116 10s[41].

In the Fife-Kinross-Clackmannan area, the North British either owned the railway lines or ran the services through working agreements. Though John Walker, a Fife man himself, worked hard to keep amicable relations with customers and commercial partners, it was only to be expected that the NBR's monopoly position would create dissatisfaction. The wagon shortage, the rate per ton-mile, and harbour dues all were contentious issues. Passenger services were also criticised. The ferries across the Forth were disliked, but so was the roundabout route via Stirling. An angry-amused letter in the *Scotsman* on 14 May described what became an epic journey from Kinross to Edinburgh, ending in the dark with unlit carriages[42], but coal haulage and coal export were by far the prime source of dispute. Having struggled through successive economic slowdowns and downturns, the North British feared over-provision of resources far more than under-provision. Enough rolling stock to meet the good times meant an expensive surplus in the bad times. Now, with the Seafield company putting its shares on the market, and the energetic Randolph Wemyss building a new coal dock at Methil, with a railway link to the North British, Burntisland's councillors were anxious to know what the NBR's policy was. John Walker sought to reassure them that, even though the NBR would work the new railway to Methil, it was not forsaking Burntisland. A Lochgelly coalowner replied that Burntisland Harbour was congested and that the NBR was being too slow in picking up loaded wagons from collieries, and discriminating in its charges. Spowart (a NBR shareholder and NBR nominee on the Burntisland Harbour board) was paying about $\frac{1}{2}d$ per ton mile while other coal shippers were being charged $2\frac{1}{4}d$[43].

Across the Firth of Forth, Bo'ness, with 6,088 inhabitants (1886) was a centre of industry as well as a port. Iron ore from Spain was already being unloaded there[44]. Leith, run by an independent harbour commission, was also seeing an expansion of trade. In June 1884 the North British paid £994 in dues for carrying over 448,000 tons of

Burntisland Docks in 1899. (*John Alsop***)**

The new dock at Silloth with the paddle tug *Solway*; she worked at Silloth dock from 1886 to 1896. (*John Alsop*)

goods on the harbour tracks in one half-year[45]. Farther east, Eyemouth was having a new harbour built and was again seeking a railway branch. The NBR agreed to work the line, when built (with the Eyemouth company paying for the junction and alterations at Burnmouth) at the usual 50% of gross receipts. A Board of Trade certificate for construction was granted on 18 August 1884. The Eyemouth Railway Company had its first general meeting in February 1885, with Meik & Co., also building the harbour, appointed as engineers, and it was resolved to take the line right to the quay[46]. Initial capital was £30,000 in £10 shares, which proved hard to raise, and the project languished. In Cumbria, the New Dock at Silloth was opened on 30 June 1885, at a cost of £90,000, with the old dock reduced to a tidal basin. Grain imports and flour and coal exports (Carr's new flour mill was erected alongside the dock in 1887) kept it busy, though by now the NBR was operating only one ship, *Albatross*, from Silloth, on the Liverpool run.

Further NBR capital was raised from June, not by a public share issue but by offering 4% convertible stock (1884) to those holding £500 or more of NBR or Edinburgh & Glasgow ordinary stock. Conversion to ordinary stock could be made at any time after 31 July 1889. At current dividend levels it was a sound proposition. In 1884 the North British paid its ordinary shareholders a dividend of 5.5% in March and 3.5% in September, making 4.5% for the year, a level sufficiently comfortable to keep attendance at the half-yearly meetings far smaller than in the crisis years. Revenue was rising three times faster than working expenses.

At this time the Dundee Suburban Railway was being promoted, and from opposing, the NBR and CR moved to agreement on jointly working it. An Act was obtained in July 1884, but the venture failed to attract investment and was eventually wound up. Edinburgh's Suburban & Southside Railway had its first train on 16 October when the directors made an inspection. It opened for goods trains on 31 October and for passengers on 1 December. Considerable alterations had been made on the south side of Waverley to accommodate a "Suburban" island platform and booking offices, placed "well forward … just outside the general station", with a new footbridge linking it to the main platforms. The main station roof was extended 100 feet west, as far as Waverley Bridge. A new west signal box controlled interlocking points and signals. The Suburban's contractor was John Waddell, and references to the line, running most of its way in a cutting through the rising ground, were complimentary: Morningside's booking office was described as a "neat little pitch-pine structure" on the over-bridge, with the waiting rooms on the platforms below[47]. The company was short-lived but profitable to its investors: in 1885 the North British purchased back the large blocks of shares, at a 5% premium[48].

In March, though a 4.5% dividend was paid again, Falshaw made some cautionary remarks about renewed recession in trade. What was to be something of a saga got under way when the chairman, commenting that the hotel site adjacent to Waverley Station had been "a ruin" for upwards of 30 years, said it was time to reconstruct it. When it was known that the NBR would run it rather than lease it out, Donald McGregor, proprietor of the

**The east end of Princes Street in the early 1890s, with the top of the Waverley Steps.
The entrance to the old coach yard and the NBR offices is just on the right of the Bridge Hotel.
The post office is just visible on the left. (*Edinburgh City Libraries*)**

Royal Hotel, began a long campaign of opposition. The North British also owned the Forth and Royal Hotels at Burntisland, the Queen's Hotel at Silloth and the Queen's Hotel in Glasgow, but had always leased them out. Claiming that railway companies had no business to run hotels, McGregor started court proceedings to force the company to sell the site. Despite his efforts to get a Court of Session interdict on the project, the Hotel Bill got the royal assent on 22 July, though with the proviso that shareholders' approval should be reconfirmed before capital was raised. John Walker, giving evidence to the Lords Committee, had said it already bore a sign, saying "North British Station Hotel"[49]. The March 1885 half-yearly meeting saw one of the rare defeats of the board by shareholders. Sheriff Orphoot of Peebles wanted the company to campaign to have the Railway & Canal Commissioners come to Scotland to resolve disputes between Scottish railway companies. The board resisted but was voted down, with the chairman protesting against shareholders "tying the Directors, while those of other companies were left free". He promised to do all they could to meet the motion, without risking the interests of the company. The immediate issue was the costs incurred in resolving the NBR's half-share in the Dundee & Arbroath Railway, but some shareholders felt that officials and directors were over-fond of expenses-paid jaunts to London[50].

The North British was part-scene of what was one of the world's longest non-stop runs in 1885. The 8.15 pm 'Night Scotsman' was credited with a non-stop run from Newcastle Central to Waverley, 124 miles 31 chains, but it appears to have made a ticket stop at Portobello, so the true distance was 121 miles 30 chains. The day express had its tickets checked at Berwick and ran straight through to Waverley[51].

The process of stock consolidation continued through the summer of 1885. A range of lien stocks including the Stobcross, Bothwell, Montrose, Port Carlisle, Silloth, Kelvin Valley (North British) and Edinburgh & Suburban, were gathered into consolidated lien stock to a value of £1,004,412 10s, bearing a fixed preference dividend of 4% per annum. The Kelvin Valley Railway was merged with the North British on 1 August, with Kelvin Valley Railway shares to receive a 4% guaranteed dividend for two years and a perpetual 5% thereafter: another good bargain for the Bairds. Apart from one train a day via Torrance, Kilsyth trains still went via Lenzie. Falshaw's warning of recession was borne out by a fall in traffic, and a querulous note was evident at the September half-yearly meeting. Defending an increase of £6,000 in salaries, Walker cited the need for additional signalmen as the block telegraph system was extended. An upgrading system for guards had also pushed up the wage Bill, but a new drive for economies was on, with the Clyde steamer service to be reduced[52].

Railway excursions were popular, with a choice of three routes southwards from Edinburgh, special offers were always available at holiday times. For the Christmas period in 1885, Thomas Cook advertised special rates for five-day excursions on the NBR-Midland route from Edinburgh to Blackburn, Bradford, Bolton, and Leeds, at 16s return in first and 8s in third; and to Liverpool, Manchester and Sheffield at £1 and 10s[53]. In 1885 it was still possible to take a steamboat from Leith to London, with the fare for the 'chief cabin' only £1 2s; second class was 16s.

The first months of 1886 saw a spate of accidents and incidents. On the night of 21-22 January a Dunfermline-Carlisle goods train was partially derailed at Gorebridge and immediately hit by the oncoming Carlisle-Sighthill goods, strewing debris all around. The southbound train was carrying oil in barrels, paper, bark, and rock salt among other merchandise. Clearing up after such happenings was invariably swift. A steam crane was sent from St. Margaret's, and between 150 and 200 men laboured all night to get the line clear by 10 am next morning. A week later they had to disinter a locomotive and goods train from a landslip at Cockburnspath and the line was reinstated within 24 hours. Another week later, the East Coast line was disrupted again by subsidence between Inveresk and Prestonpans (not the first time, and a watchman was on duty), requiring heavy re-ballasting[54]. Trade was sagging too, the weather was bad, there were strikes in the coalmines around Slamannan – gross revenue was slipping back, and operating costs rose from 47.6% of receipts (July-January 1885-86) to 48.4%. Still a dividend of 3% on the ordinary shares was managed. For the first time in decades, the North British had no Bills in Parliament.

The Glasgow City & District line, already known as "the underground railway", opened on 15 March between the Stobcross line and the City of Glasgow Union Railway just beyond College, where the old terminus was closed and a new through station built. Two island platforms formed the new Queen Street (Lower), linked by stairs and hydraulic hoists to the Upper Station. Goods trains were not allowed to use the underground section, but despite air vents, the tunnel was permanently full of smoke and the first of numerous accidents due to this

The Eastfield breakdown train, ready for action, after opening of the depot in 1904.
(*North British Railway Study Group*)

Drummond 4-4-0T No. 496, *Helensburgh*, one of three built by Neilsons in 1879. There was no cab door, only a high step-over lintel. (*Stenlake Collection*)

happened only three days after opening[55]. The North British never installed condensing equipment on its tank engines (not that it was very effective in smoke reduction). The Knightswood link was completed on 1 August. Excluding this section, the works had cost £706,763. Also on 15 March, traffic on the Stobcross line was further increased by the opening of a half-mile NBR branch to a quite imposing West End terminal station at Hyndland, which handled 46 trains a day each way for the Coatbridge/Airdrie and Hamilton lines, including sixteen to or from Edinburgh. The Glasgow City & District ran sixteen trains each way on the Maryhill-Springburn-Partick circle. All passed through Queen Street (Low Level) as did trains between College and Dumbarton, Balloch and Helensburgh. By September it handled 90 trains daily each way. At first the carriages were unlit, but protests led to the installation of a novel system of incandescent electric lighting, from a current picked up from a third rail[56]. A goods branch to Ruchill opened this year, further improving the NBR's access to industrial development in North Glasgow[57].

On 7 May, in what perhaps still remains a record, the journey from Dalkeith to central Edinburgh was accomplished in twelve minutes, by a train carrying the Prince of Wales and his entourage[58]. Standard service took 28 minutes. All passenger services to Edinburgh got a boost from the city's International Exhibition that summer, though the pressure on Waverley Station sometimes became too much. Visitors returning to Girvan recorded:

> "… on reaching the Waverley Station in Edinburgh at 4.10 pm we were shuttlecocked from one platform to another, and from one train to another; getting comfortably seated in one train, to be turned out of it at 4.40 pm because it was the 4 pm train to Glasgow; and at last … settling down with a sigh of relief in a carriage, upon which an official had stuck an 'Ayr' ticket, which started at 5 pm as the 4.20 pm train, and reached Glasgow at 7 pm."

By the time they reached Ayr, the Girvan train had long gone and the stationmaster hired a horse-drawn brake to get them home[59]. A sense of dissatisfaction with railway services was prevalent, with fares considered too high, timings inconvenient, services slow, and the responses to requests for cheaper rates often arrogant. When the magistrates of Falkirk and Grangemouth requested fare reductions between their towns and Edinburgh and Glasgow, they were told, "We do not at present see occasion to interfere with existing rates"[60], but where there

NBR warning to trespassers.
(*North British Railway Study Group*)

was competition, customers benefited. Sixty trains a day were running between Edinburgh and Glasgow, on North British and Caledonian lines.

By the autumn of 1886 economic conditions were easing somewhat and traffic was picking up. The NBR paid a 2% dividend on the ordinary shares. At this time there were 19,295 ordinary shareholders, with an average holding of £1,729. Debentures were held by 3,767 (average holding £1,793); preference or guaranteed shares by 25,861 (£1,341), and ordinary by 5,224 (£1,883). The capital amounted to £33,363,494[61]. Some shareholders were taking what the management considered an unseemly interest in the affairs of the North British Steam Packet Co. Moses Buchanan had raised the question of its profitability at the March shareholders' meeting and returned to the topic in September. The chairman left Walker to give an opaque reply: the North British had the same arrangements as with owners of other steamers, "but they did not consider it their business, in a public meeting, to disclose all their transactions"[62].

Holmes locomotive No.693, first of the "West Highland Bogies", with line inspection platform. (*John Alsop***)**

13. WALKER AND TWEEDDALE, 1887-1891

Expansion of the still-new oil shale industry was good news for the North British. In December 1886 a Bill was lodged for a branch off the Edinburgh & Bathgate Railway, near Drumshoreland, to the Broxburn Oil Company's works. By January 1887 the Linlithgow Oil Company had a line into the goods yard at Linlithgow, and twelve companies were producing 60 million gallons of crude oil a year from the shale field. But with soaring usage, competition from imported American oil was already present. The price of mineral oil, 2s 6d a gallon in the late 1870s, was now down to 5d or 6d a gallon. Coal was still king, however, and in that winter the Fife pits gained business as a result of unrest in the Lothian and Lanarkshire fields, with strikes and lockouts.

In March 1887 the 77-year old Sir James Falshaw stood down as chairman, resuming the role of deputy, and the Marquis of Tweeddale took over the chair. Tweeddale's grand social status as much as any natural acumen made him a sort of professional company director in an era when even more than now, an aristocratic title put some shine on a mundane commercial concern, and he had numerous other directorships.

Methil's new dock was opened for traffic on 5 May, and the Buckhaven-Methil railway opened on the same day. The dock had three hydraulic hoists for coal wagons, and electric lighting for night work. Brass and flute bands paraded and a wooden hall was put up to house a banquet for 300 guests, with celebration all the more cheerful for the knowledge that the Seafield project was struggling to find buyers for its stock. Leven Dock's trade plummeted[1]. In Burntisland, the oil company opened a goods line from the town, serving its own works and a new candle factory, linked to the North British at Kinghorn[2], but the main event of 1887 was the completion of the new Tay Bridge, far more solid both in appearance and in actuality than its predecessor. Its first passenger train crossed on 10 June, with directors and guests. At North Queensferry "the handsome new locomotive which was shown at the International Exhibition was waiting to convey the party"[3]. The Board of Trade's final inspection of the bridge was not until the 16th, but goods trains were running across from the 13th. Opening for passenger services came on 20 June, the first southbound train being from Dundee to Burntisland via St. Andrews and the newly-opened Anstruther line. The Newport link was restored, with a new on-shore junction at Wormit. *En route* on the 10th the directors inspected the Forth Bridge works, where 3,700 men were employed, though financial problems were hampering progress. Fowler (Sir John from 1885) kept a close watch on the works, and on 23 September 1886 he delivered an ultimatum to Arrol, that unless "adequate material changes were put in hand to maintain a better pace of progress, he would advise the directors to terminate the contract"[4]. Now Arrol told Fowler and Baker that the contract price (already revised up) was insufficient. More funds were needed to complete the bridge, just how much more he could not say, but he looked for guarantees from the company, or for the company to take over the contract. The Forth Bridge Railway had to go to Parliament to increase its authorised capital, granted in an Act of 23 June 1888.

SECOND TAY RAIL BRIDGE DUNDEE, UNDER CONSTRUCTION YEAR 1886   D 8446

Central section of the second Tay Bridge under construction, 1886. (*Stenlake Collection*)

Services over the Tay Bridge to Dundee and Aberdeen were not immediately speeded up. A traveller complained that the 6.50 am Edinburgh to Aberdeen was not timetabled to reach its destination until 11.45. The journey time of four hours and 55 minutes was ten minutes longer than the old service. Cross-county connections in Fife remained unsatisfactory: Rumbling Bridge to Kinross, 27 miles, took three hours and ten minutes by the North British[5], but passenger convenience at Portobello was improved by completion of the underpass between the Leith and main line platforms and the rebuilding of the station[6]. That summer was a busy one for the North British Steam Packet Co.'s quartet of ships working from Helensburgh, *Gareloch*, *Diana Vernon*, *Guy Mannering* and *Jeanie Deans*, with seven services to Dunoon, six to Rothesay, four to the Gareloch, two to Loch Goil, and four to the Holy Loch.

With the unrequited request for a reduction of working hours still a cause of friction and resentment, Walker made a friendly gesture when the Amalgamated Society of Railway Servants (Scotland) held its annual meeting in Dunfermline during August, laying on a free special train to give the delegates a tour of the Forth Bridge works[7]. An ordinary dividend of 2.5% was announced. At the NBR's shareholders' meeting in September, it was noted that passenger receipts were down while passenger train mileage was up by 137,000. "Not altogether satisfactory", said Tweeddale. Complaints from the floor about the level of service were brushed away as not appropriate for discussion at the meeting. The whole thing was over in 15 minutes[8], but J.Boyd Kinnear, a consistent critic of Fife services, took to public print to dismiss the chairman's claim that everything was fine. "The badness of the service, the notorious unpunctuality, the misery inflicted at the Edinburgh station and at the two piers of Granton and Burntisland, lead us to avoid any travelling for pleasure …"[9]. But Tweeddale's complacency seemed borne out by the share price, when for the first time North British £100 ordinary, at £101 15s, topped both the Caledonian, at £97 10s, and the G&SWR, at £101.

With the towers of the Forth Bridge gradually taking shape, the NBR entered a Bill for a line between a junction just west of Corstorphine Station (Saughton from 1902) and Dalmeny, of five miles and one furlong, in December 1887. Other items included amalgamation with the North Monkland Railway, with £6 of North British exchanged for every £10 of North Monkland stock; for the lease of the Newport Railway in Fife, and for a new Glasgow line between College Station and Bridgeton Cross (it was no coincidence that the Caledonian was at the time promoting the Glasgow Central Railway). The total capital to be raised was not to exceed £525,000[10].

PS *Kenilworth* at Dunoon, circa 1905, with the 'Minstrels' performing. (*John Alsop*)

In the 1880s there was concern about economic and social conditions in the West Highlands. The Napier Commission report in 1884 had stressed the need for better communications in the region, and specifically for a third west coast railhead "at some central point on the west of Inverness-shire", with state support if necessary to enable construction. Several proposals for railways resulted. One was the Clyde, Ardrishaig & Crinan, promoted in 1886, whose fate is worth comparing with that of the West Highland Railway. Unconnected to any other railway, it was to join Sandbank, by Dunoon, to Loch Fyne, with a ferry over to Furnace, where the tracks would resume, running south to a junction at Kilmichael Glassary, with one line to Crinan and another to Lochgilphead and Ardrishaig, a total length of 41 miles. A special NBR shareholders' meeting in July approved the company's proposal to work the line for 60% of gross receipts, dropping to 50%, with a highly conditional guaranteed dividend of 3.5% on the paid-up share capital, but not to subscribe funds. This was a Charles Forman scheme. Though never a director of the company, Forman exercised more influence on it than most directors. In a sense, he replaced Thomas Bouch as the NBR's consulting engineer of choice, though Forman did not always wait to be consulted; and he also worked for the Caledonian and the G&SWR. Like Bouch, he was an ardent proponent of new lines that, if taken up by a railway company, could be completed to his design and under his engineering supervision; and adept in exploiting the ever-present rivalry between the North British and Caledonian[11]. The Crinan Bill was passed in 1887, but investors kept aloof, the NBR offered no further support, and the proposal simply faded away, just while in Fort William a new campaign for a railway link to Glasgow was getting up steam. Donald Boyd and Ewen Cameron, from the local promoters, met Walker and Wieland in early February 1888, in Edinburgh. The NBR officials intimated that the company would support the proposal if the Government would contribute £300,000 towards it. Forman was again very active behind the scenes. His estimate for construction, north from Craigendoran, past Crianlarich, over Rannoch Moor, down to Fort William, then west to the township of Roshven on the shore of Loch Ailort, was £740,000. Other schemes were also being proposed. The Glenfalloch Railway, involving a line from Balloch to Ardlui and Crianlarich, and assuming joint operation by the NBR and Callander & Oban Railway companies, was withdrawn by its sponsors in March 1888[12], though the Callander & Oban Railway entered its own Bill for a Crianlarich-Ardlui line in the 1889 session.

If Lord Tweeddale had a particular expertise, it was in the mechanisms of the stock market rather than in the operational details of railway management, but Wieland was the prime architect of the North British stock conversion scheme. Unveiled in March 1888, it proposed that holders of over £100 of ordinary stock would receive, in exchange for each £100 of their existing shares, a certificate of £100 of NBR preferred stock which would carry interest at 3% per annum, and also a certificate of £100 of North British deferred stock. This latter stock would be entitled to a share of any surplus profit each half-year, once all the Preferential dividends had been paid. The company had just paid 4.25% on the ordinary shares[13], but the shareholders had seen 2% recently, and knew that bad times could come again. The scheme promised to double their holding at no cost to them and to give a regular (though not guaranteed) 3% on half of it. To critics, this was the device of "stock watering" – hugely enlarging the number of shares without increasing the actual value of the business by one penny. Deferred ordinary shares carried no voting power, but the voting power of the new preferred ordinary stock was to be as follows:

> Holdings of £500 up to £10,000: one vote for each £250 of stock.
> Holdings in excess of £10,000 to have one extra vote for each £500 of stock.

North British ordinary stock as of July 1888 amounted to £5,180,868, including £575,000 authorised but not yet issued. The Edinburgh & Glasgow ordinary stock, amounting to £2,422,485, was to be cancelled and replaced by North British ordinary deferred, making that stock up to £7,603,353[14]. Holders of Edinburgh & Glasgow ordinary shares had fared poorly ever since the amalgamation, with a 2% dividend at best and long spells with no dividend at all. But at least their dividend had been linked to the North British ordinary. Now they would receive pie in the sky, and had no reason to believe that their slice, if it materialised at all, would be a generous one. The board gave Wieland a present of 500 guineas for his work in organising the successful conversion. Wieland's inside knowledge of the worked companies' affairs perhaps accounts for his purchase – whether on his own account or on behalf of someone else – of the whole of the Glasgow, Yoker & Clydebank's new 4% debenture issues in October, £28,241 16s 1d, at a premium of 7%[15].

A dispute over terms with the Post Office had resulted in the Post Office giving six months' notice, in December 1887, of discontinuance of mail carriage by the NBR between Berwick and Edinburgh, and to stations in Fife. By this time the North British had five sorting tenders and one 'Post Office van', and carried an average of 65 tons of mail each week. The old contract, from 1882, had been for £24,500 a year, which the Post Office considered excessive, while the NBR wanted more. The Post Office offered to pay half the parcel rate for the carriage of mail bags but the North British refused. From 31 May the NBR continued to carry the mails, but with no contract, and sorting of mail on trains was stopped while a process of arbitration went on. The arbitrator, Lord Basing, awarded a new rate of £19,049 14s 6d a year for 3 years, to run from 31 May 1888; plus £12,122 16s 4½d for December 1887-May 1888. Sorting tenders resumed running through Fife only on 1 October 1888. On that date the 7 am Edinburgh-London train was withdrawn because the Post Office refused to pay for mails despatched on it[16].

On 2 July the Kilsyth & Bonnybridge Railway opened, to a junction with the Caledonian Denny branch at Bonnywater. Its act had been obtained in 1882, and the promoters, having decided to abandon it in 1885[17], eventually went ahead. A new Act of 12 July 1887 gave either the NBR or the Caledonian the right to work it, and in May 1888 they agreed to operate it as a "common line", with a joint service, and maintenance shared in alternate years. Four NBR passenger trains ran daily between Glasgow, Kilsyth and Bonnybridge. The Kilsyth & Bonnybridge Railway paid the working companies 20% of revenue on local traffic or traffic carried on to their own lines, and 40% on traffic to other companies' lines[18]. From 1908 NBR and CR staff replaced those of the KBR at stations on the line.

In a practice going back to the beginnings of public railways, regular consignors of wagon-load quantities might own their own wagons, in any number from one or two to several thousand, though (except for short trips between their own sidings in places like Coatbridge) they did not run their own locomotives on railway company tracks. These 'traders' waggons', the vast majority owned by coal companies, had the advantages for their owners of being exclusively for their own use, of attracting a lower carriage rate than railway company wagons, and avoiding possible demurrage charges. The railway in turn saved on construction and maintenance costs, and was less likely to have an excess of its own wagons during slack periods of trade. The system was not without problems: traders' wagons were not always well-maintained and might cause accidents. Railway companies liked to keep their big customers on-side (hence the 'drawbacks') and a company with its own wagon fleet was in a stronger position to defect to another line. In 1888 a Scottish Waggon Owners' Association was set up, though it does not seem to have been very active. Of course its members were commercial rivals, unwilling to share information except in times of crisis. By mid-1889 they had over 24,000 wagons[19]. During 1887, in a drive to keep its share of traffic, the North British had begun a systematic programme of 'thirling' traders' wagons. Thirling agreements were well known, binding carrier and consignor for a fixed period at a fixed rate, in return for a commitment to carry all the traffic, or an agreed minimum. In wagon thirling, the company bought a trader's wagons for cash, with priority or exclusivity for use on the trader's traffic. It maintained the wagons in good condition, and the trader paid the full carriage rate, in theory at least. Indicative of the way in which each side had a hand in the other's pocket was that in October 1888 and March 1889 two of the biggest colliery companies, Wm Baird and James Nimmo, lent the NBR £14,000 and £15,000 for five and three years respectively, at 3.5% interest (0.5% above the market rate at the time) to buy 300 mineral wagons for which orders had already been placed[20].

J.B. Kinnear returned to the attack in September 1888, noting that (despite a 4% dividend) the North British passenger receipts were going down while those of other railways were going up. He ascribed this to the state of Waverley Station and to the poor facilities in Fife, singling out the "miserable junction station of Ladybank" where expresses did not stop. Ladybank was his station – another correspondent wrote that it was easy to get a connection at Thornton[21]. The half-yearly figures showed the passenger receipts had in fact gone up by £17,259. Despite the protests of another regular combatant, the hotelier Donald McGregor, the board agreed to join with the Caledonian and Highland in building a hotel at Perth Station, which opened in August 1890. In November North British ordinary £100 shares were down to £51 10s, with the new 'ordinary preferred' at £75 17s 6d. While the Caledonian and G&SWR prices remained steady, this plunge reflected either a hostile reaction to the deferred stock scheme, or gave evidence that the often-repeated accusations of the jobbing of NBR shares were not unfounded.

Since the opening of the new Tay Bridge, the North British had exercised its running powers, sealed in the Act of 1865, over the Caledonian line to Aberdeen, but in December 1888, the Great North of Scotland Railway, which had had minimal dealings with the North British, sought a court judgement along with the Aberdeen Station Joint Committee (formed of itself and the Caledonian) that the North British was not entitled to use Aberdeen Station without the consent of the GNSR, since it was part-owner of the station, and the Act said nothing about running powers over the Great North. The NBR's solicitor, Adam Johnstone, had to contest this, while also preparing Bills, with the Parliamentary counsel, for a railway between Clackmannan and Kincardine Pier, for acquisition of the pier and abandonment of its ferry service to Higgins Neuk (this line would not become a reality until 1903) and a link line between Winchburgh and Dalmeny, giving access from the west to the Forth Bridge[22].

Through 1888, planning for the West Highland Railway (WHR) was going on, and a Bill was entered for the 1889 session. On 10 January 1889 the Lochaber landowners Cameron of Lochiel and the beer millionaire Lord Abinger met Tweeddale and other NBR directors. It was provisionally agreed that the North British would work the line for 50% of gross receipts and guarantee a dividend of 4.5% on the paid-up capital. If the WHR's 50%, after fixed costs, could not provide the dividend, the NBR would make up the deficit from 50% of the revenues derived from West Highland traffic feeding into its line. An estimate of gross receipts was based on no more than the published figures for the Callander & Oban line, whose annual earnings for 72 miles were £659 per mile. Transposed to the WHR's 101 miles, this gave a gross revenue of £66,559; and, after deduction of 50% for the NBR, a net revenue of £32,280. Rents, interest etc. would reduce this to £29,467 available for distribution to shareholders. Capital of £617,708 was assumed from the engineer's estimate, on which a 4.5% dividend would amount to £27,797, leaving a margin of £1,670[23]. It was an astonishingly casual calculation for a major enterprise – and, since the final capital requirement was over £1,000,000, and the earnings considerably less than the forecast, a recipe for financial disaster. Aware of the Callander & Oban Railway's competing Bill for a railway from Crianlarich to the head of Loch Lomond, the NBR had pre-emptively arranged for the purchase of the Lochlomond Steamboat Co. by the North British Steam Packet Co[24]. Perplexity and suspicion among ordinary shareholders, sceptical of the West Highland's ability to earn any dividend at all, would increase over the years as the NBR poured ever greater amounts into the Fort William line. Though the board never said so, the hope of ultimately extending to Inverness was the only plausible reason for departing from its long-established policy of not investing in the railways it agreed to work, though there may also have been a certain urge to demonstrate that the North British, like the Caledonian with its Oban line, was a truly "national" concern. While the Highland company would fight to the end to keep any other railway out of Inverness, it could scarcely claim that a line to Fort William and the Morar district would be a major threat, but it opposed the Bill nevertheless. On 3 July 1889, the day the Commons committee approved the Bill, a ten-year agreement was made whereby the West Highland committee and the North British Company pledged themselves not to extend beyond their intended Banavie Branch (to the Caledonian Canal). On that basis the Highland withdrew its opposition, the North British paying £500 towards its costs. On 12 August the West Highland got its Act, though the Fort William-Roshven extension was rejected by the House of Lords, which distressed the Lochaber promoters more than it did the North British management. Authorised capital was £798,000 and Wieland was appointed secretary at £500 a year, additional to his other posts. Forman's route across the wilderness of Rannoch Moor was approved, though criticised by some since it was far from the slate mines of Ballachulish, but considerably cheaper than a line through Glencoe. Formans & McCall were duly confirmed as engineers and the sole contractors for the entire length – the longest one-

A North British station, Camelon, with a Caledonian train, headed by CR 0-4-4T No. 190, built in 1891.
(*Stenlake Collection*)

company contract on any British railway project – were Lucas & Aird of London, at a price of £393,638 4s 2d. Lord Abinger cut the first sod at Fort William, on 23 October 1889. In November the NBR board agreed to buy back 19,000 £10 West Highland shares subscribed by Lucas & Aird. A letter from Wieland (NBR and WHR secretary) of 7 November affirmed:

> "… as this company is to have a pecuniary interest in the West Highland Railway, they agree, on the completion of that railway, or within twelve months, to purchase 19,000 shares and to pay interest from the date of issue at 5% per annum."

A glum note from the general accountant's office, two years later, recorded that the North British would be liable for £17,131 of interest payments on 31 October 1893[25].

The North British was also busy on other fronts. The day after the West Highland meeting of 11 January 1889, the company agreed the purchase of the Methil Docks and Railway, from the Wemyss Estate, for £225,000. A Bill in Parliament listed branches from the Stirling-Dunfermline line to Kincardine Pier, to the Camelon Chemical Works at Falkirk, and several to collieries of the Nimmo company in Monklands, as well as the raising of capital to improve the company offices and "the building fronting Princes Street known as the North British Station Hotel"[26]. This was the former Kennedy's Hotel, on the upper floors of Nos. 8 and 9 Princes Street. It had ceased to be a hotel in 1883 and housed the engineers' and police offices. The company had a completely new hotel in mind, though it let several years go by before taking action.

Newspapers in February carried large advertisements placed by the Stock Conversion & Investment Trust Ltd. Chairman of this company was the Marquis of Tweeddale, and James Hall Renton, now a West Highland director, was also on its board. The Stock Investment Trust was set up to buy existing stocks, especially in railway companies (the country's largest companies, with most shareholders) and convert them into more than one class of security. It cited the value of unconverted railway stocks in Great Britain at around £180,000,000, and estimated that conversion would raise this value by £27 million. The Taff Vale and North British Railways were cited as companies whose shares had risen in value through conversion[27].

The half-yearly report recorded a dividend of 3.25% on the company's ordinary stock. At the subsequent meeting, on 28 March, Tweeddale remarked that the dividend was equal to an annual 6.25% on the stock as it stood before the division – the highest ever paid by the NBR. Edinburgh & Glasgow ordinary shares had a 2.75% dividend. He also announced that the North Monkland Railway had been acquired, "on terms advantageous to the company". A new director was elected, in the person of Randolph Wemyss[28]. For a long time a director's minimum holding in the company's shares had been £3,000, but as a result of the division of the ordinary shares, this was raised to £5,000[29].

In July, details were published of a proposed merger of the North British with the Glasgow & South Western Railway. This surprised many people who had thought the G&SWR to be a sort of protectorate of the Midland Railway, whose chairman, Sir Matthew Thompson, was also chairman of the G&SWR, but the NBR and South Western had virtually no areas of competition and (consequently) a history of friendly relations, were joint owners of the City of Glasgow Union Railway, and were both allies of the Midland, which was very much in favour of the amalgamation. The Glasgow & South Western had 318 ³/₄ miles of line, plus 121 miles of joint line and 9 ¹/₂ of leased. On only two occasions in the 1880s it had paid a lower dividend than the North British and its record was far steadier. A combined company would have been in a very powerful position, and the share price of both rose. Naturally the Caledonian saw the merger as a threat to its future growth and prosperity and strongly opposed the proposal. Also in July the action over the NBR's use of Aberdeen Joint Station was dismissed, because the Great North of Scotland company could not bring a case without the concurrence of the Caledonian as co-owner, which was not forthcoming[30].

By the North British (Methil Harbour) Act of 12 June, the NBR became owner of the Wemyss & Buckhaven Railway and the docks at Leven and Methil, with all their equipment and machinery. A clause in the agreement specified that the Wemyss Estate should not build any railway to compete with the North British line to Methil. Burntisland was upset by the purchase of Methil, feeling its position as the company's prime port to be threatened, and there was anger in Kirkcaldy, where after a couple of bad years for the coal trade, the Seafield dock and railway scheme was still struggling to get under way. Encouraged by the Caledonian, its backers had obtained a time extension and a new name, the Kirkcaldy & District Railway[31], but its viability was always questioned, not just in North British propaganda (John Walker never lost a chance to talk it down). A *Scotsman* article pointed out that the opening of the new dock at Methil in 1887 had reduced the coal trade of Burntisland from 805,000 tons to 724,000 tons. In eight months of 1887, Methil had shipped 220,000 tons, which had risen to 409,000 tons in 1888, while Burntisland had fallen to 652,589 tons[32]. The North British was also diversifying its Forth activities by a working agreement with the Galloway Saloon Steam Packet Co., founded in 1886, the prime operator of passenger steamboats in the Firth, carrying 380,000 passengers in the 1889 season. This was perhaps in anticipation that the Galloway Saloon Steam Packet company might take over the ferries once the Forth Bridge was open. In October the NBR purchased 2,548 of the Galloway Saloon Steam Packet's total of 4,400 shares, gaining control of the business[33]. Among the assets was the pleasure pier at Portobello, where a Mr. Hübner worked the entertainments.

In September 1889, the North British paid 1.75% on the ordinary shares and 3% on the ordinary preferred. After a modest rise in 1888, share prices fell back in 1889: in September North British £100 ordinary shares were at £58 2s 6d and ordinary preferred were at £78. Shareholders at the half-yearly meeting had no worries about amalgamation with the G&SWR, but the same was not true of the Glasgow company's shareholders and rude remarks about the NBR were made at their meeting, held on the same day[34]. Meanwhile the Caledonian, still opposing the scheme, came up with the proposal that it and the NBR should jointly take over the South Western: this found no support in the other two boardrooms.

In mid-October a party of directors and guests were the first people to traverse the Forth Bridge from end to end. The steel deck was not yet complete, but a gangway was hoisted up to close the remaining gap, 150 feet above the water – it must have been an exciting walk. Three months later, on 24 January, the first train crossing was made, with Lady Tweeddale at the regulator of engine 601[35].

An Amalgamated Society of Railway Servants (Scotland) gathering in Edinburgh on 1 December maintained the long campaign for shorter hours and improved conditions. The society had written to all the Scottish railway companies, with a request for a ten hour day, higher pay, and paid holidays. John Walker returned it with the message that all memorials to directors must be sent via heads of departments. A week or so later he softened the NBR line. A special committee of directors would be appointed to look at wage applications from staff, and would also consider the society's letter[36]. The committee did not proceed with any haste, and the issue was kept alive on the men's side by local meetings at the main North British depots into 1890.

Further interesting figures were given in a report on the Fife coal trade in January 1890. The total tonnage of Fife coal moved by rail was 2,030,375 in 1886, 2,099,124 in 1887, 2,077,184 in 1888, and 2,338,958 in 1889. Coal shipments were up at Burntisland and Methil, down at Charlestown, static at Alloa and Tayport, and had entirely ceased at

Leven[37]. Increases in the depth and capacity of steamers, as well as better facilities – docks, hoists, lighting – at the bigger ports further drove trade away from the smaller tidal harbours like Kirkcaldy and Inverkeithing. At Kirkcaldy, work had finally started at the Seafield Dock (soon abandoned), a new Bill was in Parliament to link it to the Caledonian system, and in March the Caledonian company announced its intention to invest £200,000 in the scheme[38]. Of course the North British opposed. It was about to take over another Forth harbour, at Alloa, included in the company's 'omnibus' Act of 1 August 1891, and the harbour trust was dissolved[39].

On 20 February a special meeting of shareholders formally and unanimously approved the G&SWR merger; the South Western shareholders had already given a majority approval[40]. Almost £600,000 worth of the new convertible preference shares had been converted to ordinary shares, and consequently qualified for the ordinary dividend of 3.5% declared for the August 1889- January 1890 half-year, slightly above the fixed preference rate of 3%[41].

Already a familiar, if still stupendous, spectacle to people in the region (and a big attraction to day trippers), on 4 March the Forth Bridge was introduced to the wider world when, in a high wind with a choppy sea below, the Prince of Wales drove in the last rivet. Matthew Thompson, chairman of the Forth Bridge Railway Co., and John Fowler were both made baronets, Arrol and Baker received knighthoods. Every statistic was awesome: 2,767 yards in length, 330 feet tall, containing 50,958 tons of steel with $6\frac{1}{2}$ million rivets, its construction had cost the lives of 73 men, with over 500 injured. The final cost, £2,549,200, was over half as much again as the original estimate. Despite delay and overspend, bonuses of £20,000 to the engineers and £64,000 to the contractors were paid. Work was not complete on the linking lines, and the bridge did not open for through trains until Monday 2 June. On the same day the new line from Mawcarse Junction to Bridge of Earn, and the diversion round Cowdenbeath, completed the direct Edinburgh-Perth route. One writer has described construction of the bridge as "an act of economic warfare … the North British at last equalled the Caledonian operationally, and the trunk railway war would now have to evolve in new ways"[42]. The Caledonian still held Aberdeen (and the London-Aberdeen mail contract) and the "war" went on in much the same way. Although it was only a part-owner of the Forth Bridge, the North British certainly gained prestige from having two of the world's greatest bridges on its system. Through carriages from the North Eastern, Great Northern and Midland Railways might cross, but (despite their possession of running powers) it was in North British trains pulled by North British locomotives. Soon the fish merchants of Aberdeen were pressing for a fourteen to fifteen hour service to London[43]. By later that year, traffic between Edinburgh, Dunfermline and Kirkcaldy was up by 88%[44]. But the Dunfermline & Queensferry line was reduced to a minor branch.

Cowlairs Engine Shed in the 1890s. In the foreground are Drummond 4-4-0T No. 147, originally named *Slamannan*, of the 72-class, built 1882; and Holmes No. 602 (1888) of the 592-class. The Prince of Wales feathers emblem denotes that this engine drew his train at the opening of the Forth Bridge in 1890. (*John Alsop*)

Apart from its commitment to Lucas & Aird, the North British had agreed to invest £150,000 in the West Highland Company for a line as far as Fort William, and its financial clout was reflected in a boardroom rearrangement in March 1890 when Lord Tweeddale became chairman of the West Highland, with Abinger as his deputy, and Randolph Wemyss also joined its board. The NBR obtained an act on 25 July authorising it to subscribe, and guarantee interest on, WHR stock. In a gesture towards realism, the proposed West Highland dividend was cut to 3.5%. Work was pressing on: Lucas & Aird had a steamboat working on Loch Treig, 1,160 feet above sea level, and 3,000 men were employed, including 346 crofters from Skye and other islands[45].

Eyemouth's railway had failed to attract subscribers. Its capital requirement had been reduced to £22,000 in 1884, with the help of G.B. Wieland, but even he could not find a share-buyer and the line's Parliamentary deposit of £2,400 was forfeited on 30 April 1889. The company's plight seems to have prompted the wealthy Sir James Miller, an NBR director (who lived locally), to buy shares. Lord Tweeddale did likewise and both became directors, with Wieland appointed secretary in June at £250 a year. A working agreement with the NBR was confirmed, and construction of the 2.97-mile line began in July, from a junction at Burnmouth, running parallel to the main line for half a mile before turning coastwards. An ill-timed explosive blast at the junction works almost derailed the 'Flying Scotsman' on 24 October[46]. It was built as a light railway, the only substantial engineering work being a high six-piered viaduct over the Eye. The North British took a 999-year lease, at a guaranteed 4% on the capital, in March 1891[47], and it opened on 13 April, with six trains each way daily. Its local promoters had always intended it to reach the harbour, but the terminus was well short of the quays, and the NBR resisted all requests to extend it further[48]. In 1894 the Harbour Trustees entered a Bill for further works, including provision for the NBR to subscribe up to £60,000 "in respect of the advantages derived by that company from the Harbour"[49]. The NBR did not contribute. A few days after the Eyemouth lease was finalised, local landowners in the Ormiston area met NBR directors and officials to discuss a railway link of just over twelve miles from Ormiston to the village of Gifford and on to the hamlet of Garvald. Lord Tweeddale, as a large local proprietor, was very much involved. Coal, timber and agricultural supplies were seen as the mainstay of the line. By March 1891 it was agreed that the project would go forward, with a capital of £111,000, none of which was to come from the NBR, though it would work the line for 50% of gross receipts, with a guaranteed minimum return to the Gifford & Garvald Railway Company of 4% a year. The contractor James Young was willing to construct the line for £10,000 in cash and £80,000 in shares. It all seemed straightforward, but troubles lay ahead.

Despite opposition not only from the Caledonian (seventeen petitions were lodged against it by various bodies) the G&SWR amalgamation proposal was passed by the House of Commons. But it was thrown out by the House of Lords on 11 July. Parliamentary expenses for the failed merger were £14,000 for the North British alone[50].

A westbound train passes the West Lighthouse outside Tayport. Dundee Law rises on the north side of the Firth of Tay. (*John Alsop*)

Haymarket Station in the 1900s. The lack of crowds suggests it is a Saturday morning. (*Stenlake Collection*)

The North British had been slow in completing the southern Forth Bridge approaches, but this was a modest failing compared to its complete lack of preparation for additional traffic at Waverley Station. An immediate torrent of complaint arose about delays in the Edinburgh area and especially at Waverley. It was customary to attach or detach portions of trains there, and remarshal them for onward journeys, but now there were many more trains, and congestion and delays became endemic. At peak times there were chaotic scenes. A total of 188,000 wagons had been carried in the last year of the Forth ferry; now all these and more went by the bridge. Goods trains were halted for examination before crossing, adding to the delays. Partial collapse of the Winchburgh Tunnel on the Glasgow line on 17 August exacerbated the problems for a few days. Among the angriest complainers were the partner companies in the Forth Bridge Railway, for whom the newspaper reports of long delays were a public relations disaster. Not the least sufferers were the NBR staff on trains and in the station, where makeshift arrangements included an extra wooden platform. Belatedly the board began consultation with the town council about further enlargement, with Tweeddale explaining that they had thought it better to experience the results of the Forth Bridge opening before making any proposal. Now, however, "nothing short of total reconstruction" would do, and the NBR wanted to take back the Waverley Market, lay an additional two tracks through to Haymarket and place a turntable in East Princes Street Gardens[51]. Many people wanted a joint station with the Caledonian, which put in its own Bill for new Edinburgh lines, including an underground line along the George Street ridge, with a terminus on the Waverley Market site. Twenty-one CR trains a day had been running from Waverley to Larbert. Now these were transferred to the CR's 'West Princes Street' terminus[52]. William Acworth, asked by the council to comment on both companies' plans, suggested that the goods station be moved from Waverley, criticising the NBR for wanting "that the citizens of Edinburgh should sacrifice the East Princes Street Gardens in order not to make room for passengers, but for beer barrels"[53]. This would have been the time to build the goods depot on Lothian Road, but the board was not looking for further expenditure, and the beer barrels remained at Waverley, near the breweries. A Bill to authorise widening of access lines, enlargement of the station and rearrangement of streets east of the North Bridge was lodged in November. It also included a new branch line to a terminus on Leith Walk, as a response to the Caledonian scheme for a line across Leith to the eastern docks at Seafield[54].

The Forth Bridge gave Dunfermline a much-improved service to Edinburgh (congestion permitting), but the North British had never been popular in the town. It was noted that the return fare from Kirkcaldy to Edinburgh was 2s while from Dunfermline it was 3s. Following complaints Walker promised to "look into" it. Two years later nothing had happened: a new approach was made, and turned down[55]. A fresh Caledonian attempt to get a line from Larbert under the Forth and into Fife to link with the Kirkcaldy & District Railway got strong support in Kirkcaldy[56]. In September the ordinary dividend was only 1%.

'Aberfoyle for the Trossachs': a scene from the 1900s, with barefoot children among the spectators watching tourists setting off. (*North British Railway Study Group*)

The opening of the two bridges did not remove the North British Company's obligation to run ferries across the Firths of Tay and Forth, but the Tayport-Broughty and Granton-Burntisland wagon-ferries were withdrawn. The sale value of the redundant steamboats, together with their depreciation fund, was reckoned at £50,000[57]. Maintenance of the passenger and road vehicle ferries was now seen as an encumbrance and an era of complaint began between the shore communities and the North British, which wanted to divert as much traffic as possible to the railway.

Unrest among the Scottish railwaymen was coming to a head. For more than a decade they had been pressing for a reduction in working hours, with minimal concessions from the companies. Mass meetings during November at all major depots reflected frustration and anger. Another circular issued by John Walker on 15 November again implied that the working hours claim was just a cover for getting increased pay and expressed surprise that there should be a demand for a "universal maximum ten hour day" when the NBR wage levels agreed in 1883 already amounted to remuneration for a nine hour day. It ended with the meaningful remark that he always had a list of eligible men looking for jobs. This did nothing to reduce the general acclaim for strike action[58]. The men quit work on 21 December, without prior notice. James McLaren, general superintendent, denounced the action as illegal – all grades were required to give one month's notice of intention to leave the company's service – and said that the NBR had a "determined mode of dealing with recalcitrants" and would institute criminal proceedings. The numbers on strike were enough to disrupt but not to immobilise the system and there was more impact on goods than on passenger services, with Glasgow, Edinburgh and Lanarkshire as the most affected areas. At Cowlairs, Haymarket, Kipps, St. Margaret's and Dundee depots, beds were provided for 344 men and food for 688[59]. The North British placed advertisements to recruit drivers, firemen, signalmen, and guards, "to fill vacancies on the Line owing to a number of men being on strike"[60]. Public opinion was largely on the side of the railway workers, perhaps influenced by the awareness that fatigue was a frequent contributor to railway accidents, but not all were sympathetic. One Henry N. Smith wrote from Helensburgh about "the dastardly outrage which the Scotch railway servants are perpetrating". A public meeting of women supporting the railway workers was held in the Trades Hall, Edinburgh on 30 December. Though NBR officials stated that "the back of the strike is broken", pickets were still in place, and on 9 January the *Scotsman*'s reporter took from 9.50 am to 9 pm to travel from Edinburgh to Dundee, using six different trains, "but punctuality has never been a strong point with the North British in Fife"[61]. Lord Provost Boyd of Edinburgh made a vain attempt to mediate. By 15 January the NBR had taken out summonses against over 300 men for breach of contract and went on to sue the Amalgamated Society of Railway Servants (Scotland) for £20,000. In Dunfermline a meeting of 1,200 women factory workers expressed support for the strikers, then went to stage a demonstration at the Upper Station before repairing to the Union Hall "where the women and girls worked off their superfluous energy by indulging in a hearty dance with the strikers"[62]. It was claimed that on the NBR there were sixteen cases of intimidation, 25 of outrage on the person, twelve of outrages on property, and sixteen of outrages on public safety[63]. On 29 January a deputation of eight strikers met Walker, who intimated that the company would withdraw the prosecutions and the case against the union, if there was an immediate return to work. No concession was offered beyond that, but the men came back. It was unconditional surrender, but not the end of the struggle. Parliament set up a Select Committee on railway servants' hours.

14. TWEEDDALE AND CONACHER 1, 1891–1894

Strong resistance from G&SWR shareholders met the attempt to revive the NBR-G&SWR Amalgamation Bill. Orchestrated by Sir John Burns of the Burns & Laird Shipping Line, they voted it down on 4 February 1891, and the project had to be dropped. There was no dividend on NBR deferred ordinary shares for the August-January half-year, and only 1.5% for preferred ordinary. Tweeddale blamed the impact of the strike "for the entire sweeping away of the whole and more of our increased receipts"[1]. On 24 April, while in London to give evidence to a Commons committee, John Walker collapsed and died at Waterloo Station on his way to the Isle of Wight for the weekend. He was only 59 and his death was quite unexpected. Many tributes were paid to his memory and a large funeral was held on the 29th. G.B. Wieland was appointed interim manager.

Walker, since Kippendavie's death, had personified the North British to the outside world. An able negotiator and a skilful corporate strategist, he was combative against competitors but internally favoured diplomacy over confrontation. According to *The Bailie's* profilist he was "a sturdy Radical"[2], but Donald Cattanach's researches show rather that he was a shrewd capitalist, investing (as did other senior officials) in companies with which he had links through his railway work. If at bottom his ideas were set in the traditional mode that saw the company servants as a force to be controlled and made use of, his conciliatory style smoothed over the roughness of the master-and-man relationship, and probably helped to make the North British strike less violent than it was on the Caledonian, and bring it to a slightly earlier end. His almost-constant involvement in promoting new projects, and opposing other companies', took precedence over daily issues like supervision of the company's inadequate provision of rolling stock, locomotives, operational and station facilities. His death left many loose ends of plans and schemes, among them a proposal, forcefully advocated by Randolph Wemyss, for a second dock at Methil. To Wemyss's frustration, this was now put on hold.

Industrialists and the civic authorities in Partick and Scotstoun had for several years felt that the Whiteinch line was quite inadequate for the area's development support and strong local was given to the Caledonian-backed Lanarkshire & Dumbartonshire Railway's proposal to build a new line through the district, much closer to the river than the NBR-worked Glasgow, Yoker & Clydebank line. Its Bill, before Parliament in the Spring of 1891, was strongly opposed by the North British, but was passed by the Lords on 29 July. The Lanarkshire & Dumbartonshire had originally proposed joint ownership of the Whiteinch Railway but North British objections meant it was allowed only to make junctions with it and have running powers. With the prospect of Caledonian competition on the north bank, the North British belatedly sought to formalise its ownership of the Whiteinch Railway, "which they had held for many years in the names of trustees", with a Bill for its formal vesting in the company, along with provision to make it a passenger line[3]. Though passed by the Parliamentary Committee, the vesting proposal was withdrawn by the NBR, because of its unwillingness to concede joint usage of the line. Instead of invoking the running powers, the Lanarkshire & Dumbartonshire Railway decided to supplement its main line (mostly on an embankment) with its own low-level tramway, claiming the decision to be "forced upon them in consequence of the North British Company dropping the powers in their Bill of 1891 to escape the obligations of joint ownership of the Whiteinch Tramway"[4].

The summer of 1891 saw a speeding-up of the East Coast line. From 1 June the night express from London, leaving Kings Cross at 8 pm, now arrived at Waverley at 4.25 am instead of 4.45. An onward connection left at 4.32, arriving at Dundee 5.47 and Aberdeen 7.45. A Perth train left at 5.45, but there was no through service to Inverness until 7 am. Fife in general remained unimpressed by the NBR's service and bells were rung in Kirkcaldy in July 1891 when the Kirkcaldy & District Railway's Bill for a link to the Caledonian at Larbert passed the Commons. But in a clever though deeply devious move the North British counsel, Mr. Bidder, informed the Lords committee that if the Bill were rejected, the NBR was willing to take over the already-authorised lines of the Kirkcaldy & District Railway, and to contribute half the cost of building the Seafield Dock. The Lords rejected the Bill, to the fury of Kirkcaldy. At a protest meeting the Earl of Rosslyn said that "If they allowed the North British to get hold of the dock they were done for". Now the bells rang out in Burntisland, headquarters of the NBR's Fife operations[5]. Though the Caledonian was urged to re-enter the Bill, it did not do so. The NBR's cynical confidence that the other half of the dock costs would never be subscribed was justified by events. The Seafield Dock scheme was dead.

Despite council opposition, the Bill for enlarging Waverley and quadrupling the approach tracks became an Act on 5 August, with some concessions to minimise intrusion on Princes Street Gardens. On its own initiative, the council allowed a slightly wider space for the tracks, in the interests of public safety.

The Select Committee on Railway Servants' Hours heard evidence in mid-July from NBR officials. James McLaren and Matthew Holmes both testified, and could not avoid making it clear that a twelve hour day was on paper only, and that sixteen hour days were still common. Holmes admitted that locomotive crews working Sunday trains had to book off on arrival at the terminus, and book on again before the next journey, to reduce paid time at the Sunday rate. Men might have to wait for four hours between services. Questioned about signalmen's hours, McLaren gave these figures for the North British[6]:

Boxes with eight hour shifts: 122 men
Boxes with ten hour shifts: 70 men
Boxes with twelve hour shifts: 638 men
Single-shift boxes on branch lines: 56 men
Relief signalmen: 42 men

Whistlefield Station on the West Highland Line, above Loch Goil and Loch Long. (*John Alsop*)

Presumably in response to pressure from Lucas & Aird, in April 1891 the NBR board agreed to bring forward its purchase of the contractors' £190,000-worth of West Highland shares to a date not later than October 1893, "irrespective of completion of the line"[7]. Two months later, soon after a ceremonial luncheon at Loch Treig had celebrated completion of the northernmost section, the contractors brought work to a virtual halt in July in a dispute over payments. Rates had been agreed for soil and rock excavation, but now they wanted something better than the soil rate for what they called "mixed soil and rock". The case went to Dumbarton Sheriff Court and then the Court of Session, turning itself into a dispute as to whether the contract price was a "slump sum" (the WHR view) or variable (the contractors' view). Four good building months were largely lost and by 15 October the work force was down to 1,500[8]. The dispute was ultimately resolved by an out-of-court settlement (an additional £10,000 was to be paid). It was hard to get information about what was going on. When the inquiring Moses Buchanan asked about the West Highland at the September half-yearly meeting, Tweeddale blandly replied that "it was a separate concern"[9]. Continuation to the Atlantic coast had not been forgotten. The Fort William line had had no Government subsidy[10], but a line westwards would be another matter. At Fort William the West Highland, when finished, would meet deep tidal water, but fishing boats were most unlikely to make the long sail up Loch Linnhe to unload their catches. To gain the fish traffic, and to link fully into the west coast and Hebridean steamship network, a western terminus and harbour were essential. It would be expensive, and the post-Clearances population was small and impoverished, but a line to such a harbour would 'open up' the district for improvement. Though Roshven remained a possibility, a Loch Eil & Mallaig Railway committee was formed, with a line surveyed by Simpson & Wilson, of Glasgow, to Mallaig Bay. A new report in August by the West Highland Commission, including Sir James King, vice-chairman of the Caledonian Railway, noted six potential rail routes to possible harbours, including the Mallaig line, for which it recommended a Government-guaranteed dividend of 2.5% on capital of £250,000 for four years[11]. It then fell to a three-man Treasury Commission, appointed in May 1891, to pick out one scheme which would receive partial government support. Its members, General Hutchinson, chief of the Board of Trade's railway department, Admiral D.S. Nares, and Henry Tennant, ex-general manager, now a director, of the North Eastern Railway, found the task ultimately impossible. To support the Mallaig extension would preclude any development on the long stretch of coast to the north. But the West Highland was mobilising as much influential opinion as it could for the Mallaig line. In the end the commissioners supported both the Highland Railway's ten-mile extension to Kyle of Lochalsh and the projected Mallaig line. Despite a change of government in 1892, from a Conservative administration willing to shell out to a modest degree in the interest of better communications, fish supplies and – it hoped – a diminution of pressure for Highland land reform, to a Liberal one much less inclined to spend public money in this way, official backing was still promised.

Several senior officials had applied for the general manager's post, among them McDougall the goods manager. Tweeddale and Wieland listened to outside suggestions, and on 11 August an outsider was appointed, John Conacher, manager of the Cambrian Railways, at £2,500 a year. Conacher was a Scot, aged 46, whose early career had been with the Scottish Central, and had a high reputation, but the appointment caused some surprise. Moses Buchanan commented publicly on "able men in the company" being passed over. McDougall was given a substantial pay rise[12]. Conacher was certainly going to be busier on the NBR than on the largely rural Cambrian. The ordinary dividend that autumn was only 1%, traffic receipts were down, and the company, as ever, lacked enough goods wagons for efficient service. Coal traffic was most affected: Addie & Sons, coalmasters of Glasgow, obtained a ruling from the Second Division of the Court of Session that the NBR was bound to supply sufficient wagons and locomotives for their whole traffic[13]. Parliamentary expenses were very high at £37,000 for the half-year (costs of successful Bills were charged to the capital account and failed Bills charged to revenue). Floods in September, with washouts of bridges and embankments on the Waverley Route, were estimated to cost £25,000[14]. North British share prices had fallen well below the other companies' – £100 ordinary were £44 2s 6d and ordinary preferred £70 2s 6d, while Caledonian ordinary rode high at £120 and G&SWR at £103 10s[15].

During October 1891, news stories appeared about an important agreement between the North British and Caledonian companies. This was reached on 31 October[16], though elaboration of details went on, with various elements signed on 4, 5, 6 and 10 May 1892. Its key feature was a 25-year pact, the 'New Lines' or 'Peace' Agreement on future working, classifying traffic as either competitive or non-competitive. On the NBR, non-competitive traffic was reckoned at 47% of the total, on the Caledonian it was only 29%. For competitive traffic, a figure was to be set for gross joint receipts. If this figure were exceeded, 25% of the excess would be taken by each company for working expenses, and the remainder would be shared equally. It had been hoped to draw in the Glasgow & South Western also, but negotiations broke down. Most observers were pleased. The *Times* remarked that the companies "have come to their senses" and that especially on the NBR there was now a need to concentrate on "arrangements which will allow of trains being approximately punctual, and of railway servants being kept on duty for a less exhausting number of hours"[17]. But Glasgow traders did not like the

S.S. Prince George at Balloch Pier   JV 69174

PS *Prince George*, at Balloch Pier, Loch Lomond. (*Stenlake Collection*)

"combination" and the G&SWR and Midland appear to have engaged in some swift undercutting of rates. One significant effect was an end to new wagon-thirling agreements[18]. A newspaper correspondent hoped that this spirit of co-operation would bring an end to the deliberate timing of trains to make bad inter-company connections at Dolphinton and Peebles[19]. The two companies also agreed on joint ownership of the Dumbarton & Balloch Railway and the NBR's Loch Lomond steamboats. The Lanarkshire & Dumbartonshire Railway had not only got authority to build through Scotstoun and Whiteinch, but also to make a competitive line up the Vale of Leven, with its numerous "turkey-red" dyeworks. North British opposition had failed to stave this off with a Bill (given the royal assent on the same day, 5 August 1891) for improved access to the dye-works along the Leven. It was "a triumph for the Caledonian"[20], and a blow to the North British. In the end, local and shareholder objections to the duplication of facilities prevailed. The Dumbarton & Balloch Joint Railway Act was authorised on 27 June 1892, though the arrangement would not come into force until the Lanarkshire & Dumbartonshire Railway completed its line past Whiteinch. The intense railway competition on the north bank of the Clyde was spurred by the shipbuilding boom of the '90s. Clydebank, with 1,632 inhabitants in 1881, was fast becoming a substantial town. The NBR had managed to get a clause inserted in the Lanarkshire & Dumbartonshire's 1891 Act, restraining that company from opposing the extension of the Glasgow, Yoker & Clydebank Railway between Clydebank and Dalmuir[21]. A special meeting of NBR shareholders on 18 February 1892 approved this action, also the company's application to abandon the Tayport-Broughty Ferry service (later withdrawn from the Bill), its withdrawal from involvement in the Clyde, Ardrishaig & Crinan project, and to make further investment in the West Highland. Persistent questioning by Moses Buchanan drew the admission from Tweeddale that this would bring the NBR's involvement up to £375,000[22].

G.B. Wieland intimated his resignation as secretary in February, on the grounds of poor health. It was during his period as acting general manager that the peace agreement was made and he would certainly have been the NBR's prime negotiator. He was presented with three years' salary and elected a director from 17 March. John Cathles was appointed secretary of the NBR, but Wieland continued to be secretary to the associated companies, including the West Highland and Forth Bridge Railways. A *Bailie* profile at the time noted him as "somewhat imperious and arbitrary in his style" and "wonderfully careful in regard to his dress"[23].

Despite overwhelming evidence to show that railway companies routinely exceeded the twelve hour day, the House of Commons decided not to legislate on the matter. Moral pressure, it was felt, could achieve the same end. Considering the conspicuous failure of moral pressure to make the companies instal such safety measures

**The station staff at Newburgh in 1892. The man on the right may just be a passing friend.
It is perhaps unfortunate that the porter is clutching a copy of *The Idler*. (*Stenlake Collection*)**

as interlocking, block working, and continuous brakes, it was a curious decision. For the North British railwaymen, this failure was rubbed in by their manning six special trains to carry Fife and Kinross miners and their families to Perth, for the annual outing and in celebration of the first anniversary of an eight hour day in the region's collieries[24].

From 1 May, the North British abolished second class fares. The only second class traffic now was on the trains to and from England on the East Coast Route. An increase in the sale of first class tickets followed, but first class receipts actually fell by £1,100 between February and August because of a reduction in fares on some routes[25]. A shareholders' meeting on 18 August approved the raising of £1,500,000 in 4% convertible preference stock and £412,826 debentures to pay for the Waverley Station works and other projects, including £210,000 to acquire the Kirkcaldy & District Railway – for railways only: the chairman had told a previous meeting that to complete the Seafield dock would be throwing money into the sea – and the Kirkcaldy & District Railway board was re-formed with NBR directors, and Wieland as secretary[26]. The NBR's 'omnibus' Act that summer contained good news for the Eyemouth Railway. Its original deposit of £2,480, forfeited because of late completion, was to be returned, by agreement with the Treasury[27]. Overall, revenues were on the rise. Gross receipts for the half-year were £1,627,223 compared with £1,553,168 for February-July 1891; while working expenses had risen to a lesser degree, to £845,857 from £839,744. A dividend of 2.5% on the ordinary preference stock was declared[28].

Late in 1892 the North British and the Post Office were again in dispute. The current contract for mail carriage, made in 1890, was worth £30,000 a year (though a Post Office internal minute suggested that this contract had never been executed). On 31 December the NBR gave notice of termination of the contract and requested renewal at £43,000, plus £50 for the Montrose-Bervie line. The Post Office was not satisfied with the company's service, noting that the Down Night Mail, due at Stirling at 6.07 am, had been late on 66 occasions in the course of 1892, by anything between thirteen minutes and two hours eight minutes, missing the 6.20 Balloch line connection. The Post Office proposed a new charge of £32,000, including a provision of £10,000 for 'Notice and Agreement Trains'. Arbitration was invoked to settle the price. In 1892 the NBR carried 3,815 tons of mail. The cost of carrying this at half the company's standard parcel rate would be £13,216, but the arbitrator awarded ⅚ of the parcel rate, equivalent to £22,027. The £32,000 was ultimately accepted by the North British for a five-year period. The company was to provide a sorting carriage or tender for the Berwick route, and in other trains one or two third class compartments "properly fitted up with hooks and sorting boxes". In some cases it seems that the NBR carried mail by goods train, including a St. Boswells-Kelso connection with the Carlisle-Edinburgh Night Mail[29].

The North British side of Stirling Station, with the NBR's 'fish or carriage' trucks, holding carriages on this occasion. The engine looks like one of Drummond's two 2-2-2s, Nos. 474 and 475, of 1876. (*John Alsop*)

The affairs of the Gifford & Garvald Railway went into public crisis when G.B. Wieland, secretary of the company since December 1891, attempted a boardroom coup. He convened a special meeting on 1 September, at which he coolly informed the local directors that they had been replaced by others, including Randolph Wemyss and Henry Grierson, and no longer had anything to do with the company. The ousted directors took their case straight to the Court of Session, which issued an interim, then a perpetual, interdict on the interlopers usurping the position of directors of the company, and on Wieland acting as secretary; and ordered the defenders to pay the complainants' costs. Tweeddale, as chairman, can hardly have been ignorant of Wieland's intention and was not present at the meeting. He resigned from the Gifford & Garvald board on the day after the verdict. The excuse for the action was that the local directors had not formally confirmed the shareholdings necessary for them to be on the board. The actual reason appears to have been frustration with them negotiating "with themselves" over land purchase for the line[30]. The action was extraordinarily high-handed and a blatant breach of company law (the next time Wieland organised a coup, his groundwork was much better). There was no capital subscribed, and the reinstated directors asked the new contractors, Pauling & Elliot, to build the line for a combination of shares and debentures to the value of £110,000, but with no North British backing for the venture, they unsurprisingly declined.

The Royal Commission on Labour heard evidence on 1 November from Conacher, McLaren and Holmes. Conacher said that much had been done to rearrange the North British traffic to improve working hours. Though passenger train drivers sometimes worked an eighteen hour day, there had been only twelve instances in September 1892, compared with 244 in December 1890. Goods drivers had worked eighteen hour days on 122 occasions in September 1892 compared with 3,344 in December 1890. In the mineral areas, there were three classes of driver: regular passenger, regular goods, and mineral men. This third category were hired on a temporary basis according to traffic needs. The company did not offer sick pay. Conacher added that the NBR had no difficulty in finding employees[31].

An undated late-1892 memorandum from the general manager's office noted that the West Highland authorised share issue now amounted to £826,000, far in excess of the figures on which the original dividend calculation was based. On 22 December the board resolved to proceed with an amended agreement only on condition that the option be secured to the NBR of acquiring the West Highland at any time on terms not exceeding the absolute guarantee of 3.5% on the share and loans capital. It was already clear, though kept dark, that the cost of the line would be much more still. Asked by Tweeddale on 9 January 1893 to give a figure, Conacher estimated £950,000[32].

The Government's efforts to exercise a degree of control over railway rates and charges, in the Railway Rates and Charges Act of 1891, seriously underestimated the scale of the task. In common with other companies, the NBR had to compile a new rates book, giving the maximum charges, to come into force from 1 January 1893, but despite a published notice[33], it was not completed in time. There was intense agitation among shippers, and groups representing different trades and localities sought meetings, sometimes jointly with the North British and Caledonian companies. James Thompson of the Caledonian explained to a Dundee deputation, at the North British offices, that the companies were still working on the matter. He also emphasised that many rates had been reduced from 1 January, though the Board of Trade noted few significant reductions. Among the grievances of the shippers was that the railway companies now charged for the return of articles damaged in transit, if sent at owner's risk. Hitherto this had been done free and in the end the action was rescinded except for extra-fragile items. Protests continued to stream in, especially from the dairy and agricultural industries. Livestock shippers were infuriated by the withdrawal of drovers' passes. Lord Tweeddale claimed that on the NBR there was "no increase of any moment made on any part of the line". Some alterations had been made to eliminate "inequalities" and milk rates had not gone up. Many of the complaints centred on small consignments, between one and three hundredweights[34].

Amidst the larger issues, the regular officers' meetings, chaired by the general manager, kept the company's routine affairs in hand. Regular attenders were the general superintendent, with the goods manager, locomotive superintendent, chief engineer, and assistant general manager. District goods managers and traffic superintendents might be called in for specific topics, as well as such officials as the rolling stock and sack superintendents. A typical agenda, on 12 January 1893, shows the range of matters considered[35]:

1. New locomotive shed at Thornton: how to materially reduce the estimated cost of £13,754 1*s*.
2. Accommodation at Thornton for Methil Dock and Branch traffic.
3. Removal of sack store from Markinch to Kirkcaldy.
4. Sidings at Bothwell Junction. Estimated cost £6,632 2*s* 3*d*. No action to be taken.
5. Extension of sidings at Lady Lilian Pit, West Wemyss. £1,832.
6. Additional sidings for 50 wagons at Hill of Beath Colliery.
7. New sidings at Methil Dock. Deferred.
8. Other proposed new sidings: Woodend Junction, Gorgie.
9. Review of line widening at Haymarket.
10. Auchmuty Branch working (eventually, in July, it was resolved to work it with a six-wheel pug which would also shunt at Markinch).
11. Switching out of signal boxes at Milnathort and Loch Leven, at certain times.
12. Extinguishing of signal lamps in daylight.
13. Closure of Blackhall passenger station.
14. Dual brakes for 50 meat vans; old fish wagons to be fitted with Westinghouse brake and vacuum pipe.
15. Lighting at Sighthill and College Yards.
16. Defective loading of wagons.
17. Supply of refreshments to company servants in connection with cattle sales – to be further considered.
18. Review of train and engine mileage.

Items often passed through several meetings before resolution, or presentation to the board or a committee. Numerous meetings considered the problem of storing oil in signal boxes before recommending that separate corrugated-iron oil sheds be put up in all new stations, and added gradually to existing stations (meeting of 8 November 1901).

In 1892 the Glasgow Yoker & Clydebank Railway had failed to get authorisation to extend its line to meet the NBR at Dalmuir, but a new Bill was presented for 1893, with an adjusted guarantee from the NBR to the Glasgow Yoker & Clydebank Railway of 6% on capital, rather than 5.25%. It was approved by a North British shareholders' meeting on 16 February, along with a revised working agreement with the West Highland Railway – still at 50% of gross receipts, but now as a perpetual arrangement, with an absolute guarantee of 3.5% on the total share and loan capital, and any surplus to the NBR only. Tweeddale commented that this arrangement would facilitate raising of the necessary capital, and so relieve the North British and West Highland companies "from the necessity of contributing a large proportion of the capital". Moses Buchanan rose to ask why WHR ordinary shareholders should be guaranteed 3.5% for ever on that company's total outlay, while an ordinary dividend to North British shareholders could be put off year after year. The chairman "thought the arrangement was a satisfactory one from the point of view of the North British Company, and therefore he had nothing more to say about it."[36] But a handwritten memorandum from the general manager's office had noted three months before that even the 3.5% dividend would create a deficit, unless the line earned £14 per mile, a sum exceeding John Walker's already-optimistic estimate of £12 13*s* 6*d*[37]. A WHR meeting next day ratified the changes. Wieland's connections with London stockbrokers ensured, as with the Forth Bridge Railway, that very large share packages were held by these, on the security of the guaranteed dividend. Meanwhile the Bill for the Mallaig line met a technical hitch. The Government was prepared to guarantee the dividend on £260,000-worth of capital, but the figure entered in the Bill was £360,000 (the total estimated cost). Whether this was an oversight or a try-on, it resulted in hasty discussions, with the North British stepping in to guarantee the 'extra' £100,000 and a 3% guaranteed dividend. But the Bill was thrown out on Standing Orders, and had to be re-entered for 1894[38].

Also in February the North British Railway Insurance Society gave a half-yearly report. Conacher, chairman of its management committee, noted a gain of £1,030 in the period, compared with a loss of £181 in the previous half-year. In 1891, 97 Scottish railwaymen were killed on duty, of whom 94 were identified as dying from causes not beyond their own control. Fifty-nine were killed while walking, or crossing, a railway line[39]. Figures from the NBR Insurance Society show from fifteen to 20 deaths a year and many more disabling injuries.

By March the revised rate book was still incomplete, but the half-yearly report said it was being vigorously proceeded with. Meanwhile the Airdrie, Slamannan and Bathgate Coalmasters' Association complained about discriminatory increases compared with the Fife mines, and about a reduced rebate for sending coal by their own wagons. Despite some comments on depressed trade conditions, for the first time, goods traffic alone generated over a million pounds in six months: £1,025,472, with passenger revenue at £640,015. The increase of £35,024 on the corresponding half-year was largely wiped out by a jump in working expenses of £28,469 to £838,430. Ordinary preference shares got their 3% but unconverted ordinary received only 0.75%[40].

The company had switched from opposing the locally-promoted East Fife Central Railway, which had a Bill in Parliament in Spring 1893, to qualified support. It comprised two lines, from the Leven Railway to Ceres and Dairsie plus a branch from Greenside eastwards to meet the Anstruther & St. Andrews line west of Stravithie Station – 25 miles in all. Coal and lime traffic was anticipated, and capital was put at £250,000. The reason for the change of view had to do with the fact that on 14 March 1892, G.B. Wieland had acquired the estate of Letham[41], two miles north of Leven, through which the proposed line would pass. It was a speculative purchase based on the likelihood of workable coal reserves. The promoters met John Conacher in October, to receive the standard NBR answer: no investment, but a willingness to work the line if it was made. In December 1892 Wieland accepted the role of chairman of the East Fife Central committee. Conacher was also in discussion that autumn

CHAPTER FROM RAILWAY HISTORY.

The North British Railway, as seen by a newspaper cartoonist, in the 1890s. (*Author's Collection*)

with the promoters of the Aberlady, Gullane & North Berwick Railway, a line for golfers and commuters, with a capital of £66,000. Again Wieland, with two other NBR directors, was among its backers. Conacher again gave the NBR's standard reply, but also required that the Gullane-North Berwick section be dropped.

More trouble with coalmasters came in July when the NBR put up the Lothian coal rate by 2d per ton-mile. It was claimed that a verbal promise not to raise the rate had been given in 1892, but Conacher disputed this[42]. On the Gifford & Garvald there was a flicker of activity, prompted by Lord Tweeddale. A deviation of the line taking it further into his land was approved, and he rejoined the board. A new Act was obtained on 2 June 1893, but it proved impossible to raise even a reduced capital of £100,000. Wieland's fund-raising wizardry was definitely not available here. On the East Fife Central and the Aberlady, Gullane & North Berwick Railways it would be a different story. Both were authorised on 24 August[43], and Wieland was elected chairman of both boards.

J.P. Pattinson's *British Railways*, published in 1893, described the North British as the largest in Scotland "but scarcely the leading system … that position being still held by the Caledonian", and noted that the company's only trains to run at or over 45 mph were two Down trains between Edinburgh and Dundee, with most running at an average speed of 35 mph or less; and "there is probably no more unpunctual railway in the British Islands than the North British", while in general the stations were undermanned and duties "performed in the most listless manner"[44]. There was much for John Conacher to do.

In July, the East Coast dining car train was inaugurated, on Friday 21st. Running five minutes behind the 2.30pm 'ordinary' from Kings Cross, it had six carriages plus a brake van. There was a kitchen car, with a dining car on each side, which could be rearranged as drawing room cars outside meal times. A first class dinner cost 3s 6d. Forty first and 84 third class passengers were carried. From 24 July, the dining facilities were incorporated into the 2.30 pm. A different sort of passenger train was featured in the newspapers with the report on a derailment of a seventeen-coach workmen's train at Queen Street Low Level on 10 July. It was noted that the driver and fireman had been on duty for twelve hours and 40 minutes when the accident occurred[45].

A strike in the Fife coalfields pulled goods revenue down slightly in 1893 but it remained over the million-pound level for the February-August period. The North British was under pressure from Fife coalowners about loading facilities at its ports. Miners in the English Midlands were on strike at the time and demand from England was strong. They wanted more hoists at Methil and Burntisland, which had seven 'spouts' between them, of which two were said to be inefficient and drew unfavourable comparisons with the Tyne ports and Cardiff. Throughout the summer Conacher was also being hustled by Randolph Wemyss about the halted Methil No. 2 Dock project, Wemyss insisting that increased shipping accommodation was a matter of "absolute necessity"[46]. Conacher temporised, citing the low rates for coal against the investment required and referring to a planned extension of the harbour at Kirkcaldy[47]. Dismissing Conacher's arguments, Wemyss wrote on 29 September 1893 that if the North British did not act, a Bill would be promoted for a new wet dock at Methil with railway connections to the East Fife Central Railway. In November a meeting of Fife coalmasters in Edinburgh again raised the inadequacy of the NBR's provision. Scottish coal exports in 1883 had been 2,531,427 tons and in 1892 had been 4,531,384 tons, and they claimed that the railway company was failing to keep pace with the rising output. David Deuchars, assistant manager to Conacher, made no commitment on behalf of the North British[48].

Though there was a working colliery at Largoward and coal reserves had been identified on its route, the East Fife Central was a speculative line. Despite this, Wieland's influence prevailed on the North British to agree to build it, though the scheme was reduced to only the fourteen mile arm to Lochty, at an estimated cost of £104,820. The best Conacher could do was to extract a five-year guarantee from its directors that they would make up any shortfall on a 3% annual return on this investment. The directors, including Wieland, jointly signed up to this on 14 February 1894. The only one not required to sign was William Taylor, accountant of the Baird Company, who had lent Wieland the money to buy the Letham Estate[49].

Another senior official was lost to the company when James McLaren died suddenly in the guard's van of a Portobello-Edinburgh train on his way to work. Born at Polmont in 1829, he had joined the NBR as a booking clerk at Haddington aged 16. He was 64 and had "never been known to be absent from his post for more than a day or two"[50]. His place was filled by Deuchars from 23 November. G.B. Wieland, now on the board, was guest of honour at a dinner in the Waterloo Hotel on 23 November. He was presented with his portrait, by Luke Fildes RA, silver plate and a cheque for £250, which he in turn donated to the company's friendly assurance society to provide additional annuities for its two oldest members. Lord Tweeddale presided, with many compliments for Wieland's past work[51]. But Wieland was to prove a troublesome director to the chairman.

Tayport Station, with its short overall roof, looking west. The time would seem to be the late 1890s.
(Stenlake Collection)

The dispute over North British access to the station at Aberdeen was revived in 1893 by the station's Joint Committee, with the claim that the running powers over the former Scottish North Eastern Railway did not extend into the station; also that the station was too busy to fit in the NBR trains, which were causing "serious inconvenience" to the GNSR's Deeside line traffic. The committee's case had been rejected by the Court of Session, but an appeal to the House of Lords resulted in a judgement that the North British could not use the station without the consent of the Great North company, and the NBR had to apply for an Act to establish its position[52]. Other problems also beset the new management team. It was a year of coalfield strikes, and in November the miners were out in Lanarkshire, Stirlingshire and the Lothians, with a consequent shortage of coal. The position on the NBR was described as "rather alarming". With scant coal reserves, the company had diverted for its own use some wagonloads consigned elsewhere, and was being forced to pay indemnities and facing litigation. Local goods services were cut back and emergency plans for further cuts were made. The North British usually bought coal at 5s to 7s a ton at the pithead, but coalmasters could get £1 5s a ton for coal sent to England. On 28 November it was reported that work at Cowlairs had to be halted, with 2,000 men idle. Forty-two engines were out of service in the Monklands and fourteen in the Edinburgh district. With fresh supplies, Cowlairs reopened on 3 December[53].

In December 1893 and January 1894 the company sub-licensed David Wilson & Son, of Bo'ness, to operate the ferry services between North and South Queensferry and Tayport-Broughty Ferry, the steamers to be supplied at Wilson's expense. The North British had to provide an annual subsidy of £375 and also advanced money to Wilson to purchase the 32-year old vessel *Forfarshire* for the Tay route.

Waverley Station was still waiting for enlargement. A Bill for the 1894 session included a clause for extension of time to complete the works: building to be finished in 1896, widening not until 1899. The North British also agreed to contribute towards the reconstruction of the North Bridge. Now work went ahead in earnest[54]. A separate major project was the station hotel: in October six architects were invited to submit designs for a wholly new building. By 28 April 1894 an agreement had been made about Aberdeen Station with the owner-companies. The North British would pay £750 each half-year for use of the station, to be increased if the station were enlarged and would pay £7,500 to the Great North of Scotland Railway against previous usage[55].

The Newport Railway Company, with Tweeddale as chairman and Wieland as secretary, paid its usual 4.5% dividend to shareholders[56]. The North British ordinary shareholders got 1%. Working expenses, though still below the level of the 1880s, were rising, 46.09% for August 1893-January 1894 against the previous 45.58%. The half-yearly meeting on 29 March was the company's 100th. Two new directors were elected, Charles Carlow, of the Fife Coal Company, and James Parker Smith, M.P. (Liberal-Unionist) for Glasgow Partick. Almost simultaneously the Wemyss Coal Company was registered, on 17 March. Randolph Wemyss was chairman, and among the directors were Charles Carlow, and George B. Wieland (his address given as Manor House, Shepperton, Middlesex)[57]. A new pit was to be sunk, with a rail connection to the Methil line at Wemyss Castle.

Efforts were still being made by the North British to close the Burntisland-Granton ferry, opposed by, among others, Kirkcaldy Town Council, which was also trying to find a means of compelling the NBR to build the line along the Kirkcaldy shore front which had been authorised in the Kirkcaldy & District Railway Act[58]. At a special meeting on Bills, on 25 May, a short link with the Blackston line, completing the triangular arrangement at Bathgate, and a short extension to a new passenger station at Charlestown found no opposition. Tweeddale defended the £100,000 investment in the Mallaig extension, whose estimated cost was put at £388,000 including the pier. The NBR would work it for 50% of receipts, and "They would obtain a railway 40 miles long at the moderate sum of £100,000." Many discussions had been held on the Waverley expansion scheme, some mooting the abandonment of the North Bridge and the building of a replacement further east; but the town council and the NBR had agreed on a new North Bridge on the same site of three wide arches to cost around £90,000, of which the North British would contribute £30,000. The hotel proposal for Waverley was opposed, as before, by McGregor, without success[59].

An unusual case featured in the press that summer. A fireman and a driver brought assault cases against each other after a footplate fight on the 6.55 am train from Riccarton to Carlisle. While the train ran along at 30 mph, they struggled so violently that the fireman pulled out the driver's beard. It emerged that there was a history of enmity between the pair (the driver was later fined £2[60]). Riccarton's isolated community was not a harmonious one. In more typical mode, the Railway & Canal Commissioners heard a case brought by coalmasters against the North British and the Caledonian's reduction in the rebate for use of their own wagons. It emerged that many wagons were hired out by the builders. Hurst of Motherwell hired out 300 at a minimum of 3s a week and the British Wagon Co., of Rotherham, hired out 18,000 wagons. It was a highly profitable business. J.Y. Pickering, the Wishaw wagon builder, estimated a wagon's life at 20 years, with repairs. On 18 July the Commissioners ruled in favour of the railway companies[61]. By then coal deliveries were disrupted by another miners' strike, following a wage reduction, and between 30 and 40 goods guards at the Kipps yard were given notice by the company. Cowlairs Works were shut down again between 24 and 30 July. The NBR had 110 engines and 400 men idle, but kept the locomotive men on, sharing the work and pay loss. Strikes and lockouts lasted for sixteen weeks in Fife and coal output fell from 3,619,550 tons in 1893 to 2,784,019 tons in 1894. Coal brought from England up the Waverley Route kept other NBR services going[62].

In the early 1890s the Wansbeck Railway gained traffic from the construction work on Catcleugh Reservoir. At Broomhill, close to Woodburn, a siding for pipe traffic was laid, and the contractors built a narrow gauge railway from here to the dam[63].

The running shed at Cowlairs, before the opening of the depot at Eastfield. (*Stenlake Collection*)

15. TWEEDDALE AND CONACHER 2, 1894–1899

Approval of the West Highland line, with its 400 bridges, culverts and cattle creeps, was given by the Board of Trade on 3 August 1894, with the stipulation of an average speed not to exceed 25mph. The highest viaduct was in Glen Falloch, 144 feet, with a 118 feet span; the longest was of nine spans (228 yards) in the Moor of Rannoch, and the summit height at Corrour was 1,350 feet (only 134 feet lower than the Highland's summit at Druimuachdar). Matthew Holmes had produced a new 4-4-0 locomotive class for the line, twelve in 1894 with twelve to follow in 1896, and four complete new trains, each comprising a first class carriage, two thirds and a brake-van. Specially-large windows, 4 feet 6 inches by 2 feet 5 inches, were installed in the first class carriages, with "rather smaller" ones in the thirds. With steam heating, lavatories and gas-lighting, they were said to "exceed in luxury anything at present running on the North British system"[1]. William Arnott, the NBR's agent at Perth, had been appointed District Traffic Superintendent of the line north of Ardlui. Conacher had tried without success to get the mail carriage charge increased to cover the WHR. He eventually procured for the WHR a mail contract worth £350 a year for four years[2] but this did little to stem the deficit.

Services began on the 7th, three passenger trains and one goods each way daily, the best timings being 4 hours 45 minutes Down, and four hours 43 minutes Up for the 122½ miles to Queen Street. The morning Up train included a through carriage to Kings Cross. The timetable showed Inverness as a terminal point, with a Macbrayne steamer connection via the Caledonian Canal. A draft also showed a daily through train from Oban to Glasgow, which did not materialise[3]. Formal opening, by Lady Tweeddale, was on 11 August, with many guests from other companies and a great fireworks display in the evening. In the speeches, Forman praised John Walker, and G.B. Wieland's "ability and financial skill". Lord Tweeddale had some cautionary words. It was now understood that the total construction cost was around £1,100,000, and though he considered the overrun "unavoidable", he noted that "the estimate of return on capital was based upon a very much lower capital expenditure"[4]. In fact he had led the North British into a huge commitment of capital expenditure and guaranteed dividend payments, far beyond what the WHR's four trains a day each way were likely to sustain. Fort William had its railway, but there were protests over the way in which the line cut the town off from the sea front. A promenade, with a "sea fence of an ornamental character" had been mooted originally, but the text of the Act had no mention of this[5]. Only a few days before, on 31 July, the act for the Mallaig Extension had been passed, but no further progress could be made until the Government's own Guarantee Bill, assuring the line's subsidy, was passed. Political opposition from the Liberal side stopped it in 1894, and a two-year hiatus began, while the Highland Railway was building its extension to Kyle.

Meanwhile the Great Glen pact of 1889 was cracking. Prompted by reports of railway surveyors at work in the glen, the Highland company announced a plan for an Inverness-Spean Bridge line, and the West Highland promptly responded with a counter-plan[6]. A timely *Financial Times* editorial in late October remarked, "The West Highland is at best a piece of folly, from the financial point of view … it is, however, whispered in well-informed circles that the main object in view was an invasion of the Highland Railway Company at Inverness … It is clear that the Caledonian and Highland Directors do not treat the West Highland as being guaranteed by the North British for the sake of the West Highland's own sweet self." Both companies published draft Bills in the same issue of the *Edinburgh Gazette*[7]. Somewhat belatedly, the two chairmen began to patch things up. Tweeddale (who was himself a HR director) suggested that the Highland might have mistakenly assumed that the surveyors were from the NBR. Eneas Mackintosh of Raigmore, the HR chairman, replied that they had thought the surveyors were from an "independent company" and had acted because any delay would have put them at a disadvantage[8].

As part of a drive to improve the NBR's not very strong *esprit de corps*, John Conacher introduced an annual prize system for "best-kept station" in 1892. An awards list was published each August, with four classes of station. From 1895 20 first class prizes of £4, 30 second class prizes of £3, 40 third class prizes of £2 and 50 fourth class prizes of £1 were awarded[9].

In September a passenger service to Charlestown was restored, after many years, with a new terminus on a short extension beyond the harbour. Seven trains each way on weekdays (eight on Mondays) took ten minutes from Dunfermline Lower[10], and twelve back uphill. That month the unconverted ordinary dividend was 0.25% and deferred ordinary got nothing. Tweeddale blamed the coal strike – still on, though many miners were returning to work – for knocking 0.5% off the dividend. The Forth and Tay ferries were still being run by the North British, but if it was keen to divest itself of these responsibilities, there was another which it wanted to assume. English expresses between Edinburgh and Berwick were still hauled by North Eastern engines, as they had been since 1869. Re-negotiation of the rate to be paid by the North British failed to reach agreement and with the reconstruction of Waverley Station underway, the NBR felt the time was ripe for its own locomotives to haul these trains over its own line, and the agreement was terminated. The NER refused to accept this, claiming that the running powers granted them in 1862 effectively confined the North British to local services, and the NBR took the case to the Railway & Canal Commission in November[11].

The company's 'Omnibus Bill' for the 1895 Parliamentary session included the doubling of the tunnel at Dalreoch on the Helensburgh/West Highland line, new mineral branches in Fife, the take over of the East Fife Central, and a modification of the guarantee to the West Highland. Instead of paying 3.5% per annum on each £100 of capital, it would be 3% on each £116 13s 4d. West Highland authorised capital was by now £800,000. It was hoped that

Charlestown Harbour at low tide. A view taken after the opening of the passenger station in 1894.
(*Stenlake Collection*)

the East Fife Central line would be a coal feeder and the Bill provided for its vesting in the North British at a time to be agreed. On 17 January 1895 the time was set to be within one of year of the Act or on completion; with the NBR working the line at 40% of gross receipts[12], an unusually low rate. Tweeddale had said in May 1893 that the terms would be identical to the Aberlady line's, but the Aberlady terms were 50%. A contract for making the line to Lochty had been made on 6 November 1894 with John Howard, for £77,457 excluding land; the original agreed fee was reduced by £7,000 after James Carswell complained it was too high. Howard, a London contractor, had been the contractor for the abortive Seafield Dock and the Kirkcaldy & District Railway. Wieland was responsible for negotiating the termination and truncation of these projects and it may be that NBR-related contracts awarded to Howard had a compensatory aspect. In any case, he had become a friend and business associate of Wieland's[13]. Work did not begin until August 1895. Trading conditions were difficult at this time, and though passenger numbers were rising, there was a large drop of £56,053 in goods receipts in the August-February half-year. The preferred ordinary dividend was cut back to 1.5% and unconverted ordinary got nothing.

Few winters passed without snow blocks on one or more of the upland lines. The West Highland was particularly vulnerable, and the events of 21 January 1895 are not untypical. Locomotives 645 (with a large snowplough) and 663, left Cowlairs at 10.40pm to clear drifts at Crianlarich, arriving there at 5.35 next morning having cleared the line. A balllast engine and three vehicles were snowed up on the loop line. The engine was pulled out, but the vehicles were derailed, and had to be re-railed. When the snowplough engines tried to clear the loop, their wheels rode up on hard-packed snow and both left the line, at about 8 am. The breakdown train was despatched from Cowlairs. By 5 pm both engines were back on the rails. The North British tried, in vain, to get the WHR to pay extra for snow-clearing costs, adeptly fended off by Wieland in his role as West Highland secretary. There were also spats between Carswell and Arnott, divisional traffic superintendent, about who was authorised to order out the snowplough (Arnott always seemed to pinch the engineers' ballast engine)[14].

As port owners of Silloth, the company paid £890 for a 45-year old sailing vessel as a new Solway lightship[15]. At the March half-yearly meeting, the chairman defended the controversial introduction of a new eye-test for staff. A number of elderly signalmen and drivers had been dismissed for failing it, and there were accusations of victimisation. Holmgren's test for colour identification, and the Army spot test, were recommended to railway companies by the Board of Trade, but not obligatory. Defending it, Tweeddale claimed the NBR was being considerate to elderly employees who failed it, adding that 4% of the drivers and firemen were found to be colour-blind[16].

Holmes 0-6-0 No. 607 of 1888, with snowplough, photographed after introduction of the control system. Baxter notes that this engine was fitted with a tender cab in August 1915.(*Stenlake Collection*)

A party from the Kirkcaldy Field Club came to explore the cuttings of the Cowdenbeath-Invertiel Junction line in 1896. A contractor's engine heads the train.

Complaints over railway rates continued. Section 1, sub-section 3 of the Railway Rates Act enabled traders to complain to the Board of Trade about increases considered to be unfair. If the Board of Trade could not settle the matter, it went to the Railway & Canal Commission. In August, Kirkcaldy Chamber of Commerce raised a complaint over rate increases. Fully aware that the North British had put £210,000 into the Kirkcaldy & District Railway purely to snatch it from the Caledonian embrace, the Chamber also complained that the NBR was asking leave to abandon approved Kirkcaldy & District Railway plans for lines linking Kirkcaldy with the coalfield, and was seeking a delay on building the Kirkcaldy foreshore line from Seafield just to keep other companies out. Whenever they could, the Kirkcaldy shippers were diverting their traffic via the Caledonian[17]. Meanwhile on 4 July the Lords approved the NBR's Bill to absorb the Kirkcaldy & District Railway and to complete a line from Foulford Junction, on the Cowdenbeath-Thornton section, to Invertiel, just west of Kirkcaldy. This was all the NBR ever built of the projected Kirkcaldy & District Railway lines, and to add to Kirkcaldy's chagrin, the Invertiel junction faced west, directing traffic to Burntisland, rather than towards Kirkcaldy[18].

The promoters of the Mallaig extension had to sweat before a reluctant Liberal government finally set out the terms, a 3% guarantee from the Treasury on £260,000 of capital invested in the new line, plus a grant of £30,000 towards turning Mallaig into a functioning harbour – all confirmed on 7 May 1895. It was a unique commitment in a country where railways had always been expected to pay their own way. Then a further general election intervened and it was 14 August 1896 when under a new (Conservative) government, not without very considerable discussion and afterthoughts, the necessary Act was authorised. Simpson & Wilson, of Glasgow, were the engineers, and the contractors were Robert McAlpine & Sons, whose price for the 41¾-mile line with eleven tunnels, a swing bridge over the Caledonian Canal, and many bridges including the 21-arched Glenfinnan Viaduct, was £234,016 16s. G.B. Wieland remained in a peculiar position at this time, as both a North British director and secretary to the West Highland company. In the latter role he was the servant of the WHR board which occasionally asserted its own views against those of the North British board[19].

Following the heavy wobble in the Great Glen pact, the West Highland and Highland companies agreed to withdraw their competing Bills and not to re-embark on a railway between Banavie (the WHR branch to the Caledonian Canal opened on 1 June 1895) and Inverness without giving the other full notice of such intention well in advance[20]. Something similar happened south of Fort William. The Callander & Oban company had proposed to build a line from Connel Ferry north to meet the West Highland at Banavie. Given the 'New Lines' agreement between the NBR and the Caledonian, this was seen as a revival of old provocations. Legal action and

Banavie Station and quay with PS *Gondolier* about to depart, circa 1905. Engine No. 343 is one of the 'West Highland Bogies', built in 1896. (*Stenlake Collection*)

negotiations between the general managers resulted in acceptance that the Caledonian could support a line as far as South Ballachulish, leaving (for a 10-year period) the NBR free to build a line from Fort William to North Ballachulish. Joint arrangements could be made for a crossing of Loch Leven. At this time the Ballachulish slate quarries had an output of around 19,000 tons a year and employed 400 men and boys. Slate went out, and coal for the works came in, on small coastal ships[21].

During July and August 1895 the old rivalry between the East Coast and West Coast Routes boiled up in the 'Races to the North'. The reasons are not altogether clear, and may owe something to the personal character of the Great Northern and the North Eastern general managers, as well as to the earlier frustrations at Waverley. Both English companies had invested large sums in the Forth Bridge and perhaps felt that, with the shortest route between London and Aberdeen, the East Coast was entitled to provide the fastest service. The West Coast companies were not prepared to ignore a challenge. One historian called the races "grand, heroic", another "Midsummer madness"[22], and there was truth in both comments. The brief episode has been amply covered in other books and articles. What should be stressed is that the North British was at first highly reluctant to run 'racing' trains and only participated when guarantees against losses were offered by the English companies. Its locomotive dispute with the NER was still *sub judice*, and it did not want to prejudice its relationship with the Midland company. Senior East Coast officials met regularly to discuss traffic needs and plans. It was unusual for locomotive chiefs to attend, but Holmes was with Deuchars at York on 13 August 1895 when it was agreed to accelerate the 8 pm from Kings Cross from the 19th to the 23rd, then revert to the published timetable – the faster timing was not to be advertised. With a maximum loading of eight vehicles including one sleeping car, the train would arrive in Aberdeen at 5.40 am. On 20 August the officials met in Edinburgh, with Deuchars in the chair, and agreed that the line ahead of the 8 pm would be kept clear for ten minutes on the GN and NER, and for fifteen minutes on the North British. Leaving Edinburgh at 2.43 am after a three minute stop, arriving at Dundee at 3.48 and leaving two minutes later, the train would pass Kinnaber Junction at 4.31 and be in Aberdeen by 5.13 if not earlier: "the arrangement being that the NB Co. should run as much before these times as possible." That same night, the 8 pm, formed of one sleeping car, one corridor composite, two corridor thirds and two brake vans, arrived in Edinburgh 1½ minutes late, at 2.41½ am. Waverley's Stationmaster, W.H. Paton, supervised the engine change and detachment of one carriage, which took 2½ minutes. Leaving Edinburgh at 2.44 am, it arrived in Dundee exactly one hour later. Changing engines took two minutes and it left at 3.46 for a non-stop run to Aberdeen, arriving at 5.11½ am. It carried 35 passengers[23]. But the West Coast train was there already. Next day, though, the East Coast won by 14½ minutes.

Though not a racing destination, Glasgow was not neglected, and the 20 August meeting agreed to run the 10.40 pm Edinburgh-London train in two portions, the first with Edinburgh and Perth passengers; the second, at 11.00, with passengers from Aberdeen and Glasgow. This enabled the 9.05 Glasgow-Edinburgh express to leave at 9.45. The meetings more routinely discussed fish, which was carried at express speed, usually on passenger trains. Aberdeen had a fish-only express, leaving at 1.05 pm, but on 8 October 1895 the East Coast officials dropped this, opting to attach the fish trucks to the 1.25 passenger train to Edinburgh, and then to a new 6.15 pm passenger/fish train to London, arriving in Kings Cross at 3.45 am[24]. In August it was also announced that the Arbroath-Montrose line would be doubled.

When the half-yearly accounts were published in September, once again the unconverted ordinary shares got no dividend. The accounts were challenged by a *Glasgow Herald* correspondent, signing himself 'Accountant', for inaccuracies and understatement of receipts and costs. Responding to this at the half-yearly meeting on 27 September, Tweeddale explained the discrepancy between the current and previous accounts, with differing figures for receipts and expenditure:

> "It was for many years our practice to exclude from our gross revenue accounts certain receipts, amounting in all to about £24,000 a year, and to deduct them from various items of expenditure. Why this method … was adopted is not very clear".

The company had decided to discontinue the practice, hence the discrepancy. No-one sought elucidation of this opaque statement. The chairman also gave an explanation for the delay in opening the junction between the West Highland and the Callander & Oban lines at Crianlarich. A piece of land was needed whose owner refused to sell it unless the refreshment room at the West Highland station were closed and customers directed to a hotel he proposed to erect, about 150 yards away. Offers of eight times the real value of the ground had been refused, and now the company was seeking compulsory purchase powers[25]. In October a fire destroyed the stores depot at Cowlairs, causing damage estimated at £12-15,000, fortunately covered by insurance[26].

The NBR and G&SWR decided that dissolution and division of the City of Glasgow Union railway was a better option than joint ownership, with the North British taking possession of the lines north and east from College

Waverley Station and North Bridge reconstruction, circa 1896. North Eastern engines on express in foreground. (*John Alsop*)

East Junction, and converting 40% of the debenture and preference stocks of the City of Glasgow Union Railway to NBR debenture and consolidated lien stock. The City of Glasgow Union Railway ordinary stock was split 50/50, and the South Western paid the NBR an equalising amount of £45,000 (duly ratified by an Act of Parliament in July 1896). The NBR had an 'omnibus' Bill including a railway from Fort William to North Ballachulish, with a tramway link on a swing road bridge over Loch Leven to the slate quarries. The Lords passed the railway but not the tramway[27], and the company abandoned the scheme, which was never envisaged (at least by the NBR) as providing a through line between Connel Ferry Junction and Fort William. The Callander & Oban Railway's Connel-South Ballachulish line was also authorised and eventually opened in 1903.

At Burntisland an important thirling agreement was concluded on 20 February 1896, backdated to 31 October 1895 (when the negotiations began), between the North British, the Harbour Commissioners, and thirteen coal and iron companies in Fife, including Charles Carlow's Fife Coal Co. The coalmasters committed themselves to ship only from the NBR Fife ports for 21 years, and not to construct or promote new railways in Fife. The railway company bound itself not to increase dues at Methil in the duration of the agreement[28]. In Edinburgh, tuning of the great Waverley project continued, though the council was irritated by the slow progress of the main works, five months behind schedule in April 1896. On 25 May the foundation stone of the new North Bridge was laid, with Masonic pomp and ceremony[29].

Some interesting details were passed on by the chairman at the half-yearly meeting of 26 March. The company now had 23,600 shareholders. The number of third class passengers had shot up – 1,140,270 more than in the 1894-95 half-year, an increase largely ascribed to cheap weekend excursion tickets. A special charge of £2,000 was caused by the alteration of signal glasses to show red or green in darkness, rather than red or white as before. Not least, all passenger lines were now worked on the absolute block system. Working expenses were down from 49.43% of gross receipts to 46.8%. Unconverted ordinary shares got a dividend of 1.25%[30].

There can have been hardly a glen in the western Highlands which Charles Forman did not explore with the notion of building a railway through it. The mutual rivalries and suspicions of the North British and Caledonian companies were ready-made for his leverage, making each think it had better get involved before the other stole a march on it. He was involved with yet another Great Glen venture, the Invergarry & Fort Augustus Railway, which got an Act on 14 August 1896. To the Parliamentary committee, he gave his view of his own achievement: "I have in some districts made two blades of grass to grow where only one grew before, and that is, perhaps, one of the highest functions a man can perform for his country"[31]. Sponsored by local proprietors including Lord

The new Waverley Bridge of 1896. (*Stenlake Collection*)

Additional tunnel being dug beneath The Mound, Edinburgh, around 1897-8.
(*North British Railway Study Group*)

Abinger, the line was claimed as "local", linking Fort Augustus (population under 500) with the WHR at Spean Bridge, but was generally assumed to have a speculative purpose, either as a line to Inverness, or to sell out profitably to one of the big contenders. Fort Augustus was only 30 miles from Inverness. The original Invergarry & Fort Augustus Railway survey had gone as far as Invermoriston[32].

Racing rivalry was threatened again in the summer of 1896. The East Coast managers, with Conacher representing the NBR, decided that their response to the West Coast companies' demands for equal timings should be "equality in relation to distance", their London-Edinburgh route being seven miles and 24 chains shorter, and to Aberdeen sixteen miles and 30 chains shorter. Observing in June that the West Coast night train to Aberdeen had been speeded up by $\frac{1}{2}$ hour, to leave Euston at 8 pm and arrive in Aberdeen at 8 am, they retimed the 7.20 from Kings Cross, due in Aberdeen at 7.10 am, to leave at 7.45 and reach Aberdeen at 7.30. Next day they met West Coast officials and agreed to give each other a month's notice of any changes to the timetables. There was no repetition of the bravura running of 1895. Conacher was more concerned to get payment of £2,000 of East Coast guarantees against running underused trains[33].

On Saturday 20 June, around 11,000 children and adults were carried on Sunday School outings by the North British. In normal service, extensive rearrangements to the timetable were made from 1 July, with the aim of increasing efficiency and satisfying the public. Greenock commuters were encouraged to take the ferry across to Craigendoran and catch a North British train to stations right across Glasgow and on to the east. In a year of self-congratulation by the board, it was inevitable that the working hours issue should again be raised. A deputation to the management in January received no answer until June, when a circular from Conacher said that the company had made great efforts to reduce the booked time of all goods trains to a maximum of $10\frac{1}{2}$ hours a day. The shunters' request for an eight hour day was flatly refused: twelve hours, with two hours allowed for meals, was "reasonable and usual"[34]. This did nothing to placate the men, aware that meal breaks were often ignored and that booked time had little to do with actual time. Many NBR families lived in the old buildings clustered to the east of Waverley Station, and with the demolition of these properties to make way for station enlargement,

Alloa Station looking east, circa 1910. (*North British Railway Study Group*)

the company built ten tenement blocks of 120 new homes at Pleasance, of single or two apartments. The one-roomed dwellings were fitted with two wall-beds and shared a water closet between two. There were six common bathrooms, and eighteen common wash-houses with fixed earthenware tubs and clothes boilers. The number of inhabitants was 828. Two breweries had also been demolished to make room for the approach tracks from the second Calton Tunnel, and one-room dwellings "best of their kind in the kingdom" were put up to rehouse their workers. By June 1896 the Canal Street offices were also cleared and ready for demolition, with the staff dispersed in temporary accommodation. The new Waverley Bridge came into use from 28 July[35].

John Conacher made a report to the board on 16 July about the Halbeath Tramway. It had not operated since 1871 and all the rails had been lifted except for 300 yards to Inverkeithing Brickworks and 377 yards alongside the public road near Halbeath Station. Three sections were held by the NBR on leases, expiring variously in 1896, 1898 and 1938. Conacher recommended letting the leases expire, but for the NBR to keep the "main line" of around $3\,^3/_4$ miles, which was rented out to a Mr. Street[36].

With the opening, for goods and minerals, of the Lanarkshire & Dumbartonshire Railway on 1 October, the terms of the Dumbarton & Balloch Joint Railway Act of 1892 came into operation. Sale of the Loch Lomond steamers to the joint operation brought the NBR £30,000, but still, as John McGregor observes, the Caledonian's appearance in Dunbartonshire was "a major setback for the North British"[37]. A secretary-manager was appointed to run the enterprise. The line, seven miles and 24 chains long, had eleven miles ten chains of sidings, indicative of its industrial traffic. Less co-operation was seen at Crianlarich where the NBR-CR junction was still not in use. A letter from G.B. Wieland, in his persona as secretary of the WHR, advised Conacher in July 1896 that "… an agreement has been concluded with Mr. Place which will enable us to open the Crianlarich loop"[38]. The Marquis of Breadalbane suggested that the NBR was forcing traffic from the East to Fort William and Mallaig to go round via Glasgow: since the Mallaig extension was being financed by public money, this would not do[39]. The North British, which had been refused running powers between Crianlarich and Oban, was in no hurry: McDougall, the goods manager, was keen to see the junction in use, but Conacher and Deuchars were both against spending money on it[40]. By 22 December Carswell confirmed the link was complete and Major Marindin of the Board of Trade passed it for passenger use on 12 January 1897. Deuchars had suggested that a pilot engine would have to be kept at Crianlarich, but McDougall arranged for traffic exchange once a day, between 11 and 12 am, using "the ordinary goods engine"[41].

Even before work had started on the Invergarry & Fort Augustus line, the North British resumed its attempt to get to Inverness, with a new Bill for a Fort Augustus-Inverness railway, involving running powers over the Invergarry & Fort Augustus Railway. Unlike the previous Bill, which had been nominally a West Highland one, this was a NBR Bill: a powerful hint to such independently-minded members of the WHR board as Lochiel, and their secretary, of who held the purse-strings. The Invergarry company followed suit with its own Bill for an Inverness extension, and the Highland Railway also entered a Bill. This marked the peak of the "Great Glen War", but all three were rejected by Parliament[42].

Despite the NBR's investment in the Bo'ness Dock, relations with the town had deteriorated. Increased facilities were demanded, and the company's rates and charges criticised as excessive. This had much to do with the Caledonian's expansion plans for nearby Grangemouth, and the Bo'ness Commissioners' large debts. A Bill was introduced to transfer their half-share in the dock to the Caledonian, and for the Caledonian to have running powers to Bo'ness[43]. The North British (which had running powers into Grangemouth since 1867) petitioned against the Bill.

Late in November 1896 the dispute between the NBR and NER on whose engines should work the English services between Berwick and Edinburgh was on appeal in the House of Lords, the Court of Session having ruled against the North British. The NER argued that absolute control of the Anglo-Scottish traffic was essential to maintain the competitive position of the East Coast Route. It was paying the whole receipts of the Scottish section to the NBR, less a deduction of 7.48d per train-mile. In December the Lords gave a judgement requiring the NER to either get the consent of the North British or obtain an order from the Railway and Canal Commissioners confirming their right to run all the through trains. The Commissioners agreed that the NER's application should be withdrawn, and a temporary arrangement was made under which the NER ran three of the ten non-stop trains, and the NBR worked the rest. In January Lord Trayner for the Railway and Canal Commission gave judgement in favour of the North British as exercising its legal rights[44], but the North Eastern promptly re-applied for an order to allow exercise of its running powers, with an interdict against the North British "interfering" with the East Coast traffic. On 14 January the temporary arrangement expired, and the North British took over all trains from and to Berwick, with the NER making engine-changing as difficult as possible. With much public attention focused on the dispute, the NBR was on its mettle to keep time and Conacher, regularly quizzed by newspapers, claimed that the service was "better than ever" and denied that

Castlecary Station in the early twentieth century. The kilns are part of the Castlecary Fire Clay and Lime Works. (*John Alsop*)

The holiday season at Berwick in the 1900s, with a train of East Coast Joint Stock carriages under the overall roof, and trolley-loads of luggage. (*John Alsop*)

double-heading of trains was different to any other section of the line[45]. A new judgement from the Railway and Canal Commission on 10 March allowed for equal division of the services, with gross receipts payable to the North British after a 25% deduction of operating costs by the NER[46]. Still contending with the "ten hours movement", in a letter of 17 December 1896 Conacher regretted that the directors could not accede to the request, but said that the busiest yards, Carlisle, Portobello, Niddrie West, South Leith, Sighthill and Dundee, would be reorganised to work three eight hour shifts, without meal breaks. As on other railways, ambulance teams were now organised at bigger stations and depots, and a third annual competition among them was won by Portobello in April 1897[47].

Large-scale house-building on the west side of Glasgow was reflected by the erection of a passenger terminus on the Whiteinch Railway at Victoria Park, with services from 14 December 1896. Unlike Hyndland, it was a utilitarian wooden structure. The NBR's General Purposes Act of 1891 had given powers to adapt the line for passenger use, and seventeen trains ran each way to and from Bridgeton Cross. At this time the Jordanhill-Clydebank line was being doubled, and the Glasgow, Yoker & Clydebank's extension to Dalmuir opened on 8 May 1897, with a new Clydebank Station. The terminus, renamed Clydebank East, was retained and numerous Hyndland services were transferred there. The Glasgow, Yoker & Clydebank Railway was amalgamated into the North British on 15 July, with each of its shares, guaranteed a return of 6% a year from completion of the Dalmuir extension, exchanged for two NBR consolidated lien shares paying 3%. Its 4% debentures, purchased by Wieland in 1888, were exchanged for certificates of an equivalent amount of NBR stock, at the same rate of interest[48]. In the same area, what ownership of the Whiteinch Tramway section really meant became a vexed question: back in 1880 the NBR had failed to appreciate that a tramway did not have the statutory rights of a railway, and that the owners of the land could pull up the rails without offering an alternative route. The Park Yard Company, shareholders in the Lanarkshire & Dumbartonshire Railway, with its competing tramway, was demanding that the NBR lift the tram-rails where they crossed its ground. Earlier in the year the North British had re-applied to Parliament for the vesting of the Whiteinch Railway and Tramway, but withdrew the clause from its Bill because of ongoing litigation with Park Yard. The case finally went to the House of Lords who ruled in favour of the NBR in July 1898. Having established its right to maintain the tramway, the North British ceased to pursue the vesting issue, though it would recur later[49].

The dividend paid on ordinary unconverted shares for the half-year to 31 January 1897 was 1.25%. James Carswell, the chief engineer, died that month; he was replaced by his assistant, James Bell Jr., whose father had held the same post. Carswell's own son was district engineer in Glasgow[50]. At a special meeting on 6 May, shareholders approved the company's proposals to work the Newburgh & North Fife Railway at 4% per annum on its proposed capital of £180,000. The Light Railways Act of 1896 sparked numerous new or revived proposals, with old plans now projected as light railways between Arrochar and a site on Loch Fyne opposite Inveraray, and from Ormiston to the East Lothian villages of Gifford and Garvald also approved[51].

One of the general manager's tasks was to run the North British Railway Insurance Society. Going back to 1855, this body, funded by contributions from employees and company, gave regular donations to hospitals, and paid small pensions and awards for injury. Its half-yearly meeting in February 1897 recorded twelve fatal accidents (£541 18s paid out), five men permanently disabled (£64), and 342 temporarily disabled (£610). There were 8,366 members[52].

In May 1897 Parliament rejected Caledonian joint ownership of Bo'ness Dock, but allowed CR running powers "in the public interest", with the CR paying £1,000 a year to the North British. Rates at Bo'ness and Grangemouth were to be equal until the new Grangemouth Docks opened[53]. The coal trade was booming. From the strike year of 1894 Fife's output went up from 2,784,019 tons to 5,419,373 tons in 1900 and continued to rise. Also in May Randolph Wemyss gave notice to the North British of his intention to build a private railway across his estate to the docks at Methil. It was a novelty for a board member to propose to build a railway in direct competition to the NBR, but not a bombshell, since he had been discussing the idea with Conacher since October 1894. Conacher had conceded that despite the provisions of the purchase agreement of 1878, Wemyss was entitled to build a line to carry his own coal, but not that of his tenants or of other coalmasters. He was instructed by the board to inform Wemyss that his railway would have no running powers over NBR lines into Methil Docks. Wemyss interpreted the agreement differently, writing in August 1897 to Conacher that "there is nothing after the welfare of Wemyss that I desire so much as the prosperity of the North British Railway …", but he wanted control of the traffic "within the four walls of the Wemyss Estate"[54]. He was owner of the small harbour of West Wemyss which exported around 50,000 tons of coal a year but was not suitable for expansion, and was busy setting up the Wemyss Colliery Trust to acquire, by perpetual feu, the coalfields belonging to the estate. On 28 October 1897 the subscription list closed. Its directors included Randolph Wemyss, G.B. Wieland, and Henry Grierson[55]. Conacher had the task of dealing with a company that had three NBR directors on its board. In 1898 the North British carried 547,456 tons of coal from Wemyss's pits (excluding the Randolph pit) for £8,5312, generating a profit of around £4,905. This tonnage might go up, and on that basis Wemyss demanded £3,000 a year for 30 years in return for dropping his Estate Railway scheme. Conacher (in a paper written for the board early in 1899) appeared to think that was "not unfair", but because Wemyss was a director, the payment would need Parliamentary sanction, which would take time, and meanwhile Wemyss was already demanding £3,000 recompense for the delay in starting on his railway, writing to Conacher on 23 November: "Rights are Rights which admit of no compromise of principal [sic]". Around 27 November an undated letter sent by Wieland, from the Junior Carlton Club in London, to Conacher, expressed the hope that Wemyss could be appeased because otherwise he would make trouble. Conacher replied, a little stiffly, that Wemyss refused to listen to anything short of full concession even though he agreed that the NBR had made him a liberal offer; adding that he, Conacher, "will never purchase [a compromise] by sacrificing what I regard as the interests of the shareholders on a very important question." He ended by asking Wieland to make his own suggestions, but it does not seem that Wieland replied[56]. Conacher would certainly have been aware of Wieland's interest in the Wemyss Colliery Trust. Eventually, since Wemyss would not budge, the dispute was referred to arbitration.

The same trio of directors set themselves up as an opposition faction on the board, voting regularly against motions proposed by the chairman and, from later accounts, behaving in a disrespectful and even disruptive manner at meetings. The Laird of Wemyss was a wild card. Wieland was generally supposed to have taken against Conacher; Grierson's motives are more obscure, though he was a Stock Exchange speculator, and maybe expected to benefit from his association with the Wemyss Colliery Trust. Aged 71, a partner in George Gordon & Co., Glasgow shipowners, he held over £200,000 of NBR stock and until now had sat on the board for 27 years without uttering a contrary word.

Among the Newcastle-Edinburgh trains in 1897 were two carrying sorting tenders for mail, the Down services leaving Newcastle at 3.37 pm and 2.55 am, arriving at Waverley at 6.30 pm and 6.00 am; the Up services leaving Waverley at 1.50 pm and 6.30 pm, arriving in Newcastle at 11.00 and 6.38 pm. The Day Mail had three NER vehicles and in 1897 was also using NBR mail carriage No. 1, built in 1885, 28 feet 6 inches long, without automatic apparatus. The Night Mail used NBR vehicles built in 1885 and 1891, Nos. 5 and 6, both 32 feet long with a pick-up net and two arms. By 1897 automatic mail pick-up apparatus had been installed at Dunbar, Drem, Longniddry, Inveresk, Portobello, Corstorphine, Aberdour, Burntisland, Kinghorn, Dysart, Markinch, Falkland Road, Ladybank, Springfield, and Leuchars[57]. The Day Mail ended on 30 September 1908 when the London-Newcastle Travelling Post Office service was extended to Edinburgh.

In February 1897 a shareholders' meeting of the Anstruther & St. Andrews Railway had agreed to a takeover by the North British, confirmed by an Act of 15 July. Holders of the 5,700 Anstruther & St. Andrews Railway £10 ordinary shares received £3 10s per share; preference shareholders, with £55,000 of capital and a 5% dividend, had to accept NBR preference shares at 3% instead. Five passenger trains ran each way daily. Edinburgh's new North Bridge was formally opened on 15 September 1897, high above the roofs of Waverley, where the work of extension was still going on (John Conacher, in the course of a rather banal speech at the NBR's second social gathering of Edinburgh staff, on 12 January 1898, joked that a man who went to sleep, Rip van Winkle-style, for 100 years, asked when he woke up, 'Is Waverley Station finished yet?'[58]). The company's new hotel building, also under construction, was to house the offices as well, but a board meeting of 16 December 1897 voted to use all the rooms for hotel purposes. By chance, the nearby Waterloo Hotel, venue of many past meetings, was for sale, and the NBR bought it for £44,000 to use as offices, with entry from 15 March 1898.

That autumn the ordinary dividend was 1%, and NBR £100 ordinary shares were at £41 5s. Ordinary preferred, which had consistently paid their 3% since 1893, were just above par, £100 1s 3d – their highest price so far[59]. In October the NBR was back before the Railway & Canal Commissioners, in a case brought by the Caledonian, Highland and Great North companies, claiming a share of the extra nineteen mile "bonus mileage" added to fares and rates on the Forth Bridge route[60]. The Commissioners also yet again considered the issue of whose engines should work the East Coast expresses (the NER had gone back to the Court of Session, which again remitted the case to the Railway & Canal Commission) and reiterated their decision of March 1897 for equal sharing of the task[61]. The GNR and NER also unsuccessfully sought an order to compel the North British, under the terms of the NBR/E&G Amalgamation Act of 1865, to have all passenger traffic, including fish by passenger train, delivered to them at Edinburgh[62].

In the late 1890s work began on the Caledonian's line across Leith to Seafield. It was intended for passengers as well as goods, and the North British responded by starting to build the mile-long branch, authorised on 5 August 1891, to run from a junction between Abbeyhill and Easter Road, passing under the Caledonian line to a new Leith Central terminus. On 12 August 1898 its 'general purposes' act included another short Edinburgh branch, to Corstorphine. These moves disturbed the 'peace agreement' of 1891 but went ahead. A proposal at this time to extend the Whiteinch Tramway west of Scotstoun Street was contested by the Lanarkshire & Dumbartonshire, and rejected by arbitration in May 1899[63].

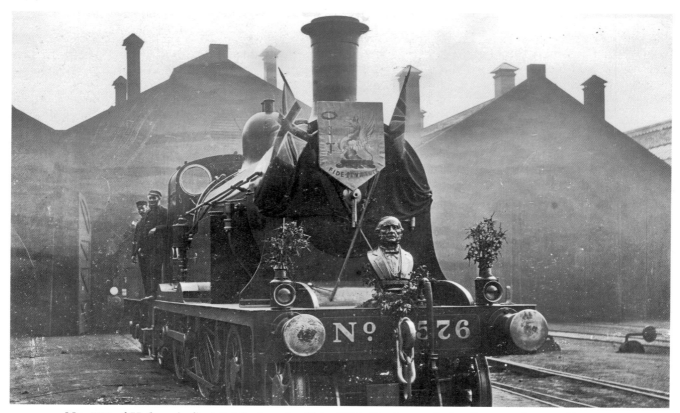

No. 576 of Holmes's first 4-4-0 class, built in 1884. It appears to be decorated as a tribute to William Ewart Gladstone, who died in May 1898, perhaps for a special train taking mourners to his state funeral in London. (*John Alsop*)

Thornton Junction, *circa* 1900. (*North British Railway Study Group*)

Since 1891 the dividend on unconverted ordinary shares had never exceeded 1.25% and had usually been under 1%, with 0% in five half-years, and frustration was building up among shareholders. At the March and September 1898 shareholders' meetings, the board was criticised on several counts. Tweeddale and his vice-chairman, Tennant, were said to have too many other directorships to pay proper attention to the North British. The board met for only one day each month. Glasgow was inadequately represented. Conacher's salary, now £4,000, was criticised as excessive[64]. The criticisms were rebuffed by the chairman, who pointed to positive actions like "almost 5,000" new wagons ordered from Cowlairs and other works[65]. In 1898-99 Edinburgh Town Council was looking for a suitable location for the Usher Hall to be built. It offered £65,000 to the North British Railway for the Port Hopetoun basin of the Union Canal, but the NBR refused. In 1869 it had sought powers to drain and sell the basin[66], long unused except for dumping rubbish, and indeed had once offered to sell it to the council, but now it intended to build a goods depot on the site at some point[67]. The locality would remain an unremunerative eyesore for years to come. North British facilities at Thornton Junction were criticised. Its island platform, with a dock at each end, and a separate Wemyss & Buckhaven platform, could be accessed only by an uncovered footbridge. Fifty passenger trains a day used it, and in 1898 it had 166,312 passengers[68]. On the plus side, the extended Waverley Station was effectively completed on 17 April, with new platforms for suburban services. (Final Board of Trade approval was not given until April 1901). In November the new general offices at 23 Waterloo Place were occupied, housing some 400 staff, some still working in unconverted former bedrooms, and a start on new offices in Glasgow was announced. John Walker was commemorated by a statue unveiled at Waverley on 15 December 1898. Lady Tweeddale, unveiling it, described Walker as an "austere personality", with "a brusque manner, but a warm heart"[69].

On 1 April the Aberlady, Gullane & North Berwick Railway, built by John Howard in little over a year, opened to Gullane, from a junction a mile and a half east of Longniddry. If the Gullane-North Berwick section had been built, a circular service via Drem would have been possible. Howard took payment in £33,000 of 4% preference shares and the full issue of Aberlady, Gullane & North Berwick debentures, £22,000. The Aberlady line was guaranteed a minimum of 4.5% per annum on its paid-up capital. A new condition had found its way into such contracts. Any shortfall between the line's earnings and the NBR's guaranteed payment would be repaid, with interest, from any future surplus[70]. The East Fife Central Railway, absorbed by the NBR on 6 July 1896, opened on 21 August as a goods-only line[71], terminating among green fields at Lochty, having climbed from 65 to 545 feet in 14½ miles. From 1910 it was adapted for passenger trains, with troop trains to Largoward in 1910 and miners' trains to Largobeath Colliery in 1913-14[72].

The Light Railways Act of 1896, simplifying the procedure for the establishing of rural lines, stimulated fresh interest in a line from Fountainhall to Lauder, first mooted as early as 1847 and again proposed in 1852[73]. The NBR had been subsidising a horse-bus connection over the hills between Lauder and Stow, but now a 10½-mile light railway from Fountainhall went ahead. The NBR put in £15,000, Berwickshire County Council £10,000, Lauder Town Council £3,000, the contractors, Dick, Kerr & Co., accepted £2,500-worth of shares as part-payment; Lords Tweeddale and Lauderdale put in £500 each, and a few Lauder citizens also bought £10 shares. With minimal facilities, the line was built for £39,811, the first light railway in Scotland. Four services each way daily became three by 1910, with an extra one on Saturdays. There never was a Sunday service. The Lauder company remained independent until 1923, paying a dividend of around 1.25% - 1.5% annually. Restored relations between the Gifford & Garvald promoters and the NBR helped to gain a light railway order on 14 July 1898 for their long-suspended branch, to cost £88,000. Tweeddale was again chairman, and Wieland found a contractor, Joseph Phillips of Westminster (a participant in the Forth Bridge builders' consortium), who was prepared to build the line in return for ownership of the shares. It was to be worked by the NBR for a remarkably low 30% of gross receipts, presumably to ensure Phillips's return on capital[74].

In September 1898 Wieland and Grierson moved a board resolution that as the previous dividend had been under 1%, and so long as a higher one was not declared, the directors should cease to take their fees, and the principal officers' salaries should be decreased, Heads of Departments should be required to propose savings, and a committee should be appointed to review their proposals. Wemyss was the only member to support, and the motion was lost. In October the board agreed to include the construction of a new access line from Bishopbriggs to Queen Street in the company's Parliamentary Bill for next session (never proceeded with). According to the minutes of the January 1899 directors' meeting, the chairman moved, and Wieland seconded, that Lord Elgin be re-appointed to a seat on the board which had not been filled since he vacated it on his appointment as Viceroy of India in 1894. There was unanimous approval (many people thought it highly likely that Elgin would become the NBR's next chairman). At the February meeting, however, Wieland, Wemyss and Grierson protested at the entry and announced their opposition to Elgin's appointment, "for reasons stated". But in March Wieland withdrew his protest. When Tweeddale proposed that the company should set aside £4,000 against bad debts, Wieland (chairman of the finance committee) moved it be increased to £11,450, because "sums outstanding at stations amount to £305,000, £26,500 up on the previous half-year". Once again he, Grierson and Wemyss were in a minority of three. It was noted that two shareholders, Henry McIver (Liverpool) and John Inglis, Glasgow shipbuilder, had put themselves forward as candidates for board seats, but the board resolved to list only the names of its own candidates in the report to shareholders. At this meeting the general manager submitted the findings of the arbitrator in the Wemyss Private Railway dispute, in favour of the Wemyss Estate[75], and discussion between the general manager and the maverick director switched to how the Wemyss Private Railway might be bought off.

Chairman, deputy chairman and officials of the NBR in 1898: No. 3 is in centre of second row; otherwise numbers read from left to right in successive rows. 1. William Montagu Hay, Marquis of Tweeddale, chairman; 2. Sir Charles Tennant, Bt., deputy chairman; 3. Matthew Holmes, locomotive superintendent; 4. David Deuchars, superintendent of the line; 5. John Conacher, general manager; 6. John Cathles, secretary; 7. A. Rutherford, chief goods manager; 8. D. Anderson, audit accountant; 9. J.J. Smith, stores superintendent; 10. J. Stewart, outdoor goods manager; 11. James Bell, engineer-in-chief; 12. G. Simpson, general accountant; 13. J. Martin, assistant secretary; 14. R. Chalmers, assistant locomotive superintendent; 15. A.B. Robertson, district traffic superintendent, Dundee; 16. James Hay, district general manager, Edinburgh; 17. A.F. Clement, telegraph superintendent; 18. John Stanley, cashier; 19. W. Andrew, assistant to general manager; 20. W. Arnott, district traffic superintendent, Burntisland; 21. A. Kidd, district traffic superintendent, Coatbridge; 22. G. Cunningham, district superintendent, Glasgow; T. Philip, district superintendent, Carlisle; G. Innes, district traffic superintendent, Fort William; 25. D.L. Anderson, district engineer, Carlisle; 26. G. Bell, district engineer, Thornton; 27. R. Boath, district engineer, Edinburgh; 28. John Gray, district engineer, Glasgow; 29. George Smith, registrar; 30. John Black, asssistant to superintendent of the line; 31. H.A. Kellow, assistant to chief goods Manager; 32. J. Steedman, Assistant to General Accountant; 33. W.F. Jackson, Rating Clerk; 34. James Allan, Police superintendent; 35. W. Binnie, plant superintendent; 36. John Lingard, horse superintendent; 37. W. Anderson, carting dept. superintendent; 38. J. Shepherd, works manager, Cowlairs; 39. J. Marshall, sack superintendent; 40. P. Aitken, canal superintendent.
(NRS, BR/NBR/4/310, reproduced with permission of BRB Residual)

NORTH BRITISH RAILWAY COY

1898

CHAIRMAN·DEPUTY·CHAIRMAN & PRINCIPAL OFFICERS

16. WIELAND'S RAILWAY, 1899–1905

A meeting was held on 12 January 1899 between a delegation of fifteen employees and the directors, on the subject of working hours. The men were received cordially, but the board, although appearing sympathetic, said they could do nothing to reduce hours unless the Caledonian Company should do the same[1]. In the course of the year it emerged that all NBR waged servants, except those in the workshops, had a weekly deduction taken from their pay, to the North British Railway Insurance Society, although the company had no legal power to do this. After a year's membership, if an employee died, his widow received £5, and there were also minimal sick pay arrangements. Until the Workmen's Compensation Act of 1897, the NBR had contributed £1,500 a year to the society. This was reduced to £750[2].

From 1 February 1899 the Caledonian Railway began to exercise its running powers to and from Bo'ness. The passenger station was extended by the North British and the platform length doubled. Large fare reductions were made. A return ticket to Falkirk went from 1s 7d to 7d, to Stirling from 3s to 1s 9d[3]. It did not last. In April negotiations between the town council and the NBR were renewed. Two tripartite agreements were made; the transfer of ownership of the harbour to the NBR; and the Caledonian to discontinue its running powers as of 1 July 1899: "being relieved of certain liabilities to the North British Company under the Act which gave them running powers to Bo'ness". The Harbour Commission was also relieved of its debts of some £480,000, taken over by the NBR. Cheap fares from Bo'ness came to a sudden end. The necessary Act received the royal assent on 6 August 1900. The amount payable by the NBR to Bo'ness Town Council was now set at £1,000 a year until the Caley opened its new dock at Grangemouth, when it would fall to £250, thereafter rising by £50 a year to a maximum of £750. The Act also provided that traffic off the Caledonian to Bo'ness would not incur a rate higher than the CR's own rates to Grangemouth and Alloa South[4]. The North British put an effort into developing the port, almost doubling its coal exports over the next ten years (402,500 tons in 1899, 752,512 tons in 1909).

At recent half-yearly shareholders' meetings, voices had been raised in complaint about the North British management, notably by one T.O. Ockleston, a Liverpool shareholder. It is unlikely that the chairman took them too seriously, but ten days before the March 1899 half-yearly meeting, a letter and circular were published which rocked the company as it had not been since the downfall of Hodgson more than 30 years before. Under Henry Grierson's name it attacked the board on six main points. The time devoted by directors to the company's affairs was "utterly inadequate", the chief officials were "virtually uncontrolled", the chairman and his deputy were directors of over 30 other companies, the directorial seat held by Lord Elgin had been held vacant for the Earl for five years; there were outstanding sums due to the company of £300,000 and candidates for directorships were not noted in company reports unless they were sponsored by the board. His attack was all the more devastating for its suddenness. Tweeddale published a reply on 17 March, claiming that Grierson's accusations were full of inaccuracies and insisting that the directors gave full attention to the company's affairs. He asked for the support of shareholders' proxy votes

2-2-2WT No. 312A, the 'Cab', between 1884 and 1895. Originally built as a 2-2-0WT by Neilson's in 1850, as No. 5, *Wee Scotland*, of the Caledonian & Dumbartonshire Junction Railway. It was sold off in 1911. (*John Alsop*)

in the imminent meeting[5]. Waterloo Place could not hold all the thousand-plus attenders on 23 March and the venue was shifted to the Music Hall. A dividend of 1.75% had been recommended on the ordinary shares, with the fixed 3% on ordinary preferred. In a lengthy address the chairman defended his board's record. Of the company's 2,776 carriages, only 37 were currently under repair; and less than 1% of the 59,446 wagons were out of service. To Grierson's criticism of the accounts, he said the amount owing from customers was equivalent to 23.75% of half a year's goods revenue, and compared well with other railways. Actual bad debt losses had worked out at around £1,800 per half-year over the past ten years. Nevertheless £4,000 had been added to the bad debt fund, bringing it up to £13,000. He accused Grierson of dodgy dealings in North British shares, of dishonourable behaviour to the board, indeed of action "little short of criminal" and pointed out that board supervision had been hardly more than nominal when Walker was manager and – significant pause – Wieland was secretary. Ockleston rose to repeat the claim that the railway was being run by its officials and not by the board. He objected to the consolidation of preferred stocks, and to the company's battle over "immaterial things" with the North Eastern instead of collaborating with it in making the Northumbrian lines work effectively and profitably. Despite Grierson's circular, the directors' report and accounts were carried unanimously. But the opposition had yet to fire its main guns. Five directors were due for re-election: Boase, Elgin, Jordan, H.G. Younger, and C.J. Wilson. Amid uproar over how the election should be conducted, Ockleston proposed four alternative candidates: John Inglis, Henry MacPherson, John Howard, Henry McIver, adding that his friends were willing to accept H.G. Younger (whose family brewery was a major customer). Eventually voting papers were distributed, and counted by NBR clerks. After a two hour adjournment, Cathles announced the result. Younger topped the poll, followed by the four opposition candidates. Grierson and his allies had assembled 55,599 proxies, 14,472 more than the board. Tweeddale and Tennant announced that, having lost the confidence of the shareholders, they were resigning from the board[6].

Personal feelings, ambitions and gains aside, the *coup* – impossible without the participation of the Liverpool shareholders – appears to have been partly driven by an old shareholder fear, particularly among English shareholders, that the company was being run too much by its executives in the interest of the service, and insufficiently controlled by its directors in the interest of the share price and the dividend. But the personal

Rhu Pier on the Gareloch, with PS *Lady Clare* departing. (*John Alsop*)

aspects cannot be overlooked. Strong hints are evident of a move to block Lord Elgin's return to the board and potential chairmanship (as chairman of the finance committee, he had had some differences with Wieland). Personal dislikes between the conspirators and Tweeddale (and Conacher) were emphasised by Randolph Wemyss in a later letter[7]. The motive of the Baird Trustees, largest single shareholders, who withheld £1,750,000 worth of support from Tweeddale, remains unclear, though Wieland had cultivated personal relationships with several of their most senior figures. A member of the Baird family, John, was a Tweeddale supporter. Having joined the board in March 1889, he resigned on 9 June[8]. What is plain is that Wieland, Grierson and Wemyss, in league with Ockleston and his associates, made a combination whose effectiveness Tweeddale and the other directors fatally underestimated (Tweeddale might have remembered the Gifford & Garvald episode: Wieland had evidently learned from it). Whether the new board would make a difference remained to be seen. The *Scotsman* commented that "the conduct of the railway will be eagerly watched"[9]. As far as running a railway was concerned, Tweeddale's board could point to many achievements and improvements, from the accomplishment of the West Highland (to some, of course, that was a non-achievement) to the laying of new sidings, and extensive modernisation, from 92-lb steel rails (from 1896) to train-tablet working on numerous lines. Conacher's management had done much to improve efficiency, customer relations and staff morale.

The new board decided not to meet formally until 6 April and Wieland was quoted as saying he had no desire to be the chairman. The affair scarcely affected the share price, though NB £100 deferred ordinary were already at a depressed £45 10s[10]. Business went on as usual, with the summer train service announced on 30 March, including a new fast express between Queen Street and Elie, leaving Glasgow at 3.45 pm and returning from Elie at 6.40 next morning, arriving in Queen Street at 9 am. On 6 April, Sir William Laird and ex-Provost Moncur of Dundee were elected to the board and Laird was immediately made chairman, with Grierson as deputy. The directors' allowance was fixed at £4,100. Directors coming in to sign cheques or documents received an additional £100, and all received a two guineas per night allowance for away attendances[11]. The new finance committee, chaired by Wieland as before, recorded that a loan of £606,700 to the West Highland company was still outstanding, though a loan from the Galloway Saloon Steam Packet Co. of £10,500 seems to have been repaid. Short-term loans came to almost £1,000,000: £450,000 from the Bank of England, on seven days' notice, £200,000 from the Union Bank and the same amount from the British Linen Bank, £100,000 from the Distillers' company, £8,000 from the Champion Reef Gold Company, and £15,000 from R.&R. Clark[12]. A few days after the revolution, at "a ceremony of more than ordinary interest" Lady Tweeddale cut the first sod of the Gifford & Garvald Railway, on 8 April. Lord Tweeddale's speech made only the briefest of references to the North British, which was unrepresented[13].

Having been elected on the basis that directors should direct, the new regime had to make its presence felt, and there was plenty to do. Main line surfacemen were granted 1s a week extra pay and men with more than a year's service were given entitlement to two days paid holiday a year. Complaints still flowed in about the Tay and Forth ferries: "All carts, horses and carriages are compelled to go round by the Forth Bridge". A speculative company's proposal for a Dundee & Broughty Ferry Light Railway (effectively a tram-line) had to be resisted; negotiation of the handover of Bo'ness Harbour to the North British was accomplished by Conacher, with the NBR making no commitment as to improved facilities at the docks[14]. Two of the ousted directors had been partners in the North British Steam Packet Co. and were replaced by Henry McIver and H.G. Younger, with a new deed of co-partnership drawn up. Sale of the Loch Lomond steamers to the Dumbarton & Balloch joint line had brought in a credit balance of £13,900, which was transferred to a reserve fund to which the NBSP's operating loss of £5,847 for 1898 was charged[15] (the loss had been ascribed to the NBR's request that four steamers, rather than the usual two, be kept in operation on the Clyde through the winter months). In May, 2,548 shares in the Galloway Saloon Steam Packet Co. were transferred to the NBSP partners, leaving a rump of 150 shares standing in the names of Henry Grierson, George Bradley Wieland, Thomas Aitken and M.D. Galloway, "under back letters to the company." The steamboat company, always a tail wagged by the North British dog, meekly accepted an agreement made by Conacher with the CR and G&SWR to withdraw advertising of steamer services from the Glasgow newspapers[16]. In Glasgow, Prince's Dock, on the south bank, had been open since 1897, with tramway access from the General Terminus Quay, but in June, the NBR, Caledonian and South Western went ahead with the Prince's Dock Joint Railway, from the CR-G&SWR Govan Branch. Its cost, £170,000, was to be divided two-fifths each to the North British and Caledonian, and one-fifth to the South Western[17].

On the north shore of the Firth of Forth, Randolph Wemyss had won game, set and match – the arbitrator had decreed on 10 March that he was free to build his private railway and to carry his tenants' coal on it as well as his own. At the board meeting on 11 May, Wemyss temporarily left the room while his colleagues resolved that the company would pay him £3,000 a year from 1 November 1899 for 30 years or as long as he or his successors refrained from constructing it, so long as receipts from the Wemyss Estate to the NBR remained above £12,000; if less than £12,000, the £3,000 to be proportionately reduced. Parliamentary approval was needed for this, and provision was made to give Wemyss £3,000 if this was refused. On 16 May Wemyss resigned from the board and sold his NBR shares[18]. At the board meeting of 25 May it was reported that he had declined the £3,000 offer. His terms were now 30% of the gross receipts for 30 years, with a minimum payment of £3,000 a year. A meeting between Sir William Laird and Wemyss appeared to get a compromise agreement, which was then repudiated in a letter from his solicitors[19]. On 22 June 1899 the board agreed that there was no point in pursuing the matter. The Wemyss Private Railway went ahead.

It is possible that when Conacher was hired, Wieland thought he would be an efficient but unassertive manager content to execute the board's will. In fact he was as strong a manager as Walker and with a rather stricter view of corporate and personal business ethics. Randolph Wemyss found it impossible to bully Conacher and made further waves in June, with a newspaper letter which openly attacked him. Referring to Tweeddale's chairmanship as "a dishonest regime", he claimed that Wieland had made the peace agreement of 1891 with the Caledonian, which Conacher had inherited, and that he (Wemyss) and Conacher had had "serious differences of opinion" over NBR policy in Fife, where unnecessary capital had been spent in some places and injudicious savings made in others. Of the £305,000 in outstanding charges, he reckoned £35,000 to be irrecoverable, with a total deficiency of £40-50,000 far eclipsing the £13,000 provision. Feeling his position had been made impossible, Conacher resigned on 22 June, with effect from 1 July, writing to Laird:

> "Dear Sir William, As it is apparent to me that I will not be able to work in harmony with the board of directors as now constituted, I beg to resign my appointment as general manager."[20]

That evening he wrote to his son:

> "My dear Charlie, The papers will have told you of my resignation. Matters came to a pass yesterday when the new men decided to give me an opportunity of resigning. I told them I would not resign, as I had not failed in my duty to the company and told them if they desired me to go they must terminate the engagement. Eventually terms for retirement were arranged under which I am to receive £5,000 for giving them during the next twelve months any information or assistance they can reasonably ask for …"[21].

Several directors, including Charles Carlow, as well as public sympathy, were on his side:

> "judging by outward and visible signs, no better manager of a railway than Mr. Conacher has ever held office"[22].

NBR ordinary shares slipped back to £42, but from Liverpool, Ockleston wrote to describe the NBR's former management as "a quagmire", and suggesting it was obvious that Conacher had to go. Conacher made a reply via a friend, contesting only a couple of points of detail, but adding that both he and Lord Tweeddale had told Wemyss he ought to resign over the private railway plan[23]. Conacher's £5,000 was to be paid half on 1 July 1899 and half on 1 July 1900. A month after resigning he represented the NBR at a Parliamentary inquiry into new dock schemes on the south bank of the Clyde[24]. The board lost little time in appointing William Fulton Jackson as the new manager, at £1,500 a year[25]. Aged 43, he had been head of the rates & charges department for 22 years, a trusted aide to Wieland, with an intimate knowledge of the NBR system. Accusations and recriminations went on through the summer and into the autumn. Tweeddale claimed that he, not Wieland, was the instigator of the 1891 peace agreement; Wemyss denied it. Meanwhile, Conacher was ready to "court the fullest possible inquiry" into his conduct as manager[26]. An ousted director, Charles Wilson, also pushed for an enquiry, accusing the new men of undisclosed Stock Exchange connections and dealings in NBR shares: "Dealers can make a profit whether stock rises or falls", and asking if it was legal for Wieland to remain as paid secretary of the West Highland, Forth Bridge, Eyemouth, and Newport Railway companies. Grierson sent

W.F. Jackson, general manager of the NBR from 1899 to 1918
(*Glasgow Museums*)

a further circular to the shareholders in September, justifying the actions of the new board, and claiming that £56,000 had to be found to meet bad debts, "reserves for the Loch Lomond steamers", etc. Probably with Grierson himself in mind, among others, the *Financial News* was more concerned about new, or renewed, malpractices:

> "… remembering, as we do, the early information that was obtainable in the old and unregenerate days of the company, and the curious stories that used to be current as to the significance of the lowering or raising of the blinds in the boardroom when the directors were deciding upon the dividend to be declared, we cannot avoid the suspicion that someone was enabled to profit by inside knowledge that was not open to the public. We trust, however, that it is not the prelude to a resumption of the discreditable incidents that used to occur before Mr. Conacher undertook the management, and that we shall not again hear of wholesale gambling in the company's stocks by the company's officials[27]."

A pleasant interlude in this cross-fire was the Cowlairs families' outing to Berwick on 22 September, with some 8,000 people carried in nine trains. Music, dancing, and sea trips on the company's PS *Forth* were among the attractions. Matthew Holmes presided over an excursion committee dinner for 80 in the Kings Arms Hotel, including Macpherson and Grierson.

Both sides were preparing for the half-yearly meeting due on 28 September. Tweeddale and Tennant kept up their attack in a letter published on the 25th, criticising the injustice done to Conacher, and the appointment of the inexperienced Jackson; and, in relation to the alleged £56,000, pointing out that G.B. Wieland had been chairman of the finance committee. On the 28th, Laird announced that the board had commissioned the NBR auditors, Mackenzie & Guild, to ascertain the true state of the accounts as of 1 January 1899 and they had found matters in "a grave state". Large sums had been paid as drawbacks (rebates) out of unpublished traffic receipts without the knowledge of the board. The provision for bad debts etc. was £48,000 less than required, and £56,000 would have to be written off over the next two half-years. Wilson made a long speech, still asking for an inquiry into the change of management, but the rug was pulled from under him when Ockleston revealed he had written to the new board asking for a seat; and the meeting voted against any inquiry[28]. Wilson had played his hand badly. His letters to Conacher show his awareness of Wieland's ability to manipulate NBR affairs but he failed to bring home an attack, writing to Conacher on 29 September: "It only remains for you to verify the secret History of the North British Railway Coy as displayed from the inside, including the doings in sidepaths of Wieland Wemyss and Howard" – but Conacher did not take up the suggestion. He had been given a copy of the auditors' report and followed it up by pointing out that, had the same new-found method of treating "certain items as immediate liabilities" and disregarding "certain credits hitherto relied upon", the accounts of July 1891 would have shown a large deficiency – Mackenzie & Guild were the auditors then too. He claimed that the drawbacks were a system initiated by Walker, and that the only sum unaccounted for in the accounts of January 1899 was £5,408[29]. But the new board was firmly entrenched, and Jackson swiftly imposed himself as a general manager for whom no detail was too trivial, and rules and regulations were Holy Writ.

For most of its customers and the travelling public, of course, the internal affairs of the North British were of limited interest and they were more concerned with the service the company provided. Ten years on from the post-Forth Bridge *débacle*, the new Waverley Station was at last a cause for pride, with a *Railway Magazine* article describing its 23-acre extent stretching eastwards over the old Trinity College Church and Physic Garden sites, with 11.5 acres glazed over, its double access roads from the Waverley Bridge, the nineteen platforms with a total length of 4,460 yards, its vast cellars with their foot-warmer heaters, its telegraph office where 40 ladies dealt with 4,000 messages daily; its East Cabin with "the largest signal frame ever constructed", holding 260 levers; its 300 staff and 630 trains a day, all presided over by the long-serving Mr. Paton[30]. Canal Street and the old offices no longer existed. Work on Waverley would go on into 1904, but other needs had to be passed over. Failure to keep pace with the increase of coal production in Fife meant a shortage of siding space as well as of locomotives and wagons – there was no refuge siding for mineral trains between Dunfermline and Thornton Junction. Accidents still happened: one Singer-bound workmen's train ran into the back of another in the smoky tunnel between Queen Street and Charing Cross, killing five people and injuring twenty on 28 March 1900. On a better note, at the end of July the 'Flying Scotchman' was to be a corridor train, and the long-established 20-minute luncheon stop at York was abolished. Its East Coast Joint Stock carriages, some built at Cowlairs, made a "veritable train de luxe". The first class diner, with eighteen places, was 60 feet 6 inches long; the third class diner, with 42 places, was 62 feet 11 inches. The vehicles were linked by Gould's patent auto-couplings (the NBR, GNR, Great Central and North Eastern had been collaborating in experiments on this[31]), and an internal alarm chain was fitted. The North Eastern Railway laid on Britain's first six-coupled express locomotive. Nevertheless, there was more

Eyemouth Station and River Eye, a Valentine's view taken circa 1907.

argument: Lord Balfour of Burleigh had to be called on to settle whether the train (10 o' clock from Kings Cross) should be timed to arrive in Edinburgh at 6.15 pm (as wanted by the NER) or 6.30 (as wanted by the NBR and GNR). He went for the shorter time despite the fact that this broke the East Coast and West Coast agreement on timing (and the NBR commented that the NER was frequently late anyway[32]). This was a pot-and kettle remark. The NBR was notoriously unpunctual and a hoary joke suggested it dated from the sixth day of Creation, when God made "all creeping things". The dispute over NER running powers was still simmering, but in the winter of 1900-01 the North British expressed readiness for an amicable settlement[33].

The Aberlady, Eyemouth and Newport companies were absorbed on 6 August 1900 by virtue of an Act which also authorised a goods branch to Bainsford, off the Grahamston line, and ownership of Bo'ness Harbour. The Newport and Aberlady final dividends were 4.5% on ordinary stock and 4% on preference; shareholders were to receive North British debenture and lien stock to give "no more and no less" according to Laird[34]. But a shareholder, James Calder, protested that the market value of NBR stock exchanged with that of the Aberlady company (chairman G.B. Wieland) was £123,885, against a capital of £66,000 and loans of £22,000, netting a profit of at least £80,000 for Aberlady investors – chiefly John Howard, now a North British director[35].

In December 1900 W.F. Jackson presided at the fifth Edinburgh employees' soirée, at the Music Hall in George Street. His speech was standard stuff, praising the staff's loyalty, tact, energy and ability, and adjuring them to be justly proud of the company. The new management was as deft as its predecessor in fending off claims for shorter hours. A reply in March to new representations on the subject expressed the sympathy of the directors, but they regretted that action was impossible[36]. Among the workers it remained the vital topic, and local and area meetings continued the agitation.

Henry Grierson chaired the half-yearly meeting on 21 March 1901, and had a mixed story to tell. Receipts were up by £100,000 and train mileage was down by 80,000, but costs were up by £130,000, and various works had to be put off "till better times" came. He partly blamed an increase in coal and coke prices that had cost the company £70,000. The sum owed by the West Highland company to the NBR, which would reach £1,206,463 by June 1902[37], was not mentioned. The ordinary shares received a dividend of 0.25%. People might well have wondered what the point of the great shake-up of 1899 was, if this was the achievement. One item in the NBR's costs was £5,816 16s 10d for the salvaging and repair of the steamer *Redgauntlet*, which had hit a reef off Arran on 16 July 1899 and

The concrete viaduct at Morar, photographed in 1914. (*John Alsop***)**

Mallaig Station soon after completion, with West Highland Bogie No. 346 (1896), and Holmes 0-6-0 No. 793, built in 1900 and not withdrawn until 1967. Midland and East Coast Joint Stock carriages. (*John Alsop*)

had to be 'lifted'. This would otherwise have been a severe burden for the steamer company's partners. But the North British deducted £500 4s 9d from NBSP half-yearly earnings on the Silloth-Liverpool route because of the renewal of an agreement with the LNWR on traffic between Carlisle and Liverpool, backdated to 1 February 1900[38].

The 41-mile Mallaig Extension was opened on 1 April, the first train leaving Edinburgh at 4.30 am, and reaching Mallaig at 11.45, where two steamers for Skye and Lewis waited at the new 600 feet pier. An Up train left Mallaig for Glasgow at 7.20 am, arriving in Queen Street at 1.55 pm, three minutes ahead of time[39]. Robert McAlpine, the contractors, had made extensive use of concrete in the works, including the curving 21-arch viaduct at Glenfinnan. There were eleven tunnels, the longest being 330 yards. Total cost was £550,000, of which the North British was bearing £290,000 (rather than Tweeddale's "bargain" £100,000). Though complaints arose about the adequacy of the steamer service, the WHR went into active competition to capture the herring traffic, chartering a steamer in May to bring the catch from Stornoway to Mallaig, and emphasising its seven hour advantage to Edinburgh over the Highland line from Kyle of Lochalsh[40]. Charles Forman, not involved with the extension, had died on 8 February, aged only 48. His achievements, including the West Highland line, and the Glasgow Central Railway, are real and enduring, yet his unrealised schemes are far more numerous[41].

Sir William Laird resigned as chairman on 18 April[42], and on 2 May G.B. Wieland was unanimously elected as his successor. With his long and intimate knowledge of the company and its workings, he had been the real driving force on the new board, and his elevation meant no change of direction. For the North British, as for other railway companies, the new century presented a vital issue – how to operate profitably. It was not so much a problem as a predicament. The company had a very large capital – all the share issues since 1844, all the combined and consolidated stocks of the merged companies, had owners who awaited their twice-yearly dividends. Modifications of working hours, and overtime pay, had pushed up the wages Bill. Similar reforms in the mining industry had increased the price of coal. A thousand miles of track and over 650 stations and goods depots needed constant expenditure. Rising industry standards, driven by the wealthier English companies, and customer demand, required investment in better carriages and bigger engines. All this had to be paid for from the company's revenues, which were simultaneously being eroded by tramway systems in the urban districts, creaming off passengers and profits from suburban services. If income was insufficient, could charges not just be increased? But the Railway & Canal Traffic Act (1894) had placed the onus on railway companies to prove the reasonableness of any increase in rates made from 31 December 1892. Rates for coal haulage would be one of the main areas of contention in the 1900s. From 1 January 1900 the NBR, G&SWR and Caledonian had all increased their coal rates by around 5%. A coalition of coalowners took the case to the Railway & Canal Commissioners in June 1901. The Baird empire, in which Sir William Laird was still a partner, was not a party to the coalowners' case, but a share of the costs was paid by the Fife Coal Co., of which Charles Carlow was a director, as well as of the NBR. Giving evidence, W.F. Jackson claimed that higher working costs made the increase essential. In 1900, the NBR had carried 4,757,738 tons of merchandise, 4,248,246 tons of other minerals, and 14,764,074 tons of coal[43]. Hearings went on until October, when the Commissioners decided that the railways had not established their case. The increase was countermanded, leaving the coal companies free to reclaim the amounts overpaid[44].

Kirkcaldy and Inverkeithing Harbours, with no investment from the North British, remained peripheral to the greatly-expanding coal traffic from Fife pits, but after five years of level-pegging with Burntisland between 1890 and 1895, Methil had begun to gain the lead. In 1895 it shipped 727,564 tons and Burntisland shipped 726,815 tons. By 1900 Methil was shipping 1,685,628 tons compared with Burntisland's 983,588. Dysart and Charlestown, unable to take the bigger ships coming into use, shipped 72,186 and 62,558 tons respectively in 1900, but neither improved on these figures in the 1900s, and Charlestown, which had shipped 140,025 tons in 1877 compared to Methil's modest 50,000 tons, now declined rapidly[45].

Competition on Anglo-Scottish traffic to Edinburgh remained strong, and a new Midland-North British dining-car service was introduced, giving an 8½ hours journey time from Waverley to St. Pancras. The inaugural train left Edinburgh at 9.25 am on 1 July with 27 passengers, of whom 12 were booked through to London. The northbound train left London at 9.30 am and was due in Edinburgh at 6.05 pm (the 'Flying Scotsman's' timing was 10 am to 6.15 pm). Over a longer route, the new service offered a real challenge. The first northbound service left Carlisle ten minutes late, but the NBR, using No. 738, "one of Mr. Matthew Holmes's latest express engines", brought it into Waverley only half a minute behind time. The maximum noted speed was 58 mph – that morning, however, the 'Flying Scotsman' managed to arrive at 6.03 pm. But on 8 July the Midland train was first in Edinburgh, punctually at 6.05 pm, followed by the West Coast train at 6.07 (eight minutes early) and the 'Flying Scotsman' at 6.09 (six minutes early[46]).

On 2 July the Lauder Light Railway opened. The Marquis of Tweeddale was chairman of the Lauder company and the North British was represented only by David Deuchars. Another long-delayed opening, even closer to Tweeddale's seat at Yester, near Gifford, was that of the Gifford & Garvald line, as far as Gifford, on 14 October, at a cost of £99,330 3s 10d. The extension to Garvald was never attempted. The NBR was to work the line, paying £3,600 a year, and had three directors out of five on the board (one of them was W.F. Jackson, who supplanted Tweeddale as chairman – a very Wieland-ish appointment), though the company would remain independent until 1923. Two trains a day ran each way between Gifford and Ormiston (three on Saturdays).

Train mileage was still being cut down – by 150,000 miles in the February-July half-year, despite many special trains to the very successful Glasgow International Exhibition; and Wieland expressed his desire to minimise capital expenditure, which "has been the bane of the North British". Surprisingly perhaps, a project close to his

Oxton, April 1901. The Board of Trade Inspector's train, first on the line. (*John Alsop*)

Locomotive No. 18 was built in 1872 to work Leith Docks. (*John Alsop*)

heart was the new North British Station Hotel, rising alongside Waverley Station, and consuming large amounts of capital as it did so[47]. Chairman Wieland speedily resolved a wrangle with the ex-directors of the East Fife Central Railway. The coal reserves had proved to be inadequate, and the line had never paid its way. Its final cost was £132,463 and the receipts between August 1898 and August 1899 were only £1,124 4s 7d, far short of the NBR's guaranteed minimum of 3% on capital, £3,973 18s. Since October 1899 the NBR had been pressing the guarantors (including Wieland) to pay the shortfall, which by June 1900 amounted to £7,136. A laconic NBR board minute of 8 August 1901 recorded an agreement with the guarantors, whose content is not known but which almost certainly relieved them of their debt[48].

Edinburgh's ports, Granton and Leith, were owned respectively by the Duke of Buccleuch and Leith Burgh, and the railway companies paid tollage for their use. Leith Docks had expanded greatly, with the Albert Dock (1869) and the Edinburgh Dock (1881) and through the 1890s the North British was under pressure from the coalmasters to provide better access, but, perhaps because of preoccupations with Bo'ness and Fife, took no action. In 1901 four Lothian coal companies promoted their own Bill for a set of railways linking their pits with a new harbour to be built just west of Cockenzie. Despite having insisted its facilities were sufficient, the North British quickly introduced its own Bill for the same lines, with the purchase of the tiny harbour at Cockenzie[49]. Both Bills were withdrawn because of landowners' opposition, and a fractious relationship between the NBR and the coalowners continued, while the output of the coalfield steadily rose.

A special shareholders' meeting approved a Bill for the NBR to take over the North British Steam Packet Company, and the raising of £150,000 for the provision and maintenance of steamers at Craigendoran and Silloth[50]. On 22 July 1902 the NBR duly obtained an act to run its own steamship service on the Clyde, though it was prohibited from scheduled services to Inveraray, Ardrishaig, Campbeltown and the West of Arran. Lachlan Gilchrist, secretary of the North British Steam Packet since October 1899, was appointed steamer superintendent (marine superintendent from 1906[51]).

The short Corstorphine Branch opened on 2 February, and the former Corstorphine Station on the Glasgow line was renamed Saughton[52]. In this case the railway killed off a tram line, Corstorphine-Edinburgh. But it was only a horse-tram. A few miles to the west,] Asylum was a new vast institution some way from the village of that name. Its governing board decided that a branch railway from the Edinburgh-Bathgate line was essential to make

Bangour Station and branch train. The fireman of the Drummond 4-4-0T, No. 75, built in 1882 as *Sunnyside*, is breaking up the massive coal lumps. (*North British Railway Study Group*)

access easier for patients, staff and visitors. A bargain was made with the North British, guaranteeing a minimum income to the railway company of £1,500 a year. A correspondent estimated the traffic's value at £300 a year, with a £1,200 annual loss to the hospital board, and wondered whether the management or the patients had made the deal. On the Edinburgh-Glasgow line, a group of entrepreneurs approached the NBR with a proposal to build a Behr monorail[53]. Parliament had already authorised a Manchester-Liverpool high-speed monorail in 1901, but Board of Trade stipulations effectively stifled the project.

J. Boyd Kinnear, a long-time campaigner for better service in Fife, was still lambasting the NBR for poor facilities. At Collessie Station, his milk churns and everything else had to be hoisted up from ground level because the company had refused to build a loading bank. He vowed to switch to road transport as soon as possible[54].

On 16 October the North British Hotel opened its doors to customers. Ten storeys high from its basements at platform level, with ten Otis lifts, its architect, J. Hamilton Beattie, who died before completion, considered it "a free rendering of the Renaissance period". The president of Edinburgh's Cockburn Association, having damned the new Caledonian Hotel at the foot of Lothian Road as needing blowing up with gunpowder or dynamite, gave a welcome to the NBR's massive pile, "really a handsome building" though out of place in its location[55]. G.B. Wieland had taken personal charge of stocking the wine cellars[56]. Carpeted throughout by Charles Jenner & Co., with palm lounge and ballroom, it catered not only for tourists and visitors but for the better class of commercial traveller, with a writing room and special rooms for stock display[57]. 'Bachelor suites' could be rented by single businessmen. Its manager, F.T. Burcher, was general manager of all NBR hotels and refreshment rooms. Strangely, no director nor official of the NBR attended the ceremonial dinner given by the contractors on the 15th. The toast to the North British Railway had to be answered by Hugh Mayberry, a Glasgow accountant with strong Caledonian connections. The NBR remained coy about the hotel's cost, reckoned by the *Scotsman* to be around £380,000 apart from the site and furnishings[58]. Down in the station, an electrically-worked train arrival indicator had been installed earlier in the year, and an improved version with bigger lettering, patented by David Wells, assistant telegraph superintendent, was put up for south and west trains in December, with the claim that there was "No such apparatus in operation elsewhere"[59].

The Amalgamation Acts of the 1860s were still invoked on occasion: the Caledonian Railway was taken to the Railway Commissioners by the North British because it refused to send coal from Bannockburn Colliery to Aberdeen via the NBR even though the consignors wished to do so. The Caley claimed that it was "local traffic of the Caledonian" and so ineligible under the act, but the North British won its case[60]. Both companies were soon back with the long-running wrangle over connections at Perth, the NBR complaining that the Caledonian did not wait even when passengers were seen running for the train. The CR responded that the North British should run its trains to time. The Commissioners ruled that the Caledonian must delay departure of its Crieff trains for up to five minutes if the NBR connection was late, or for longer if the NBR train was actually signalled. Other trains should also be held if the North British arrival was signalled[61].

One of the projects stalled or delayed was the railway between Kincardine and Dunfermline. In January 1903 the NBR applied for an extension of time on the act for the line, facing opposition from the local authorities, who suspected that the company had no intention of completing it. The contract for construction was finally let in March 1904. At the March 1903 half-yearly meeting, Wieland informed the shareholders that the company had no new extension schemes in view. He also observed that the NBR's wage Bill had risen by £280,000 over the past ten years, but staff numbers had increased considerably, to around 19,000. Still, working expenses at 50% of gross revenue were, he said, less than on any other of Britain's five largest railway companies[62]. The deferred ordinary dividend was 2.5% – the highest level it would attain through the 1900s. By now there were 33,841 shareholders, with an average holding of £1,788, 8,552 held debentures (average holding £1,871), 25,861 held preferred or guaranteed stock (£1,341), and 5,224 ordinary stock (£1,883). The company's total capital was £60,528,728[63]. In May Matthew Holmes retired, a sick man with only a few months to live, and William Paton Reid, already effectively in charge, took over, though not formally confirmed as locomotive superintendent until June 1904[64]. A new engine shed was almost complete at Eastfield, replacing the cramped depot at Cowlairs: the NBR's largest, with fourteen tracks and room for 84 engines, it came into use in September.

The Invergarry & Fort Augustus Railway, seven years from its Act, was ready to open. A Parliamentary Committee was considering the Highland company's Bill for working the line, with the North British hotly opposing, on the ground that the Highland was purely concerned to keep it out of Inverness. Jackson told the committee that the NBR was willing to work the Invergarry & Fort Augustus Railway at cost, but not at a loss. The Highland's Bill was approved by the Lords, with a clause that nothing in it should prejudice the NBR's right to build a line to Inverness[65] and services from Spean Bridge began on 22 July. While rural services were growing, competition from Glasgow tramcars resulted in the withdrawal of the circular 'omnibus' trains from Springburn from 12 January 1903. The capacious new Leith Central opened on 1 July – a four-platform terminus set above street-level, with overall roof, and shops below. Direct trains to Waverley ran every half hour, taking six minutes.

Leith Central Station, post 1905. Leith's electric trams pass by. (*Stenlake Collection*)

Since Leith's and Edinburgh's trams ran on separate systems, traffic was quite heavy and from 1 October an hourly circular service was inaugurated, using a link-line at Lochend (authorised on 6 August 1900) to run via Portobello, the suburban line and Waverley. Goods traffic got a boost from the opening of the joint line to Prince's Dock on 17 August, giving the North British access to the south bank of the Clyde, by way of running powers on G&SWR and joint G&SWR-Caledonian tracks.

More waterworks construction prompted the laying of a siding for contractors' supplies on the Northumberland Central line, from February 1902. A station was applied for and the NBR agreed to spend £180 on a temporary platform. The station opened on 12 January 1903, named first White House, then Fontburn. The signalman at Whitrope Tunnel box was appointed stationmaster at £60, with neither a house nor lodging allowance[66].

For all Jackson's reputation as a martinet, Prussian-style discipline was not always in evidence. The report on a collision at Lochmill Siding, between Manuel and Linlithgow, established that five men had been in the main-line box with the signalman, "smoking, talking and playing games". The 5.25 express from Aberdeen had run into a goods on the same line, and the signalmen at Lochmill and Manuel were held to blame[67].

For the half-year to 31 January 1904, the deferred ordinary dividend was 2.25%.

Gross revenue	To 31 January 1904	To 31 January 1903
Passengers	£866,524	£861,281
Goods/minerals	£1,358,349	£1,363,499
Miscellaneous	£63,698	£59,789
Total	£2,287,671	£2,284,570
Working expenses	£1,157,353	£1,164,253[68]

Only a heavy hand on working expenses was enabling the dividend to stay above 2%. Good-ish news for the shareholders meant constraint on the wages and working hours issue, and agitation continued.

At the half-yearly meeting on 22 September, the deferred ordinary dividend was down to 1.75%; and with shareholders criticising a lack of detail in the accounts, Wieland shed some light on the company's financial position. The sum of £669,000 was owed to various banks, and interest in the half-year amounted to £16,000, paid from revenue. Between mid-1901 and mid-1904 the NBR had spent £1,800,000 on new lines and siding capacity, and he reiterated his wish for the capital account to be closed. The sum of outstanding customer accounts was £260,000 (John Conacher might have been forgiven a bitter laugh). The company still had various unconsolidated stocks at 6%, 5% and 4.5%, but he felt it had ample capital, including £400,000 of unissued preference stock. With surprising frankness, he told the meeting that the NB hotel was "not a great success – built on too large a scale." It was, however, a success "in the sense and for the purpose for which it was built, which was to give access to East Coast and Midland traffic." At the end of the chairman's remarks, an anonymous clergyman rose to call him "a gallant old hero of railway warfare" and advised fellow-proprietors to put all their cash into North British stock. Replying, Wieland said "he could hardly second the recommendation to buy North British stock at present. These were troublous times"[69]. On 8 September NBR £100 preferred ordinary shares were at £79 and deferred at £43 6s 8d.

Getting fish to the London market was always a topic for the East Coast managers' meetings. Four-wheeled vans whirled along at high speeds were now disapproved of. The traffic managers wanted six-wheelers, with refrigeration. To guarantee early arrival of Aberdeen fish at Billingsgate, the NER now required that 70%, and the GNR 50%, of the fish trucks should be fully braked, and the rest piped. Deuchars could not guarantee this, as the NBR was passing on traffic from the Great North and the Highland, and pointed out that the Caledonian did not suffer from such a stipulation. He was willing to put on a fish-only train from Aberdeen for the next season, leaving at 2pm, if the North British would be remunerated for any losses caused by delay. A previous attempt to run this train had failed because the fish merchants received no compensation for delays and as a result had switched their custom to the West Coast[70].

The boom in Clyde shipbuilding and the enlargement of Scottish ports for export shipping also had an impact on imports. Iron ore was being imported from Spain in increasingly large quantities, but other materials were also coming in. When a new cement works was opened at Cousland, on the Ormiston line, with its own siding and a tramway into the works, it was noted as an attempt to compete with cheap imported cement[71].

John Charles Montagu-Douglas-Scott, Earl of Dalkeith, then Duke of Buccleuch, chairman of the NBR from 1905 to 1912. (Glasgow Museums)

At the March 1905 shareholders' meeting, the Earl of Dalkeith stood in for Wieland, who was at Menton, on the way back from Egypt. He died there on 26 March, aged 67. A *Financial News* obituary remarked that "In Edinburgh Mr. Wieland never achieved popularity; but it is fair to admit that under his presidency the North British improved on the prosperity that began in the Tweeddale and Conacher *régime*"[72]. Wieland remains an enigmatic figure, a man who built up power and influence (and wealth) behind the scenes but who eventually as chairman became the company's public face. A master-schemer with a touch of mischief, his letters often make belittling comments on men whom he felt he could manipulate or out-manoeuvre. Having brought about a boardroom coup on the basis that directors should direct, he spent most of his latter years in the south of England, though attending meetings regularly. His great talent was in ensuring that share flotations were taken up speedily and fully. This was achieved primarily through deals with London stockbrokers, rich in cash and looking for a safe return. The effect was to load the North British with ever-weightier commitments in the form of guaranteed preference dividends, often (as with the West Highland) not sustained by earnings. As chairman he failed to maintain a sufficient level of investment to assure future services. Private speculations in coal, land, cigars and wines attest to his interest in wealth and the good things that go with it. He enjoyed passing on share tips to friends and associates and had no hesitation in profiting from his own position. Through association with Renton and Howard, he was also drawn into various enterprises, like the Ayrshire & Wigtownshire Railway, that had nothing to do with the North British, but he also worked hard for the North British over three decades[73].

Lord Dalkeith was elected as chairman. Aged 41, he had had an unusual education for an aristocrat, having joined the Navy aged 13 and served for ten years. He took a keen interest in the company's affairs both as chairman and (from 1912) vice-chairman, maintaining that role, latterly as Duke of Buccleuch, until the NBR's end. As befitted a former naval person, he was a practical, hands-on, chairman compared to his predecessor – interested in the locomotives and technical systems which to Wieland were perhaps undesirable if unavoidable aspects of what he preferred to see as a great abstraction, a financial construct, but Dalkeith was fully convinced of the North British's need to rein in its costs, and tight control on expenditure continued.

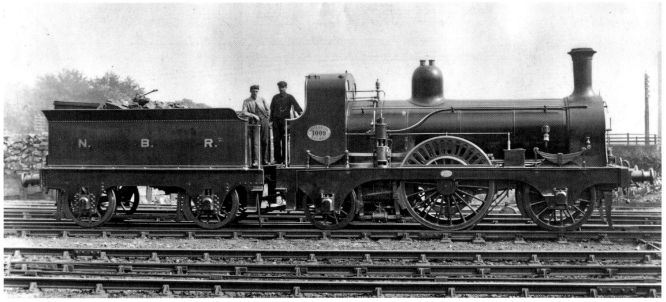

The much-rebuilt 2-2-2 No. 1009, in the early 1900s. Originally No. 55, constructed as a Crampton engine in 1849 by E.B. Wilson & Co. (*North British Railway Study Group*)

17. DALKEITH AND WHITELAW, 1905–1913

Labour M.P.s at Westminster made an issue of the state of workmen's trains in the spring of 1905, and Jackson gave evidence on the NBR's behalf to a Select Committee. There were 205 carriages set aside for such trains, including eight first class (for foremen), and 15 composites. Women-only compartments were provided. The North British carried over 1,000,000 work-people a year between Queen Street, Yoker, Clydebank, Kilbowie (Singer works), Carntyne, Shettleston and Easterhouse. Jackson denied that any of the NBR carriages lacked windows or window-straps and said he had no complaint about vandalism or violence (Singer trains had a vigilance committee). Like the Caledonian general manager Robert Millar, he considered that boys were much worse[1]. A different kind of service was introduced on 14 June when two 23-seater Arrol-Johnson charabancs were put on the road between North Berwick and Gullane, where the railway link had never been laid. Built by Mo-Car of Paisley, under the supervision of W.P. Reid, at £560 each, they were solid-tyred, and made twelve runs daily, each way, giving access to seven golf courses. At the end of October the vehicles were moved to Fort William, for an experimental service to North Ballachulish. They returned to East Lothian from 2 July 1906[2]. Bangour Hospital's 2½ mile line opened in May at a cost of over £30,000, but saving an estimated £18,500 in carrying materials for the new hospital buildings[3]. William Paton, "prince of station-masters" retired from Waverley Station in June, and was presented with a testimonial and £1,575 by the Secretary of State for Scotland, the Marquis of Linlithgow, who confessed himself one of a new breed, the railway enthusiast: "I had railway fever upon me as a boy"[4].

Still claiming that the Fife coalfields were under-provided with shipping capacity, Randolph Wemyss promoted a Bill for a new dock at Buckhaven[5] The NBR opposed it on the grounds of the 1878 agreement, insisting that existing facilities could cope. Output that year was 7,241,439 tons. Wemyss alleged that John Walker had undertaken to have the dock at Methil enlarged, which the NBR had not done, and offered to transfer his Bill to the North British. Search in the records found a document signed by Walker and Wemyss on 26 December 1888, but without a word about enlarging Methil. The Bill was thrown out by the House of Lords, but the NBR was less successful in opposing a Bill for a tramline between Edinburgh and Dalkeith, whose preamble was approved by the Commons[6]. Even with no new projects of its own to push through, the company spent £7,800 in opposing other companies' Bills. Dalkeith, as new chairman, had to confront one legacy of Wieland's unwillingness to spend capital. Since 1901, merchandise and mineral traffic had risen by 17%, 3,700,000 tons, but the NBR had built no new main line locomotives and had added only nine shunting engines. At the September half-yearly meeting he said that "considerable addition must at once be made to our engine power"[7]. It was carrying capacity, rather than dock capacity, that the company lacked.

Another of the many new tramlines that the North British had to contend with was the Laird of Wemyss's Leven-Kirkcaldy public tramway of 1906, the NBR having turned down his suggestion that it should sponsor the venture[8]. On 14 March, however, the North British announced a plan for a new dock at Methil. Docks took several years to construct and the company was taking a gamble on the continuing rise in coal output. A *Scotsman* article on the same day estimated that the present Fife docks could handle up to 6½ million tons (4,629,100 tons were exported in 1905), and, noting the very low carriage charges to Methil, queried whether the NBR could make a profit from a dock extension there. Wemyss expressed his confidence that "contrary to supposition" the NBR would make money out of the new dock, but later in the year re-launched his own Bill for a dock at Buckhaven[9]. At the half-yearly meeting on 22 March Dalkeith clarified how new engines would be paid for, with £13,500 to be taken from half-yearly revenue for a locomotive and coach Fund. With the opening of the line to Kincardine on 2 July, Dunfermline gained a new railway link just at the time a district tramway scheme was being promoted (against NBR opposition). Four passenger trains went each way daily, with five on Saturdays. The three intermediate stations, lit by gas, were commended as "commodious". On the same day a three hour express service was introduced between Edinburgh and Aberdeen, as the NBR's response to the Caledonian's 'Grampian Corridor' train of 1905. Known as the "block trains", there were two each way, leaving Edinburgh at 11 am and 3.20 pm, and leaving Aberdeen at 9.30 am and 6.55 pm. Glasgow connections left for Edinburgh at 10.20 am and 2.40 pm. Journey time from Edinburgh was reduced by 40 minutes; from Glasgow by 56 minutes[10]. Some hiccups marked the start. The new 'Atlantic' locomotive on the inaugural train was taken off at Dalmeny, ostensibly because suitable turntables had not yet been installed at Dundee and Aberdeen. Not all the new carriages were ready: some "ordinary" ones had to be used[11]. The new carriages had vestibule connections, steam heating, hot water (winter only), and electric light. Though criticised by some shareholders as excessively lavish, these trains were a success, but south of Edinburgh, there was over-provision. Some Midland services in the 1900s were under-used to the extent that between 1903 and 1907 the MR paid £5,000 to the North British for maintaining the Edinburgh portion of the 1.30 pm St. Pancras-Glasgow, and over £6,000 for the overnight 'Highland Express', little-used despite having through carriages for Fort William and Aberdeen[12]. The Fort William service was formed of two carriages detached at Waverley from the St. Pancras train and attached to the East Coast train from Kings Cross, leaving at 4.30 am for Glasgow, formed of two sleeping cars, a corridor coach and a NBR six-wheeler. In the summer of 1906 the Midland carriages came off at Cowlairs and were taken as a separate train ahead of the 5.50 am Queen Street-Fort William[13].

Faced with continued petitions for reduced working hours, the board, through Jackson, wrote to the North British United Grades Movement secretary on 28 June, refusing any general cut in hours, but adding Methil, Burntisland and South Leith yards to the eight hour shift system, and making a few further minor concessions[14].

**No. 323 of Holmes's 317-class (1903) passes a shunting 0-4-0, perhaps No. 358, the last
0-4-0 tender engine to run in Britain (withdrawn 1925). The time is between 1903 and 1911,
when the two Wheatley 0-4-0s were fitted with cabs. (*John Alsop*)**

In August the North British United Grades Movement merged with the Amalgamated Society of Railway Servants (from 1892 a UK-wide union).

W.F. Jackson acted as a witness for all the Scottish railway companies before the House of Commons Select Committee on Land Value Taxation (Scotland) in November 1906. This was his prime area of expertise and he defended the companies' position with skill and statistics. Railway companies were by far the biggest individual rate-payers to local authorities in Scotland. He cited the values or rentals for the year up to Whitsunday 1907 as £672,146 for the North British, £642,809 for the Caledonian, £292,076 for the G&SWR, £76,309 for the GNSR, and £43,045 for the Highland. He pointed out that by act of Parliament, railway land could only be used for railway purposes and so had no development value. Jackson's testimony helped, or ensured, the exclusion of railways and canals from the Land Values Bill of 1907[15].

Heavy snowfalls disrupted East Coast services in late December 1906. On the 28th – an ill-omened date for the North British – the 7.37 am Aberdeen train from Waverley could not get beyond Arbroath, and after a long wait there was shunted on to the Up line and returned towards Dundee, the engine running tender-first. The telegraph wires were down, the block system inoperative, and a blizzard was raging, with the train being worked on the 'caution' system. At Elliot Junction, where it was due to stop, it crashed into a Caledonian local train which had left Arbroath only ten minutes before it. Thirteen people died on the scene and the final toll of dead was 22. George Gourlay, driver of the express, was arrested at home next day. Though he attracted much public sympathy, he was found guilty of culpable homicide by a 10-5 jury majority, chiefly because he had assumed a signal which seemed clear *was* clear, and had approached the station at an unduly fast speed, but the jury recommended "the utmost leniency". He was sentenced to five months' imprisonment[16]. The company had backed and defended him throughout and on his release immediately restored him to his job.

On 3 March 1907, Charles Carlow addressed the annual festival of railway employees at Methil. Referring to the "coal boom" of the time, he said the railways were "under a cloud", partly because of demands for improved hours "and all that kind of thing" and partly because of demands from the Board of Trade for more safety precautions and from the travelling public for more luxury. To make the concessions asked for by the staff would cost the company £100,000. But there was only £118,000 available to pay even the current low dividend rates, 1.75% and 1%. "Remember the poor shareholder", he adjured his possibly unreceptive audience. In fact the dividends announced a few days later were the usual 3% on ordinary preferred, with 0.5% on deferred ordinary. North British stock fell to £32 17s 6d for £100 ordinary and the preferred ordinary sank to £69 12s 6d[17].

Fort Augustus Station, with West Highland Bogie No. 55. (*Stenlake Collection*)

Fort Augustus Pier Station when new. Scarcely-used, it was closed in 1933. (*John Alsop*)

By 1907 the Highland company, confident of its monopoly in Inverness, was no longer prepared to lose money on the Invergarry & Fort Augustus line. The North British took over the service on 1 May, with a three year agreement to work the railway for 60% of its gross revenue, with a minimum take of £2,000.

Complaints about NBR services still cropped up from time to time in newspaper correspondence columns, citing delays, dirty carriages, even "services planned with a malicious ingenuity to baffle travellers"[18]. While it is impossible to know to what extent these letters reflected a general opinion, it is likely that, given the age of much of the rolling stock and locomotives and the ever-stronger drive for economy in working expenses, that there was a good deal of justification for the complaints. Paradoxically, others complained about the top end of service, criticising "fancy trains" with dining car staff "in blue and gold" like high-ranking naval officers. These complainers were more likely to be writing as shareholders than as passengers, and also picked on the relationship between railways and coalmasters, noting that the railways had had to repay £100,000 to the coal shippers after failing to justify the rate increase of 1900. On the North British, the calibre of the directors was questioned, as was the board's predilection for "appointing" new directors[19]. Such comments tended to arise in times of falling receipts and low dividends, and Dalkeith's speech to the half-yearly meeting on 21 March was a catalogue of problems: snow, the Elliot crash, higher labour costs, the burden of rates, ever-greater competition from trams and motors, etc. He pledged more co-operation with the Caledonian and yet further cost-cutting[20], but sometimes the company's own attitude is questionable: in response to a question asked in Parliament as to whether the Board of Trade was aware that the Caledonian and North British timed trains at Crianlarich for the greatest inconvenience and delay to transfer-passengers, the board replied that the companies had assured it that every effort was made to be convenient but requirements of local traffic and steamship connections were a problem[21]. "Local traffic" on both the Callander & Oban and West Highland lines might have raised a hollow laugh in certain quarters.

At Clydebank the new Rothesay Dock was inaugurated on 25 April 1907, served jointly by the North British and Caledonian. Meetings from 22 February had thrashed out the mode of working, agreed on 11 April. Initially, one engine was to work the dock lines between 7am and 5pm, supplied in alternate years by each company, but this soon proved insufficient[22]. Wemyss's Buckhaven Dock Bill was again rejected, but Parliament passed the NBR's Methil Bill, with certain provisos including that it must complete the work as soon as possible. Dalkeith promised "no undue delay"[23]. Wemyss contrived to get the North British Bill re-contested in the Commons and eventually

Singer Station, Kilbowie, after 1907. (*Stenlake Collection*)

a settlement was made, including compensation to the Wemyss Coal Co. for coal measures below the dock, which could not be worked, and a half penny per ton rate for coal coming in on Wemyss's own railway until the quantity should reach 5,000,000 tons a year[24]. Glasgow's second goods station on the College site opened on 1 August 1907, alongside the G&SWR station. Hailed as the largest goods depot in Scotland, its main building was of brick, 500 feet long and 321 broad, with three levels plus a basement, and a mile of track inside the building alone. Electric cranes were installed. The official name was to be High Street but it was generally known as 'College'. Perhaps it was not quite as ready as supposed, since by the 15th, some of the staff transferred from Sighthill had been moved back, along with some of the 'sundry' or lighter traffic[25]. More work was going on west of the city, where part of the Helensburgh line, including Kilbowie Station, (renamed Singer from 4 November) was being deviated ³/₄ of a mile to the north to make room for expansion of the huge Singer factory, including a works terminal of three island platforms with six tracks, which opened on 3 November.

At the half-yearly meeting of the North British Railway Insurance Society on 26 August 1907 it was revealed that expenditure had exceeded income. Discussions with the North British board (taking in also the effects of the Workmen's Compensation Act from 1 July 1907) included a request for an extra contribution of a penny per member per week. The directors regretted that this was impossible, but agreed to increase the company's annual payment to £1,000 (about a shilling a year for each employee) so long as it was matched by members' contributions. These were raised to 6*d* a week, with boys of 14 or less paying 4*d*[26]. The board also passed a resolution making 65 the official retirement age for salaried staff. The North British wage Bill for the half-year to July 31 was £25,000 up and the amount available for dividend £30,000 down. An increase in revenue of £80,000 had been swallowed up by increased costs and charges[27]. Some reductions in winter steamer services followed, with passengers from Craigendoran to Rothesay having to change to a Caledonian ship at Dunoon[28]. All railway events were happening against a backdrop of menacing newspaper headlines, 'Rail Crisis', 'Strike Threat', as the union prepared for a Britain-wide showdown. The industrial climate had been worsening through the year, with the railway companies refusing to acknowledge the existence of the Amalgamated Society of Railway Servants, the Society threatening a strike for recognition and better working conditions, and the companies making preparations to minimise its effect, including a training scheme for potential 'blackleg' workers[29]. At the last minute, on 6 November, a strike was averted by the president of the Board of Trade, David Lloyd George, whose proposal of conciliation committees within each company to resolve pay and hours issues was accepted by both sides. Management and (elected) men would be members, and an arbitration system would be set up to deal with any impasses. The North British board was reported as being "generally favourable" to the scheme[30].

Following inter-company discussions, passenger fares went up in late November, especially weekend tickets. The excursion fare between Edinburgh and Glasgow, 5s (first) and 3s (third) was abolished and the standard fares of 7s 6d and 4s 3d applied. Rises in coal prices and other cost increases were blamed. North British and Caledonian directors and officials held two meetings in a single week to discuss elimination of wasteful duplication.

The reluctance of a jury to blame railwaymen for failures which might be ascribable, or partly ascribable, to their working conditions, was evident when a 'Not Proven' verdict was returned against Driver Ekvall, whose heavily loaded excursion train had run into a light engine at Coatbridge on 30 September. One person was killed and 50 injured. Ekvall had been arrested, but the jury blamed the North British for entrusting the train to a goods driver, even though he had fourteen years' experience. A Board of Trade inquiry, published after the trial, found the driver primarily responsible[31].

At the very end of the year it was announced that the North British and Caledonian companies had made an important agreement, to be effected in 1908. Details of the 50-page document were understood to include the pooling of all competitive goods and passenger traffic within Scotland and the rationalisation of competitive services. From the Laird of Wemyss came an immediate letter to the press expressing concern that healthy and beneficial competition would be throttled. Meanwhile the Scottish Railway Shareholders' Association claimed credit, as a pressure group, for bringing the agreement about[32]. The split of revenues was agreed at 55.12531% to the CR and 44.87469% to the NBR on coaching services, and 52.50306% to the CR and 47.49694% to the NBR on goods services. Between 1909 and 1914, the CR would pay the North British a total of £102,835 under this division. Among other provisions the NBR was to pay £2,500, then £250 a year until May 1911, for use of the jointly-owned line between Dalreoch Junction and Cardross. The Caledonian was to pay the NBR £750 plus £75 a year for use of the old Monkland & Kirkintilloch line between Gartsherrie and Garnqueen North, until it should build its own link (this was never constructed). Both companies pledged themselves not to acquire, lease or work the G&SWR, GNSR or Highland Railways. Traders' season and return tickets would be valid on both systems. The Agreement was effective from 1 February 1908 and due to last 20 years, with ten year's notice of termination[33]. A joint committee and 'standing arbitrator' were to supervise the arrangements. Long schedules of stations and sidings for joint operation were compiled[34]. Service reductions began in February with the cutting of two Glasgow-Aberdeen trains, each way; of one train each way from Edinburgh to Glasgow (Hyndland), and one Stirling-Edinburgh service. During February the NBR also signed up to the Government provisions for conciliation boards, shortly before the deadline. Lloyd George held an informal inquiry that month into the British railway service: W.F. Jackson was the only Scottish railway representative[35].

No. 420 of Wheatley's second 4-4-0 class, built at Cowlairs in 1873 and rebuilt in 1887, at Waverley with a train for Glasgow (Hyndland). (*John Alsop*)

In March, Cowlairs Works was put on a five-day week, with a reduction of 5¼ hours (and commensurate drop in pay) until further notice. Protests about service cuts came from Aberdeen fish traders and the chamber of commerce, but the board was unmoved. The company was struggling to make ends meet, and the ordinary dividend in March 1908 was only 0.25%. The half-yearly report made the reasons clear:

Gross revenue	to 31 January 1908	to 31 January 1907
Passengers	£917,470	£888,047
Goods	£1,475,522	£1,454,687
Miscellaneous	£58,878	£61,293
Total	£2,449,571	£2,402,028
Working expenses	£1,393,75	£1,339,383

The modest rise in revenue was outweighed by the increase in operating costs. The shareholder might have seen the million-pound-plus difference between gross revenue and working expenses as all eligible for distribution in dividends, but other charges, including interest payments and taxes, rapidly reduced it. At the March half-yearly meeting, Dalkeith announced that the company had issued £1,450,000 of 4% preference stock, offered at a premium of 1.1%, and that the directors were satisfied with the take-up. He ascribed the rise in working costs wholly to a £55,000 increase in the cost of coal. The agreement with the Caledonian would include closure of competing stations where one could handle the traffic, with joint staffing of the surviving station. The 'New Lines' agreement of 1891 would be extended to run concurrently with the new treaty, and a joint committee of directors would supervise both. In reply to criticism of the West Highland's lack of revenue, he admitted it was "not a happy subject." Andrew Macdonald, spokesman of the Scottish Railway Shareholders' Association, raised a question which would soon assume great importance: wagon demurrage. This related to the length of time customers retained company wagons on their sidings, often far longer than the day or so it might take to load or unload them. The loss of wagon usage was theoretically chargeable but usually ignored or written off. At this meeting Charles Wilson of Hawick, member of a family long connected with the NBR, an ex-director and champion of John Conacher, was elected to the audit committee[36].

A look at some of the traffic committee's 'housekeeping' in 1908 sheds some light on the attitudes, particular issues and problems of the time. Board committees tried to watch over everything. Dining Car receipts and costs were reported monthly. For December 1907 they were: receipts £453, expenditure £361, profit £92. Convictions for crime on the line were also reported; in January 1908 they were: theft seven; trespass fourteen, drunk four, malicious mischief two, travelling without a ticket two, breach of the peace two. Other convictions in the course of the year were for vending heather, indecent behaviour, arson, and throwing stones at telegraph insulators. The company employed travelling squads of ticket examiners, who appear to have more than paid for themselves: receipts from 1 January to 30 June were £721 16s 11½d, while they cost £293 1s 8d. 'Pension' payments were decided: Mrs. Sneddon, after 41 years as gatekeeper at Clackmannan, was awarded 2s 6d a week. With the Government's Old Age Pension scheme (for 70 plus) anticipated in 1909, the board resolved that when retired servants could get a state pension equal to or greater than the company's grant, the company payment would be stopped, though "none shall be worse off than at present"[37]. When the district superintendent at Fort William resigned in October, he was not replaced. The board also formed a sub-committee to report on the future management of the Galloway Saloon Steam Packet Co., and the formation of a steamboat committee for all matters to do with the steamers[38].

	1908	1907
Salaries & Wages	£144,427	£150,085
Fuel, lighting	£19,076	£19,805
Clothing	£2,289	£1,340
Printing & stationery	£7,709	£6,168
Horse shunting etc.	£4,375	£4,760
Wagon covers, ropes	£6,887	£10,328
Joint station expenses	£2,940	£2,850
Miscellaneous	£3,786	£3,756
Solway buoys and lights	£177	£236
Total	£191,666	£199,328

A reduction of £7,662 was achieved, but the board wanted more, and not just from traffic. A special meeting of directors was convened on 14 October to look at what had been effected so far, and was not satisfied that the officials had done enough, "in view of the present position of the company". The strictest economy was insisted on, and Jackson produced a report listing further savings, including some made jointly with the Caledonian. They included dropping canvassers, saving £5,740 on passenger costs and £4,300 on goods. The Cowlairs workshops, already shut on Saturdays, would now close between 12 noon on Friday and 9.45 am on Monday, saving £13,060 in wages. The running department would save £2,073 in wages because of service reductions, and £29,314 in using less, and cheaper, coal. Other engineering workshops would close on Fridays as well as Saturdays, though this would save only £4,983 because of various exceptional costs. The telegraph department would cut its costs by £200, and the steamers by £1,760. Salary reviews for stationmasters, usual at the end of the year, were deferred. Jackson appended a suggestion that the cuts really went beyond what was desirable except for the present especially stringent conditions: "The fact should be borne in mind that this Company's business has all along been conducted on more economical lines than apply to most other Railway Companies." He warned of possible staff protests, and, if the working hours were to be unduly prolonged, "the Board of Trade, who have already made it known that they are by no means satisfied with the conditions existing on this Company's system, will be induced to press more strongly for reductions in actual working hours."[39].

In May the Edinburgh International Exhibition opened. Not as grandiose as its nineteenth century predecessor, it still attracted many visitors, and the NBR set up a temporary station by the site near Saughton as well as using the existing Gorgie Station for special trains. Its main contributions to the display were a model of the new Atlantic-type locomotive *Aberdonian*, and another of the PS *Waverley*, its biggest and most recent steamship.

Inter-company co-operation had its limits. The Caledonian refused running powers to the NBR over any part of the Lanarkshire & Dumbartonshire tramroads in Scotstoun, and the North British had to arrange for construction of its own lines, with a wayleave not to exceed £2,000[40]. On 14 July the Court of Session rejected the NBR's appeal against the Railway Commissioners' refusal to sanction a lower rental for its use of Aberdeen Joint Station[41]. A Provisional Order under the Private Legislation Proceedings (Scotland) Act of 1899 was sought in August for the amalgamation of the West Highland Company with the NBR; also for taking over the Invergarry & Fort Augustus Railway and to empower the Forth Bridge Railway to raise £100,000 of new capital. In 1902 all West Highland Railway debenture and other stock guaranteed by the North British had been converted to 3% NBR debentures. By 30th June, 1907, the total of West Highland indebtedness to the North British stood at £2,351,725, including the values of the converted shares and debentures[42]. Far from being an independent concern, it was a ball and chain attached to the North British. A Scottish Railway Shareholders' Association circular that month regretted there had been little abatement of Clyde steamer services, and shared a more general feeling that the new NBR-Caledonian agreement had not achieved a great deal. In particular the Scottish Railway Shareholders' Association considered it had failed by not covering Anglo-Scottish traffic[43]. The still-prickly nature of the relationship between the two companies is illustrated by the more than year-long correspondence between Jackson and Guy Calthrop of the CR to agree the nature and cost of NBR locomotive facilities at the Caledonian's new Ferryhill Depot at Aberdeen[44].

No. 868 *Aberdonian*, first of the 'Atlantics'(1906). (*North British Railway Study Group*)

Both the Caledonian and the Glasgow & South Western combined with the North British on the issue of demurrage charges, which came to the fore in the summer of 1908. Delays to wagons had always been a cause of argument and the North British had always been more liable to charge demurrage than the other companies. In 1896 a Bo'ness timber merchant declared a preference for the Caledonian because "demurrage is not so readily asked for"[45], but charges had never been systematically enforced. Now on 1 August the companies jointly issued a circular informing all customers that from 1 February 1909, demurrage charges on wagons and tarpaulin sheets would be enforced. After two days, for every day or part-day, 1s 6d would be charged for wagons up to 16-ton capacity, 2s for 16-20 tons and 3s for 20 tons-plus. Even traders' own wagons would not be wholly exempted. A "siding rent" of 6d a day would be charged for these if they remained for more than two days on a railway company's siding. The companies reserved the right to ask a consignor for written confirmation that demurrage charges, if incurred, would be paid. But "the Companies do not undertake to supply waggons or sheets at the time, or of the number ordered."[46] The announcement sparked fury from the shippers, who denounced it as a way of increasing carriage rates by the back door. Objectors claimed that delays were often caused by the railway company failing to provide a locomotive when asked for, or having insufficient siding capacity at the docks, and pointed out that modern ships had greater capacity and took longer to load. The railway companies remained unmoved. Speaking for them all, Sir Charles Renshaw of the Caledonian said there would be a "Board of Control" to deal with individual cases[47].

At this time there was some enthusiasm among shareholders for a NBR-Caledonian merger, which was not reflected on the respective boards. Then in September the North British announced there would be no dividend on ordinary preferred and deferred shares. The Scottish Railway Shareholders' Association promptly demanded a Committee of Inquiry into the company's affairs and the board recorded its "surprise" at this. Both sides set about canvassing for proxy votes in anticipation of the imminent half-yearly meeting[48]. But the meeting, on 24 September, despite Macdonald's charge that some directors' interests were at variance with those of the company, saw the board's report accepted. Dalkeith had pointed to the general recession in trade, combined with rising prices, and pledged to enforce the demurrage charges[49].

Ferry services between Granton and Burntisland were reduced to five a day, each way, on weekdays and two on Sundays, an action immediately challenged by Fife County Council as a breach of statutory obligations under the Act of 1842 which stipulated that there should be eight sailings each way daily, and three on Sundays[50]. Trying to cut out other peripheral costs, the NBR repeated an attempt previously made in 1900[51] to officially close down the silt-filled harbour at Leven, with its Provisional Order immediately opposed by the Wemyss Estate and other local interests. A large curtailment of services was made in late October, with over 100 weekday trains and 20 Sunday trains withdrawn and a consequent wave of protests from the towns affected, Grangemouth, Falkirk, Bathgate, Dunfermline, Bo'ness and others. Some services were restored after visits from local deputations to the board[52]. In November the Railway & Canal Commissioners reserved judgement on the NBR's Aberdeen line claims against the Caledonian. For the company's work force, the Caledonian agreement meant job losses. All work at Grangemouth Docks was to be done by the CR, and a new grievance was born[53]. Before the end of the year, wage cuts were being made. Overtime rates for surfacemen went down from time plus a half to time plus a quarter, and there were pay reductions in the goods department. These now had to be approved by sectional conciliation boards, and go to arbitration if necessary[54]. A freezing spell at the turn of the year, with blizzards, snowdrifts and blockages, meant further loss of revenue.

The large North British stations were generally open places. Tickets were collected on the trains, at ticket platforms just outside, except at holiday times and Saturday evenings; but the company was being urged by some shareholders to introduce platform tickets, both to reduce overcrowding in the stations and as a source of extra income[55]. The directors took no action on this. Revenues on both passenger and goods services were still falling and they were more concerned to stem the losses than to invest in ticket machines.

Demurrage remained a burning issue, and as February approached, a crisis atmosphere developed. There was a general refusal to sign up to the conditions set out in August 1908 and their legality was challenged. Iron and steel companies said they might have to close down. It seemed that the very existence of Scotland's mining, heavy industries and docks was being put at risk[56] by the enforcement of a modest set of charges. There was more than a dash of moral blackmail in the reaction. Private meetings between major customers and the railway companies failed to get the policy changed. In a circular published on 21 January the companies again asserted that "Detention of wagons has been unreasonable and unfair". Hoping to break the deadlock, the Board of Trade organised a conference on 5 February, without result. By then, some collieries had to stop production because no wagons had been supplied. The railway companies were open to changes in detail, such as charging 1d per ton of wagon capacity per day rather than the proposed flat rates. They also agreed not to charge consignors for

Cowlairs Incline: splicing a cable, with brake wagons behind. (*John Alsop*)

delays caused by consignees. The North British also offered a "substantial discount" to customers who actually signed up to pay demurrage charges[57], but these were few. It was a stand-off – if the railways did not supply wagons to the non-payers, they would lose their own basic income as well as cause an economic disaster. Negotiations continued, wagons were supplied, and the NBR kept a record of all charges, but even by 3 February it was noted "more empty waggons seem available"[58].

An ordinary dividend of 0.25% in March did little to reassure the Scottish Railway Shareholders' Association, though it expressed satisfaction that the North British had reduced train miles by 500,000 and managed to get its working expenses down from 55.36% to 53.75% of gross revenue. Compensation payouts for the Elliot Junction smash amounted to £44,000. The chairman explained that the NBR had not joined the Caledonian and G&SWR in a pooling arrangement for steamer services because there was little competition between the respective routes[59]. In June the Railway & Canal Commision finally issued a judgement on the Kinnaber-Aberdeen claim, reiterating that the NBR should receive £600 a year from the Caledonian out of the 'residue' of revenues on the line, as from 16 July 1907. The NBR had argued for an equal division of the residue, though it had only 283 yards of owned track on the route compared to the CR's 38 miles[60].

The cable-worked 1 in 42 incline from Queen Street to Cowlairs had always been a source of frustration to the traffic department, and long before 1900 locomotive tractive and braking power could have coped with the incline. In the 1900s, planning for a change became more purposeful, and after a year's trial of locomotive-only usage, the cable system was finally ordered to be dismantled in September 1909. Powerful new 0-6-2 tank engines were available for banking trains up the hill. Each day 450 trains used Queen Street and abolition of the cable improved the station's efficiency. Work was also completed at Portobello, where the 'clay hole' had always been a problem. A wide bed of clay here was worked by the firm of Turner & Co., with a long history of wrangles with the North British over subsidence. Turners claimed that clay was a mineral which they were entitled to extract, but the NBR said it was earth. After renewed subsidence of the railway embankment in 1904, the NBR obtained a judgement from the Court of Session that clay was not a mineral, and sued Turners for £1,150[61]. The case went to the House of Lords on appeal, and Turner & Co. were finally interdicted from working the clayfield close to the railway. Graigentinny and Portobello West Yards were remodelled for greater efficiency in train-marshalling. The whole work was done for less than the estimate, Dalkeith told the half-yearly meeting on 23 September[62].

In the continuing demurrage battle a further Board of Trade conference on 19 August proved fruitless. But at the NBR's half-yearly meeting, Dalkeith observed that many more wagons were now in circulation. Indeed they had "several thousand" lying idle. The number awaiting repair was 5,998 compared to 1,438 a year earlier, which suggests that many of the retained wagons had been in poor condition[63]. In November the railway companies sent details of the arrears of demurrage charges incurred by coal and iron and steel companies to the Board of Trade, and asked for arbitration. But the consignors refused arbitration and demanded that the issue go to the Railway & Canal Commissioners, claiming that the companies' circular of August 1908 was illegal and unenforceable, that demurrage had always been built into the carriage rate, and the proposed extra charge was unreasonable and excessive[64].

Edinburgh Town Council was pressing the North British to do something about the derelict state of the Union Canal basin at Port Hopetoun. The Canal was earning £1,730 a year but costing £2,250 to run. Still with designs on building a goods depot on the site, the NBR was reluctant to spend money on clearing it up, and opposed an Edinburgh Town Council Provisional Order for improvement of the canal district[65]. Internally, the conciliation boards failed to agree on the company's wage reductions and Sir Francis Hopwood was appointed to arbitrate on the issue. By 13 November a settlement had been established with all grades except goods guards, shunters, and locomotive men. Hopwood's judgement did not concede a great deal to the employees, imposing a ten hour day and a 60 hour week (the company had wanted a twelve hour day with two hours for meals). The long-established trip system, which had paid certain long-distance engine crews thirteen days' pay for 12 days' work, was abolished[66]. Locomotive men were to be promoted by merit, not seniority in service. The minimum overtime rate was to be time plus one fifth from 1 April 1910 to 31 March 1912; thereafter time plus a quarter (the company had wanted to pay overtime at the standard rate). The rule about retirement at 65 applied only to salaried staff. In December the board agreed that all waged servants aged 72 and over should be required to retire as from 1 June 1910[67].

In February 1910 the railway companies brought their own claims on unpaid demurrage charges before the Railway & Canal Commission, against a range of large customers. The North British joined with the other companies in trying to block the use of traders' wagons, claiming that its own wagon stock was sufficient for the needs of traffic. This further annoyed the shippers. Although only a proportion of coal and mineral traffic was carried in traders' own wagons (unlike England, where most of it was) they considered it another attempt to extort extra payment. During the dispute the question of "thirled waggons" also arose – the terms on these gave the original owner certain rights, including first call on availability, and no demurrage charge. The ten coal companies leading the opposition reckoned that they had 14,679 wagons of their own, plus 7,993 thirled wagons, the latter nearly all with the North British, which had made numerous thirling agreements in 1887 while competing for coal traffic against the Caledonian. Every thirling agreement was slightly different to the others, and the Commissioners wisely chose not to bring them into the demurrage dispute[68].

Having passed on an ordinary dividend in September 1909, one of 0.25% was declared in March 1910. Carlow stepped down as vice-chairman, replaced by William Whitelaw, but remained a director. His Fife Coal Company had just obtained a contract to supply the NBR with 60,000 tons of coal at 8s 3d a ton[69]. Despite economic stringency, the board had an inspection saloon built, on two 4-wheel bogies, of four compartments, with a small kitchen[70]. Hopwood's award was described by the board as a "disconcerting" addition to working expenses, and in June, protest meetings were being held about the company's interpretation of it, which ignored the ten hour day stipulation though it accepted the 60 hour week. Among the locomotive men, feelings ran high. Most were now members of a specialist union, the Amalgamated Society of Locomotive Engineers and Firemen (ASLEF), founded in 1881. The NBR refused to take the issue to the Central Conciliation Board until all internal procedures had been exhausted. When an ASLEF deputation went to meet North British directors on 9 August, the Amalgamated Society of Railway Servants was infuriated and called it a betrayal of the principle of collective bargaining. Finally the employees' side of the Central Conciliation Board met the NBR management on 25 August, and the belated common-sense solution was adopted of asking Sir Francis Hopwood to say what he had meant on the ten hour/60 hour issue. Meanwhile, some

William Whitelaw, chairman of the NBR from 1912 to 1923
(*Glasgow Museums*)

Dysart Station: a tinker family attracts the attention of the railway police. (*John Alsop*)

concessions were made to the enginemen. They would get a full fortnight's pay even if the hours actually worked fell short of 120; drivers on the routes from Edinburgh to Aberdeen and Carlisle would go up from 7s to 7s 6d daily, and firemen from 4s to 4s 4d. There would be an additional allowance for the nineteen crews of the Atlantic locomotives. Other main-line drivers would be advanced to 7s 3d a day, and firemen to 4s 2d. The men accepted this as remedying the "worst grievances", while the company claimed that NBR drivers were the best-paid in the country[71].

From 17 May, exhaustively and expensively, the demurrage case was argued in front of the Railway Commissioners. In one way, the railways' policy was working – deployment of wagons was already much freer; but demurrage charges were still resisted. Traders' wagons remained an issue. Giving evidence in November, Jackson stated that the North British had 32,500 traders' wagons on its lines, out of a total given by him of 68,254, and that he was not aware of any trader being refused permission to put on wagons[72].

In the course of 1908 the North British had removed a discount on harbour charges available to regularly-calling ships at Methil. The Burntisland Harbour Commissioners, NBR-dominated, did the same. 'Coal trimming' charges had been reduced at Bo'ness and Grangemouth, but not at the Fife ports. Complaining about this and failing to get satisfaction, the Lochgelly Coal & Iron Co. raised an action in the Court of Session against the NBR and Burntisland Harbour Commission, for breach of the 1896 Burntisland agreement. The court found in favour of the North British, and the Lochgelly company appealed to the House of Lords, an action which would not be resolved until 1913. At that time the coal trade was intensely active, with 59 collieries active in Fife, but also having to be highly competitive in price. The pits at Fordell, with their own private tramway, were shipping 85,000 tons a year, more than Dysart or West Wemyss, through the tiny harbour of St. David's, on Dalgety Bay[73].

A dispute between the Newburgh & North Fife Railway and the North British was raised before the Court of Session in December. For the NBR the attraction of the line was that it provided a Perth-Dundee route independent of the Caledonian. It had been agreed on 5 and 6 April 1907 that the Newburgh & North Fife Railway company would build the line and the NBR would maintain and work it in perpetuity, collecting the revenues and paying 50% of the gross to the Newburgh & North Fife Railway. If this revenue should be insufficient to match a 4% per annum return on the North Fife paid-up capital, the North British would make up the difference from its own resources. The line had opened on 25 January 1909. Its authorised capital was £180,000, with borrowing powers of £60,000, but details of a dubious deal emerged. Unable to raise the capital, its board had made an agreement with a speculative outfit, the Engineering Electric Construction Syndicate Ltd, also known as Arbuthnot, Latham & Co., which contracted to build the line for £240,000. The NBR managers claimed that this agreement was illegal, and reckoned the syndicate, which promptly subcontracted the work for £130,000, had made at least £60,000 profit. The £240,000 was to cover a double line, but only a single line was laid. There was no likelihood of earnings meeting the £9,600 a year needed to pay 4% on £240,000, and the North British refused to pay towards a dividend on any capital in excess of £180,000. The Newburgh & North Fife Railway directors had paid the Syndicate only £10,600 in cash, with £109,400 in ordinary shares, £60,000 in preference shares, and £60,000 in debentures. The Court of Session decided that it could not act since the arbitration clause in the working agreement had not been invoked, and the case went to the Commissioners of Railways & Canals[74].

The Commissioners had just given judgement in the demurrage case, essentially backing the railway companies' action, though making one or two reductions in the proposed charges. A request by one group of coalowners to have their coal moved only in their own wagons was refused[75], and the dispute now subsided, helped by an improvement in economic conditions. By October 1912, there was no longer an excess of empty wagons[76]. In March 1912 it was recorded that the North British had earned £18,600 in demurrage charges and siding rent for the period prior to August 1911[77]. The traders had a right to feel aggrieved – as long as the railway companies were locked in competition, demurrage had been largely ignored. They had been encouraged to buy or hire their own wagons to make up for railway company shortages at times of peak demand. But the new climate of co-operation and combination had changed all that. There was a real gain for both sides, however, in greater efficiency of wagon usage. It is likely that this spurred the North British to further efforts, with its control system.

In February Sir Francis Hopwood confirmed that he had meant a 60 hour week and not a week of six ten hour days, a ruling welcomed by the company[78]. With trading conditions gradually improving, an ordinary dividend of 1.25% was declared in March 1911, though Lord Dalkeith pointed out that recent awards had put the wage Bill up by £73,000, and the reduction of the working week from 72 to 60 hours had meant an increase in staff numbers and in overtime pay. The affairs of the Invergarry & Fort Augustus Railway were taking up board time, and NBR money. Its directors had proposed to close it down from 31 January 1911, rather than share half the company's deficit with the North British, but the NBR persuaded them to hold off[79].

**Newburgh Station staff, early twentieth century, with a fine array of
NBR publicity material behind. (*John Alsop*)**

Reid 'Glen' class No. 266 *Glen Falloch*, built 1913, heads another 'Glen' at Fort William with a Glasgow train. *Glen Falloch* was in service until 1960. (*John Alsop*)

At the end of 1907, the NBR superannuation fund had had a deficit of £150,000, caused by more pensions payable from 1904 as a result of the retirement at 65 rule and a change in payments: pensions based on average salary for the final seven years of service rather than the average of the individual's entire period of service. Just over 3,000 salaried staff were in the scheme. A new Provisional Order was now sought, providing for members to contribute 2.5% of salary, to be matched by the company. No pension was to exceed two thirds of the average salary in the fifteen years prior to retirement, with a minimum amount of £40 a year[80]. The NBR Insurance Society, for waged staff, was in disarray. Its members passed a vote of no confidence in its management. The board offered to put the society on a firm footing, but only after it knew what its obligations would be under the forthcoming National Insurance Act[81].

If the enginemen had been pacified in the autumn of 1910, the surfacemen were not. Especially among the 800 or so in the Western District, dissatisfaction with pay and conditions was rife. On 20 May 1911 they asked for an extra 1s a week on the current pay of 19s- £1, a reduction of the working day to nine hours, and for the company to provide a shovel once a year (men had to provide their own shovels). The NBR refused, and on 11 June 300 men went on strike between Dalmuir and Lenzie, returning on the 17th after Jackson agreed to meet a deputation if they went back to work, but the company conceded nothing. The conciliation board had made a five-year award on 11 June 1909, and new arrangements could not be considered for three years. On 1 August 1911 the men intimated the intention of striking from the 12th. Their demands were now a 2s a week pay-rise, an eight hour day, six days' paid holiday a year, and holiday passes for travel. The Amalgamated Society of Railway Servants, having accepted the conciliation board scheme, did not back the men, who seceded to form their own union[82]. Trouble also arose at Silloth, where dockers went on strike, complaining of getting 7s 6d for a ten hour day while dockers in other Cumberland ports got 8s for a nine hour day. These disputes reflected a wider unrest among railway workers, with threats of national strike action. The 1909 settlement had proved to be only a temporary palliative, though Scottish railwaymen were said to be less militant than those in England. Representatives of the Scottish railway companies met in the North British offices and Dalkeith issued a statement to say that they abided by the Conciliation Scheme and expected the Board of Trade to support them. Events moved fast. While the companies planned for keeping food supplies moving, coping with the summer tourist traffic, and getting troops to protect men who stayed at work, the Government proposed a Royal Commission on railway pay and conditions. The unions rejected this and North British men in Edinburgh and Glasgow voted on 18 August for an immediate strike. It was over almost before it had begun, with a settlement made over the weekend, involving relatively minor concessions but seen as a move towards forcing the companies to recognise the unions; and the men returned to work (a company notice intimated that all men on strike reporting for their next shift of regular duty would be reinstated in their posts), except for the Western District surfacemen, who hung on for two more days before being assured that they were included in the general settlement. On 29 August W.F.

Lindores Station on the North Fife Line, circa 1910. (*Stenlake Collection*)

Jackson circulated the directors' thanks to the staff: "nearly the whole of the company's staff continued to perform their duties"; and nine days' extra pay (at half-rate) was awarded to non-strikers among the Western District surfacemen[83]. To the Royal Commission on the Working of the Conciliation Scheme, Jackson said it was working well; the NBR directors far preferred arbitration to union recognition, which he described as a "national calamity"[84].

David Deuchars retired on 16 September after 36 years with the North British, having joined the Dundee & Arbroath Railway in 1861 at the age of 15. At a smoking concert on 28 November he was presented by his colleagues with a French clock and silver candelabra, and at a customers' testimonial dinner on 8 December he received a cheque for £300. Directors of the NBR were notably absent, as was W.F. Jackson[85]. Deuchars had been superintendent of the eastern district as well as overall superintendent of the line; now the tasks were divided and John Black became general superintendent with no district responsibility. The *Glasgow Herald* observed that he had been much involved in procuring economic working[86]. It had been known since September that company clerks were to have a new pay scale. A deputation met the directors and managers on 22 September to discuss it. The cost of living had gone up by 20% in fifteen years and it was estimated that a clerk with a wife and three children had a family budget of 57s 6d a week, or £147 a year. The tone of these discussions was quite different to those of wage negotiations. In November an unnamed NBR official dismissed the railwaymen's national programme for a minimum adult wage of 27s 6d per week as "prohibitive"[87].

Better facilities brought the need for better maintenance and the NBR invested in new cleaning arrangements. Static pump vacuum cleaning for carriages was installed at Bridgeton Cross and in a new cleaning shed at Craigentinny. Portable cleaners were purchased for the Fife and Northern districts. It was noted that the first cleaning of a carriage by vacuum removed from 8 to 9lbs of dust[88].

Minor lines with aspirations beyond their means continued to be troublesome. From 31 October the NBR withdrew services on the Fort Augustus line and protracted negotiations followed with the owners, the Board of Trade, and Inverness County Council. More annoying to the NBR management was the Newburgh & North Fife Railway, which took the North British before the Railway Commissioners, claiming breach of agreement, neglect, bad service, and diversion of traffic to the NBR's own lines, and demanding £15,000 in damages. There was a case to answer – the new harmony with the Caledonian had certainly reduced the company's interest in the North Fife line as an alternative route from Perth to Dundee and St. Andrews. In evidence to the Commissioners, Jackson claimed the North British service was "reasonable", and that the proprietors having made a bad bargain now wanted the NBR to take over their line "on prohibitive terms"[89]. In January 1912 the Railway & Canal Commission found against the North British for inadequate service and failure to advertise the Newburgh & North Fife line. The NBR had to keep open the south junction at St. Fort and run goods trains over the line when it provided the shortest route. It also had to pay the Newburgh & North Fife's costs[90]. This was not to be the end of the story.

In January 1912 the new salary scale for clerks was announced, at £15 for 1 year of service, rising to £60 on six years', and £100 after fifteen years. Having expected considerably better, the recipients were not at all happy and protest meetings followed, but the North British was firmly locked into controlling costs. A miners' strike in February-April forced the company to cut train and steamer services and in March notices were issued that men would be employed on a day-to-day basis – hastily altered to short-time working when it was pointed out that the NBR Insurance Society's membership was valid only for full-time employees. The society made a bid for independence as an 'Approved Society' under the National Insurance Act, but, apparently under company pressure, rescinded this decision in April and remained under the company's wing. In fact the society was totally insolvent and it was agreed with the company that members should pay 4*d* a week, to cover pensions only, with the company matching that sum. The NBR would also maintain existing pensions, though at a reduced level. Payments of sickness, accident and death benefits would stop from the end of the year. Apart from the company's and independent societies, a voluntary aid scheme also existed; an annual Railway Guards' concert in Edinburgh raised money for the permanent sick and injured, and widows' and orphans' funds (in February 1914 it was a joint NBR-Caledonian concert).[91]

Nationwide, the railwaymen secured a victory when the Railway Commissioners, in response to complaints, brought forward the termination date of current pay arrangements made under the Conciliation Scheme from March 1915 to 1 July 1913. New conciliation boards would meet half-yearly and their remit was widened. North British traffic receipts in the first week of March were £36,300 down on the equivalent week in 1911, and excursion trains were run only if the promoters of the trip could provide the necessary locomotive coal[92]. Service cuts reduced competitiveness with tram routes, soon after the North British had introduced "zone tickets", giving unlimited travel within designated zones for a low fare: Edinburgh was divided into eight zones. As with workmen's trains, company liability in the case of accident was limited to £100 per passenger[93]. For the half-year to January 1912, an ordinary dividend of 1.5% was announced. Accounts for the year of 1912 would cover only eleven months, as the Railway Companies (Accounts and Returns) Act of 1911 changed the railways' accounting year to January-December.

In the course of a decade, the North British had done virtually nothing to improve the service offered to collieries in the Lothians. As their output became ever greater, the coal companies again promoted a Bill for their own railway system, this time not involving a new harbour, but focused on better facilities at Leith. Current production was around three million tons a year, and the Royal Commission on Coal Supplies had estimated the reserves at 3½ Billion tons[94]. The demurrage dispute spurred the coalmasters on: they wanted their own railways and their own wagons. Among opponents to their Bill was Lord Dalkeith, who with triple interests in collieries, railways and Granton Harbour, which had shipped 463,000 tons of coal in 1911, might have wondered which finger to lick[95]. The Lords threw out the Bill on 21 June, but the coalmasters did not accept defeat.

Paddle steamers *Jeanie Deans* andthe Caledonian's *Queen Empress* at Rothesay. (*Stenlake Collection*)

18. WHITELAW AND BUCCLEUCH, 1913–1918

At the half-yearly meeting in March 1913 Lord Dalkeith announced he was stepping down as chairman, swapping posts with his deputy, William Whitelaw. The new chairman, aged 44, was well integrated into the structure and culture of Scotland's industrial oligarchy. A son of Alex Whitelaw, his grandmother had been Janet Baird, eldest child of a remarkable family. His cousin John Baird had joined the NBR board in 1888. Sir William Laird and A.K. McCosh were both partners in Bairds. Since 1902 Whitelaw had been chairman of the Highland Railway, but now stood down though he remained a director[1].

With the miners gradually returning to work during April, suspended services were restored. But the West Highland line was down to one train a day, each way. Under Whitelaw, the economy drive went on, and the tight grip on costs was not relinquished. W.F. Jackson informed the passenger guards that he was asking the conciliation board to reduce their wages by 2s a week. Leith remained a focus of dissatisfaction for the coalmasters. By 1913, it was shipping out 2,230,000 tons of coal a year, compared to around half a million tons in the mid-1890s, and they introduced a fresh Bill for their own Lothian railways. This year, however, despite its claims that the delays arose at the collieries, and that the collieries tried to get their coal sent to Leith Docks before the steamer arrived, causing unnecessary congestion[2], and insistence that its current facilities were adequate, the NBR published proposals for new lines "to take account of future development" east of Edinburgh. In 1912 Jackson had claimed that the company could not find extra space at Leith. Now, a deal with the Caledonian secured six acres of land and an engine shed at Seafield (the CR line of 1903 had not been a success). The South Leith Branch was to be double-track, as was the Macmerry line as far as Smeaton Junction. A new line would run to the north of Portobello Station and marshalling yard, connecting the Leith Branch to the main line at Monktonhall, also connecting with the Macmerry and Ormiston lines and the suburban line; and new spur lines to collieries would be laid[3].

A new summer passenger train was introduced on June 3, the 'Lothian Coast Express', leaving Queen Street at 3.50pm (Monday-Friday), with eight carriages, two for Gullane, four for North Berwick including a refreshment car, and two for Dunbar, which was reached at 5.45. It left Dunbar at 7.55 am, reassembling itself at Drem and Longniddry, to reach Glasgow at 9.49. Another new train was introduced on 1 July, for the summer only, between Glasgow and Crail, the 'Fifeshire Coast Express'.

In October 1912 agreement was finally reached with Edinburgh Town Council on the semi-derelict Port Hopetoun Basin. The canal, which extended to Lothian road, with an arm to Port Hamilton, would now terminate just beyond Fountainbridge. The council would undertake the development of the site and the NBR (which had once refused £60,000) accepted a payment of £25,000[4].

Methil Docks, showing lines leading up to the coal hoists, in the 1900s. The ship on the right is from Sundsvall, Sweden. (*Stenlake Collection*)

Whitelaw's first half-yearly meeting as chairman had glum figures to contemplate. The ordinary dividend was 0.5%, due in part to the effects of the coal strike. Opposition to the coalmasters' Lothian Railways Bill had cost £13,000, and demurrage charges had so far brought in only £8,111. Noting the employees' claim that the Government had promised that railway companies could raise their charges in order to finance better pay and working hours, he pointed out that the Government had done nothing to legislate on this. On a more sanguine note he said that the new Methil Dock would shortly open: Fife coal output had risen from 2,459,395 tons in 1887 (year of the first Methil dock) to 9,037,790 tons in 1911[5].

At this time, of course, railways still had a virtual monopoly of inland transport – hence national concern over strikes. Commerce and industry were increasingly dependent on regular deliveries and rapid transit. A digest of the NBR's express goods services in autumn 1912 shows its longest through train to be Sighthill-Edinburgh-Riccarton-Hexham-Newcastle, leaving Glasgow at 9.30 pm and in Newcastle at 7.10 am. Another long runnner was the Balloch-Carlisle, via Edinburgh and Hawick. The Waverley Route carried five trains from Glasgow, three from Dundee, and one each from Falkirk, Coatbridge and Edinburgh, with reciprocal northbound services. The 'Second Sighthill and Carlisle Goods' was notable for running the 98 miles and fifteen chains from Carlisle to Edinburgh in three hours and five minutes, its only stop at St. Boswells, for water. The load was 30 wagons and a brake van. The Glasgow-Tweedmouth express goods covered 103¾ miles via Coatbridge and the Edinburgh suburban line in 185 minutes, including a thirteen minute halt at Niddrie West. It took 22 vehicles to Niddrie, and 30 on from there, all with traffic for York and stations beyond[6].

Arbitration on passenger guards' pay for a 60 hour week gave a starting rate of 23s for main line guards, with 25s on the Edinburgh-Glasgow and Aberdeen-Edinburgh-Carlisle routes, rising to 29s. Branch line guards' rates were from 23s to 28s. Goods depot workers still had a twelve hour day but each day was to stand on its own, and extra hours would receive the overtime rate. Porters, cleaners and lampmen got a pay rise of 1s a week, with a minimum rate of 18s, for a 60 hour week, with overtime to be paid at time plus ¼[7]. Stationmasters, whose salaries had been static for some years, showed unusual militancy this winter, meeting in Edinburgh to record dissatisfaction with a "very unsatisfactory reply to a petition for the redress of grievances", giving a few minor concessions, and raising the minimum pay level from £60 to £65, but offering no pay for Sunday duties. Their own North British Agents' Asssociation was wound up, and they opted to join the national Railway Clerks' Association[8].

Methil's No. 3 Dock was opened by the Countess of Dalkeith on 22 January 1913. The new locomotive No. 400, *The Dougal Cratur*, festooned with flags and shields, pulled the first train into the dock area, and guests transferred to *Redgauntlet*, the first ship to enter the dock. The builders were Robert McAlpine & Co., and the cost was £750,000 plus about £50,000 for the extensive new sidings at Kirkland, north of Leven. The engineer was Benjamin Hall Blyth, whose partnership had designed all three Methil docks[9]. In all, the North British spent £1,387,000 on Methil and Leven between 1889 and 1913, with a further £800,000 on Burntisland[10]. The celebrations may have deen dampened by the judgement from the House of Lords in the appeal from the Lochgelly Coal & Iron Co. over the claimed breach in the 'Burntisland Agreement' of 1896. The Lords found against the North British and ordered it to pay the complainants' costs[11]. The agreement was revised, accepting that the (raised) charges pertaining at 24 March 1910 would remain in force until 31 October 1922, unless Grangemouth and Bo'ness should reduce their dues, in which case the NBR dues would also be reduced. The North British had to pay "forthwith" £47,500 to the coal companies in reparation. *Redgauntlet* had been on the Forth since 1909, transferred to the Galloway Saloon Steam Packet Co. At this time the North British fleet consisted of *Talisman*, *Dandie Dinmont*, *Lucy Ashton*, *Kenilworth*, *Waverley* and *Marmion* on the Clyde and *William Muir* on the Forth, plus two lightships, three dredging vessels, ten barges and five boats[12].

Because of the Government subsidy the Board of Trade kept a record of services and accounts on the Banavie-Mallaig section. The summer service was three daily passenger trains each way, and one goods, with an extra passenger service on Saturdays. In winter it was two passenger trains and one goods, each way. Costs routinely exceeded revenues[13]:

	1902	1903	1907	1913
Passengers	£5277	£4991	£5220	£5644
Parcels	£1524	£1494	£1843	£3169
Livestock	£208	£231	£173	£259
Parcel post & mail	£93	£114	£188	£297
Goods & minerals	£1255	£1467	£2035	£2753
Total	£8357	£8297	£9569	£12,122
Operating costs	£19,358	£14,789	£15,227	£16,168

PS *Talisman*, painted white for cruising, leaves Rothesay on a calm evening. (*Stenlake Collection*)

**Cupar in 1910. A Holmes 693-class 4-4-0, No. 231 (built in 1896) pulls in with a
Dundee-bound stopping train.** (*John Alsop*)

To improve the tourist appeal of the West Highland line, a new train was unveiled in April 1913. Designed by W.P. Reid and built at Cowlairs, it was formed of corridor carriages, one first-third composite, and two brake thirds, lit by gas and steam-heated. The end compartments had end-windows so that the scenery could be admired. In the same month passenger fares were raised by 1-5%, to offset increased operating costs[14]. The Lauder Light Railway made overtures for a takeover by the NBR but at its half-yearly meeting on 30 April, H.G. Younger informed its shareholders that this was not possible – the commitments of the North British were too great. No dividend was paid on ordinary deferred shares[15]. But the NBR was persuaded to restart services on the Fort Augustus Railway. In 1912 the company had offered to buy the line for £22,500 but on 21 March Dalkeith told the NBR shareholders that the Invergarry & Fort Augustus Railway had refused. By 1913 it was willing, and for £27,500 (additional £5,000 contributed by the county) the line became North British property through an Act of 28 August 1914. It had cost £344,000 to construct.

Scottish coal extraction would reach its peak in 1913, with a total of 42.5 million tons. In June the Lords again rejected the Lothian coalmasters' Bill, but passed the NBR Bill[16]. The North British showed some willingness to compromise, agreeing to build fourteen of their lines within two years and to allow collieries' own wagons – but gave a flat refusal on reducing carriage rates. By September Hugh Symington of Glasgow had contracted to build the new lines, six miles plus sidings, and including 30 bridges, for £170,000[17]. A simultaneous battle was going on before the Railway & Canal Commission. In November 1912 the North British had appealed against the adverse ruling in the case of the Newburgh & North Fife Railway. The Court of Session remitted the case to the Railway & Canal Commission. Argument centred on the extent of the Newburgh & North Fife Railway's paid-up capital: counsel for the North British claimed that the Newburgh & North Fife Railway had no paid-up capital at all[18].

Leuchars Station was burned down, allegedly by suffragettes, at the beginning of October. Cupar Town Council made a bid for the junction site to be transferred there[19], but the station was rebuilt, to a more commodious design than the old one, and services were improved, with through carriages to St. Andrews on two trains a day from Edinburgh, and one from Glasgow[20]. On 30 October M.P. Galloway, manager of the Saloon Steamer Company, died. His business had declined under NBR dominion, with its earnings drawn off as "loans" to the North British, and three of its ships sold off. A new vessel, *Roslin Castle*, had been added in 1906 but was sold to the Admiralty in 1908 and replaced by the NBR's 14-year old *Redgauntlet*. John G. Galloway was authorised to run the company until permanent arrangements were made, but they never were. A proposal to buy the paddle steamer *Slieve Bearnagh* was rejected by the NBR board in February 1914[21].

**Celebration at Port Carlisle of the first steam service, on 6 April 1914. The engine is
Drummond 0-6-0T No. 22, of the 165-class, built in 1878, and originally named *Langholm*.
"Alas! the dear old Dandy's reign is o'er; But in fond hearts that homely horse-drawn waggon
Remains a 'coach of state' for evermore!" (lines from a contemporary postcard). (*John Alsop*)**

Firemen at Thornton Depot went on strike in January 1914, in protest against men being brought in from the Perth shed, some of whom superseded locals in 'seniority'. The company resisted this attempt to go back to pre-1909 practice. Piecemeal improvements to working conditions went on. A board meeting on 12 February approved three days' holiday a year without loss of pay for goods guards, shunters and locomotive men. The now-annual shareholders' meeting on 26 February was informed of increased wage costs of £117,000 and a coal Bill up by £110,000. The ordinary deferred dividend was 1.25%. A practice begun in August 1857 ended when the Port Carlisle Railway's horse-drawn 'dandy car' made its last run to Drumburgh on 4 April, and a tank engine took over.

Extensions were completed at Cadder Yard, near Bishopbriggs, in January. There were 34 sidings, with capacity for 1,800 wagons. 2,200 wagons could be detached and re-marshalled in 24 hours, with 200 trains arriving or departing. Two pilot engines were permanently employed shunting on the Up side, with a third in reserve (Up, on the Glasgow-Edinburgh line, was towards Edinburgh). William Fraser, engineer-in-chief, also confirmed progress on the new Kirkland Yard, outside Leven, on a new loop and sidings at Inverkeithing, and new engine sheds at Polmont and Dunfermline Upper[22]. These improvements tied in to a grander plan. A meeting of officials and directors on 25 February[23], with Whitelaw in the chair, received a report on various English control centres from Charles Stemp (who had joined from the Great Eastern Railway as outdoor assistant superintendent in 1907), with full details of a proposed NBR system. It arranged for control offices, for the Eastern District at Edinburgh, for the combined Monklands and Western Districts at Lenzie, and for the Fife and Northern Districts including Dundee, at Burntisland, with a central office in Edinburgh. Traffic districts and headquarters were now Southern (Hawick), Central (Edinburgh), Western (Glasgow), North Western (Glasgow), and Fife & Northern (Burntisland). The initial cost of establishing control offices in the Western & Monklands, Central and Fife districts was £28,737, but it was reckoned that in the Western & Monklands districts alone, the saving should equal 25 locomotives in a year. Engines required a 'head-marker' – there were eighteen codes using white and purple lights or discs – and large-size numbers painted on the tender for quick recognition. The control system was first installed in the Central District and was fully operative from 15 September. Telephone and telegraph linked individual signal boxes direct to Control, where a table 18 feet long by 3 feet 6 inches wide was set out with bands of steel to represent the running lines. On this the operators moved 'tickets' (tabs) to represent the positions of trains and told the signalmen which trains to allow first. Information included the availability of guards and engine crews, and details of ships in dock, with their arrival and departure dates. A later note on the control system listed its aims as designed to obviate unnecessary running of light engines or engine-plus-van; congestion at collieries and in yards; holding up of trains in loops and refuge sidings; and excessive hours of trainmen. The telephone network was vital to this, especially for wagon management and for liaison with the loading quays[24]. Central control had a control-master, an assistant control-master, three controllers, three clerks, five telegraph-telephone boys, and two general clerks. Three eight hour shifts were worked daily, and the office closed only between 10 am and 6 pm on Sundays. 'Control' took over the chief goods manager's responsibility for the general running of goods trains, allocated rolling stock (eliminating the job of plant & rolling stock superintendent), and the distribution of locomotive coal. District inspectors' responsibility for arranging wagon deliveries and pick-ups was transferred to Control[25].

At the end of January 1914 the Railway & Canal Commissioners gave a decision in the long-running dispute between the Newburgh & North Fife and North British companies. It fixed the amount of Newburgh & North Fife capital on which the NBR should pay its share of guarantee at £137,965. If the net revenue due to the Newburgh & North Fife was not enough for a 4% dividend (£5,518) then the NBR was to make it up from the mileage proportion accruing to it on its own system from traffic originating on the Newburgh & North Fife[26]. This was a neat solution, rebuffing the Newburgh & North Fife Railway's exaggerated claim but putting an onus on the North British to make something out of the line.

With the outbreak of the First World War, from 5 August 1914 the Regulation of the Forces Act (1871) was invoked to place all railway companies under Government control. North British excursion and special trains were immediately cancelled and arrangements made instead for trains to effect the general mobilisation of troops. On 14 August 70 troop specials passed through Waverley Station. The NBR was designated "secretary company" to liaise with the military authorities and pass information to the other Scottish railway companies, with a direct telephone line from the superintendent's office to Scottish Command[27]. An ambulance train, ordered by Scottish Command on 6 August, was ready within 24 hours, with four vestibuled parcel vans converted into ward cars with 96 suspended cots, two brake thirds for 'sitting cases', a composite first/third for staff, and a dining car. This set was held in reserve but later two naval ambulance trains (not of NBR stock) ran between Edinburgh, Chatham and Plymouth[28]. A dividend announcement was postponed (when made on 19 September, it was to notify 0% on deferred ordinary). Appeals for military volunteers were being answered in large numbers. The NBR undertook to keep on paying half the salary of single men, and $^4/_5$ of that of married men, who joined the colours (with company approval); and to keep their jobs open, "as far as possible". In those early days there was much expectation that it would all be over by Christmas.

The 1871 act provided for full compensation to railway companies for any losses or injuries suffered while under Government control, and it was agreed that the accounts of 1913 should be taken as a base, except when the net receipts for the first half of 1914 were less than the first half of 1913, in which case the sum payable was to be reduced in the same proportion. All Government traffic – men and freight – was to be carried without any direct charge being made or any accounts rendered. No allowance was made to cover increased interest payments on account of new investments and new capital expenditure since the war began. This point was afterwards met by an arrangement that the Government should pay interest at 4% on all new capital invested by the railways since August 4, 1914, on new lines, branches, terminals, equipment, or other facilities put into use since January 1, 1913.

Newcastleton, August 1914 – a special train is just leaving with newly-mobilised territorial troops.
(*North British Railway Study Group*)

A company circular in September 1914 set out revised traffic districts and their headquarters: Southern (Carlisle), Central (Edinburgh), Western (Glasgow), North-Western (Glasgow), Fife (Burntisland) and Northern (Dundee). This was a re-arrangement made in connection with the extension of the train control system to the Western District, with its office at Coatbridge, from 18 October[29]. The Burntisland control office opened on 1 October.

Only the expectation of an early end to the war can explain the decision in October 1914 to contract with A.&J. Inglis for a big new steamer for the Galloway Company. To cost £27,500 (partly offset by the intended sale of *Edinburgh Castle*) and be capable of eighteen knots, it was for 'deep sea' trips and cruises as far as St. Andrews. Plans for competition from other operators, and customers' impatience with the old vessels, prompted the change in policy. To be named *Duchess of Buccleuch*, it was commandeered by the Admiralty while still on the stocks. Even more surprising is the ordering of *Fair Maid*, from the same yard, for the Clyde routes, in 1915. It too was converted on the stocks to a minesweeper. Launched in December 1915, it was sunk by a mine in November 1916.

Railwaymen generally were exempted fron conscription, but as in other railway companies, North British staff were encouraged to join the Railway Volunteer Force, intended for mobilisation in the event of invasion. Eligible men were listed but the corps was never embodied[30]. By February 1915, with prices of virtually all commodities rising fast, agitation about railway workers' wages was growing. On the 21st the Board of Trade arranged a conference of Scottish railways at the NBR offices, where it was agreed that during the period of Government control all wage earners over eighteen would get 3*s* a week war bonus if earning less than 30*s* a week; if earning more than that, a 2*s* bonus. The companies considered these payments to be working expenses chargeable to the Government, but it later emerged that they would have to bear 25% of it themselves. William Whitelaw accused the Government of unilaterally changing the terms of its agreement with the railway companies[31].

By the end of 1915 Queen Street's reconstruction was completed, except for the four 30cwt electric luggage lifts, which were held over and not finished until after the war. The frontage on West George Street was adapted to provide a new main entrance and a new two-level parcels department was set up on the east side of the station. The new Lothian lines went into use from 30 September 1915, though the link from Meadows Junction, on the South Leith Branch, to the Caledonian sidings at Seafield was not laid until 1916. Whitelaw remarked to the February 1916 a.g.m. that under state control these lines were providing great value to the coalowners and the Government at the expense of the NBR deferred shareholders[32], but in 1917 the Government agreed to pay 4% interest on such costs, backdated to December 1912[33]. Cowlairs Works, like other railway works, was partly used

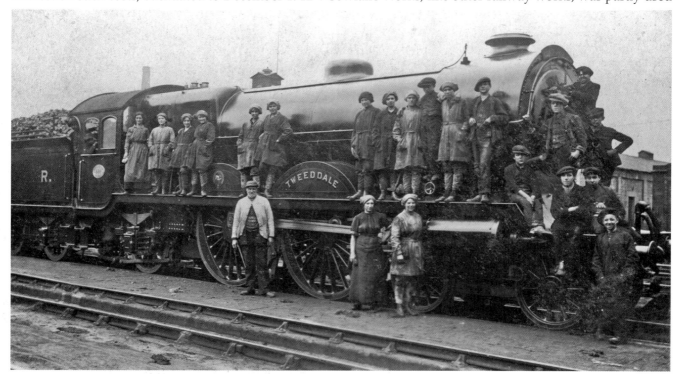

Women cleaners outnumber the men in this image from the 1915-18 period. Reid 4-4-2 No. 880
***Tweeddale* was one of the first batch of Atlantics, in 1906. (*Stenlake Collection*)**

Stobs Camp. (*John Alsop***)**

for war purposes[34], but seventeen new locomotives were built there during 1915, and in the second half of the year 29 passenger carriages, 42 other coaching vehicles, 240 mineral wagons, 40 timber wagons, 20 refrigerated meat vans, 40 cattle wagons, 160 covered vans and ten goods brakes were added to the stock[35]. In 1915 the Gask coal branch in Fife also carried material to and from a naval stores base at Lathalmond. Despite pressure on services, 25 North British engines were shipped to France for military service. In addition, two went to the Highland Railway.

Between Partick and Clydebank now lay a district of intense industrial and commercial activity. In 1891 eight works had fronted the Clyde in the area. By 1914 there were fifteen major ones, and a further twelve inland from the river, including the Albion Motor Works and six iron foundries. In addition Glasgow Corporation had established a huge cattle lairage at Merklands Quay. All had sidings from the Whiteinch or the Lanarkshire & Dumbartonshire tramways. In November an application for a Provisional Order, preliminary to a Bill, was again made for the vesting of the Whiteinch Tramway in the North British[36]: but opposition from the Caledonian and from shipyards and other customers led to its withdrawal[37].

Major stations, bridges and piers had military guards, and occasionally spies or suspect persons were arrested. There was excitement at Dunoon on 25 March 1915 when a man with a camera was taken off the *Talisman*. He had an American passport, and was taken into military custody[38]. On the Clyde, eventually only *Lucy Ashton* and *Dandie Dinmont* remained to run a much-restricted NBR service, with the other ships requisitioned by the Admiralty. All Firth of Forth steamer excursions were stopped with the outbreak of war, and the Forth was restricted to military shipping. Burntisland was taken over as an Admiralty port. In February 1916 an extraordinary news item appeared: William Whitelaw and William Jackson, as chairman and a commissioner of Burntisland Harbour Commission, had appeared before the sheriff at Cupar on a charge of hindering the national war effort by detaining the steam lighter *Briton* on 26 October 1915, when it was urgently required for conveying ammunition to the fleet. The case was remitted to the Court of Session, where further details emerged. As the harbour was owned by the NBR, dues for its use were still payable, but the Admiralty was in arrears. Unpaid dues for the *Briton* amounted to 19s 2d, and the company was unwilling to let it go until all arrears were cleared. Naval officers were despatched to the head office and acceded to Whitelaw's and Jackson's request to show "a technical display of force" in taking the boat, to clarify that the NBR was not conceding its claim. Despite this, the admiral in command had insisted on prosecution. The jury took only five minutes to give a 'Not Guilty' verdict and the case caused considerable public indignation[39]. Whitelaw had a less successful brush with military authority when he procured for his chauffeur, not a NBR employee, a railwayman's badge of exemption from military service. The sheriff sent the man (as he had wanted) to the Army[40].

Back in 1886 the NBR (and the Caledonian) had agreed a special rate for transport of oil products of the Broxburn Oil Co. Similar deals had been done with other Scottish oil-producers, but the NBR/Broxburn agreement was the only one still legally enforceable. Trouble came when the Anglo-American Oil Company complained to the Railway & Canal Commissioners in 1915 that its local competitors were getting favourable treatment. The Commissioners found for Anglo-American, and North British entered a Bill to have the discretionary rate for the Broxburn company terminated[41], but when it agreed to pay £50,000 compensation for the loss of privilege, the other Scottish producers complained, unsuccessfully, to the House of Lords. Rates for oil transport went up despite an attempt by seven Scottish producers to block the rise[42]. The Scottish shale reserves were by now yielding only 15-20 gallons per ton, compared to 35 gallons in the 1880s, and despite the German U-boats, imports of American motor spirit were flooding in.

Zeppelin airships made raids over Edinburgh and south-east Scotland in April-May 1916. Station staff were put on look-out, and the telephone network was invaluable. A bomb hit the NBR-owned County Hotel in Lothian Road, Edinburgh on 2 April, injuring one person. An armoured train was placed on the NBR for use north of Edinburgh, its formation being a gun-truck at each end, each with a support van, and an 0-6-2T engine in the middle. A regulator was fixed at each end, linked to the locomotive via an "intermediate regulator valve", a military driver and fireman were provided, and a company traffic officer accompanied the train. The gun trucks (running on Caledonian-provided 30-ton boiler trolleys) carried a twelve pounder gun and Maxim machine guns[43]. The train was built at Crewe. At Gretna Township just west of Gretna Green, a vast munitions factory was established, with railway access from the converging CR, G&SWR and NBR lines[44], and the NBR's Longtown-Gretna Branch (only two daily trains each way) was wholly taken over for its use. From 22 September 1916 to October 1918 the NBR moved 70,000 tons of cordite explosive from new sidings at Longtown. Occasionally, 'Jellicoe' trains from South Wales to Grangemouth, with coal for the Grand Fleet, were diverted via the NER and Berwick, and from 21 May 1917 the notorious 'Misery' naval train from Euston to Thurso ran via Hawick and Inverkeithing in order to serve Rosyth. Its winter timetable that year was[45]:

Euston dep. 3 pm	Thurso dep. 11.45 am
Carlisle dep. 9.40 pm	Perth dep. 10.25 pm
Hawick dep. 11.00 pm	Inverkeithing dep. 11.35 pm
Edinburgh dep. 12.38 am	Edinburgh dep. 12.31 am
Inverkeithing dep. 1.11 am	Galashiels dep. 1.33 am
Perth dep. 2.20 am	Carlisle dep. 3.20 am
Thurso arr. 12.45 pm	Euston arr. 10.05 am

The board's February 1916 report noted that to cope with wartime traffic, the Granton line was being doubled. It also recorded that the new goods and parcel accommodation at Queen Street was complete, apart from the electric hoists. At the annual meeting on 24 February, Whitelaw cautioned the shareholders that Government control did not guarantee a dividend. It merely confirmed that the net revenue from traffic working, as of 1913, would be maintained. Moving into extraordinary meeting mode, the proprietors approved a proposed Order for vesting the Whiteinch Tramway in the NBR, the purchase of Mutter, Harvey & Co., station carters, for £63,677, from 1 July 1916; and ended with cheers for their chairman[46]. Despite this, the Whiteinch Tramway never became a statutory North British line.

From 5 June the NBR, CR, and G&SWR combined to operate a pooled wagon scheme that involved 103,366 vehicles. Special-use wagons, covered vans and multi-wheeled wagons were excluded, as were traders' wagons, often still dumb-buffered despite all resolutions to abolish them. The NBR provided 49,000 wagons, of which 6,868 were marked "for local use only". A common user wagon office was set up in the NBR's Glasgow offices under a Control Committee, and staffed by two clerks from each company. On 8 December 1916 37 goods managers met to devise a scheme for the Railway Executive covering some 300,000 four-wheeled wagons. From 2 January 1917 the Highland and Great North companies joined in the Scottish scheme, and there was liaison with the general wagon pool of English and Welsh railways. Common use was also made, and monitored, of company tarpaulins and ropes. By May 1918 the scheme included virtually all wagon types except vacuum-fitted covered vans. Despite efforts from the railway companies, traders' wagons remained outside the pool. Their owners had made difficulties about joining in, and just before the proposed inclusion date of 5 February, the Board of Trade decided that it was "impracticable"[47].

Wartime austerity measures meant the withdrawal of dining cars on the East Coast expresses from 1 May 1916[48] though the NBR continued to run diners on some Scottish services. Late in the year drastic service reductions, and increased fares, were being rumoured. At the NBR's annual concert in the Music Hall (for the Red Cross) on

15 December Whitelaw confirmed that some stations would close: "Railway Companies had got their orders". That month John Black retired as superintendent after 51 years with the company. Born in 1847, he claimed to remember open seatless trucks for "Irish labourers" in the NBR's early years. His job was divided, with William Strang as commercial superintendent and Charles Stemp as operating superintendent. On 22 December it was announced that 59 North British stations would close from 1 January – 34 of them wholly, ten would have workmen's trains only, and 24 would have workmen's trains, goods trains, or both. Fares, unchanged since 1913, now went up by 50%, and all reduced fare facilities were withdrawn except for workmen's fares, theatrical companies, bands and concert parties, as well as naval and military forces and police when on duty[49], with the small consolation that all tickets were interavailable. Some concessions were still made. 'Zone tickets' were introduced in the Edinburgh and Glasgow areas and 'easy payment' spread terms were available to season ticket buyers. In a rationalisation of long distance services, Glasgow-Kings Cross trains were axed. The new year was also marked on 3 January by a major accident half a mile east of Ratho, when a packed twelve coach Edinburgh-Glasgow express ran into a light engine. Thirteen people were killed, and many others injured[50]. The toll might have been worse had the train not been formed of recently-built bogie carriages. The subsequent inquiry ascribed the crash to a long-established though irregular method of working whereby an engine was allowed to make use of the adjacent main line to move to the other end of its train, when standing on a loop line. The inspector noted that a similar accident had occurred at the same place on 18 December 1911 and considered it "inexplicable" that the practice had been allowed to continue[51].

In February 1917 the deferred ordinary dividend was 0.5%. The North British was already having trouble with the Government over claims under the 1914 agreement. In 1915 large sums had been spent on wagon repairs made necessary by war work and it had claimed over £90,000 in repayment. This had been questioned, and the matter was only resolved at the beginning of December. The preferred ordinary dividend of 3% had been held back because of this but was now paid[52]. The NBR was also seeking to make the Post Office pay for wayleave on all the telegraph poles installed on its system since 1885, despite the fact that perpetual wayleave right was covered by the annual £2,250 paid by the Post Office. The Court of Session found for the NBR, but the Post Office appealed to the Lords, who found against the North British[53]. In August a 10% "temporary increase" in pay for all railway workers earning under £500 a year was imposed by the Railway Executive[54]. In 1917, the NBR was again accused of discriminatory charging, this time by the Anglo-American Oil Co., which won on appeal against having to pay higher rates than Scottish oil companies. British Petroleum made a similar claim and received damages. Virtually all the Scottish oil companies opposed the NBR/Caledonian rate

Reid 'Scott' class No. 413 *Caleb Balderstone*, built in 1914, at Haymarket.
This engine ran until 1958. (*John Alsop***)**

**Reid Atlantic No. 872, *Auld Reekie* (built 1906) leaves Waverley on a west- or north-bound train.
A NBR coffin wagon is on the left. (*Stenlake Collection*)**

increases in 1917, but a case by the Broxburn Oil Co. was dismissed, and the others were settled out of court[55]. Another new industry was established on the NBR system with the bauxite plant of the British Aluminium Company at Burntisland in 1917.

In December 1917 W.F. Jackson announced his intention to retire, because of poor health. The company's longest-serving general manager, appointed in 1899, he had long since lived down the derogatory comments about being Wieland's puppet and had been a respected if austere figure. A fervent Christian and a strong supporter of the YMCA, he has been criticised for a narrow and inflexible attitude[56], but off-duty at least, he had some humour, owning a succession of dogs called 'Snark' and with occasional jokey poses among his many photographs (his albums are now in the Glasgow University Archive)[57]. Most of his shots are of holidays, as far afield as Sweden and Egypt, very few feature North British scenes. In May 1918 James Calder, his assistant, was appointed general manager. He was a child of the North British, born in 1869 at Blackhall Station where his father was agent.

A company report on goods department war service recorded that the NBR had transported heavy guns to Silloth and Reedsmouth for testing on artillery ranges. Beardmores also tested hundreds of field guns brought by rail to Inchtarff Siding, close to Gavell on the Kilsyth line. Among exceptional items carried were listed: anchors, aeroplanes (complete and crated), airship cars, cranes, funnels, masts, buoys, propellers, tank hulls, traction engines, and masts. Prior to August 1914 no women had been employed in the department. During the war 534 were taken on, in clerical and manual posts. By 1918 the NBR was employing around 1,300 women, compared to 119, mostly gatekeepers and cleaners, in 1914. The company served new military airfields at East Fortune, Drem, Aberdour, Donibristle, Turnhouse, Crail, Leuchars, Dundee (seaplanes) and Montrose (from 1913). Donibristle had its own railway from a jetty by the East Ness, Inverkeithing, linked to the NBR main line at Donibristle Siding for the transfer of fuel and stores[58]. At Stobs a rail-served prisoner-of-war camp was set up, later converted into a hospital for wounded prisoners – German prisoners, brought to the camp and dispersed to other locations, accounted for 500,000 trips. The increase in loaded wagons dealt with at exchange points between 1914 and 1918 was 65%, with the greatest rise on the East Coast line at Berwick:

	NBR to NER	NER to NBR
April 1914	9,430	5,963
April 1918	22,531	16,659

In the war years the NBR hauled 1,290,000 tons of coal from Berwick to East Coast ports. It also ran Ayrshire coal trains between Corkerhill (G&SWR locomotive depot) and Grangemouth, carrying around 380,000 tons – 38,000 wagon-loads[59].

The branch line to Rosyth opened on 1 January 1918 and 20 trains a day carrying workmen and sailors ran there from Edinburgh (Inverkeithing had a further ten). Over 4,000 workmen commuted from Edinburgh to the dockyard[60]. Portobello's iron pier was sold for scrap at £2,180, condemned by decrepitude and wartime restrictions on its use. By 1918, NBR passenger services were reduced by almost 45% compared with 1914, and as far as the general public was concerned, the outlook was for further restrictions, confirmed by William Whitelaw at the annual meeting on 22 February. The deferred ordinary dividend announced for 1917 was only 0.75%. In response to the Government-awarded pay increases to railway staff, which had a direct impact on the amount available for dividend, the Scottish Railway Shareholders' Association had reorganised itself as the Scottish Shareholders' Protection Association, and Whitelaw welcomed this "with the utmost satisfaction"[61].

Following the Armistice on 11 November 1918, there was a period of intense activity as the forces were demobilised, with rail-served dispersal camps set up at Kinross, Duddingston and Georgetown (the last served mainly by the Caledonian), followed by a longer period of winding down as services and installations required for the war effort were terminated, dismantled or sold. 4,836 North British staff had joined up, out of 24,625, and 775 had been killed in action[62]. Now most of the survivors took up their old jobs again. The Railway Executive continued to control the national system, and the wartime wagon-pooling arrangement, which had led to much greater efficiency in wagon use, was maintained.

In 1918 passions could still be roused about which was Scotland's "premier line". A writer in *Railway & Travel Monthly* advanced the claim of the NBR: longest mileage, greatest capital investment, most locomotives, largest engine (a dubious claim this), largest station (Waverley) and largest marshalling yard (Portobello), largest dock owner, only one to possess two trunk routes to England, and only company to adopt the control system[63], but this kind of comparison was becoming irrelevant in a context of war-worn systems and the expectation of large-scale rationalisation of Britain's railway system.

Haddington Station in the 1900s. The number of the engine, 1059, shows it is on the duplicate list. It looks like a Hurst 80-class 0-6-0 of 1861-67. (*John Alsop*)

19. LAST YEARS, 1919–1923

At the annual meeting on 22 February 1919, Whitelaw gave some details of wartime Government traffic carried free under the guarantee arrangements. During 1918 NBR stations forwarded 750,000 tons of merchandise, 322,000 tons of coal and 172,000 tons of other mineral traffic. 136,000 officers' travel warrants were collected, and over one million from other ranks. He reckoned all this as worth some £1 ³/₄ million to the company. Surviving requisitioned ships now returned for refit: *Marmion, Talisman*, and *Kenilworth*; with *William Muir* about to be handed back. *Waverley* was not returned until February 1920. Noting that the Railway Executive Committee had ordered the companies to implement an eight hour day (48 hour week) from 1 February, Whitelaw advised the NBR shareholders to join the SRSPA, in order to protect their interests in an effective pressure group.

Fire at engine sheds was always a hazard. Fort William's had burned down in 1918 and was rebuilt incorporating a new dormitory for enginemen, but a more disastrous blaze, starting in an oil store, engulfed Eastfield locomotive shed on 28 June 1919. Forty engines were in the wooden-roofed shed, and though most were moved out, sixteen were destroyed[1]. From 1 February 1919 the 65-minute service between Waverley and Queen Street was restored. From 2 June 1919 the summer service to Crail was reinstated, as the Fife Coast Express. Leaving Crail at 7.15 am, it reached Queen Street at 9.40; the return service left Queen Street at 4.05 pm and was in Crail by 6.27. There was a similarly-timed Edinburgh service, 7.25 am from Crail, arriving Waverley 9.14, with a return train from Waverley at 4.50 pm, arriving in Crail 6.38. The Lothian Coast Express from Glasgow to North Berwick, Aberlady and Gullane – the only scheduled train to run non-stop through Waverley Station – was also restored, leaving Queen Street at 4.15 pm and in North Berwick by 5.53, while its morning service left North Berwick at 8.10 and was in Glasgow by 9.50[2].

To railway directors and shareholders, the improvements in railway workers' pay and conditions since 1914, during the period of Government control, seemed extraordinary, though much else had changed dramatically in those years and the railwaymen were at best keeping pace with employees in other industries. Bjut the railway companies' earnings were not rising to match. In 1913, the North British wage Bill, excluding salaried staff, was 24.5% of receipts; in 1919 it was 36.25%. The proportion of receipts allocated to dividend fell from 27% in 1913 to 14.25% in 1919[3]. No wonder Whitelaw advised the shareholders to join their 'union'. Another telling statistic was that in 1913 there had been 8,610 claims made for goods lost or pilfered on the North British; in 1919 the number was 28,144[4]. The spirit of the times had changed in many ways. The "railway servant" years were gone and despite higher pay and shorter hours, the workers remained militant and suspicious of the intentions of their employers and of the Government. A national strike was called, to start at midnight on 26-27 September, and the North British men responded immediately. The company estimated that 80% were out[5]. There was picketing on a large scale and many instances of violence. Detonators were placed on lines still in use, windows were broken in signal cabins and stones thrown at trains. At Inverkeithing a sleeper laid across the line was pushed aside by a locomotive. Traffic was worked on a time-interval system because of the absence of signalmen. Though the strike was a sudden one, the company reacted swiftly with emergency arrangements, and many volunteers, included demobilised soldiers, came forward. Over 200 men were housed in Waverley Station, and 500 naval ratings with "kits and hammocks" were despatched from Rosyth to Edinburgh and Glasgow. A 'strike bulletin' produced in Glasgow had a defiant tone. A meeting of strikers at Waverley saw "Ranks as solid as Arthur's Seat", and Springburn was described as "now a naval base"[6]. Volunteer porters, generously tipped by travellers, earned £1 or more a day and assumed that this was normal. At Fort William, where "a small number of extremists" were said to be, rails were found loosened on the line. A national settlement was made on 5 October, and with promises of mediation and a new wage offer to come, the men returned to work[7].

The Committee on Rural Transport (Scotland) reported in July 1919. It noted that the Falkland Light Railway had failed to raise enough capital, and that the Treasury and Fife County Council had agreed to support it, but the war had intervened. The committee recommended the scheme and also (in a supplementary report) an extension of the Gifford Branch to Garvald and on to meet the main line near Dunbar. Neither scheme was taken further, however[8].

W.P. Reid retired in December, to be replaced by two men, Walter Chalmers, the chief draughtsman, with the new title of chief mechanical engineer, and John P. Grassick, district superintendent at Eastfield, as superintendent of locomotive running. In March 1920 Reid was awarded a CBE. Charles Stemp also received a CBE to add to the OBE he had been awarded in 1918 – in both cases for their contribution to the war effort[9]. The traffic committee, meeting in January 1920, proposed to order 3,000 new wagons, including 100 swivel-bar wagons, 50 14-ton pig-iron wagons, and 500 sixteen ton mineral wagons for locomotive coal. The eventual order approved by the locomotive & stores committee in February, though large, was more modest (1913-level prices quoted: the balance between these and 1920 prices was to be charged to the Government):

> 50 dual-fitted fish vans at £237 apiece
> 10 horse boxes at £280
> 4 vestibule firsts at £1,750
> 2 saloon thirds at £1,300
> 4 vestibule brake vans at £798
> 8 vestibule thirds at £1,552
> 5 bogie thirds (9 compartments) at £1,013

– all to be built at Cowlairs. In addition, 395 assorted vans and wagons were ordered, at a cost of £48,050 – including 145 sixteen-ton mineral wagons, 200 ten-ton covered vans, 25 six wheel 20-ton brake vans, and 25 fifteen-ton covered vans, all to be built at Cowlairs except for the mineral wagons. Further engines were ordered, two superheated additions to the Atlantics, at £4,300 each, and fifteen 0-6-0 goods with 19½ in cylinders, at £2,734 each (ten fitted with Westinghouse brake equipment) to be delivered by 31 December 1920, and another ten 19½ in goods engines (£2,734) plus six superheated passenger tank engines at £3,100, to be delivered by 30 June 1921[10]. Twenty locomotive boilers at £2,930 each were ordered from Beardmores. These were again 1913 prices – the real price was quoted for an additional five 0-6-0s ordered in April, at £11,750 apiece[11]. In February the North British Steam Packet Co. was wound up, with its assets and balance of £26,592 15s 2d transferred to the NBR Company. In 1919 the steamers had generated revenue of £44,891 18s 2d against costs of £48,579 6s 6d, the only profitable months being April-August.

The burst of buying helped to push the company's short-term loans up to £1,455,737 8s 9d by March 1920. Other decisions included the ordering of a 55 feet turntable for Riccarton Junction and the installation of track circuiting at Canal Junction, Carlisle. In February Trinity House permitted the long-established Solway Lightship to be replaced by a lighted buoy, and the two light vessels 'Solway Lightship' and *Tobin* were put up for sale[12]. In a sign of the times, the traffic committee purchased four reconditioned 32 hp Albion three ton lorries from the War Department, at £845 each, to be charged to the capital account of J.&P. Cameron. Camerons were in effect a NBR subsidiary, with a long-standing loan of £26,592 15s 2d[13]. Later in the year a traffic sub-committee for the Cameron cartage business ordered an Overland motor car at £472 3s, and a pony, harness and trap to be added to the loan, plus the cost of the lorries[14]. Apart from the Cameron loan, the company's horse renewal and provision account stood at a notional capital cost of £25,000 (in 1914 the NBR had 685 horses; by 1921 it would have 559, plus ten motor vehicles charged to the horse account[15]). In May a letter from the Ministry of Transport gave orders for an increase in the 'floating' war bonus, because of the increase in the cost of living. From 1 April until the next adjustment in June, an additional £5 per annum was paid to male clerical staff, workshop staff, and station masters earning up to £350. Inclusive of the bonus element, a senior driver was now earning £234 a year, and a

Queen Street Station interior, around 1920. Reid Atlantic on Aberdeen express. (*John Alsop*)

foreman £270. Among the officials, James Calder, general manager, received £2,050 (half what Walker and Conacher had been paid), James Watson, solicitor, £3,300, W.A. Fraser, engineer-in-chief, £1,700, John Martin, chief accountant, £1,450, James McLaren, secretary, £1,050, Charles Stemp, operating superintendent, £1,550, Walter Chalmers, chief mechanical engineer, £790 (same rate as a district engineer; W.P. Reid as locomotive superintendent had been on £1,600), J.P. Grassick, locomotive running superintendent, £720, J.E. Ryan, hotels manager, £1,050[16]. Ryan's empire embraced the North British Hotel in Edinburgh, with the North British Grill Room and Bar, the Princes Street Grill Room, and the Waverley Steps Restaurant and Bar; the Glasgow hotel and refreshment room at Queen Street, and company-run refreshment rooms at Berwick, Dundee, Ladybank, St. Boswells, and Thornton, as well as a laundry at Joppa. Disappointingly for day-trippers and Sunday school children, there were no special excursion trains that summer. Both the NBR and the Caledonian said they had no facilities for running such services, though reluctance to pay overtime rates may have been a factor[17].

It was by now well-known that the Government intended to consolidate Britain's hundred-plus railway companies into a mere four or five. On 16 July the chairmen and vice-chairmen of all five Scottish railways wrote to Sir Eric Geddes, Minister of Transport, stating that the official claims of economies in the proposed grouping of their companies were exaggerated; protesting about the inclusion of employees on boards of management, and suggesting that the degree of government control was equivalent to nationalisation without purchase[18]. This was very much a Whitelaw theme. He wrote in *Modern Transport* that the Scottish companies should be grouped with their "English allies", citing the Forth Bridge Company as a model of co-operation. In his view, the rise of motor traffic reduced the railways' local functions and they should concentrate on long distance traffic[19]. By the end of August the short term loans had been reduced to £775,520 3s 10d, of which £400,000 was due to the British Linen Bank. At Glasgow the Royal Hotel was converted into company offices, and part of the Waverley Restaurant in Edinburgh was also taken over. The age of bureaucracy had arrived.

Through 1919 and 1920 the management had to give attention to the ferry services. From 1 August 1918 the subsidy to David Wilson & Son had to be raised to £1,000 a year to cover their losses, and from July 1919 Wilson's business was acquired by the Leith Salvage & Towage Co., which found it equally difficult to run the services profitably. Rates were already at the statutory maxima. The ships were old, decrepit, and too small for the new motor traffic. The Leith company demanded a subsidy of £3,000 a year for Queensferry alone, and John G. Galloway of the Galloway Saloon Steam Packet was asked to find a company to take over the service, but

Forth Ferry *Dundee* at South Queensferry. A 1926 photograph but North British in all respects. (*John Alsop*)

reported that "no-one would buy these old boats almost at any price". In August the NBR purchased the elderly PS *Dundee*, formerly owned by Wilson, for £4,850, in anticipation of direct working of the Queensferry service[20]. By 14 November 1920 the Leith Salvage & Towage contract was ended by mutual agreement, and the NBR reluctantly resumed direct working. Costs immediately went up since the seamen got higher pay as railway employees, while their working hours were reduced.

In January 1921 the company asked for powers to raise £1 million of capital, presumably to reduce its dependence on loans. A dividend of 1.25% on deferred ordinary shares was announced, then suspended because the Government was keeping back £430,000 of moneys claimed by the company. Under state control it had become standard practice for the railway companies to claim each month for any shortfall between their estimated net receipts for the previous month and the equivalent month in 1913. In December 1920 the NBR had a deficit of £425,598, compared with a surplus of £190,596 in December 1913, and so claimed £616,194, of which the Ministry of Transport paid only £186,194. The chairman's tone was becoming increasingly angry, and a furious speech to the annual shareholders' meeting on 25 February denounced the behaviour of the Ministry of Transport, claiming that it had welshed on the agreement with the railways. The Government, he said, was seeking to ruin the railways in order to buy them up "at scrap value". For almost two years the case would be batted between the Railway Commissioners and the Court of Session. The central issue was that in 1920 the NBR claimed £1,835,068 for repairs and partial renewal of rolling stock, while in 1913 the same items had cost only £297,583. In previous years also the NBR had claimed above the 1913 figure. The company called these figures 'misleading' because the 1920 claim included arrears of charges from preceding years because the work had had to be contracted out; and "the condition of the rolling stock as a whole was much worse than in 1913", needing greater and more frequent repairs. The Ministry did its utmost to evade the central issue, arguing (in vain) that the case could not be heard in Scotland, then (equally vainly) that the Minister's decision was "not examinable" by a court of law. The North British took its case to the Railway & Canal Commission, who made an interim order in March for the Ministry to pay the £430,000[21]. The Ministry promptly appealed to the Court of Session.

In April and May there was a miners' strike and their union invoked the "triple alliance" of colliers, railwaymen and dock workers for support. Many railway workers were disinclined to join in, and on 26 April there was a battle at Thornton Junction between strikers and non-strikers. Fifteen people were convicted of "mobbing, rioting and looting", and 95 for theft[22]. Back in July 1920 the NBR had 62,494 tons of coal 'in bing' (around four weeks' requirement) but now stocks were almost exhausted, with 483 tons in bing and 3,906 tons in wagons. A special purchase of 33 wagon-loads cost the company £2 5*s* a ton for hard coal and between £3 6*s* and £4 for coke (approximately double the usual rates). Three locomotives were to be tested on the Cowlairs Branch with oil-burning apparatus. But train services were cut back by 60%, and the workshops were reduced to a four day week[23]. By August, only one engine, 0-6-2T No. 859, was to continue with oil firing for a short time. Against this stormy background the Railways Bill was published on 12 May. Despite the wishes of the companies, the Scottish railways were to be grouped together in two companies: NBR and Great North; and Caledonian-G&SWR-Highland, along with their associated independent lines, in the NBR's case the Edinburgh & Bathgate, Forth & Clyde Junction, Newburgh & North Fife, Gifford & Garvald, and Lauder Railways. This was considered necessary because Scottish rates and fares were lower than in England and Wales, and would be regraded upwards if amalgamation with English companies were allowed. The way was left open for amendments[24], and these were not slow in coming. Scottish chairmen and general managers met at the NB Hotel on 13 May, and Whitelaw issued a statement that the Government's proposed "lump sum" of £51 million for the railways was a poor substitute for the guarantee of August 1914, and that the Bill would be ruinous for the Scottish railways.

A fire at the St. Margaret's workshops on 16 May spread to the roundhouse. Most of the locomotives were got out, but two were badly damaged and the roundhouse was destroyed. The cost of restoration at 1913 prices was to be debited to the workshops fire insurance fund (£25,773 13*s*) with the excess charged to the Government, as had been done for the Eastfield fire in 1919[25]. Meanwhile an extraordinary general meeting of NBR shareholders, loyal to the chairman despite their withheld dividend, on 3 June passed a unanimous protest against the Railways Bill[26].

On 31 May the Court of Session sent the £430,000 case back to the Railway Commissioners for resolution. Under pressure from Lord Mackenzie of the Railway & Canal Commission, the counsel for both sides reached a compromise figure, but the Ministry of Transport refused to accept it and by 21 June the case was back before the Commissioners. A Ministry official confirmed that in their view the NBR was overcharging. Given Whitelaw's outspoken views on Government policy towards the railways, the company was not held in great esteem at the Ministry of Transport. Nor was it likely that the North British would understate its claims on the Ministry, but every item in the huge Bill could be justified, with "large deliveries of repaired and renewed stock" and provision for end-of-year liabilities pushing it up. Against the Ministry's claim that the NBR stock was in better condition in 1920 than in 1913, James Calder testified that on 31 January 1913 the NBR had 1,058 locomotives, of which 57 were under or awaiting repair. By 1917 this number had risen to 113, and by 1920, when the company had 1,135

Reid 0-6-2T No. 859, built 1909. This engine was fitted with double-spring front buffers for banking trains on the Cowlairs incline. (*Stenlake Collection*)

Glenfarg Station. (Stenlake Collection)

locomotives in commission, the number was 194 – leaving fewer effective engines than in 1913[27]. The Commissioners decided in favour of the North British and the Government immediately launched another appeal. By July it was withholding a further £550,000-worth of NBR monthly claims. Once again the case went back to the Court of Session[28].

From April the Border Counties line was used again for night working, with the loops at Kielder, Falstone, Bellingham, Wark and Wall switched out. This cost £2,995 but would save £1,079 a year in signalmen's wages. On 6 July some improved and accelerated summer services were announced, including the "Fifeshire, Lothian Coast, Peebles-shire and East of Fife Expresses", though the restaurant car on the Fifeshire Coast Express was withdrawn[29]. Britain's longest through service, from Aberdeen to Penzance, 785 miles via Sheffield, Nottingham, Oxford and Bristol, was introduced in October. Two tests of 'foreign' locomotives were made in 1921, both concerned with goods haulage. On 12 January the GWR 2-8-0 No. 2846 was tried on Glenfarg. In September a North Eastern 3-cylinder locomotive was borrowed. It took a 754-ton coal train up the Glenfarg line, seven miles at an incline of 1 in 75, in 33 minutes. This suggests interest in developing a powerful goods engine for the NBR's main line mineral traffic, though no prototype was built[30].

Government control of the railways ended on 15 August 1921. Four days later the Railways Act set out the future for the railway companies. They would be amalgamated into four large concerns, with an Eastern group comprising the Great Northern, Great Eastern, Great Central, North Eastern, North British, Great North of Scotland, and numerous smaller companies. Interim working arrangements would be made, and the North Eastern was to draw up a draft formula for the merger. A joint committee was formed, with William Whitelaw and R.H. Tennant representing the North British. An explicit condition was that the companies bound themselves to accept a proportion of a total sum of £60 million as a full discharge of all obligations incurred by the Government during the period of state control. The NBR board still had its outstanding claims, including £555,000 for the first five months of 1921 on top of the £430,000 previously retained, and had already decided to suspend all dividend payments until they were paid. It also sought to impose pay cuts, and maintained a list of "employees to be dispensed with and not to be replaced"[31].

Following a NBR board decision on 3 June, in September the Galloway Saloon Steam Packet Co. was wound up, and its assets of £31,995 6s 6d, of which £30,000 were in Burntisland Harbour debentures, were handed to the NBR (placed in the interest suspense account[32]). By this time the Galloway Saloon Steam Packet Co. owned only one ship, *Duchess of Buccleuch*, converted to a minesweeper and returned by the Admiralty, but not returned to service. Pleasure steamers on the Firth of Forth had not resumed after the war. The Clyde steamers were running at a loss: even in June 1921 their revenue was £4,068 14*s* 7*d*, against expenses of £8,322 5*s* 2*d*[33]. The ferries also continued to be a problem, with the Commercial Motors Users' Association pressing via the Ministry of Transport for more sailings, and capacity for heavier lorries – the current *gross* weight limit was only four tons. The Ministry dictated the ferry rates, at a level considerably less than the NBR proposed. Between December 1920 and May 1921 the Granton-Burntisland Ferry carried 264 lorries, 51 ambulances, and sixteen carts, compared to 29 lorries, no ambulances and 66 carts in the same period 1912-13[34]. Still, £100 a year was found to subsidise the steamer service on Loch Shiel, and the NBR leased the pier at Glenfinnan.

Sir Eric Geddes gave a public explanation on 27 August of the Government's case against the North British, based on the companies' 1913 levels of spending. In 1913 the NBR had one of the lowest levels of spending on rolling stock maintenance and repair. Then in 1921 its claim exceeded the 1913 level by more than any other company: to the extent of £1,762,749 at current prices, or £728,024 at 1913 values. The Government was not satisfied that this excess was due to abnormal circumstances or to excessive wear and tear[35]. In November the Court of Session struck down the Railway & Canal Commission ruling that the Ministry should pay up. This was purely on a point of law and not the end of the saga – with Government control now ended, the court said the NBR's claim should be included in the final settlement of claims relating to wartime operations, "in which the Railway & Canal Commissioners had full powers in the event of differences arising." The North British once again withheld its deferred ordinary dividend[36], and a circular sent to shareholders explained that the company's right to recover the £430,000 (plus deductions from the January-August claims now amounting to £690,000) was unaffected. How far withholding of the dividend was necessary, and how far the company was using its shareholders to put pressure on their M.P.s, is a nice point, but they were undoubtedly supportive of their chairman. In December the NBR was informed that it would be receiving £1,192,988 in the first tranche of the £60 million to be distributed to railway companies, leaving £28,864 in suspense. The current half-yearly dividends were now paid. The sum was revised up to £1,296,120, the highest of any Scottish railway company. Another £22,264 12*s* 7*d* was received as the NBR's share of the Forth Bridge Railway's payout[37]. In its last days, the company was so flush with cash that it lent £100,000 to Edinburgh Town Council and £250,000 to Glasgow[38].

The division of "competitive receipts" agreed between the Caledonian and the North British in 1907 had been suspended during the period of Government control. It resumed from 15 August 1921, but in November, in view of the impending amalgamations, the Caledonian gave notice of termination as from 31 January 1932. At the end of 1922 the CR paid an excess of £4,434, but the North British paid an adjustment of £8,440 going back to wrongly declared coal traffic in 1909. In 1923 the CR paid £36,674.

In 1921 the North British had over 650 stations. In Glasgow it had 26 goods stations, seven in Edinburgh, seven in Coatbridge and three in Leith. Wagon-weighing machines were installed at 69 locations. In Greenock, far out of its own territory, it rented part of Lynedoch goods station from the G&SWR (the NBR had eight siding connections in the Greenock area). Altogether some 324 sidings were in use, into industrial and commercial sites ranging from oil refineries to munitions works, and guano processors to breweries. Most were quite short, though they might stem from a branch several miles long, like the Hopetoun mineral branch that left the Edinburgh & Bathgate line near Uphall Station, bisecting Uphall Village, running north to Ecclesmachan, then east almost as far as Winchburgh, to the large Hopetoun Oil Works. It had fourteen mineral or industrial sidings[39].

New trouble opened on the labour front in January 1922 when the Scottish railway companies made a joint application to the London-based National (Railway) Wages Board for revision of wages and working conditions. They wanted an end to the eight hour day. It was stated that the NBR had 31.33% more employees in the locomotive running department than in 1913. In 1913 wage-cost per engine mile was 2.63; by 1921 this had risen to 11.55*d*. The wages board refused to rescind the eight hour day but did permit a sliding scale of wage reductions. Its two Scottish members, James Calder, and David Cooper of the G&SWR, issued a minority report in favour of immediate decreases in wages and increase in working hours (the North British wage Bill had risen from £1,660,154 in 1913 to £6,023,148 in 1921[40]). High Street Goods Station suffered a huge fire on 20 January, in which five people were killed, with an estimated £1 million of damage. "A dropped light" by an unknown person was identified as the cause[41]. The basement held whisky stocks valued at £1 million, which were not affected. Among other events of 1922 may be noted the unveiling on 12 March of the NBR war memorial at Waverley Station, by the Duke of Buccleuch, who reflected that "it is the destiny of our race to govern other races" – and to pay the price. At the fire-prone St. Margaret's the tarpaulin maintenance shop was burned down on 2 April, with £50,000 worth of damage. Platform tickets were finally introduced across the system from 14 September, at the cost of a penny, except at Waverley, Queen Street and Dundee, where it was 3*d*[42].

In May the NBR put in a total claim against the Government to the Railway Commissioners for £1,755,707. The Government contested the amount and details were requested[43]. A massive exercise resulted in the North British providing an account for the entire period between 5 August 1914 and 15 August 1921, totalling £13,978,491. After negotiations and adjustments this was reduced to £12,576,788 3s 5d. Mr. Bell of the NER played a vital role as a middleman between the two sides, with constant correspondence and numerous meetings with John Martin, the NBR's accountant[44]. A degree of confidence in the outcome is suggested by orders for six locomotive boilers at £2,930 each, with the North British Locomotive Co., and ten shunting tank engines with Robert Stephenson & Co., at £4,123 apiece[45], but in September once again the deferred ordinary dividend was held over. Finally, on 4 November, a settlement with the Ministry of Transport was made, and the delayed dividends were paid. At an extraordinary general meeting on 17 November, Whitelaw explained how the dispute over the withheld £430,000 had developed, until by August 1921 it embraced two separate issues:

1. The withholding by the Ministry of Transport of a total of £1,120,000 claimed for the 1920-21 period.
2. A claim by the Ministry alleging that the NBR had been overpaid approximately £1 million in previous years, based on the mysterious explanation that the Ministry regarded the NBR as a "provision" company, not as a "programme" company.

Now Item one was conceded and would be paid in full. Item two had been negotiated down to a figure of £405,000, which the NBR would repay to the Government[46]. A somewhat different explanation and set of figures was given to the House of Commons by the Parliamentary Secretary to the Ministry of Transport:

> "The North British Railway Company claimed a sum of £10,681,243 in respect of maintenance and renewal of rolling stock during the period of control, mainly upon the ground that, because they had spent or were committed to the expenditure of that amount, they were, under the arrangements, entitled as of right to recoupment out of public funds. This principle has throughout been contested on behalf of the Government, and justification has been required for the amount claimed in excess of the normal. In pursuance of this principle payment of sums which the company claimed during 1921 on account of the compensation ultimately payable was refused on the ground that no justification had been shown for charging them against the taxpayer … The Government maintained a consistent attitude

Kirkcaldy Station: the tall building on the left is part of the Caledonia Linoleum Works. (*John Alsop*)

Holmes 4-4-0 No. 262 of the 633-class (1894), in original condition, takes on water beneath the landmark clock at Cowlairs. (*Stenlake Collection*)

throughout the litigation, and it was only when the company submitted figures and statistics in justification of expenditure in excess of the normal that an arrangement became possible. That part of the arrangement in which the taxpayer is directly interested is the reduction of the claim from £10,681,243 to £9,790,545. Of this difference, £405,000 represents sums expended during control and withdrawn from the claim, and £485,698 represents sums claimed, which the Government contended were discharged by the lump sum payable under the Railways Act. The methods by which the company propose to allocate and dispose of the further sum, which upon this reduction the Government was enabled to pay, is not a matter in which the taxpayer is interested. I am glad that this difficult matter has been amicably settled"[47].

Government departments, of course, never behave unreasonably or adopt bullying tactics … On the whole, it was a victory for the North British, and a tribute to the tenacity it had shown against officialdom and obstruction,and Whitelaw received well-earned cheers on 17 November[48]. By then it was known that he was to be chairman of the new East Coast group, the London & North Eastern Railway. The shareholders had no reason for dissatisfaction. After some haggling over the value of deferred ordinary stock, the board approved the amalgamation terms on 25 August. Debenture holders received the equivalent in LNER debentures; consolidated lien and preference No. 1 got the equivalent in LNER guaranteed stock; other preference, and preferred ordinary, also received the equivalent; and deferred ordinary received £10 in LNER preferred ordinary and £40 in deferred ordinary for every £100 of their NBR stock. Ten directors were to lose their positions, and £13,000 was set aside as their compensation (agreed after a challenge and a vote, by 95 to 50[49]). Two reminders of past dramas arose in the last days. An offer (unspecified) from the Admiralty was accepted for its use of Burntisland Harbour, and a claim from the estate of Randolph Wemyss (he had died in 1908 but his spirit had lived on) for £80,581 less 5%, for coal uncut beneath Methil Dock, was settled.

On 1 January 1923 the North British Railway ceased to be an independent company. Only a few residual actions remained. A final dividend, declared on 16 February, paid 3% on preferred ordinary and 1% on deferred, and the last board and annual meetings, with no business to discuss, were held on 2 March. In those 78 years, less than a long human lifetime, so much had happened, so many millions expended, so many men, women and children had been involved, for good or ill, in the company's affairs – but few regrets were expressed. After all, for most people it was a seamless transition into the LNER[50]. The years of nostalgia, and of historical inquiry into the North British company's affairs, still lay ahead.

20. THE NORTH BRITISH IN CONTEXT

This short chapter shows some non-public aspects of the North British and looks at the ways in which the company was perceived.

By the 1900s over 50,000 people had a direct involvement with the North British, half as employees, half as shareholders, though the great majority of the shareholders owned only a modest amount of stock. This was very similar to the Caledonian company and anyone who also reads the history of the Caledonian will be struck by the parallels between the two: the same early expansiveness, the same defensiveness, the same crises at much the same time. The managers of both were learning how to run a big joint-stock company – a new entity in itself – that also happened to be a railway company, with power previously undreamt-of to change the life of communities and the entire country. The North British was like those large-jawed fish or snakes capable of ingesting a creature larger and less aggressive than themselves. From its first years, take-overs marked it as a successful predator and the amalgamation with the Edinburgh & Glasgow confirmed it. Yet – as the embittered shareholders of the E&G were to discover, the huge jaws masked a frame that was rickety and infirm. Throughout most of its history, the North British lived beyond its income, spending excessive amounts on Parliamentary Bills, lawsuits, engineering surveys, and in opposing schemes that might hem it in or take some of its traffic, while almost constantly seeking to minimise the day-by-day costs of track and station improvement, and provision of locomotives and rolling stock. Ultimately it became Scotland's largest railway company but it never outlived that sense of being stretched beyond its natural capacity.

The presence of the North British in the literature of its time is scanty in the extreme. Scotland had no Emile Zola to record the heroism, pride, degradation and awfulness of industrial life. Janet Hamilton (1795-1873) was a rare poet in confronting the changing scene:

> The loch is lonely noo nae mair;
> Whaur heather, broom and bracken
> Ance clad the muir, the yellow corn
> By wastlin' winds is shaken;
> And Johnnie's cot the iron hoof
> O' railroad desecration
> Has trampit down – see, there's the line,
> And there's the railway station.
> From *A Lay of the Loch and the Muirlan'*

Refreshment stop: Crianlarich Station around 1910. (*Stenlake Collection*)

Occasional references are mildly humorous or satirical:

"The train for Fort-William stopped for a reputed five minutes at Crianlarich …" and Jimmy Swan and a fellow commercial traveller got off for some refreshment. "They entered a place in the station where the same was indicated, and found themselves before a counter covered with teacups and bell-shaped glasses", and ordered beer and sandwiches.
"'Licensed drinks in the refreshment room farther along the platform,'" said the lady, and they made haste to it, ordering "'Two lagers and a brace of sandwiches.'
'We have no eatables here… You'll get sandwiches at the other refreshment room farther along the platform.'
'Great Scot,' said Jimmy, 'could you not combine both shops and have a regular refreshment room, the same as they have on the Continent? It might be wicked, but it would be handy.'
'This is not the Continent; it is Crianlarich,' said the lady tartly…"[1]

The North British never put a dining car on the West Highland and Crianlarich's refreshment stop was well-used. The dual facilities may be apocryphal, but the story also pinpoints the railways' somewhat furtive attitude to alcohol sales in a country where the temperance movement waged perpetual war against the demon drink. Canal Street in Edinburgh was well-known for its spirit-shops before the North British came on the scene, and one half-suspects that part of the company's aim in ending their leases was to divert custom to its own premises.

As noted elsewhere, the North British considered its enforced contributions to local and national taxes much too great already. Its charitable giving was small and mostly to its own staff. It did give annual donations to several hospitals, but the stream of casualties due to workplace injury was evidence of its need for the hospitals' support. Though its staff were often accused of brusqueness in dealing with members of the public, the company could make gracious gestures. In February 1875 farmers Ferrier and Dunn, at Falahill, were given first class passes for a year for their help in digging out snow-blocked trains[2]. Employees' exertions in such situations were taken for granted. In the twentieth century, the company displayed greater appreciation of special actions by staff: in October 1911, for example, two porters each received ten guineas (and silver watches from the Carnegie Fund), for pulling a fallen luggage trolley out of the way of an express and for bodily hoisting a drunk man off the line in front of a train[3].

In most places where there was a concentration of staff, an annual soirée was held, with speeches from invited guests followed by music and dancing. They were paid for by the participants, with any surplus going to the local hospital or another charity. Annual outings were subsidised by the company – North Berwick was popular, where sea trips on a Galloway steamer could be included. Most employees only had a couple of days' paid holiday (in contrast to the senior officials who could apply for more generous "leave"), and any other time off, whatever the reason, was unpaid. The oldest outside-interest group, apart from the libraries, appears to be the North British Rowing Club, on the Union Canal in Edinburgh, started in 1876 for "gentlemen" on the staff, and which survived until 1939[4]. In Edinburgh, a literary society was started on 10 December 1900, meeting weekly in the superintendent's conference room (Deuchars was a vice-president) for talks or debates. One of the first was 'Should the State Control the Railways?' The motion was carried by thirteen votes to eleven. W.F. Jackson spoke on 'The Advantages and Disadvantages of Travelling' in 1901 and Lord Dalkeith addressed them on 'The Influence of Naval Power in the Development of the British Empire' in 1905. In June 1901 33 members had a day trip to Dollar, in a saloon attached to the regular trains. A magazine was published for a time; in December 1901 it included 'The Materialist Element in the Development of Society', by 'Marxian', and a critical article on the Boer War by 'Vincit Veritas'. The directors, mostly staunch Conservatives, can hardly have approved of such contributions. From around 1880 to 1890 there was a North British Railway Musical Society which gave choral performances as well as organising musical picnics and canal trips. Ladies might join but the rules stated that "the business of the Society is to be conducted by the Male Members exclusively". In December 1923 its residual funds, punctiliously kept for 33 years, were distributed to needy ex-employees[5].

The NBR's employees did not have a single or unanimous view of their company. For many, perhaps, the perspective did not extend beyond the stationmaster or foreman, who might be a good leader or a bully. There is little evidence of attitudes, apart from the comments at meetings by trade union activists which were naturally critical, since there was much to criticise. Even here, a distinction might be made between the company, which embraced everyone, and its management. And some officials, like Conacher and Deuchars, appear to have tried with some success to foster a positive sense of North British identity. Thomas Middlemass's memoir *Mainly Scottish Steam* recalled his father "who in his capacity as a goods guard, served the North British Railway, and scorned the Caledonian Railway, with equal devotion". Middlemass called it "a quixotic semi-pugnacious loyalty", noting that men like his father found no difficulty in equating an inborn inability to doff their caps and a genuine pride in being a "company servant"[6]. Even so, the men of his father's generation (born in 1870) cut their teeth in the strike of 1890 and had no illusions about the company's attitude to its work force.

Leaderfoot Viaduct. (*John Alsop*)

As far as the travelling public was concerned, the North British rarely appeared to deserve praise. The comments on unpunctuality are so frequent as to suggest that it was endemic, perhaps exacerbated by a shortage of station staff. Its long-lived carriages were not admired by their users, but it had more dining cars than most railways, and can claim to have inaugurated the sleeping car. Unlike some other companies, the Caledonian being a notable example, it had few buildings of architectural distinction. The great exception was the North British Hotel of 1902, which thanks to its good proportions and its clock tower quickly established itself as an admired landmark in a city intensely conscious of its historic appearance. Some fine bridges were built, like Charles Jopp's Leaderfoot Viaduct. Unfortunately the Tay Estuary did not lend itself to the design of a lofty and eye-pleasing bridge (as witness also its road bridge), and the Forth Bridge, magnificent as it is, is not an exclusively North British creation. North British engineering in the early years was hampered by perpetual shortage of funds, but later, to those who saw beyond façades and waiting-rooms, from the 1870s onwards in Waverley Station, and in Queen Street's arched roof, it was equal to any rival in Britain. And in its last full decade, it embraced the best of current technology to develop its Control systems.

Any image of railway stations from the late Victorian period onwards shows a plethora of advertisements, both for the railway service and for other businesses. Outdoor advertising was expanding hugely. For the railway companies it was a useful source of income, but Edinburgh Town Council took exception to the way in which Waverley Station's walls were "hidden by posters" and sought powers to control advertising, even on railway property. The Union Billposting Company applied for an interdict against the council removing hoardings, though it agreed to remove them during King George V's visit to the city, "without prejudice"". The North British also had its own posters, and published or sponsored guidebooks to its routes. Sales promotion in semi-concealed forms was also popular. The NBR published *Epistles of Peggy*, at 3*d*, a set of artless letters in which Peggy sends her impressions of travel through Scotland with "the Pater", going nowhere unless the NBR goes too: "You do not tire of Scotland when you travel by the North British Railway". They were aimed at selling tickets to tourists rather than crafting a company image for home consumption. But the NBR had its admirers. Will H. Ogilvie's spontaneous poetic tribute to *Borderer* (see preliminary pages) though misnumbering No. 881, shows an appreciation of the railway, and the train, as something heroic in a landscape of hills and valleys, savouring the contrast between city platforms and the engine hurrying its train through a picturesque countryside to which its green paintwork and trail of steam add an admirable element of human presence and endeavour, rather than detracting from a natural scene (in contrast to the earlier Janet Hamilton)[8]. The glamour of comfortable long-distance transport had wide popular appeal, and the North British green livery, with W.P. Reid's use of resonant names for the express engines, played up well to this enthusiasm. For visitors especially, travelling on the main lines in comfortable modern carriages, through attractive scenery, crossing mighty bridges, skirting North Sea cliffs or Atlantic beaches, the North British offered a very different prospect than it did to those who had to make cross-country journeys or wait at remote junctions for a late local train whose maximum speed was fifteen or twenty miles an hour.

Reid superheated 400-class No. 419, *The Talisman,* **built 1914, with a fish train.**
(*North British Railway Study Group***)**

21. POWER AND PROVISION

Rather than simply repeat technical details available elsewhere, this chapter complements the main text by tracing the NBR's somewhat patchy progress towards a modernised and larger fleet of locomotives, wagons and carriages able to cope with increasingly intensive and heavy traffic. More detailed information may be found in specialist books and journals, notably Baxter's *British Locomotive Catalogue Vol. 6*, G.W.M. Sewell's *North British Locomotives: A Design Survey*, and John Thomas's *The North British Atlantics*, and in numerous articles by Euan Cameron and others in the North British Railway Study Group's Journal[1].

On 28 August 1844 the newly-incorporated NBR placed orders via John Miller for 26 locomotives to work the line, all of them from R.&W. Hawthorn of Newcastle and Leith, at £1,650 each. Numbers 1-16 were passenger engines and 17-26 were goods; all of 0-4-2 wheel formation, based on the Stephenson 'Patentee' design of 1833, and with few differences between the types other than that the passenger engines had 5 feet 6 inches driving wheels, and the goods engines 4 feet 6 inches. Delivery began from September 1845 and some of the earlier engines were hired to the Edinburgh & Glasgow. In January 1846 Robert Thornton joined as the NBR's first locomotive superintendent, from the E&G Haymarket Depot[2]. Hawthorns built all but one of the 71 locomotives acquired before and during his term of office. The exception was No. 55, built in 1849 by E.B. Wilson of Leeds, to the patent design of Thomas Russell Crampton. As a 'Crampton' it survived only to 1855 when it was rebuilt as a conventional locomotive by Robert Stephenson & Co. in Newcastle. Under Thornton the company acquired seven 2-2-2 locomotives, 26 0-4-2, fifteen 2-4-0 and 22 0-6-0, all tender engines. The 0-6-0s were intended for goods and mineral haulage, in three classes of progressively greater tractive power. Nos. 27-32, built in 1846, had driving wheels of 4 feet 3 inches diameter and 15 x 24 inch cylinders. In Nos. 47-54, built in 1848, the cylinders were enlarged to 18 x 24 inches, and these dimensions were kept in Nos. 64-70 (1850-52), which had 4 feet 9 inches driving wheels. Thornton's successors William Smith and Edmund Petre built no new engines but struggled to keep the Hawthorns in action. At the end of July 1850 the company owned 64 engines and 216 passenger carriages (70 first, 70 second, 60 third, 26 composite). It had 1,968 goods/mineral wagons, 98 cattle trucks, 24 horse-boxes, 28 luggage vans, 21 carriage trucks, two powder vans and 32 ballast trucks: 2,173 in total[3]. By 31 July 1854 the number of engines had risen to 71. There were 219 passenger carriages (70 first, 70 second, 61 third, and eighteen composite), 2,223 goods/mineral wagons, 56 covered vans, 134 cattle trucks, 24 horse-boxes, 39 luggage vans, 21 carriage trucks, two powder vans and 42 ballast trucks. No brake vans are noted in either year[4]. Assuming 32 of the locomotives to have been built as goods engines, there was one to every 70 open wagons in 1854, a ratio which suggests that many wagons were static much of the time.

From January 1855 William Hurst brought with him the four 0-4-2 engines acquired from the Lancashire & Yorkshire Railway, Nos. 72-75. He tackled the problems of St. Margaret's vigorously, rebuilding two and making heavy repairs to thirteen of his stud of run-down Hawthorn engines in his first six months and was authorised to build two 2-2-2 well-tank engines for the Selkirk and Jedburgh lines, numbered 31 and 32. Operative from January 1856, these were the first locomotives built at St. Margaret's, and were followed by a class of 0-4-2WT, fourteen built between 1857 and 1864, all but one at St. Margaret's. Lack of main line power meant hiring six engines from the GNR in 1854-55, though the NBR sold off three of its 1846-vintage 0-6-0 goods engines in 1855. A census of rolling stock at 31 January 1857 gave the following numbers (brackets show additional units noted as "non-effective"):

Locomotives 55 (17), Tenders 61 (7), first class carriages 72 (8), second class 65 (5), third class 57 (5), Composite 18 (0), Covered vans 99 (5), Mineral wagons 2,250 (93), Cattle wagons 137 (1), Horse boxes 25 (1), Passenger guard's vans 17 (1), Goods guard's vans 24 (1), Carriage trucks 20 (1), Powder vans 2 (0), Ballast wagons 22 (0), Horse carriages 1 (0).

In 1859 the North British took over use of two 2-4-0 tender engines and a 2-4-0 tank of the Port Carlisle and Silloth companies. Numbered 101-2 and 100, these continued to work their own lines. In the 1850s, new carriages might be partly made from old ones. When an axle of a brake third on the 6.30 am Leith-Portobello train broke on 6 June 1862, it was found that though the carriage was seven years old, the axle was around fourteen years old[5]. Other than two small 0-4-2WT engines, no increase in provision was made between 1857 and 1860, when the new stock ordered in September 1859 began to be delivered. By the end of 1861, six new 2-4-0 passenger engines, seven 0-6-0 goods engines, and three 0-4-2 tanks were added.

The Edinburgh, Perth & Dundee merger of July 1862 brought in that company's locomotive stock, including engines originally built for the Granton and Fife companies: thirteen 0-4-2, nine 0-4-0, two 2-2-0, six 2-2-2, 23 0-6-0, and three saddle tanks, two 0-4-0 and one 2-4-0. They were allocated numbers between 111 and 167. The NBR also gained 1,743 wagons, and the Burntisland works, opened by the Edinburgh & Northern in 1848, which remained useful because of the lack of direct rail connection. There was also the small Edinburgh Leith & Granton repair shop at Heriothill in Edinburgh. By the end of 1862, the year in which the Border Union and Border Counties lines opened, five engines had been scrapped or sold and 27 had been added, though of the 150 engines now at the NBR's disposal, over a third were pre-1850 and even if in working order were of limited power for the traffic of the 1860s. New engines were essential. Hurst developed a 2-4-0 class, of which 24 were built by Neilson's and Dübs of Glasgow, with a variety of modifications, between 1861 and 1868, as Nos. 90-95, 341-346, and 382-393. For the fast-expanding mineral and merchandise traffic he introduced a series of 0-6-0s, beginning with two built at St. Margaret's in 1860 and a third in 1861, Nos. 76-78, and another 57 between 1861 and 1867 built by Hawthorns, Dübs, and Robert Stephenson & Co. of

0-6-0 No. 159A was built at Burntisland for the Edinburgh, Perth & Dundee Railway as No. 49, in 1862. Rebuilt by Holmes, it was transferred to the duplicate list in 1886 and withdrawn in 1896.
(*North British Railway Study Group*)

No. 21A at Cowlairs, some time between 1885 and 1895, when it was renumbered 843. Built in 1846 by R.&W. Hawthorn as an 0-4-2 tender engine, it was converted in 1867-68. (*John Alsop*)

Newcastle. Though varying in detail, all had 5 feet driving wheels. Cabs did not exist, only a 'weatherboard'. St. Margaret's also built four short-wheelbase 0-4-0 engines in 1865-66, for working twisty colliery lines. Hurst's contribution was thus substantial and some of his later engines remained active until 1909-10. The last of the handful of locomotives to be built at Burntisland was No. 108, in 1864, final one of Hurst's twelve 0-4-2WT class introduced in 1857. From 1861 the North British was hiring wagons to supplement its stock, not only from the Scottish Waggon Co. – a hire-purchase deal in January 1863 brought 500 coal wagons from the Metropolitan Wagon Co., at £13 10s a year for five years, after which they became NBR stock[6].

With the establishment of the North British Steam Packet Co. in 1864, the locomotive superintendent, already responsible for the ferryboats, also had the steamers to maintain. Amalgamation with the Edinburgh and Glasgow Railway in August 1865 brought 120 locomotives, including those of the Monkland Railways and E&G subsidiary companies, most of them less than ten years old, though with a couple of veteran 0-4-2s of 1846. The NBR now also possessed the Cowlairs Works, established in 1841. Though Cowlairs had built few locomotives before 1862, it had more space for development than St. Margaret's. At this juncture the locomotive stock, 326 in all, was formed as follows (including locomotives taken into stock and given numbers by the North British: the E&G had also listed fourteen engines which Hurst found to be "dead"):

	Built pre-1855	Built 1855-65
0-4-2	54	34
0-4-0	14	27
2-2-0	6	8
2-2-2*	29	0
2-4-0	19	23
0-6-0	38	37
0-4-0 tanks	2	9
0-4-2 tanks	0	16
2-4-0 tanks	2	5
2-2-2 tanks	1	2
Total	165	161

*Among these was ex-Caledonian & Dumbartonshire Junction No.5, built in 1850 as a 2-2-0; rebuilt 1858; converted into the NBR Inspection Saloon ('The Cab') in 1868; rebuilt again in 1882 and 1895, and sold in 1911[7].

By the end of 1865 many though not all the locomotives of 1847-50 had been rebuilt, which generally meant a new boiler and often new or re-bored cylinders, and some small locomotives were converted to tank engines. In that year the NBR owned 8,330 wagons, with approximately 5,000 more to come from the E&G and Monkland companies. Traders' wagons at this time may have numbered around 13,000. But the company needed 1,350 sprung-buffer coal tip wagons, 850 open sprung-buffer wagons, 100 iron-bar wagons, and 25 goods brake vans. Passenger stock was also needed: 100 third class carriages, plus 60 old firsts to be converted to third, 65 first-second class composite, and 25 guard's vans[8].

Edinburgh & Glasgow passenger engines had names, but the NBR removed them. Numbering policy had begun as a straightforward numerical sequence from No. 1, and to a degree this was maintained to the end. But once a locomotive was scrapped or placed on the duplicate list (normally when its value had been written down to zero in the accounts) its number was likely to be applied to a new engine. Thus there were three No. 1s at different times, and most numbers were reused at least once. The position was further complicated by the allocation of blocks of numbers to locomotives of merged companies, again with numbers often being reused when locomotives were withdrawn.

In 1866 thirteen 2-4-0, eight 0-60 and one 0-4-0 engines were added to the stock, plus two 0-4-0ST engines bought from the Benhar Colliery Co., and an 0-6-0ST banking engine ordered from Dübs by the E&G just before the merger (two more were ordered by the NBR for 1867; they worked up to 1920 and 1921). Hurst was ordered in April 1866 to delay all locomotive construction and as the company's financial crisis deepened, to reduce his staff. Samuel Johnson, the ex-E&G locomotive superintendent, resigned in August, and arranged for five of the 2-4-0s currently building at Neilsons to be sold to his new employer, the Great Eastern. Hurst was given six months' notice from 31 August. His departure coincided with that of most of the directors.

Thomas Wheatley, from the LNWR Works at Wolverton, occupied the hot seat from 1 February 1867. Economy was, as ever, the watchword for the locomotive department, and Wheatley was a no-frills designer. A further four E&G-designed 2-4-0s were delivered, two from Beyer Peacock of Manchester and two from Cowlairs, by early 1867. Otherwise, only six engines were added in 1867, two 0-4-0s bought from Balquhatston Colliery, Glasgow; one 0-6-0, No. 251, from Cowlairs, and three more delivered in December by Neilson's, part of an order for twelve that continued into 1868. By mid-1867 the wagon stock had risen to 16,461[9], though this figure was revised down by January 1868 after a count of E&G and Monklands rolling stock. In September 1867 Kippendavie claimed that the company was doing more work with fifteen fewer engines[10]. This was not the case, as none were withdrawn, though a large number may have been out of service.

Wheatley's 0-4-0 of 1868, originally No. 358, at Carmyllie around 1900. It was rebuilt in 1902. (*John Alsop*)

In 1869 the Leslie Railway's solitary 0-4-0 was added to NBR stock as No. 157. In 1870, of the company's 390 engines, specifically passenger designs accounted for only 70 or so. These were for main line duties: on secondary lines like the Forth & Clyde Junction and Border Counties, the same engines pulled goods and passenger trains, often in mixed formation. In 1870 92 pre-1850 locomotives were still listed, though eighteen were withdrawn in the course of that year.

Much of Wheatley's activity centred on keeping the older locomotives going, since the NBR could not afford to replace them wholesale. By the end of 1869, he was able to concentrate building at Cowlairs, which turned out 22 new locomotives in 1870 apart from rebuilds. They were badly needed, as in the February-July 1871 half-year, traffic exceeded the corresponding period in 1870 by 250,000 tons (minerals), 60,000 tons (merchandise), and 650,000 passengers; and 48 locomotives were awaiting repairs. While some old carriages had been replaced, carriage stock had not been increased since 1867. Nor had the wagon fleet. As a result of withdrawal of old vehicles, Kippendavie told shareholders that there would be fewer in 1872, though assuring them that "carrying capacity would be as great as ever it was on the North British"[11].

Altogether 135 0-6-0 tender engines were built during Wheatley's eight-year tenure, often incorporating parts from withdrawn engines as well as their numbers. Over half were built at Cowlairs, nine at St. Margaret's, and the others at Neilson's and Dübs. Most of those built prior to 1872 were rebuilt in the late 1880s and the 1890s; 38 were still at work in 1923. There were also 36 0-6-0 saddle-tanks, including six to work on the train-ferry ramps, four 0-4-0, twelve 2-4-0, and two 0-4-0ST. His most famous contribution was his "bogie coupled", the first inside-cylinder, inside-frame 4-4-0 locomotives. Their solid bogie wheels were cast in Bochum, Germany. Two were built in 1871 and four, slightly larger, in 1873, all at Cowlairs, intended for express passenger service, and equipped with the typically minimal cabs of the time. The first one, No. 224, famously went down with the Tay Bridge, was salvaged, and rebuilt temporarily in 1885 as the NBR's only compound-expansion engine. The class was not wholly satisfactory, proving unequal to hauling the Midland trains over the Waverley Route.

Following Wheatley's departure at the end of 1874, Dugald Drummond, once a foreman at Cowlairs, now returned as chief. Wheatley had evidently expanded the works and Drummond, fortunate to coincide with one of the NBR's more prosperous periods, supervised the building of new erecting and carriage shops. He began the practice of naming North British passenger engines, though in an unimaginative manner, using station names. Until now the company had relatively few tank engines, almost all very small. In his nine years Drummond built 66 tank engines and 147 tender engines, a considerable modernisation, the number of tanks reflecting the extension of branch workings and shunting duties. Thirty-three of them were 4-4-0Ts, and though the dimension of driving wheels varied from 6 feet (Nos. 494-6, for fast Helensburgh trains) to 4 feet 6 inches (25 0-6-0T) all were built to haul passenger or mixed traffic. For express trains, after a flirtation with a pair of 2-2-2 engines with 7 feet driving wheels, Nos. 474-5, he introduced a more powerful 4-4-0 class, twelve strong, led by No. 476 *Carlisle* (not 479 *Abbotsford*, which is shown in the official photograph) built by Neilsons, though the need for modifications delayed their full introduction. The backbone of NBR motive power was strengthened by 133 0-6-0 engines, coming in a steady flow from Cowlairs, Neilson and Dübs from 1866, most of them lasting for a few years beyond the end of the North British in 1923. Drummond withdrew or scrapped eighteen engines. He was the first NBR engineer to design a sheltering cab for engine crews, and also put the NBR among the first companies to begin use of the Westinghouse continuous air brake. By January 1878 the NBR had fifteen engines and 137 other vehicles fitted with the Westinghouse brake, with 140 more carriages being fitted[12]. Under Board of Trade pressure, carriages were also being fitted with continuous footboards. In October 1878 the NBR had 624 with footboards and 712 without, but these were being added "as they come to be renewed". At the same time, platform heights – often minimal when first built – were being raised, "as opportunity offers"[13]. During the Drummond period, amalgamations and long leases brought four 2-4-0 engines from the Forth & Clyde Junction Railway into NBR stock as Nos. 401-4 in August 1871, two 2-4-0 and two 0-4-2 engines of the Peebles Railway in July 1876; five 0-4-0s of the Leven & East of Fife Railway in August 1877, and four 0-6-0 tank engines of the Glasgow, Bothwell, Hamilton & Coatbridge in August 1878. Goods traffic built up rapidly in 1870-75 and over 500 eight ton mineral and 250 general merchandise wagons were added, though not enough to match demand. An indication of new traffics was the conversion of twelve of "the best covered waggons" to carry American fresh meat[14].

Drummond resigned in July 1882, and Matthew Holmes, chief inspector in the locomotive department, was immediately appointed locomotive superintendent, and would hold the post for 21 years. A practical engineer, Holmes carried on where Drummond had left off, making modifications which were prompted by experience. These included the replacement of Ramsbottom safety valves by the lock-up type on all engines after the

Drummond 2-2-2 No. 475 *Berwick* built by Neilson & Co. in 1876. (*John Alsop*)

mysterious boiler explosion of No. 465 at Dunbar on 1 September 1882. Instead of Drummond's straight-sided cab, Holmes employed a rounded-top cab design similar to that introduced by Patrick Stirling on the G&SWR. He also removed the names of engines. In 1883, the North British had more than 30,000 wagons: almost 50% more than in 1873, while the locomotive stock had risen to 573, but mineral tonnage had doubled. While the use of traders' wagons makes it impossible to reckon a precise locomotive/wagon ratio, it is clear that the position was worse in 1883 than it had been ten years earlier. A Parliamentary report noted that the NBR carried around 41% of coal transported in Scotland in 1885: 7,058,551 tons, out of 17,051,245. Monklands was by far the prime field, with 4,320,636 tons; Fife was 1,900,497, Lothians 702,666, Canonbie 37,618, Plashetts 16,981 and other areas 86,243 tons[15]. Traffic requirements of the time are indicated by the fact that from 1882 to 1890 only eighteen express passenger engines were added, compared to 54 0-6-0 goods. Six passenger 4-4-0s appeared in 1884, to work between Edinburgh and Glasgow, and a further twelve, of slightly enlarged design and with 7 feet driving wheels, in 1886: the first one, No. 592, was displayed at the Edinburgh International Exhibition that year.

In 1889 and 1901 four 0-4-0ST engines were bought in, one from the Gartness Coal & Iron Co., two from the Methil Dock Co., and the last from Wood, the Whiteinch haulage contractor[16]. In all Holmes built 204 0-6-0 engines between 1883 and 1900. All had 5 feet driving wheels; the first group (1883-87) had 17x26 inch cylinders; from 1888, beginning with No. 604, they had 18x26 inch cylinders and slightly larger boilers, the aim being to increase their tractive power. In addition virtually all the Wheatley 0-6-0s were rebuilt in the 1890s, from 1898 a start was made on rebuilding Drummond's, giving the NBR a stock of 452 engines for its main mineral and general goods traffic. By 1899 the company had some 60,000 wagons, or 132 per locomotive, at a time when 30 was a full train-load. Clearly many stood idle, whether empty or loaded, though at any time, a large number would be on colliery and ironworks lines worked by owners' engines. Many goods engines were fitted with Westinghouse brakes to work passenger stock at busy times. In 1892 20 Wheatley 0-6-0 "coal engines" were converted into tanks for shunting duties, and a new design of 0-6-0T for heavy shunting in the new marshalling yards was introduced in 1900-01, 40 in all.

At the half-yearly meeting on 27 September 1894 a shareholder made an unfavourable comparison between the NBR's rigid, noisy six-wheel carriages and the smooth-running bogie coaches in use on the Caledonian. The chairman did not respond[17]. Renewal and expansion of the coaching stock was going ahead at a much slower rate than the rise in passenger numbers. New passenger engine requirements in the 1890s were answered by the twelve strong 693-class 4-4-0s of 1894 to work the West Highland Railway, with twelve more in 1896. Their traffic was mostly passenger trains and fish specials, and the class was felt to be under-powered. Only seven survived into LNER ownership. Holmes introduced three sets of broadly similar 4-4-0 express locomotives between 1890 and 1903, 54 in total, most of which did not appear until 1895 and after, though twelve of the 633-class were completed in the Forth Bridge year of 1890. In 1896 the Caledonian claimed the headlines with its new 'Dunalastair' 4-4-0 class, and it is interesting to compare the dimensions of J.F. MacIntosh's 766-class and Holmes's 729-class, both of 1898:

	Driving wheels	Boiler	Boiler Pressure	Cylinders	Total Heating Surface
766	6 feet 6 inches	57.25x136.5 inches	175psi	19x26 inches	1381.2 sq ft
729	6 feet 6 inches	56.125x132 inches	175psi	18.25x26 inches	1350 sq ft

The differences are not great, but the dimensions are significantly larger than those of Holmes's preceding 693-class of 1894. His final 317-class 4-4-0 of 1903 slightly exceeded the CR's 900-class both in total heating surface and overall weight.

Cowlairs Works, mechanical headquarters of the NBR system, was visited by the *Railway Magazine* in July 1900. By that time the works covered 25 acres, though it still also housed a locomotive running shed. The inquirers noted a large iron foundry, an "old locomotive" working the air-blast plant, fourteen coke-fired crucibles in the brass foundry, gas-driven sewing machines in the upholstery shop where tablet pouches, cushions, despatch bags, etc., were made, and observed "asbestos-coated wooden lagging" round the boiler of a locomotive in the erecting shop. The smithies had steam hammers, there was an 850-ton hydraulic press, and much in the way of compressed-air driven machinery. A narrow-gauge railway ran inside the works. On Matthew Holmes's office walls they saw a picture of Engine 224, gradient profiles on the line, wall graphs of fuel consumption for 1888-89 and of costs per 100 miles of fuel, oil, tallow, and enginemen's and cleaners' wages. Twelve draughtsmen worked in the drawing office. Holmes was also responsible for 3,887 employees in the running department and 3,174 in maintenance, with a wage Bill of £366,336 a year, an average of slightly less than £1 a week (though a good proportion would be boys of 14 up), and informed the visitors that the company had 776 engines, 2,887 carriages, and 62,101 wagons. The works' building capacity was reckoned at 24 engines, 143 carriages and 1,732 wagons in a year.

Reid Atlantic No. 881 *Borderer* (1906), possibly the NBR's fastest engine. (*Stenlake Collection*)

No. 882 of W.P. Reid's first 4-4-0 class (1906), dressed up for an Eastfield locomotive department excursion in September 1911. King George V's coronation was in June, which may explain the prominent crown. (*Stenlake Collection*)

The table at the end of this chapter shows a modest increase in wagon numbers between 1900 and 1905, but the increase in load capacity was significant. In March 1903, G.B. Wieland noted that more large mineral wagons, twelve ton and sixteen ton, were being built, to cope with expanding traffic (mineral traffic was up by 800,000 tons). W.P. Reid took over at Cowlairs in May 1903. Following the substantial building programme of Holmes's last years, new building was scaled back and no new locomotives appeared until the end of 1905, though rebuilding of Drummond 0-6-0s continued. From 1905, with Lord Dalkeith as chairman and the shipbuilder John Inglis heading the locomotive committee, the locomotive side was taken firmly in hand by the board, with an openness to new technology. In 1905 the 0-6-0 No. 636 was hired to Beardmore's to test a combined steam and compressed air superheater, as was, briefly, the Atlantic *Dunedin* in 1906. Despite the prevailing climate of economy, a new building programme was considered essential and put in hand. This included a major innovation for the NBR, a 4-4-2 engine with outside cylinders and a high-sided Belpaire firebox, intended for fast, heavy expresses. Reid had offered 4-4-2 and 4-6-0 designs; the directors chose the Atlantics. Only just fitting within the NBR's tight height limit of thirteen feet, fourteen were built by the recently-formed North British Locomotive Company (no relation to the NBR) and delivered in July-August 1906. The history of this class, with the two years of difficulties after its introduction – largely due to the engineer's complaints about their effect on the track – has been told in detail by John Thomas[18]; but eventually they served well, into the late 1930s with a further six added in 1911 and two more, superheated from the start, in 1921. They did not herald a general NBR move to outside cylinders and Belpaire fireboxes: other new classes preserved the traditional appearance, though of increased dimensions and tractive effort. Also in 1906 Reid introduced a mixed-traffic 'Intermediate' 4-4-0 with 6 feet driving wheels, Nos. 882-893, with large 4,235-gallon tenders, able to run non-stop over the Waverley Route. The time-lapse between these and the next 4-4-0 class was due to lack of money – this was at the height of enforced economies – but on 8 December 1908 a board committee met at Cowlairs and approved designs for an express passenger engine, a passenger tank, an improved 'Intermediate' and a goods engine. It advised the board that 100 new engines would be needed over the next four years, at a total cost of £286,220, and recommended that 80 should be charged to revenue and 20 to capital[19]. In the event, 170 engines would be built between 1909 and 1912, 60 of them at Cowlairs. Six express 4-4-0s were built by NBL in 1909, reintroducing names, taken from Sir Walter Scott and his novels, with ten more from Cowlairs in 1911. Cowlairs also built twelve more 'Intermediate' mixed-traffic versions, with 6 feet coupled wheels in 1909-10; and from September 1912 'Superheated Scotts' appeared, 22 built up to August 1915 and five more in 1920, all at Cowlairs; most of them serving until the

Reid 8-class 0-6-0 No. 297, built at Cowlairs in 1918. This engine was in service until December 1966.
*(**North British Railway Study Group**)*

end of 1950, with No. 412 *Laird o' Monkbarns* not withdrawn until June 1966. While the 'Intermediates' were nameless, a superheated version beginning with No. 149 *Glen Finnan*, bore the names of western glens. Thirty-two were built, all at Cowlairs, between 1913 and 1920; No. 256, *Glen Douglas*, is preserved. By 1908 all passenger engines were equipped for steam heating of trains, as were many of the goods engines. A new 0-6-0 design, the 848-class, appeared from June 1906, ten delivered that month by North British Locomotive, 14 from Cowlairs between July 1906 and January 1909; another 30 from North British Locomotive Company in 1909-10, and 22 from Cowlairs between 1910 and 1913.

By 1906, the wagon stock was noted as 67,849, including registered traders' wagons. Wagon weight and capacity were increasing – on 19 October 1911 the locomotive & stores committee decided that in each successive half-year, 250 new sixteen ton mineral wagons would be added, and the equivalent number of dumb-buffer wagons would be sold off or scrapped. With the inauguration of the control system in 1913, locomotive numbers were painted in large size on the tenders, to help identification. Reid also introduced a power-classification code, to help the controllers select appropriate engines for trains. The list initially went from A to R, omitting O and Q. A to G denoted goods engines, with A for the powerful 0-6-2T 858-class[20], of which 65 were built between 1909 and 1917, with a further 20 in 1920-23. B to F was for 0-6-0 types. H to R denoted passenger and mixed-traffic engines, with the 'Atlantics' as H and I depending on whether they were superheated or not.

To cope with heavier train-loads, a superheated 0-6-0 known as the S-class, with No. 8 as the lead engine, was introduced from December 1914. Twenty-five were built at Cowlairs in 1914-18, 69 by North British Locomotive Company in 1918-21, and a further ten at Cowlairs in 1921. Many of these engines were still at work into the 1960s. The locomotive committee organised several comparative tests of this class with engines of other companies, at different times, one of them in June 1917 against an NER 0-8-0; another against a Great Western 2-8-0, on Glenfarg bank, in January 1921 and a NER 3-cylinder 0-8-0 in August of the same year. In an earlier test in 1910 No. 881 *Borderer* was tried on the LNWR's Shap Fell against an 'Experiment' class 4-6-0. *Borderer* may have held the NBR speed record, since maxima of 80mph are said to have been recorded on this occasion[21]. On 27 May that year 'Intermediate' 4-4-0 No. 867 turned in a better performance in a test on the Highland line between Blair Atholl and Druimuachdar Summit than the host company's 4-6-0 *Skibo Castle*.

Despite the heavy wartime traffic noted in Chapter 18, the North British was able to cope due to the creation of the "Wagon Pool" and the limitations placed on passenger services (though these resulted in severe overcrowding on many trains). In 1917, 22 Holmes 0-6-0 engines of 1888-91 were transferred to France to work military supply trains. After their return to the NBR in 1919 they were named after generals and battles (and 'Ole Bill'); No. 673 *Maud* is preserved. Two engines were also lent to the Highland, and reluctantly returned by it. Between 1914 and the end of 1919 91 new engines were built, 75 being 0-6-0s, but

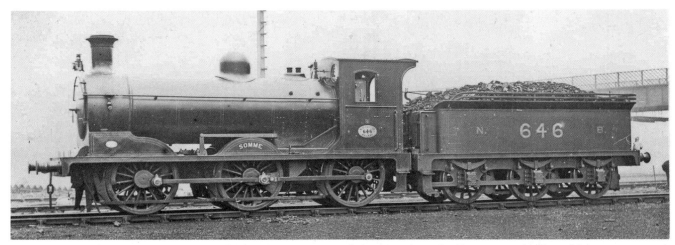

One of the war engines, Holmes 0-6-0 No. 646 of the 604-class, built 1891, re-boilered in 1913.
(*North British Railway Study Group*)

the locomotive stock generally was in a very run-down condition as a result of heavy work and limited opportunity for maintenance and repair.

On 31 December 1919 Reid retired, to be succeeded by the long-serving chief draughtsman Walter Chalmers, with the new title of chief mechanical engineer. In his brief term of office, Chalmers oversaw the construction of the final two Atlantics, Nos. 509-10, and also bought a small four-wheeled petrol-engined shunter to replace the horse at Kelso. This was the NBR's only non-steam locomotive. Despite the stygian and dangerous fumes of the Glasgow 'Underground', electric traction never seems to have been seriously considered, though discussions went on between 1901 and 1906 about electric assistance to replace the Cowlairs rope[22].

The livery of North British engines has exercised researchers over the years. At different times, under different locomotive superintendents, changes were made, though it is not always clear whether the superintendent had a free hand or was carrying out the wishes of the locomotive committee or its chairman. The basic colour of all North British engines was green, in various shades at different times, some described as brown, ochre or dark yellow; and with different linings and details of numbering and lettering, until 1915, when goods engines began to be painted glossy black[23].

The following table sets out some basic statistics relating to NBR 'power and provision' in the 50 years up to the end of 1922, using information from company Reports and Parliamentary Returns (which do not always correspond precisely). A variety of permutations can be worked out from these figures, though it must be borne in mind that traders' wagons are not counted in (unless noted). Nor is non-revenue mileage (shunting, empty stock movements, etc.).

NBR Power and Provision

Year	Track Miles	Engines	Passenger Coaches	Other Passenger Train Vehicles	Wagons	Other Vehicles	Passenger Journ
1870	789	390	831	272	16,216	103	9,435,061
1875	851	453	1176	390	22,355	152	11,309,515
1883	1006	573	1310	444	32,465	144	19,119,535
1890	1086	648	1644	470	45,224	144	29,117,884
1900	1242	801	1956	988	62,516	192	39,100,225
1905	1305	847	2002	1168	64,022	307	39,719,549
1913	1370	1058	2623 a	1203 c	60,356	3277 d	43,141,196
1922	1377	1074	2358 b	1218	55,806	3164 d	32,051,156

a- Including 15 restaurant, 15 Sleeper and 2 miscellaneous coaches.
b- Including 22 restaurant and 15 sleeper coaches.
c- Including 5 post office, 290 luggage, 224 cart, 215 horse and 419 miscellaneous vehicles.
d- Including locomotive coal.

Auchendinny Station, on the Penicuik Railway (opened 2 July 1872). (*Stenlake Collection*)

Gross Passenger Receipts	Passenger Train Miles	Minerals Tons	Minerals Gross Receipts	Merchandise Tons	Merchandise Gross Receipts	Goods Train Miles
£602,230	3,121,911	5,163,674	£402,226	1,806,584	£508,388	3,972,553
£839,942	3,641,637	7,179,655	£609,254	2,242,271	£676,914	4,725,081
£960,790	5,032,780	10,297,839	£767,163	3,291,458	£803,156	6,248,496
£1,059,735	7,268,058	11,950,067	£850,450	3,795,703	£838,851	7,137,555
£1,614,728	9,142,620	18,382,418	£1,335,507	4,646,734	£1,152,298	8,775,108
£1,779,278	9,548,768	21,042,895	£1,452,511	4,996,073	£1,253,080	8,448,036
£1,603,882	9,201,087	22,746,217	£1,416,719	5,030,720	£1,794,118	8,416,053
£2,369,700	8,479,560	22,803,953	£3,098,293	5,011,426	£2,834,848	6,478,899

TIMELINE FOR THE NORTH BRITISH RAILWAY AND ASSOCIATED LINES

Dates of incorporations and amalgamations, authorisations, etc. are the dates on which the relevant act received the royal assent, unless otherwise noted. Opening dates are dates of the first public service.

1820s

1824 Monkland & Kirkintilloch Railway incorporated, 17 May.
1826 M&KR opens, October. Edinburgh & Dalkeith and Ballochney Railways incorporated, 5 May.
1828 Ballochney Railway opens, 8 August.

1830s

1831 Edinburgh & Dalkeith Railway opens, St. Leonards-Dalhousie.
1832 E&D branch to Fisherrow opens.
1835 Edinburgh & Glasgow Railway prospectus published.
      Slamannan Railway authorised, 3 July.
1836 Edinburgh, Leith & Newhaven Railway authorised, 13 August.
      Dundee & Arbroath Railway Act, 17 May.
1838 Edinburgh & Glasgow Railway Act, 4 July.
      Edinburgh & Dalkeith Leith Branch opens.
1839 'Great North British Railway' promoted, February.

1840s

1840 Slamannan Railway opens between Ballochney Railway and Union Canal at Causewayend, 5 August.
1841 Edinburgh & Glasgow Railway sets up Cowlairs Works.
      Report of Smith-Barlow inquiry into Anglo-Scottish route.
      Wilsontown, Morningside & Coltness Railway authorised.
1842 Edinburgh & Glasgow Railway opens, Queen Street-Haymarket, 21 February.
      Edinburgh, Leith & Newhaven Railway opens, Scotland Street-Trinity, 31 August.
      Provisional committee for NB Railway formed, with John Learmonth as chairman, Charles Davidson as secretary, January.
1843 NBR's revised prospectus for an Edinburgh-Berwick line, November.
1844 NBR Act receives royal assent, 4 July. John Learmonth is first chairman.
      Meadowbank (St Margaret's) locomotive works set up. Edinburgh Leith & Newhaven renamed Edinburgh, Leith & Granton Railway.
1845 Edinburgh & Dalkeith Railway purchase authorised 21 July; completed October.
      Edinburgh & Hawick Railway authorised 21 July, bought by NBR. Caledonian, Edinburgh & Northern, and East of Fife Railway Acts.
      Wilsontown, Morningside & Coltness Railway opens from Newmains (Chapel Colliery) to Longridge.
1846 NBR line to Berwick completed: formal opening 18 June, public service from 22nd.
      Edinburgh, Leith & Granton Railway opens between Trinity and Granton, 2 February.
      E&G line between Haymarket-North Bridge Station opens, formally, 3 August (goods only).
      Acts for Stirlingshire Midland Jct, Edinburgh & Bathgate, Glasgow Airdrie & Monkland Jct, Caledonian & Dumbartonshire Jct, and Stirling & Dunfermline Railways, 25 June and 16 July; also for lines from Slamannan Railway-Bo'ness.
      Robert Thornton appointed NBR locomotive superintendent.
1847 Waverley Bridge Joint Station (E&GR and NBR) and Canal Street Station (Edinburgh, Leith & Granton Railway) open 17 May; Granton Pier extension, June.
      NBR Musselburgh Branch opens from Fisherrow line, 16 July.
      EL&G and Edinburgh & Northern merger Act, 27 July. Slamannan Railway linked to Edinburgh & Glasgow Railway at Manuel.
      Monkland & Kirkintilloch, Ballochney and Slamannan Railways converted to standard gauge, 26-7 July.
      Edinburgh & Bathgate Railway Act passed. Newcastle & Berwick Railway completed, becomes the York, Newcastle & Berwick.
1848 Temporary bridge between Tweedmouth and Berwick opens for goods (10 October) and passengers (15 October).
      Edinburgh & Northern Railway completed between Burntisland and Ferryport-on-Craig, 17 May, and Ladybank-Perth (Hilton Junction), 18 July; also Thornton-Crossgates.

Monkland Railways formed from Monkland & Kirkintilloch, Ballochney and Slamannan Railways, 14 August.
Edinburgh & Glasgow Railway opens Lenzie-Campsie Branch, 5 July; leases Edinburgh & Bathgate Railway, and absorbs Union Canal Co.

1849 Edinburgh & Hawick Railway completed to St. Boswells, 18 February, and Hawick, 29 October.
Tweedmouth-Sprouston Branch of York, Newcastle & Berwick Railway opens, 27 July.
Tranent Colliery Branch opens, 11 December.
Duns Branch opens, 13 August.
Edinburgh & Bathgate Railway opens from Ratho Jct to Bathgate, 12 November (goods only).
Edinburgh & Northern renamed as Edinburgh, Perth & Dundee Railway, April.
Stirling & Dunfermline and Edinburgh Perth & Dundee Railways link between Dunfermline and Crossgates opens, 13 December.
Wilsontown, Morningside & Coltness Railway amalgamates with Edinburgh & Glasgow, 28 July.

1850s

1850 Kelso Branch opens (to Wallace Nick), 7 June; North Berwick Branch 17 June. Royal Border Bridge formally opened 29 August.
Train-ferries begin operation across the Firth of Forth, 7 February.
Edinburgh & Bathgate Railway opens line between Longridge and Bathgate, 30 March.
Aberdeen Railway completed, 1 April.
Caledonian & Dumbartonshire Jct Railway opens between Bowling and Balloch, 15 July.
Miller retires, Charles Jopp appointed chief engineer, on a consultancy basis.

1851 Kelso Branch extended to Maxwellheugh (7 January) and NBR-YN&B joint line Maxwellheugh-Sprouston opens, 1 June.
Train-ferries begin operation across the Firth of Tay, 28 February.
Monkland Railways open Causewayend-Bo'ness.
Stirling & Dunfermline Railway opens Alloa-Tillicoultry line.
St. Andrews Railway Act, 3 July.
Thornton resigns, November; William Smith appointed NBR locomotive superintendent.

1852 St. Andrews Railway opens, 29 May. Stirling & Dunfermline Railway opens, 1 July.
Leven Railway Act, 17 June.
Learmonth resigns, May; James Balfour becomes second chairman; Davidson dismissed; James Nairne appointed secretary.
Henry Chaytor briefly general manager, then Thomas Rowbotham.

1853 Passenger services begin on Edinburgh & Bathgate Railway.
Peebles Railway incorporated, 8 July.
Port Carlisle Railway incorporated, 4 August.
Forth & Clyde Junction Railway Act, 4 August.

1854 Leven Railway opens, Thornton-Leven, 3 July.
North Eastern Railway formed. East of Fife Railway Act passed, 23 July.
Border Counties Railway Act, 1 July.
Selkirk & Galashiels Railway Act, 31 July.
Port Carlisle Railway opens 22 May (goods), 22 June (passengers).
Calton Tunnel accident, 9 December.
Edmund Petre replaces Smith as locomotive superintendent, March-December; William Hurst appointed 15 December.

1855 Peebles Railway opens, 4 July. Monkland Railways opens lines from Bathgate (Monklands) to Blackston Junction and to Cowdenhead, June and November.
Glasgow Dumbarton & Helensburgh Railway incorporated 15 August.
Jedburgh Railway Act, 25 May. East of Fife and Fife & Kinross Railways incorporated, 16 July.
Richard Hodgson becomes third chairman.

1856 Selkirk & Galashiels Railway opens, 5 April. Jedburgh Railway opens, 17 July.
New 'English and Scotch Traffic Agreement' operative from 1 January.
SMJ and Aberdeen Railways merge as Scottish North Eastern, 29 July.
Forth & Clyde Junction Railway opens between Stirling and Balloch, 26 May. Carlisle & Silloth Bay Railway opens, 4 September.
West of Fife Mineral Railway incorporated 14 July.

1857 East of Fife Railway opens between Leven and Kilconquhar, 8 July.
Leslie Railway and Kinross-shire Railway Acts, 7 July and 5 August. Fife & Kinross Railway opens from

Ladybank to Strathmiglo.

Dock Street Station (Dundee East) opens (Dundee & Arbroath Railway).

James McLaren appointed passenger superintendent.

1858 Border Counties Railway opens from Hexham to Chollerford, 29 August.

Fife & Kinross Railway opens from Strathmiglo to Kinross, 15 March.

Glasgow, Dumbarton & Helensburgh Railway opens, 31 May. West of Fife Mineral Railway opens from Whitemyre Jct to Steelend and Roscobie, 25 June.

Stirling & Dunfermline Railway is vested in the Edinburgh & Glasgow.

Devon Valley Railway Act, 23 July.

James Bell appointed engineer-in-chief, January.

1859 NBR acquires Selkirk & Galashiels Railway, 29 July.

Monkland Railways opens from former Ballochney Railway at Clarkston Wester Monkland, to Stepends Colliery.

E&G opens Blackhall Jct-Shotts. Border Union Railway Act, 21 July. Wansbeck Railway Act, 8 August.

NBR acquires Selkirk & Galashiels Railway, 29 July.

Silloth Dock opens, 3 August.

Charlestown Railway Company incorporated 8 August.

1860s

1860 NBR acquires Jedburgh Railway, 3 July, and Border Counties Railway 13 August.

Kinross-shire Railway opens Lumphinnans-Kelty-Kinross, 20 June. Monkland Railways opens between Stepends Junction and Cowdenhead.

Montrose & Bervie Railway incorporated, 3 July.

1861 Carlisle-Hawick line opens from Carlisle to Scotch Dyke (goods 12 October, passenger 29 October).

East of Fife and Leven Railways merge to form Leven & East of Fife Railway, with Anstruther extension authorised, 22 July; and West of Fife Mineral Railway, Charlestown Railway, and Elgin Railway merge to form West of Fife Railway & Harbour Co. Kinross-shire Railway merges with EP&D, 1 August.

NBR leases Peebles Railway, 11 July; Galashiels & Peebles line authorised, 28 June.

Alva Railway Act, 22 July.

Blane Valley Railway Act, 6 August. Glasgow & Milngavie Junction Railway Act, 1 August.

Monkland Railways opens from Brownieside Jct to Greenside Jct via Airdrie South, 10 May (goods).

Leslie Railway opens from Markinch, 1 February.

1862 NBR absorbs West of Fife Railway & Harbour Co., and Edinburgh Perth & Dundee Railway (with Fife & Kinross Railway), 29 July.

Hawick-Carlisle line opens, 1 July (goods from 23 June). Monkland Railways opens Westcraigs Jct-Shotts, 5 February.

Leases of Port Carlisle Dock & Railway and Carlisle & Silloth Bay Railway & Dock, 3 June.

Leadburn, Linton & Dolphinton Railway, and Ormiston Branch Acts, 3 June. Berwickshire Railway Act, 17 July.

North Eastern Railway gains running powers between Berwick and Edinburgh.

Bathgate-Airdrie South passenger service via Brownieside Jct from 11 August.

Wansbeck Valley Railway opens, Scots Gap-Morpeth, 23 July.

Edinburgh & Glasgow Railway takes over the Glasgow Dumbarton & Helensburgh and Caledonian & Dumbartonshire Junction companies, 14 August.

1863 NBR granted powers to acquire the Queensferry crossing, and Edinburgh–Dunfermline–Perth line authorised, 28 July.

Glasgow & Milngavie Junction Railway opens, 20 April.

Leven & East of Fife Railway extended to Anstruther, 1 September.

Berwickshire Railway opens between Duns and Earlston, 16 November.

Devon Valley line opens from Kinross to Rumbling Bridge.

Alva Railway opens, 11 June.

Esk Valley Railway Act, 21 July.

Wansbeck Railway Act: amalgamates with NBR, 21 July.

Northumberland Central Railway Act, 28 July.

NBR Steamboats Act, 28 July. Alloa Dock opens, 13 November.

1864 Canonbie-Langholm Branch opens, 18 April.

Leadburn, Linton & Dolphinton Railway opens, 4 July.

Peebles Railway extended to Innerleithen, 1 October. City of Glasgow Union Railway incorporated, 29 July.

NBR acquires Silloth Bay Steam Navigation Co., January.

North British Steam Packet Co. formed.

1865 Edinburgh Vegetable Market and Station Enlargement Act, 29 June.

Edinburgh & Glasgow Railway absorbs Monkland Railways 31 July, and merges with NBR, 1 August (Act of 4 July).

First Forth Bridge Act, 4 July. 'Scotch Territorial Agreement' with Caledonian, 12 May. Blane Valley Extension Act, 5 July.

Coatbridge-Glasgow line Act, 4 July.

Wansbeck Railway completed to Reedsmouth Jct, 1 May.

Berwickshire Railway opens from Earlston to Ravenswood Jct (St Boswells), 2 October. Montrose-Inverbervie Railway opens, 1 November.

1866 Plan for reconstruction of Waverley Station accepted, 23 July. Ratho-Kirkliston-Dalmeny line opens, 1 March.

Peebles Railway extension from Innerleithen to Galashiels opens, 18 June.

Leadburn, Linton & Dolphinton Railway absorbed by NBR, 16 July.

Blane Valley Railway (Lennoxtown-Killearn) opens for goods, 5 November.

Monktonhall-Thorneybank line opens (goods only).

NBR leases Forth & Clyde Jct and Esk Valley Railways, 16 July.

Newport Railway Act, and NBR/Devon Valley Amalgamation Act, 3 August.

Addiewell Oil Refinery Branch opens.

James Nairne dies, 26 March, John Walker appointed secretary, 12 April.

Committee of Inquiry report, November: Hodgson resigns, John Beaumont is temporary chairman until election of John Stirling, December.

Hurst dismissed, Rowbotham resigns.

1867 Esk Valley Railway opens to Polton, 15 April.

Blane Valley Railway opens for passengers, 1 July.

Anstruther-St Andrews Railway opens, 1 June.

Smeaton Jct-Ormiston goods branch opens. NBR buys Queensferry ferry service.

NBR and Caledonian form Grangemouth Branch Joint Committee.

NBR and Caledonian linked at Dolphinton, 1 March.

Broxburn Railway Act, 12 August.

Thomas Wheatley appointed locomotive superintendent, 1 February.

Samuel L. Mason appointed general manager April.

1868 NBR-Caledonian Joint Purse agreement, from 1 February.

Piershill-Trinity line opens, Canal Street Station (Edinburgh) closes, 22 May.

Dalmeny-South Queensferry Branch opens.

Ormiston line extended to Macmerry.

Cameron Bridge-Buckhaven Railway opens, 20 December.

NBR absorbs 'Baird's Railway' at Coatbridge, 13 July.

Telegraph Act: NBR receives £100,000.

1869 Camps minerals branch opens from Uphall.

Tillicoultry Branch extended to Dollar, 1 May.

Anglo-Scottish traffic agreement ends, 30 June.

NER exercises running rights to Edinburgh, from 1 June.

1870s

1870 Coatbridge (Sunnyside Jct)-Glasgow line opens to Gallowgate, 19 December.

Northumberland Central Railway opens from Scots Gap to Rothbury, 8 October (public opening 1 November).

Thorneybank-Hardengreen Jct opens.

Tay Bridge Act, 1 August.

Penicuik Railway and Edinburgh, Loanhead & Roslin Railway incorporated, 26 June.

1871 Coatbridge-Gallowgate line extended to College Station, Glasgow, 1 February.

Devon Valley Railway opens between Rumbling Bridge and Dollar, 15 April.

Coatbridge deviation completed, 7 August (goods) and 23 October (passengers).

NBR absorbs the Esk Valley Railway, 13 July, and leases the Forth & Clyde Junction Railway, from 1 August.

NB board agrees to merger with Caledonian Railway.

Arbroath-Montrose line authorised, 18 July.

1872 CR merger plan fails.

Penicuik Railway opens from Hawthornden, 2 September.

NBR takes over Leslie Railway and Northumberland Central Railway, 18 July.

Macmerry line gets passenger trains, 1 May.

Whiteinch Railway and Tramway incorporated, 1 July.

North Monkland Railway Act, 18 July.

1873 NBR absorbs Glasgow & Milngavie and Broxburn Railways, 28 July.

Sleeping car introduced, 31 July.

Forth Bridge Railway Co. incorporated, 5 August.

Dunfermline & Queensferry Railway, and Kelvin Valley Railway (Maryhill-Kilsyth) Acts, 23 July.

Edinburgh, Loanhead & Roslin Railway opens to Loanhead, 6 November, for mineral traffic.

John Walker resigns as secretary and joins board.

G.B. Wieland appointed secretary, July.

James McLaren appointed general superintendent.

1874 Sixteen people die in collision at Manuel, 27 January.

Edinburgh, Loanhead & Roslin Railway opens to Roslin for all traffic, 23 July.

Glasgow, Bothwell, Hamilton & Coatbridge Railway Act, 16 July.

Whiteinch Railway and Tramway opens, 8 October; Stobcross line on 20 October.

Waverley Station redesign completed.

Mason resigns, August; John Walker resigns from board to become general manager.

Wheatley resigns, October (effective 31 January 1875).

1875 City of Glasgow Union Railway opens between Shields Jct and Springburn, 16 August.

Midland Railway opens to Carlisle for goods (2 August).

Devon Valley Railway absorbed by NBR, from 1 January.

NBR takes 50-year lease of Forth & Clyde Junction Railway, from 1 August.

Dugald Drummond appointed locomotive superintendent, February.

1876 Midland Railway opens passenger services via Carlisle, 1 May, with through trains to Edinburgh (Waverley).

Berwickshire, Penicuik and Peebles Railways absorbed by NBR, 1 August (Act of 13 July).

Burntisland No. 1 Dock opens, 1 December. Kilsyth Railway Act, 13 July.

1877 Leven & East of Fife and St. Andrews Railways absorbed by NBR, 1 August. Glasgow, Bothwell, Hamilton & Coatbridge Railway opens from Shettleston to Hamilton, for goods, 1 November.

Edinburgh, Loanhead & Roslin Railway extended to Glencorse, 28 June, amalgamated with NBR from 31 July.

Kilsyth Railway vested in Kelvin Valley Railway, 17 May.

Dunfermline & Queensferry Railway opens, 1 November.

Queen Street Station Act 17 May, rebuilding begins, to 1888.

Queen's Dock, Glasgow, opened, August.

1878 Tay Bridge passed for use, 5 March; opened for passenger traffic, 1 June.

North Monkland Railway opened, February. Glasgow, Bothwell, Hamilton & Coatbridge Railway opens for passengers, 1 April, with Bothwell Jct-Whifflet link line 1 November (goods) amalgamated with NBR, August.

Dunfermline-North Queensferry line opens, 1 April.

South Queensferry-Port Edgar branch opens, 1 October.

Newport Railway opens, 12 May.

Kelvin Valley Railway opens between Birdston Jct (Kirkintilloch) and Kilsyth, 1 June.

Rail link to Alloa Dock.

Edinburgh, Loanhead & Roslin line extended from Glencorse to Penicuik Gasworks, 30 June.

CR reopens Glasterlaw fork to facilitate NB Arbroath-Aberdeen traffic.

Glasgow, Yoker & Clydebank Railway Act, 4 July.

1879 Bothwell Jct-Whifflet link line opens for passengers, 1 May.

Newport-Wormit Railway completed, 12 May.

KVR opens between Torrance and Maryhill for goods, 1 June, for passengers, 1 October.

NBR absorbs the Glasgow, Bothwell, Hamilton & Coatbridge Railway, 2 August (Act of 21 July).

Tay Bridge collapses, 28 December.

James Bell Sr retires; James Carswell appointed engineer-in-chief.

1880s

1880 Dundee & Arbroath Railway becomes joint NBR-Caledonian line, 1 February.

NBR absorbs Port Carlisle Dock & Railway and Silloth Bay Railway & Dock companies, also Arbroath & Montrose Railway, Act of 12 August (effective date 1 August).

Strathendrick & Aberfoyle Railway Act, 12 August. Anstruther & St. Andrews Railway, and Edinburgh Suburban & Southside Jct Railway Acts, 26 August.

Whiteinch Railway acquired by NBR in trust.

Queen's Dock, Glasgow, completed, 20 March.

1881 Arbroath-Kinnaber Jct line opened throughout for goods, 1 March. New Tay Bridge Act, 18 July. Montrose & Bervie Railway vested in NBR, 18 July. Blane Valley Railway absorbed. Wemyss-Buckhaven line opens, 1 August, operated by NBR.
Bo'ness Dock opens, 3 December.

1882 John Stirling dies, Sir James Falshaw becomes chairman.
Drummond resigns, 27 July; Matthew Holmes appointed locomotive superintendent.
NBR opens Craigendoran Pier, 15 May.
Strathendrick & Aberfoyle Railway opens, 1 October; Glasgow, Yoker & Clydebank Railway opens, 1 December.
Kinross-Bridge of Earn line Act, 3 July.
New Forth Bridge Act, 12 July.
Glasgow City & District Railway, and Kilsyth & Bonnybridge Railway Acts, 10 August.
NBR-Caledonian 'peace agreement', December.

1883 New Montrose viaduct completed, May 1.
First through NBR passenger trains, Edinburgh-Aberdeen.
Strathendrick & Aberfoyle Railway opens, 2 October.
Anstruther & St. Andrews Railway Act and Seafield Dock & Railway Act, 16 July.

1884 Edinburgh Suburban & Southside Junction Railway opens for goods, 31 October; passengers, 1 December.
Eyemouth Railway incorporated, 18 August.

1885 Partick-Yorkhill line opens, 2 February.
Marshall Meadows deviation, Berwickshire.
NBR absorbs Kelvin Valley and Edinburgh Suburban & Southside Junction Railways, 1 August (Act of 22 July).
Silloth New Dock opens, 30 June.

1886 Glasgow City & District line opens from Yorkhill to High St, opening of Queen Street (Lower), 15 March; Kingswood North-South line 1 August.
Hyndland Branch opens, 15 March. Silloth Battery Extension line built.

1887 Marquis of Tweeddale becomes chairman; Falshaw vice-chairman, March.
New Tay Bridge opens, 13 June (goods), 20 June (passengers).
Wemyss & Buckhaven Railway extended to Methil, and Methil No. 1 Dock opens, 5 May.
Glasgow City & District circular route opens, 1 February.
NBR takes over GC&D company, 5 July.
East of Fife Railway completed between Anstruther and St. Andrews, 1 June.

1888 Kilsyth & Bonnybridge Railway opens, 2 July, a NBR-Caledonian 'common line'.
NBR leases Newport Railway, 16 May, backdated to 1 January, and absorbs North Monkland Railway on completion, 31 July.
'Races to the North' in July-August.

1889 West Highland Railway Act, 12 August.
NBR acquires Lochlomond Steamboat Co., 1 February, and Wemyss & Buckhaven Railway with Leven and Methil docks, 26 July.
NBR-Highland Railway Great Glen agreement. NBR Station Hotel Act, 8 July.
NBR-G&SWR merger proposed.

1890s

1890 Forth Bridge opening ceremony, 4 March.
Connecting lines from Dalmeny to Saughton Jct and Winchburgh Jct open, 2 June; also Cowdenbeath loop line and Glenfarg line from Mawcarse Jct to Bridge of Earn.
Contest with CR for amalgamation with G&SWR.
Agreement with CR on Glasgow, Edinburgh and Aberdeen traffic receipts.
Eyemouth Railway absorbed, 1 August.
Scottish railway strike, December 1890-January 1891.

1891 Eyemouth Railway opens, 13 April.
NBR absorbs Blane Valley and Strathendrick & Aberfoyle Railways, 5 August, also Alloa Dock, and Whiteinch Railway, 1 August.
Floods damage bridges on Waverley line, September.
New Lines Agreement with Caledonian Railway, 31 October.
NBR acquires control of Galloway Saloon Steam Packet Co., October.
Invergarry & Fort Augustus Railway Act, 14 August.
John Walker dies, 24 April; John Conacher appointed general manager, 11 August; takes up duties 2 November.

1892 Bridgeton Cross Branch opens, 1 June.
Dumbarton & Balloch Joint Line Act, 20 June.
G.B. Wieland resigns as secretary, joins board.
John Cathles appointed secretary, 17 March.

1893 Duplicating of Haymarket and Mound tunnels, Edinburgh.
Kincardine Branch opens, 18 December.
Glasgow, Yoker & Clydebank Extension Act, 27 July; East Fife Central Railway and Aberlady, Gullane & North Berwick Railway Acts, 24 August.
McLaren dies; David Deuchars appointed superintendent of line, 23 November.

1894 West Highland Railway opens to Fort William, 7 August (official ceremony 11 August).
Mallaig Extension Act, 31 July.
Reconstruction of Waverley Station begins.
Charlestown Branch extended to new station for passenger service, 1 September.
NBR-NER dispute on Anglo-Scottish trains begins.

1895 WHR Banavie Branch opens for all traffic, 1 June.
Garngaber Junction Railway (Waterside Jct-Bridgend Jct) opens, 4 December.
Kirkcaldy & District Railway and East Fife Central Railway absorbed by NBR, 6 July.
'Races to the North' in August. Prince's Dock, Glasgow, opened 10 September.

1896 NBR takes control of Burntisland Docks.
Pact with Fife coalowners.
NBR opens Kirkcaldy & District Railway, Foulford Jct-Invertiel Jct., 3 March.
City of Glasgow Union Railway divided: NBR takes over Springburn-College East Jct line, 20 July.
Lanarkshire & Dumbartonshire Railway opened.
Joint Committee formed by NBR, CR and L&D to operate services between Dumbarton East Jct and Balloch Pier, 1 October.
Victoria Park (Whiteinch) passenger service starts, 14 December.
Invergarry & Fort Augustus Railway Act, 14 August.
Points and signals interlocking complete on NBR system.
NBR-Caledonian peace agreement committee re-established.

1897 Glasgow, Yoker & Clydebank Railway opens Clydebank Jct-Dalmuir Jct for goods traffic, 8 May, amalgamates with NBR, 15 July.
Abbeyhill Extension and second Calton Hill Tunnel, Edinburgh.
Link line between Bathgate Upper and Lower Stations opens.
Link to CR at Crianlarich opens, 20 December.
Methil No. 2 Dock opens.
GY&C and Anstruther & St. Andrews Railways amalgamate with NBR, 1 August (Act of 15 July).
James Carswell dies; James Bell Jr appointed engineer-in-chief.

1898 Waverley Station enlargement completed, 17 April.
Aberlady, Gullane & North Berwick Railway opens, to Gullane, 1 April.
East Fife Central Railway (Cameron Bridge-Lochty) opens as goods line, August.
Colliery lines opened in Cardenden area.
NBR (General Powers) Act authorises Kincardine-Dunfermline line, 12 August.
Lauder Light Railway and Corstorphine branch authorised, 30 June.
Gifford & Garvald Light Railway Order, 14 July.

1899 Tweeddale resigns, Sir William Laird becomes chairman.
Conacher resigns, June. William F. Jackson promoted to general manager.
NBR acquires former Waterloo Hotel, Edinburgh, as head office.
Dumbarton-Balloch line and Loch Lomond steamers jointly owned with Caledonian Railway.
Wemyss Private Railway authorised, September.

1900 – 1909

1900 Collision at Charing Cross, Glasgow: seven people killed, 28 March.
NBR absorbs Aberlady, Gullane & North Berwick, Newport, and Eyemouth Railways, and takes control of Bo'ness Docks, 6 August.
Methil No. 2 Dock completed, January.

1901 WHR Mallaig Extension opens, 1 April.
Lauder Light Railway opens, 2 July.
Gifford & Garvald Light Railway opens from Ormiston to Gifford, 14 October.

Cadder Marshalling Yard opens, October.

Central Goods Shed, Sighthill, opens.

Laird resigns, April. G.B. Wieland becomes chairman. Wemyss Private Railway opens.

1902 Burntisland New Dock opens.

Corstorphine Branch opens, 1 February.

North British Steam Packet Co. amalgamated with NBR, 22 July.

North British Station Hotel, Edinburgh, opens, 15 October.

1903 Holmes resigns, 7 May; W.P. Reid "in charge" at Cowlairs.

Leith Central Branch opens, 1 July.

Prince's Dock Joint Railway (Joint NBR, G&SW, CR) opens, 17 August.

NBR drops circle service on former CGU line.

NBR rebuilds Queen's Hotel, Glasgow, as North British Hotel.

Invergarry & Fort Augustus Railway opens (worked by HR), 22 July.

1904 Two motor cars bought for North Berwick-Gullane service, 8 September.

Possil-Saracen Works Goods Branch opens, 1 December.

Glasgow High Street Goods Station opens.

Eastfield Locomotive Depot opens, September.

Reid confirmed as locomotive superintendent, 2 June.

1905 Wieland dies, 26 March. Earl of Dalkeith becomes chairman.

Flood damage to Waverley and West Highland lines, June.

1906 Kincardine-Dunfermline line opens, 2 July.

NBR takes over Bangour Railway.

Portobello Marshalling Yard extended.

'Atlantic' express locomotives introduced.

Elliot Junction collision, 22 persons killed, 28 December.

1907 NBR takes over working of Invergarry & Fort Augustus Railway, 1 May.

Kilbowie diversion and Singer Station open, 3 November.

High Street Goods Station, Glasgow, opens, 1 August.

Rothesay Dock, Clydebank, opens, 25 April. Rosyth Dockyard Railway opens.

Lethans Colliery Branch extended from Steelend.

Act for third Methil Dock, 2 August.

1908 NBR absorbs the West Highland company, 31 December.

Rope haulage on Cowlairs Incline discontinued, 31 October.

Bainsford Branch, Falkirk, opened.

Final NBR-CR peace agreement.

1909 Newburgh & North Fife Railway opens, 25 January.

Fortisset Colliery branch opens (Monklands), also Lochore-Redford Branch (Fife).

James Bell Jr retires; Charles J. Brown appointed engineeer-in-chief.

1910 – 1923

1910 William Whitelaw elected vice-chairman.

1911 Invergarry line closed, 31 October.

Deuchars retires, 30 September, John Black appointed superintendent of line.

Charles Brown resigns; William Fraser appointed engineer-in-chief.

1912 Cowdenbeath-Invertiel Jct goods line opened.

Cadder Yard completed.

Whitelaw elected chairman, 7 March; Dalkeith is vice-chairman.

1913 Methil No. 3 Dock opens, 22 January.

Control system introduced in Lothian District, 15 September.

NBR reopens the Invergarry line, 1 August.

NBR Lothian lines Act, 15 August.

1914 NBR acquires the Invergarry Railway, 28 August.

Steam traction begins on Port Carlisle Railway, 4 April.

Railway Executive control from 5 August.

Western District control centre operative from 18 October.

1915 Rosyth Dockyard Station opens, 1 July.

'Lothian lines' open, Portobello West to Monktonhall, 30 September.

1916 Meadows Jct-Seafield link opened, Edinburgh.

South Leith and Inverkeithing yards extended.

John Black retires.

1917 Collision at Queensferry Junction, 12 fatalities, 3 January.

Charles Stemp promoted to operating superintendent; William Strang is commercial superintendent.

Many stations close as wartime economy measure.

Longtown Yard laid out.

1918 Jackson retires, James Calder appointed general manager.

Cathles retires, James McLaren appointed secretary.

William Strang dies, Matthew Strang appointed commercial superintendent.

1919 Link line from Cowdenbeath loop line to Lumphinnans Central Jct opened.

Donibristle Airfield Branch, January.

Dining car services resume, 1 February.

Fire at Eastfield Depot damages 19 engines, 28 June.

National railway strike, 27 September-5 October.

W.P. Reid retires, 31 December.

Silloth-Liverpool steamer service is terminated.

1920 Walter Chalmers appointed chief mechanical engineer, 1 January.

1921 Bangour Railway closes, 30 July.

Government control of railways ends, 15 August.

Railways Act passed, 19 August.

NBR contest with Ministry of Transport on compensation payments.

Galloway Saloon Steam Packet Co. is wound up.

1922 Fire at College Goods Station kills 5, 19 January.

Burntisland Harbour is vested in the NBR.

Final settlement of dispute with Ministry of Transport, November.

1923 NBR is merged into the London & North Eastern Railway, 1 January.

Last shareholders' AGM, 2 March.

APPENDIX 1

The North British Railway: A Waged Staff Profile in 1901

These figures, supplied by departmental heads for the Board of Trade, cover more than 10,000 staff and give a picture of the position before the reforms of the 1900s. Dockyard, canal and engineering workers are not included, nor are ancillary staff in locomotive depots.

	Category	Number	Weekly Pay	Annual Paid Holidays
1	Signalmen (8hrs)	295	20s-26s	3 days
	Signalmen (10 hrs)	252	20s-26s	3 days
	Signalmen (12 hrs)	630	20s-26s	3 days

Total number 1,312 including relief and spare men. Waverley E. and W. and Queen Street High Level men get additional 1s weekly. Overtime and Sunday pay at ordinary rate. Cord vest, trousers and cap issued yearly, pilot jacket biennially.

	Category	Number	Weekly Pay	Annual Paid Holidays
2	Train Register boys	60	10s-13s	3 days

Clothing provided as for signalmen.

	Category	Number	Weekly Pay	Annual Paid Holidays
3	Passenger Guards	274	21s-28s	3 days

Branch guards' maximum 27s. Edinburgh/Glasgow to Aberdeen/Carlisle, 2s extra. Conductor guards on Midland route, 45s with no allowances; on East Coast Route 38s plus 2s 6d overnight allowance. Main line uniform: coat and vest with two pairs tweed trousers and cap, annually. Top coat and waterproof triennially. Branch lines: Jacket and vest, one pair cord and one pair tweed trousers and cap, annually. Top coat and waterproof triennially. Daily hours: twelve maximum. Overtime/Sunday rate not specified.

	Category	Number	Weekly Pay	Annual Paid Holidays
4	Bankheadmen	2	32s and 33s	3 days

Employed at Cowlairs. Pilot jacket, vest, tweed trousers and cap annually. Top coat triennially.

	Category	Number	Weekly Pay	Annual Paid Holidays
5	Ticket collectors	152	19s-26s	3 days

Two grades, first class get 22-24s; second class get 19-21s. Coat, vest, trousers and cap annually. Topcoat biennially. Twelve hour day with two hours allowed for meal. Overtime not specified.

	Category	Number	Weekly Pay	Annual Paid Holidays
6	Porters	943	8s-35s	None

Most are paid 17-19s. Cord suit and cap provided annually. Sunday pay as on other days. Twelve hour day with two hours allowed for meals. Overtime paid only in exceptional circumstances.

	Category	Number	Weekly Pay	Annual Paid Holidays
7	Carriage cleaners	143	7s-25s	None

Most are paid 18s. Cord suit and cap provided annually. No overtime, but a day's pay given for any period of work on Sunday.

8	Lampmen	118	9s-25s	None

Most are paid 18-19s. Cord suit and cap annually, oilskin suit triennially. No overtime arrangements.

9	Parcel checkers	9	19s-23s	None

Pilot jacket, vest, cord trousers and cap annually. Sunday work at ordinary rate.

10	Parcel deliverers	51	20s-24s	None

Employed in Edinburgh, Leith and Glasgow. Most are paid 24s. Jacket, vest, cap and two pairs trousers annually, top coat biennially. No fixed hours and no overtime pay.

11	Van boys	37	5s-12s	None

Most are paid 9s. Pilot jacket, cord vest and trousers, and cap, annually, top coat biennially. No fixed hours and no overtime pay.

12	Passenger shunters	43	18s-30s	None

Edinburgh, 21 men: eight hour day, start rate 24s rising to 30s after six years.
Queen Street, two chief shunters at 26s, two shunters at 20s and 26s, two assistant shunters at 20s and 21s. Other stations, sixteen shunters at 18s-20s.
Jacket, vest, two pairs cord trousers and cap annually; top coat, leggings and waterproof triennially. Sundays and overtime paid at ordinary rate.

13	Shunters	279	21s-30s	None

Eight hour yards: 159 men at Leith Walk, South Leith, Portobello, Niddrie West, Carlisle, Dundee, Thornton, Kipps, College, Bathgate Upper. Other yards 12 hours. Stoker jacket and vest, 2 pairs cord trousers, and cap annually. Stoker top coat, brown waterproof and 1 pair leggings triennially. Overtime in week at ordinary rate; Sunday work at time plus a half.

14	Goods guards	896	24s-30s	None

Distribution: Eastern District 181, Southern 51, Northern 47, Fife 101, Western 224, Monkland 287, West Highland 5. Uniform as for shunters. Overtime in week at time plus one fifth; Sundays at time plus a half.

15	Marshalmen	67	26s-35s	None

Twelve hour day. Clothing, overtime and Sundays as for goods guards.

16	Pilot guards	19	20s-21s	None

Jacket, vest and trousers annually, waterproof biennially.
Twelve hour day, no overtime pay, Sunday work at ordinary rate.

17	Yard pointsmen	30	17s-21s	None

Cord suit and cap annually, waterproof and leggings triennially. Twelve hour day, no overtime pay, Sunday work at ordinary rate.

18	Ropemen and brakesmen	22	21s-28s	None

Employed at Cowlairs, ten hour day. First brakesmen are paid 25s-28s; second brakesmen and ropemen 21s-25s. Pilot jacket and vest, two pairs trousers and cap annually; top coat, brown waterproof and leggings triennially. Sundays at ordinary rate, overtime not normally worked.

19	Gatekeepers	179	0s-19s	None

36 have free house and no pay; 63 have house plus 1s-5s, nine have house plus 8s-10s, 53 have house plus 11s-15s, eighteen have no house and are paid 15s 6d-19s. Clothing for men: cap only. No clothing provided for women. No overtime pay, Sunday pay only for special services.

20	Waiting room attendants	211	5s-18s	None

166 have house and up to 5s a week; 28 have house plus 5s 3d-10s; 17 have no house, 10s 6d-18s. No clothing supply specified. No overtime pay.

	Category	Number	Weekly Pay	Annual Paid Holidays
21	Water closet attendants	14	5s-18s	None

Twelve hour day. Jacket, vest, trousers and cap annually. No overtime pay.

	Category	Number	Weekly Pay	Annual Paid Holidays
22	Cloak room attendants	15	14s-22s	None

Twelve hour day. Pilot suit and cap annually. Sunday at ordinary rate, no overtime pay.

	Category	Number	Weekly Pay	Annual Paid Holidays
23	Miscellaneous	97	4s-30s	See details

Includes 50 flagmen, one piermaster, one dandy driver, East Coast car attendants (only ones in this category to get paid holiday, three days), and one night foreman, at 30s.

	Category	Number	Weekly Pay	Annual Paid Holidays
24	Locomotive men	2,478	3s 6d-7s (daily)	None

At 1 February 1902 there were 1,263 drivers and 1,215 firemen. Payment on a basis of 72 hour weeek of six days except in case of triple-shift yards with eight hour days. Time reckoned from signing on to signing off. Nine hours allowed between duty stints. Drivers' rate starts at 4s 6d daily on pug or pilot engine, up to 7s daily on main line 'long road' trips; firemen 3s 6d - 4s. Overcoat and jacket provided in alternate years. Holidays allowed but no payment. One family pass per annum allowed.

	Category	Number	Weekly Pay	Annual Paid Holidays
25	Goods porters	1,184	18s-30s	See details

Twelve hour day with two hours for meals. Starting rate 18s-20s; up to 30s for foremen, yardsmen, and weighers at principal stations. Clothing unspecified. Holidays: "men allowed two or three days a year with full pay if circumstances permit". One family pass per annum.

	Category	Number	Weekly Pay	Annual Paid Holidays
27	Permanent way men	not noted	17s-46s	See details

66 hours per week (ten hours Mon.-Fri., 6 hrs Sat.). In winter, dawn to dusk. In tunnels, work during night 11 pm - 6.30 am with short meal break. Wages vary slightly between divisions, Western highest. Minimum is 17s for all surfacemen; maximum 46s for an inspector on Western Division. Clothing not specified. Tunnel workers and flying squad get extra 1s. Men provide their own shovels. For examining line on Sundays, Northern & Central & Border Divisions allow half-day's pay; Western gives full day. Other Sunday work paid at double time, and weekday overtime at time plus a half, in all divisions. Two days holiday with full pay and free family pass. Inspectors in Northern Division get one week's paid holiday.

APPENDIX 2

Ships of the North British Railway, North British Steam Packet Co., Lochlomond Steamboat Co., and (from 1891) Galloway Saloon Steam Packet Co.

NBR ships had red funnels with black top, 1862-1902. From 1902 a white band was interposed between the red and black. GSSP steamers had yellow funnels. Tonnages are gross registered tons. Lochlomond Steamboat vessels were jointly owned by NBR, L&D, and CR (D&B Joint Line Committee) after 1 October 1896, and had red funnels with black tops.

SS *Doddington*. Built 1830. Owned by Silloth Bay Steam Navigation Co., taken over by NBR on 16 January 1864. 60 tons. Weekly run to Annan. Scrapped 1866.

PS *William Adam*. Built 1838 by Menzies & Co., Leith. 38 tons. Acquired by NBR 1865. Sold for scrap 1866.

Solway Lightship. Built 1840 by Wm. Bell, Carlisle. 80 tons. Acquired by NBR 1864. Supplemented by *Tobin*, 1895 and used sporadically until 1920, then converted into a 'lemonade bar' at Skinburness.

PS *Granton*. Built 1846 by Maxton & Co., Leith, for Edinburgh & Northern Rly. 196 tons. Ferry for Granton-Burntisland, transferred to NBR 1862. Scrapped 1875.

PS *Burntisland*. Built 1846 by Maxton & Co., Leith, for E&NR. 196 tons. Ferry for Granton-Burntisland, transferred to NBR 1862. Scrapped 1875.

PS *Forth*. Built 1846 by Hawarden Iron Co., Liverpool, for E&NR. 209 tons. Ferry for Granton-Burntisland, transferred to NBR 1862. Coal hulk in 1876, scrapped 1879.

PS *Auld Reekie*. Built 1847 at Blackwall, for E&NR. 163 tons. Passenger ferry Granton-Burntisland. Transferred to NBR 1862. Moved to Tayport-Broughty Ferry after bridge collapse, 1880. Returned to Firth of Forth 1887, under licence to David Wilson. Sold 1890.

PS *Thane of Fife*. Built 1847 at Blackwall, for E&NR. 163 tons. Passenger ferry Granton-Burntisland. Transferred to NBR 1862. Moved to Tayport-Broughty Ferry after bridge collapse, 1880. Newport-Dundee from 1887, under licence to David Wilson. Sold 1890.

PS *Ariel*. Built 1847 by John Reid & Co., Port Glasgow. 207 tons. Bought 10 September 1862 for NBR, registered by Robert Young. Silloth-Dublin and Silloth-Liverpool. Sold 1868.

PS *Express*. Built 1848 at Blackwall for E&NR. 269 tons. Tayport-Broughty Ferry. Moved to Granton 1877. Broken up 1879.

PS *Queen*. Built 1849, for Silloth Bay Steam Navigation Co. 132 tons. Taken over by NBR on 16 January 1864, but sold on in March.

PS *Leviathan*. Built 1849 by Robert Napier, Govan, for Edinburgh Perth & Dundee Rly. Train ferry, for Granton-Burntisland. Transferred to NBR 1862. Scrapped 1890.

PS *Robert Napier*. Built by Robert Napier, 1850, for EP&DR. Train ferry for Tayport-Broughty Ferry. 216 tons. Transferred to NBR 1862. Moved to Granton May 1878, returned to Tay January 1880-June 1887. Scrapped 1888.

Tobin. Built Liverpool 1850, perhaps for T. Tobin & Co. 171 tons. Acquired by NBR from Mersey Docks & Harbour Board 1895 for use as a Solway lightship. Sold or scrapped in 1920-21.

PS *Nymph*. Built 1851 in Liverpool. 91 tons. Bought by NBR 1857 for Queensferry service. Scrapped 1890.

SS *Silloth*. Built 1856, Port Glasgow, for Silloth Bay Steam Navigation Co., taken over by NBR on 16 January 1864. 247 tons. Sold 1879.

PS *Carrier*. Built 1858 by Scotts, Greenock, for EP&DR. Tayport-Broughty Ferry train ferry. 243 tons. Moved to Granton 1877. Sold 1882 to Samuel L. Mason.

PS *Prince of Wales*. Built 1858 by Laurence Hill, Port Glasgow, for Lochlomond Steamboat Co. Transferred to NBSP 31 October 1888, then 1 October 1896 to D&B Joint Line Committee. 1901 became coal hulk at Newry.

PS *Forfarshire*. Built 1861 by Gourlay Bros., Dundee, for Scottish Central Railway. Transferred successively to Caledonian Rly, Dundee Harbour Trust, David Wilson, Leith Salvage & Towage Co., and NBR 13 November 1920. On Queensferry route 1893-1922. Broken up 1922.

PS *Balbirnie*. Built 1861 by H. Morton & Co., Leith, for EP&DR. 533 tons. Train ferry primarily on Tay route, Forth route from 1887. Transferred to NBR 1862. Scrapped 1890.

PS *Prince Consort*. Built 1862 by Cairds, Greenock, for Lochlomond Steamboat Co. 169 tons. Transferred to NBSP 31 October 1888, then 1 October 1896 to D&B Joint Line Committee. Scrapped 1899.

PS *Arabian*. Built 1863 on Tyne for NBR directors as Silloth tug. 69 tons. Also did Annan run. Transferred to NBSP Co. 1866, sold 1886.

PS *Waverley* (I). Launched May 1864 by Mitchells, Walker on Tyne. 564 tons. Ordered for NBSP Co. Dublin service but rejected late 1866 and sold on by builder.

PS *Carham*. Built 1864 by A.&J. Inglis, Glasgow. 158 tons. Registered in name of Richard Hodgson and three others. Ran Silloth-Dumfries then transferred to Helensburgh 1867. Sold to Dingwall & Skye Railway, June 1871.

SS *Dunlop* and *Black Dwarf*. Steam lighters acquired 1864 to participate in trade from Silloth to Greenock and north and east of Scotland. Further details unknown.

PS *Waverley* (II). Launched 16 May 1865 by A.&J. Inglis, Glasgow. 593 tons. Two funnels. Intended for Silloth-Dublin route but too big. Sold to L&SWR 1868.

PS *Kinloch*. Built 1865 by A.&J. Inglis, Glasgow, for NBR. 585 tons. First of NBR's own train ferries, for Granton-Burntisland. Scrapped 1890.

SS *Kittiwake* (I). Built 1866 by Thos. Wingate, Whiteinch, Glasgow. 321 tons. Silloth-Liverpool, then replaced *Ariel* on Dublin route. Broken up 1882.

PS *Meg Merrilees* (I). Built 1866 by A.&J. Inglis for NBSP Co. 213 tons. For Helensburgh-Ardrishaig, but too big; sold 1868.

PS *Dandie Dinmont* (I). Built 1866 by A.&J. Inglis for NBSP Co. 215 tons. For Helensburgh-Ardrishaig but laid up 1866 and transferred 1868 to Granton-Burntisland and Tayport-Broughty Ferry passenger services. Back to Clyde 1869. Sold 1885.

PS *Lord Aberdour*. Built 1866 by Aitken & Mansel, Whiteinch, Glasgow, for Donald McGregor and John Galloway. 130 tons. Acquired by GSSP Co. 1886. Scrapped 1900.

PS *James Cox* (ex-*George Crow*). Built by Mitchell & Co., Low Walker, 1867. 24 tons. Purchased by NBR for Tay route 1878 and name changed. Sold 1884.

PS *Gareloch/Wemyss Castle*. Built 1872 by A.&J. Inglis. 209 tons. Replaced *Carham* at Helensburgh. Transferred to GSSP Co. on Firth of Forth as *Wemyss Castle*, January 1891. Sold for scrap, 1906.

PS *Dundee*. Built 1875 by W. Simons & Co., Renfrew, for Dundee Harbour Trust. 264 tons. Acquired by David Wilson 1918, NBR in 1920, and moved to Queensferry route. Passed to LNER, 1923.

SS *John Beaumont*. Built 1876 by Key & Sons, Kinghorn, for NBR. 165 tons, screw at each end. For Queensferry route, sank 18 December 1878, refloated and refitted as PS, 1879. Sold 1890 to Captain Arthur for same route, leased to David Wilson 1893, sold on, 1890.

PS *John Stirling*. Built 1876, Key & Sons, for NBR. 427 tons. For Granton-Burntisland passenger service. Sold 1892.

Rhoda and *I*, dredging vessels, acquired 1876, further details unknown.

PS *Guy Mannering* (ex-*Sheila*). Built 1877 by Caird & Co., Greenock, for Gillies & Campbell. 225 tons. Acquired by NBR 1882 and renamed *Guy Mannering* 1883. Craigendoran-Rothesay service. Sold 1894.

SS *Albatross*. Built 1878 by Ramage & Ferguson, Leith. 366 tons. For Silloth-Liverpool route, transferred to Clyde 1905, returned to Silloth. Sold 1919.

PS *William Muir*. Built 1879 by Key & Sons, for NBR. 364 tons. For Granton-Burntisland route. Sole ship on route after Forth Bridge opened. Minesweeper 1914-16. Transferred to LNER, 1923.

PS *Midlothian*. Built 1881 by Ramage & Ferguson, for NBR. 920 tons. Last and biggest of the train ferries. Withdrawn 1890 and scrapped.

PS *Meg Merrilees* (II). Built 1883 by Barclay Curle, Glasgow for NBSP Clyde service. 244 tons. Rejected by NBSP Co. as too slow.

PS *Lord Morton*. Built 1883 for GSSP Co. 220 tons. Sold to Admiralty April 1918.

PS *Queen*. Built 1883 by Caird & Co. for Lochlomond Steamboat Co. 233 tons. Transferred to NBR 31 October 1888; 1 October 1896 to D&B Joint Line Committee. Registered in name of J. Brown 1904, H. Grierson 1906. Sold for scrapping April 1911.

PS *Jeanie Deans* (I). Built 1884 by Barclay, Curle for NBSP to replace *Meg Merrilees*. 234 tons. Sold 1896.

PS *Stirling Castle* (I). Built 1884 by S.&H. Morton, Leith, for GSSP Co. 160 tons. Sold 1898.

PS *Diana Vernon*. Built 1885 by Barclay, Curle for NBSP Clyde service. 154 tons. Sold 1901.

PS *Edinburgh Castle*. Built 1886 by Scotts, Kinghorn, for GSSP Co. 158 tons. Sold to Admiralty April 1918.

PS *Solway*. Built 1886 by Ramage & Ferguson. 103 tons. Silloth tug, replacing *Arabian*. Sold 1896.

PS *Tantallon Castle* (I). Built 1887 by S.&H. Morton, Leith, for GSSP Co. 240 tons, enlarged to 257 tons 1895. Sold 1898.

PS *Lucy Ashton*. Built 1888 by T.B. Seath, Rutherglen, for NBSP Clyde service. Registered in name of Robert Young. Transfer to NBR 1902, and in service to 1923.

PS *Empress*. Built 1888 by Shanks & Bell, Yoker, for Lochlomond Steamboat Co. 229 tons. Transferred to NBR 31 October 1888. Transferred to D&B Joint Committee 1 October 1896. Registered in name of J. Brown 1904, H. Grierson 1906. Passed to LNER 1923.

PS *Lady Rowena*. Built 1891 by S. McKnight, Ayr, for NBSP Co. 362 tons. Craigendoran-Arrochar route. Transferred to NBR 1902, sold 1903.

PS *Lady Clare*. Built 1891 by J.M. McArthur, Paisley, for NBSP Co. 257 tons. Replaced *Gareloch* on Loch Long, then Craigendoran-Greenock route. Transferred to NBR 1902, sold 1906.

PS *Redgauntlet*. Built 1895 by Barclay, Curle, for NBSP Co. 277 tons. Transferred to NBR 1902, then to GSSP Co., 1909 to replace *Roslin Castle*. Minesweeper 1914-17. Sold 1919.

PS *Dandie Dinmont* (II). Built 1895 by A.&J. Inglis for NBSP Co. 218 tons. Craigendoran-Arrochar route. Transferred to NBR 1902. Lengthened 1912. Passed to LNER 1923.

SS *Kittiwake* (II). Built 1896 by Scott & Sons, Bowling, for NBSP Co. in name of Henry Grierson. 366 tons. Silloth-Liverpool run. Sold 1919 to Dundalk & Newry Steam Packet Co.

PS *Talisman*. Built 1896 by A.&J. Inglis for NBSP Co. 279 tons. Transferred to NBR 1902. Minesweeper 1915-19. Passed to LNER 1923.

PS *Petrel*. Built 1897 by J.P. Rennoldson, South Shields. 170 tons. Silloth tug, replacing *Solway*. Transferred from NBSP Co. to NBR 14 March 1919, passed to LNER (scrapped 1949).

PS *Kenilworth*. Built 1898 by A.&J. Inglis, for NBSP Co. 330 tons. Transferred to NBR, 1902. Used on day cruises, painted white, from 1909. Minesweeper 1914-19. Passed to LNER 1923.

PS *Prince George*. Built 1898 by A.&J. Inglis for D&B Joint Committee. 256 tons. Loch Lomond service. Passed to LNER 1923.

PS *Princess May*. Built 1898 by A.&J. Inglis for D&B Joint Committee. 256 tons. Loch Lomond service. Passed to LNER 1923.

PS *Waverley* (III). Built 1899 by A.&J. Inglis, for NBSP Co. 449 tons. Minesweeper 1915-20. Passed to LNER 1923 (sunk at Dunkirk, 1940).

PS *Stirling Castle* (II). Built 1899 by Scotts, Kinghorn, for GSSP Co. 271 tons. Sold 1907.

PS *Tantallon Castle* (II). Built 1899 by Scotts, Kinghorn, for GSSP Co. 333 tons. Sold 1901.

PS *Princess Patricia* (ex-*Shakespeare*). Built 1905 by Thornycrofts, Southampton for London County Council; purchased by D&B Joint Committee for Loch Lomond, 1914. 120 tons. Passed to LNER 1923

PS *Marmion*. Built 1906 by A.&J. Inglis, for NBR. 403 tons. Loch Long and Arrochar routes. Minesweeper 1915-18. Passed to LNER, 1923.

SS *Roslin Castle*. Built 1906 by Hawthorns, Leith, for GSSP Co. 129 tons. Sold to Admiralty March 1908.

PS *Prince Edward*. Built 1911 by A.&J. Inglis, for D&B Joint Committee. 310 tons. Loch Lomond service. Passed to LNER, 1923.

Dredger *Almond*. Built 1914 by Fleming & Ferguson, Paisley, for NBR. 309 tons. Bucket dredger based at Bo'ness from 1919. Passed to LNER 1923 (scrapped 1963). It had two hopper barges acquired second-hand, *Southborough* and *Cornwall*.

PS *Fair Maid*. Built 1915 by A.&J. Inglis, for NBR. 304 tons. Requisitioned by Admiralty 1915 as minesweeper, sunk 13 November 1916. Never used by NBR.

PS *Duchess of Buccleuch*. Built 1915 by A.&J. Inglis for GSSP Co. 450 tons. Taken over by Admiralty 1915-18. Only ship still registered to GSSP Co. in 1920. Scrapped 1923.

BIBLIOGRAPHY
1. ORIGINAL DOCUMENTS

Glasgow University Archive Service (GUAS)
John Patrick Library, Kirkintilloch, J.F. MacEwan Collection (McE)
National Archives of Scotland (NAS)

Post Office Archives, London (POST)
St Andrews University Library, C.J.A. Robertson Collection (St. AND.)

2. OFFICIAL PUBLICATIONS

Edinburgh Gazette (*Ed. Gaz.*)
Hansard

London Gazette (*Lond. Gaz.*)
Parliamentary Papers (PP)

3. NEWSPAPERS, JOURNALS, SERIAL PUBLICATIONS, ETC

Aberdeen Weekly Journal (*Abdn. Jnl.*)
The Bailie
Bradshaw Shareholders' Guide, 1867, 1883
Caledonian Mercury (*Cal. Merc.*)
Cumberland News
Daily News
Dundee Courier & Argus (*Dund. Cour.*)
Glasgow Herald (*Glas. Her.*)
Glasgow News
Herapath's Railway Journal (Herapath)
Leeds Mercury
Lloyds Register of Shipping
Marine News
Morning Chronicle
Morning Post

Newcastle Courant (*Newc. Cour.*)
North British Railway Study Group Journal (*NBRSGJ*)
North British Shipping & Railway Journal
Railway Gazette (*RG*)
Railway Intelligence
Railway & Canal Historical Society Journal (*RCHS*)
Railway Magazine (*Rly. Mag.*)
Railway News
Railway Times (*RT*)
Scotsman (*Scmn.*)
Scottish History Review
Scottish Railway Gazette (*SRG*)
The Times
Transport History (*TH*)
York Herald

4. PAMPHLETS AND ARTICLES

BRB (British Railways Board). *100 Years of the Sleeping Car*. London 1973
Cameron, Euan, *Development of the North British Passenger Locomotive in the Victorian Era*. Gosforth, 1995
Douglas, John Monteath, *The North British Railway* (1878)
Geddie, John, *Souvenir of the Opening of the North British Station Hotel, Edinburgh*. Edinburgh 1902

North British Railway. *Epistles of Peggy*. 1903
North British Railway: Rules & Regulations 1898
North British Railway. Working Timetables, 1888-1922
Graphic 'Sketch of the North British Railway', by 'A Losing NB Shareholder'. Wm Paterson, Edinburgh, 1870
Worling, M.J., *A Brief History of the Edinburgh & Dalkeith Railway*. Dalkeith 1988

5. MANUSCRIPTS AND THESES

Cattanach, Donald, G.B. *Wieland of the North British Railway*.

Hargrave, J.F. (1991) *Competition and collusion in the*

British railway track fittings industry: the case of the Anderston Foundry, 1800-1960 (Durham E-Theses On-line)

6. BOOKS
1. BOOKS ON THE NORTH BRITISH AND ASSOCIATED RAILWAYS

Brotchie, A.W., *The Wemyss Private Railway*. Witney, 1998
Brown, A., *Craigendoran Steamers*. Johnstone, 1979
Deayton, A., *Steamers of the Clyde: North British and LNER*. Stroud, 2000
Douglas, Hugh, *Crossing the Forth*. London, 1964
Ellis, C. Hamilton, *The North British Railway. London*, 1955
Hajducki, A.M., *The North Berwick and Gullane Branches*. Oxford, 1992
Hajducki, A.M., *The Haddington, Macmerry and Gifford Branch Lines*. Oxford, 1994
Hajducki, A.M., and Simpson, A., *The Lauder Light Railway*. Oxford, 1996

Hajducki, A.M., Jodeluk, M., and Simpson, A., *The St. Andrews Railway*. Usk, 2008
Hajducki, A.M., Jodeluk, M., and Simpson, A., *The Anstruther & St. Andrews Railway*. Usk, 2009
Hurst, Jeff, *The Glencorse Branch*. Usk, 1999
Jenkins, S., *The Rothbury Branch*. Oxford, 1991
Koerte, A., *Two Railway Bridges*. Basel, 1990
McGregor, John, *100 Years of the West Highland Railway*. Glasgow, 1994
McGregor, John, *The West Highland Railway: Plans, Politics and People*. Edinburgh, 2005
Sewell, G.W.M., *The North British in Northumberland*. Braunton, Devon, 1992

Sewell, G.W.M., *North British Locomotives: A Design Survey*. Bardon Mill 2002

Thomas, John, *The West Highland Railway*. Newton Abbot, 1965

Thomas, John, *The North British Railway*, 2 vols. Newton Abbot, 1969, 1975

Thomas, John, *The North British Atlantics*. Newton Abbot, 1972

White, Stephen, *Solway Steam. Carlisle*, 1984

Wood, Lawson, *The Eight-Minute Link*. Eyemouth, 1990

2. OTHER BOOKS

Acworth, William, *The Railways of Scotland*. London, 1890

Acworth, William, *The Railways and the Traders*. London, 1891

Addyman, John F. (ed.), *A History of the Newcastle & Berwick Railway*. Northallerton, 2011

Alderman, Geoffrey, *The Railway Interest*. Leicester, 1973

Atkins, C.P., *The Scottish 4-6-0 Classes*. London, 1976

Bagwell, Philip S. *The Railway Clearing House in the British Economy, 1842-1922*. London, 1968

Bagwell, Philip S., *The Transport Revolution from 1770*. London 1994

Barnes, E.G., *The Midland Railway. London*, 1968

Baxter, David and Mitchell, Peter (eds.), *British Locomotive Catalogue 1825-1923, Vol. vi.* Southampton, 2012

Biddle, Gordon, *Historic Railway Buildings*. Oxford, 2003

Bowtell, Harold D., *Dam Builders' Railways*. Brighton, 1994

Bremner, David, *The Industries of Scotland*. Edinburgh, 1869

Brodie, Ian, *Steamers of the Forth*. Newton Abbot, 1976

Brotchie, A.W., and Jack, H., *Early Railways of West Fife*. Catrine, 2007

Brown, J.L., and Lawson, I.C., *History of Peebles*. Edinburgh, 1990

Bruce, W.S., *The Railways of Fife*. Perth, 1980

Cairncross, A.K., *Home & Foreign Investment, 1870-1913*. Cambridge, 1953

Campbell, R.H., *Scotland Since 1707: The Rise of an Industrial Society*. Edinburgh, 2nd ed., 1985

Campbell, R.H., and Dow, J.B.A., *A Source Book of Scottish Economic & Social History*. Oxford, 1968

Chacksfield, J.E., *The Drummond Brothers*. Usk, 2005

Checkland, S.G., *Scottish Banking: A History 1695-1973*. London, 1975

Cobb, M.H., *The Railways of Great Britain: A Historical Atlas*, 2nd ed., Shepperton, 2006

Cummings, A.J.G, and Devine, T.M., *Industry, Business and Society in Scotland since 1700*. Edinburgh, 1994

Cunningham, A., *Mining in the Kingdom of Fife*. 2nd ed. Dunfermline, 1913.

Deas, Francis, *The Law of Railways as Applying to Scotland*. Edinburgh 1873

Dobbin, Frank, *Forging Industrial Policy: the United States, Britain and France in the Railway Age*. Cambridge 1994

Ellis, C. Hamilton, *British Railway History*, 2 vols. London, 1974

Ellis, C. Hamilton, *Four Main Lines*. London, 1950

Foxwell, E., and Farrer, T.C., *Express Trains, English & Foreign*. London, 1889

Fraser, W.H., and Maver, Irene, *Glasgow, Vol ii, 1830-1912*. Manchester, 1996

Galt, William, *Railway Reform: Its Importance and Practicability*. London, 1865

Gourvish, T.R., *Mark Huish and the LNWR*. Leicester, 1972

Grinling, Charles H., *History of the Great Northern Railway*. London 1903

Hamilton, J.A.B., *Britain's Railways in World War I*. London, 1967

Haws, Duncan, *Merchant Fleets: British Railway Steamers, Scottish & Irish Companies*. Hereford, 1994

Highet, Campbell, *The Glasgow & South-Western Railway*. Lingfield, 1965

Highet, Campbell, *Scottish Locomotive History, 1831-1923*. London, 1970

Hoole, Ken, *Illustrated History of the East Coast Joint Stock*. Sparkford, 1993

Hull, Edward, *Our Coal Resources at the End of the Nineteenth Century*. London, 1897

Johnston, C., and Hume, J.R., *Glasgow Stations*. Newton Abbot, 1975

Johnston, Ronald, *Clydeside Capital, 1870-1920*. Phantassie, 2000

Kellett, J.R., *The Impact of Railways on Victorian Cities*. London, 1969

Lambert, R. S., *The Railway King*, new ed. London, 1964

Lewin, H.G., *The Railway Mania*. London, 1936

Lloyd's Register of Shipping, 1899-1900; 1922-23

McKean, Charles, *Battle for the North*. London, 2006

Marshall, Peter, *The Scottish Central Railway*. Usk, 1998

Marshall, Peter, *Burntisland:Fife's Railway Port*. Usk, 2001

Martin, Don, *The Monkland & Kirkintilloch and Associated Railways*. Kirkintilloch, 1995

Mason, Roger and McDougall, Norman, *People and Power in Scotland: Essays in Honour of T.C. Smout*. Edinburgh, 1992

Mavor, James, *The Scottish Railway Strike 1891: A History and Criticism*. Edinburgh, 1891

Measom, George, *Official Illustrated Guide to the N.E., N.B., E.&G., S.C. and Other Railways*. London, 1861

Middlemass, Thomas, *Mainly Scottish Steam*. Newton Abbot, 1973

Mowat, Sue, *The Port of Leith*. Leith, 1994

Muir, Augustus, *The Fife Coal Company: A Short History*. Dunfermline, 1952

Oxford Dictionary of National Biography. Oxford, 2004

Paget-Tomlinson, E., *The Railway Carriers*. Lavenham, 1990

256

Paterson, A.J.S., *The Golden Age of the Clyde Steamers.* Newton Abbot, 1969

Pattinson, J.P., *British Railways.* London, 1893

Pratt, Edwin A., *Railways and Nationalisation.* London, 1908

Pratt, Edwin A., *British Railways and the Great War*, 2 vols. London, 1921

Puxley, Chris, *The Port of Silloth, 1859-2009.* Bristol 2009

Quick, Michael, *A Chronology of Railway Passenger Stations in Great Britain.* Oxford, 2009

Ransom, P.J.G., *The Victorian Railway and How It Evolved.* London, 1996

Reed. M.C. (ed.), *Railways in the Victorian Economy.* Newton Abbot, 1969

Robertson, C.J.A., *The Origins of the Scottish Railway System, 1722-1844.* Edinburgh, 1983

Ross, David, *The Highland Railway, 2nd ed. Catrine,* 2010

Ross, David, *George & Robert Stephenson: A Passion for Success.* Stroud, 2010

Ross, David, *The Caledonian: Scotland's Imperial Railway,* Catrine, 2013

Scottish Industrial History: A Miscellany. Edinburgh, 1978

Scrivenor, Harry, *Railways of the United Kingdom.* London, 1849

Sherrington, C.E.R., *The Economics of Rail Transport in Great Britain*, 2 vols. London, 1928

Simnett, W.E., *Railway Amalgamation in Great Britain.* London, 1923

Slaven, A., and Checkland, S., *Dictionary of Scottish Business Biography.* Aberdeen, 1993

Smith, Alexander, *County of Fife (3rd Statistical Account of Scotland).* Edinburgh 1952

Smith, W.A.C., and Anderson, P., *An Illustrated History of Glasgow's Railways.* Oldham, 1993

Snodgrass, Catherine P., *County of East Lothian (3rd Statistical Account of Scotland).* Edinburgh, 1953

Tatlow, Joseph, *Fifty Years of Railway Life in England, Scotland and Ireland.* London, 1920

Thomas, John, *The Springburn Story.* Dawlish & London, 1964

Thomas, John, *A Regional History of the Railways of Great Britain, Vol vi* (revised Alan J.S. Paterson). Newton Abbot, 1984

Thomas, John, and Turnock, David, *A Regional History of the Railways of Great Britain, Vol xv.* Newton Abbot, 1989

Williamson, James, *The Clyde Passenger Steamer.* Glasgow, 1904

Wilson, Harold, *The Travelling Post Offices of Great Britain and Ireland.* Derby, 1996

Wrottesley, J., *The Great Northern Railway, Vol 1.* London, 1979

NOTES AND REFERENCES
1. LEARMONTH'S RAILWAY 1, 1842-1844

1. *Scmn.*, 7 February 1824. The business was transferred to Russell & Macnee (Russell having been Learmonth's manager) in January 1838 (*Scmn.*, 21 January 1838).
2. *Scmn.*, 23 November 1836.
3. *Scmn.*, 6 February 1839.
4. *Scmn.*, 9 February 1839, GNBR prospectus (no mention of the Tyne and Tweed crossings).
5. *Scmn.*, 24 July 1839.
6. Quoted in *Cal. Merc.*, 2 May 1840.
7. Ross, *George and Robert Stephenson*, 178f.
8. *Cal. Merc.*, 4,18,27 March; 3, 17 April 1841.
9. *Scot. Hist. Rev.*, vol. 57, no. 164, October 1978. Robertson, C.J.A., 'Railways and the Sabbath'.
10. Edinburgh Town Council withdrew its original objections to this station, under certain conditions. See *Scmn.*, 9 April 1839.
11. *Scmn.*, 18 February, 1 March, 21 June 1837; E&G Act, 4 July 1838.
12. *Cal. Merc.*, 4 March, letter from Theodore Rathbone; 17 April; *Scmn.*, 27 February 1841.
13. NAS.BR/NBR/1/1, adjourned meetings on 18 and 19 January 1842.
14. NAS.BR/NBR/1/1, sub-committee, 25 January 1842.
15. *Cal. Merc.*, 12 February, 10 March, 1842.
16. The railway killed the general trade of small harbours. In 1843 Dunbar had seventeen trading vessels; in 1899 none, though it was still exporting potatoes by sea in 1914. See Snodgrass, *East Lothian*, 52.
17. NAS.BR/NBR/1/1, provisional committee, 14 February 1842.
18. *Cal. Merc.*, 10 February 1842.
19. NAS.BR/NBR/1/1, report to the provisional committee, 15 June 1842.
20. NAS.BR/NBR/1/1. Report by provisional committee to subscribers. October 1842.
21. NAS.BR/NBR/1/1, report by Learmonth on meeting with Hudson, 19 May 1843.
22. NAS.BR/NBR/1/1, July 1843; *Cal. Merc.* 12 August 1843.
23. NAS.BR/NBR/1/1, provisional committee, 3 August 1843.
24. *Cal. Merc.*, 30 September 1843.
25. *Scmn.*, 26 August, report of E&G half-yearly meeting; 13 September 1843.
26. *Cal. Merc.*, 16 November 1843.
27. NAS.BR/NBR/1/1, sub-committee, September and October 1843.
28. NAS.BR/NBR/1/1, report of meeting on 27 October 1843. *Scmn.*, 10 January 1844.
29. *Leeds Mercury*, 27 January 1844.
30. *Glas. Her.*, 1 April 1844.
31. NAS.BR/NBR/1/1. sub-committee minutes, 12 March 1844.
32. *Glas. Her.*, 22 April 1844, *Cal. Merc.* 25 April 1844.

CHAPTER 1 CONTINUED

33. NAS.BR/NBR/1/1, sub-committee's report, 23 June 1844.
34. *York Herald*, report of special meeting, 11 May 1844 NAS.BR/NBR/AP/S/178. See also Lambert, *The Railway King*, 272.

35. *York Herald*, 1 August 1846.
36. NAS.BR/NBR1/1, sub-committee, 11 January, 2 February 1844.

2. LEARMONTH'S RAILWAY 2, 1844-1847

1. *Scmn.*, 14 September 1844.
2. *Scmn.*, 28 December 1844.
3. NAS.BR/NBR/1/1, sub-committee's report, 23 June 1844.
4. Mowat, *The Port of Leith*, 346. Its oft-repeated designation as "the Innocent Railway" is false; see fatal accident report in *Edinburgh Courant*, 29 March 1832; also Worling, *Brief History of the Edinburgh & Dalkeith Railway*.
5. NAS.BR/NBR/1/1, sub-committee, 27 June 1844.
6. *Scmn.*, 28 December 1844.
7. *Cal. Merc.*, 19 December 1844.
8. *Glas. Her.*, 7 July, *Scmn.*, 5 July 1845.
9. *Scmn.*, 1 November 1845.
10. *Scmn.*, 20 August, *Cal. Merc.*, 21 August, *Lond. Gaz.*, 3240, 26 October 1845.
11. *Glas. Her.*, 22 December 1845.
12. *Lond. Gaz.*, 2312, 5 July 1844.
13. *Scmn.*, 12 March 1845.
14. *Scmn.*, 28 August 1844; *Lond. Gaz.*, 2389, 30 June 1846.
15. *Cal. Merc.*, 12 February 1846.
16. *Cal. Merc.* 19 February 1846. See also PP 1847 (164). Report of the Commissioners of Railways, 396.
17. This emerged at the E&N half-yearly meeting on 31 August 1846. Learmonth had not told the E&N directors that he was effectively the major shareholder in the Edinburgh & Perth. *Cal. Merc.*, 3 September 1846.
18. *Cal. Merc.*, 14 May 1846.
19. *Cal. Merc.*, 24 May 1846.
20. *Cal. Merc.*, 21 May 1846.
21. *Cal. Merc.*, 20 May 1846.
22. See *NBRSGJ*, No. 118, March 2013, 18ff, Rodgers A. and Cattanach D., '*Waverley: A History*'.
23. *Scmn.*, 8 July 1846.
24. *Cal. Merc.*, 22 June 1846.
25. *Scmn.*, 20 June 1846.
26. See John Black's reminiscence, chapter18.
27. *Scmn.*, 12 August 1846.
28. NAS.BR/NBR/1/3, Directors' meeting, 29 July 1846
29. *Cal. Merc.*, 31 and 6 August 1846.
30. NAS.BR/NBR/1/3. Directors' meeting, 24 and 25 June 1846.
31. NAS.BR/NBR/1/3, abstract balance sheet, 27 August 1846; *Cal. Merc.*, 31 August 1846.
32. *Scmn.*, 22 August 1846, report of E&G shareholders' meeting at Liverpool.

33. *Cal. Merc.*, 7 September 1846. NAS. BR/NBR/1/3. Directors' meetings, 20 May, 16 September 1846.
34. The old St. Margaret's Well, moved in 1859, was adjacent.
35. NAS.BR/NBR/1/3, Directors' meetings, 2, 16 and 23 September; Finance committee, 27 October 1846.
36. *Cal. Merc.*, 24 September 1846.
37. *TH*, vol 7 no. 1, March 1974.Robertson, C.J.A., 'The Cheap RailwayMovement in Scotland', 3.
38. *Cal. Merc.*, Report of Committee of Inquiry, 2 August 1849.
39. *Scmn.*, 11 November 1846.
40. Advertisements in *Scmn.*, 1 August, 9 September, 4 November 1846; PP 1881 (374): Scott's evidence to Select Committee on Railways.
41. NAS.BR/NBR1/3, Directors' meeting 30 November 1846; *Cal. Merc.*, 3 and 10 December 1846.
42. NAS. BR/NBR/8/1212. Peddie, incidentally, or a man of identical name, was one of the two auditors of the British Guarantee Association (chairman John Learmonth).
43. *Scmn.*, 27 February 1847, half-yearly report.
44. NAS.BR/NBR/1/3, Directors' meetings of 6, 20, 25 January and 3 February 1847.
45. Lambert, *The Railway King*, 203.
46. *Newcastle Courant*, 15 January 1847.
47. See for example *Cal. Merc.*, 8 February 1847.
48. NAS.BR/NBR/1/3, Law committee, 8 March 1847.
49. *Cal. Merc.*, 12 July 1847.
50. *Cal. Merc.*, 30 September 1847.
51. NAS.NB/BR/1/3. Goods traffic committee, 20 December 1847.
52. *Cal. Merc.*, 9 September 1847.
53. NAS.BR/NBR/1/3. Capital account, 26 February 1847.
54. NAS.BR/NBR/1/3. Directors' meetings, 17 March, 2 June 1847.
55. NAS.BR/NBR/1/3. Directors' meeting, 2 June 1847 authorised £1,111 3s to be paid.
56. NAS.BR/NBR/1/3, Directors' meetings, 28 July, 25 August, 1 September, 25 October 1847.
57. *Cal. Merc.*, 16 March 1848.
58. *Cal. Merc.*, 22 November 1849. There is no evidence of his profiting further; similar inventions were probably being made by others.

3. LEARMONTH'S RAILWAY 3, AND INTERREGNUM, 1848-1855

1. NAS.BR/NBR/1/3. Directors' meeting, 1 December 1847.
2. *Cal. Merc.* 1 May 1848.
3. *SRG*, 4 March 1848.
4. *Lond. Gaz.*, 3240, 28 October 1845; 4507, 14 November 1846; *Scmn.*, 5 January 1848.
5. *Cal. Merc.*, 11 May, 23 October 1848. The General Post Office was built on the Shakespeare Square site from 1859.
6. *Scmn.*, 4 July 1846.
7. PO Minutes 26 September 1848, quoted in Wilson, *The TPOs*, 179.
8. *Cal. Merc.*, 23 October 1848.
9. Vamplew, *Scottish Industrial History*, 'The North British Inquiry of 1866', 149, notes that the NBR was among the first Scottish railways to introduce preference shares.
10. *Cal. Merc.*, 12 March; *Glas. Her.*, 11 May, 1849.
11. *Scmn.*, 25 August 1849. Russell & Macnee moved to 106 Princes Street.
12. *Cal. Merc.*, 27 September 1849, comments at the half-yearly shareholders' meeting.
13. NAS.BR/NBR/1/4. Directors' meeting 7 February 1849.
14. NAS.BR/NBR/1/4. Finance committee, 4 December 1849; Directors' meetings, 28 February, 19 March, 4 April 1850.
15. NAS.BR/NBR/1/5.
16. *Morning Post*, 15 May 1850.
17. PP. Report of Commissioners of Railways, 1850.
18. NAS. BR/NBR/8/1212. This was a contract for coal carriage: the NBR directors were described as "Trustees on behoof of the North British Railway".
19. Hajducki, *The North Berwick & Gullane Branches*, 20; C.J.A. Robertson in *TH*, vol. 7 no. 1, 8.
20. NAS.BR/NBR/1/5. Directors' meeting 26 July 1850.
21. *Cal. Merc.*, 8 July 1850.
22. NAS.BR/NBR/1/5. Directors' meeting, 15 August 1850.
23. NAS.BR/NBR/1/5. Directors' meetings 23 and 31 August 1850.
24. Grinling, *Great Northern*, 96.
25. NAS. BR/NBR/1/5. Directors' meetings 8 and 31 September; *Scmn.*, 20 November 1850, 19 February 1851. The lines were never laid, however.
26. Directors' half-yearly report, quoted in *Daily News*, 10 September 1850.
27. *Scmn.*, 18 September 1850.
28. *Dund. Cour.*, 2 April 1851. This was probably the only time the train ferries took carriages with passengers.
29. *Scmn.*, letter of 19 May 1852.
30. *Ed. Gaz.*, 469, 13 June 1861.
31. NAS.BR/NBR1/5. Directors' meetings, 13 June, 31 July 1851.
32. A temporary terminus was at Maiden Lane from 7 August 1850 until Kings Cross was opened on 14 October 1852.
33. Full details of these Agreements in Gourvish, *Mark Huish & the LNWR*.
34. *Scmn.*, 24 September 1851.
35. *Scmn.*, 20 October 1852.
36. NAS.BR/NBR/1/5. Directors' meetings, 3 and 28 November 1851.
37. *Daily News*, 8 January 1852.
38. NAS.BR/NBR/1/5. Directors' meeting, 19 February 1852. *Ed. Gaz.*, 999, 19 November 1852.
39. *SRG*, 10 January, 28 February 1852.
40. *SRG*, 13 March 1852.
41. *Cal. Merc.*, 11 March 1852.
42. *SRG*, 20 March 1852.
43. NAS.BR/NBR/1/5. Directors' meeting, 23 April 1852.
44. NAS.BR/NBR/1/5. Directors' meeting 22 May 1852.
45. NAS.BR/NBR/1/5. Directors' meeting 28 May 1852.
46. NAS.BR/NBR/1/5. Directors' meeting 28 May 1852.
47. *Cal. Merc.*, 30, *Scmn.*, 28 August 1852.
48. See *TH*, vol. 7, no. 1, March 1974. Robertson, 'The Cheap Railway Movement', 16.
49. *Cal. Merc.*, 28 October 1852.
50. PP.Reports to Lords of the Privy Council for Trade, 1854, p. 28; Wrottesley, *The GNR*, i, 209.
51. *Ed. Gaz.*, 984, 16 November 1852.
52. *Cal. Merc.*, 10 March 1853, Directors' half-yearly report.
53. NAS. BR/NBR/1/7. Directors' meeting, 11 March 1853.
54. Wrottesley, *The GNR*, i, 83.; Wilson, *The TPOs*, 185.
55. *Cal. Merc.*, 15 September 1853, Directors' half-yearly report.
56. *Scmn.*, 12 and 19 November 1853.
57. NAS.BR/NBR/1/7. Directors' meetings, 21 April, 19 May 1854.
58. PP. Report from the Select Committee on the Conveyance of Mails by Railways, 1854.
59. NAS.BR/NBR/1/7. Directors' meetings, 1, 2, 15 December 1854.
60. NAS.BR/NBR/1/7. Directors' meetings, 17 November, 2 December 1854.
61. NAS.BR/NBR/1/7. Directors' meeting, 23 February 1855.

4. HODGSON'S RAILWAY 1, 1855-1858

1. *Cal. Merc.*, 19 and 22 March 1855.
2. PP. Report to Lords of Privy Council for Trade, 1856, 9.
3. Half-yearly report, 20 March 1855; Wrottesley, *The G.N.R.*, i, 88.
4. PP. Returns of Parliamentary Expenses Incurred by Railway Companies, to 1859.
5. *Cal. Merc.* 29 March 1855.
6. NAS.BR/NBR/1/7. Directors' meeting, 20 July 1855. The NBR negotiated on behalf of the East Coast companies with the Prison Board, see for example PP. 17th Report of the General Board of Directors of Prisons in Scotland, 1856, 7.
7. NAS. BR/NBR1/7. Locomotive committee, 6 March 1856.
8. *Cal. Merc.*, 13 September 1855.
9. *Cal. Merc.* 11 October 1855.
10. *Scmn.*, 16 January 1856.
11. *Cal. Merc.*, 26 January 1856; *Ed. Gaz.* 1036, 14 November 1856.
12. *Cal. Merc.*, 15 February 1856.
13. Bagwell, *The Railway Clearing House*, 251f. It suspended membership for a time in 1867. See also Gourvish, *Mark Huish*, 297f, for breakdown of revenues between routes.
14. *Cal. Merc.*, 27 March 1856.
15. *Cal. Merc.*, 3 September 1856.
16. *Scmn.*, December 29, 1855.
17. *Newc. Cour.*, 31 March 1854.
18. *Newc. Cour.*, 27 February; NAS. NB/BR/1/8 Directors' meeting, 1 January 1857.
19. In 1873 the book room was taken over for office space; but the library continued to exist and by 1899 had 3,177 items catalogued, covering a wide range of fiction, general topics, and technical subjects; but avoiding politics and economics. There had also been a library at Cowlairs from 1850.
20. NAS. BR/NBR/1/8. Directors' meeting; Works committee, 1 January 1857.
21. *Glas. Her.*, 25 February 1857.
22. NAS. BR/NBR/1/8. Directors' meeting, 13 February 1857.
23. *Glas. Her.*, 9 July 1856, quoting Board of Trade report.
24. NAS.BR/NBR/1/8. Loco committee 25 June, Directors' meeting 26 June 1857. As the number of carriages was the same in January 1858, it seems there was no sale.
25. NAS. BR/NBR/1/8. Directors' meeting, 13 February 1857.
26. POST 32/14B. NAS.BR/NBR/1/8. Directors' meeting, 1 May 1857.
27. NAS. BR/NBR/1/8. Directors' meeting, 28 August 1857.
28. *Ed. Gaz.*, 14 November 1856; *Newc. Cour.*, 27 February 1857.
29. Tomlinson, *The NER*, 578.
30. *Cal. Merc.*, 18 August 1857.
31. *Cal. Merc.*, 16 September 1857.
32. Thomas, *NBR*, i, 86.
33. *Newc. Cour.*, 4 September 1857; *Ed. Gaz.*, 27 November 1857.
34. *Cal. Merc.*, 7 November 1857: perhaps the first reference to the Caledonian as "the true line".
35. *Cal. Merc.*, ibid.
36. NAS.BR/NBR/1/9. Director's meeting, 25 July 1860.
37. NAS. BR/NBR1/7. Urgency committee, 27 December 1865; Directors' meetings 29 January 1856 and 12 March 1857.
38. NAS.BR/NBR/1/8. Half-yearly accounts, 31 January; Directors' meeting 19 August 1858.
39. *Cal. Merc.*, 3 September 1856.
40. NAS. BR/NBR/1/8. Directors' meeting 25 October 1857.
41. NAS.BR/NBR/1/8. Directors' meetings, 25 June, 9 July 1858.
42. PP. 3rd Report of Postmaster General, 1858.

5. HODGSON'S RAILWAY 2, 1858-1861

1. *Ed. Gaz.*, 1086. 17 November 1857.
2. PP. Minutes of Proceedings of Committee 13 on Railway Bills, 1858.
3. *Cal. Merc.*, 11 August 1858.
4. *Cal. Merc.*, 1 September 1858; NAS.BR/NBR/1/8. Directors' meeting 30 July 1858.
5. NAS. BR/NBR/1/8. Directors' meeting 19 August 1858.
6. Mowat, *Port of Leith*, 351. NAS. BR/NBR/1/8. Directors' meetings 26 March 1858.
7. NAS. BR/NBR/1/9. Half-yearly meeting, 4 September 1858; *Cal. Merc.*, 6 September 1858.
8. *Cal. Merc.* 13 November 1858.
9. *Rly Mag*, vol. 4, January-June 1899, 331. Robert Cochrane, 'Centenary of the Waverley Route.'
10. *Cal. Merc.*, 1 December 1858.
11. NAS. BR/NBR/1/9. Directors' meeting, 11 February 1859.
12. PP. Report on Railway & Canal Bills for 1859.
13. *Scmn.*, 19 January 1859.
14. *Cal. Merc.*, 21 January 1859.
15. NAS.BR/NBR/1/9. Directors' meeting, 4 July 1859.
16. NAS. BR/NBR/1/9. Directors' meeting, 11 February 1859.
17. Tomlinson, *NER*, 578.

18. NAS. BR/NBR/1/8. Directors' meeting, 18 September 1857. In fact the Carlisle companies were virtually bankrupt and had no funds, see White, *Solway Steam*.
19. *Scmn.*, 25 March 1859.
20. *Glas. Her.*, 25 March 1859; *Cal. Merc.*, 1 June 1859.
21. *Cal. Merc.*, 16 April 1859. *Ed. Gaz.*, 26 July 1859.
22. *Morning Chronicle*, 16 August 1859.
23. Ellis, *British Railway History*, i, 335.
24. *Scmn.*, 6 January 1860 has a letter of complaint.
25. NAS. BR/NBR/1/9. Directors' meeting, 17 August 1859; Urgency committee, 5 September 1859.
26. NAS. BR/NBR/1/9. locomotive superintendent's report, 31 July; directors' meetings, 16 September 1859, 29 September; 14 October 1859.
27. NAS. BR/NBR/1/9. Directors' meetings, 20 April, 15 September, 9 November 1860; 31 January 1861.
28. NAS. BR/NBR/1/9. Locomotive committee, 9 November; directors' meeting, 30 November 1859; Locomotive committee, 21 March 1860.
29. *Scmn.*, 29 May 1860.
30. *Scmn.*, 24 May 1860.
31. Quoted in Bruce, *The Railways of Fife*, 33.
32. *Scmn.*, 21 December 1860.
33. NAS. BR/NBR/8/1212.
34. *Scmn.*, 16 and 23 March 1860, report of half-yearly meeting on the 22nd; 27 September, report of half-yearly meeting on the 26th.
35. *Newc. Cour.*, 2 March 1860.
36. *NBRSGJ*, No. 83, 10ff. D. Yuill, 'Carrying Coals to Leith & Granton', Pt 2.
37. NAS. BR/NBR/1/9. Half-yearly report, 26 September 1860.
38. NAS. BR/NBR/1/9. Directors' meeting, 9 November 1860.
39. NAS. BR/NBR/1/9. Directors' meeting, 18 December 1860.
40. *SRG*, 24 March, 25 August 1860.
41. NAS. BR/NBR /1/9. 14 June 1860; NBR1/10. 17 May, 11 June 1861.
42. NAS. BR/NBR/1/9. Directors' meeting, 20 November 1860.
43. Hoole, *Illustrated History of the E.C.J.S.*, 10; Wrottesley, *Great Northern*, i, 136.
44. NAS. BR/NBR/1/9. Directors' meetings 18 December 1860, 9 January and 19 February 1861; *Glas. Her.*, 3 August 1864.
45. NAS. BR/NBR/1/10. Directors' meeting, 11 June 1861.
46. *Scmn.*, 4 January 1861.
47. NAS. BR/NBR/10. EGM, 9 August 1861.
48. *Scmn.*, 31 January 1861; see also Brown & Lawson, *History of Peebles*, 19ff.
49. Referring to *Railway Times* items on 29 October 1859 and 2 February 1861, C.J.A. Robertson surmised that the decision of the Peebles company to lease its line was "prompted in part by the realisation that its six Bouch-designed timber bridges were only three years younger than those at St. Andrews", which had had to be replaced.
50. *Scmn.*, 11 May, 17 May, 12 June 1861.
51. PP. Report of Select Committee on the Berwick Election, 1861.
52. *Scmn.*, 2 September 1861.
53. *Scmn.*, 27 April; NAS. BR/NBR/1/10. Special meeting 12 November, 1861.
54. NAS. BR/NBR/1/10. Directors' meeting, 30 August 1861.
55. NAS. BR/NBR/1/10. Special meetings 12 and 29 November, 1861.
56. *Cal. Merc.*, 16 September 1861.
57. *Cal. Merc.*, 19 September 1861, 'Returns of Scotch Railways'.
58. *Cal. Merc.*, 28 September 1861.
59. *Cal. Merc.*, 13 November 1861, report of special meeting on 12th.

6. HODGSON'S RAILWAY 3, 1861-1864

1. Measom, *Official Illustrated Guide*, 210, 214, 326, 375.
2. NAS. BR/NBR/1/10. Directors' meeting 10 January 1862.
3. NAS. BR/NBR/1/10. Directors' meeting and half-yearly meeting 21 March 1862.
4. NAS. BR/NBR/1/10. Wharncliffe meeting, 23 May 1862.
5. NAS. BR/NBR/1/10. Directors' adjourned meeting, 13 June 1862.
6. *Scmn.*, advertisement, 1 July 1862.
7. See Sewell, *The NBR in Northumberland*, 20.
8. *Ed. Gaz.*, 10 June 1862, 970; Bradshaw *Railway Shareholders' Guide*, 1867.
9. Quoted in White, *Solway Steam*, unpaged.
10. *Scmn.*, 2 August 1862.
11. Tomlinson, *NER*, 618.
12. NAS. BR/NBR/1/10. Directors' meeting 12 July, 3 October 1862.
13. *Cal. Merc.*, report of special meeting, 5 May 1862.
14. *Cal. Merc.*, 19 March 1862, report of EP&D half-yearly meeting.
15. *Scmn.*, 23 January 1863.
16. *Cal. Merc.*, 1 September; NAS. BR/NBR/1/10. Directors' meeting 6 September 1862.
17. *Glas. Her.* 22 December 1862.
18. *Glas. Her.*, *Belfast Telegraph*, 4 May 1863.
19. *Cal. Merc.*, 23 and 29 September 1862, report of half-yearly meeting.
20. NAS. BR/NBR/1/11. Half-yearly report, March 1863.
21. NAS. BR/NBR/1/10. Directors' meeting, 14 November 1862.

CHAPTER 6 CONTINUED

22. *Glas. Her.*, 18 April 1863; *Cal. Merc.*, 21 September 1864, report of half-year meeting.
23. Hodgson Hinde's name was changed for inheritance reasons. The circumstances of his departure from the Caledonian board may have contributed to his brother's animus against that company: see Ross, *The Caledonian*, 56.
24. *Newc. Cour.*, 27 March 1863.
25. *Newc. Cour.*, 28 August 1863.
26. *Cal. Merc.*, 12 June 1863.
27. *Scmn.*, 11 May, 5 June 1863.
28. *Glas. Her.*, 22 July 1863.
29. *Cal. Merc.*, 25 September 1863.
30. *Cal. Merc.*, 16 October 1863.
31. *Ed. Gaz.*, 1465. 24 November 1863.
32. *Cal. Merc.*, 4 January 1864.
33. *Ed. Gaz.*, 24 November 1863.
34. NAS.BR/NBR/1/14. Memorandum from R. Hodgson to investigation committee, 10 October 1866. The S.B.S.N. Co. was not formally wound up until March 1882. See *Lond. Gaz.*, 1013, 7 March 1882.
35. *Newc. Cour.*, 26 February 1864.
36. NAS. BR/NBR/1/12. 40th half-yearly report, 23 March 1864.
37. NAS.BR/NBR/1/12. Directors' meeting, 11 May 1864.
38. NAS. BR/NBR/1/12. Directors' meetings, 29 April, 22 July 1864.
39. *Scmn.*, 4 July 1864.
40. *Cal. Merc.*, 31 October 1863.
41. NAS. BR/NBR/1/12. Urgency committee 20 May, Directors' meeting 27 May 1864.
42. *Glas. Her.*, 4 June 1864.
43. *Dund. Cour.*, 10 June 1864.
44. *Cal. Merc.*, 1 July 1864.
45. *Gas. Her.*, 1 July; *Cal. Merc.*, 21 September 1864; PP. Report from the Board of Trade to the House of Commons on Railway & Canal Bills, 1865.
46. *Glas. Her.*, 9 August 1864.
47. *Dund. Cour.*, 18 August 1864. Though some sources say Carlisle (Canal) then closed to passengers, Silloth services are advertised as departing from there at least until August 1865. See *Belfast Telegraph*, 30 August 1865.
48. *Cal. Merc.*, 21 and 28 September 1864.
49. NAS. BR/NBR/1/12. Directors' meeting, 2 September, 5 August 1864.
50. NAS. BR/NBR/1/12. Director's meeting 2 September; finance committee 15 September 1864.
51. NAS. BR/NBR/1/12. Directors' meeting 7 June, Locomotive committee 21 June and 18 August; directors' meetings 16 September, 22 July, 19 August 1864.
52. NAS BR/NBR/1/12. Directors' meeting, 10 November 1864.
53. NAS. BR/NBR/1/12. Directors' meeting, 9 November 1864.
54. NAS. BR/NBR/1/12. Directors' meetings 25 November and 9 December; Loco Committee, 8 December 1864.

7. HODGSON'S RAILWAY 4, 1864-1866

1. NAS.BR/SNR/1/1, 15 November, 17 December 1864; BR/SNR/1/2, 24 and 30 March, 16 June 1865.
2. *Cal. Merc.*, 9 May 1865.
3. *Cal. Merc.*, 2 January 1865.
4. *Cal. Merc.*, 6 March 1865.
5. *Cal. Merc.*, 20 and 24 March 1865.
6. *Scmn.*, 28 April 1865, report of EVR half-yearly meeting.
7. Tomlinson, *NER*, 618.
8. *Cal. Merc.*, 20 May 1865.
9. *Ed. Gaz.*, 11 July 1861, 861.
10. *Dund. Cour.*, 28 September 1865.
11. *Scmn.*, 17 August 1865.
12. The railway companies generally built houses of better standard than miners' housing.
13. NAS. BR/NBR/1/13. Directors' meetings, 17 and 18 August 1865.
14. The NBR never built the station, renting part of the former Newcastle & Carlisle goods station, then, from early 1871, the new NER Forth Banks Goods Station.
15. NAS. BR/NBR/1/13. Directors' meeting, 1 September 1865.
16. *Cal. Merc.*, 16 and 25 August 1865. *Scmn.*, 10 March 1866, 13 January 1868.
17. NAS. BR/NBR/1/13. Directors' meeting 28 September, 26 October 1865. Since the 1840s there had been a 'North British Hotel' in Glasgow, adjacent to Queen Street Station but not a NBR property.
18. NAS.BR/NBR/1/13. Directors' meeting 28 September, Loco Committee 11 October 1865.
19. NAS. BR/NBR/1/13. Extraordinary general meeting, 12 October 1865.
20. *Cal. Merc.*, 22 May 1865, reporting extraordinary general meeting of E&G Railway.
21. *Glas. Her.*, 28 September 1865.
22. *Glas. Her.*, 31 August 1865.
23. NAS. BR/NBR/1/13. Directors' meeting 28 September 1865.
24. *Cal. Merc.*, 29 September 1865.
25. *Glas. Her.*, 7 October 1865.
26. *Glas. Her.*, 11 November 1865.
27. *Scmn.*, 2 October 1865.
28. *Cal. Merc.*, 14 and 20 December 1865.
29. PP. Report by PMG to Treasury Upon Complaints as to Fife Mails, 3 May 1866;

Wilson, *The TPOs*, 185. Incidentally, unless a locomotive stop at Berwick were still included, this must have meant a NER engine took the train through to Edinburgh.

30. *Glas. Her.*, 13 December 1865.
31. *Cal. Merc.*, 1 January 1866.
32. *Glas. Her.* 1 February 1866.
33. Mowat, *Port of Leith*, 363.
34. *Cal. Merc.*, 17 February 1866.
35. NAS. BR/NBR/1/13. Clothing committee, 8 February 1866.
36. NAS. BR/NBR/1/13. Half-yearly meeting 23 March 1866.
37. *Scmn.*, 10 March, *Glas. Her.*, 17 March 1866, directors' half-yearly report.
38. *Cal. Merc.*, 28 April 1866.
39. NAS. BR/NBR/1/13. Directors' special meeting 9 March, urgency committee, 29 March 1866.
40. *Glas. Her.*, 28 May, 13 June; *Dund. Cour.*, 21 June, 1866. NAS.BR/NBR/1/14. Memorandum from R. Hodgson to investigation committee, 10 October 1866.
41. NAS.BR/NBR/1/14. Directors' meeting, 23 June 1866.
42. NAS.BR/EDB/23/5. *Cal. Merc.*, 26 June 1866.
43. *Cal. Merc.*, 16 and 25 June, *Glas. Her.*, 27 July; *Dund. Cour.*, 16 August 1866.
44. *Dund. Cour.*, 11 August 1866.
45. *Glas. Her.*, 18 August 1866.
46. *Lond. Gaz.*, 5815, 24 November 1865.
47. *Glas. Her.*, 22 August 1866.
48. *Cal. Merc.*, 28 September 1866.
49. *Glas. Her.*, 20 October 1866.
50. NAS. BR/NBR/1/14. Directors' meeting, 1 November 1866.
51. *Glas. Her.*, 2 November 1866.
52. Quoted in *Cal. Merc.*, 5 November 1866.
53. *Glas. Her.*, 7 November 1866.
54. *RT*, 3rd August, 1867.
55. Letter in *Glas. Her.*, 17 November 1866.

8. THE KIPPENDAVIE YEARS 1, 1866-1870

1. *Cal. Merc.*, 18 December 1866.
2. Neele, *Reminiscences*, 473.
3. *Abdn. Jnl.*, 16 January 1867.
4. NAS. BR/NBR/1/14. Directors' meeting, 16 March 1867.
5. NAS.BR/NBR/1/14. Directors' meeting 21 December 1866.
6. *Scmn.*, 15 November 1866, Lythgoe's testimony to committee.
7. *Glas. Her.*, 3 May 1864, *Cal. Merc.* 21 January 1865, 22 January and 21 November 1866.
8. NAS.BR/NBR/1/14. Directors' meeting 4 January 1867.
9. He is however buried at Warriston Cemetery, Edinburgh.
10. NAS.BR/NBR/1/14. Directors' meeting 4 January; *Scmn.*, 23 March 1867.
11. *Ed. Gaz.*, 20 and 23 November 1866.
12. The NBR was usually careful to maintain good relations with the G&SWR, and vice versa.
13. *Leeds Mercury*, 4 May 1867.
14. *Pall Mall Gazette,* 1 June; *Glas. Her.*, 5 June 1867.
15. *Scmn.*, 7 June 1867.
16. See Jenkins, *The Rothbury Branch*, 25f.
17. Half-yearly report, *Glas. Her.*, 12 September; *Morning Post*, 23 September 1867.
18. *Glas. Her.*, 1 October 1867.
19. *Scmn.*, 30 March 1868, Walker's evidence for Forth Bridge Bill; 13 March 1869, Trustees' meeting convened to approve deal.
20. *Daily News*, 21 October 1867.
21. *Glas. Her.*, 21 September 1867, report of half-yearly meeting; Neele, *Reminiscences*, 161.
22. *Ed. Gaz.*, 1396, 26 November 1867.
23. *Glas. Her.*, 23 January 1868.
24. GUAS.UGD 8/1/21. Stobcross Branch.
25. *Glas. Her.*, 1 February 1868.
26. *Glas. Her.*, *ibid*.
27. *Scmn.*, 21 May 1868.
28. *Scmn.*, 16 May 1864.
29. *Scmn.*, 6 March, 21 May, 1867; 10 July, 13 October 1869. Quick, *Stations*, Leith.
30. *Abdn. Jnl.*, 11 March 1868.
31. *Morning Post*, 24 March; *Glas. Her.*, 28 March, 1868: Half-yearly report and half-yearly shareholders' meeting.
32. *Dund. Cour.*, 13 May 1868.
33. *Glas. Her.*, report of special meeting, 30 May 1868.
34. *Glas. Her.*, 11 and 21 August 1868.
35. *Glas. Her.*, half-yearly report, 22 September; half-yearly meeting, 1 October, 1868.
36. *Dund. Cour.*, 24 December 1868.
37. Brotchie & Jack, *Early Railways of West Fife*, 195.
38. *Glas. Her.*, 27 February 1869.
39. *Scmn.*, 2 March 1869.
40. *Glas. Her.*, report of CGU half-yearly meeting, 21 April 1869.
41. *Glas. Her.*, 3 June 1869.
42. *Glas. Her.*, 10 May 1869.
43. *Glas. Her.*, *ibid*.
44. *Glas. Her.*, 13 and 16 July 1869.
45. Tomlinson, *NER*, 638f.
46. *Glas. Her.*, 6 August 1869, report of special shareholders' meeting.
47. *Glas. Her.*, 29 September 1869, report of half-yearly meeting on 28th.
48. *Glas. Her.*, 13 November 1869.
49. *Ed. Gaz.*, 1465, 23 November 1869.
50. *Dund. Cour.*, 15 January 1870.
51. PP 1870 (341). Select Committeee on Railway Companies, 105.

CHAPTER 8 CONTINUED

52. *Dund. Cour.*, 31 January 1870. Presumably people simply got off on the track, as there was no station by the loch-side.
53. *Glas. Her.*, 17 and 18 February 1870.
54. *Glas. Her.*, 22 February 1870.
55. POST 32/33A.
56. *Glas. Her.*, 4 August 1870.
57. *Ed. Gaz.*, 9 August 1870.
58. *Glas. Her.*, 29 March and 1 April 1870.
59. Bagwell, *The Railway Clearing House*, 58.
60. *Scmn.*, 23 April 1870.
61. *Glas. Her.*, 29 August 1870.
62. See PP 1872 (364).
63. *Glas. Her.*, 6 September 1870.
64. *Morning Post*, half-yearly report, 23 September 1870.
65. *Glas. Her.*, 30 September 1870, report of half-yearly meeting.
66. *Glas. Her.*, 10 November 1870.

9. THE KIPPENDAVIE YEARS 2, 1870-1873

1. *Glas. Her.*, 16 June 1870. See also *RCHS Journal*, July 2012, pp25-35: John Duncan, 'Local Taxation and the Victorian Railway Companies'.
2. *Dund. Cour.*, 15 September 1870.
3. *Glas. Her.*, 4 August 1870.
4. *Glas. Her.*, 31 January 1871.
5. *Glas. Her.*, 17 March 1871, report of special meeting on Bills.
6. *Glas. Her.*, 17 March and 1 August 1871.
7. *Glas. Her.*, 7 August, 23 October 1871.
8. GUAS.UGD 8/1/42, Prospectus of North British, Arbroath & Montrose Railway; *Illus. London News*, 29 July 1871.
9. *Glas. Her.*, 29 September 1871.
10. *Glas. Her.*, 4 November 1871.
11. PP. 1871 (C.438). Post Master General's 17th Report.
12. *Railway Magazine* June 1914. T. Moffat, 'Railways in Fife', 394ff.
13. *Glas. Her.*, 2 December 1871.
14. *Ed. Gaz.*, 24 November 1871, 841.
15. *Glas. Her.*, 16 and 28 December 1871.
16. *Scmn.*, 9 January 1872. *Dund. Cour.*, 25 January; *Glas. Her.*, 2 and 7 February 1872.
17. *Glas. Her.*, 23 March 1872.
18. *Glas. Her.*, 23 February 1872; *Bradshaw's Shareholder's Guide*, 1883.
19. See *Newc. Cour.*, 1 March 1872.
20. *Birmingham Post*, 26 February, *Dund. Cour.* 1 March 1872.
21. *Scmn.*, 14 March 1872.
22. *Glas. Her.*, 23 March 1872.
23. *Scmn.*, 30 March and 27 April, 1872.
24. *Scmn.*, 11 May 1872.
25. *Glas. Her.*, 6 June 1867.
26. *Scmn.*, 29 May, 3 June, 1 October 1872.
27. See Sewell, *The NBR in Northumberland*, 82.
28. Bradshaw's *Shareholders' Guide*, 1883, 252-3.
29. POST 32/33A (1870-73).
30. *Scmn.* 24 August 1872.
31. *Scmn.*, 13 and 17 September 1872, PP 1873, (C.832), Railway Returns for 1872, 36.
32. An explosion here on 22 October 1890, not caused by the railway, severely damaged the corrugated iron 'tunnel'; see PP. Report by HM Inspector of Explosives, 1890-91.
33. *Ed. Gaz.*, 26 November 1872, 796.
34. *Ed. Gaz.*, 753ff, 22 November 1872.
35. NAS. BR/NBR/4/300.
36. *Glas. Her.*, 13 and 27 January 1873.
37. *Glas. Her.*, 8 February 1873; BRB, '100 Years of the Sleeping Car'.
38. NAS.BR/NBR/1/20. Loco & stores committee, 8 and 30 January, works committee 30 January, 1874.
39. *Glas. Her.*, 23 March 1873.
40. NAS.BR/NBR/4/181, circular to shareholders of 19 March 1873.
41. Neele, *Reminiscences*, 161.
42. NAS.BR/NBR/1/20. Directors' meeting, 14 March 1873.
43. *Glas. Her.*, 10 June 1873.
44. See Kellett, *The Impact of Railways on Victorian Cities*, 239ff., quoting Glasgow Reference Library MS correspondence D397154, 25 September 1893. 1873 passenger figures are extrapolated.
45. NAS.BR/NBR/1/20. Loco & stores, 1 and 29 May 1873.
46. *Ed. Gaz.*, 21 November 1873.
47. *Glas. Her.*, 14 June 1873.
48. NAS.BR/NBR/1/20. Traffic committee, 18 December 1873.

10. THE KIPPENDAVIE YEARS 3, 1873-1877

1. *Glas. Her.*, 12 and 13 June 1873.
2. NAS.BR/DQ/1/1. Directors' meeting 4 August 1873.
3. NAS.BR/DQ/1/1. Directors' meeting, 12 September 1873.
4. NAS.BR/NBR/1/20. Directors' meeting, 30 September 1873.
5. *Dund. Cour.*, 27 August 1873.
6. *Glas. Her.*, 23 September 1873.
7. *Glas. Her.*, ibid.

264

8. NAS.BR/NBR/1/20. Works committee,
   16 October, finance committee, 4 December, 1873.
9. NAS.BR/NBR/1/20. Directors' meeting
   4 July 1873.
10. NAS.BR/NBR/1/20. Directors' meeting,
    8 January, 1874; traffic committee, 17 April, 1873.
11. *Glas. Her.*, 9 January 1874.
12. *Glas. Her.*, *Dund. Cour.*, 29 January 1874.
13. *Glas. Her.*, 10 February 1874.
14. *Glas. Her.*, 19 March 1874. Thomas, *NBR* i, 181,
    notes the very high turnover of signalmen. In
    busy locations it was an intensely demanding
    and poorly rewarded job.
15. NAS.BR/NBR/1/20. Directors' meeting
    22 January 1874.
16. *Glas. Her.*, 1 April 1874.
17. *Dund. Cour.*, *Glas. Her.*, 6 March 1874.
18. NAS.BR/DQ/1/1. Directors' meeting
    1 June 1874.
19. *Glas. Her.*, 20 June 1874.
20. NAS.BR/DQ/1/1. Directors' meeting
    23 October 1874
21. NBR press advertisements bore Mason's name
    to 31 July, Wieland's, as secretary, to
    14 September, and Walker's from mid-September.
    It has been speculated that Mason was eased
    out to give Walker the job; but the time interval
    suggests otherwise.
22. Cattanach, *Wieland*, 22.
23. *Glas. Her.*, 22 September, *Scmn.*, 1 October, 1874.
24. Cunningham, *Mining in the Kingdom of Fife*, 25.
25. *Glas. Her.*, 5 September 1874.
26. *Glas. Her.*, 9 December 1874.
27. NAS.BR/LIB/S/6/224, Douglas's pamphlet;
    and NBR/1/22, directors' meeting,
    21 October 1874.
28. NAS. BR/NBR/4/300.
29. GUAS. UGD.8/9/14/1, Whiteinch Railway.
30. See Ross, *Caledonian*, 110.
31. *Glas. Her.*, 22 and 25 February; *Glas. Her.*,
    31 March 1875.
32. NAS. BR/NBR/1/22. Loco committee,
    30 March 1875.
33. NAS. BR/NBR/1/22. Directors' meeting
    25 February 1875. Wilson, *The TPOs*, 185.
34. *Glas. Her.*, 16 March 1875.
35. NAS. BR/DQ/1/1. Directors' meeting,
    30 March 1875.
36. NAS. BR/NBR/1/22. Traffic committee,
    13 May 1875.
37. *Northern Echo*, 5 July 1875.
38. *Glas. Her.*, 10 September 1875.
39. *Glas. Her.*, 23 July 1875.
40. *Scmn.*, 5 November 1875 describes the Pullman
    car. The old roof was transferred to Kipps, to
    cover the yard between the sawmill and the
    smithy. NAS. BR/NBR/1/22. Loco committee,
    26 August 1875.
41. Houses: NAS.RHP 16201 for design; *Glas. Her.*,

27 January 1875, Fraser & Maver, *Glasgow*, ii,
123. Works: NAS. BR/NBR/1/22. Loco committee,
5 and 24, directors' meetings 26 August,
30 September 1875. *Glas. Her.*, 5 November 1875.
42. *Ed. Gaz.*, 23 November 1875, 824.
43. *Glas. Her.*, 4 February 1875, report of Special
    meeting on Bills, 3 February. This line would
    not be built until 1890.
44. *Glas. Her.*, 8 March, *Scmn.* 22 March, 1875.
45. As permitted by an Act of Parliament, 1875.
46. *Scmn.*, 8 October 1875.
47. NAS. BR/NBR/1/22. Directors' meeting
    3 March; *Glas. Her.*, 26 May 1876.
48. *Scmn.*, 9 June, 26 May, 19 December 1876.
    See also McE, T25/3/33.
49. For 'Flying Scotchman' see *Scmn.*, 10 February,
    1873; For 'Flying Scotsman' see *Scmn.*, 15 August
    1888. NAS. BR/NBR/1/22. Loco committee,
    13 April and 8 June 1876.
50. NAS. BR/FBR/1/1. Half-yearly report,
    August 1876. The £16,768 was the paid-up
    portion of the £134,000 specified in the NBR
    (Fife Railways) Act 1876.
51. *Scmn.*, 23 June 1876.
52. *Scmn.*, 11 December 1876.
53. *Newc. Cour.*, 19 January 1877.
54. *Scmn.*, 2 December 1876.
55. *Lond. Gaz.*, 4005. 14 July 1876.
56. PP. Returns by Railway Companies for the
    six months ending 31 December 1878.
57. *Scmn.*, 28 December 1876.
58. *Dund. Cour.*, 1 January and 5 February 1877.
59. NAS. BR/NBR/1/24. Works committee,
    10 May 1877.
60. *NBRSGJ*, No. 36, December 1988, A.A. Maclean,
    'The South Queensferry Branch', 3ff.
61. NAS. BR/DQ/1/1. Special shareholders'
    meeting, 15 February 1877.
62. *Dund. Cour.*, 16 and 30 March 1877.
63. NAS. BR/LIB/S/6/224.
64. *Dund. Cour.*, 13 July 1877.
65. *Dund. Cour.*, 7 August 1877.
66. *Abdn. Jnl.*, 1 October 1877.
67. *Scmn.*, 24 October 1876.
68. NAS. BR/NBR/1/24. Traffic committee
    23 August, 14 September 1877.
69. *Dund. Cour.*, 23 November 1877.
70. *Dund. Cour.*, 25 September 1877.
71. NAS. BR/NBR/1/24. Traffic committee,
    31 May, 2 August; loco committee
    8 November 1877.
72. Brotchie & Jack, *Early Railways*, 199, 201, 204.
73. *Lond. Gaz.*, 6518. 23 November 1877. The branch
    was still supplying a bottle works in the 1900s.
74. NAS. BR/NBR/1/24. Works committee,
    29 November; finance committee and
    directors'meeting, 20 December 1877.
75. NAS. BR/NBR/1/24. Directors' meeting,
    10 January 1878.

11. THE KIPPENDAVIE YEARS 4, 1877-1881

1. Registered in the NBR (Additional Works & Powers) Act, 1877.
2. *Scmn.*, 1 April 1878.
3. NAS.BR/NBR/1/24. Directors' meeting 16 March 1878. The council claimed that the NBR had no legal right to erect a building here.
4. NAS.BR/NBR/1/24. Meetings on 21 February 1878.
5. McE., T/25/3/32.
6. *Abdn. Jnl.*, 5 February 1878.
7. *Abdn. Jnl.*, 30 April 1878.
8. NAS.BR/NBR/1/24. Loco committee, 24 May 1878; *Scmn.*, 15 June 1878.
9. *Scmn.*, 1 June 1878.
10. *Scmn.*, 11 June 1887.
11. *Abdn. Jnl.*, 4 September 1878; PP 1878-9, 5th Annual Report of the Railway Commissioners.
12. *Scmn.*, 4 June 1878.
13. NAS.BR/NBR/1/24. Half-yearly report, February; board meeting 17 September 1878.
14. *Scmn.*, 26 June 1878.
15. NAS.BR/NBR/1/26. Loco & stores committee, 15 August, works committee, and directors' meeting 16 August 1878.
16. Hoole, *ECJS*, 100. Two more, *Columba* and *Iona*, were in use from 20 April 1880. The Pullmans were withdrawn in December 1901.
17. NAS.BR/NBR/1/24. Works committee, 4 July 1878.
18. NAS.BR/NBR/1/26. Loco & stores committee, 12 September, works committee and directors' meeting, 12 and 13 September, 1878; see also BR/NBR/4/300.
19. NAS.BR/NBR/1/26. Special directors' meetings, 5 and 8 October, finance committee, 17 October 1878.
20. NAS.BR/NBR/1/26. Directors' meeting 12 December 1878.
21. *Scmn.*, 7 December 1878.
22. See PP. 1878 (C.2157).
23. The new dock was to cost £105,000. It does not appear that the NBR took any action, despite reminders from the town council. *Dund. Cour.*, 5 May 1879.
24. NAS.BR/NBR/1/26. Directors' meeting 17 July 1879.
25. In 1898 the stock was withdrawn and replaced by new vehicles built by the Midland Railway. See NAS.BR/NBR/1/46. Loco & Stores Committee, 22 September 1898.
26. NAS.BR/NBR/1/26. Directors' meeting 28 August 1879. *Scmn.*, 29 August 1879.
27. NAS.BR/NBR/1/26. Directors' meeting, 12 September 1879. *Scmn.*, *Dund. Cour.*, 26 September 1879. As Donald Cattanach observes, *Wieland*, 29f, 'insider dealing' was not then illegal but was regarded with deep disfavour.
28. NAS. BR/FBR/1/1. board meetings 6 August and 2 September 18; BR/NBR/1/26. Directors'

meeting, 6 November 1879.
29. *Abdn. Jnl.*, 7 October; NAS.BR/NBR/1/26. Directors' meeting, 16 October 1879.
30. *Leeds Mercury*, 8 October 1879.
31. NAS.BR/NBR/1/26. Directors' meeting, 16 October 1879.
32. *Scmn.* 17 February quoted one minister: "The Lord of the Sabbath kept back the hurricane just until the Sabbath-breaking train was reaching that part of the bridge which was weakest …".
33. NAS.BR/NBR/1/26. Special meeting of directors, 31 December 1879.
34. *Dund. Cour.*, 28 December 1879
35. *Dund. Cour.*, 17 January 1880; Koerte, *Two Railway Bridges*, 111. McKean, *Battle for the North*, 354n, notes an article by P.J.A. Burt in *Weather*, vol. 59, Dec. 2004 which concludes that "the storm which brought down the bridge was not that severe".
36. *Glas. Her.*, 27 January 1880.
37. NAS.BR/FBR/1/1. board meeting, 12 January, Report February 1880.
38. *Scmn.*, 2 and 4 March 1880.
39. *Glas. Her.*, 5 March, *Dund. Cour.*, 9 March, *Scmn.*, 19 March 1880; NAS.BR/NBR/1/26. Directors' meeting, 17 March 1879.
40. NAS.BR/NBR/1/26. Finance committee, 18 March 1880.
41. NAS.BR/NBR/1/26. Directors' meetings, 14 and 27 May 1880.
42. NAS.BR/NBR/1/26. Finance committee, 27 May 1880.
43. In 1881 a Committee of Inquiry into Wind Pressure on Railway Structures settled on 56lb/sq foot.
44. See for example, McKean, *Battle for the North* 218f.
45. *Scmn.*, 11 August and 15 September 1880.
46. *Scmn.*, 16 July 1880.
47. Cattanach, *Wieland*, 71. He also notes that William Laird, a Baird director, received £300 commission for the placing of ESSJR debentures. In this way Wieland cemented his personal relationships with men of position and influence.
48. NAS.BR/FBR/1/1. board meetings 9 and 13 July, 4 and 26 August, 23 September 1880.
49. *Scmn.*, 24 September 1880. Barlow was consultant engineer to the Midland Railway.
50. GUAS.UGD 8/9/14/1, Whiteinch Railway.
51. *Scmn.*, 1 November 1880.
52. *Scmn.*, 18 December 1880. A meeting between the Harbour Trust and the NBR talked in terms of strengthening rather than reconstruction (*Scmn.*, 31 December 1880), but ultimately W.H. Barlow provided a new design.
53. *Scmn.*, 29 December 1880.
54. NAS.BR/FBR/1/1. Half-year report and special meeting, 13 January 1881.

12. WALKER'S RAILWAY, 1881-1887

1. *Glas. Her.*, 24 January and 4 March 1881.
2. *Glas. Her.*, 26 February 1881.
3. In March 1882 the liquidators were due to pay the NBR £23,145 16s plus accrued interest of £13,259 12s 6d; see *Scmn.*, 2 March 1882.
4. *Glas. Her.* 1 April 1881.
5. According to Sir Henry Oakley of the Great Northern, giving evidence on the Kirkcaldy & District Railway Bill, *Glas. Her.*, 21 July 1891.
6. NAS.BR/FBR/1/1. board meeting and e.g.m., 11 July 1881.
7. *Glas. Her.*, 30 September 1881.
8. Thomas, *Springburn Story*, 124f.
9. *Scmn.*, 5 January, 10 March 1882.
10. Cattanach, *Wieland*, 47, 49; *Scmn.*, 2 April, 10 September 1881.
11. *Scmn.*, 10 December 1879; *Glas. Her.*, 5 December 1881.
12. NAS.BR/FBR/1/1. board meetings 30 September and 5 November 1881.
13. Quoted in Acworth, *The Railways and the Traders*, 137.
14. *Scmn.*, 6 May 1882. *Sheila* was renamed *Guy Mannering*.
15. See Thomas, *NBR*, ii, 68.
16. NAS.BR/NBR/1/24. Directors' meeting, 14 June 1878.
17. McGregor, *The West Highland Railway*, 29.
18. *Abdn. Jnl.*, 2 June 1883.
19. *Glas. Her.*, 1 December 1882.
20. *Glas. Her.*, 14 February 1883.
21. See PP, Private Bill Legislation Expenses, 1886.
22. *Scmn.*, 3 and 15 March, 10 May, 11 September 1882; *Glasgow News*, 4 January 1886.
23. *Scmn.*, 15 September 1882. See also Chapter 21.
24. *Glas. Her.*, 17 January 1883.
25. *Scmn.*, 8 November 1882.
26. *Scmn.*, 4 and 26 December 1882.
27. PP, Railway Bills for session 1883.
28. POST 32/47A. Letter from Walker to Baines, 30 November 1882.
29. *Scmn.*, 22 January 1883.
30. *Glas. Her.*, 25 January, *Scmn.*, 25 January, 9, 13 and 19 February, 1883.
31. *Dund. Cour.*, 20 February 1883.
32. *Scmn.*, 17 March 1883.
33. *Glas. Her.*, 5 January 1883.
34. *Dund. Cour.*, 9 February 1883.
35. *Dund. Cour.*, 8 March 1883.
36. *Glas. Her.*, 14 September 1883.
37. *Glas. Her.*, 1 June 1883.
38. *Scmn.*, 1 and 15-16 June 1883.
39. Brotchie, *The Wemyss Private Railway*, 33.
40. *Glas. Her.*, 2 November and 5 December 1883, *Scmn.*, 1 March 1884.
41. *Scmn.*, 25 December 1883.
42. *Scmn.*, 14 May 1883.
43. *Scmn.*, 9 and 12 January 1884.
44. *Scmn.*, 26 April 1866.
45. *Scmn.*, 14 June 1884.
46. PP 1883 (248). BoT Report on Applications Made under the Railways Construction Facilities Act 1864; *Scmn.*, 23 February, 1885.
47. *Scmn.*, 15 and 17 October 1884.
48. Cattanach, *Wieland*, 69ff. As Cattanach says, it had been a good investment. Wieland, as secretary of the Suburban company, was paid £2,500.
49. *Scmn.*, 3 July 1885. In 1914 the NBR also recorded an interest in the County and Crown Hotels, Edinburgh, the Royal and Ivanhoe Hotels, Glasgow, the Star & Garter at Linlithgow, and the Harrow Inn, Dalkeith. (NAS. BR/NBR/RAC/S/1/138). By then it also had the Lovat Arms at Fort Augustus, which was put up for sale in October 1921 (NAS. NBR/1/74. Estate committee, 20 October 1921) and approved the sale of the North Berwick Hotel, by the 'North British Hotel Co.', to the sitting tenant in 1922 (NAS. *Ibid.*, finance committee, 15 December 1922).
50. *Scmn.*, 27 March 1885, report of half-yearly meeting.
51. *Rly. Mag.*, February 1900, 108. W.J. Scott, 'An Account of the 8.15 pm "Night Scotsman".'
52. *Scmn.*, 1 October 1885.
53. *Scmn.*, 21 December 1885.
54. *Scmn.*, 23 and 27 January, 8 February 1886.
55. *Glas. Her.*, 18 March, 29 September 1886; 13 July 1899, Conacher's evidence at the Prince's Dock committee.
56. The system was patented by H.S.P. Carswell, "an assistant engineer at Cowlairs" (*Scmn.*, 18 August 1886); son of James Carswell. It was removed in November 1901.
57. *Glas. Her.*, 29 September 1886.
58. *Scmn.*, 8 May 1866.
59. *Scmn.*, 6 August 1886.
60. *Scmn.*, 14 September 1886.
61. PP 1886 (219). Return of Railway Stockholdings.
62. *Scmn.*, 24 September 1886.

13. WALKER AND TWEEDDALE, 1887-1891

1. *NBRSGJ*, No. 82, Spring 2002, 27: Alan Simpson notes that in 1887 Leven had 203 ships calling, totalling 13,965 tons; in 1888 only 29, totalling 1,654 tons.
2. *Scmn.*, 6 May and 1 June 1887.
3. *Scmn.*, 11 June 1887. This was the 4-4-0 No. 592, completed in April 1886.
4. NAS. GD/330/295. Letter from Fowler to Arrol.
5. *Scmn.*, 11 July 1887.
6. *Scmn.*, 2 June 1887.
7. *Scmn.*, 19 August 1887.
8. *Scmn.*, 23 September 1887.
9. Letter to *Scmn.*, 26 September 1887.
10. *Lond. Gaz.*, 6160, 18 November 1887.
11. NAS.BR/CAC/3/2; see also McGregor, *West Highland*, 36.
12. NAS.BR/NBR/1764/1; *Scmn.*, 16 March 1888. John McGregor points out (communication to author) that the Caledonian camp considered the upper Loch Lomond and Loch Fyne area to be properly theirs, by virtue of the C&O line.
13. *Scmn.*, 22 March 1888.
14. *Scmn.*, 10 August 1888.
15. Cattanach, *Wieland*, 106f; he also notes, 19, that Wieland had masterminded a split of the E&G preference (ordinary) stock in autumn 1876.
16. *Scmn.*, 31 January 1888; POST 32/54A, 57B.
17. *Glas. Her.*, 5 February 1885.
18. *Scmn.*, 28 March 1885, 12 and 19 May 1888; McE., T/25/3/33.
19. *Glas. Her.*, 19 June 1889. This section is also indebted to *NBRSGJ*, No. 012, Ed McKenna, 'Thirled Wagons on the NBR', 11ff.
20. *NBRSGJ*, McKenna, *op. cit.*, 14.
21. *Scmn.*, 19 and 25 September 1888.
22. *Scmn.*, 25 December 1888.
23. NAS.BR/NBR/8/1764/1.
24. *Scmn.*, 12 January 1889.
25. NAS.BR/NBR/1764/3.
26. *Lond. Gaz.*, 6464, 23 November 1888.
27. *Scmn.*, 4 February 1889.
28. *Scmn.*, 29 March 1889.
29. *Scmn.*, May 8 1889; announced at a Wharncliffe meeting to consider Bills.
30. *Scmn.*, 26 July 1889.
31. *Scmn.*, 25 April 1888.
32. *Scmn.*, 22 August 1889.
33. *Scmn.*, 30 July 1889; *Marine News*, vol xxiv, No. 11, November 1970, 386ff. Somner, G.H., 'The Galloway Saloon Steam Packet Co.'
34. *Scmn.*, 25 September 1889.
35. *Scmn.*, 16 October 1889; 25 January 1890.
36. *Scmn.*, 2 and 16 December 1889.
37. *Glas. Her.*, 7 January 1890.
38. *Glas. Her.*, 13 February, 25 March 1890.
39. *Scmn.*, 8 September 1891.
40. *Glas. Her.*, 21 February 1890.
41. *Glas. Her.*, 16 and 28 March 1890, half-yearly report and meeting.
42. McKean, *Battle for the North*, 303.
43. *Abdn. Jnl.*, 14 March 1890.
44. *Glas. Her.*, 1 October 1890.
45. *Glas. Her.*, 16 August 1890.
46. *Scmn.*, 25 October 1889.
47. *Scmn.*, 21 March 1891.
48. *Scmn.*, 27 July 1887; *Glas. Her.*, 30 May 1890; *Morning Post* 14 April 1891; Wood, *The Eight-Minute Link*.
49. *Ed. Gaz.*, 1323, 23 November 1894.
50. *Scmn.*, 12 July, *Glas. Her.*, 1 October 1890, half-yearly report.
51. *Glas. Her.*, 1 October 1890.
52. *Glas. Her.*, *ibid*.
53. Acworth, pamphlet, 1890.
54. *Lond. Gaz.*, 6561ff, 25 November 1890.
55. *Scmn.*, 16 July 1892.
56. *Glas. Her.*, 16 September 1890.
57. *Glas. Her.*, 22 September 1890.
58. *Glas. Her.*, 24 November 1890.
59. PP. Hansard, 3rd Series, Vol. 351, Lords, 6 March 1891.
60. *Glas. Her.* 22, 23, 26 December 1890.
61. *Scmn.*, 10 January 1891; *Glas. Her.*, 30 and 31 December 1890.
62. *Scmn.*, 15 and 28 January 1891.
63. PP. Hansard, *op. cit*.

14. TWEEDDALE AND CONACHER – 1, 1891-1894

1. *Scmn.*, 27 March 1891, report on half-yearly meeting.
2. *Bailie*, 21 January 1891.
3. *Scmn.*, 4 February 1891.
4. NAS. BR/NBR/4/300.
5. *Scmn.*, 25 June and 22 July 1891; *Dund. Cour.*, 22 July, 14 August 1894; *Glas. Her.*, 4 July 1895.
6. *Scmn.*, 15 July 1891.
7. NAS. BR/NBR/8/1764/3. Directors' meeting, 16 April 1891.
8. *Glas. Her.*, 11, 22, 29 July, 5 August, 15 October 1891.
9. *Scmn.*, 30 September 1891.
10. Ewen Cameron had asked for one but Lord Lothian, Secretary of State, had refused. NAS.BR/NBR/8/1764/1.
11. *Scmn.*, 19 August 1890.
12. *Scmn.*, 12 August 1891, and report of half-yearly meeting, 30 September 1891.
13. *Scmn.*, 17 March 1892.
14. *Scmn.* and *Abdn. Jnl.*, 30 September 1891.
15. *Scmn.*, 7 November 1891.
16. *Glas. Her.*, 2 November 1891.
17. *Times*, 28 October 1891.

18. NAS.BR/NBR/1/378. See also *NBRSGJ*, McKenna, *op. cit.*, 18.
19. *Scmn.*, 3 and 9 November 1891.
20. *Glas. Her.*, 17 June 1891.
21. *Glas. Her.*, 18 June 1892.
22. *Scmn.* and *Dund. Cour.*, 19 February 1892.
23. *Bailie*, 30 March 1892.
24. *Scmn.*, 6 May and 7 June 1892.
25. *Abdn. Jnl.*, 30 September 1892.
26. *Scmn.*, 19 August and 30 September; *Dund. Cour.*, 19 February, 1892.
27. *Glas. Her.*, 30 April 1892.
28. *Scmn.*, 22 September 1892.
29. POST 11/22 and 32/70A.
30. *Scmn.*, 9 and 23 December 1892; Cattanach, *Wieland*, 74ff.
31. *Scmn.*, 2 November 1892.
32. NAS. BR/NBR/8/1764/1 and 1764/2.
33. *Lond. Gaz.*, 7425, 16 December 1892.
34. *Glas. Her.*, 2 February, 3 and 15 March 1893.
35. NAS. BR/NBR/1/398.
36. *Glas. Her.*, 17 February 1893.
37. NAS.BR/NBR/8/1764/1. Memo dated 17 November 1892.
38. *Dund. Cour.*, 11 March, *Glas. Her.*, 15 March 1893.
39. *Dund. Cour.*, 28 February 1893.
40. *Glas. Her.*, 23 March 1893.
41. Cattanach, *Wieland*, 121ff.
42. *Glas. Her.*, 23 July 1893.
43. *Lond. Gaz.*, 4825, 25 August 1893.
44. Pattinson, *British Railways*, 117ff.
45. *Leeds Mercury*, 24 July, *Glas. Her.*, 29 July 1893.
46. Letter to Conacher, 14 July 1893, quoted in Brotchie, *The Wemyss Private Railway*, 39ff.
47. A private scheme which did not materialise. See *Dund. Cour.*, 3 March 1893.
48. *Glas. Her.*, 8 November 1893.
49. Cattanach, *Wieland*, 125ff. It is not clear whether Taylor was acting for Bairds or on his own account.
50. *Dund. Cour.*, 31 October 1893.
51. *Scmn.*, 24 November 1893.
52. *Abdn. Jnl.*, 14 November, *Glas. Her.*, 15 November; *Lond. Gaz.*, 6593, 21 November 1893.
53. *Dund. Cour.* and *Glas. Her.*, 28 November; *Glas. Her.*, 4 December 1893.
54. *Scmn.*, 26 May 1894.
55. *Abdn. Jnl.*, 24 and 28 April, 1894.
56. *Dund. Cour.*, 18 January 1894.
57. Dunfermline Sunday Press, 24 March 1894.
58. *Dund. Cour.*, 16 May 1894.
59. *Glas. Her.*, *Scmn.*, 26 May 1894.
60. *Illustrated Police News*, 16 June 1894.
61. *Glas. Her.*, 29 June and 19 July 1894.
62. *Glas. Her.*, 24 July 1894.
63. Bowtell, *Dam Builders' Railways*, 87, ref. to NBR Works Committee, March 1894.

15. TWEEDDALE AND CONACHER – 2, 1894-1899

1. *Glas. Her.*, 29 June and 13 August 1894.
2. NAS. BR/NBR/1764/5.
3. NAS.BR/NBR/8/1764/2.
4. *Glas. Her.*, 13 August 1894.
5. *NBRSGJ*, No. 26, January 1986. John McGregor, 'Fort William'.
6. *Scmn.*, 14 September 1894.
7. *F.T.*, 30 October 1894; *Ed. Gaz.*, 1287, 20 November 1894.
8. NAS. BR/NBR/1764/6. Letters of 3 and 6 December 1894. The "independent company" was the Invergarry & Fort Augustus, whose surveys, made by Charles Forman, went well beyond the supposed terminus. John McGregor (letter to author) suggests that the NBR may have suspected some complicity between the Highland's action and the C&O company's scheme for a Connel Ferry-Banavie line.
9. *Dund. Cour.*, 22 August 1894, 16 September 1895.
10. A new (1890) station just west of Comely Park; the original station was renamed Dunfermline Upper at the same time.
11. *Glas. Her.*, 19, 24, 28 September, *Dund. Cour.*, 28 November 1894.
12. *Ed. Gaz.*, 20 November 1894.
13. Cattanach, *Wieland*, 128, inclines towards the cronyism theory. In 1891-92 Wieland and Howard were involved with J.H. Renton in the purchase, as a speculation, of the Girvan & Porpatrick Junction Railway, ultimately sold to the G&SWR.
14. NAS. BR/NBR/1764/2. Report from Matthew Holmes, 22 January 1895; works committee 21 November 1895.
15. *Glas. Her.*, 29 March 1895. See Appendix 3, *Tobin*.
16. *Dund. Cour.* 11 March, *Glas. Her.*, 29 March 1895.
17. *Glas. Her.*, 8 May 1895.
18. *Dund. Cour.*, 5 July 1895.
19. Cattanach, *op. cit.*, 98.
20. NAS. BR/NBR/8/1764/4. Great Glen Agreement, 13 February 1895.
21. NAS.BR/NBR/8/1764/3. Report from Arnott to Conacher, 19 December 1895.
22. Ellis, *British Railway History*, ii, 31; Thomas, *NBR*, ii, 44ff.
23. *Glas. Her.*, 22 August 1895. The fastest Edinburgh-Dundee service in 2012 took 64 minutes; the fastest Dundee-Aberdeen service 71 minutes, with three stops.
24. NAS.BR/NBR/1/367. Minutes of EC Meetings.
25. *Glas. Her.*, 24, 25, 28 September 1895.
26. *Glas. Her.*, 28 October 1895. See also Note 8 above.
27. *Abdn. Jnl.*, 20 May 1896.
28. NAS.BR/NBR/4/373.

29. *Scmn.*, 1 April, 25 May 1896.
30. *Scmn.*, 27 March 1896.
31. *Scmn.*, 9 May 1896.
32. McE. T25/3/24.
33. NAS. BR/NBR/1/367. EC Traffic meetings, 29 May, 17 and 18 June, 24 November 1896. W.J. Scott in *Railway Magazine*, February 1900, 108, recorded that an East Coast-West Coast meeting at Euston in 1896 had agreed on a slow-down: "At the stroke of a pen Aberdeen was wafted 35 miles or so further from London than it had been since August of the year before."
34. *Scmn.*, 6 July 1896.
35. *Scmn.*, 16 and 17 September; 28 July 1896.
36. NAS. BR/NBR/8/1212. The last rails were finally lifted in 1904.
37. BR/NBR/4/373; McGregor, *West Highland*, 13.
38. NAS. BR/NBR/1764/1. Letter of 17 July 1896.
39. *Scmn.*, 19 September 1896.
40. NAS. BR/NBR/1764/1. Memoranda of 22 and 25 July 1896.
41. A thick file of correspondence on this junction, strategic in location but very minor in commercial importance, and its operating arrangements, is in NAS. BR/NBR/1764/1.
42. *Ed. Gaz.*, 1122, 20 November; 1213, 24 November 1896. See also McGregor, *West Highland*.
43. *Lond. Gaz.*, 24 November 1896, 6553.
44. *Scmn.*, 27 November, 17 December 1896; *Glas. Her.*, 8 January 1897.
45. *Dund. Cour.*, 28 January, *Glas. Her.*, 29 January, 1897. The northbound night express left Berwick at 2.57 am and was due at Waverley at 4 am. Frequently the NBR brought it in three minutes early, doing the 57.5 miles in an hour. Its standard consist was a six wheel brake and a composite carriage for Glasgow, sixwheel brake, composite carriage, bogie sleeping car, bogie vestibule third for Aberdeen; six wheel brake for Perth; six wheel composite (with sleeping accommodation) and six wheel vestibule third for Inverness; and a brake van. Total weight c180 tons. (*Railway Magazine*, February 1900. W.J. Scott, 'An Account of the 8.15 pm 'Night Scotsman', 115).
46. *Glas. Her.*, 11 March 1897.
47. *Scmn.*, 28 December 1896; *Dund. Cour.*, 26 April 1897.
48. *Glas. Her.*, 6 February, 15 December 1897.
49. NAS. BR/NBR/4/300. *Glas. Her.*, 8 April, 19 July 1897; 21 June, 29 July 1898.
50. *Scmn.*, 21 January 1897.
51. *Glas. Her.*, 7 May 1897.
52. *Scmn.*, 23 February 1897.
53. *Scmn.*, 4 May 1897.
54. NAS.BR/NBR/SPC/9/2/1.
55. *Scmn.*, 26 October 1897.
56. Documents in NAS.BR/NBR/SPC/9/2/1.
57. Wilson, *The TPOs*, 185f.
58. *Scmn.*, 13 January 1898.
59. *Dund. Cour.*, 17 September 1897.
60. *Glas. Her.*, 1 October 1897.
61. *Scmn.*, 26 and 27 January 1898. In 1904, by mutual agreement, the NER resumed running of the expresses.
62. PP. ninth Annual Report of R&CC, 1898.
63. NAS. BR/NBR/4/300.
64. *Scmn.*, 25 March, 23 September 1898. Walker (and Wieland as interim general manager) had been paid the same amount.
65. *Scmn.*, 25 March 1898.
66. *Ed. Gaz.*, 1468, 23 November 1869.
67. *Scmn.*, 13 August 1898.
68. PP. Commons Paper 1 August 1899, Sir Francis Marindin's Report on Thornton Junction.
69. *Rly. Mag.*, November 1898, 501; *Scmn.*, 16 December 1898. The statue is currently stored by Glasgow Museums Resource Centre.
70. *Abdn. Jnl.*, report of NBR e.g.m., 26 May 1893.
71. General manager's Circular GM90, though *The Pall Mall Gazette*, 16 August 1898, noted it as already open.
72. See *NBRSGJ*, No. 19, April 1984. N.R. Ferguson, 'Pre-Grouping Traffic on the EFCR', 15; and No. 53, D. Stirling, 'Passengers on the EFC Line', 4.
73. *Cal. Merc.*, 25 October 1852.
74. See Hajducki & Simpson, *The Lauder Light Railway*; *Scmn.*, 23 September 1897.
75. NAS.BR/BNR/1/46. Directors' meetings, 22 September, 20 October 1898, 12 January, 9 February, 9 March 1899.

16. WIELAND'S RAILWAY, 1899-1905

1. One delegate reported that the chairman had seemed willing to grant the concession "but the manager whispered in his ear and he said, 'Oh, I make no pledge'." *Scmn.*, 13 January, 6 February 1899.
2. PP 1899 (C.9203). Home Office Report on Shop Clubs; evidence from John Laing, secretary of NBR Insurance Society.
3. *Scmn.*, 2 February 1899.
4. NAS.BR/NBR/4/373. *Scmn.*, 25 August 1899.
5. *Scmn.*, 17, 18 March 1899.
6. *Scmn.*, 24 March 1899.
7. *Scmn.*, 20 June 1899.
8. *Scmn.*, 30 March, 7 April 1899.
9. *Scmn.*, 7 April. 199.
10. *Scmn.*, 25 March, 1899.
11. Cattanach, *Wieland*, 152, quoting NAS. BR/NBR/HOT/4/43, notes that the drinks laid on for directors' meetings were whisky, sherry, brandy, claret and port.
12. NAS.BR/NBR/1/46. Directors' meeting 6 April 1899.
13. *Scmn.*, 10 April 1899.
14. *Scmn.*, 22 April, 19 and 25 May, 1899.
15. NAS.BR/NBS/1/2. Meetings of 6 April and 12 January 1899; 15 December 1898.
16. NAS.BR/NBS/1/2. board meeting, 25 May 1899.
17. *Glas. Her.*, 9 and 14 June 1899.
18. NAS.BR/NBR/1/46.
19. *Scmn.*, 20 June 1899.
20. NAS.BR/NBR/1/46. Directors' meeting, 22 June 1899.
21. NAS.BR/SPC/9/1. Conacher Papers.
22. *Scmn.*, 27 June 1899.
23. *Scmn.*, 5 July 1899.
24. *Glas. Her.*, 13 July 1899.
25. NAS.BR/NBR/1/46. Directors' meeting 6 July 1899. A minority of six voted in favour of delaying his appointment.
26. *Scmn.*, 6 July, 1 August 1899.
27. *Financial News*, 15th September, 1899, quoted in Cattanach, *Wieland*, 30.
28. *Scmn.*, 29 September 1899.
29. *Scmn.*, 5 October 1899.
30. *Rly. Mag.*, February 1900, 117ff.
31. Alderman, *The Railway Interest*, 174.
32. *Scmn.*, 31 July and 17 November 1900.
33. *Scmn.*, 9 February 1901, report of NER half-yearly meeting on the 8th.
34. *Scmn.*, 23 February 1900.
35. *Scmn.*, *ibid.*
36. *Scmn.*, 5 March 1900.
37. Cattanach, *Wieland*, 89.
38. NAS.BR/NBS/1/2. Management meetings 27 September and 22 November 1900.
39. *Scmn.*, 2 April 1901.
40. *Scmn.*, 7 May 1901.
41. McGregor, *The West Highland*, 249, lists Forman's principal schemes, including a mountain railway to the summit of Ben Nevis.
42. Laird died on 14 August, and his seat was taken by Andrew K. McCosh, also from the senior ranks of Baird partners. His son, of the same name, became a director in December 1919.
43. *Scmn.*, 6 and 10 June 1901.
44. *Scmn.*, 31 October 1901.
45. Figures from Cunningham, *Mining in the Kingdom of Fife*, 72.
46. *Scmn.*, 2 and 9 July 1901.
47. Back on 16 March 1883 he had submitted plans for alterations to the old Kennedy's as the North British Station Hotel.
48. I am indebted to Cattanach, *Wieland*, 121ff, for elucidation of the EFCR history.
49. *Ed. Gaz.*, 1314ff and 1320ff, 19 November 1901. A branch to Cockenzie was never built.
50. *Scmn.*, 27 December 1901, 31 January 1902
51. *Scmn.*, 3 July 1931.
52. *Scmn.*, 3 February 1902.
53. *Scmn.*, 6 and 16 May, 1902.
54. *Scmn.*, 10 October 1902. Threats of this kind would would become increasingly frequent.
55. *Scmn.*, 30 November 1901.
56. NAS.BR/NBR/1/44. Hotel committee 8 April 1899; an offer from James McDougall & Son of Bollinger's extra quality 1893 champagne is "referred to Mr. Wieland".
57. Geddie, *Souvenir of the Opening*, 39.
58. *Scmn.*, 14 and 16 October 1902.
59. *Scmn.* 31 December 1902.
60. *Scmn.*, 16 November, 15 December 1902.
61. *Scmn.*, 24 April 1902.
62. *Scmn.*, 27 March, 1903.
63. PP 1902 (400). Return of Railway Stockholdings.
64. This probationary period was not unusual for an 'inside' promotion. The same happened with his contemporay J.F McIntosh on the Caledonian.
65. *Scmn.*, 2 May, 1 July 1903.
66. Bowtell, *Dam Builders' Railways*, 129. The station closed on 3 October 1921, then was reopened as an unmanned halt.
67. *Scmn.* 12 January 1904.
68. Half-yearly report, *Scmn.*, 16 March 1904.
69. *Scmn.*, 23 September 1904.
70. NAS. BR/NBR/1/367. EC managers' meeting 27 October 1904.
71. *Scmn.*, 6 January 1905.
72. *Financial News*, 28 March 1905.
73. Cattanach, *Wieland*, 107ff (W.F. Jackson was secretary of this company for 20 years). The opening chapters trace Wieland's early life as the son of a London vaudeville actor: an unusual background for a future railway chairman.

17. DALKEITH AND WHITELAW, 1905-1913

1. *Scmn.*, 26 May 1905.
2. See Hajducki, *The North Berwick & Gullane Branches*, 85; *Scmn.*, 12 June 1905. In April 1907 the original vehicles were traded in for two new ones, but the service was dropped from autumn 1910.
3. *Scmn.*, 18 May 1905. A private line worked by the NBR, it would be closed in 1921.
4. *Scmn.*, 24 June 1905.
5. *Ed. Gaz.*, 330, 28 March 1905.
6. *Scmn.*, 21, 22 and 25 July 1905.
7. *Scmn.*, 22 September 1905.
8. Smith, *County of Fife*, 559.
9. *Scmn.*, 14 March, *Ed. Gaz.*, 316, 20 March, *Scmn.*, 17 March; *Ed. Gaz.*, 1244, 23 November 1906.
10. *Rly. Mag.*, July 1906, 32.
11. *Scmn.*, 2 and 3 July 1906.
12. Barnes, *Midland Railway*, 264.
13. *Rly Mag.*, September 1906, 284.
14. *Scmn.*, 23 July 1906.
15. *Scmn.*, 6 November 1906, 8 August 1907.
16. *Scmn.*, 13 March 1907.
17. *Scmn.*, 4, 8 and 9 March 1907.
18. *Scmn.*, 1 June 1906.
19. *Scmn.*, 14 and 15 March, 6 July 1907.
20. *Scmn.* 22 March 1907.
21. *Glas. Her.*, 11 July 1907.
22. NAS. BR/NBR/3/27. In the three months ending 30 September 1922 the NBR recorded 3,170 hours of engine power at the dock, and the CR 2,282 1/4 hours.
23. *Scmn.*, 3 May 1907.
24. *Scmn.*, 17 and 20 July 1907.
25. *Glas. Her.*, 2 and 13 August 1907.
26. *Scmn.*, 27 August 1907.
27. *Scmn.*, report of half-yearly meeting, 27 September 1907.
28. *Scmn.*, 2 October 1907.
29. *Scmn.*, 23 October 1907.
30. *Scmn.*, 8 November 1907.
31. *Scmn.*, 10 December 1907.
32. *Scmn.*, 31 December 1907, 1 January 1908; *Glas. Her.*, 1 January 1908.
33. In anticipation of the 1923 mergers, on 7 November 1921 the Caledonian gave ten year's notice, accepted by James McLaren (company secretary) for the NBR on the 8th.
34. NAS.BR/CAL/3/12.
35. *Scmn.*, 7 and 18 February 1908.
36. *Scmn.*, 27 March 1908.
37. NAS.BR/NBR/1/425. Directors' meeting, December 1908.
38. NAS.BR/NBR/1/425. Directors' meeting, 18 June 1908.
39. NAS.BR/NBR/1/425. Directors' meeting, 31 October 1908.
40. NAS.BR/NBR/1/425. Directors' meeting 14 May 1908.
41. *Glas. Her.*, 15 July 1908.
42. Cattanach, *Wieland*, 89.
43. *Scmn.*, 18 August 1908.
44. Ross, *Caledonian*, 171
45. *Scmn.*, 7 May 1896.
46. Advertisement in *Scmn.*, 4 August 1908.
47. *Scmn.*, 19 December 1908.
48. *Scmn.*, 9, 11, 18 and 19 September 1908.
49. *Scmn.*, 25 September 1908.
50. *Glas. Her.*, 30 October 1908.
51. *Ed. Gaz.*, 20 November 1900, 1138.
52. *Scmn.*, 7, 21 and 23 October, 7 November, 29 December 1908.
53. *Scmn.*, 5 October 1908.
54. *Scmn.*, 30 November, 5 December 1908.
55. *Scmn.*, 6 January 1909.
56. *Scmn.*, 16 January 1909.
57. *Scmn.*, 16 and 22 January, 5 and 6 February, 19 March 1909.
58. *Scmn.*, 3 February 1909.
59. *Scmn.*, 19 March 1909.
60. *Glas. Her.*, 12 June 1909.
61. *Scmn.*, 4 July 1904.
62. *Glas. Her.*, 28 September 1909.
63. *Scmn.*, 24 September 1909.
64. *Scmn.*, 11 November 1909.
65. *Scmn.*, 28 October 1909, 29 January 1910.
66. See *Scmn.*, 10 July 1891: Matthew Holmes described the system to the Select Committee on Railwaymen's Hours.
67. NAS. NBR/BR/1/60. Directors' meeting, 16 December 1909.
68. *Scmn.*, 12 February, 1910. See also *NBRSGJ*, No. 102, December 2006. Ed McKenna, 'Thirled Wagons on the NBR'. W.F. Jackson told the Railway & Canal Commissioners that he disliked thirling agreements and had made none during his twelve years as general manager.
69. *Scmn.*, 4 and 18 March 1910; NAS. NBR/BR/1/60. Loco committee, 3 March 1910.
70. Noted in *R&T Monthly*, No. 96, April 1918, article on NBR, 205ff.
71. *Scmn.*, 5 September 1910.
72. *Scmn.*, 8 November 1910.
73. Cunningham, *Mining in the Kingdom of Fife*, 77.
74. *Glas. Her.*, 12 December 1910, 23 February 1911.
75. *Scmn.*, 24 January 1911.
76. *Scmn.*, 11 October 1912.
77. *Scmn.*, 22 March 1912.
78. *Scmn.*, 23 February 1911.
79. *Scmn.*, 25 October 1910, 24 March 1911.
80. *Scmn.*, 24 March 1911.
81. *Scmn.*, 23 August 1910, 17 May and 29 August 1911.
82. *Glas. Her.*, 12 and 17 June, 11 August 1911; *Scmn.*, 1, 11 and 16 August 1911.
83. *Scmn.*, 18, 19, 21, 22 and 29 August, 8 September 1911.

84. *Scmn.*, 26 September 1911.
85. *Glas. Her.*, 9 December 1911. Perhaps there were still reservations about public tributes to NBR officials. But Deuchars had been the obvious candidate as Conacher's successor in 1899, and he and Jackson may not have been friends.
86. *Scmn.*, 29 November, 16 September; *Glas. Her.*, 30 September 1911.
87. *Scmn.*, 2 November 1911.
88. *Rly. Mag.*, September 1911.

89. *Scmn.*, 6 December 1911.
90. *Scmn.*, 29 November and 6 December 1911, 29 January 1912.
91. *Scmn.*, 13 February, 30 April, 18 June, 20 September 1912; 25 February 1914.
92. *Scmn.*, 11 and 15 March 1912.
93. *Rly. Mag.*, April 1912, 265f. Shareholders complained that the fares were too low, see *Scmn.*, 24 March 1911.
94. *Scmn.*, 8 May 1912.
95. *Scmn.*, 20 June 1912.

18. WHITELAW AND BUCCLEUCH, 1913-1918

1. See *Dictionary of Scottish Business Biography*, ii, 323ff.
2. *Scmn.*, 11 May 1912
3. *Ed. Gaz.*, 1205ff, 19 November 1912.
4. *Scmn.*, 15-19 October 1912.
5. *Scmn.*, 20 September 1912, report of half-yearly meeting.
6. *Rly. Mag.*, October 1912, 391ff.
7. *Scmn.*, 4,6,7 November 1912.
8. *Glas. Her.*, 3 February 1913.
9. *Scmn.*, 23 January 1913. Blyth's eponymous father founded the partnership in 1848. B.H. Blyth II followed Forman as the NBR's preferred engineer.
10. Cunningham, *Mining in the Kingdom of Fife*, 50.
11. *Scmn.*, 12 February, 2 April 1913.
12. NAS. BR/NBR/4/429/1.
13. PP. BoT Annual WHR Report, 1904, 1914.
14. *Scmn.*, 26 April 1913.
15. *Times*, 1 May, *Scmn.*, 8 August 1913.
16. *Scmn.*, 10 June 1913.
17. *Scmn.*, 22 September 1913.
18. *Scmn.*, 18 July 1913.
19. *Scmn.*, 3 October 1913.
20. *Glas. Her.*, 11 November 1912.
21. NAS. BR/GSP/1/2.
22. *Scmn.*, 19 February 1914.
23. NAS.BR/NBR/4/373.
24. NAS.BR/NBR/4/373. See also *Railway Magazine*, January 1914. Moffat, Tom, 'The Control System on the NB Railway', 1ff.
25. See for example Working Timetable for Southern District, 1908: 'Special Goods Train from South Leith at about 4.50 am for Polton and Whitehill Collieries: District Inspector to arrange.'
26. *Scmn.*, 31 January 1914.
27. Pratt, *British Railways & the Great War*, i, 1055.
28. Pratt, *op. cit.*, 573.
29. NAS.BR/NBR/4/373. Circular GM 268, 5 September 1914.
30. Pratt, *op. cit.*, i, 820.
31. *Scmn.*, 22 February 1915, 25 February 1916.

32. *Scmn.*, 25 February 1916.
33. *Scmn.*, 23 February 1917.
34. Pratt, *op. cit*, i, 606.
35. Baxter, *BLC*, vi, 208, 211; *Scmn.*, 16 February 1916.
36. *Ed. Gaz.*, 1787, 23 November 1915.
37. NAS. BR/NBR/4/300.
38. *Glas. Her.*, 26 March 1915.
39. *Scmn.*, 12, 23 and 24 February 1916.
40. *Scmn.*, 17 October 1916.
41. *Ed. Gaz.*, 1787, 23 November 1915.
42. *Scmn.*, 18 June 1915, 9 and 16 May 1916, 14 June 1917.
43. Pratt, *op. cit.*, i, 810.
44. More details are given in Ross, *Caledonian*, 181.
45. Pratt, *op. cit*, i, 392, 472, 490, 508.
46. *Scmn.*, 16 and 25 February 1916. .
47. *Glas. Her.*, 10 January, 3 February 1917.
48. *Scmn.*, 20, 26 April 1916.
49. NAS.BR/NBR/4/373. NBR Circular R.429., 29 December 1916.
50. *Scmn.*, 4 January 1917.
51. *Scmn.*, 12 July 1917.
52. *Scmn.*, 23 February 1917, report of annual meeting.
53. *Scmn.*, 28 March, 19 May 1917.
54. *Scmn.*, 23 August 1917.
55. PP. R&CC 28th Report, 1917, 29th Report 1918.
56. See Thomas, *NBR*, ii, 28f.
57. GUAS. W.F. Jackson Photographic Albums.
58. See OS 25in map, 1925. Leuchars and Montrose had siding access.
59. NAS.BR/NBR/4/373. Documents 216/3761, 217/400 and 218/4965.
60. *Scmn.*, 29 January 1918.
61. *Scmn.*, 23 February 1918, report of a.g.m.
62. *Scmn.*, 13 March 1922. This number does not include those who resigned in order to join up, after railwaymen were exempted from military service.
63. K. Paton in *Railway & Travel Monthly*, No. 94, vol xvi, February 1918.

19. LAST YEARS, 1919-1923

1. *Scmn.*, 30 June 1919.
2. *Scmn.*, 29 May 1919. The Dunbar portion was not included.
3. *Scmn.*, 21 February 1920; figures quoted at NBR annual meeting on 20th.
4. *Scmn.*, *ibid.*
5. *Scmn.*, 29 September 1919.
6. GUAS. 47/4/1. 'Glasgow District Railwaymen's Strike Bulletin No. 7', Saturday October 4.
7. *Scmn.*, 29 September, 2, 4 and 6 October 1919.
8. PP. Cmnd 227, 987.
9. *Lond. Gaz.*, 30 March 1920, *Ed. Gaz.*, 9 January 1918.
10. NAS.BR/NBR/1/72. Traffic committee, 15 January and 19 February, loco & stores committee, 20 February 1920.
11. NAS.BR/NBR/1/72. Loco & stores committee, 9 April 1920.
12. Steamers committee, 7 May 1920. *The Cumberland News*, 25 September 2009, has an article on the Solway lightships.
13. NAS.BR/NBR/1/72. Finance Committee, 12 March, traffic committee, 15 January, works committee 5 February 1920.
14. NAS.BR/NBR/1/72. Traffic sub-committee, 24 September 1920.
15. NAS.BR/NBR/4/207.
16. NAS.BR/NBR/1/72. Directors' meeting, 7 May 1920.
17. *Scmn.*, 20 August 1920.
18. *Scmn.*, 23 July 1920.
19. *Scmn.*, 27 August 1920.
20. NAS. BR/NBR/8/1767/2. Letter from Galloway to Calder, 26 July; minutes of steamers committee, 27 August 1920.
21. *Scmn.*, 31 January, 12, 22 and 26 February, 16 March 1921.
22. NAS.BR/NBR/1/74. Traffic committee, 30 June 1921.
23. NAS.BR/NBR/1/72. Loco & stores committee, 6 May and 25 August; *Scmn.*, 14 and 27 April, 3 May 1921.
24. *Scmn.*, 13 May 1921.
25. NAS.BR/NBR/1/72. Locomotive & stores committee, 3 June; *Scmn.*, 17 May 1921.
26. *Scmn.*, 4 June 1921.
27. Of course this included the Eastfield and St. Margaret's losses – hardly wartime wear and tear.
28. *Scmn.*, 1, 16, 20, 21, 22, 23 June 1921.
29. NAS.BR/NBR/1/72. Loco & stores committee, 7 April 1921..
30. NAS.BR/NBR/1/74. Loco & stores committee 6 May; *Scmn.*, 6 July, 10 September, 3 October 1921.
31. NAS.BR/NBR/1/74. Special meeting of directors, 29 July, directors' meeting 26 August 1921.
32. NAS. BR/GSP/1/2.
33. NAS.BR/NBR/1/74. Directors' meeting, 23 September, traffic committee, 25 August, 1921.
34. NAS. BR/NBR/8/1767/1.
35. *Scmn.*, 27 August 1921, quoting reply to Sir William Raeburn M.P..
36. *Scmn.*, 10 and 23 November 1921.
37. NAS.BR/NBR/1/74. Directors' meeting, 7 April, Finance committee 28 July 1922.
38. Finance committee, 22 September 1922.
39. NAS.BR/NBR/4/207. See OS 6in map for 1895. It also shows (contrary to Cobb's *Atlas*) that the two Broxburn branches were linked by c1890, as the 'Drumshoreland and Winchburgh' line.
40. *Scmn.*, 26 January, 25 February 1922.
41. *Scmn.*, 21 January, 10 February 1922.
42. *Scmn.*, 13 March, 3 April, 14 September 1922.
43. *Scmn.*, 17 May 1922.
44. NAS.BR/NBR/4.207 contains a substantial set of accounts, all checked by the NER accounts department.
45. NAS. BR/NBR/1/74. Locomotive committee, 2 and 30 June, 1922.
46. *Scmn.*, 18 November 1922.
47. *Hansard*, Commons, 7 December 1922, vol 159 cc2040-2W.
48. *Scmn.*, 18 November 1922.
49. NAS.BR/NBR/1/74. Directors' meeting 15 December 1922; *Scmn.*, *ibid.*
50. When British Railways was formed, in 1948, 652 former North British engines were still running.

20. THE NORTH BRITISH IN CONTEXT

1. Neil Munro, 'Rankine's Rookery', from *Jimmy Swan, The Joy Traveller.*
2. NAS.BR/NBR/1/22. Traffic committee, 4 February 1875.
3. *Scmn.*, 20 October 1911.
4. *NBRSGJ*, No. 83, Spring 2002.
5. NAS. BR/NBR/1/365; BR/NBR/4/283; BR/NBR/1/407.
6. Middlemass, *Mainly Scottish Steam*, 24, 25.
7. *Scmn.*, 14 April, 17 July 1911.
8. NBR engines were also said to have a "musical whistle": see *Rly. Mag.*, January 1912, Bowman A.K., '*Expresses of the North British Railway*', 24ff.

21. POWER AND PROVISION

1. The chapter also draws on A.A. Maclean's article 'North British Railway Wagons' in *NBRSGJ* No. 44, of June 1991.
2. NAS.BR/NBR/1/3. Directors' meeting, 20 May 1846.
3. NAS. BR/NBR/1/5. Half-yearly report, September 1850.
4. Half-yearly report, September 1850; NAS.BR/NBR/1/7. Directors' meeting, 31 August 1854. Four vans were converted to brake vans in 1850.
5. PP. Reports of Accidents, May-June 1862.
6. *NBRSGJ*, No. 44, June 1991, 12ff. A.A. Maclean, *op. cit.*
7. See Baxter, *BLC*, vi, 139. It was illustrated in *Rly. Mag.*, April 1898, 297.
8. NAS. BR/NBR/1/13. Directors' meeting 28 September 1865.
9. Directors' report, 31 July 1867.
10. *Glas. Her.*, 12 September 1867.
11. *Glas. Her.*, 29 September 1871.
12. PP. 1868 (C.1963), Continuous Brakes: Returns of Railway Companies.
13. PP 1878-79 (C.2243). Correspondence Relative to Continuous Footboards and Platform Heights.
14. NAS. BR/NBR/1/24. Loco committee, 29 March 1877.
15. PP. Railway Returns on Coal Traffic, 1886. The NBR's record of registered traders' wagons is preserved from 1885 onwards (NAS.BR/NBR/5/81-86): most are coal wagons but paper, lime, linen and flax wagons are also recorded. See also *NBRSGJ*, No. 44, Maclean, op. cit.
16. McE., T25/3/1. He also notes a further Whiteinch 0-4-0ST, given NBR No. 1250, never on the Capital list, and sold to Finlaysons of Airdrie in 1920.
17. *Scmn.*, 28 September 1894.
18. Thomas, *The North British Atlantics*.
19. NAS.BR/NBR/1/425.
20. *Rly. Mag.*, April 1898, 292, calls No. 858 'Hercules', a playful reference to the E&G's 0-6-0WT No. 21 *Hercules* of 1844, originally intended to pull trains up the Cowlairs Incline.
21. Highet, *Scottish Locomotive History*, 217, 173.
22. See Johnston & Hume, *Glasgow Stations*, 81, 85.
23. *NBRSGJ*, No. 96, Summer 2005 has an authoritative article on NBR liveries by Allan Rodgers.

INDEX

Towns and villages are in the general index, but for specific references to stations, see under 'Stations'. Locomotive and ship references are grouped under 'Locomotives' and 'Ships'. Timeline entries are not indexed. References to illustrations are in bold type.

Methil Docks, 128, 134, 139, 140, 145, 153, 162, 167, 180, 186f, 197, **203**, 204, 222, 232
Metropolitan Wagon Co., 229
Midland Rly, 31, 65, 66, 79, 83, 97, 103, 105, 108, 111, 121, 140, 141, 180, 187
Midland Scottish Joint Stock, 113, 264
Middlemass, Thomas, 225
Miller, John, 20, 21, 22, 23, 26, 27, 227
Miller, Sir James, 142
Millerhill, 90, 98
Ministry of Transport, 215, 217, 218, 221
Mocatta, Maurice, 99f
Monkland & Kirkintilloch Rly, 24, 62
Monkland Railways, 62f, 66, 228
Monktonhall, 54, 56, 78
Montgomery, Sir Graham, 49f
Montrose, 90, 91, **120**, 121, 127
Montrose & Bervie Rly, 90, 91, 120, 121, 149
Morar, **178**
Morningside (Edinburgh), 65, **119**
Morningside (Lanarkshire), 64, 68, 74, 88
Morpeth, 48, 55, 105
Motor service, 186
Muir, William, 76
Munro, Neil, 224
Musselburgh, 26, 29, 35, 46, 49
Mutter, Harvey & Co., 210

N

Nairne, James, 40, 55, 72
Napier Commission, 136
National Bank, 55
Neilsons, 104, 105, 106, 110, 228, 230, 231
Newall continuous brake, 52
Newburgh & North Fife Rly, 166f, 197f, 200, 205, 207
Newcastle, 20, 42, 48, 55, 59, 67, 70, 108, 167, 203, 261
Newcastle & Berwick Rly, 25, 28, 30
Newcastle & Carlisle Rly, 20, 42, 55
New Lines agreement, 67, 110
Newhaven, 21
Newport on Tay, 113, 134
Newport Rly, 113, 135, 154, 178
Niddrie, 30, 46, 203
'Night Scotsman', 130, 269
Nimmo, James, & Co., 138, 139
North Berwick, 25, 28, 30, 34, 45, 225
North Berwick Hotel Co., 52
North Bridge, 21, 22, 25, 26, 29, 30, 35, 36, **37**, **58**, 155, **161**, 162, 168

North British Railway:
　'best-kept station', 157
　board crises, 36, 41, 73, 74f, 172f
　dispute with Government, 211, 217, 218ff, 221f
　emblem, **19**
　shareholders' committees, 33, 71, 75, 83, 96
　financial situation, 32, 58, 78, 80f
　formation, 21, 23
　'Grouping', 218, 219, 222
　joint purse with CR, 79f
　merger with E&G, 61f, 66f
　offices, 22, 38, 39, 68, 139, 164, 168, 216
　opening, 26
　'premier line', 213
　relations with traders, 70, 125, 147, 151, 152, 153, 159, 179, 194ff, 201
　staff clubs, 225
　stock conversions, 136
　stock jobbing, 82, 113, 114, 115, 138, 176, 265

North British Agents' Association, 203
North British, Arbroath & Montrose Rly, 87, 90, 107, 127
North British Locomotive Co., 221, 234, 235
North British Railway Insurance Society, 152, 167, 172, 190, 199, 201
North British Steam Packet Co., 60, 77, 81, 133, 135, 138, 175, 181, 215, 229
North Eastern Rly, 38, 40, 42, 43, 45, 48, 49, 52, 55, 59, 83, 86, 94, 105, 111, 118, 121, 141, 157, 160, 165, 168, 177f, 262, 269
North Monkland Rly, 93, 110, 135, 140
North Queensferry, 52, 97, **142**
Northumberland, 49
Northumberland Central Rly, 59, 79, 92, 93, 102, 184

O

Oban, 124, 156
Ockleston, T.O., 172ff, 176
Octuple Agreement, 35, 42
Ogilvie, Will H., 226
Ormiston, 54, 56, 63, 66, 78, 90, 142, 180, 184
Orr Ewing, John, 67, 76, 89

P

Pasley, General, 26
Paton, W.H., 160, 177, 186
'Peace Agreement' (1891), 147, 159, 192
Peddie, Donald, 28, 51, 257
Peebles, 25, 27, 37, 51, 58, 73, 148
Peebles Rly, 37, 40, 49f, 51, 52, 61, 65, 68, 85, 103, 105, 231, 260
Penicuik, 26, 51, 64, 65, 90
Penicuik Railway, 90, 94, 99, 103, 105
Penzance, 219
Perth, 25, 30, 39, 42, 54, 60, 63, 66, 85, 86f, 96, 113, 121, 122, 138

Dollar Station (opened on 3 May 1869) on the Devon Valley line, around 1910. (*Stenlake Collection*)

Fort William Station (opened on 7 August 1894) around 1903. (*Stenlake Collection*)

Fountainhall Station, opened on 4 August 1848, was the junction for Lauder from 2 July 1901.
A north-looking view, with the branch train. (*Stenlake Collection*)

The branch terminus at Langholm opened on 18 April 1864 and the buildings were enlarged in 1894. This 1935 view still displays the North British scene. Engine shed and water tank base (with its water-level gauge) form an integrated structure. (*John Alsop*)

Back cover: An 0-4-2 engine of Hurst's 90-class, built between 1861 and 1868, banks a coal train up to the north end of the Forth Bridge, in the 1890s. (*North British Railway Study Group*)